Serverless computing in Azure with .NET

Design, build, test and automate deployment, and more

Sasha Rosenbaum

BIRMINGHAM - MUMBAI

Serverless computing in Azure with .NET

First published: August 2017

Production reference: 1160817

Published by Packt Publishing Ltd.
Livery Place
35 Livery Street
Birmingham
B3 2PB, UK.

ISBN 978-1-78728-839-3

www.packtpub.com

Credits

Author
Sasha Rosenbaum

Reviewers
Donna Malayeri
Mikhail Veselov

Commissioning Editor
Aaron Lazar

Acquisition Editor
Chaitanya Nair

Content Development Editor
Rohit Kumar Singh

Technical Editor
Vibhuti Gawde

Copy Editor
Pranjali Chury

Project Coordinator
Vaidehi Sawant

Proofreader
Safis Editing

Indexer
Francy Puthiry

Graphics
Abhinash Sahu

Production Coordinator
Nilesh Mohite

Foreword

Push it down the stack.

Abstract it away to a third-party.

Focus on what's unique to my application.

This book is about the next important step in our never-ending journey to build more sophisticated and scalable applications with less effort and fewer lines of code. If there has been a unifying thread to my career, it's been the relentless pursuit of not worrying about as many aspects of my applications as possible.

To put serverless computing in perspective, consider how your own interaction with the stack has changed over the years. Has it moved in the upward direction?

Did you ever have to worry about an actual data center? That got abstracted into colocation services. What about the physical servers in those managed racks? They went the way of cloud-based VMs. How about configuring, patching, and networking those VMs? On Azure, that got pushed down into cloud services so we could just publish our code and scale at will. But then even the application frameworks got encapsulated into specialized services for mobile backends, websites, asynchronous job processing, and more.

So at this point in the journey, we have a nicely dialed-in platform where we have VMs, but they are so preconfigured and loaded up with useful frameworks that you don't need to think about them that much. However, you may still be creating fairly elaborate projects with more plumbing code than what feels quite right.

Serverless computing is a jump forward from that. The big idea is that you can just write a collection of useful functions (or methods or microservices) with no application container whatsoever. They become available in the cloud at an infinite scale (and low cost) to be invoked at will. The potential to cull and simplify mid-tier code is significant.

I happened to work with this model recently, and it was an eye-opener. My company has an elaborate application implemented on Azure Cloud Services. We had a need to integrate with an external authentication provider whose API was most conveniently accessed via a Node.js library. Having C#.NET skills in house, we were not looking forward to spinning up a new service application to do the Node work. Then we found Azure Functions.

We were able to write a series of 10-line routines that did what we needed, expose them via a RESTful endpoint, and call them from our existing application in a day. We did this without thinking about building a new service or deploying new VMs or considering how it would scale out.

This is just a tip of the iceberg scenario, but it got me thinking about how to architect our services as functions going forward. This will certainly help us spend less time and effort building things, but the elastic properties of how this scales and is paid for are really interesting. Scalability is provided at the function level. There are no underlying VMs in

your account that you need to ramp up or down. Your functions simply run when invoked and you pay for the execution thereof. It's a much more cost-effective model as there are literally no idle resources from your point of view.

Serverless is clearly an exciting new tool for forward thinking architects and developers alike.

All this backstory brings us to your author, Sasha Rosenbaum. I'd like to tell you why I think she's an important voice on the topic at hand. We met at a consultancy specializing in custom software development for the Azure platform. Shortly after she joined, it became clear that she could fearlessly take on any new technology, figure it out quickly, and apply it for customers with all the attention to detail and pride in the work that you could ever want. So I, somewhat selfishly, made sure that she worked on all my projects because I knew the chance of success was going to be 100%.

I personally witnessed her grok and apply tools as diverse as Azure Cloud Services, App Services, and SQL Databases; .NET MVC, Web API, and Entity Framework; hybrid native application development for iOS and Android, Python running on IoT devices, and interactive video. All these over a two-year period! Then a short year after I left the company, she had added DevOps expertise to the list and was booking speaking engagements on the topic.

I mention this because Azure Functions are nascent, with limited real-world examples to draw experience from. You want your guide to not only have really dug into the details, but also to have a breadth of experience from which to put the new technology into perspective. You need help figuring out where it might (or might not) add value to your situation.

I can assure you that Sasha is the right person for the job. She has just the right mix of inquisitive, theoretical, and pragmatic to bring actionable insight to the serverless computing conversation.

I hope you find this book as useful for your work as I have, and I hope that you appreciate the mountain of work and dedication that Sasha put into creating it.

Steve Harshbarger

President and CTO of Monj

About the Author

Sasha Rosenbaum helps Microsoft clients migrate their infrastructure and applications to the cloud, working as a technology solutions professional on the global black belt team. She covers a broad range of products and services available on the Azure platform, and helps clients envision, design, and deploy cloud based applications.

Sasha has been working with Azure since its early days, helping companies on their journey to the cloud, as a consultant. She has a computer science degree from Technion, Israel's Institute of Technology, one of the top 20 CS departments in the world.

Sasha is passionate about the DevOps movement, helping companies adopt a culture of collaboration. Sasha is a co-organizer of the the DevOps Days Chicago conference.

You can visit Sasha's personal blog and follow her on Twitter (@DivineOps).

I would like to express sincere gratitude to my technical reviewers, Donna Malayeri and Mikhail Veselov, for their feedback and insights. Additional thanks goes to Packt for this tremendous opportunity, as well as the entire Packt editorial team that worked with me, for their dedication and effort throughout the publishing process.

Finally, I would like to thank Lou for his unwavering support, which helped me see this project to completion.

I hope you will enjoy this book!

About the Reviewers

Donna Malayeri is a program manager on the Azure Functions team, where she is responsible for the developer experience and the Visual Studio tooling. She previously worked on products such as Azure Mobile Services, Reactive Extensions (Rx), Visual F#, and Scala. She holds a PhD in programming languages from Carnegie Mellon University. In her spare time, she enjoys amateur improve and beadwork. You can follow her on Twitter at `@lindydonna`.

Mikhail Veselov is a professional software developer with over 12 years' experience in .NET-related products. His work with cloud-based applications started in 2011, with various projects completed since that time. He holds two degrees'--in math and computer science--from the Saint-Petersburg State University. He is also a big fan of the bass guitar and origami. You can ask him any question at `vmatm@ya.ru`.

I want to thank all my teachers and people who helped me in my career, especially the Saint-Petersburg Computer Science Center. Personal thanks go to my family, who gave me support in every moment of my life, and to all my friends all over the world.

www.PacktPub.com

For support files and downloads related to your book, please visit www.PacktPub.com.

Did you know that Packt offers eBook versions of every book published, with PDF and ePub files available? You can upgrade to the eBook version at www.PacktPub.com and as a print book customer, you are entitled to a discount on the eBook copy. Get in touch with us at service@packtpub.com for more details.

At www.PacktPub.com, you can also read a collection of free technical articles, sign up for a range of free newsletters and receive exclusive discounts and offers on Packt books and eBooks.

https:/ / www. packtpub. com/ mapt

Get the most in-demand software skills with Mapt. Mapt gives you full access to all Packt books and video courses, as well as industry-leading tools to help you plan your personal development and advance your career.

Why subscribe?

- Fully searchable across every book published by Packt
- Copy and paste, print, and bookmark content
- On demand and accessible via a web browser

Customer Feedback

Thanks for purchasing this Packt book. At Packt, quality is at the heart of our editorial process. To help us improve, please leave us an honest review on this book's Amazon page at `https://www.amazon.com/dp/1787288390`.

If you'd like to join our team of regular reviewers, you can e-mail us at `customerreviews@packtpub.com`. We award our regular reviewers with free eBooks and videos in exchange for their valuable feedback. Help us be relentless in improving our products!

Table of Contents

Preface

Dear reader,

I firmly believe that time is the most valuable resource we have. Thank you for choosing to spend your time with me, learning about Azure serverless compute.

It is hard to believe how far cloud technologies have come in the last decade. serverless compute is a type of technology that was unimaginable just a few years ago and is now rapidly gaining popularity. With the rise in popularity, it is timely to think where serverless compute fits into application development in general. This book aims at providing a hands-on guide to implementing .NET-based Azure serverless functions as well as looking at the bigger picture of designing and maintaining serverless applications.

With this rapid technology advancement, it is only fitting, perhaps, that even during the time of writing of this book, the Azure serverless technology was enhanced a number of times. Every effort has been made to keep the book's content as current as possible. Please keep this in mind as you read, and do not hesitate to reach out if the text needs further revision.

I would like to express sincere gratitude to my technical reviewers, Donna Malayeri, and Mikhail Veselov, for their feedback and support. Additional thanks goes to Packt publishing for this tremendous opportunity, as well as the entire Packt editor team that worked with me, for their dedication and effort throughout the publishing process.

Finally, I would like to thank Lou for his unwavering support that helped me see this project to completion.

What this book covers

Chapter 1, *Understanding the Serverless Architecture*, discusses the features of serverless computing and the type of workloads that are best suited to be hosted in it.

Chapter 2, *Getting Started with Azure Environment*, provides us with a solid introduction to the Azure serverless computing environment and walks us through the deployment of our first Azure Functions application.

Chapter 3, *Setting Up the Development Environment*, gives us an understanding of how to develop a serverless computing application on a local computer using Visual Studio and, then, deploy it to Azure.

Chapter 4, *Configuring Endpoints, Triggers, Bindings, and Scheduling*, explores more advanced options to configure function triggers and input/output parameters as well as to configure custom routes for HTTP-triggered functions.

Chapter 5, *Integrations and Dependencies*, covers more about Azure Functions integrations and dependencies. We will describe how to share common code between different functions in the same Function App and the advantages of doing so.

Chapter 6, *Integrating Azure Functions with Cognitive Services API*, shows you how to use JavaScript, HTML, and CSS to develop a mobile application and how to set up the environment to test run this mobile application.

Chapter 7, *Debugging Your Azure Functions*, discusses the process of debugging the serverless functions. We will discuss both local and online debugging processes, and how to enable cloud-triggered functions to be debugged locally.

Chapter 8, *Testing Your Applications*, walks us through testing best practices in detail and covers the process of testing Azure Functions, focusing primarily on unit and integration testing using the MSTest framework.

Chapter 9, *Configuring Continuous Delivery*, reviews the benefits of using source control, and the benefits of continuous integration and delivery approaches in software development.

Chapter 10, *Securing Your Application*, reviews the different layers of application security as it pertains to serverless computing. We will review the authentication, authorization, and key management of Azure Functions in detail, and provide the steps for configuring different authentication and authorization types.

Chapter 11, *Monitoring your Application*, explains how to monitor the Azure serverless compute performance and application health using Azure native tools.

Chapter 12, *Designing for High Availability, Disaster Recovery, and Scale*, discusses the three major design considerations of building a reliable application: the application's high availability, disaster recovery readiness, and the ability to scale on demand and be prepared to handle high or fluctuating load.

Chapter 13, *Designing Cost-Effective Services*, discusses the pricing of Azure Functions. You will learn how to estimate the cost of serverless computing in Azure. We will also review the pricing of the other PaaS services used in the TextEvaluation application as a function of the expected user traffic load.

Appendix A, *C# Script-Based Functions*, reviews C# script-based functions and discusses the two main implementation differences between script-based and precompiled functions.

Appendix B, *Azure Compute On-Demand Options*, gives a brief overview of additional Azure services that provide compute on-demand capabilities and discusses the different workload types that are best suited for each one.

What you need for this book

This book requires the following two things:

- Access to a Microsoft Azure subscription (a trial account is sufficient)
- Visual Studio 2017 IDE (any edition)

Who this book is for

This book is for the following professionals:

- Software engineers looking for a hands-on guide on .NET-based Azure Functions
- Application architects looking to understand the pros and cons of serverless architecture
- IT professionals looking to understand Azure serverless compute operations management from networking, security, monitoring, and continuous delivery standpoints

Conventions

In this book, you will find a number of text styles that distinguish between different kinds of information. Here are some examples of these styles and an explanation of their meaning. Code words in text, database table names, folder names, filenames, file extensions, pathnames, dummy URLs, user input, and Twitter handles are shown as follows: "Since the `text` variable was not previously defined, the log output will now display a compilation error." A block of code is set as follows:

```
{
"IsEncrypted": false,
"Values": {
"AzureWebJobsStorage":"DefaultEndpointsProtocol=https;
AccountName=textsentimentstorage;AccountKey=<full account
key>",
"AzureWebJobsDashboard": "DefaultEndpointsProtocol=https;
AccountName=textsentimentstorage;AccountKey=<full account key>"
}
}
```

When we wish to draw your attention to a particular part of a code block, the relevant lines or items are set in bold:

```
[default]
exten => s,1,Dial(Zap/1|30)
exten => s,2,Voicemail(u100)
exten => s,102,Voicemail(b100)
exten => i,1,Voicemail(s0)
```

Any command-line input or output is written as follows:

```
Install-Package Microsoft.Azure.Webjobs.Extensions.ApiHub -pre
```

New terms and **important words** are shown in bold. Words that you see on the screen, for example, in menus or dialog boxes, appear in the text like this: "If you do not have any subscriptions listed, click on **add subscription** to add a new Pay-As-You-Go subscription, and follow the creation wizard."

Warnings or important notes appear like this.

Tips and tricks appear like this.

Reader feedback

Feedback from our readers is always welcome. Let us know what you think about this book-what you liked or disliked. Reader feedback is important for us as it helps us develop titles that you will really get the most out of. To send us general feedback, simply e-mail feedback@packtpub.com, and mention the book's title in the subject of your message. If there is a topic that you have expertise in and you are interested in either writing or contributing to a book, see our author guide at www.packtpub.com/authors.

Customer support

Now that you are the proud owner of a Packt book, we have a number of things to help you to get the most from your purchase.

Downloading the example code

You can download the example code files for this book from your account at `http:/ / www. packtpub. com`. If you purchased this book elsewhere, you can visit `http:/ / www. packtpub. com/ support` and register to have the files e-mailed directly to you. You can download the code files by following these steps:

1. Log in or register to our website using your e-mail address and password.
2. Hover the mouse pointer on the **SUPPORT** tab at the top.
3. Click on **Code Downloads & Errata**.
4. Enter the name of the book in the **Search** box.
5. Select the book for which you're looking to download the code files.
6. Choose from the drop-down menu where you purchased this book from.
7. Click on **Code Download**.

Once the file is downloaded, please make sure that you unzip or extract the folder using the latest version of:

- WinRAR / 7-Zip for Windows
- Zipeg / iZip / UnRarX for Mac
- 7-Zip / PeaZip for Linux

The code bundle for the book is also hosted on GitHub at `https:/ / github. com/ PacktPublishing/ Serverless- computing- in- Azure- with- Dot- NET`. We also have other code bundles from our rich catalog of books and videos available at `https:/ / github. com/ PacktPublishing/` . Check them out!

Errata

Although we have taken every care to ensure the accuracy of our content, mistakes do happen. If you find a mistake in one of our books-maybe a mistake in the text or the code-we would be grateful if you could report this to us. By doing so, you can save other readers from frustration and help us improve subsequent versions of this book. If you find any errata, please report them by visiting `http:/ / www. packtpub. com/ submit- errata`, selecting your book, clicking on the **Errata Submission Form** link, and entering the details of your errata. Once your errata are verified, your submission will be accepted and the errata will be uploaded to our website or added to any list of existing errata under the Errata section of that title. To view the previously submitted errata, go to `https:/ / www. packtpub. com/ books/ content/ support` and enter the name of the book in the search field. The required information will appear under the **Errata** section.

Piracy

Piracy of copyrighted material on the Internet is an ongoing problem across all media. At Packt, we take the protection of our copyright and licenses very seriously. If you come across any illegal copies of our works in any form on the Internet, please provide us with the location address or website name immediately so that we can pursue a remedy. Please contact us at `copyright@packtpub.com` with a link to the suspected pirated material. We appreciate your help in protecting our authors and our ability to bring you valuable content.

Questions

If you have a problem with any aspect of this book, you can contact us at `questions@packtpub.com`, and we will do our best to address the problem.

1
Understanding Serverless Architecture

This chapter provides a theoretical introduction into serverless computing, and the types of workloads it is best suited for.

In this chapter, we will cover the following topics:

- The features of serverless computing
- Serverless compute best practices
- Serverless computing advantages and disadvantages
- The types of services and applications that are a good fit for serverless

Being a technical person, you might be tempted to skip the theory and dive into practice. It is highly advised, however, that you read the next few pages before diving into implementation details.

What is serverless?

Being an emerging trend in the technology world, serverless computing is rapidly gaining popularity. The most wide-spread definition of serverless at this point is driven by the arrival of technologies such as AWS Lambda, Azure Functions, IBM OpenWhisk, and Google Cloud Functions:

> **Serverless computing** *is a code execution model where server-side logic is run in stateless, event-triggered, ephemeral compute containers that are fully managed by a third-party.*

This definition of serverless is synonymous with **Functions as a Service** (**FaaS**). We will use these terms interchangeably in this book.

In different programming languages, we may encounter the terms "function", "procedure", and "method" referring to different types of routines performing a task. In this context, the term function is not programming language specific, but rather conceptual:

*In programming, a **function** is a named section of a program that performs a specific task.*

Ironically, serverless computing does not actually run without servers. Rather, it involves outsourcing the server provisioning and management to a third-party.

Nearly all existing serverless computing technologies are provided by major public cloud vendors. The sheer scale of today's public cloud vendors allows for the following two things that make serverless more attractive than ever before:

- **Realizing the cost benefits of the economy of scale**: For any specific development team, or even organization, it would be difficult to reach the scale at which outsourcing parts of the application to separately managed compute containers provides worthwhile cost benefits. At public cloud vendors' scale, serverless compute becomes inexpensive because the compute power allocation is balanced across thousands of servers and billions of executions, with each specific client application peaking at different times. The nature of software-defined data centers also allows for more efficient server allocation.
- **Minimizing the adverse effects of vendor lock-in:** The modern IT world is rapidly coming to a consensus that the benefits of public cloud outweigh the disadvantages of any vendor lock-in that comes with it. With many IT services moving to public cloud, it becomes easier and more beneficial to leverage a cloud provider for hosting serverless applications.

 With the arrival of Azure Functions Runtime, you can truly run your functions on any server, whether in the cloud or in an on-premises data center, eliminating the vendor lock-in concerns.

By now, you are probably familiar with some variation of a "shared responsibility" diagram outlining the differences between IaaS, PaaS, and SaaS. Let's add a visual to show where **Functions as a Service** (**FaaS**) fits in:

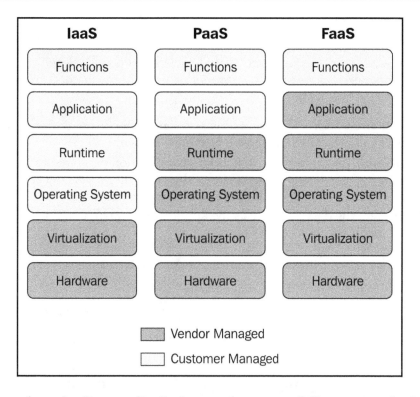

As you can see from the diagram, FaaS takes vendor responsibility one step further, abstracting away the application context along with the physical hardware and virtual servers.

For this reason, despite the book title, I, personally, think that the term serverless is not completely accurate, and the actual architectural approach we are working with would be better described by the term **Applicationless**.

Azure serverless

The Azure serverless offering is called Azure Functions.

The implementation details of serverless computing differ by vendor, and it is difficult to overview the serverless computing features without being vendor-specific. This book is dedicated to Azure Functions, and thus will focus on Azure-specific features whenever there is difference between vendors.

Architecture

To illustrate where serverless computing would come into your application, let's take a look at a classic three-tier architecture. In this commonly used approach, the application is broken down into the following tiers:

- **Presentation Tier:** The presentation tier handles the user interface and typically operates as a thin client on a web or mobile device.
- **Logic Tier:** The logic tier, also known as application tier, handles the functional process logic and the business rules of the application. This tier can serve one or more presentation tier clients and scale independently.
- **Data Tier:** The data tier persists the application data in databases or file shares and handles the data access layer.

Any of these tiers can be further expanded and broken into separate services. For a deeper dive into three-tier architecture, please visit the following link:

`https://en.wikipedia.org/wiki/Multitier_architecture#Three-tier_architecture`

A basic three-tier architecture can be presented as the diagram below:

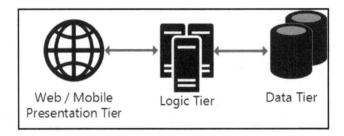

With the introduction of serverless computing, all, or parts of your application's logic tier can be replaced by serverless computing containers, or FaaS.

Depending on an application, functions can handle all of the business logic, or work jointly with other types of services to comprise the logic tier.

A basic three-tier architecture with the logic tier fully handled by functions can be presented as the following diagram:

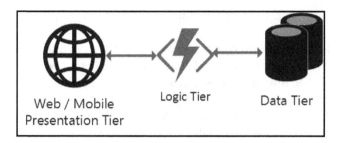

It is crucial to note that not all types of functionality typically handled by the business logic tier are well suited for FaaS. To see which functionality can be replaced by FaaS, let us discuss the inherent features of serverless computing.

Inherent features

The following list outlines the inherent features of serverless computing, which also dictate the implementation best practices. In some cases, the best practices are imposed by the serverless provider, while in others they remain a developer responsibility.

Asynchronous

Serverless computing is event-triggered and asynchronous by nature. It is therefore important to use non-blocking, awaitable calls in functions.

Stateless

Serverless computing is inherently stateless, meaning that no state should be maintained on the host machine. This also means not sharing state between any parallel or sequential function executions. Any required state needs to be persisted to a database, a file server, or a cache.

In recent years, the stateless approach was made popular by the Twelve-Factor methodology, and many applications have already been refactored to use stateless web and logic tiers. The following quote is from the Twelve Factor App Methodology, factor 6:

> **VI. Processes**
> *Execute the app as one or more stateless processes*
> **Twelve-Factor processes are stateless and share nothing.** *Any data that needs to persist must be stored in a stateful backing service, typically a database.*

To learn more about the Twelve-Factor Methodology, please visit `https://12factor.net`.

While the Twelve-Factor Methodology is increasingly popular, and makes applications easy to deploy and scale, the restriction of local state is not always a good thing. The main benefit of local state is the low latency of access, and some applications cannot attain optimal performance without it. As an example, when building an application used to trade in a financial market, persisting state to a database or even a cache can become extremely costly. Applications that require local state would not be a good fit for serverless computing. To learn more about stateful alternatives, please look into Azure Service Fabric stateful services:

`https://docs.microsoft.com/en-us/azure/service-fabric/service-fabric-reliable-services-introduction`

Note that some of the serverless computing vendors completely prevent you from accessing the host machine. With Azure Functions, you do have read/write access to the host machine's virtual D drive, however, it is highly recommended that you don't use it to persist state.

Idempotent and defensive

To ensure consistency, serverless computing functions should be idempotent.

Mathematically, a function is idempotent if, whenever it is applied twice to any value, it gives the same result as if it were applied once, that is, $f(f(x)) \equiv f(x)$.

To give a simple example of a non-idempotent function, imagine a function with a task of calculating a square root of the input number. If the function is run a second time on an input value that has already been processed, it will result in an incorrect output, as $\sqrt{(\sqrt{(x)})} \neq \sqrt{(x)}$. Thus, the only way to ensure that the function remains idempotent is making sure that the same input isn't processed twice.

In an asynchronous, highly parallelized environment ran by ephemeral compute containers, we need to work extra hard to ensure that execution errors will not impact all of the subsequent events. What happens when a function crashes midway through encoding a large media file? What happens if a function tasked with processing 100 rows in a database crashes before finishing? Will the remainder of the input remain unprocessed, or will its already processed part be re-processed?

To ensure consistency, we need to store the required state information with our data, allowing a function to exit gracefully if no more processing is required. In addition, we need to implement a circuit-breaker pattern to ensure that a failing function will not retry infinitely. To learn more about the circuit-breaker pattern, please visit the following link:

```
https://docs.microsoft.com/en-us/azure/architecture/patterns/circuit-breaker
```

Azure Functions in particular have some built-in defensive mechanisms that you can leverage. For instance, for a storage queue triggered function, a queue message processing will be retried five times in case of failure, after which it will be dropped to a poison-message queue.

Execution restrictions

In comparison to a traditional application, a FaaS environment has two very important execution restrictions: the length of time the function can run and the time it takes to start the first function execution after a period of inactivity.

Limited execution time

In a FaaS environment, the runtime of each particular function execution should be as short as possible.

Some vendors impose hard limits on the functions' execution time, limiting the runtime to a few minutes. These limits impose a certain style of programming, but can get cumbersome to deal with.

Azure Functions are offered under two different hosting plans: a Consumption plan and an App Service plan. The Consumption plan scales dynamically on-demand, while an App Service plan always has at least one VM instance provisioned. Because of the different approaches to resource provisioning, these plans have different execution constraints.

Under the App Service plan there is no limit on the function execution time.

Under the Consumption plan there is a default limit of 5 minutes, which can be increased up to 10 minutes by making a change in the function configuration.

Even under the App Service plan, however, it is highly recommended to keep the function execution time as short as possible. A long running function can be broken down into shorter functions that each perform a particular task.

For very long running and/or compute-intensive work, consider a different type of **Compute as a Service** -Azure Batch. You can refer to the following link for more information on Azure Batch:

`https://docs.microsoft.com/en-us/azure/batch/batch-technical-overview.`

Startup latency

In a FaaS environment, the functions should be kept as light as possible. Loading many explicit or implicit external dependencies (when a library you reference loads many additional modules it relies on) can increase the function load time and even cause timeouts. Thus, functions should keep their external dependencies to a minimum.

In addition, in most FaaS environments, functions face a significantly increased cold start latency. After a period of inactivity an unused function goes idle. The next time the function is loaded, compute and memory will need to be allocated to it, external dependencies will need to be loaded, and, in the case of compiled languages like C#, the code needs to be re-compiled. All of these factors can cause a significant delay in function startup time.

In Azure C# based functions specifically, the cold start problem has been alleviated with the release of .NET Class Library based functions, since the functions are precompiled and can be loaded more quickly. In addition, when running under the App Service plan (rather than a Consumption plan), the cold start problem is eliminated.

Advantages of serverless computing

The advantages of FaaS can be grouped into a few categories.

Some of the advantages exist in most PaaS environments, however, they may be more pronounced in a FaaS environment.

Some of the advantages are similar to the advantages of the Microservices architecture, in which the application is structured as a collection of loosely coupled services, each of which handles a particular task. To learn more about Microservices architecture, please visit `http://microservices.io/patterns/microservices.html.`

Lastly, some of the advantages are specific to the FaaS environment only.

Scalability

Serverless computing makes it very easy to scale the application out by provisioning more compute power as required, and deallocating it when the demand is low. This allows developers to avoid the risk of failing their users during peak demand, while also avoiding the cost of allocating massive standby infrastructure.

This makes serverless computing particularly useful for applications experiencing inconsistent traffic. Let's take a look at the following examples:

- **An application used during sporting events**: In this case, your application is likely to experience highly variable traffic loads, with a significant difference between high and low traffic. Serverless can help mitigate the complexity and cost of providing adequate service.

- **A retail application**: It is common for retail applications to experience extremely high loads during holiday seasons or during marketing campaigns. While these loads are predictable, they often differ so significantly from the day-to-day load, that maintaining the required standby infrastructure can get very costly. Serverless can eliminate the need for standby infrastructure.

- **A periodic social media update application**: Imagine an application which posts an update to a Twitter feed once every hour. This application requires very little compute power. In the traditional IT world, such an application would typically run on two servers to ensure resiliency, which is extremely wasteful from the compute power standpoint. Deploying multiple applications to the same server can often become problematic for operational/organizational reasons, and in most organizations, the on-premises compute power is heavily underutilized (on-premises, teams tend to significantly over-provision hardware because it is quite difficult to add more compute power in the future). Serverless computing fits very well to solve this problem.

It is important to note that the scalability advantage exists in every PaaS service, however, with serverless computing, the scaling typically is completely dynamic and handled by the vendor. This means that while in a typical PaaS service, you will need to define metrics (such as high CPU or memory utilization) and, to an extent, define the scaling procedure (such as a number of additional nodes to provision or whether or not the application needs to scale back down after the demand decreases) with serverless computing, the vendor will simply allocate additional compute to your function based on the number of requests coming in.

Pay-As-You-Go

In serverless computing, you only pay for what you use. The Pay-As-You-Go model is likely to result in cost savings in most cases (remember the underutilized infrastructure), and becomes particularly beneficial in the inconsistent traffic scenarios described in the previous section. The model also means that any speed optimization of your service translates directly into cost savings.

Pay-As-You-Go is also an advantage of any PaaS service, however, most PaaS services do not get as granular in allocating compute power.

While the translation of execution time to cost is a lot more direct in an FaaS environment, it is wise to calculate whether or not the dynamic compute allocation is actually the best pricing model for your application. We will discuss cost-effective services design in more detail in `Chapter 13`, *Designing for High Availibility Disaster Recovery and Scale*.

Reduced operational costs

In a serverless computing environment, you do not need to provision, manage, patch, or secure servers. You are outsourcing the management of both the physical hardware and the virtual servers, operational systems, networking, and security to the serverless computing vendor. This provides cost savings in the following two ways:

- Direct infrastructure cost
- IT operations cost

This advantage also exists in any PaaS services, and for a FaaS service it may actually not be as straightforward as it seems. While there are very clear cost benefits to not managing servers, it is important to remember that operations typically cover a lot more than server management, including tasks such as application deployment, monitoring, and security. More on this in the next section.

Speed of deployment

Serverless computing makes it incredibly easy to go from an idea to execution. Whether proving the business value of an idea or needing a sandbox to test a scenario, the ease of creating new business logic layer with serverless computing provides an excellent ability to test drive your minimal viable product.

Independent technology stack and updates

Similar to Microservices architecture, FaaS forces a pattern of breaking the logic layer into smaller, task-specific services. This provides the following tangible benefits:

- **Versioning the services independently of one another**: In a monolithic application, changing even a small part of business logic will trigger a redeployment of the entire monolith. In a FaaS environment, each function handles a particular task, and thus the implementation of each function can be changed independently, as long as the contract with the services upstream and downstream of the function is maintained. This can have a tremendous effect on the agility and flexibility of the application update process.

- **Freedom to use a different technology stack for each service**: In a monolith application, the developer is committed to a particular technology stack, whether or not it is well suited for the task at hand. In a FaaS environment, the developer is free to implement each task in the way best suited for the job, and most serverless computing vendors provide a number of different languages/platforms to choose from. If part of your application can benefit from Python's powerful tooling for processing regular expressions, you can easily deploy a Python-based Azure Function along with your C#-based functions, either packaged in the same Function App or separately. This freedom can greatly improve code efficiency and simplicity.

 In Azure Functions, specifically, the continuous delivery setup deploys the entire Function App, not a single function, so in cases where a function needs to often change independently, it is best if it is deployed as a separate Function App. We will discuss the Function versus Function App topic in more detail in the next chapter.

Integration with the cloud provider

Existing serverless frameworks are closely integrated with other services offered by the same public cloud vendor. They make it easy to trigger the functions based on events in other cloud services and store the outputs in cloud data stores. They are hosted on the same infrastructure, which makes for minimal latency. As such, serverless functions are ideal for augmentation of other cloud services with bits of custom code performing tasks that aren't offered as a fully managed service.

Open source

While they are fully managed by the Microsoft engineering, Azure Functions are an open source offering based on the Azure WebJobs SDK, which means that as a developer you could contribute quality code and help develop required features or resolve issues.

To learn more about Azure Functions and the Azure WebJobs SDK, visit `https://github.com/Azure/Azure-Functions`.

Disadvantages of serverless computing

The following section outlines the current disadvantages of leveraging serverless computing.

Some of these disadvantages arise from additional complexity of the application architecture. Others stem from the lack of maturity of current serverless environments tooling and the problems that come with outsourcing parts of your system.

Distributed system complexity

Similar to the Microservices architecture, serverless introduces increased system complexity and a requirement for network communication between application layers. The added complexity centers around the following two main aspects:

- **Implicit interfaces between services**: As discussed earlier, functions make the application changes easier by allowing for separate versioning of services. This, however, introduces an implicit contract between different parts of the system, that could be broken by one of the sides. In a monolith application, breaking changes can be easily caught by the compiler or integration testing. In a FaaS environment, a developer could make a breaking change without impact awareness.

- **Network and queueing**: In a FaaS environment, parts of the application communicate with each other using HTTP requests or queueing mechanisms. This introduces additional latency, adds a dependency on queueing services, and makes handling errors and retries significantly more complex.

Potential load on downstream components

When relying on the inherent dynamic scalability of the serverless computing for the business logic layer, it is easy to miss the potential overload on the downstream components such as databases and file stores. During the design and testing phases of the application development, it is crucial to verify that downstream components are able to handle the potential high load created by the dynamic scaling of the serverless computing tier.

Potential for repetitive code

The assumption of the three-tier architecture is that the business logic tier can serve multiple different clients, such as various web and mobile devices, different consumer APIs, and so on. When the entire business logic tier is moved into serverless computing, certain functionality is likely to be moved upstream to client applications. This can introduce a situation in which each client application is implementing the same functionality.

Different operations

As we've discussed, the server administration and scaling out is fully handled by the serverless computing vendor. However, this benefit comes with a trade-off. You are still fully responsible for testing, deploying, and monitoring your application. You are also responsible for the application security, as well as for ensuring that it will perform correctly and consistently at scale. With serverless computing, you may be presented with a new set of tools for managing all of the preceding tools that may not integrate well with your current ops stack. Needing to train your team on the new tool stack can be a drawback.

Security and monitoring

With serverless computing offers being new, their security and monitoring tools are also new and often very specific to the serverless environment and the particular vendor. This introduces new complexity into the process of managing operations for the application overall, adding a new type of service to manage. Security and monitoring of Azure Functions will be discussed in depth in Chapter 10, *Securing Your Application* and Chapter 11, *Monitoring Your Application*.

Testing

Testing can become more difficult in a serverless environment due to the following few aspects:

- For the purposes of Integration testing, it is sometimes difficult to replicate the full cloud-based flow on a testing machine.
- The more distributed the system becomes, the more dependencies and points of failure are introduced, and the harder it becomes to test for every possible variation of the flow
- Load testing becomes an even more crucial aspect of testing the application, as some issues may only arise at scale

We will discuss testing of serverless applications in more detail in Chapter 8, *Testing Your Azure Functions*.

Vendor control

Unlike vendor lock-in, vendor control implies that by outsourcing a big part of your operations management to a third-party, you also relinquish control over how these operations are handled. This includes the service limitations, the scaling mechanism, and the potential optimization of hosting your application.

In addition, the vendor has the ultimate control over the environment and tooling, deciding when to roll out features and fix issues (although in the case of Azure Functions, you can help fix issues by contributing to the open source project).

Vendor lock-in

Despite the theoretical portability of implementation code used in functions, the surrounding features and tooling make it relatively difficult to deploy the application with another vendor.

For Azure Functions, specifically, Microsoft has recently released the Azure Functions Runtime, which allows you to run functions on your own server. With Azure Functions Runtime, you can run functions on-premises or even in a different public cloud, which allows you to avoid vendor lock-in. For more information, visit https://docs.microsoft.com/en-us/azure/azure-functions/functions-runtime-overview.

Multitenancy

Just a few years ago, multitenancy used to be on top of the list of concerns of organizations considering leveraging the public cloud. However, multitenancy is also what enables public clouds to become more cost-effective and more innovative than private data centers. In particular, the cost benefits of dynamically allocated serverless computing arise from the economy of scale, which is made possible by utilizing the same infrastructure to serve many different client applications at different times.

At present, most organizations have accepted that public cloud vendors are committed to ensuring that as a customer, you will get the same security isolation and dedicated resources allocation in a public cloud as you would in a single-tenant environment.

Vendor-specific limitations

Some disadvantages of serverless computing are vendor-specific and luckily do not apply to Azure Functions. We will overview them briefly here, as you may see references to them online:

- **Environment configuration**: In some serverless computing environments, it is difficult to set environment-specific variables (for instance, `dev`/`test`/`prod` settings) for each function. In Azure Functions, each Function App has a `local.settings.json` file that defines configuration settings in a manner similar to traditional .NET applications. In an Azure environment, these settings are located in the Function App. This also means that the recommended approach is to deploy `dev`, `test`, `prod`, or other environments into separate Function Apps. More on the concept of Function Apps will be covered in `Chapter 2`, *Getting Started with Azure Environment*.

- **Local development tools and debugging**: With most serverless computing vendors, there is a noticeable lack of local development tools for functions. The lack of local tools can make it significantly harder to debug or troubleshoot the application. With C# precompiled Azure Functions, the Visual Studio development tools are on par with the rich development environment of traditional .NET applications.

- **Service grouping**: With some serverless computing vendors, it is not possible to deploy functions that are part of the same applications as a group, which places more load on the deployment team. Azure Functions allow you to deploy functions, even those written in different languages, together as a part of the same Function App, or separately as part of different Functions Apps.

- **Execution time limit**: Under the Consumption plan, the default function execution time limit is currently 5 minutes, and can be extended to 10 minutes. Under the App Service plan, there is no hard execution time limit on a function execution. Thus, when you need a longer-running function, you can choose the App Service plan (although this has cost and dynamic scaling implications).

- **Cold start issues**: Under the Consumption plan, after a period of idleness, functions may experience cold start issues while the infrastructure is being provisioned. Under the App Service plan, functions get at least one dedicated instance at all times, and hence there are no cold start issues. Thus, when you need the function to start up quickly after a period of idleness, you can choose an App Service plan.

- **Separate API Gateway configuration**: With some serverless computing vendors, an API Gateway may be required to gain access to your functions via HTTP requests. With Azure Functions, the function endpoint URL is automatically provisioned for every HTTP triggered function, making the configuration significantly simpler. The endpoint URL is encrypted with TLS and can also be easily configured to utilize different types of authentication. More on the endpoint configuration and security will be covered in the later chapters of this book.

To read more on some of the serverless computing advantages and disadvantages, please review this excellent post by Mike Roberts at `https://martinfowler.com/articles/serverless.html`.

Applications

Given all of the things outlined in this chapter, it becomes clear that for most applications, it is easier to view FaaS as a component augmenting your overall application architecture, rather than an environment completely handling the business logic layer.

The following types of workloads are best suited for a serverless environment:

- Asynchronous
- Event-driven
- Stateless
- Fast

The following types of workloads will benefit the most in serverless environment:

- Characterized by variable load
- Requiring massive horizontal scale
- Event-driven
- Augmenting other cloud services
- Standalone (needing a different toolset or version than the rest of the application)

For the right type of workload, serverless computing provides excellent benefits. Serverless computing can bring significant cost savings (discussed in more detail in Chapter 13, *Designing High Availibility, Disaster Recovery, and Scale*) and the advantages of completely dynamic scaling based on load.

Summary

In this chapter, we discussed the features of serverless computing and the type of workloads that are best suited to be hosted in it. In the following two chapters, we will dive into an implementation of our first serverless function.

We will start in the next chapter with an overview of Azure cloud and tooling and proceed to deploy our first "Hello world" function using Azure Functions Portal.

2
Getting Started with the Azure Environment

This chapter will cover the full setup and configuration of the Azure serverless computing environment (Azure Functions) and deploying our first "Hello World" application into it.

The first part of this chapter will cover the basics of getting access to the Microsoft Azure Cloud. If you are already familiar with Microsoft Azure and have access to an Azure account and a subscription, you may choose to skip to Azure serverless computing section.

During the course of this chapter, we will cover the following topics:

- Learning how to set up a new Azure account and subscription and accessing the Management Portal
- Understanding the Azure serverless computing environment
- Deploying an HTTP-triggered Azure Function using the Functions Portal
- Understanding environment settings and the definition of a function
- Learning how to clean up Azure resources

As discussed in the previous chapter, serverless computing offers are vendor-specific. While the architectural concepts may be the same across different vendors, the technical tools each vendor provides may differ greatly. In this chapter, we will cover some of the Microsoft Azure Cloud design and features which are important to understand when getting started with Azure serverless computing.

Microsoft Azure Cloud

Azure is a public cloud computing platform powered by Microsoft. Microsoft Azure was first made available to the public in February 2010. Azure data centers are currently available in 40 regions across many countries and are expanding at a rapid rate. Azure offers a variety of IaaS, PaaS, and SaaS products. In addition to native Azure products and services, thousands of third-party products can be hosted on the Azure platform.

In this book, we will focus on a native Azure service called the Azure Functions, which is Microsoft's primary offer for serverless computing.

The Azure Functions is a **Functions as a Service (FaaS)** offering. As discussed earlier, in a typical **Platform as a Service (PaaS)** offering, you are responsible for managing your application and data layers, while the vendor manages the hardware, middleware, OS, servers, and networking. In a FaaS environment, the vendor also manages the application context, and you can focus solely on implementing a particular function - writing code that accomplishes a specific goal.

Azure account

An Azure (billing) account is an account that is used for billing and management purposes of Azure subscriptions. An Azure account grants access to the Azure Billing portal, where you can create and manage Azure subscriptions. There are two types of Azure accounts, personal and organizational:

- **Personal account**: If you are accessing Azure for personal use, you will need to create an Azure Billing account prior to creating a subscription. In this case, an Azure account can be created using a personal Microsoft account (former live ID). A Microsoft account can be created using *any* e-mail provider. You can sign up for a free Microsoft account at https://account.microsoft.com.
- **Organizational account**: If you are getting access to Azure through an organization, you may or may not have access to the billing portal. Even if you don't have access to billing, you can still get access to Azure resources by being granted permissions over one or more Azure subscriptions.

Here are a few different ways in which you can get access to an Azure account and subscription for development purposes:

- Sign up for a free personal trial account using a personal Microsoft account.

- Create a personal Pay-As-You-Go account using a personal Microsoft account.

- Use an MSDN subscription monthly Azure benefit which comes with a certain amount of monthly Azure credit. You can use a Microsoft account or an organizational account that has access to an MSDN subscription.

- Use a corporate Azure account (an organizational account).

If you are going to use a personal Azure account, please visit this page to get started `https://account.windowsazure.com`.

If you intend to use an organizational Azure account, contact your administrator to request access.

Azure subscription

An Azure subscription is a logical grouping of Azure resources for billing and access management purposes. While an Azure account gives you access to the Azure Billing portal, an Azure subscription gives you access to an Azure Management Portal, where you deploy Azure compute resources. You can have many Azure subscriptions under the same Azure account.

Note that your Azure usage will be billed per subscription. In a corporate environment, separating applications between subscriptions is the easiest way to provide a chargeback to the appropriate business unit.

For the purpose of this book, we will stick to free service tiers whenever possible to minimize Azure compute costs, but we will still incur some costs for using the cloud compute power. A free trial Azure account should be sufficient to implement all the examples in this book, as long as you do not trigger millions of executions.

Subscription constraints

Depending on the type of resource or service, there may be a quota on the number of resources that can be deployed into a single subscription. For instance, there is a limitation on the number of cores and the number of storage accounts in the subscription. There are both soft and hard limits. By default, the subscription is deployed with the soft limit, which can then be increased up to the hard limit by calling Microsoft support.

During the development covered in this book, we will never exceed any default limits. In production environments, however, especially for large scale applications, the subscription limits are very important for planning.

Refer to `https://docs.microsoft.com/en-us/azure/azure-subscription-service-limits` for more information on subscription constraints.

Creating a subscription

Let's create an Azure subscription by performing the following steps:

1. After you have created your Azure account, sign into the Azure Billing Portal at `https://account.windowsazure.com` and click on **subscriptions** to see the list of all the subscriptions you have access to:

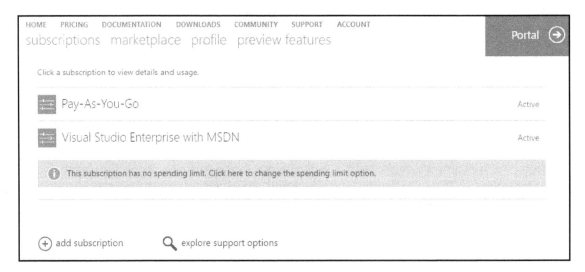

2. If you do not have any subscriptions listed, click on **add subscription** to add a new Pay-As-You-Go subscription, and follow the creation wizard.

3. After the subscription has been created, you can sign in into the the Azure Management Portal to access Azure compute resources.

Azure Management APIs

Azure resources can be managed through two APIs: the older classic (Azure Service Manager) API and the new Azure Resource Manager API. The recommended deployment model/API is the new Azure Resource Manager API, and most new features and services are only being released for the new API. In this book, we will stick to using the Azure Resource Manager API. When using online documentation, note which deployment model/API is referenced so that you can avoid confusion.

One of the most important differences between the APIs lies in access control. In the Azure Resource Manager API, it is possible to grant granular access from subscription level down to a single resource level and assign different access roles from the reader to the owner of the resource. In the classic API, the access is granted as an all-or-nothing administrative access at a subscription level.

API access

Both Azure management APIs can be accessed in a number of ways. In the API descriptions below, the provided links cover only the Resource Manager API, since this is the recommended API.

The access methods are as follows:

- **Azure Management Portal - GUI**: This is the control option we will use in most examples in this book.

- **REST API**: The Azure REST API allows developers to deploy and manage Azure resources using REST calls. To learn more, visit `https://docs.microsoft.com/en-us/azure/azure-resource-manager/resource-manager-rest-api`.

- **PowerShell**: PowerShell is a command-line shell and scripting language that allows you (among other things) to manage Azure resources. To learn more, visit `https://docs.microsoft.com/en-us/azure/azure-resource-manager/powershell-azure-resource-manager`.

- **Azure CLI 2.0**: Azure CLIs are cross-platform command-line tools that can be run on Windows, Linux, or Mac and used to manage Azure resources. To learn more, visit `https://docs.microsoft.com/en-us/azure/azure-resource-manager/xplat-cli-azure-resource-manager`.

- **Azure SDKs**: Azure SDKs allow developers to manage Azure resources in code in a number of programming languages. To learn more, visit `https://docs.microsoft.com/en-us/azure/#pivot=sdkstools`.

- **Azure Resource Manager Templates (in Resource Manager API only)**: These are covered in the section that follows.

Most of the examples in this book will be given using the Azure Management Portal. However, it is important to keep in mind that the portal is calling the Azure Resource Manager API behind the scenes, and the same management actions can be performed using any of the tools mentioned. While the GUI is easy to use, especially during the first learning stages, the other management tools are invaluable when it comes to automation.

The Azure Resource Manager API

The Azure Resource Manager API is an API designed for use on a massive scale, which makes it easier to parallelize management operations. The Azure Resource Manager API has an object-oriented approach, and treats every resource in Azure as an object. These resources can be nested or connected together when needed.

For instance, in the Azure IaaS realm, you can host a virtual machine (VM) that has a network interface (NIC), which has a public IP, on a Virtual Network (VNet) in Azure. The VM, the NIC, the public IP, and the virtual network are all resources that can be managed together or independently through the Azure Resource Manager API.

Resource groups

The resources can be grouped into **resource groups**, which provide logical containers for all related resources. The grouping of resources into resource groups is up to you--you can choose to group them by application, by resource type, by environment, and so on.

Resource groups are also a logical container in terms of **Role-Based Access Control (RBAC)**, which allows you to assign management roles (owner, contributor, reader, and so on) to users or user groups. RBAC roles can also be assigned at subscription or even specific resource levels.

Azure Resource Manager templates

Any resource in the Azure Resource Manager API can be defined as a JSON template. An Azure Resource Manager template is a declarative JSON file, which defines the Azure resources in a resource group and the dependencies between them. You can define an entire application in an Azure Resource Manager template and deploy it to Azure as a whole. Azure Resource Manager templates can be very useful for building continuous deployment pipelines.

To learn more, visit `https://docs.microsoft.com/en-us/azure/azure-resource-manager/resource-group-overview#template-deployment`.

Azure Management Portal

The Azure Management Portal is the GUI portal that provides access to Azure resources. Here, you can deploy and manage resources in all the subscriptions you have access to. We will use the Azure Management Portal to deploy the serverless computing application. To browse to the Azure Management Portal, navigate to `https://portal.azure.com`

Upon the first sign-in, your portal landing page will look as shown in the following screenshot. The main dashboard and the left management pane are fully customizable. You can pin the services you use often to the main dashboard. You can also unpin resources or customize the tile size. To learn more, visit `https://docs.microsoft.com/en-us/azure/azure-portal/azure-portal-dashboards`.

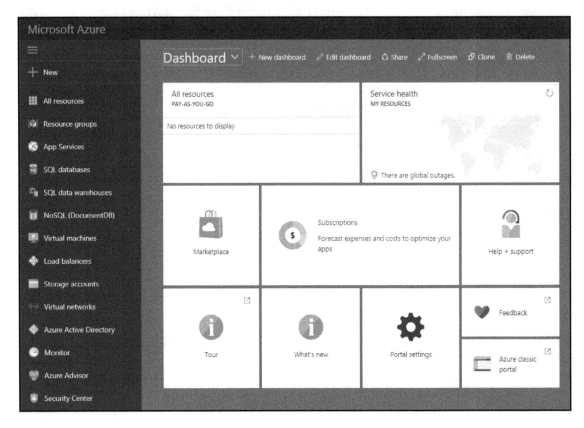

In the left-hand side pane, you can also "star" the types of services you browse often to make them stay on the panel. You can also click on browse (arrow icon) on the bottom of this pane and type the service name into the free text search.

Azure serverless computing

The Azure serverless computing offering is called Azure Functions.

Azure offers a number of other "compute-on-demand" services in which you aren't required to manage servers, such as Azure WebJobs and Azure Batch. These services are not Functions as a Service, and are best suited for background or batch processing. These services will be covered in the `Appendix A`, *Azure Compute On-Demand Options*.

Hosting Plan

There are two options for hosting plans for the Azure Functions: the **Consumption Plan** and the **App Service Plan**.

With an **App Service plan**, you host the application on Azure App Service.

In general, App Service is a Platform as a Service offering for hosting web or mobile applications on Azure. If you have a web development background, you can think of App Service as an IIS as a service. When deploying a .Net Web Application (as we will see in `Chapter 3`, *Setting Up the Development Environment*, when deploying a results dashboard), you will only need to take care of your application code. The Azure platform will take care of everything from IIS and down, including OS, patching, virtualization, hardware, high availability, and scale. The environment can be scaled manually, on schedule, or based on metrics (such as high CPU), and the platform will seamlessly provide more instances to host the application.

In the context of the Azure Functions on an App Service plan, App Service serves as a container to host the application with one or more functions. An advantage of using an App Service plan is that it has dedicated compute resources. This helps avoid the issues with the delay of loading a cold function from storage and removes execution time limits for long-running functions.

The **App Service Plan** option also enables a number of additional features, which will be covered in later chapters. The disadvantages of the App Service plan are the higher pricing and the lack of a truly dynamic scale.

With a **Consumption plan**, the compute for your functions is allocated dynamically. This means that your application can scale rapidly to numerous compute instances when there is a spike in demand, and it can scale down to zero servers when no executions are required. With a Consumption plan, you are billed at a very low cost, on per-execution basis.

Function App

A Function App can be comprised of one or more individual functions that are hosted together. These functions do not have to be of the same type or even written in the same language.

When deploying functions from source control or a continuous delivery pipeline, the Function App represents the smallest deployment unit (i.e. the separate functions in the Function App cannot be deployed independently).

Azure Function

An Azure Function consists of function code and configuration. The function code is what is going to be executed when the function is triggered. The function configuration defines, among other things, the function's input and output bindings. The input bindings determine when and how the function code will be triggered.

Deploying a function

In this section, we will walk through the step-by-step deployment of our first serverless Azure Function using the Azure Management Portal.

Creating an Azure serverless environment

To create your first Azure Function, navigate to Azure Management Portal at `https://portal.azure.com`. In the left-hand side pane, navigate to **New** | **Compute** | **Function App**. The parameters in the following screenshot will be explained next:

Let's take a moment to elaborate on the Function App deployment parameters.

The App name parameter

The App name parameter is the DNS prefix that your application will be assigned. Once deployed, your application will be publicly routable via `[YourAppName].azurewebsites.net`. The name (DNS prefix) needs to be unique within the `azurewebsites.net` domain.

Note that a custom domain name can be assigned to your application. We will cover the custom domain name configuration in `Chapter 10`, *Securing Your Application*.

In Azure serverless computing, HTTP-triggered functions are automatically assigned a public endpoint and do not require an API Gateway. The `https://[YourAppName].azurewebsites.net` URL will be the base URL for your functions' endpoints.

In this book, we will be working on a text sentiment analytics application, hence we will choose `TextEvaluation` as the application name. Note that you will have to choose a different name or append a suffix if the name you want to use already exists.

The Subscription parameter

The Azure subscription under which your application will be deployed.

The Resource Group parameter

A resource group is a logical grouping unit for Azure resources. It is a logical container that makes it easier to access and manage related resources. Resource groups are also indicated in your billing statements, making it easier to identify which application/environment the charge is for.

For the purposes of this book, all the resources we provide belong to the same application and environment, and will be deployed into the same resource group. Let's call this resource group "serverless".

The Hosting Plan parameter

As mentioned earlier, the Azure Functions have two options for hosting: the Consumption plan and the App Service plan.

The Consumption plan is the default pricing plan, which is billed based on resource consumption and the number of executions. Resource consumption is measured in gigabyte-seconds and is calculated by multiplying the average memory size used by the function by the time in seconds it takes to execute. The plan comes with 400,000 gigabyte-seconds and 1 million executions a month for free with every subscription, which is very useful for `dev/test` environments. The Consumption plan will scale on demand to fit the needs of your application.

An App Service plan is billed based on the plan tier (Free, Shared, Standard, or Premium) and the number of instances deployed, regardless of compute execution time. While the App Service plan can be scaled up or out, in the case of the Azure Functions, it will be less dynamic than the Consumption plan.

In addition to the preceding billing, the standard storage rates apply, however, storage is typically a minimal part of the overall bill, as storage prices are very low. We will cover planning the cost in more detail in Chapter 13, *Designing for High Availability, Disaster Recovery, and Scale* . You can also visit https://azure.microsoft.com/en-us/pricing/details/functions for more details.

Both the Consumption plan and the App Service plan allow for parallel execution of functions. If the demand for the function exceeds the capacity of a single thread, new threads will be added. The scaling of the App Service plan is limited by the plan tier and the number of instances, while the scaling in the Consumption plan is dynamic.

The functions pricing structure may change in the future. The up-to-date retail pricing is available online.

The Location parameter

This is the location of the data center in which your application will be deployed. While Azure public endpoints are reachable from anywhere around the world, you should pick a location that is in closest geographical proximity to your application's users to reduce latency.

When deploying a large-scale global application, you may also replicate it in multiple data centers. We will cover application's geo-replication in Chapter 13, *Designing for High Availability, Disaster Recovery, and Scale.*

The Storage parameter

The storage account is the Azure Storage where your application assets will reside.

To create the storage account, click on the **Storage account** arrow and then select **New** and pick a name for it. Naming storage accounts can become tricky, as the name needs to be unique within the Azure Storage domain. The name needs to be between 3 and 24 characters, containing lowercase letters and numbers only. By default, Azure will provide a unique name by appending a random string to the name of your service.

The Automation options link

As mentioned earlier, every resource in Azure is described as a JSON template. These templates can be parameterized and reused to deploy the same resources in different environments.

The Automation options link allows us to explore and download the Resource Manager template that is generated to deploy the Function App resource. This template can later be reused to deploy the same resource (Function App) again. This template can also be downloaded after the resource has been deployed by navigating to **Resource** | **Automation options**.

To learn more, visit `https://docs.microsoft.com/en-us/azure/azure-resource-manager/resource-manager-export-template`.

Deploying the application

After filling all the parameters your Function App requires, you can also check the **Pin to dashboard** checkbox if you want the application to appear on your main dashboard in Azure portal.

After validating that all the parameters are correct, click on **Create**.

It may take a few minutes for your service to get deployed.

Functions Portal

Functions Portal is a part of Azure Management Portal that provides a rich development environment for the Azure Functions.

C# based the Azure Functions are currently offered in two flavors: a "script-based" function and a "precompiled" function.

Precompiled functions are created in Visual Studio using a class-library-based project and offer traditional .NET development experience.

C# script-based functions are deployed from Functions Portal and based on .csx "C# script" files. With functions based on .csx, the development process is more similar to developing in a script language like Node.js.

This chapter will describe creating and configuring a "script-based" function using the Functions Portal.

For the remainder of the book after this chapter, we will work with precompiled functions development using Visual Studio, as it provides richer development experience and a more natural integration with testing frameworks and source control.

Deploying Azure Functions online

Once the Function App is deployed, the Management Portal will redirect you to the "Functions Portal" page. Let's explore the following steps to deploy an Azure function online:

1. When you navigate to **Functions | Add** (plus sign), it will open a Quickstart page. We will skip the Quickstart deployment so that we can drill into all the options available.
2. On the bottom of the page, select **Custom function** under **Get started on your own**.
3. Set **Language** as **C#**, and select **Scenario** as **API & Webhooks**.
4. Choose the **HttpTrigger - C#** template, which will create a new function from an HTTP trigger template, with an automatically assigned HTTP endpoint.
5. Choose a name for your function. This name will become a part of your function's endpoint URL. This name needs to be unique in the Function App, but not across different Function Apps.

6. Select **Anonymous** under **Authorization level**. Different authorization mechanisms will be covered in detail in `Chapter 10`, *Securing Your Application*. For the time being, we will choose "anonymous", meaning that our HTTP endpoint will be accessible to anyone on the public URL that is automatically generated for your function:

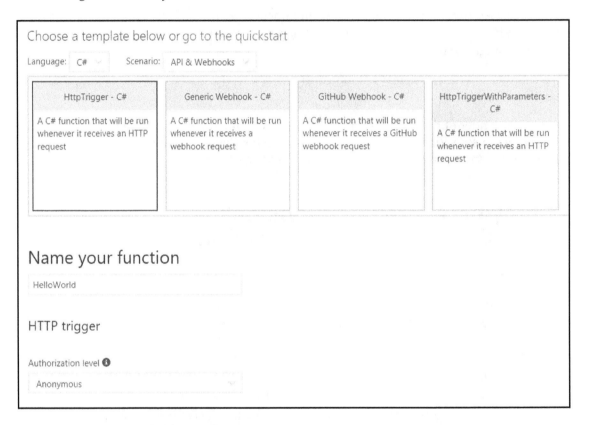

7. Click on **Create**.
8. After the function is created, you will be redirected to the Functions Portal development UI. The following screenshot is taken with **Test** and **Logs** panes enabled. You can click the respective buttons in the portal to display or hide these panes:

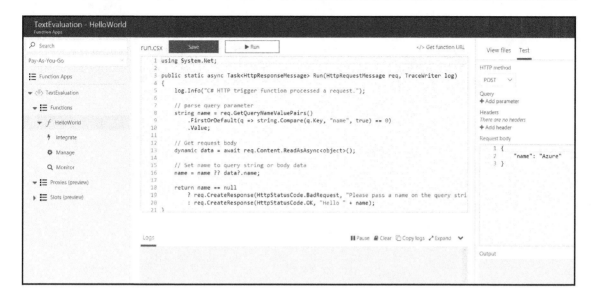

Function files

If you click on the **View files** button in the top-right corner, you will see the files library that contains the code and configuration used in your function. The required files will be auto generated from the template when you pick the function type. You can also add or upload new files and delete the files from the bottom of the **View files** pane.

These files are hosted in your App Service environment under `D:\home\site\wwwroot\[YourFunctionName]`. There is also a `host.json` file which is located in the `wwwroot` directory and contains the runtime configuration shared by all the individual functions in your Functions App.

The HTTP-triggered function template that we have created comes with the following two auto generated files that you can see in the next section. They are the `run.csx` file that contains the function code, and the `function.json` file that contains the function's configuration. We will elaborate on the differences between script-based and precompiled functions in `Appendix A`, *C# Script-Based Functions*.

The function.json file

The function.json file contains function configuration settings. The runtime uses function.json to determine which types of events to listen to, and how to pass data in and out of the function:

```
{
  "bindings": [
    {
        "authLevel": "anonymous",
        "name": "req",
        "type": "httpTrigger",
        "direction": "in"
    },
    {   "name": "$return",
        "type": "http",
        "direction": "out"
    }
            ],
    "disabled": false
}
```

As you can see in the preceding code, the configuration generated by the template we chose contains two bindings, which are an HTTP trigger input binding and an HTTP output binding. You may notice that the authorization type is defined on the input binding. We will elaborate on different types of bindings in Chapter 4, *Configuring Endpoints, Triggers, Bindings, and Scheduling*.

The "disabled": false setting specifies that the function is currently enabled. This setting gives you the ability to disable the function at any point without deleting it (for instance, to prevent incurring compute charges).

The run.csx file

The run.csx file contains the function code. This is the C# code that will be executed every time the function gets triggered. A CSX file is a C# script file, a type that was introduced recently. In C# script, a method may exist outside a class, which allows for execution of a standalone function.

Note that when working with "precompiled" functions (starting from the next chapter) we will be working with traditional CS class files, rather than CSX script files. Currently, when you create a new function online, it defaults to a CSX C# script-based function, and when you create a new function project from Visual Studio 2017, it defaults to a "precompiled" class-library based Function App.

Based on the type of function we choose, the portal will generate the following HTTP-triggered function code for us to begin with:

```csharp
using System.Net;

public static async Task<HttpResponseMessage>
Run(HttpRequestMessage req, TraceWriter log)
{
    log.Info("C# HTTP trigger function processed a request.");

    // parse query parameter
    string name = req.GetQueryNameValuePairs()
    .FirstOrDefault(q => string.Compare(q.Key, "name", true) == 0)
    .Value;

    // Get request body
    dynamic data = await req.Content.ReadAsAsync<object>();

    // Set name to query string or body data
    name = name ?? data?.name;

    return name == null ? req.CreateResponse
    (HttpStatusCode.BadRequest, "Please pass a name on the
    query string or in the request body") : req.CreateResponse
    (HttpStatusCode.OK, "Hello " + name);
}
```

Let's see how this code works. This function is built to respond to an HTTP endpoint trigger. It expects a parameter called `name` in either the query URL or the query body. If it gets a string value, such as `World` for the `name` parameter, it will then return an HTTP response with `status OK (200)` and a "Hello World" message. If it does not, it will return an HTTP status of `Bad Request (400)` and a `Please pass a name on the query string or in the request body` message.

HTTP endpoint

This function also has a publicly accessible HTTP endpoint, that is auto generated based on the function name and the Functions App name we've used. All endpoints are automatically configured to use HTTPS rather than plain HTTP, meaning that the traffic will be encrypted with TLS. This is especially important if you authenticate the function with a key, as this means the key won't be passed in clear text.

Let's explore the HTTP endpoint by performing the following steps:

1. To get the endpoint URL, click on **Get function URL** preceding the function code:

 Since we set the **Authentication level** to **Anonymous**, no API key or any other form of authorization currently needs to be provided to access the endpoint from the public internet.

2. Let's go ahead and browse to the function URL:

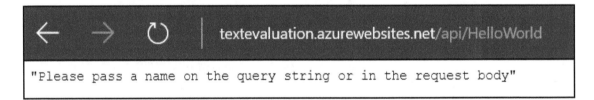

As expected, we got an error message, as we did not provide the name parameter in either the URL or the body of the HTTP request.

3. Let's fix the issue by providing the name parameter in the URL string by appending substring ?name=Serverless!:

Congratulations! You have just deployed your first, public facing, serverless computing function!

Exploring the Functions Portal

In this section, we will explain the different features and tools available in the Functions Portal.

The Test pane

In addition to testing the endpoint from the browser, we can also use the Functions **Test** pane by clicking on the **Test** icon in the top-right corner. The **Test** pane provides us with the ability to test HTTP request types other than GET, such as POST, PUT, or HEAD, and provide the request body, query parameters, and headers. It also has the **Output** pane, which displays the HTTP response status code and content:

To test with the **Test** pane, let's go ahead and change the value of the `name` parameter from `Azure` to `Serverless` and click on the **Run** button on top.

You will see the `Status: 200 OK` message, and the `"Hello Serverless"` message appears in the **Output** window.

Function logs

The Functions Portal also provides the view of function logs. There are two **Logs** windows that you can enable: one on the bottom of the **Test** Pane on the right and the other on the bottom of the development console. These panes will display the same output:

```
Logs                                         ‖ Pause  ⬛ Clear  ⧉ Copy logs  ↗ Expand  ⌄

2017-05-22T01:48:51.082 Function started (Id=2b4a890f-a1a4-4d76-be2d-276ce0c4e433)
2017-05-22T01:48:51.082 C# HTTP trigger function processed a request.
2017-05-22T01:48:51.082 Function completed (Success, Id=2b4a890f-a1a4-4d76-be2d-276ce0c4e433, Duration=0ms)
```

The logs will display the `Trace` function along with what is called a function `Pulse` when the function was started, whether or not it completed successfully, and so on. Each log entry has a detailed timestamp.

 The function pulse might be deprecated in the future.

The **Logs** pane comes with a few options such as **Clear**, **Copy logs**, or **Expand**. You can also pause the function execution from the **Logs** pane if you have decided that you need to make changes mid-execution.

Error output

To see how the console displays an error, we can change the parameter we supplied in the **Request body** section from `name` to `text`:

Request body

```
1 {
2        "text": "Serverless"
3 }
```

Output

Status: 400 Bad Request

```
"Please pass a name on the query string or
in the request body"
```

As expected, we got the `400 Bad Request` error code, and also the `Please pass a name on the query string or in the request body` error message.

Note that the **Logs** window is still displaying the output indicating that the function completed successfully. This is because even though an error message was returned due to wrong input, no error has occurred in the function itself:

```
2017-01-14T16:39:35.928 Function started (Id=49b724d2-2e3d-4b85-
9aaa-4ffd8dcef948)
2017-01-14T16:39:35.928 C# HTTP trigger function processed a
request.
2017-01-14T16:39:35.928 Function completed (Success, Id=49b724d2-
2e3d-4b85-9aaa-4ffd8dcef948)
```

To demonstrate the output in case of an exception in the function code, let's change the `name` variable in line 16 to `text`, as follows:

```
15      // Set name to query string or body data
16      text = name ?? data?.name;
```

Since the `text` variable was not previously defined, the log output will now display a compilation error.

Function App settings

As this chapter provides an introduction to the Azure environment and building your first Function App, we will not elaborate on all of the advanced configuration, which will be covered in the following chapters. The next few pages will discuss some of the advanced settings and tools that are most relevant when getting started.

In the new Functions Portal, when you click on the Function App itself, you will see a configuration view broken down into four tabs -- **Overview**, **Settings**, **Platform features**, and **API Definition**.

In **Settings**, you can configure a number of advanced features.

Application Settings

Clicking on **Application Settings** will lead you into the **Application Settings** blade which contains environment variables and application settings that would be stored in a `Web.config` file in a typical .NET web application. We will use these settings in future chapters to configure the Function App settings.

Application Settings also appear under the **Platform features** tab.

Daily Usage Quota

Under the Consumption plan, Daily Usage Quota lets you configure the amount of memory in gigabyte-seconds that your application is allowed to consume in one day. The application will stop after the quota is reached and won't allow any more calls for the current day.

As the Consumption hosting plan comes with 400,000 gigabyte-seconds (GB-s) a month, if you do not want to exceed the free tier, you can configure approximately 1/31 of that, or 13,000 GB-s per day (assuming that you only have one function in your App Service environment):

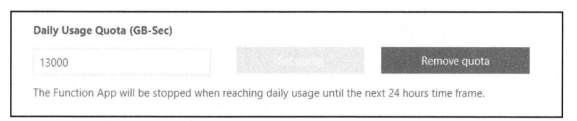

If you exceed the quota, the "disabled" setting in the function.json file will turn to true, and in the **Administrative** pane, you will get an error message outlining that your function has been disabled because it has exceeded the daily quota.

If your function is triggered by an HTTP request, the users of your application will get the following message when trying to make a request to it:

```
Error 403 - This web app is stopped.
The web app you have attempted to reach is currently stopped and
does not accept any requests. Please try to reload the page or
visit it again soon.
```

You can re-enable the application by removing the quota.

The runtime version

The runtime version is the version of the Azure Functions (WebJobs SDK) runtime that is being used to run your Function App. You can specify the runtime version you want to use. ~1 will specify the latest version.

The Function App edit mode

You can choose to set your Function App edit mode to read-only, to prevent any changes to your deployed application. This can help prevent configuration drift.

Host keys

HTTP triggered functions can leverage API keys to secure access. Host keys are the keys shared by all the functions in the Function App (in addition, there are function keys specific to each function).

Host and function keys will be covered in depth in `Chapter 10`, *Securing Your Application*.

Slots

Deployment slots enable publishing your application from your continuous delivery pipeline into a staging environment, which can be subsequently promoted to the production environment with near-zero downtime (by doing a DNS swap).

Deployment slots will be covered in more detail in `Chapter 9`, Configuring Continuous Delivery.

Proxies

Proxies allow you to add endpoints to your Function App that are implemented by another resource. This also allows you to break an API into multiple Function Apps, while still presenting a cohesive API surface to your consumers.

To read more about proxies, visit `https://docs.microsoft.com/en-us/azure/azure-functions/functions-proxies`.

The Platform features pane

In the **Platform features** pane, you can configure advanced settings that are available in the Function App as part of an App Service plan. Some of the features will be available only under an App Service plan, while others are available under both the **App Service Plan** and the **Consumption Plan**. We will cover a number of features available on the following list shown in the screenshot. Additional features will be covered in more advanced chapters of this book.

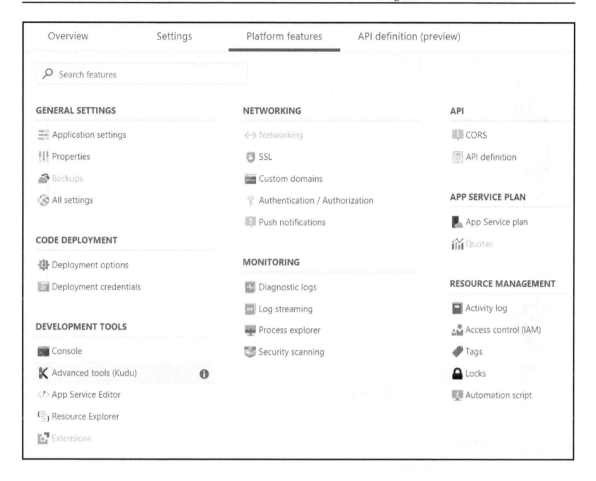

App Service Editor

Clicking on the **App Service Editor** button will open a new browser tab, as shown in the following screenshot. Opening the App Service Editor allows you to develop your application using Visual Studio online. In addition to editing the specific function files such as `function.json` and `run.csx`, which you can do in the function editor, you will also be able to browse the entire application folder structure and modify the `host.json` file and any additional project files you may have created.

> If you edit the `function.json` file of a Function App under the **Consumption Plan** in the **App Service Editor**, the triggers will only be synchronized after the Functions Portal is refreshed and the change is reflected there.

Take a look at the following screenshot for a better view:

Dev Console

Dev Console is a CMD console available with any Azure App Service environment, including the Azure Functions.

Dev Console gives you limited access to `D:\home\site\wwwroot` of the VM on which your App Service environment is hosted. Dev Console *does not* give you administrative access to the virtual machine, allow you to install software, or even browse to any other disks on the VM. It will allow you to browse, create, delete, or modify files under the `D:\home` directory. To demonstrate this, we can explore the folder structure and create a new file, as shown in the following screenshot:

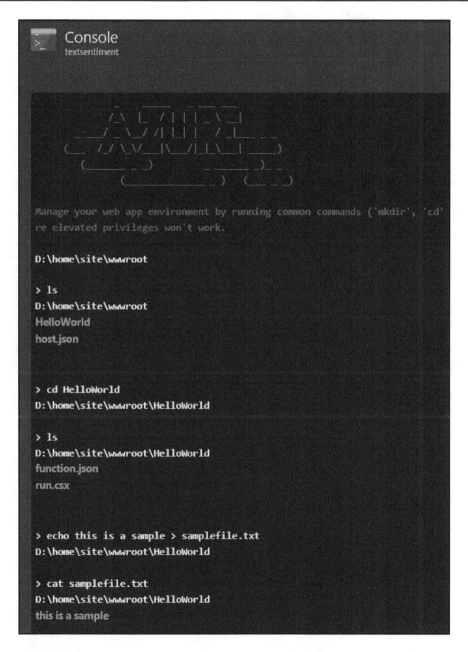

You will notice that the `samplefile.txt` file that we've just created now appears in **View files/App Service Editor**.

Resource Explorer

As discussed earlier, everything in Azure Resource Manager API is a resource, and everything can be defined as a JSON template. To view your Azure Functions as JSON, you can click on **Resource Explorer** or browse to `https://resources.azure.com` and drill down to your Function App, which will be under the following path:

```
https://resources.azure.com/subscriptions/[YourSubscriptionID]/resourceGroups/
[YourResourceGroup]/providers/Microsoft.Web/sites/[YourAppName]
```

The application can be accessed and also modified from here. To modify the application, check the **Read/Write** button on top (not displayed in the screenshot) and the blue **Edit** button. For instance, changing line 19 to "enabled": false, will disable your functions from running:

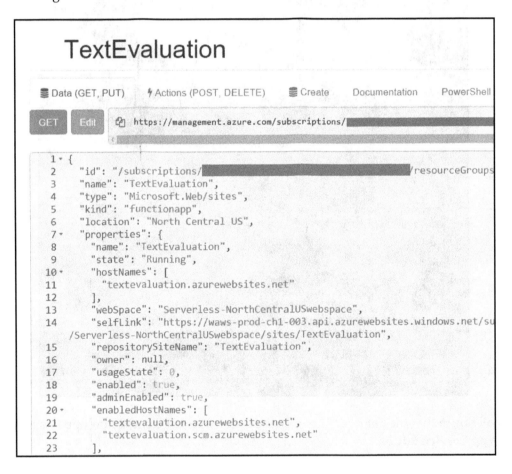

Having access to the JSON template of your resource can be useful as at any time it will give you read or even write access to more settings than what is currently available in the GUI portal. In addition, since your application can also be deployed using a JSON template, this is where you can copy the initial template from. This feature makes it easy to clone the application between different environments, such as dev/test/prod.

Clean up Azure resources

If you have been experimenting with deploying different resources, you may want to delete some of them to keep things organized and to avoid being charged for resources you don't use. This section will describe the procedure of resource deletion at various levels. Be careful--the delete procedure is **irreversible**.

Deleting a function

One way to delete a specific function inside the Function App, is to delete it from the function's app **Functions** list as shown in the following screenshot:

Alternatively, you can also delete by navigating to **Functions State** | **Manage** | **Delete function**:

Deleting the Function App

To delete the entire Function App, go to the application's **Overview** page and click on the **Delete** button on the right-hand side, as shown in the following screenshot:

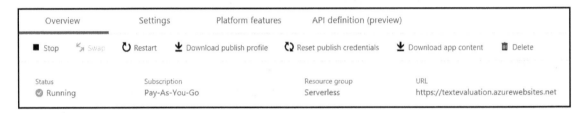

Deleting the resource group

To browse to the entire resource group, navigate to the main portal **Dashboard** ∣ **Resource Groups** ∣ [YourResourceGroupName].

You can right-click on the resource group name and select **Delete**. A confirmation box will prompt you to enter the resource group name, and display the list of existing resources under the resource group you are deleting. Remember, after confirmation, the delete action is **irreversible**.

Exploring further options

As you may have noticed, there are a number of panes in the left pane such as **Integrate**, **Manage**, and **Monitor**, as well as a number of settings in **Function Advanced Settings**. We will cover all of these in later chapters, as the book progresses to the respective subjects.

Summary

This chapter provided us with a solid introduction to the Azure serverless computing environment and walked us through the deployment of our first Azure Functions application.

In this chapter, we covered the basics of Microsoft Azure cloud and created our first serverless computing environment and a "Hello World" function. We also walked through application settings and environment configuration.

In the next chapter, we will walk through creating an Azure Functions project in Visual Studio and deploying it to our existing Azure environment. We will also set up two other application components: the database and the Web UI to demonstrate a real-world example of serverless computing utilization.

3
Setting Up the Development Environment

In this chapter, we will walk through a Visual Studio development environment setup for Azure Functions, and also start developing the text sentiment application.

During the course of this chapter, we will cover the following topics:

- Set up the development environment with Visual Studio 2017
- Set up the Azure Functions project
- Create a Function App with a sample text scoring function
- Deploy the application to Azure
- Set up the database to store the scoring results
- Set up a web-based dashboard to display the scoring results
- Tie the serverless compute, the database, and the web tiers together

By the end of this chapter, we will have a simple application comprised of the following components:

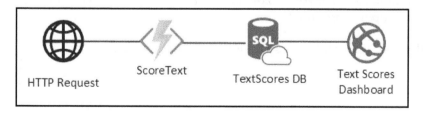

Configuring the development environment

In this part of the chapter, we will go through the configuration of the development environment for the Azure Function App project in Visual Studio.

When we create functions online in the Functions portal, we create C# script `.csx` based functions. C# script code files have certain features that differ from traditional C# code, which will be highlighted in the `Appendix A`, *C# Script-Based Functions*.

When we create functions in Visual Studio, we are developing "precompiled" functions. The functions are built in a traditional class-library project, and compiled into a library (DLL). The entire library is then published as a Function App, accompanied by a `function.json` file for each function.

Development in Visual Studio offers full access to IntelliSense, unit testing, and integration with source control repositories and continuous delivery tools, and thus is preferable to the online experience.

Downloading and installing Visual Studio

Azure Functions tools are available for Visual Studio 2017 Update 3 or later. Lets download and install Visual Studio by performing the following steps:

1. Download Visual Studio Community for free from the link `https://www.visualstudio.com/vs/community`, or use any of the paid editions. (Please verify that your development machine meets the minimal installation requirements).
2. Configure Visual Studio to use C# as the main language during installation.
3. Check Web and Azure workloads in VS installer. This will install the Azure SDK and the Functions SDK.
4. Sign in to Visual Studio with the same Microsoft or organizational account that you used to create your Azure environment. This will make it easier to publish your applications into the same Azure subscription.

Your Visual Studio IDE is now ready to use for Azure Functions.

Creating the project

After you have installed the Azure SDK and Azure Function tools for Visual Studio, the Function App template will appear in the Visual Studio project templates. To create a new Functions project, perform the following steps:

1. Navigate to **File** -> **New** -> **Project**:
2. In Templates, select **Visual C# -> Cloud -> Azure Functions** as shown in this screenshot:

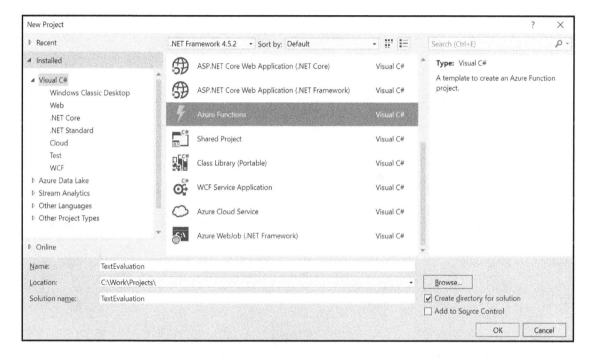

3. After you click **OK**, a new Function App project will be created. As a reminder, a Function App is a container that can host one or more individual functions.

4. Open the **Solution Explorer** pane by clicking on **View -> Solution Explorer**. In **Solution Explorer**, you will see the new Function App project structure as seen in this screenshot:

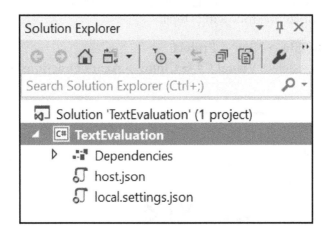

Function App Configuration Files

You will notice that the newly created project does not automatically contain a function. The files in the project tree are the files that define the entire project's configuration and settings, and will apply to all functions added to the project. The following two files are important to note:

- `local.settings.json`
- `host.json`

The local.settings.json file

The `local.settings.json` file is an analogue of the `app.config` file in a conventional .Net application. This file contains the configuration settings for your application that can be published to **App Settings** in your Azure Function App environment.

The `AzureWebJobsStorage` and `AzureWebJobsDashboard` settings define the connection to the data storage and the logs storage accounts respectively. By default, they are set to the same value. All functions, except the HTTP triggered ones, currently require these connection strings to point to Azure even when the function is run locally. This is because the Functions Runtime uses Azure queues to schedule all triggers other than the HTTP trigger.

To run your local Function App against the Azure environment that we created in the previous chapter, we need to propagate the `AzureWebJobsStorage` and `AzureWebJobsDashboard` settings from your Function App in Azure to your local Visual Studio environment.

To do so, navigate to **Functions Portal** -> `<Your Function App Name>` -> **Platform Features** -> **Application Settings**. You will see the settings with the corresponding names, and you can copy and paste them back into your project's `local.settings.json`, as shown in the following sample `local.settings.json` file:

```
{
  "IsEncrypted": false,
  "Values": {
    "AzureWebJobsStorage":"DefaultEndpointsProtocol=https;
    AccountName=textsentimentstorage;AccountKey=<full account
    key>",
    "AzureWebJobsDashboard": "DefaultEndpointsProtocol=https;
    AccountName=textsentimentstorage;AccountKey=<full account key>"
  }
}
```

It is important to note that `local.settings.json` file is local (as the name suggests), and is not used by the Azure runtime. When we add additional settings, such as connection strings, in the local environment, the same settings will need to be propagated to the **Function App Settings** in the portal. The ability to configure different settings in the local and Azure environments is useful because the environment settings values typically differ between the development machine and Azure .

Currently, when you publish the function app from Visual Studio, the `local.settings.json` file does not get published. You *can* publish the `local.settings.json` using Functions Core Tools. To learn more, please visit `https://docs.microsoft.com/en-us/azure/azure-functions/functions-run-local#a-namepublishapublish-to-azure`.

The host.json file

The `host.json` file is the metadata file defining the configuration settings for your entire Functions App (as opposed to a specific function). This is the file that we saw in the `D:\home\site\wwwroot` directory in `Chapter 2`, *Getting Started with Azure Environment*.

At the moment, our `host.json` file is empty. We will elaborate more on the kinds of settings that will be defined here in `Chapter 4`, *Configuring Endpoints, Triggers, Bindings and Scheduling*.

Creating the function

Let's take a look at the following steps to create the function:

1. In **Solution Explorer**, right-click the project, choose **Add** -> **New Item** -> **Azure Function**, and enter `ScoreText` in the name. This will be the name of the `.cs` file that defines the function.
2. In the next dialog, fill the following parameters:
    - **Function type**: **HttpTrigger**
    - **AccessRights**: **Anonymous**
    - **FunctionName**: `ScoreText`

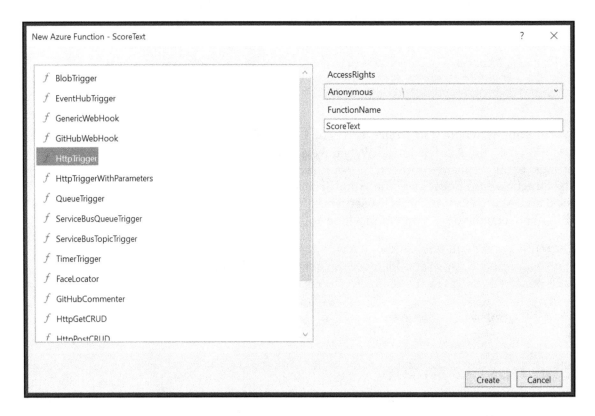

3. Click on **Create**.

    You will see the `ScoreText.cs` file appear in the project tree.

Running the function locally

The function code is provided next. The auto-generated code implements the same behavior as we've seen in the `HelloWorld` function created online, however, you will notice a few differences in code. The differences exist because the online function was a C# script (CSX) based function.

The Visual Studio "precompiled" function template has references to a number of system libraries and the `Azure.WebJobs` libraries, and the function's `Run` method is annotated with attributes. The `FunctionName` attribute indicates to the compiler that the `Run` method is a function entry point in the Function App class-library. The `HttpTrigger` attribute allows us to provide the trigger settings based on which the `function.json` file is generated. When the project is compiled, the `Microsoft.Net.Sdk.Functions` library converts the attribute settings into the `function.json` file, which is placed in the function directory (under `bin`)

Let's run the function locally by performing the following steps:

1. Open the `ScoreText.cs` file in **Solution Explorer**. You will see the following auto-generated code:

```
using System.Linq;
using System.Net;
using System.Net.Http;
using System.Threading.Tasks;
using Microsoft.Azure.WebJobs;
using Microsoft.Azure.WebJobs.Extensions.Http;
using Microsoft.Azure.WebJobs.Host;

namespace TextEvaluation
{
 public static class ScoreText
 {
   [FunctionName("ScoreText")]
 public static async Task<HttpResponseMessage>
 Run([HttpTrigger(AuthorizationLevel.Anonymous, "get", "post",
 Route = null)]HttpRequestMessage req, TraceWriter log)
 {
   log.Info("C# HTTP trigger function processed a request.");

   // parse query parameter
   string name = req.GetQueryNameValuePairs()
   .FirstOrDefault(q => string.Compare(q.Key,
   "name", true) == 0)
   .Value;
```

```
    // Get request body
    dynamic data = await req.Content.ReadAsAsync<object>();

    // Set name to query string or body data
    name = name ?? data?.name;

    return name == null
    ? req.CreateResponse(HttpStatusCode.BadRequest, "Please pass a
    name on the query string or in the request body")
    : req.CreateResponse(HttpStatusCode.OK, "Hello " + name);
    }
  }
}
```

2. Click on **Build -> Build solution** to build the application.
3. Browse to the new function's files in the /bin/Debug/net461/ScoreText under the project directory and review the generated function.json file. The code is as follows:

```
{
    "bindings": [
    {
        "type": "httpTrigger",
        "methods": [
            "get",
            "post"
        ],
      "authLevel": "anonymous",
      "direction": "in",
      "name": "req"
    },
      {
        "name": "$return",
        "type": "http",
        "direction": "out"
      }
    ],
      "disabled": false,
      "scriptFile": "..\\bin\TextEvaluation.dll",
      "entryPoint": "TextEvaluation.ScoreText.Run"
}
```

4. Notice the two additional settings, `scriptFile`, which is pointing to the relative location of the `DLL` that the function was compiled to, and `entryPoint`, which specifies the entry point of the `Run` method in that `DLL`.

5. To run your application locally, make sure that you have selected the **Debug** mode, and then click on **Start** to run the application.

6. The project will start on your development machine, and you will see the following output in Function Core Tools:

```
Listening on http://localhost:7071/
Hit CTRL-C to exit...
[5/22/2017 12:46:39 AM] Reading host configuration file 'C:\Work\Projects\TextEvaluation\TextEvaluation\bin\Debug\net461\host.json'
[5/22/2017 12:46:40 AM] Loaded custom extension: SendGridConfiguration from ''
[5/22/2017 12:46:40 AM] Generating 1 job function(s)
[5/22/2017 12:46:40 AM] Starting Host (HostId=niichavo-2120180320, Version=1.0.10955.0, ProcessId=14212, Debug=False, Attempt=0)
[5/22/2017 12:46:41 AM] Found the following functions:
[5/22/2017 12:46:41 AM] Host.Functions.ScoreText
[5/22/2017 12:46:41 AM]
[5/22/2017 12:46:41 AM] Job host started
[5/22/2017 12:46:41 AM] Executing HTTP request: {
[5/22/2017 12:46:41 AM]     "requestId": "55e12ee6-db73-45f5-b460-b56f69982c03",
[5/22/2017 12:46:41 AM]     "method": "GET",
[5/22/2017 12:46:41 AM]     "uri": "/"
[5/22/2017 12:46:41 AM] }
[5/22/2017 12:46:41 AM] Executed HTTP request: {
[5/22/2017 12:46:41 AM]     "requestId": "55e12ee6-db73-45f5-b460-b56f69982c03",
[5/22/2017 12:46:41 AM]     "method": "GET",
[5/22/2017 12:46:41 AM]     "uri": "/",
[5/22/2017 12:46:41 AM]     "authorizationLevel": "Anonymous"
[5/22/2017 12:46:41 AM] }
[5/22/2017 12:46:41 AM] Response details: {
[5/22/2017 12:46:41 AM]     "requestId": "55e12ee6-db73-45f5-b460-b56f69982c03",
[5/22/2017 12:46:41 AM]     "status": "OK"
[5/22/2017 12:46:41 AM] }
Http Function ScoreText: http://localhost:7071/api/ScoreText
Debugger listening on [::]:5858
```

7. By default, your function is up and running on localhost, on port `7071`.

8. To see your function in action, open your browser, browse to the function's endpoint, and append the name parameter, `http://localhost:7071/api/ScoreText?name=Local Environment!` as follows:

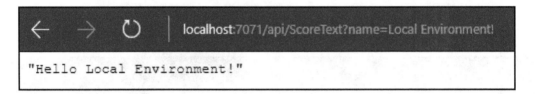

Congratulations! You now have a development environment that allows you to develop and debug your serverless functions locally!

Deploying the application to Azure

Now that we have verified that the application is running correctly locally, we are ready to publish it to our Azure environment.

The following section will show how to publish the function using Visual Studio. You can also publish the function using Function Core tools. To learn more, please visit `https://docs.microsoft.com/en-us/azure/azure-functions/functions-run-local#a-namepublishapublish-to-azure`.

We will use the same Azure Function App that we set up in Chapter 2, *Getting Started with Azure Environment*. If you don't already have an existing Function App, you can set up a new one in the publishing dialog. Let's take a look at the following steps to deploy the application to Azure:

1. In **Solution Explorer**, right-click on the `TextEvaluation` solution, and select **Publish...**:

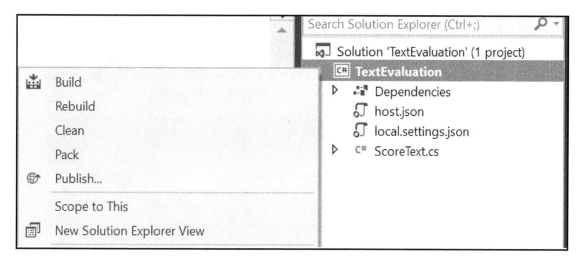

2. A publishing dialog will open. Select **Azure Function App** and then select the **Select Existing** option as shown in the following screenshot:

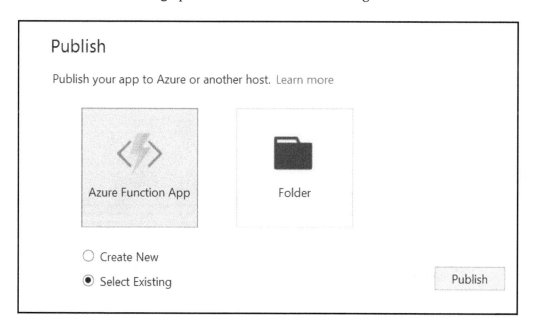

3. Visual Studio will automatically connect to the Microsoft or organizational account that you are signed in with, and retrieve the Azure subscriptions you have access to. Choose the appropriate subscription under the **Subscription** option and resource group from the **View** drop-down menu. Then choose the Azure Function App that we created in the previous chapter:

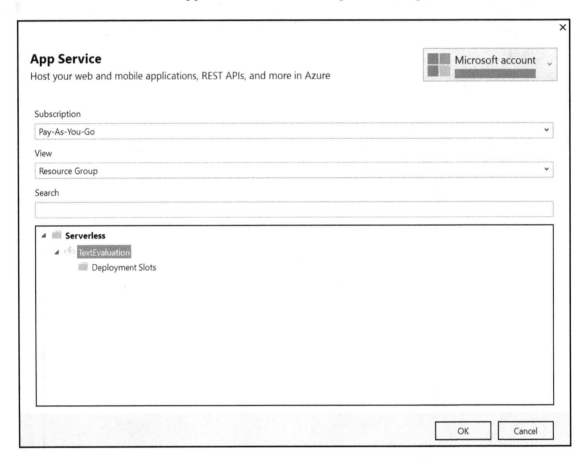

4. Click on **OK**.

5. Visual Studio will retrieve the details of the Function App, and populate a publishing profile as seen in the following screenshot:

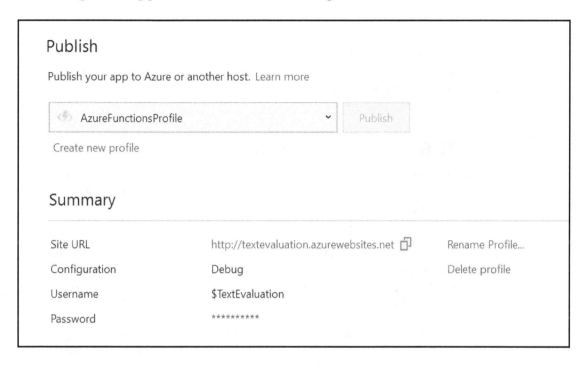

6. Once you are ready, click on the **Publish** button. The publishing process may take a few minutes.

   You will see the output in the **Output** window as shown in the following screenshot, indicating whether the publishing process succeeded:

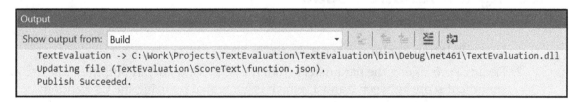

7. Browse to the Azure portal, and navigate to **App Services** -> TextEvaluation -> **Function App** to see the new function added to the function list (you may need to hit refresh for the list to update).

Note that the existing `HelloWorld` function was not replaced, since we have given our new function a different name.

8. You can browse to the new function URL, `https://<YourFunctionApp>.azurewebsites.net/api/ScoreText`, or use the **Test** Pane to verify that the function works as expected on the public URL.

Modifying the text scoring function

In the previous section, we created a new function using Visual Studio, and published it to our existing Azure Function App. Now that you understand the basics, we can start working on the application code.

In this book, we are working on creating a text sentiment analysis application that utilizes Azure serverless computing to process text input from external sources. As we go through this process step by step, we will add new input sources, such as file upload. Later, we will describe how to integrate the scoring function with one of the Azure Cognitive Services APIs to return a meaningful text sentiment score.

In this chapter, we will start by extending our serverless computing function to integrate with a database and a web dashboard. To keep things simple, we will keep the function's trigger as an HTTP request, and extend it to return a text score to simulate the results that we will later get from the Cognitive Services API. For the time being, the text sentiment score we return will be a random double between 0 and 1.

Updating the function code

Let's take a look at the following steps to update the function code:

1. Using **Solution Explorer**, open `ScoreText.cs`.
2. Remove processing the parameters from the body, and add an output of a text sentiment score between 0 and 1, which is generated by using the C# Random function, as shown in the following code sample:

```
using System;
namespace TextEvaluation
{
  public static class ScoreText
  {
```

```
[FunctionName("ScoreText")]
public static async Task<HttpResponseMessage>
Run([HttpTrigger(AuthorizationLevel.Anonymous, "get", "post",
Route = null]]HttpRequestMessage req, TraceWriter log)
{
    // parse query parameter
    string name = req.GetQueryNameValuePairs()
    .FirstOrDefault(q => string.Compare(q.Key, "name", true) ==
0)
    .Value;
    if (name == null)
    {
      log.Error($"Name parameter missing in HTTP request.
      RequestUri={req.RequestUri}");
      return req.CreateResponse(HttpStatusCode.BadRequest,
      "Please pass name parameter the in query string");
    }
    // Generate random text score between 0 and 1
    var score = new Random().NextDouble();
    //Return the text score in HTTP response
    return req.CreateResponse(HttpStatusCode.OK, "The text
    sentiment score is " + score);
    }
  }
}
```

3. Click on **Run** to verify that the function will compile and run without an error.

4. Browse to the function URL, `http://localhost:7071/api/ScoreText?name=Test Document`, and submit the required parameter to verify that the function returns the expected (randomized) text score result.

   The output is a random score between 0 and 1, as shown in the following screenshot:

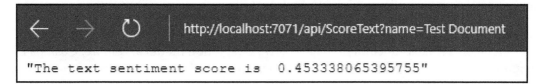

Republishing the function to Azure

Now that we are sure our function is working as expected, we can republish it to the Azure environment. The publishing profile we've created in a previous step will let us publish the function to the same environment in a single click.

After republishing the function, you can verify that the it works as expected by browsing to its public endpoint, as follows:

You can also test the function after publishing by using the Test pane in the functions portal.

Storing the results

Now that we have a function generating a text sentiment score, we need to create a data store to hold the processing results. In this book, we will use a Microsoft SQL Server database as the datastore, as it is most commonly used in .Net application development.

We will deploy our SQL database in a PaaS SQL server in Azure. Using a PaaS service will allow us to deploy a database in the cloud, while the hosting server configuration, high availability, backup, and so on will be taken care of by the Azure platform.

Note that the Azure Functions serverless environment allows for integration with many more types of data stores, including NoSQL table storage, Cosmos DB, and other types of external databases, as well as triggering various APIs with function outputs.

Cosmos DB is a new globally-distributed Azure PaaS database, that supports multiple different models such as document, tables, key-value, graph model and more. Cosmos DB integrates really well with Functions. To learn more about Cosmos DB, visit `https://docs. microsoft.com/en-us/azure/cosmos-db/introduction`.

Setting up the SQL PaaS database in Azure

As mentioned in the previous section, the Azure SQL database is a Microsoft SQL Server based database that is available as a service in Azure. To deploy a new Azure SQL database, go to the Azure portal, and perform the following steps:

1. Navigate to **New -> Databases -> SQL Database**.
2. Fill in the following parameters:
   - **Database name**: This parameter represents the name of the database.
   - **Subscription**: In this parameter, choose the appropriate subscription from the drop-down menu.
   - **Resource group**: In this example, we will choose the existing serverless resource group so that we can see all of the resources related to our application organized together. In your environment, you may choose to organize resources differently (for instance, put all of your databases in the same resource group).
   - **Select source**: Choose **Blank database** to create a new empty database.
   - **Server**: Click into the server blade to configure a new SQL server (elaborated further in this section).
   - **Want to use SQL elastic pool?**: Choose **Not now** (this setting becomes relevant when managing multiple databases).

- **Pricing tier**: In this parameter, choose **Basic** for the cheapest database option. This will give us 2 GB of storage and 5 DTUs, which is, in most cases, sufficient for dev environments (in a production environment, it is recommended to select **Standard** and above for a bigger size and significantly improved performance).
- **Collation**: Keep the default option, as seen in the following screenshot:

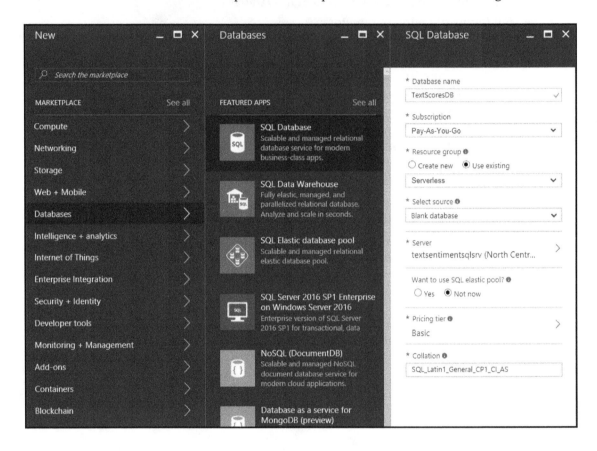

Creating the SQL Server

Let's take a look at the following steps to create the SQL Server:

1. In the database options blade, navigate to **Server** -> **Create** to create a new server, and fill in the following parameters:
   - **Server name**: The name prefix must be unique within the `database.windows.net` domain. The name can contain lowercase letters, numbers, and dashes, and cannot exceed 63 characters.
   - **Server admin login**: Provide an SQL administrator name. This name cannot start with a number, contain non-alphabetic characters, or be identical to one of the reserved names or roles in the SQL server
   - **Password**: Provide an SQL administrator password. The password must comply with minimal strength requirements.
   - **Location**: Choose the same location that you have deployed your Azure Functions App to (putting a database in a different region than the application may cause latency). As we are going to use this database during local development as well, choose a location that is geographically close to you.
   - **Latest update**: Select **Yes**.
   - **Allow azure services to access server**: Check this option. This setting is on by default, and it signifies that any IPs within the Azure IP ranges will be whitelisted in the SQL firewall rules. In a production environment, you may want to turn this setting off, and whitelist a more specific set of IPs.

2. After filling in all the required parameters, click on **Select** in the SQL Server blade.

3. Click on **Create** in the SQL database blade. After a few minutes, your new database will be deployed.

   As you can see in the next screenshot, the SQL Azure database provides a rich environment with many features such as **Geo-Replication**, **Transparent data encryption**, and **Monitoring alerts** readily available. This book does not aim to cover Azure SQL in detail. You can learn more about SQL Azure features at `https://docs.microsoft.com/en-us/azure/sql-database`:

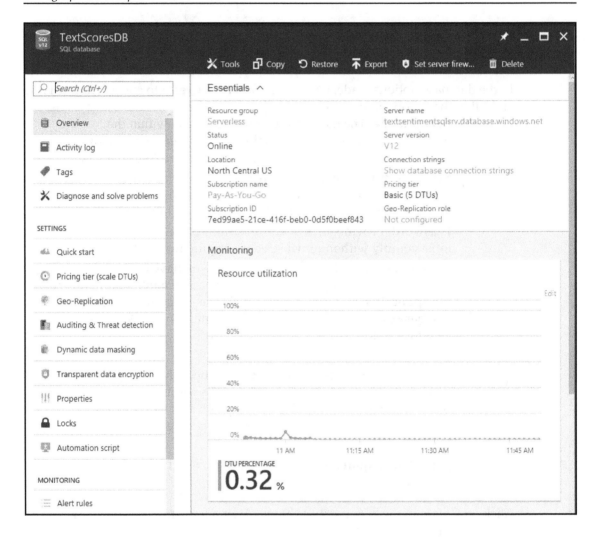

Managing the SQL database from Visual Studio

There are multiple ways to connect to and manage your SQL Azure database, including SQL Management Studio and Azure management portal itself. In this book, we will use the Visual Studio SQL Server tools, since we already have Visual Studio installed and configured.

Take a look at the following steps to learn to connect and manage your SQL Azure database:

1. To connect to your new `TextScoresDB` from Visual Studio, click on **View -> SQL Server Object Explorer**. In the SQL server object explorer, click on the **Add SQL Server** button (server with a plus icon).

2. Now navigate to **Browse -> Azure**. As long as you are signed in to Visual Studio with the same account that has access to your Azure subscription, you will see the `TextScoresDB` database that we have created in the previous section on the list along with all the other SQL Azure databases you have access to.

3. Click on `TextScoresDB` to have the connection parameters fill in automatically.

4. Enter the SQL administrator password you used when creating the SQL server. Check the **Remember password** option:

5. Click on **Connect**.

   Since all non-Azure-based IP ranges are automatically blocked by the SQL server firewall, you will receive the following prompt. This is a prompt to create a firewall rule on the SQL server to allow your development machine IP access the server:

6. In the dialog shown in the preceding screenshot, you will see your computer's public IP automatically filled in. If you are on a secure network, click on **OK** to whitelist your client IP to access your SQL Azure database.

7. You are now connected to the Azure SQL server we've deployed, and can modify the databases on it.

Note that if your client IP changes in the future, and you need to remove or modify the whitelist rules, you can do so in the Azure portal. To access the firewall rules, navigate to **SQL Databases** -> `TextScoreDB` -> **Overview** -> **Set server firewall...** (in the top pane), as shown in the following screenshot:

You will see the following blade, which allows you to add or remove firewall rules apart from allowing or disallowing general access for Azure based services. The view will also display your current public IP, and allow you to whitelist it with one click on the **Add client IP** button in the top pane if it is not already listed:

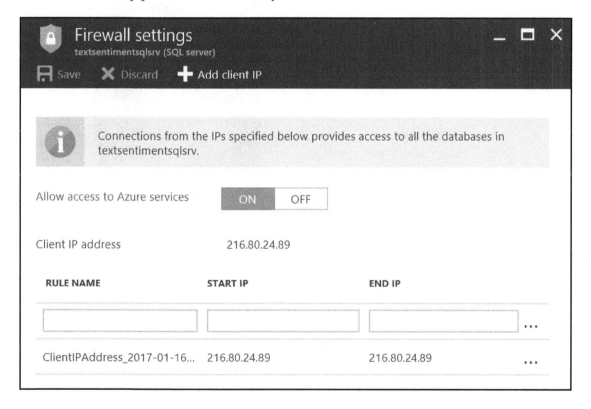

Creating the DocumentTextScore table

After your Azure-based SQL server has loaded in the SQL server explorer in Visual Studio, you can expand the view to browse specific databases, tables, and columns.

 You can also run SQL queries online, in a query editor in the Azure portal. To browse to the query editor, go to **<Your Database> -> Tools** (on the **Overview** tab) **-> Query editor**. From here, you can simply run any SQL query, just as you could from Visual Studio or SQL Server Management Studio, although you cannot browse the structure of your tables and columns.

To create a new table in the `TextScoresDB` database in Visual Studio, follow these steps:

1. To add a new table, right-click on the database name, and choose **New Query...** as follows:

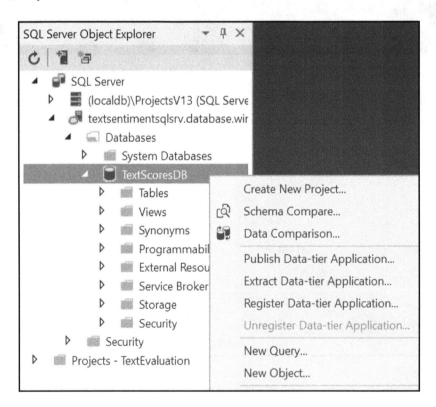

2. In the SQL query window that opens, enter the following code. This code will create a new SQL table named `DocumentTextScore`, which has four columns: int `ID`, which is an Identity column, string `DocumentName`, [Date] `DATETIME` (with the default value of the current UTC date and time), and float (double) `TextSentimentScore`:

```
CREATE TABLE DocumentTextScore
(
    ID INT IDENTITY(1,1) PRIMARY KEY,
    DocumentName VARCHAR(255) NOT NULL,
    [Date] DATETIME NOT NULL DEFAULT GETUTCDATE(),
    TextSentimentScore FLOAT NOT NULL
);
```

3. Click on **Execute** (the green button in the top-left corner). After executing, you will see a **Query executed successfully** status message in the output window.

4. Now that we have created a table, we can insert some test values into it. To insert the first row into the table, execute the query that follows:

```
INSERT INTO DocumentTextScore (DocumentName,
TextSentimentScore)
Values ('First Document', 0.42786)
```

5. To verify that the data was inserted, execute the next query to select all rows from the `DocumentTextScore` table:

```
SELECT * FROM DocumentTextScore
```

You will see the current table structure and data in the **Output** window:

Integrating the ScoreText function with the SQL database

Now that we have created our SQL Server database, it is time to configure our Azure Function to store the output in the `DocumentTextScore` table.

In this book, we will use an inherent feature of Azure Functions, which allows us to define the SQL connection as an output binding. To do so, we will use a new library called ApiHub SDK, which allows us to interact with an SQL database as if we were interacting with an external API. This approach makes it easier for us to swap the connection out for a different type of data store if required in the future.

Lets execute the following steps to integrate the `ScoreText` function with the your SQL database:

1. To add the SQL table as the output, go to Functions Portal -> `ScoreText` -> **Integrate** -> **Outputs** -> **+ New Output**:

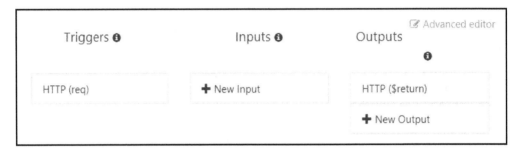

2. You will see a list of different output options available, including different types of databases and APIs. To configure a connection to Azure SQL, choose **External Table connection**, and click on **Select** as shown in this screenshot:

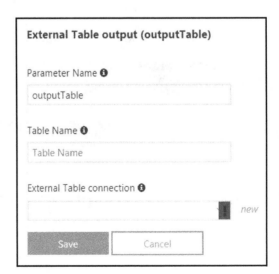

3. Click on **new** next to the **External Table connection** input, and configure the required connection settings.

4. Choose the following settings for the first blade:
    - **API**: Choose SQL Server from the drop-down menu and then navigate to **Connection** -> **Create New** -> **DisplayName**
    - **SQL Server name**: Fill in the full name (URL) of the Azure SQL Server we have created in previous steps, you can find the URL of your server under **SQL Databases** -> TextScoresDB -> **Overview** -> **Server Name**
    - **SQL Database Name**: Fill in the name of the database we have created, TextScoresDB
    - **Username**: Provide the SQL administrator name, in our example, sqladmin
    - **Password**: Enter the SQL administrator password you've chosen

5. Click on **OK**.

6. Click on **OK** twice to create the connection string.

7. In the new prompt that opens, configure the required values:
    - **Parameter Name: outputTable**
    - **Table Name:** DocumentTextScore

8. Leave the **Data Set Name** and **Entity ID** options unchanged.

9. Click on **Create**.

10. The new connection string to our Azure SQL database has been created and stored in the Function App settings under the name **sql_SQL**. We can use this connection in our function code online, however, since this value isn't automatically propagated back to the Visual Studio project, we will need to copy and paste it manually into the local.settings.json file to use it in the local project.

11. To copy the value, browse to **Function App** -> **Platform features** -> **App Settings** and scroll down to find the connection string that was generated:

sql_SQL	Endpoint=https://logic-apis...	☐ Slot setting	...

12. Let's change the setting's name to a more readable `azureSQL` instead of **sql_SQL** that was generated by default, as shown in the following screenshot:

```
azureSQL                        Endpoint=https://logic-apis...
```

13. Then click on the setting's value, select all, and copy. In Visual Studio, open `local.settings.json` in the `TextEvaluation` project. Add the `azureSQL` key as shown in the following code, and copy-paste the entire endpoint value, as follows:

```
{
    "IsEncrypted": false,
    "Values": {
    "AzureWebJobsStorage": "",
    "AzureWebJobsDashboard": "",
    "azureSQL": "Endpoint=https://logic-apis-northcentralus
    .azure-apim.net/apim/sql/<SqlGuid>/;Scheme=Key;
    AccessToken=<YourAccessToken>"
    }
}
```

14. In addition to the connection string, a new output binding was also defined for the `ScoreText` function, which you can see if you navigate to `function.json`. When working with Visual Studio, the `function.json` is auto generated based on the function's signature, and hence, to create the output binding locally, we will need to add the new output parameter decorated with the appropriate `WebJobs` attribute to the function signature. To do so, we first need to install the ApiHub Sdk NuGet packages.

15. In Visual Studio, navigate to **Tools -> NuGet Package Manager -> Package Manager Console**, and run the following command:

```
Install-Package Microsoft.Azure.Webjobs.Extensions.ApiHub -pre
```

This last command will install the WebJobs ApiHub extension, and the ApiHub SDK packages.

16. In Visual Studio, open the `ScoreText.cs` file. Add the using statement for ApiHub, and change the function signature to the following:

```
using Microsoft.Azure.ApiHub;
namespace TextEvaluation
{
```

```
public static class ScoreText
{
  [FunctionName("ScoreText")]
  public static async Task<HttpResponseMessage> Run(
     [HttpTrigger(AuthorizationLevel.Anonymous, "get", "post",
     Route = null)]HttpRequestMessage req,
     [ApiHubTable(connection: "azureSQL", TableName =
     "DocumentTextScore")]ITable<TextScore> outputTable,
     TraceWriter log)
```

The attribute decorating the `outputTable` parameter is what tells Visual Studio how to generate the output binding in `function.json`.

We are now ready to connect to the new output table, both in our local and the online function environment.

When working with online C# script-based `.csx` functions,the process of adding a reference to a NuGet library is different. If you are working with C# script functions, please refer to the `Appendix A`, *C# Script-Based Functions*.

Modifying the function to store results in SQL

Now that we've added the connection string, the binding, and the dependency to the function configuration, it is time to make changes to the function code by executing the following steps:

1. First, right-click on `TextEvaluation` -> **Add** -> **Class**, and add a `TextScore.cs` class with the following code:

    ```
    public class TextScore
    {
        public string DocumentName { get; set; }
        public double TextSentimentScore { get; set; }
    }
    ```

2. Now we can add the code to store the new score in the database after it has been generated by calling the `CreateEntityAsync(entity)` method on the `outputTable` parameter:

    ```
    // Generate random text score between 0 and 1
      var score = new Random().NextDouble();
      var textScore = new TextScore() { DocumentName = name,
      TextSentimentScore = score };
    ```

```
//Store the text score record in the database
await outputTable.CreateEntityAsync(textScore);
log.Info($"Randomized text score function returned a score of
{score}. RequestUri={req.RequestUri}");
```

3. After you've completed the changes, compile and run the new code.

4. If you navigate to the project's folder, /bin/Debug/net461/ScoreText, you will find function.json that contains the new output binding:

```json
{
  "bindings": [
    {
      "type": "httpTrigger",
      "methods": [
        "get",
        "post"
      ],
      "authLevel": "anonymous",
      "direction": "in",
      "name": "req"
    },
    {
      "type": "apiHubTable",
      "connection": "azureSQL",
      "tableName": "DocumentTextScore",
      "direction": "out",
      "name": "outputTable"
    },
    {
      "name": "$return",
      "type": "http",
      "direction": "out"
    }
  ],
  "disabled": false,
  "scriptFile": "..\\bin\TextEvaluation.dll",
  "entryPoint": "TextEvaluation.ScoreText.Run"
}
```

5. Browse to the function URL to make sure the function works correctly as shown in the following screenshot:

6. Now that the function has been configured to store the text sentiment score results in the database, we can run the `SELECT *` query on the `DocumentTextScore` table again to see all the scores that our testing has generated:

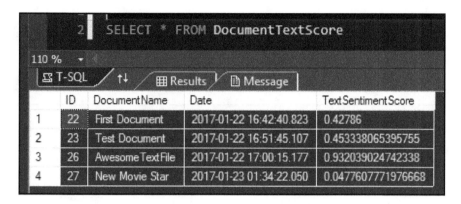

	ID	Document Name	Date	Text Sentiment Score
1	22	First Document	2017-01-22 16:42:40.823	0.42786
2	23	Test Document	2017-01-22 16:51:45.107	0.453338065395755
3	26	Awesome Text File	2017-01-22 17:00:15.177	0.932039024742338
4	27	New Movie Star	2017-01-23 01:34:22.050	0.0477607771976668

7. Once you have verified the code correctness, right-click on the project, and select **Publish** to republish the function to Azure. You can then refresh the function portal to see that the updated code has been loaded, and browse the function's Azure-based URL endpoint to make sure that the scores are stored in the database as expected.

In the production environment, you, typically, have different databases for Dev/Test/QA, and so on, and your development database is often local. In this book, however, we will continue using an Azure SQL database during development to demonstrate that the same function code can run locally on your machine and in your Azure Functions environment.

Setting up a web dashboard for scoring results

The last step of setting up our development environment is to set up a visual dashboard to display the results of our text processing. There are many ways to create such a dashboard. To stick with the theme of this book, we are going to create one as an ASP.NET Core web application, that is hosted on Azure App Service.

Azure App Service is a PaaS environment geared towards web, API, and mobile backend applications (App Service can also be used to host functions under the App Service plan). One way to think of App Service for a .Net web application is as an IIS as a service.

Lets take a look at the following steps:

1. To start a new project in Visual Studio, navigate to to **File -> New Project -> .NET Core -> ASP.NET Core Web Application**. Enter the application name, folder location, and solution name for the new project. Let's call the new project `TextScoreDashboard`:

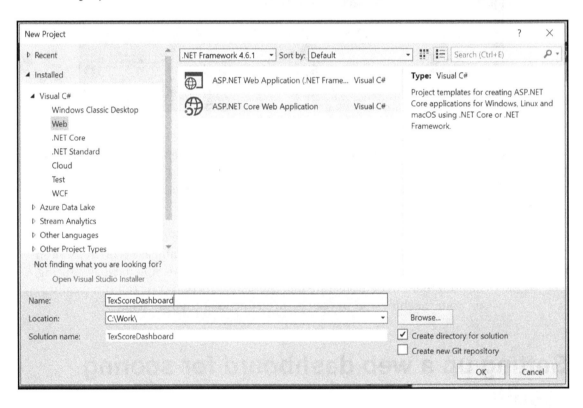

2. Click on **Next**, and, in the next step, select **Web Application**. Click on **Next** again. A new **ASP.Net Core Web Application** project will be created from the template. The application will contain an MVC web application template code, and some default `.cshtml` pages.

3. After the project has been created, right-click the project and click on **Publish** to create the Azure environment for the project:

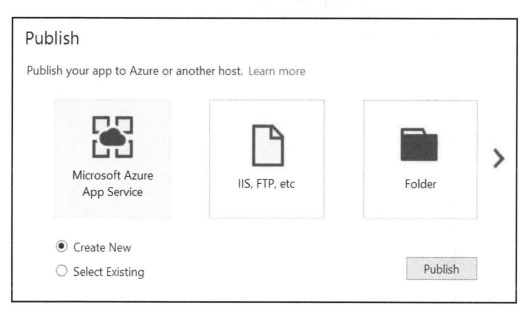

4. In the next dialog, configure the App Service for the new application.

5. Click the **New** button next to **App Service Plan**, and fill the required configuration as follows:

   - **App Service Plan**: Choose the name for the new App Service plan. It is good practice to identify the type of resource in the name for easier readability.
   - **Location**: Choose the same Azure region that your Functions App and your database are in.

- **Size**: Choose the **Free** tier. The free tier comes with limited resources and no SLA, however, in most cases, it is sufficient for dev environments:

6. Click on **OK**. In the next form, fill in the required fields as follows:
   - **Web App Name**: The name needs to be unique within the `azurewebsites.net` domain. This is the public domain name, which is assigned to your web application, and automatically becomes routable. In our example, it will be `TextScoreDashboard.azurewebsites.net`. (You can assign an additional custom domain to the web application if required. Custom domain assignment is covered in Chapter 10, Securing your Application).

- **Subscription**: Select the subscription that your other resources are located in.
- **Resource Group Name**: Choose the same resource group that your other resources are located in.
- **App Service Plan**: Choose the plan name you have created in the previous dialog. When you click on create, the App Service plan and the App Service itself will be created in Azure.

 If you chose a **Plan** tier other than **Free**, you will start getting billed for it upon creation.

7. Let us verify that the application works locally. To do so, run the application in Visual Studio using **IIS Express:**

8. By default, it will start on `http://localhost:7158/`, and you will see the template home page of an ASP.NET Core application:

Connecting the ASP.Net Core Web Application to the database

The first step for displaying our function results in the web application is to connect the application to the Azure SQL database that we've created in the previous section. To do this, we will use Entity Framework to generate the model from the existing database.

Installing Entity Framework dependencies

Let's take a look at the following steps for installing Entity Framework dependencies:

1. First, we will need to install the Entity Framework packages that our project will require. To do so, from the `TextScoreDashboard` project in Visual Studio, navigate to **Tools** -> **NuGet Package Manager** -> **Package Manager Console**.

2. Now run the following install-package commands:

```
Install-Package Microsoft.EntityFrameworkCore.SqlServer
Install-Package Microsoft.EntityFrameworkCore.Tools
Install-Package Microsoft.EntityFrameworkCore.Design
Install-Package Microsoft.EntityFrameworkCore.SqlServer.Design
```

3. To verify that all the packages were installed, navigate to `[ProjectName]` -> **References** -> **.NETCoreApp** , and see the package references in the list, as seen in the following screenshot:

```
▷  Microsoft.EntityFrameworkCore.Design (1.1.0)
▷  Microsoft.EntityFrameworkCore.SqlServer (1.1.0)
▷  Microsoft.EntityFrameworkCore.SqlServer.Design (1.1.0)
▷  Microsoft.EntityFrameworkCore.Tools (1.1.0-preview4-final)
```

Get the SQL Azure connection string

Now we need to connect to the database, and generate the model in the dashboard project, which can be done by executing the following steps:

1. Get the database connection string. The easiest way to get the full, well-formatted SQL Azure database connection string is to go to the Azure portal and navigate to **SQL Databases** -> `Database Name` -> **Properties** -> **Show database connection strings** -> **ADO.NET** as seen in the following screenshot:

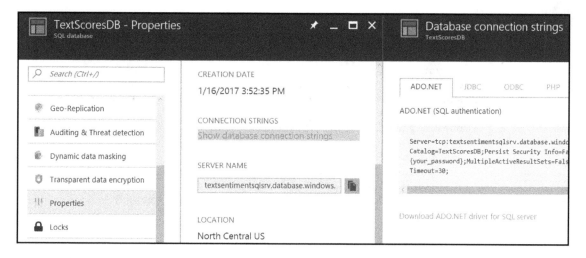

2. Copy the full connection string as follows:

```
Server=tcp:textsentimentsqlsrv.database.windows.net,1433;Initial
Catalog=TextScoresDB;Persist Security Info=False;User ID=
{your_username};Password={your_password};
MultipleActiveResultSets=False;Encrypt=True;
TrustServerCertificate=False;Connection Timeout=30;
```

3. Replace the values of `your_username` and `your_password` with the appropriate credentials.

4. Now, to generate the model from the database, in Visual Studio browse to **Tools -> NuGet Package Manager -> Package Manager Console**, and run the following command (insert the proper full connection string value):

```
Scaffold-DbContext "<full connection string>"
Microsoft.EntityFrameworkCore.SqlServer -OutputDir Models
```

5. If you get an error about the `Scaffold-DbContext` command not being defined, please close and re-open Visual Studio, and then rerun the command.

Updating the generated database context

Lets execute the following steps to update the generated database context:

1. Running the `Scaffold-DbContext` command will generate two classes under ProjectName Models. Those two classes are `TextScoreDBContext.cs` and `DocumentTextScore.cs`.

2. The `DocumentTextScore.cs` file will define a `DocumentTextScore` partial class with public properties based on the SQL `DocumentTextScore` table columns:

```
using System;
using System.Collections.Generic;
namespace TextScoreDashboard.Models
{
    public partial class DocumentTextScore
    {
        public int Id { get; set; }
        public string DocumentName { get; set; }
        public DateTime Date { get; set; }
        public double TextSentimentScore { get; set; }
    }
}
```

3. The `TextScoreDBContext.cs` file will define `DbContext`, and the model builder for the entity as follows:

```
using System;
using Microsoft.EntityFrameworkCore;
using Microsoft.EntityFrameworkCore.Metadata;
namespace TextScoreDashboard.Models
{
    public partial class TextScoresDBContext : DbContext
    {
        public virtual DbSet<DocumentTextScore>
        DocumentTextScore { get; set; }
        protected override void OnConfiguring
        (DbContextOptionsBuilder optionsBuilder)
{
 #warning To protect potentially sensitive information in your
 connection string, you should move it out of source code.
 See http://go.microsoft.com/fwlink/?LinkId=723263 for guidance
 on storing connection strings.
        optionsBuilder.UseSqlServer(@"<full connection
        string>");
}
protected override void OnModelCreating(ModelBuilder
modelBuilder)
{
    modelBuilder.Entity<DocumentTextScore>(entity =>
    {
        entity.Property(e => e.Id).HasColumnName("ID");
        entity.Property(e => e.Date)
            .HasColumnType("datetime")
            .HasDefaultValueSql("getutcdate()");
```

```
entity.Property(e => e.DocumentName)
    .IsRequired()
    .HasColumnType("varchar(255)");
        });
    }
  }
}
```

4. We will need to make a few changes to this file, and the project, to make sure that ASP.Net Core can load the database at runtime.

Dependency injection

The code in the previous section does not conform to the ASP.NET Core best practices. The best practice is to register the new service (DbContext) during application startup, and inject it into the classes that are using it, such as MVC controllers, using Dependency Injection rather than initializing the context inline in the TextScoresDBContext class. To learn more about Dependency Injection, view the documentation at https://docs. microsoft.com/en-us/aspnet/core/fundamentals/dependency-injection.

Let's take a look at the following steps:

1. To change the code to conform to best practice, open TextScoreDBContext.cs, and replace the following lines of code:

```
protected override void OnConfiguring(DbContextOptionsBuilder
optionsBuilder)
{
  #warning To protect potentially sensitive information in your
  connection string, you should move it out of source code. See
  http://go.microsoft.com/fwlink/?LinkId=723263 for guidance on
  storing connection strings.
  optionsBuilder.UseSqlServer(@"<full connection string>");
}
With the lines below
public TextScoresDBContext (DbContextOptions
<TextScoresDBContext> options)
: base(options)
{ }
```

The full code in TextScoreDBContext.cs after the change is as follows:

```
using System;
using Microsoft.EntityFrameworkCore;
using Microsoft.EntityFrameworkCore.Metadata;
```

```
namespace TextScoreDashboard.Models
{
    public partial class TextScoresDBContext : DbContext
    {
        public TextScoresDBContext
        (DbContextOptions<TextScoresDBContext> options)
        : base(options)
        { }
    public virtual DbSet<DocumentTextScore> DocumentTextScore {
    get; set; }
    protected override void OnModelCreating(ModelBuilder
    modelBuilder)
    {
      modelBuilder.Entity<DocumentTextScore>(entity =>
      {
         entity.Property(e => e.Id).HasColumnName("ID");
         entity.Property(e => e.Date).HasColumnType("datetime")
         .HasDefaultValueSql("getutcdate()");
         entity.Property(e => e.DocumentName)
         .IsRequired()
         .HasColumnType("varchar(255)");
      });
    }
  }
}
```

2. Now, to initialize the service at application startup, open `Startup.cs` (in the main project tree). At the top of the file, add the following using statements:

```
using Microsoft.EntityFrameworkCore;
using TextScoreDashboard.Models;
```

3. Add the following lines in the `ConfigureServices` method:

```
public void ConfigureServices(IServiceCollection services)
{
        var connection = Configuration.
        GetConnectionString("azureSql");
        services.AddDbContext<TextScoresDBContext>(options =>
        options.UseSqlServer(connection));
```

4. Finally, add the `azureSQL` connection string that we are using in `Startup.cs` to the `appsettings.json` file (don't forget the comma before the code block!).

This is not the same connection string that we have used in the Azure Function application project, but the ADO.Net connection string we have used to create the model in the ASP.Net Core project. If you are used to the classic ASP.NET application, this pattern of adding a connection string will be slightly different from the well-defined block in `web.config`. However, the idea is exactly the same.

```
"ConnectionStrings": {
        "azureSql": "<full connection string>"
}
```

Creating the web UI

In the previous section, we configured the model, and initialized DbContext using the connection string to our SQL Azure `TextScoresDB` database. Now that the database is accessible in our web application, we can generate the MVC controller and view to display the text score results.

This book will not describe the .Net MVC architecture in any detail, but it will give you the instructions on creating the code needed to display the function results in the web UI.

Creating the MVC controller

As the first step, we will need to add an MVC controller. We will inject `DbContext` into the controller via the dependency injection so that we can have access to `TextScoreDB` when the controller loads. Then we will add an `Index` action to the controller, and pass the records stored in the `DocumentTextScore` table to the `Index` MVC view as a model.

Lets create the MVC controller by executing the following steps:

1. Right-click on **Controllers** and click on **Add -> New Item -> MVC Controller**.
2. Modify the controller code to look like the following:

```
using System.Linq;
using Microsoft.AspNetCore.Mvc;
using TextScoreDashboard.Models;
namespace TextScoreDashboard.Controllers
{
    public class DocumentsController : Controller
    {
        private TextScoresDBContext _context;
        public DocumentsController(TextScoresDBContext context)
        {
```

```
            _context = context;
        }
        public IActionResult Index()
        {
            return View(_context.DocumentTextScore.ToList());
        }
    }
}
```

In this example, we are not going to define any CRUD operations, as we are not going to update or create new database records from the web application. The controller will only have one action dedicated to presentation.

Creating the MVC view

Finally, we will create the MVC View to present the table with the text score results in the web UI by performing the following steps:

1. To add the folder named `Documents` (corresponding to the controller named `Documents`), right-click on **Views** and navigate to **New Folder...** ->`Documents`.

2. To add the `Index` view, right-click on `Documents` folder and navigate to **Add** -> **New Item** -> **MVC View Page** -> `Index.cshtml`.

3. Modify the code to look like the following:

```
@model IEnumerable<TextScoreDashboard.Models.DocumentTextScore>
@{
    ViewBag.Title = "Document Scores";
}
<h2>Document Scores</h2>
<div class="main-content">
    <table class="table">
        <tr>
            <th>Document Name</th>
            <th>Date</th>
            <th>Score</th>
        </tr>
        @foreach (var item in Model)
        {
            <tr>
                <td>
                    @Html.DisplayFor(m => item.DocumentName)
                </td>
                <td>
                    @Html.DisplayFor(m => item.Date)
                </td>
                <td>
```

```
                @Html.DisplayFor(m => item.
                TextSentimentScore)
            </td>
        </tr>
    }
    </table>
</div>
```

In the preceding code, you will notice that we pass IEnumerable of the DocumentTextScore table records as the model to the view. Then we use a foreach method to iterate through all records in the model, and create an HTML table holding the MVC display templates for each of the values in the item table record. Once the data from the database is loaded, this view will create an HTML page displaying all the records in the DocumentTextScore SQL table.

Changing the application home page

Now that we have the MVC controller and view ready to load the database content, we need to change the application landing page, and its main layout from the generic template code generated by Visual Studio, to our TextScoreDashboard application code.

All we want on the application landing page right now is a link to the Documents view, where we can browse the text scores.

Let's see how we can change the application home page by performing the following steps:

1. To modify the landing page, navigate to **Views** -> **Home** -> Index.
2. Replace the existing code with the following:

```
@{
    ViewData["Title"] = "Home Page";
}
<h2>Text Sentiment Scores Dashboard</h2>
<div class="main-content">
    <ul>
        <li>
            @Html.ActionLink("Document Scores", "Index",
            "Documents", null, null)
        </li>
    </ul>
</div>
```

3. On the main layout, we will replace the unnecessary links with a link to the Document Scores page, and make minor styling changes.

4. To change the main application layout, go navigate to **Views** -> **Shared** -> `_Layout.cshtml`.

5. Under the `<body>` element, change the code to look like the following (Careful! The following code is not the full file code--only the parts that have been changed.):

```
<body>
    <div class="navbar navbar-inverse navbar-fixed-top">
        <div class="container">
            <div class="navbar-header">
                <button type="button" class="navbar-toggle"
                data-toggle="collapse" data-target=".navbar-
                collapse">
                    <span class="icon-bar"></span>
                    <span class="icon-bar"></span>
                    <span class="icon-bar"></span>
                </button>
            <a asp-area="" asp-controller="Home" asp-
            action="Index" class="navbar-brand">Dashboard</a>
                </div>
                <div class="navbar-collapse collapse">
                    <ul class="nav navbar-nav">
                        <li><a asp-area="" asp-
                        controller="Documents" asp-action="Index">
                        Document Scores</a></li>
                    </ul>
                </div>
            </div>
        </div>
    </div>
    <div class="container body-content">
        @RenderBody()
        <footer>
            <hr />
            <p>&copy; 2017 - TextScoreDashboard</p>
        </footer>
    </div>
</body>
```

6. We have made all the changes required to load and display the text score results from our SQL Azure database in our web application. Let's compile and run the application locally.

7. After you run the project and open the `http://localhost:7158` page in your browser, you should see the following web page:

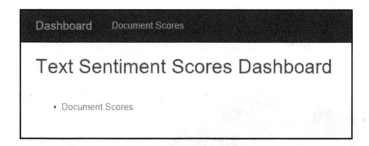

8. To browse from the application landing page to the Document Scores dashboard, click on the **Document Scores** link in the main content area, or in the top navigation bar.

You will see the list of the scores that our testing has generated so far, as seen in the following screenshot:

Dashboard	Document Scores	

Document Scores

Document Name	Date	Score
First Document	1/22/2017 4:42:40 PM	0.42786
Test Document	1/22/2017 4:51:45 PM	0.453338065395755
AwesomeTextFile	1/22/2017 5:00:15 PM	0.932039024742338
New Movie Star	1/23/2017 1:34:22 AM	0.0477607771976668

Publishing to Azure

Now that we have a fully functional web application that we can run locally, we can also publish it to Azure. The publishing process is nearly identical to the publishing process of the Azure Functions App. That is because we are using the same process called "Web Publish", and publishing to the same type of environment which is PaaS App Service.

Let's publish our web application by performing the following steps:

1. To get started, right-click on project name and click on **Publish...** as shown in the following screenshot:

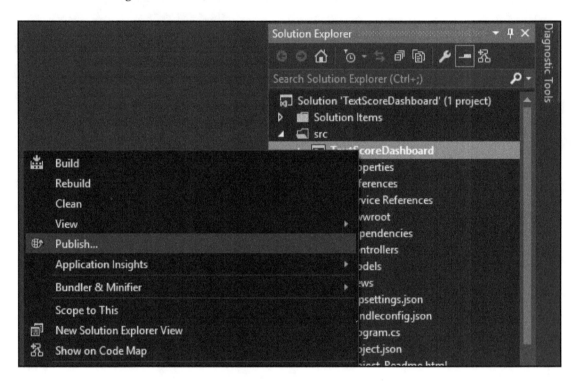

   In the dialog that opens, you will notice that we are in the last stage of the publishing process. That is because we have already tied the application to an Azure App Service environment when we first created the project, and all the configuration settings have been pre-filled for us.

2. If you need to modify any of the environment/publishing details, you can click on the **Preview** button to go back to the previous steps. If you wish to publish the application to the environment we've already established, simply click on the **Publish** button:

The first deployment may take a few minutes while the content is being uploaded and the environment is being configured.

3. After the deployment completes, navigate to your Azure application URL--in our example, http://textscoredashboard.azurewebsites.net, and smoke test the application. You will see the same score results dashboard that you were accessing locally.

The web application we've deployed is now publicly available on http://textscoredashboard.azurewebsites.net.

This book will not review App Service features of Web Apps any further, only the features that pertain to Azure Functions. For more information on Azure Web Apps, please refer to `https://docs.microsoft.com/en-us/azure/app-service-web/app-service-web-overview`.

Tying it all together

Now that we have configured the local development environment, and deployed the Azure serverless computing function, the database, and the web tier, we are ready to take full advantage of the serverless computing power. The integration with the web tier and the database will provide us with a comprehensive view of the text scoring results while we work to flesh out the advanced features of our text sentiment score application.

Summary

This chapter gave us an understanding of how to develop a serverless computing application on a local computer using Visual Studio, and then deploy it to Azure. In addition to that, we've learned how to use the results of our serverless computing process in other tiers of the application.

In this chapter, we have set up a development environment with Visual Studio 2017, created a Function App, and deployed it to Azure. We have set up a SQL Azure database to store the results of our serverless computing process. We then set up a web dashboard deployed as an Azure Web App to display these results.

Thus we have created the three common application tiers: the data tier, the logic tier in serverless compute, and the presentation tier, as shown in the following diagram. This allowed us to create the first basic version of the text sentiment score application:

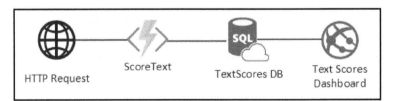

In the upcoming chapters, we will build upon the existing code to develop the advanced text sentiment scoring capabilities in our application.

4
Configuring Endpoints, Triggers, Bindings, and Scheduling

In the previous two chapters, we used a number of input and output bindings to interact with our serverless functions. In this chapter, we will elaborate on the different types of bindings, and learn to configure event triggers for serverless computing.

During the course of this chapter, we will cover the following topics:

- Understanding the input and output bindings of the function
- Configuring the function endpoints
- Triggering serverless functions based on an event
- Setting up a function to process a file upload to the Blob storage
- Creating a scheduled function

By the end of this chapter, we will have added a number of components to our application, which are illustrated in the following diagram:

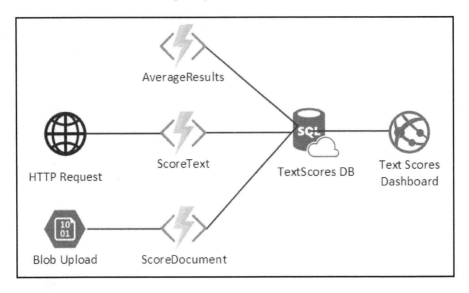

Triggers and bindings

The concept of triggers and bindings is central to Azure serverless computing. We have used triggers and bindings in the previous chapters by using function templates. In this chapter, we will elaborate on the bindings' structure, and the different options currently available in Azure serverless computing.

Triggers

A trigger is an event used to trigger your function code. Previously, we have defined functions triggered by HTTP requests. A variety of other triggers are available, and we will give examples of the most popular ones in this chapter.

Each function is limited to a single trigger. The function trigger must be defined in a binding in `function.json`, or through a trigger attribute in the function's signature in the Visual Studio functions project.

The function trigger must be selected from the supported list (the current list is provided further in the chapter). Defining custom triggers may become available in the future.

Binding

Binding specifies the metadata for your function trigger, input or output, and is defined in the `function.json` file. For precompiled functions, the `function.json` file is generated at compilation time by parsing the attributes in the function's signature.

While there is only one trigger per function, there is no limit to the number of input and output bindings. Currently, the binding type must be selected from the supported bindings list; however, defining custom bindings will be supported in the future.

Let us explore some examples of the three possible binding types.

Trigger binding

All trigger bindings have at least three following elements. Let's explore them in the following code snippet:

```
{
        "name": "name of the trigger parameter in function
        signature",
        "type": "trigger type",
        "direction": "in"
}
```

Take a look at the following three elements depicted in the preceding code snippet:

- `name`: This element is the name used for the trigger parameter used in the function signature. You can browse the code of the `ScoreText` function we've created in the previous chapter to see that the trigger name defined in the `function.json` file, `"name": "req"`, corresponds to the first parameter in the function signature in ScoreText.cs, `HttpRequestMessage req`. This parameter allows us to access the data supplied by the trigger in our function code.
- `type`: This element represents the trigger type, such as `httpTrigger` or `timerTrigger`.
- `direction`: The direction is set to `in` for a trigger binding.

Depending on the specific trigger, a number of additional settings may be required or optional. We will go into some of them in more detail. Please refer to the specific trigger documentation for more information on the attribute types.

The currently available trigger types are listed at the following link:

```
https://docs.microsoft.com/en-us/azure/azure-functions/functions-triggers-
bindings
```

The list of .NET attributes for precompiled functions and their documentations can be found at `https://docs.microsoft.com/en-us/azure/azure-functions/functions-dotnet-class-library`.

Input binding

As we've just seen, trigger binding also defines the first input parameter for your function. On top of that, you can add other bindings to specify additional input parameters. As you will see in the table later in this chapter, certain types of bindings can serve as input, but not as triggers.

Every input binding has the settings of name, type, and direction, with direction value is set to `in`. The rest of the settings will depend on the type of binding you use. Most input-only bindings will also have a connection string, which allows them to connect to an external data store from which the data is coming.

As an example, we will use an input-only binding used for Azure Storage Queue, as shown in the following code:

```
"bindings": [
    {
        "type": "queueTrigger",
        "queueName": "<Name of the storage queue to poll>",
        "connection": "<Name of app setting with connection string>",
        "direction": "in",
        "name": "<Name of input parameter in function signature>"
    }
```

In a precompiled function, this binding will be defined using the attributes in the function's signature as follows:

```
[FunctionName("MyQueue")]
    public static async Task Run([QueueTrigger("<queueName>",
    Connection = "<connection>")]string <name>, TraceWriter log)
```

Please refer to the documentation online to learn more about binding specific arguments for each available input binding type. All currently available bindings are listed at the following link `https://docs.microsoft.com/en-us/azure/azure-functions/functions-triggers-bindings`.

Output binding

Output binding defines the output of your function. Serverless function outputs are most commonly defined by calls to external APIs. As the function execution is triggered asynchronously, the output should not be returned directly to the service that triggered the function. The output must be submitted to another API to trigger a new event, or store data in some form of persistent data store.

All output bindings will have the settings of name, type, and direction, with direction value set to out. The rest of the settings depend on the binding type. Certain types of bindings are available as output only.

As an example, we will use an output-only binding to the Twilio SMS API as shown in the following code snippet from function.json:

```
{
    "type": "twilioSms",
    "name": "<Name of output parameter in function signature>",
    "accountSid": "TwilioAccountSid",
    "authToken": "TwilioAuthToken",
    "to": "<Can be parametrized/dynamic: phone number SMS is sent
    to>",
    "from": "<Phone number SMS is sent from>",
    "direction": "out",
    "body": "<Can be parametrized/dynamic: message text>"
}
```

In a precompiled function, this output binding will be defined by using the following TwilioSms attribute (the following example also includes a queue trigger input binding):

```
[FunctionName("QueueTwilio")]
public static SMSMessage Run([QueueTrigger("myqueue", Connection =
"AzureWebJobsStorage")] JObject order,
[TwilioSms(AccountSidSetting = "<accountSid>",
AuthTokenSetting = "<authToken>",
To = "<to>", From = "<from>", Body = "<body>")] out SMSMessage
<name>,TraceWriter log)
```

The following table shows the list of currently available bindings for triggers, inputs, and outputs (the availability of the trigger or binding might be dependent on the programming language of the function). In the following table, a V signifies if a binding is available as a trigger, input, or output, or a combination of the preceding. Please also refer to the online documentation, as new binding types are being added frequently:

Type	Trigger	Input	Output
Schedule	V	NA	NA
HTTP (REST or webhook)	V	NA	V*
Blob storage	V	V	V
Event Hubs	V	NA	V
Storage Queues	V	NA	V
Service Bus Queues	V	NA	V
Storage Tables	NA	V	V
Mobile Apps Tables	NA	V	V
CosmosDB (DocumentDB)	NA	V	V
Notification Hubs push notifications	NA	NA	V
Twilio SMS Text	NA	NA	V
External Table (SQL, SharePoint, SalesForce, DB2, and so on)	NA	V**	V**
External File (Filesystem, FTP, Dropbox, and so on)	V**	V**	V**

* HTTP output binding requires an HTTP trigger.

** External Table and External File are still in preview at this time.

Advanced bindings

Azure functions also support two more advanced types of binding: parameter binding and binding at runtime. In this book, we will not cover these types of bindings. Please refer to the following links to learn more:

Parameter binding: `https://docs.microsoft.com/en-us/azure/azure-functions/functions-triggers-bindings#parameter-binding`

Binding at runtime: https://docs.microsoft.com/en-us/azure/azure-functions/
functions-triggers-bindings#advanced-binding-at-runtime-imperative-binding

Endpoints

A function endpoint is the publicly available URL on which you can access the function.

In Azure serverless computing (unlike in some serverless offers provided by other vendors), HTTP(s) endpoints are assigned automatically to all the functions that have an HTTP or a Webhook trigger, without a need for an API Gateway. By default, the function is assigned an endpoint constructed in the following manner, based on your application and function name:

```
http://<YourAppName>.azurewebsites.net/api/<FunctionName>
```

Custom routes

To change the domain part of the URL (http://<YourAppName>.azurewebsites.net), you can configure a custom domain for your Function App, which we will describe in more detail in Chapter 10, *Securing Your Application*. This change will apply to all the functions defined under the Function App.

To customize the default api route prefix, you can add the following code to the host.json file (main project tree):

```
{
    "http": {
        "routePrefix": "textapi-v1"
    }
}
```

You can also specify an empty route prefix, such as "routePrefix": "", to simply remove the api prefix from the URL.

This change will apply to all the functions under the Function App.

To define a custom route for the part of the URL of a specific function (`<FunctionName>`), you can modify the URL by adding a `route` property to your function's input trigger binding definition. The following route is constructed according to the web API routing standards, and defines a custom route, plus two parameters, with parameter types of string and nullable integer:

```
"bindings": [
{
  "authLevel": "anonymous",
  "name": "req",
  "type": "httpTrigger",
  "direction": "in",
  "methods": [ "get" ],
  "route" : "documents/{directory:alpha}/{id:int?}"
},
```

In this example, you can now access the function using the following URL, and the function will receive two parameters:`directory = english`, and `id = 101`:

```
http://<YourAppName>.azurewebsites.net/api/documents/english/101
```

You can then use the parameters submitted in the URL by defining them in the function's signature, and accessing their values in the function code. For this example, the precompiled function signature would be as follows:

```
public static async Task<HttpResponseMessage> Run(
  [HttpTrigger(AuthorizationLevel.Anonymous, "get",
  Route = "documents/{directory:alpha}/{id:int?}")]
  HttpRequestMessage req, string directory, int? id, TraceWriter
  log)
```

Please see more information regarding constructing web API routes at this link:

```
https://www.asp.net/web-api/overview/web-api-routing-and-actions/attribute-
routing-in-web-api-2#constraints
```

Allowed methods

By default, an HTTP trigger function binding generated online does not have a `methods` attribute, meaning that the function responds to all HTTP methods. As we have seen, an HTTP trigger function generated in Visual Studio will specify GET and POST as allowed methods by default. You can restrict the methods allowed on a specific function to the methods of your choosing by adding a `methods` attribute with a list of allowed methods in the `function.json` file:

```
"methods": [ "post", "put" ]
```

Which can be achieved by specifying them on the trigger attribute in the function's signature in a precompiled function, as follows:

```
[HttpTrigger(AuthorizationLevel.Anonymous, "get", "post", Route =
null)]HttpRequestMessage req
```

Now, if an unallowed method is called in the function endpoint, the function will respond with a 405 "Method Not Allowed" response.

API definition

Function App API definition (currently in preview) allows you to write an OpenAPI 2.0 (formerly, Swagger) definition inside a Function App. OpenAPI is a widely accepted industry specification, standardizing how REST APIs are described. The OpenAPI metadata produces a machine-readable definition that can be consumed by Microsoft and third-party software such as Postman or Runscope.

The API definition feature allows you to create the swagger.json metadata file hosted in your Function App. Once the metadata is generated, it is accessible via https://<YourFunctionApp>.azurewebsites.net/admin/host/swagger?code=<ApiKey>.

To learn how to generate an API definition, please visit https://docs.microsoft.com/en-us/azure/azure-functions/functions-api-definition.

Proxies

Azure Functions Proxies (currently in preview) allow you to specify the endpoints on your Function App that are implemented by another service. Among other things, this allows you to break your API implementation into multiple Function Apps, or add additional endpoints served by a different web API app while still presenting a single cohesive API to the end user.

Proxies also allow you to modify requests and/or responses, creating a transformation. These transformations can be static, or may use variables provided by the route template parameters, request and response parameters (such as request headers), or application settings.

To learn how to configure function proxies, please visit https://docs.microsoft.com/en-us/azure/azure-functions/functions-proxies.

Securing the endpoints

The examples we've seen up until now created functions available on a public endpoint, and required no authentication or authorization. If your function accesses protected data, it is paramount to secure the function endpoint.

By default, all the function endpoints on a default domain (a subdomain of `azurewebsites.net`) provided by Azure use HTTPS, combining HTTP protocol with **Transport Layer Security** (**TLS**) encryption (still commonly referred to as the older protocol name, SSL), so that the data transferred to and from the function cannot be "sniffed" over the internet connection. TLS, in combination with endpoint authorization (function keys), helps ensure that your function can only be triggered by authorized users. To learn more about HTTPS, visit `https://en.wikipedia.org/wiki/HTTPS`.

If a custom domain is assigned to a Function App, you will need to add an SSL certificate for the domain, and enable SSL encryption on the function endpoint.

We will elaborate more on SSL encryption and types of Function endpoint authorization in `Chapter 10`, *Securing Your Application*.

Blob Storage trigger

One of the prominent use cases for serverless computing is file processing. A function can be triggered upon file upload to a particular data store to do immediate manipulations on the data. This allows for asynchronous processing, and eliminates the need to be polling or traversing the data store in search of new data. In this manner, you can kick off a media encoding process, an image compression process, or, in our example, a text sentiment analysis on a text file after the user uploads a file.

To set up a function triggered by a file upload to the Azure Blob Storage, we will first need to create a storage account.

Creating a storage account for document upload

Let's create a storage account for document upload by performing the following steps:

1. To create a Blob storage account, in the Azure portal, navigate to **New** (plus icon) -> **Storage** -> **Storage Account** as shown in the following screenshot:

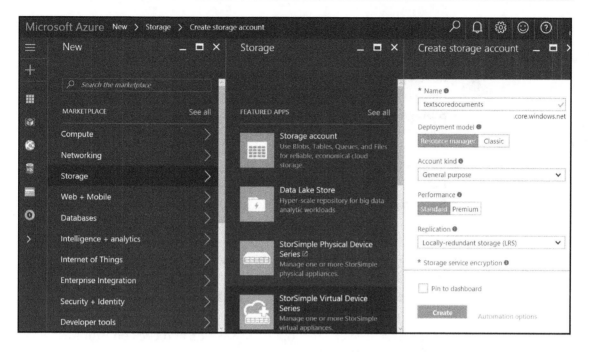

2. In the new blade, fill in the following required settings:

- **Name**: Type in the storage account name. In this example, we will name the account `textscoredocuments`. The name allows only for lowercase letters and numbers, must be between 3 and 24 characters in length, and unique within the `core.windows.net` Azure storage domain.

- **Deployment model**: Choose the **Resource manager** model. This specifies that we are using Azure Resource Manager API to create the account.

- **Account kind**: Choose the **General purpose** option. This will allow us to create all four types of storage such as Blobs, Files, Queues, and Tables within the storage account. A general purpose account is required for function blob triggers.

- **Performance**: Choose the **Standard** option. Premium storage has better performance; however, it is also higher priced. For file storage purposes, the Standard storage tier is sufficient in most cases.

- **Replication**: Choose the **locally-redundant storage (LRS)** option. Locally-redundant storage is replicated three times within the same Azure data center for resiliency purposes, which is sufficient for development environment purposes. In production applications, you may choose to use one of the geo-redundant storage types.
- **Storage service encryption**: Choose **Enabled**. This allows for encryption of data at rest, and has no implications for the storage performance or cost.
- **Secure transfer required**: Choose **Enabled**. This requires the data in transit to be transferred over HTTPS only.
- **Subscription**: Choose the subscription that your other resources are in.
- **Resource group**: Choose the resource group that your other resources are in.
- **Location**: Choose the geographic location that your other resources are in.
- **Pin to dashboard**: Check to get the storage account "pinned" to the main portal dashboard.

3. After the account has been created, open the account, and click on **Blobs** as shown in the following screenshot:

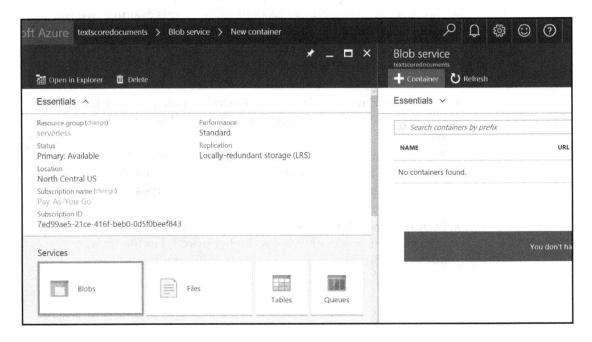

4. In the **Blob service** blade, click on the **Container** button to add a new blob container. A blob container is equivalent to a file folder that you use to organize files. We will create the new container that our Blob-triggered serverless function will be "watching" for blob uploads.

5. In the new container blade, fill in the following required parameters:
   - **Name**: This field represents the container name. This name can only contain lowercase letters, numbers, and hyphens. We will name the container `documents`.
   - **Access type**: Choose **Private**. Access type defines if the blobs in the container are publicly accessible for the **Read** or **List** permissions.

6. Click on **Create**.

Getting the storage connection string

To trigger the function based on the file upload to storage, we will need the storage account connection string. The connection string is dependent on the account name and the account key. Azure storage generates two access keys by default to allow "rolling" the keys without interruption of access to storage. The keys are used to authenticate access, and should be stored securely.

Let's take a look at the following steps to get the storage connection string needed for the blob triggered function:

1. To get your storage account connection string, navigate to **Storage account -> Storage account name -> Access keys**.

2. Click on the **...** button next to **key1**, and then click on **View connection string**. This is the connection string we will use when creating the function. Copy the connection string from the popup:

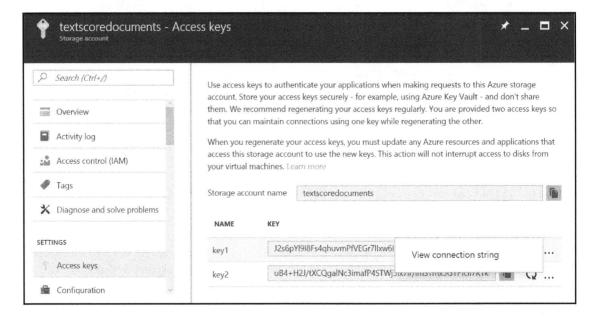

Creating a Blob trigger function

Now we are ready to create our **Blob Trigger** function. Let's perform the following steps to create it:

1. In the Visual Studio project, right-click on the `TextEvaluation` project name, and then click on **Add -> New Item -> Azure Function.**
2. In the **Name** field, type `ScoreDocument`.
3. Fill in the required parameters as follows:
   - **Function Type**: Select **BlobTrigger** in this field.
   - **FunctionName**: This will be the new function name. Enter `ScoreDocument`.
   - **Connection:** Enter `blobStorageConnection`. We will define the connection string in `local.settings.json` after the function is created.

- **Path:** This is the name of the Blob storage container that the function will be "watching" for new blob uploads. Enter `documents/{name}`, the name of the container we have just created, plus the blob name pattern. Having the `{name}` in the path will allow us to access the blob name using a `name` variable (see the function code on the next page). We could also create very specific name patterns to look for a particular name structure, or a specific file extension. For example, the following path would mean that the function only gets triggered when a document with file extension `.txt` is uploaded:

```
"path": "documents/{name}.txt",
```

 To learn more about name patterns, visit the following link: `https://docs.microsoft.com/en-us/azure/azure-functions/functions-bindings-storage-blob#pattern`.

4. Click on **Create:**

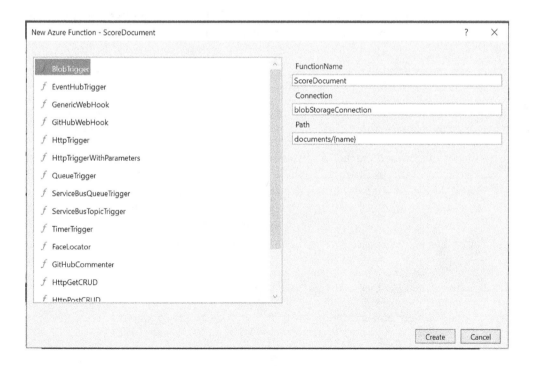

5. After the new function is created, click on **Build -> Rebuild Solution**, and then navigate to the project folder, `/bin/Debug/net461/ScoreDocument`.

6. Open the `functions.json` file. You will see the following code. As explained in the previous section, this binding defines a Blob trigger with the function trigger `name` being set to `myBlob`. There are also two additional settings: the document path and the name of the storage connection string:

```
{
  "bindings": [
  {
    "type": "blobTrigger",
    "connection": "blobStorageConnection",
    "path": "documents/{name}",
    "direction": "in",
    "name": "myBlob"
  }
  ],
  "disabled": false,
  "scriptFile": "..\\TextEvaluation.dll",
  "entryPoint": "TextEvaluation.ScoreDocument.Run"
}
```

7. The connection string named `blobStorageConnection` now needs to be added to the project configuration. To achieve that, browse to the `local.settings.json` file. Add the new setting, as follows. In the setting value, paste the full connection string that you copied from the Azure Storage account, except for the trailing semicolon:

```
"blobStorageConnection": "DefaultEndpointsProtocol=https;
AccountName=textscoredocuments;AccountKey=<FullAccountKey>"
```

8. As we mentioned earlier, all but HTTP triggered functions require the connection to Azure WebJobs Storage, which is not set automatically in local projects. If you haven't done so before, to get the connection strings, in Functions Portal, navigate to your `[Your Function App]` **-> Platform features -> Application Settings**, and copy the `AzureWebJobsStorage` and `AzureWebJobsDashboard` settings to your `local.setting.json` file as follows:

```
"AzureWebJobsStorage":"DefaultEndpointsProtocol=https;
AccountName=textevaluationstorage; AccountKey=
<FullAccountKey>",
"AzureWebJobsDashboard":"DefaultEndpointsProtocol=https;
AccountName=textevaluationstorage; AccountKey=
<FullAccountKey>",
```

Function code

Let's take a look at the following steps to create the function code:

1. In the project tree, browse to the `ScoreDocument.cs` file.
2. Let's replace the generated code with the following code.

   The following function code assumes that the uploaded file is a text file that can be processed using `StreamReader`. Upon execution, the file content will be stored in the `blobContent` variable, while the file name will be stored in the `name` parameter. (The code is kept short for clarity. In production code, we would also need to perform input validation).

   The code is as follows:

   ```
   public static class ScoreDocument
   {
     [FunctionName("ScoreDocument")]
     public static async Task Run(
         [BlobTrigger("documents/{name}", Connection =
         "blobStorageConnection")] Stream myBlob, string name,
         TraceWriter log)
     {
         var blobContent = new StreamReader(myBlob).ReadToEnd();
         log.Info($"C# Blob trigger function Processed blobn
         Name:{name} n Size: {myBlob.Length} Bytes");
     }
   }
   ```

3. To see the function in action, place a breakpoint at the opening bracket, then compile and run the function. You will see the Functions Core Tools window load. The new function is running and ready to react when triggered.

Triggering the function

Now that the function is up and running locally, we need to trigger its execution by uploading a text file to the `documents` container in our Blob storage account. Document upload can be done through the portal, or using a desktop application called Azure Storage Explorer. At the moment, we will walk through an upload example using Azure portal, and will describe the usage of Storage Explorer in Chapter 7, *Debugging Your Azure Functions*. To learn how to use Storage Explorer, please visit `https://docs.microsoft.com/en-us/azure/machine-learning/machine-learning-data-science-move-data-to-azure-blob-using-azure-storage-explorer`.

In the portal, file upload can be done by performing the following steps:

1. To upload a new file, navigate to **Storage accounts** -> [Your Account Name] -> **Blobs** -> `documents`, and click on the **Upload** button as seen in this screenshot:

2. In the **Upload blob** blade that opens, click on the folder icon to browse to a file from your computer.
3. Keep the **Blob type** field as `Block blob`, and the **Block size** field as `4 MB`. Click on **Upload**:

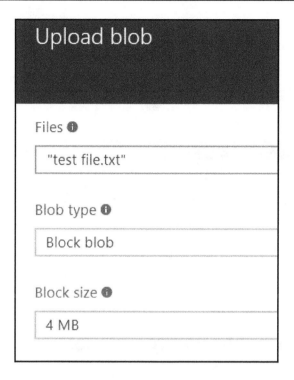

4. Shortly, you will see the new file appear in the file list in the `documents` container.

5. Since the function host is currently running on your local machine, the `ScoreDocument` function will be triggered upon file upload to the `documents` container. It may take a few moments before the function gets triggered. The triggering process is *not* real time in case of Blob Storage (it is real time for all other available triggers).

You may re-upload the same file multiple times, and the function will get triggered every time, as it watches out for new file versions along with new files.

6. After the function gets triggered, your breakpoint will fire. In Visual Studio, in the **Locals** window, you can explore the current values of the function parameters:

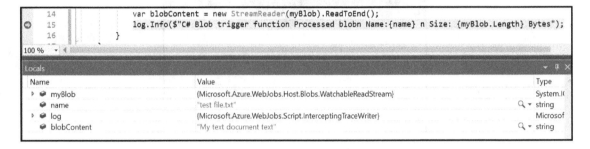

7. Click on **Continue** in Visual Studio to continue the function execution.
8. Switch back to the Functions Core Tools window, and you will see the log output indicating that the `ScoreDocument` function executed successfully.

Updating the function to process text

Now that we have verified that the function gets triggered successfully upon file upload, we can build upon the code we have developed in the previous chapter to tie the new `BlobTrigger` function to the database. We will, essentially, use the exact same code we've developed for the `ScoreText` function, but now apply it to the text file uploaded to storage.

 We are still using a randomized score rather than processing an actual text sentiment. The actual sentiment processing, which generates a meaningful score, will be added in `Chapter 6`, *Intregrating Azure Functions with Cognitive Services API*.

To update the function, execute the following steps:

1. In the `ScoreDocument.cs` file, add a `using` statement for `ApiHub`, and add the same `ApiHubTable` parameter that we used in the `ScoreText` function signature. The modified code will store the uploaded document score in the same `DocumentTextScore` SQL table. Examine the following code example:

```
using System.IO;
using Microsoft.Azure.WebJobs;
using Microsoft.Azure.WebJobs.Host;
using System.Threading.Tasks;
using Newtonsoft.Json.Linq;
```

```
using Microsoft.Azure.ApiHub;

[FunctionName("ScoreDocument")]
public static async Task Run(
[BlobTrigger("documents/{name}", Connection =
"blobStorageConnection")] Stream myBlob,
[ApiHubTable(connection: "azureSQL", TableName =
"DocumentTextScore")] ITable<TextScore> outputTable,
string name, TraceWriter log)
{
    var blobContent = new StreamReader(myBlob).ReadToEnd();

    // Generate random text score between 0 and 1
    double score = new Random().NextDouble();
    var textScore = new TextScore()
    {
        DocumentName = name,
        TextSentimentScore = score
    };

    //Store the text score record in the database
    await outputTable.CreateEntityAsync(textScore);
    log.Info($"Document scoring function processed a text file " +
        $"\"{name}\" and returned a score of {score}");

}
```

2. To trigger the function locally, click on **Start** to run the project.

3. In Azure portal, upload a new text file to the `documents` container in the storage. When the function gets triggered, you will see the following log output:

```
[5/27/2017 6:15:00 PM] Executing 'Functions.ScoreDocument'
(Reason='New blob detected: documents/test file.txt',
Id=1e0be07a-6906-4766-8474-7032a8ef1297)
[5/27/2017 6:15:00 PM] Function started (Id=1e0be07a-6906-4766-
8474-7032a8ef1297)
[5/27/2017 6:15:00 PM] Randomized text score function processed
a blob file test file.txt and returned a score of
0.531259265044359
[5/27/2017 6:15:00 PM] Function completed (Success,
Id=1e0be07a-6906-4766-8474-7032a8ef1297, Duration=61ms)
[5/27/2017 6:15:00 PM] Executed 'Functions.ScoreDocument'
(Succeeded,Id=1e0be07a-6906-4766-8474-7032a8ef1297)
```

4. When ready, publish the project to Azure using the same process that you learned in `Chapter 3`, *Setting Up the Development Environment,* either using Visual Studio or Functions Core Tools.

5. After you have published the code, and added the `blobStorageConnection` connection string to the Function App application settings, your function is ready to execute in Azure. To trigger the function in Azure, stop your local project, and upload a new file to the `documents` container in the storage.

6. To see the invocation logs, in Functions Portal, browse to the `ScoreDocument` function, and then navigate to **Monitor**. You will see both local and online invocation logs here, since the local function is tied to the same WebJob Host. Clicking a specific invocation record will allow you to see the invocation details as well as the function logs.

 Application Insights is the recommended monitoring tool for Azure Functions, and it will eventually completely replace the **Monitor** tab. We will walk through Application Insights setup and configuration in `Chapter 11`, *Monitoring your Application*

The Monitor logs are seen in the following screenshot:

Timer trigger

To create a serverless function that executes on a specific schedule, we need to use the timer trigger. A timer trigger is an event, which triggers the function execution periodically, based on a specific schedule. To demonstrate a scheduled function, we will create a new function to run every minute and average our scoring results.

There are certainly easier ways to average scoring results, however, we are using averaging to showcase a scheduled process.

Prior to creating the function, let us explain how to define the function's schedule.

CRON expression

In Azure Functions, a binding for a timer trigger will look like the following, where the schedule is defined by a CRON expression:

```
{
    "name": "name of the trigger parameter in function signature",
    "type": "timerTrigger",
    "direction": "in",
    "schedule": "CRON Expression"
}
```

A CRON expression is a string, typically, used to define a schedule for a routine in job schedulers on Unix-like systems. A CRON expression is defined by six fields: `{second}`, `{minute}`, `{hour}`, `{day}`, `{month}`, and `{day of the week}`.

A `*` symbol in a CRON expression is an indicator for "every", such as every day, every hour, every day of the week, and so on. A `/` in the expression can be used to define the step values. For instance, `*/5` in the minutes field would mean every 5 minutes. Commas are used to separate values in a list, and hyphens are used to define ranges.

Here are some schedule examples to help illustrate the concept:

- To have the function triggered every hour of every day, define `"schedule": "0 0 * * * *"`
- To have the function triggered every 10 minutes from Sunday through Friday, define `"schedule": "0 */10 * * * 0-5"`
- To have the function triggered at 11:15 on Monday and Wednesday, define `"schedule": "0 15 11 * * 1,3"`

To learn more about CRON expressions, visit the following link: `https://en.wikipedia.org/wiki/Cron#CRON_expression`

For Azure Functions, the time zone used when executing the CRON expression is UTC. You can set the schedule to reflect your local time zone by using the UTC offset of your local time zone (for example, CST time zone in US has a UTC offset of -6). If you wish to change the time zone of the schedule itself, you can define an application setting in the Function App called `WEBSITE_TIME_ZONE`, and set the value of the time zone according to the Microsoft Time Zone Index that can be found here:

```
https://msdn.microsoft.com/library/ms912391.aspx
```

Implementing the average result function

Let's take a look at the following steps for implementing the average result function:

1. To create a new scheduled function, right-click on the project, and navigate to **Add -> New Item -> Azure Function**. Select the following options:

   - **Type**: `Timer Trigger`
   - **Name**: `AverageResults`
   - **Schedule**: `"0 0 * * * *"`--as explained in the previous section, this will trigger the function every hour on top of the hour

   The generated function code in `AverageResults.cs` will be as follows:

   ```
   [FunctionName("AverageResults")]
   public static async Task Run([TimerTrigger("0 0 * * *
   *")]TimerInfo
   myTimer, TraceWriter log)
   {
       log.Info($"C# Timer trigger function executed at:
       {DateTime.Now}");
   }
   ```

   When you compile the function, the following timer trigger binding will be defined in the `function.json` file:

   ```
   {
     "type": "timerTrigger",
     "schedule": "0 0 * * * *",
     "useMonitor": true,
     "runOnStartup": false,
     "direction": "in",
     "name": "myTimer"
   }
   ```

2. Now to make use of the function to average the scoring results, we need to add both input and output binding references to the SQL tables.

3. First, let's add a new table to our Azure SQL database. In Visual Studio, in SQL server object explorer, right-click on the `TextScoresDB` database, and select **New Query...**. Paste the following code into the query window, and click on **Execute**:

```
CREATE TABLE AverageDocumentScore
(
   ID INT IDENTITY(1,1) PRIMARY KEY,
   DocumentCount INT NOT NULL,
   AverageScore FLOAT NOT NULL,
   [Date] DATE NOT NULL DEFAULT GETUTCDATE(),
);
```

This preceding code will add a new empty `AverageDocumentScore` table to our existing Azure SQL database.

4. Now we can add parameters (bindings) for both `DocumentTextScore` and `AverageDocumentScore` SQL tables to the function. Note that, in the case of `AverageDocumentScore`, we will use the same binding to both get data from the table, and store the outcome in it (essentially, the same binding works as both input and output binding).

5. Since we are using the same Azure SQL database, we already have the `azureSQL` connection string defined in the `local.settings.json` file, and don't need to re-add it.

Before looking into the complete function code, let us explain two technical aspects of the implementation.

Defining the SQL table binding

There are two different ways in which we can use to access SQL table records using the `ApiHub.SDK` library:

1. Defining the binding using a POCO object

   Using a **Plain old CLR object (POCO)** object lets you explicitly define a class that has all, or a subset of properties defined in the SQL table.

2. Defining the binding using JObject

Using JObject (defined in the `Newtonsoft.Json.Linq NuGet` library) lets you define the entity as a JSON object. With JSON object, you can add properties during runtime, which allows for more flexibility with the object type.

In the previous example, we used a POCO object to define the entities of the `DocumentTextScore` SQL table in `ApiHub.SDK` binding.

When accessing the `AverageDocumentScore` SQL table, we will use JObject to define the entity in the binding. This will allow for more flexibility, as we are using the same binding to both get the input from, and send the output to the same SQL table.

To use JObject, we will define the function parameter as `ITable<JObject> averageTable`. A single entity we get from the `AverageDocumentScore` table will then look as follows:

```
{
    "@odata.etag": "",
    "ItemInternalId": "a974ab5b-4b8e-45e6-b63c-dfa9b6fefdce",
    "ID": 31,
    "DocumentCount": 16,
    "AverageScore": 0.4697681,
    "Date": "2017-02-19"
}
```

And the new JObject instance to be stored back in the SQL table can be constructed on the fly in the following manner :

```
// Create new score entity as JObject
var scoreAverage = new JObject {
    new JProperty("DocumentCount", count),
    new JProperty("AverageScore", average)
};
```

Finding an existing entity

To ensure that we are not storing an average score every time the function runs, we need to have a unique identifier for the average. For `AverageDocumentScore` table, we chose the date as the unique property. Thus, only a single average score will be stored for each day, and this score will be updated if the function re-runs.

To ensure that we are not storing duplicates, we need to find the entity (SQL table row) if it already exists. Loading all the data stored in the `AverageDocumentScore` table and then searching for existing entities on a particular date can become a very "costly" operation as the table grows. To avoid doing that, we are going to use the `query` parameter of the `ListEntitiesAsync()` method, which will execute against the SQL table, and filter out the entities we are not interested in. The query is an oData query. As an example, a query looking for all entities where City equals Chicago would be defined in the following manner:

```
var addresses = await table.ListEntitiesAsync(query:
Query.Parse("$filter=City eq 'Chicago'"));
```

More information regarding constructing an oData query can be found at http://www.odata.org/documentation/odata-version-2-0/uri-conventions/.

In our function code, we are looking for all the entities created on a particular date. Since we pass the query in a string, the data type must be represented in a certain literal form. The following code lets us look for all entities on today's date:

```
var today = XmlConvert.ToString(DateTime.Now,
XmlDateTimeSerializationMode.Utc);
var query = "$filter=Date eq Date(" + today + ")";
var entities = await averageTable.ListEntitiesAsync(query:
Query.Parse(query));
```

Information regarding representation of different data types in oData query can be found at http://www.odata.org/documentation/odata-version-2-0/overview/.

Full Function Code

For the sake of readability, the following code does not check for any errors or edge cases. In a production system, you should add exception and edge case handling in case of unexpected input and so on.

The following is the full AverageResults function code:

```
using System;
using System.Linq;
using Microsoft.Azure.WebJobs;
using Microsoft.Azure.WebJobs.Host;
using Microsoft.Azure.ApiHub;
using Newtonsoft.Json.Linq;
using System.Xml;

namespace TextEvaluation
{
 public static class AverageResults
 {
   [FunctionName("AverageResults")]
   public static async Task Run(
   [TimerTrigger("0 * * * * *")]TimerInfo myTimer,
   [ApiHubTable(connection: "azureSQL", TableName =
   "DocumentTextScore")]ITable<TextScore> scoresTable,
   [ApiHubTable(connection: "azureSQL",
   TableName = "AverageDocumentScore")]
   ITable<JObject> averageTable, TraceWriter log)
 {
   log.Info($"Average score function executed at:
   {DateTime.Now}");
   // Calculate the average score for all existing documents
   var scores = await scoresTable.ListEntitiesAsync();
   var average = scores.Items.Average(p =>
   p.TextSentimentScore);
   var count = scores.Items.Count();

   // Create new score entity as JObject
   var scoreAverage = new JObject {
     new JProperty("DocumentCount", count),
     new JProperty("AverageScore", average)
   };

   // Get the average score record for today's date from
   // AverageDocumentScore SQL Table
   var today = XmlConvert.ToString(DateTime.Now,
     XmlDateTimeSerializationMode.Utc);
   var query = "$filter=Date eq Date(" + today + ")";
   var entities = await
     averageTable.ListEntitiesAsync(query: Query.Parse(query));

   if (entities.Items.Count() == 1)
   {
     // Update the entry if it exists
```

```
        log.Info($"Updating average sentiment score " +
          $"for today to average={average}");

        var entityId = entities.Items[0]["ID"].Value<string>();
        await averageTable.UpdateEntityAsync(entityId,
        scoreAverage);
    }
    else
    {
        // Create new entry
        log.Info($"Creating new average sentiment score " +
          $"for today average={average}");
        await averageTable.CreateEntityAsync(scoreAverage);
    }
    }
    }
    }
}
```

To test the function, run it locally.

You can verify whether the new entries are being created in the AverageDocumentScore SQL table, by calling the following query on the SQL table from **Visual Studio -> SQL Server Object Explorer**:

```
select * from AverageDocumentScore
```

 If you encounter the error "Response status code does not indicate success: 400 (A value must be provided for item.)" while attempting to save the new record, please downgrade the version of the Newtonsoft.Json NuGet package to 9.0.1. At the time of this writing, this is the latest compatible version.

After verifying that the function works, publish it to your Azure environment. After you are done with your initial testing, you may want to change your function's schedule to run more sparingly (for instance, once daily at midnight) to prevent running over the free execution quota.

You can also completely disable the function by adding the Disable property to the trigger attribute, as in the following code, or by choosing **Disable** in the function state in the **Functions portal Manage** tab.

```
[FunctionName("AverageResults")]
[FunctionName("AverageResults")]
public static async Task Run(
[TimerTrigger("0 0 0 * * *"), Disable]TimerInfo myTimer,...
```

Summary

This chapter allowed us to explore the more advanced options to configure function triggers and input/output parameters as well as to configure custom routes for HTTP-triggered functions. We saw two detailed examples of common function triggers, and described the different approaches to access SQL table records.

In the course of this chapter, you learned more about function triggers, and input and output bindings, and saw how to configure custom routing to a function's HTTP endpoints. To put our learning into practice, we created a new text processing function triggered by file upload to storage, and an averaging function that is run on a specific schedule.

In the next chapter, we will proceed to discuss how to integrate our function code with third-party services by setting up text ingestion from a Twitter feed.

5
Integrations and Dependencies

In previous chapters, we started working on an implementation of a text sentiment analysis application using Azure serverless computing. We built a number of functions and discussed the process of setting up triggers as well as input and output bindings.

Standalone functions will work great in some cases, however, in most applications, we will need to integrate the serverless computing with other types of services to achieve the results we require. In this chapter, you will learn more about Azure Function integrations and dependencies and leveraging additional cloud services where applicable. We will discuss some of the most common scenarios, including the following:

- Integration with Logic Apps to process a Twitter feed
- Integration with Service Bus
- Sharing code between different functions in the same Function App
- Adding references to the NuGet packages and other external libraries

Leveraging Logic Apps will allow us to create simple workflows prior to triggering functions, without the need to re-implement common scenarios from scratch in the custom code.

The integration with Service Bus will illustrate how asynchronous incoming messages can be stored in a highly scalable message queue until the serverless computing units are ready to process them.

Finally, the referencing NuGet packages and sharing code between functions will allow us to leverage thousands of available NuGet libraries and avoid code repetition.

By the end of this chapter, we will expand our application with two more functions and some additional integrations, as is reflected in the following diagram:

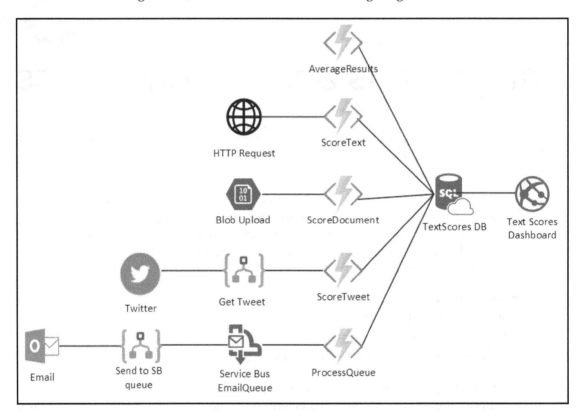

Processing a Twitter feed

In this section, we will use a function to read and process a Twitter feed. Twitter exposes a REST API that, among other things, allows developers to search for tweets that include certain words or expressions. You can register an application with Twitter, and create custom code to call the Twitter Search API. To make things easier, in this book, we will use Azure Logic Apps to streamline the process of integrating with Twitter.

Azure Logic Apps provide a simplified way to implement common workflows without writing custom code. When creating Logic Apps, you can choose from a list of triggers and actions to execute, add conditional statements, and design multi-step workflows. Logic Apps provide hundreds of built-in triggers and actions, and over a hundred connectors to third-party SaaS applications.

Logic Apps offer a powerful way to implement common scenarios, and the integration between Logic Apps and Functions allows to add custom code into the workflow.

To implement Twitter feed processing, we will add a Logic App to search for new tweets and then trigger an Azure Function when the Logic App is executed.

We are now implementing the following part of the overall diagram that we saw at the beginning of this chapter:

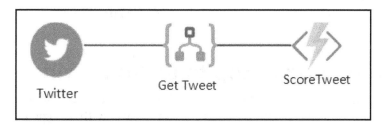

Creating a WebHook Trigger function

Let's create the Azure Function that will process the tweets by performing the following steps:

1. In Visual Studio, right-click on the `TextEvaluation` project and navigate to **Add -> New Item -> Azure Function**.
2. In **Type**, choose `GenericWebHookCSharp`, and in the name field, enter `ScoreTweet`.
3. Once the template is generated, replace the function code in `ScoreTweet.cs` with the following code.

The function will be triggered by an HTTP WebHook from the Logic App and get the tweet body in JSON format. This code will leverage the `Newtonsoft.Json` library to deserialize the tweet from JSON:

```
using System;
using System.Net;
using Newtonsoft.Json;
public static async Task Run(HttpRequestMessage req,
TraceWriter log)
{
    string jsonContent = await req.Content.ReadAsStringAsync();
    dynamic data = JsonConvert.DeserializeObject(jsonContent);
    log.Info($"Function triggered by tweet: {data.TweetText},
    username: {data.UserDetails.UserName}");
}
```

4. After the function is ready, publish it to your Azure Functions environment.

Creating the Logic App to search Twitter

As mentioned earlier, Logic Apps provide a simplified way to implement common application workflows in the cloud. Anything implemented with a Logic App can also be implemented in custom code, however, the Logic Apps allow us to save time and effort by making the implementations of common scenarios available out of the box.

Now that our WebHook function is published and available in our subscription, we can create the Logic App to process a Twitter feed and then trigger the function.

To create the Logic App, execute the following steps:

1. Log in to the Azure Portal and navigate to **New -> Web + Mobile -> Logic App -> Create**.
2. Fill in the required parameters:
     - **Name**: Enter `TwitterFeedReader`
     - **Subscription**: The same subscription your other resources are in
     - **Resource Group**: The resource group your other resources are in
     - **Location**: The same location your other resources are in

   It will take a few moments for the Logic App to get created.

3. Once the Logic App is created, you will be redirected to the **Logic App Designer**. From the list of common triggers, select **When a new tweet is posted**:

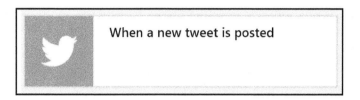

4. You will be prompted to sign in to your Twitter account:

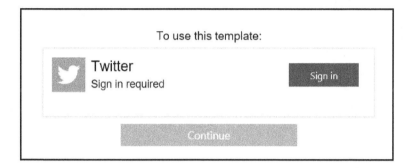

5. Sign in with your Twitter credentials and then click on **Authorize App**. This process will create and authorize an application in Twitter, which will generate an authorization key. Behind the scenes, the Logic App will call the Twitter Search API with a search keyword we are about to configure (more information about the Search API can be found at `https://dev.twitter.com/rest/public/search`). The whole integration process will be completely transparent to us.

6. In the dialog that opens, enter `serverless` as the search text.

7. Under **How often do you want to check for items?** click on **Edit**. Keep the frequency at **Minute** and change the interval to **30** minutes.

> This configuration means that the Logic App will be triggered every 30 minutes, and it will scan Twitter for new tweets that contain the word `serverless`.

8. Click on **Save**.
9. Now that we've added the first step in the Logic App flow that will search Twitter, we need to add the second step to process the tweets using the Azure Function we've created earlier. To do so, navigate to **New step** -> **Add an action** -> **Azure Functions** -> **Choose an Azure function** -> `TextEvaluation` -> `ScoreTweet`.
10. Click on the **Context object** option to be passed to the function and select **Body** to pass the entire body of the tweet into the function.

> Properties from all previous steps are listed in each step, allowing us to select the values we need. Passing the body of the tweet will allow us to pass all the information pertaining to the tweet in the JSON format:

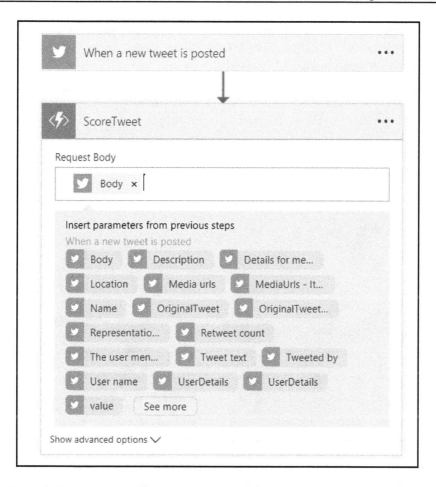

11. Click on **Save**.

12. Now that we've created the flow, you can click on **Run Trigger** in the Logic App Designer to trigger the app. (You could also wait for the app to be triggered on schedule as defined in the trigger step). If the keyword you are searching for is rare, you can tweet from your own account to test the flow. If the keyword is popular, you are likely to find other people's tweets.

To see that the app has executed successfully, browse to app **Overview** tab (`Logic apps -> TwitterFeedReader -> Overview`). You will see one or more runs, depending on how many tweets the search was able to find:

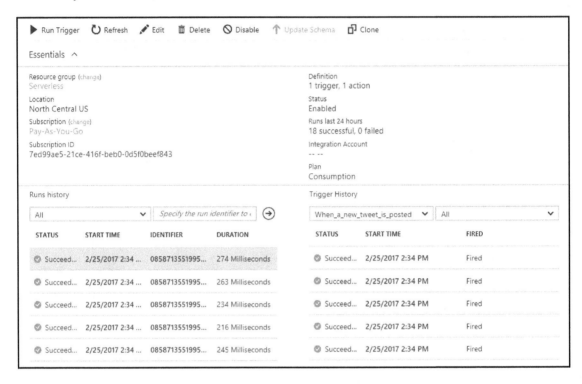

Click on a specific run to see the run details. Click on the **When_a_new_tweet_is_posted** step to see the headers and explore the tweet body that was sent as a payload from the first to the second step.

You can also click on **See Raw Outputs** on the right-hand side to see the tweet Body in JSON format.

If a certain run failed or stalled, you can investigate the error here.

Switch to the Azure Functions portal to verify that the `ScoreTweet` function is being triggered and run successfully. You will see the tweet that triggered the run in the function's Logs window:

```
2017-02-25T21:53:02.527 Function started (Id=ff964012-7826-476a-
bacb-1ec5fafc2d79)
2017-02-25T21:53:02.699 Function triggered by tweet: #Serverless compute is
so much fun! :) #AzureFunctions, username: DivineOps
```

This simple flow just allowed us to create a basic application for analyzing a Twitter feed.

 It is highly recommended to disable the Logic App when it's not in use. While each execution price is low, searching for common keywords can trigger millions of executions, which can result in high overall charges.

Now that we can successfully gather relevant tweets, we need to add the sentiment processing to the function code. We will continue to use the random score generator we've used in previous chapters, however, we will now leverage our ability to share code between all functions in the Function App to avoid the error-prone process of copy-pasting the same code.

Sharing code between functions

As we've seen previously, it is fairly common to need to share code between functions. In the first two examples in this book, we copy-pasted the code that does the text processing. Now, as we move forward and introduce more and more possible inputs, we may want to plug them into a unified processing unit instead of following the error-prone copy-paste process.

A great advantage of encapsulating a common functionality used by the functions in a separate class is the improved testability of the code. The new class will generally have a single responsibility, which can be tested with a suite of unit tests. The test class can rely on Dependency Injection, which is not yet available in function implementation itself. Dependency Injection makes it easier to "mock" any of the external components used in the code. To learn more about Dependency Injection, visit `https://en.wikipedia.org/wiki/Dependency_injection`

Furthermore, the separation of concerns makes it easier to swap the concrete class for a different implementation if needed down the line, allowing us to avoid tight coupling with a specific data store or external API.

The process of sharing code differs greatly between precompiled functions and the C# script-based functions. With a precompiled function, the code sharing is no different than in any C# class library. In C# script-based functions, each function is compiled into a separate assembly in memory (rather than a single assembly for the entire Function App). Thus code sharing must be done through using a #load directive, which imports the code from another file source.

Since C# script-based functions are currently not very popular, we will not overview the code sharing process for C# script-based functions here. Please refer to the `Appendix A`, *C# Script-Based Functions* for a detailed walk through on how to share code in C# script-based functions.

In precompiled functions, sharing code works the same as in any traditional .NET application.

To share code between functions, add an `EvaluateText.cs` class to the project. At the moment, we are still using a random text score. In the next chapter, however, when we integrate the Cognitive Services API to do the text sentiment evaluation, we will only need to replace the scoring implementation in the shared code, rather than changing it separately in each function.

In Visual Studio, right-click the `TextEvaluation` project, and create a new `EvaluateText.cs` class with the following code :

```
using System;
public class EvaluateText
{
 public double ScoreTextSentiment(string text)
 {
    // Generate a random text score between 0 and 1
    double score = new Random().NextDouble();
    return score;
 }
}
```

After you have added the class to the project, modify the `ScoreTweet` function to use the shared code. This function will now extract the tweet text from the JSON payload and pass it on to the `ScoreTextSentiment` method in the `EvaluateText` class:

```
using System;
using System.Net;
using Newtonsoft.Json;
using System.Threading.Tasks;

public static async Task Run(HttpRequestMessage req, TraceWriter
log)
{
   string jsonContent = await req.Content.ReadAsStringAsync();
   dynamic data = JsonConvert.DeserializeObject(jsonContent);
   var tweetText = data.TweetText.ToString();
   var user = data.UserDetails.UserName.ToString();

   //Call shared code to score the tweet text
```

```
var score = new EvaluateText().ScoreTextSentiment(tweetText);
log.Info($"Scored tweet: {tweetText}, user: {user}, sentiment
score: {score}");
}
```

Publish the function to your Azure environment.

Now that we have updated the function, we need to verify that the code runs as expected. To do so, you could trigger the Logic App with a new tweet. Alternatively, you could post a request directly to the ScoreTweet function in the functions portal, using a request body from one of your previous tweets.

Post a tweet and track the logs in the Functions portal to see that the code works as expected:

```
2017-03-04T18:53:39.875 Function started (Id=8b266666-e491-40a9-
8d1d-36ed1fbe4231)
2017-03-04T18:53:39.875 Scored tweet: Running #serverless
functions :), user: DivineOps, sentiment score: 0.716230769975218
2017-03-04T18:53:39.875 Function completed (Success, Id=8b266666-
e491-40a9-8d1d-36ed1fbe4231)
```

Now we have successfully added a Twitter feed to the list of inputs to our Azure Function app and enabled a shared module to process text from different sources. In the same way as described, we could easily plug in additional social media or company internal data streams and use a unified approach in shared code to process the data.

Integrating with a Service Bus queue

When speaking of integrations with other services and APIs, it is important to give an example of integrating Azure Functions with Azure Service Bus.

Even though Azure Functions scale on demand, they are designed to run and scale asynchronously. While in some cases it makes sense to trigger a function immediately when an event takes place, in others, it is important to introduce middleware that can decouple the creator of the event from its consumer, and allow them to scale at different rates, while ensuring that none of the events are left unprocessed. Azure Service Bus provides a set of message-oriented middleware technologies that can be used for reliable message queuing.

One of the typical scenarios in which we would want to leverage Service Bus Queues is a scenario of temporal decoupling. The sender, or multiple senders, will add new messages to the queue, and the receiver will pick the messages up as soon as it has available compute resources. This enables Service Bus clients to send and receive messages at a different rate and provides a highly scalable data store for the unprocessed messages in the meantime.

A Service Bus Queue has a first-in, first-out (FIFO) mechanism, which means that the messages are processed by the receivers in the same order in which they have arrived, and each message is processed once. When you create a Service Bus Queue triggered Azure Function, it receives a new message in the PeekLock mode, which allows for two-step message processing. The function calls `complete` upon successful processing of the message or `abandon` if the processing failed. Failed message processing is then retried (five retries are attempted by default). If the function exceeds the PeekLock timeout, the lock on the message is automatically renewed. The Service Bus PeekLock mode also allows for DeadLetterQueue support for messages that could not be processed.

To read more about the PeekLock mode and other details on Service Bus queueing, visit `https://docs.microsoft.com/en-us/azure/service-bus-messaging/service-bus-performance-improvements#receive-mode`.

In addition to Queues, Azure Service Bus also provides Topics and Relays to support subscription-based and bi-directional communication flow. Azure Functions offer out-of-the-box triggers for Queues and Topics.

Email processing using Service Bus

To show an example of integration with Service Bus, we need a system that generates asynchronous messages that can be dropped in a queue. Since we are working with text, we will use email as an example of such a system. In real-life scenarios, Service Bus messages are rarely text-based. Typical message examples would include a message with a description of a job submitted from one part of the system to another or messages with telemetry from IoT devices.

In this chapter, we will build a flow that will pick up email messages from an Office 365 Outlook account, drop them in a Service Bus Queue, and then pick them up for processing. (Note that Office 365 is simply used as an example).

To implement the flow, we will use a Logic App to pick up email messages and drop them in the Service Bus Queue, and then a Service Bus Queue-triggered Azure Function to pick up and process the messages. As in the previous example, the Logic App simply provides a convenient way for us to integrate with Outlook and get the incoming email messages without writing custom code.

 This particular example requires that you have an Office 365 account. If required, you can sign up for an Office 365 trial at `https://portal.` `office.com/Signup/MainSignup15.aspx?Dap=FalseQuoteId=79a957e9-` `ad59-4d82-b787-a46955934171ali=1.`

We are now implementing the following part of the overall diagram in the beginning of this chapter:

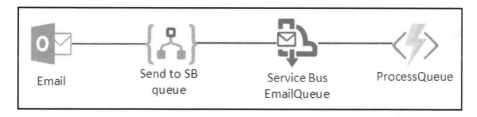

As we are describing a very simple architecture, it may seem that the Service Bus Queue is superfluous in the flow, since we know that the Logic App could be triggering the Azure Function directly. Remember, however, that this architecture allows us to scale the different parts of the system independently of one another.

For instance, we could now plug in multiple senders, aggregating email messages from completely different email clients into the same Service Bus Queue. When working with Service Bus Topics, we could also use different receivers to process different types of messages based on the criteria we choose. We could also change the sender or receiver part of the system independently, without impacting the other side. Lastly, if the receiving part of the system is unable to scale to process the load (for instance, if we have a quota on the function's resource consumption, as was described in `Chapter 2`, *Getting Started with Azure Environment*), the Service Bus Queue will hold the messages until the receiver is ready (to see quotas and limitations on Service Bus scaling, visit `https://docs.microsoft.com/en-` `us/azure/service-bus-messaging/service-bus-quotas`).

Creating a Service Bus queue

To create a new Service Bus namespace and new Email Queue, execute the following steps:

1. Log in to the main Azure Portal. Navigate to **New** -> **Service Bus** -> **Create**.
2. Fill in the required parameters as follows:
   - **Name**: Enter `TextSentimentSb`
   - **Pricing Tier**: Select `Basic`
   - **Subscription**: The same as existing resources
   - **Resource Group**: The same as existing resources
   - **Location**: The same as existing resources
3. After the Service Bus namespace is created, we will need to add the Email Queue. To do so, click on **Add Queue**.
4. In the name field, enter `emailqueue`. Keep the rest of the parameters at default values:

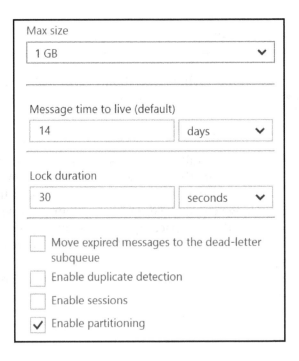

Configuring the access permissions

To access Service Bus resources from other services, such as Functions or Logic Apps, we need to set up access permissions. In Service Bus, access permissions are configured using shared access policies. Shared access policies allow us to define the access rights for the entire Service Bus namespace, or separately for each service. After the access policy is configured, it generates a key-based connection string that will be used for the access.

By default, Service Bus will create a new `RootManageSharedAccessKey` policy which has management permissions over the entire namespace. We could continue using this policy, however, for security purposes, it is important to define the access policies with the least sufficient privileges. This means that we want to define a policy on the specific Email Queue scope rather than the entire Service Bus and give it the minimum permissions --Send or Listen, rather than Manage.

In the case of Azure Functions, we currently must configure the access policy at the root level (the entire Service Bus namespace). For the Logic App, we will create an access policy at the Queue level. To learn more about Service Bus access policies, visit `https://docs.` `microsoft.com/en-us/azure/service-bus-messaging/service-bus-sas#shared-access-` `policy.`

Listen Access Policy for the function

The minimal permission we need in the function is a Listen permission over the Service Bus namespace (currently cannot limit it to a particular queue).

To create the Listen Access Policy which we will use in the Azure Function, execute the following steps:

1. Navigate to **Service Bus Overview -> Shared Access Policies -> Add**.

2. Enter the **Policy name** as `ListenPolicy`, and check the **Listen** permission only:

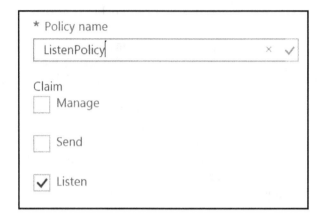

3. When the policy is created, we will need to copy the Email Queue connection string that we will use to access this queue in our function.

4. To copy the connection string, navigate to **Service Bus Namespace -> Shared Access Policies -> ListenPolicy -> Primary Connection String**. The connection string will be in the following format:

```
Endpoint=sb://<YourSbNamespace>.servicebus.windows.net/;
SharedAccessKeyName=ListenPolicy;SharedAccessKey=
<YourAccessKey>
```

We will use this connection string in the Azure Function.

Send Access Policy for the Logic App

The minimal permission we need in the Logic App is the Send permission over the `emailqueue` queue. As mentioned, we want to assign the policy to the `emailqueue` queue rather than the entire namespace to limit the scope of access permissions to the minimum required.

To create the access policy for the Logic App, execute the following steps:

1. To create a new, `emailqueue`-specific **Send** policy for the Logic App, navigate to **Service Bus Namespace -> Queues -> emailqueue -> Shared Access Policies**.

2. Click on **Add** and enter the policy name, `EmailQueueSendPolicy`, and check the **Send** permission only.

3. After the policy is created, to copy the connection string, navigate to **Queues -> emailqueue -> Shared Access Policies ->** `EmailQueueSendPolicy` **-> Connection String -> Primary Connection String**. The connection string will be in the following format:

```
Endpoint=sb://<YourSbNamespace>.servicebus.windows.net/;
SharedAccessKeyName=EmailQueueSendPolicy;SharedAccessKey=
<YourAccessKey>;EntityPath=emailqueue
```

We will use this connection string in the Logic App.

Creating the function

Now that we have a Service Bus Queue set up, we are ready to create an Azure Function to receive the messages from the queue.

To create the function, execute the following steps:

1. To do so in Visual Studio, right-click on `TextEvaluation` project and click on **Add -> New Item -> Azure Function** and add a `ProcessQueue` function.

2. Fill in the required parameters as follows:
   - **Type**: `ServiceBusQueueTrigger`
   - **Access rights**: **Listen**
   - **FunctionName**: `ProcessQueue`
   - **Connection**: `serviceBus`
   - **Queue name**: `emailqueue` (lowercase)

3. Click on **Create**.

4. Add the setting for the Service Bus connection string to the root level `ListenPolicy` to `local.settings.json`:

```
"serviceBus": "Endpoint=sb://textsentimentsb.servicebus
.windows.net/;SharedAccessKeyName=ListenPolicy;
SharedAccessKey=<FullAccessKey>"
```

If you leave the connection attribute empty, the Functions Runtime will assume that there is a Service Bus connection string in App Settings named `AzureWebJobsServiceBus`.

5. Modify the `ProcessQueue.cs` file to change the function input parameter name to `emailBody`:

```
using Microsoft.Azure.WebJobs;
using Microsoft.Azure.WebJobs.Host;
using Microsoft.ServiceBus.Messaging;

namespace TextEvaluation
{
 public static class ProcessQueue
 {
 [FunctionName("ProcessQueue")]
 public static async Task Run(
 [ServiceBusTrigger("emailqueue", AccessRights.Listen,
 Connection = "serviceBus")]string emailBody, TraceWriter log)
 {
    log.Info($"C# ServiceBus queue trigger function processed
    message: {emailBody}");
 }
 }
```

6. Compile the function. Upon compilation, the following trigger binding will be created in `function.json`:

```
"bindings": [
{
  "type": "serviceBusTrigger",
  "connection": "serviceBus",
  "queueName": "emailqueue",
  "access": "listen",
  "direction": "in",
  "name": "emailBody"
}
```

7. When ready, publish the function to your Azure environment.

8. After publishing, you will also need to add the `serviceBus` connection string by navigating to **Platform features -> Application Setting**, or publish it by running the `func azure functionapp publish <FunctionAppName> --publish-local-settings -i` command from Functions Core tools.

9. Once the function is deployed to Azure, it will automatically pick and process all messages in the Service Bus `emailqueue`. To prevent the function from picking up all messages as soon as we create them, so that we can observe the process in a controlled manner, we can temporarily suspend the function. We will then re-enable the function once we have messages in the queue. To suspend the function, browse to **Functions Portal**, click on **Manage** and switch **Function State** to **Disabled**:

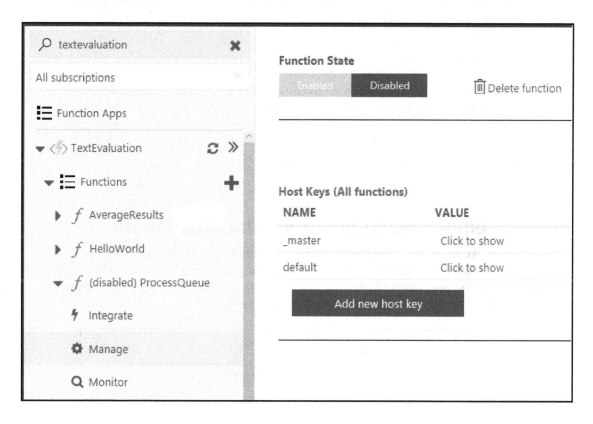

Other Service Bus configuration options

Azure Functions provide a number of other integration options with Azure Service Bus. We will not overview them in detail in this chapter, but we are providing references to learn more:

- **Configuring single-threaded processing**: By default, the Functions Runtime will process multiple Service Bus messages concurrently. You can force the function to process only a single queue or topic message at a time by setting `serviceBus.maxConcurrentCalls` to 1 in `host.json`. To learn more, visit `https://docs.microsoft.com/en-us/azure/azure-functions/functions-bindings-service-bus#trigger-behavior`.
- **Configuring Service Bus as an output binding**: In addition to using Service Bus as an input trigger, you can also use Service Bus Queues and Topics as an output binding. In this case, the function will become the sender of the messages to the queue. As an example of using the output binding, visit `https://docs.microsoft.com/en-us/azure/azure-functions/functions-bindings-service-bus`.

Sending email messages to Service Bus Queues

As a reminder, we have just configured the **Service Bus Email Queue**, and the `ProcessQueue` function, as can be seen in the following diagram. Now, we will configure the first block in the application flow--the Logic App that picks email messages from an Outlook account and drops them in the Service Bus Queue:

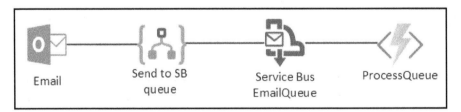

To create the Logic App, execute the following steps:

1. In Azure **Portal**, navigate to **New** -> **Logic App** -> **Create**.

2. Fill in the required parameters as follows:
   - **Name**: Enter `EmailQueuing`
   - **Subscription**: Use the same subscription we've used for our other resources
   - **Resource Group**: Select **Serverless**
   - **Location**: Use the same location we've used for our other resources

3. When the Logic App is created, you will be redirected to **Logic App Designer**.

4. From common triggers, pick **When a new email is received in Outlook.com**.

5. Sign in with your Office 365 account and then click on **Continue**. Select the **Inbox** folder to track new emails coming into your inbox, and define an interval to check for new emails. In this example, we will keep the interval at 3 minutes, which means the Logic App will be triggered every 3 minutes to check for new incoming emails:

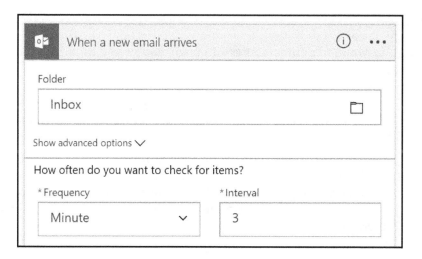

6. Click on **Save**.
7. Click on **New Step**.
8. In **Choose an action**, select **Service Bus** and then pick **Send message** from the drop-down menu that opens:

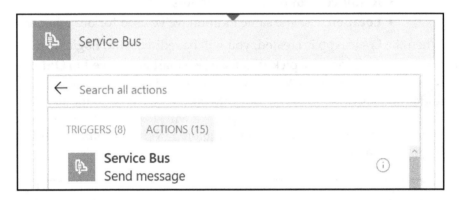

9. Click on **Manually enter connection information** and fill in the following settings:
    - **Connection Name**: Enter `ServiceBusEmailQueue`
    - **Connection String**: Paste the connection string of the Service Bus `EmailQueueSendPolicy` that we've created in the previous step.

If you click on **Browse current subscription** and select your Service Bus from the list, the portal will only allow you to choose from access policies defined at the Service Bus level (rather than queue level). The manual process is also useful when connecting to a Service Bus in a different subscription.

The following screenshot shows the **Manually enter connection information** view:

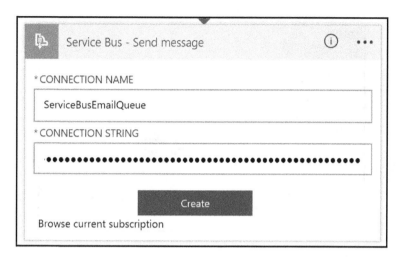

10. Click on **Create**.
11. In the **Send Message** action step that gets created, fill in the following parameters:
    - **Queue/Topic name**: Enter **emailqueue (queue)**
    - **Content**: In the **Content** box, select **Body** from the list of parameters available

- Leave the rest of the configuration parameters empty, as shown in the screenshot:

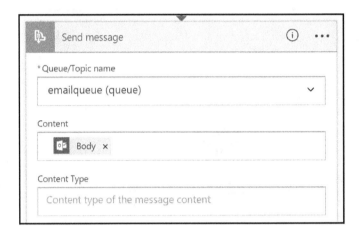

12. Click on **Save**.

Testing the Service Bus flow

To test the full flow, perform the following steps:

1. In **Logic App Designer**, click on **Run** to trigger the Logic App.
2. Send an email to your Outlook account.
3. You will see the Logic App being triggered, and sending a message to the Service Bus emailqueue. You can click on either of the action steps of the Logic App to see more details and browse the input and output parameters:

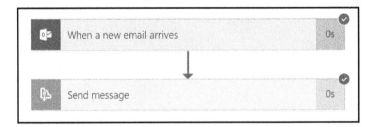

4. To check whether the message has indeed reached the email queue, in Azure Portal, navigate to Browse -> **Service Bus** -> **emailqueue** -> **Overview**.

5. In the queue overview, you will see the queue summary, and you'll see that we currently have a single active message in our queue.

Note that if your `ProcessQueue` function was not disabled, the message might be picked up and processed by the function faster than you browse to the message queue, in which case you will see zero active messages count:

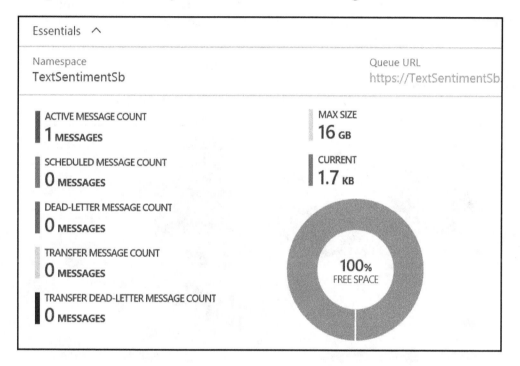

6. To test the message being processed, browse to the **Functions Portal** and re-enable the function in the **Manage** tab.

7. After a few moments, the function will get triggered and you will see its execution in the **Monitor/Logs** tab.

8. Switch back to the Service Bus `emailqueue` overview. You will now see that there are zero active messages in the queue.

We now have a flow that allows an Azure Function to pick up and process messages from a Service Bus Queue.

.NET dependency

Azure Functions are transitioning to running on .NET Standard 2.0, which is a specification that bridges the gap between different versions of .NET runtimes, notably .NET Framework and .NET Core.

.NET Standard allows developers creating custom libraries (such as different NuGet packages) to target one base library to run across all .NET platforms. For the application developers, .NET Standard will ensure that most third-party libraries will be available on every base platform, so that there is no significant difference between libraries available on .NET Framework and .NET Core, for instance.

.NET Standard is not an implementation of .NET runtime, but rather a specification that other runtime implementations, such as .NET Framework and .NET Core can conform with. The idea behind .NET Standard is highlighted in the following diagram:

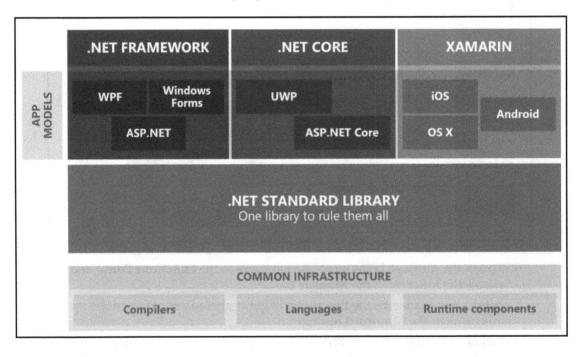

You can refer to the following image source:

```
https://blogs.msdn.microsoft.com/dotnet/2016/09/26/introducing-net-standard/
```

Running on .NET Standard means that the same function project will be able to run both on Functions Runtime (Windows based) and the planned .NET Core Functions Runtime (Linux and macOS) with no code changes. Effectively, this makes Functions Runtime OS agnostic.

Functions Runtime, in turn, provides a way to deploy the serverless compute any server you own (on-premises or even in a different public cloud), essentially making Azure Functions vendor agnostic.

To learn more about Functions Runtime, visit `https://azure.microsoft.com/en-us/blog/introducing-azure-functions-runtime-preview/`.

Adding NuGet libraries

In C# precompiled functions, adding NuGet libraries is the exact same process as in any traditional .NET application. In C# script-based functions (available when deployed online in the Functions Portal) the process is significantly different.

Since C# script-based functions are currently not very popular, we will not elaborate on the process here. Please refer to the `Appendix A`, *C# Script-Based Functions* for a detailed walk-through on how to add NuGet dependencies in C# script-based functions.

Summary

In this chapter, we've learned more about Azure Functions integrations and dependencies. We have described how to share common code between different functions in the same Function App, and the advantages of doing so.

We walked through an example integration with Azure Service Bus, a message queueing component commonly used when leveraging serverless compute. We have also showed an example of leveraging Logic Apps to easily integrate with external data streams, such as Twitter.

In the next chapter, we will integrate our application with the Microsoft Cognitive Services text sentiment analysis API to gain real insight into the positive/negative sentiment of the text submitted as input to the various functions we've created.

6
Integrating Azure Functions with Cognitive Services API

In this chapter, we will integrate our functions with the Microsoft text sentiment analytics API and thus implement the key functionality of the full text sentiment analysis application implementation. We will cover the following topics:

- Designing and implementing a text sentiment API call to analyze text
- Expanding on the usage of shared code to encapsulate common functionality
- Plugging the new results into the database and the Web UI

From the overall application standpoint, we are adding the last major component to our architecture, as shown in the following diagram:

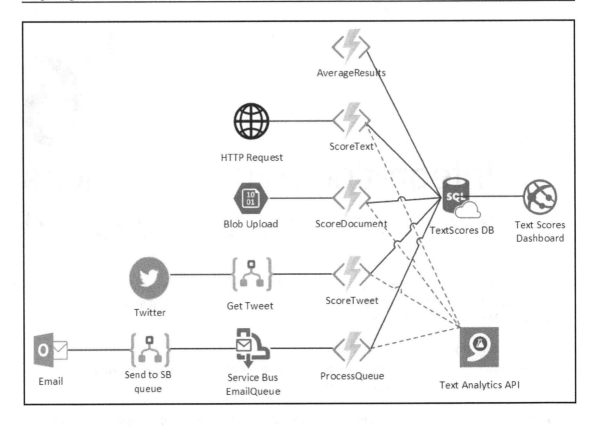

Using Microsoft Cognitive Services APIs to analyze text

Microsoft Cognitive Services provide over a dozen different APIs for working with text, speech, images, videos, and more. Those APIs offer insights such as emotion recognition or speech intent recognition. Cognitive Services leverage Machine Learning and the wide range of knowledge gained by Microsoft while developing products such as Office and Bing. Cognitive Services APIs aim to arm developers with insights from enterprise-grade artificial intelligence tools by using a few simple lines of code. The complete list of currently available APIs is available at `https://www.microsoft.com/cognitive-services/en-us/apis`.

In this book, we will leverage one of the Microsoft Cognitive Services APIs, the text sentiment Analytics API. This API allows a user to submit text, and provides a sentiment score of the text in the 0 to 1 range, with 0 being the most negative and 1 being the most positive possible score.

As an example, the sentence "The crowd was extremely unhappy" will receive a negative sentiment score of ~0.13, while the sentence "Everything is awesome" will receive a positive sentiment score of ~0.99. In between the two extremes, many utterances are likely to be scored as neutral. A score of 0.5 is considered objectively neutral, and scores between 0.35 and 0.65 can be considered neutral depending on context.

One of the possible applications of text sentiment analytics API is to assess the market's perception of your brand. The API allows developers to assess the overall sentiment of texts such as product reviews or company mentions on Twitter, making it possible to leverage artificial intelligence for market research.

Creating a Cognitive API account

In addition to the sentiment analysis, the Text Analytics API also provides capabilities of topic detection, key phrase detection, and language detection. In this chapter, we will focus on the use of sentiment analysis specifically. All of the Text Analytics APIs are available online for free testing at `https://www.microsoft.com/cognitive-services/en-us/text-analytics-api`.

Beyond a simple one-time test, we need to create an Azure Cognitive Service API account to leverage the APIs. When creating an account, we will need to specify the type of the API we're leveraging, since many diverse APIs are available. Let's explore the following steps to create our Cognitive API account:

1. In Azure portal, navigate to **New -> Cognitive Services API**, and then click on **Create**.
2. Fill in the required parameters:
   - **Account name**: Type `TextAnalyticsApi` in this field
   - **Subscription**: Select the subscription where your resources are deployed
   - **API type**: Select **Text Analytics API (preview)**
   - **Location**: Choose the location where your other resources are deployed

- **Pricing tier**: Select **F0 (5K Calls per 30 days)** under this field (a free tier allowing for up to 5,000 calls per 30 days)
- **Resource group**: Select the resource group where your other resources are deployed

3. As shown in the following screenshot, you will need to click on **Enable** to agree to the terms and conditions of using the Cognitive Services APIs. Consenting to the form grants Microsoft permission to use information gained from your usage of Cognitive APIs to further train and improve these APIs.

 You currently need to be an account (billing) administrator on the subscription to have the rights to enable the service).

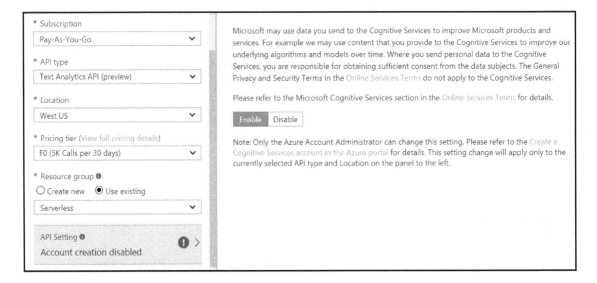

4. Check the **Pin to dashboard** checkbox to make the API account appear on the main dashboard.
5. Click on **Save** and then click on **Create**.
6. Once the API account is deployed, click on **Keys** and copy the primary key that we will use to access the API.

Text sentiment API usage

The following section relays the Cognitive Services APIs documentation that can be found at the following link: `https://docs.microsoft.com/en-us/azure/cognitive-services/cognitive-services-text-analytics-quick-start#task-2---detect-sentiment-key-phrases-and-languages`

Before diving into the function implementation, let's describe the expected input and output of the Microsoft text sentiment analytics API. To submit a call to the API, we need to submit an HTTP POST to the following endpoint:

```
https://westus.api.cognitive.microsoft.com/text/analytics/v2.0/sentiment
```

Note that the endpoint is not account dependent.

To authenticate against the API, we need the following headers. The API key is the key we acquired from API keys in the previous step:

- `Ocp-Apim-Subscription-Key`: <your API key>
- `Content-Type`: application/json
- `Accept`: application/json

The text we submit to the API needs to be broken down into separate "documents" and needs to be submitted as a JSON "document" list, adhering to the following structure:

```json
{
  "documents": [
{
  "language": "en",
  "id": "1",
  "text": "First document"
},
...
{
  "language": "en",
  "id": "100",
  "text": "Final document"
}
]
}
```

When constructing the JSON payload, it is important to keep in mind the following text sentiment analytics API limits:

- The maximum size of a single "document" that can be submitted is 10 KB, and the total maximum size of submitted input is 1 MB. No more than 1,000 documents may be submitted in one call. Rate limiting exists at a rate of 100 calls per minute.
- When submitting short snippets of text, we can submit each as a single API call, or potentially aggregate multiple text snippets (defined as multiple "documents") into a single API call to avoid exceeding the rate per minute limit.
- When submitting longer texts, it is recommended that the text be split into sentences for a more accurate sentiment analysis.
- When approaching texts with more than a 1,000 sentences in length, a different text splitting procedure (breaking the text into the maximum 10 KB pieces) may be considered. Alternatively, the longer texts, especially texts exceeding 1 MB in size, may require multiple API calls to be scored.

The response we will get from the text sentiment analytics API will be in the following format, where we are getting a sentiment score corresponding to each separate "document":

```
// Sentiment response
  {
"documents": [
{
  "id": "1",
  "score": "0.934"
},
...
{
  "id": "100",
  "score": "0.002"
},
]
}
```

If the "documents" represent separate text snippets, each sentiment score stands on its own.

When aggregating the results for text segments belonging to the same text, the simplest approach would be to average the scores. Alternatively, you can exclude neutral sentences or give them less weight in the aggregate, to make the positive/negative tendency of the overall text more prominent in the aggregate score.

Based on this documentation, you can see that different use cases may require different approaches to constructing the text sentiment analytics API payload, depending on the expected average text length and the relative weight you wish to give the neutral parts of the text. In this chapter, we will take the "middle ground" approach that will allow us to score both short and long texts using the same implementation. In production environments, consider your particular use case when choosing the API call implementation procedure.

The text sentiment analytics API call implementation

To implement the call to the Text Sentiment Analytics API from the Function App, we will leverage the shared code to avoid code duplication. We will modify the EvaluateText class we have implemented in the previous chapter to call the API and return a meaningful sentiment score rather than using a random double score value.

To implement the procedure, let's first add the following two settings to the `local.settings.json` file so that we can access them across all the functions in the Function App:

```
"textSentimentApiUrl": "https://westus.api.cognitive.microsoft.com/
text/analytics/v2.0/sentiment",
"textSentimentApiKey": "<You API key>"
```

 When publishing the application, remember to add the settings to the **App Settings** in the portal.

Now, let's modify the `EvaluateText` class to make an asynchronous call to the API.

You may need to add a reference to the `System.Configuration` assembly. To do so, in the project tree, right-click on **Dependencies** and then click on **Add Reference**. In this, type `System.Configuration` into the search box and add the latest version.

Please take a look at the first part of the `EvaluateText` class code:

```
using System;
using System.Threading.Tasks;
using System.Net.Http;
using System.Net.Http.Headers;
using Newtonsoft.Json;
```

```csharp
using System.Configuration;
using System.Collections.Generic;
using System.Linq;
using System.Text;

namespace TextEvaluation
{
  public class EvaluateText
  {
    private readonly HttpClient _client;

    public EvaluateText(HttpMessageHandler messageHandler = null)
    {
      if (messageHandler == null)
      {
        _client = new HttpClient();
      }
      else
      {
        _client = new HttpClient(messageHandler);
      }
    }

    public async Task<double> ScoreTextSentiment(string inputText)
    {
      // Generate random text score between 0 and 1
      var score = await CallTextSentimentApi(inputText);
      return score;
    }

    <implementation code>
  }
```

The `HttpClient` method is defined as an instance variable in the `EvaluateText` class for testability purposes, which will be discussed in Chapter 8, *Testing Your Azure Functions*.

Now let's dive into the API call implementation code.

Following is the code of the `CallTextSentimentApi` method. The method loads the API URL and the API Key from the application settings, using `ConfigurationManager`. The method then creates and configures the `HttpClient` instance, which will be used to call the API. It then calls the `ConstructJsonPayload` method to construct the payload from the input text, converts the payload into a byte array and submits it to the text sentiment Analytics API. Lastly, the method calls the `CalculateScore` method to calculate the overall score based on the API response. The implementation of the `ConstructJsonPayload` and `CalculateScore` methods will be provided next.

Take a look at the `CallTextSentimentApi` method code:

```
public async Task<double> CallTextSentimentApi(string inputText)
{
  // Get the API URL and the API key from settings
  var uri =
ConfigurationManager.AppSettings["textSentimentApiUrl"];
  var apiKey =
ConfigurationManager.AppSettings["textSentimentApiKey"];

  // Configure the HttpClient request headers
  _client.DefaultRequestHeaders.Add("Ocp-Apim-Subscription-Key",
apiKey);
  _client.DefaultRequestHeaders.Accept.Add(
    new MediaTypeWithQualityHeaderValue("application/json"));

  // Create the JSON payload from the input text
  var jsonPayload = ConstructJsonPayload(inputText);

  byte[] byteData = Encoding.UTF8.GetBytes(jsonPayload);
  var content = new ByteArrayContent(byteData);
  // Add application/json header for the content
  content.Headers.ContentType = new
MediaTypeHeaderValue("application/json");

  // Call the Text Sentiment API to get the scores
  var response = await _client.PostAsync(uri, content);
  var jsonResponse = await response.Content.ReadAsStringAsync();

  //Calculate the average score
  var overallScore = CalculateScore(jsonResponse);
  return overallScore;
}
```

Constructing the payload

As discussed in the preceding section, the text sentiment analytics API expects the payload to be broken down into a potentially large number of relatively small "documents". When working with short snippets of text, such as tweets or SMS messages, the entire message can be submitted for scoring as a single document. As we move to work with larger texts, the text needs to be split up to avoid reaching the 10 KB limit of a single document. As we move to work with even larger texts, the total input limit of 1 MB per API call also needs to be taken into consideration.

In our implementation of constructing the payload, we will implement a one-size-fits-all approach, which will allow us to process text of any size.

We will leverage the Newtonsoft.Json library to serialize objects to a JSON payload, and hence, we will first need to define the class structure that conforms to the hierarchy expected by the text sentiment analytics API.

We will use the same class structure to serialize the request and deserialize the response, and hence we will define properties required for both input and output of the API. The double "score" in the document class, and "errors" list in the documentList class will be used to deserialize the response.

The following code snippets define the three classes:

- document.cs: Let's explore the document class in the following code snippet:

```
public class document
{
  public string id { get; set; }
  public string text { get; set; }
  public double score { get; set; }
}
```

- error.cs: Let's explore the error class in the following code snippet:

```
public class error
{
    public string id { get; set; }
    public string message { get; set; }
}
```

- `documentList.cs`: Let's explore the `documentList` class in the following code snippet:

```
public class documentList
{
    public List<document> documents { get; set; }
    public List<error> errors { get; set; }
}
```

Now that we've defined the class structure based on the text sentiment analytics API documentation, we can implement the `ConstructJsonPayload` method.

As recommended by the documentation at `https://docs.microsoft.com/en-us/azure/cognitive-services/cognitive-services-text-analytics-quick-start#task-2---detect-sentiment-key-phrases-and-languages`, the method will split the text into single sentences, assign them consecutive string IDs, and add each one as a separate document to the API payload. Then, it will serialize the resulting object to a JSON string and return it to the main `CallTextSentimentApi` method described in the preceding section.

Note that we are making an assumption that the `inputText` parameter has up to 1,000 sentences, and that it's total size does not exceed 1 MB. If the text is longer, in this implementation, the remaining portion of it will be discarded without scoring. If you are working with longer texts, a better-suited procedure should be designed.

The following method also assumes a well-formed input text that can be broken into sentences by periods and uses the `String.Split(...)` method to break the text up. Depending on your expected input, a different splitting procedure, or more input validation may be needed.

Take a look at the code of the `ConstructJsonPayload` method:

```
public string ConstructJsonPayload(string inputText)
{
    // Remove new line characters
    inputText = inputText.Replace(Environment.NewLine, String.Empty);
    // Split the input text into sentences
    var sentences = inputText.Split(new char[] { '.' },
StringSplitOptions.RemoveEmptyEntries);

    // Create the list of documents, and add sentences to the list
    var list = new List<document>();
    // Limit the document list at 1000, Text Sentiment API
limitation.
    for (int i = 0; i < sentences.Count() && i < 1000; i++)
    {
        list.Add(new document
```

```
          {
            id = i.ToString(),
            text = sentences[i]
          });
    }
    // Create the payload class
    var docs = new documentList() { documents = list };
    // Serialize the payload to JSON
    var json = JsonConvert.SerializeObject(docs);
    return json;
}
```

Calculating the overall score

As with constructing the payload, calculating the score can be defined in more than one way. The simplest approach is to average the score between all of the sentences in the text.

Another approach would be to create a weighted average of the text score, by disregarding the neutral sentences (scored between 0.35 and 0.65 or a narrower range) or giving them a lower weight than the strongly positive or negative sentences. When the standard average is used, the overall positivity or negativity of the text might be muffled by the neutral sentences in the text. Giving more weight to strongly positive or negative statements might closer approximate the human perception than an unweighted average does. You can read more about the concept of the weighted average at this link: https://en.wikipedia.org/wiki/Weighted_arithmetic_mean.

You could also consider calculating the median sentence score instead.

In the following implementation of the `CalculateScore` method, we will use the standard (unweighted) average score of all sentence scores:

```
 public static double CalculateScore(string jsonResponse)
{
  // Deserialize the response from JSON
  var documentScoreList =
JsonConvert.DeserializeObject<documentList>(jsonResponse);
  // Calculate and return the average text score across different sentences
  var averageTextScore = documentScoreList.documents.Average(p => p.score);
  return averageTextScore;
}
```

Using Sentiment Analysis in Azure Functions

To see the Sentiment Analysis method that we've developed in action, let's execute the scoring on two different types of text.

A short text analysis example

As the first test, let's call the new scoring method in the `ScoreTweet` function.

As mentioned earlier, you could potentially send the entire tweet as a whole, or even a list of up to a 1,000 tweets in a single call to the text sentiment API. In our implementation, we will break the tweets, however short, into separate sentences, and average the scores.

The full `ScoreTweet.cs` code is included in the following code snippet for completeness:

```
using System.Net.Http;
using Microsoft.Azure.WebJobs;
using Microsoft.Azure.WebJobs.Host;
using Newtonsoft.Json;

namespace TextEvaluation
{
public static class ScoreTweet
  {
    [FunctionName("ScoreTweet")]
    public static async Task Run([HttpTrigger(WebHookType =
    "genericJson")]HttpRequestMessage
    req, TraceWriter log)
  {
    string jsonContent = await req.Content.ReadAsStringAsync();
    dynamic data = JsonConvert.DeserializeObject(jsonContent);
    var tweetText = data.TweetText.ToString();
    var user = data.UserDetails.UserName.ToString();

    //Call shared code to score the tweet text
    var score =
      await new EvaluateText().ScoreTextSentiment(tweetText);

    log.Info($"Scored tweet: {tweetText}, " +
      $"user: {user}, sentiment score: {score}");
  }
  }
}
```

With these changes, we are finally ready to gain meaningful insight into our input text.

After the code changes are complete, publish the function to your Azure environment (do not forget to update the Function App settings to include the new settings of API URL and key!).

To test the new procedure, you can either re-enable the **Logic App** option to do the keyword-based Twitter search or trigger the `ScoreTweet` function directly. You can use the following example tweet to submit a request to the function:

```
{
    "TweetText": "Loving the serverless compute :-)",
    "TweetId": "841105860118138880",
    "CreatedAt": "Mon Mar 13 01:57:18 +0000 2017",
    "CreatedAtIso": "2017-03-13T01:57:18.000Z",
    "RetweetCount": 0,
    "TweetedBy": "DivineOps",
    "MediaUrls": [],
    "TweetLanguageCode": "en",
    "TweetInReplyToUserId": "",
    "Favorited": false,
    "UserMentions": [],
    "OriginalTweet": null,
    "UserDetails": {
    "FullName": "Sasha Rosenbaum",
    "Location": "Chicago, IL",
    "Id": 444131405,
    "UserName": "DivineOps",
    "FollowersCount": 1000,
    "Description": "",
    "StatusesCount": 1000,
    "FriendsCount": 1000,
    "FavouritesCount": 1000,
    "ProfileImageUrl": ""
    }
}
```

Once the function executes successfully, you should see the following logs in the **Logs** pane:

```
2017-05-28T21:13:42.545 Function started (Id=7a48e9ed-c5c8-4331-
b092-17289556ce79)
2017-05-28T21:13:42.545 Function completed (Success, Id=7a48e9ed-
c5c8-4331-b092-17289556ce79, Duration=0ms)
2017-05-28T21:13:43.792 Scored tweet: Loving the serverless compute
:-), user: DivineOps, sentiment score:0.949561040962202
```

A long text analysis example

To test the procedure while analyzing significantly longer texts, we will use the ScoreDocument function that we've developed in Chapter 3, *Setting Up the Development Environment*. This will allow us to upload a text of any length to Blob Storage as a text file, and test how well our procedure works to estimate an overall score of a longer text.

As examples of positive and negative leaning texts, we will use a positive and negative review of a product.

Let's take a look at the following steps:

1. For an example of a negative review, let's create a document named negativeReview.txt and paste the following text into it:

   ```
   The quality of the product was terrible, it was made of really
   cheap materials. The delivery was 2 days late. When I called
   customer service, I had to listen to elevator music for 25
   minutes, and the representative was rude. When the product
   finally arrived one of the widgets was cracked, so I had to
   send it back and wait on hold again to get a refund. I would
   never buy this product again.
   ```

2. For an example of a positive review, let's create a document named positiveReview.txt and paste the following text into it:

   ```
   The product is awesome! I've been using it for 3 months, and I
   already can't imagine what I would do without it! The colors
   are very pretty, I got it in blue and green. I got a lot of
   compliments after wearing it. Also, I called the customer
   service about getting it gift wrapped for my sister's birthday,
   and they were super friendly and helpful. I would definitely
   recommend getting this product.
   ```

3. Now, let's update the ScoreDocument.cs file to call the ScoreTextSentiment method in the EvaluateText class. (The commented TODO item in the code refers to the result storing procedure implemented later in this chapter). Update the ScoreDocument with the following code:

   ```
   using System.IO;
   using Microsoft.Azure.WebJobs;
   using Microsoft.Azure.WebJobs.Host;
   using Microsoft.Azure.ApiHub;
   using System.Threading.Tasks;

   namespace TextEvaluation
   ```

```
{
  public static class ScoreDocument
  {
    [FunctionName("ScoreDocument")]
    public static async Task Run(
    [BlobTrigger("documents/{name}", Connection =
    "blobStorageConnection")]Stream myBlob,
    [ApiHubTable(connection: "azureSQL", TableName =
    "DocumentTextScore")]ITable<TextScore>
    outputTable, string name, TraceWriter log)
  {
      var blobContent = new StreamReader(myBlob).ReadToEnd();
      //Call shared code to score the document text
      var score = await
        new EvaluateText().ScoreTextSentiment(blobContent);

      //TODO: Store the text score record in the database
      log.Info($"Document scoring function processed a text file " +
        $"\"{name}\" and returned a score of {score}");
  }
 }
}
```

4. Run the function locally to test the scoring of uploaded documents.

 When running this function locally, it is helpful to disable the existing online function deployment to prevent multiple processes competing to analyze the same uploaded documents. To do so, browse to Azure Functions Portal and go to your Function App in ScoreDocument and navigate to **Manage -> Function State,** then click on **Disabled**.

5. As described in Chapter 3, *Setting Up the Development Environment*, the ScoreDocument function will be triggered every time a new document is uploaded into a particular Blob container in a particular Azure **Storage account**. To trigger the function, in the Azure portal, navigate to **Storage accounts ->** textscoredocuments **-> Blobs ->** documents **-> Upload a document**.

6. Browse and upload the negativeReview.txt file into the storage account. Observe the function being triggered, and the negative score obtained:

```
[5/28/2017 9:19:18 PM] Executing 'Functions.ScoreDocument'
(Reason='New blob detected: documents/negativeReview.txt',
Id=aead1e6e-bb3a-4aac-b9db-e10d153cea14)
[5/28/2017 9:19:19 PM] Function started (Id=aead1e6e-bb3a-4aac-
b9db-e10d153cea14)
```

```
[5/28/2017 9:19:24 PM] Document scoring function processed a
text file "negativeReview.txt" and returned a score of
0.205427933032018
[5/28/2017 9:19:24 PM] Function completed (Success,
Id=aead1e6e-bb3a-4aac-b9db-e10d153cea14, Duration=5070ms)
[5/28/2017 9:19:24 PM] Executed 'Functions.ScoreDocument'
(Succeeded, Id=aead1e6e-bb3a-4aac-b9db-e10d153cea14)
```

7. Repeat the same upload procedure to upload the `positiveReview.txt` file.
   Observe the function being triggered and the positive score obtained:

```
[5/28/2017 9:24:41 PM] Executing 'Functions.ScoreDocument'
(Reason='New blob detected:
documents/positiveReview.txt', Id=dc811a69-2925-4084-b132-
d74946a8effc)
[5/28/2017 9:24:41 PM] Function started (Id=dc811a69-2925-4084-
b132-d74946a8effc)
[5/28/2017 9:24:42 PM] Document scoring function processed a
text file "positiveReview.txt" and returned a score of
0.926892325552445
[5/28/2017 9:24:42 PM] Function completed (Success,
Id=dc811a69-2925-4084-b132-d74946a8effc, Duration=1350ms)
[5/28/2017 9:24:42 PM] Executed 'Functions.ScoreDocument'
(Succeeded, Id=dc811a69-2925-4084-b132-d74946a8effc)
```

As you can see, we are getting meaningful sentiment scores from the API for both short and long input texts.

Storing the function results

We previously implemented the result storing procedure in each function separately. In most applications, different functions will serve unrelated purposes and may call different external APIs or store the results in different data stores. In some cases, however, the functions are accessing the same data store in a similar fashion. In such cases, there may be value in implementing this procedure in a shared method to prevent code repetition. Of course, how much code can be reused and how much value the shared method may provide depends on the use case.

Let's demonstrate such a "shared" procedure for storing the data in our SQL Azure database. Keep in mind that the output binding for the table still needs to be defined in each function, but using JObject as the object type allows us to generalize a significant part of the code. We will define a common `StoreOutput` class to handle the data store.

Since we are treating SQL databases as an external API, this shared code allows us to implement error handling, possible retry logic, and logic to avoid duplications.

 The following `StoreOutput` class is defined a static class because it provides a "library" type method that isn't associated with a particular object. The `EvaluateText` class we've described earlier was defined as a non-static class because it instantiates `HttpClient`, and the instantiation is easier to test with Dependency Injection. The choices of static vs non-static class aren't prescriptive.

The `StoreOutput` class itself looks as follows:

```
using System.Linq;
using System.Threading.Tasks;
using Newtonsoft.Json.Linq;
using Microsoft.Azure.ApiHub;
using Microsoft.Azure.WebJobs.Host;

namespace TextEvaluation
{
    public static class StoreOutput
    {
        //TODO: add implementation
    }
}
```

Now we can implement the data storing method. This method will have input parameters of the function output as JObject, a reference to the `outputTable`, a reference to the function trace log , and finally an optional parameter of `nameProperty`.

The `nameProperty` is a parameter of type string, that will allow us to compare the new output record with existing records, so that we can update a record if it already exists. We will use a filter query, similar to what we've used in Chapter 4, *Configuring Endpoints, Triggers, Bindings, and Scheduling* to find existing records.

If the `nameProperty` parameter is submitted, the `StoreOutputSQL` method will look for existing entities for which the value of the `nameProperty` parameter is the same as the value in the `output` parameter. If the `nameProperty` parameter is omitted, or if there are no entities that match the `nameProperty` value, the method will create a new entity based on the `output` parameter.

Refer to the `StoreOutputSQL` method implementation in the following code snippet:

```
public static async Task StoreOutputSQL(JObject output,
ITable<JObject> outputTable, TraceWriter log,
string nameProperty = null)
{
   // If updating existing entities is required
   if (nameProperty != null)
   {
      // Get property value
      var entityName = output[nameProperty].Value<string>();
      // Construct comparison query
      var query = "$filter=" + nameProperty +
          " eq '" + entityName + "'";
      //Get existing entities
      var entities = await
        outputTable.ListEntitiesAsync(query: Query.Parse(query));

      if (entities.Items.Count() == 1)
      {
         // Update the entry if it exists
         log.Info($"Updating existing row in output table");
         var entityId = entities.Items[0]["ID"].Value<string>();
         await outputTable.UpdateEntityAsync(entityId, output);
      }
      else if (entities.Items.Count() == 0)
      {
         log.Info($"Creating new row in output table");
         await outputTable.CreateEntityAsync(output);
      }
      else
      {
         // More than one existing entity - shouldn't be possible
         // Handle error
      }
   }
   else
   {
      log.Info($"Creating new row in output table");
      await outputTable.CreateEntityAsync(output);
   }
}
```

Every function that uses this shared code will need a separate binding for `outputTable` in the function's signature (and hence in the `function.json` file). The output binding will have the same attributes and values, except for the specific output table name.

Since we already have the appropriate binding and reference for the `ScoreDocument` function, we will only need to update the code in the `ScoreDocument.cs` file to call the shared code method. Note that we have switched to using the JObject instead of a `TextScore` POCO object.

The full updated code for the `ScoreDocument` function is provided for completeness:

```
[FunctionName("ScoreDocument")]
public static async Task Run([BlobTrigger("documents/{name}",
Connection = "blobStorageConnection")] Stream myBlob,
[ApiHubTable(connection: "azureSQL",
TableName = "DocumentTextScore")] ITable<JObject> outputTable,
string name, TraceWriter log)
{
   var blobContent = new StreamReader(myBlob).ReadToEnd();

   //Call shared code to score the tweet text
   var textScore = await
EvaluateText.ScoreTextSentiment(blobContent);

   // Create new score entity as JObject
   var documentScore = new JObject {
      new JProperty("DocumentName", name),
      new JProperty("TextSentimentScore", textScore)
   };

   //Store the text score record in the database
   await StoreOutput.StoreOutputSQL(documentScore, outputTable, log,
"DocumentName");
      log.Info($"Document scoring function processed a text file " +
         $"\"{name}\" and returned a score of {textScore}");

}
```

After updating the code, run the project, and re-upload the `positiveReview.txt` file to the Blob Storage account. The "create" flow for storing the result in the output table will execute, and the function output will be as follows:

```
Executing 'Functions.ScoreDocument' (Reason='New blob detected:
documents/positiveReview.txt', Id=c2ef6477-1fa0-4a30-ac2a-
51ca9ccf0d86)
Function started (Id=c2ef6477-1fa0-4a30-ac2a-51ca9ccf0d86)
Creating new row in output table
```

```
Document scoring function processed a text file
"positiveReview.txt" and returned a score of 0.926892325552445
Function completed (Success, Id=c2ef6477-1fa0-4a30-ac2a-
51ca9ccf0d86)
Executed 'Functions.ScoreDocument' (Succeeded, Id=c2ef6477-1fa0-
4a30-ac2a-51ca9ccf0d86)
```

Let us re-upload the same document again. Now the "update" flow will execute, and the scoring result will be stored in the same SQL table row. If the file text was changed, we would then store the new sentiment score after the document re-upload. The function's output is as follows:

```
Executing 'Functions.ScoreDocument' (Reason='New blob detected:
documents/positiveReview.txt', Id=ba6e8aa7-fe13-4f74-bdc0-
1eeb9a5782b5)
Function started (Id=ba6e8aa7-fe13-4f74-bdc0-1eeb9a5782b5)
Updating existing row in output table
Document scoring function processed a text file
"positiveReview.txt" and returned a score of 0.926892325552445
Function completed (Success, Id=ba6e8aa7-fe13-4f74-bdc0-
1eeb9a5782b5)
Executed 'Functions.ScoreDocument' (Succeeded, Id=ba6e8aa7-fe13-
4f74-bdc0-1eeb9a5782b5)
```

When you are ready, republish the function to your Azure environment (and re-enable it using the **Manage** tab).

Storing tweet score results using the shared code

Let us now store the tweet scores in SQL using the same shared code implementation.

Note that in this application, we are using Azure SQL Database to store the tweet data. You may also consider using a non-relational database, such as CosmosDB, as a more suitable data store for social media data. When choosing a data store, it is important to consider the volume of the incoming data and the speed at which it may change.

Creating the TweetTextScore table

Since we didn't previously save the tweet scores at all, we will need to create a new SQL table.

Let's explore the following steps to create the `TweetTextScore` table:

1. Open the Visual Studio SQL Server Explorer and connect to the `TextScoreDB` database (alternatively, browse to Azure Portal and then navigate to **SQL Databases** -> `TextScoreDB` ->**Tools** -> **Query Editor**).

2. In the new query window, run the following code to create the `TweetTextScore` table that will store the tweet text and it's score:

```
CREATE TABLE TweetTextScore
(
    ID INT IDENTITY(1,1) PRIMARY KEY,
    [Date] DATETIME NOT NULL DEFAULT GETUTCDATE(),
    Username VARCHAR(255) NOT NULL,
    TweetText VARCHAR(255) NOT NULL,
    TextSentimentScore FLOAT NOT NULL
);
```

3. After the table is created, insert the following row for testing purposes:

```
INSERT INTO TweetTextScore (Username, TweetText,
TextSentimentScore) Values ('DivineOps',
'Everything is awesome in Serverless compute!', 0.8567)
```

Updating the ScoreTweet function

Now we can leverage the shared code in the `ScoreTweet` function.

We will add the new `outputTable` parameter to the function's signature, and use the shared `StoreOutputSQL` method to store the new entities. Using JObject will allow us to define the new entity we need to store during runtime. We will pass `TweetText` as a `nameProperty` parameter, so that tweets with the same tweet text won't be stored twice.

Note that we do not need to add any settings in the `local.settings.json` file, since the `TweetTextScore` table is in the same Azure SQL database we are already referencing in the project.

The full updated code for the `ScoreTweet` function will look like the following:

```
using System.Net.Http;
using Microsoft.Azure.WebJobs;
using Microsoft.Azure.WebJobs.Host;
using Microsoft.Azure.ApiHub;
using Newtonsoft.Json;
using Newtonsoft.Json.Linq;
```

```
namespace TextEvaluation
{
 public static class ScoreTweet
 {
    [FunctionName("ScoreTweet")]
    public static async Task Run([HttpTrigger(WebHookType =
    "genericJson")]HttpRequestMessage req, [ApiHubTable
    (connection:"azureSQL", TableName = "TweetTextScore")]
    ITable<JObject> outputTable, TraceWriter log)
 {
    string jsonContent = await req.Content.ReadAsStringAsync();
    dynamic data = JsonConvert.DeserializeObject(jsonContent);
    var tweetText = data.TweetText.ToString();
    var user = data.UserDetails.UserName.ToString();

    //Call shared code to score the tweet text
    var score = await
       new EvaluateText().ScoreTextSentiment(tweetText);

    // Create new score entity as JObject
    var tweetScore = new JObject {
      new JProperty("Username", user),
      new JProperty("TweetText", tweetText),
      new JProperty("TextSentimentScore", score)
    };

   //Store the text score record in the database
   await StoreOutput.StoreOutputSQL(tweetScore, outputTable, log,
   "TweetText");

   log.Info($"Scored tweet: {tweetText}, " +
      $"user: {user}, sentiment score: {score}");

   }
  }
}
```

When ready, publish the function to Azure, and post a new tweet to verify that the scoring result is stored correctly in the database.

Reflecting the new results in the Web dashboard

We have shown how the result storing procedure can be utilized across multiple functions. Now let's tie our database back to our TextScoreDashboard Web UI.

As with any MVC application, we will need to add the Model-View-Controller for the new database table to the `TextScoreDashboard` application to be able to view the tweet scoring results in the web application.

Updating the model from database

Since we are building the application using a "database first" approach, let's first update the application model classes from the database. As in Chapter 3, *Setting Up the Development Environment*, we will use a scaffolding command, for which we will perform the following steps:

1. Open the `TextScoreDashboard` project in Visual Studio.
2. Navigate to **Tools** -> **Nuget Package Manager** -> **Package Manager Console**.
3. Run the following command.

   You will notice the `-Force` flag. This flag is needed to force the regeneration of the model classes from the database, replacing the existing classes we've generated previously.

   The command is provided below:

   ```
   Scaffold-DbContext "<database connection string>"
   Microsoft.EntityFrameworkCore.SqlServer
   -OutputDir Models -Force
   ```

Updating controllers and views

Let's execute the following steps for updating controllers and views:

1. In your project tree, browse to the `Controllers` folder and add the following `TweetsController` class. This controller will load the DB context and populate the tweet scores list. The controller class code is below:

   ```
   using System.Linq;
   using Microsoft.AspNetCore.Mvc;
   using TextScoreDashboard.Models;
   namespace TextScoreDashboard.Controllers
   {
     public class TweetsController : Controller
     {
       private TextScoresDBContext _context;
       public TweetsController(TextScoresDBContext context)
       {
   ```

```
      _context = context;
   }
   public IActionResult Index()
   {
      return View(_context.TweetTextScore.ToList());
   }
 }
}
```

2. Under the `Views` folder, add a folder called `Tweets`.

3. In the `Tweets` folder, add a view called `Index.cshtml` with the following Razor code that will populate an HTML table with the tweet scores list from the SQL table:

```
@model IEnumerable<TextScoreDashboard.Models.TweetTextScore>
@{
    ViewBag.Title = "Tweet Scores";
 }
<h2>Tweet Scores</h2>
<div class="main-content">
<table class="table">
<tr>
<th>Username</th>
<th>Tweet Text</th>
<th>Score</th>
</tr>
@foreach (var item in Model)
{
   <tr>
   <td>
     @Html.DisplayFor(m => item.Username)
   </td>
   <td>
     @Html.DisplayFor(m => item.TweetText)
   </td>
   <td>
     @Html.DisplayFor(m => item.TextSentimentScore)
   </td>
   </tr>
}
</table>
</div>
```

4. To make the new view accessible from the main page, navigate to **Views** -> **Home** -> `Index.cshtml` and add the link to the new view:

```
<h2>Text Sentiment Scores Dashboard</h2>
<div class="main-content">
<ul>
<li>@Html.ActionLink("Document Scores", "Index", "Documents",
null, null)</li>
<li>@Html.ActionLink("Tweet Scores", "Index", "Tweets", null,
null)</li>
</ul>
</div>
```

5. Finally, add the following minor modification to the `_Layout.cshtml` file. Navigate to **Views** -> **Shared** -> `_Layout.cshtml` to display the new link on the main navigation bar of the application (the following code is a small excerpt from the full `_Layout.cshtml` file, not the full file):

```
<aasp-area="" asp-controller="Home" asp-action="Index"
class="navbar-brand">Scores</a>
</div>
<div class="navbar-collapse collapse">
<ul class="nav navbar-nav">
<li><aasp-area="" asp-controller="Documents" asp-action=
"Index">Documents</a></li>
<li><aasp-area="" asp-controller="Tweets" asp-action
="Index">Tweets</a></li>
</ul>
</div>
```

6. When you're ready, publish the application to your Azure Web App environment.

7. Browse to `http://<YourAppName>.azurewebsites.net/Tweets` to see the tweet score results:

Scores	Documents	Tweets

Tweet Scores

Username	Tweet Text	Score
DivineOps	Everything is awesome in serverless compute!	0.8567
DivineOps	Loving the serverless compute :-)	0.8760291

The same principles that we've used in the preceding can be used to plug the `ScoreText` and `ProcessQueue` function results into the database/web UI. In this book, we will not cover this process to avoid repetitive content.

Summary

In this chapter, we have implemented the integration of Azure Functions with the Microsoft Cognitive Services text sentiment analytics API. This integration allowed us to leverage the depth and breadth of Microsoft knowledge based on historical data, Machine Learning, and artificial intelligence to analyze the sentiment of input text.

We also expanded on the approach of using shared code across multiple Azure Functions to encapsulate functionality that is needed across the board, and we integrated the new results from a Twitter feed and document analysis with our Web UI dashboard.

During the previous four chapters, we walked through how to design and build a full text sentiment analytics application for analyzing text documents and tweets based on Azure serverless compute (Azure Functions), with a SQL Azure database as a data store and .NET Core Web application as a GUI.

As reflected in the architecture diagram in the beginning of this chapter, the application is comprised of multiple components, each relying on a different type of Azure Function. The application utilizes the Text Analytics API across the board.

During the course of these chapters we have also described additional options for triggers, input and output bindings, and alternative data stores that can be easily leveraged when using functions. Covering a broad spectrum of tools in our toolbox allowed us to show the great power of the cloud that a developer can harness when working with serverless compute.

In the next two chapters, we will focus on the developer experience when using Azure serverless compute, describing the debugging and testing process when working with Azure Functions.

7
Debugging Your Azure Functions

In the previous chapters, we walked through the steps of building a simple text sentiment analysis application using Azure serverless compute. In this chapter, we will discuss the process of identifying and resolving code defects prior to publishing your functions.

During the course of this chapter, the reader will learn the following topics:

- Logging capabilities and best practices
- Handling errors in a serverless environment
- Debugging functions locally
- Debugging functions in the cloud

Software debugging

Software debugging is an iterative activity involving execution testing and code correction. It differs significantly from implementation testing, which will be covered in the next chapter. Implementation testing is aimed at demonstrating the application's correctness, and can be performed in various ways, some of which might not even involve code execution. Debugging, on the other hand, is aimed at locating and correcting code defects.

Debugging is a multi-step process, which can be outlined by the following process diagram:

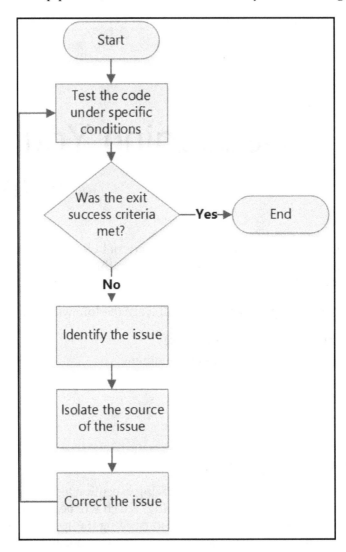

As seen in the preceding diagram, the process starts with executing the code under a particular set of conditions, and with a specific end result in mind. The list of possible start conditions used in debugging typically covers the common success and error cases. During debugging, it is important to verify that the code handles errors gracefully in common scenarios, such as incorrect input or inaccessible data store. This means that the "success criteria" in the preceding diagram may also include graceful error handling.

High-level programming languages such as C# tend to offer a rich development environment with built-in elaborate debugging tools, and a very smooth debugging experience. In serverless compute, however, debugging may get more complicated. By nature, serverless compute is asynchronous, event-driven, and highly parallelized, which makes isolating errors more difficult. The ability to debug functions locally is of great help, however, it allows for debugging only a single function execution at a time. In an environment such as this, effective logging becomes crucial to the process of isolating errors.

The second challenge of debugging in serverless compute is the process of triggering the functions on demand. We will discuss the process of triggering all types of functions later in this chapter.

Logging events

In any application, logs are a very useful debugging and monitoring tool, however, they become even more crucial in serverless compute. As we will see in this chapter, it is not always easy to debug the functions locally, and it isn't always easy to simulate parallel execution of functions when they are triggered at scale. Given the asynchronous, cloud-based, and highly parallelized nature of the serverless code, the `log` statements become one of our most powerful tools for identifying and correcting errors.

Azure Function templates come preconfigured with the `TraceWriter log` parameter, which is based on the `Microsoft.Azure.WebJobs.Script.Intercepting.TraceWriter` class, implemented in the WebJobs SDK.

The usage of the `TraceWriter` class is not limited solely to functions and WebJobs. You can start leveraging the `TraceWriter` class in other parts of your application (such as Web UI) by installing the WebJobs NuGet package. This would allow you to log events consistently across multiple tiers of the application.

In addition, Functions now support the `ILogger` interface, implemented in the `Microsoft.Extensions.Logging NuGet` library. The `ILogger` interface offers better support for structured logging, allowing you to pass objects in the log message. You can easily switch from using `TraceWriter` to using `ILogger`, by simply passing `ILogger` as a parameter in the function's signature. To learn more, please visit `https://github.com/Azure/azure-webjobs-sdk-script/wiki/ILogger`.

In this chapter, we will continue using the `TraceWriter` log to log events during the debugging process. Switching the implementation to use the `ILogger` interface would be nearly seamless.

Both `TraceWriter` and `ILogger` integrate natively with Application Insights, which is the recommended monitoring tool for Azure Functions. In `Chapter 11`, *Monitoring Your Application*, we will explore this integration in detail.

Logging best practices

Given the importance of logging in serverless compute, it's worth going over the best practices of logging. In the previous chapters, we did not devote much time to logging, and did not focus on making the logs "production ready". In this chapter, we will spend more time on how to implement application logging and error handling.

Logging adequately

The one thing that is almost as bad as not logging at all, is logging too much. When every event in an application is logged, and nearly every code line has a `log` statement attached to it, the logs quickly become noise. If an application generates hundreds of exceptions a second, and every exception is sent out as an e-mail alert, people will quickly start ignoring these alert messages altogether, ignoring the critical errors along with the less critical ones. In addition, unless the `log` statements are properly tagged and easy to classify, mining through these logs can be very difficult.

In addition to mining difficulties, logging has a "cost", and can impact your application performance if overused.

Unfortunately, there is no hard rule on which events are "worthy" of logging, as it highly depends on your application. During the development phase, you may choose to err on the side of logging too much, and then weed out some of the logs when the application reaches production.

Logging with context

While it is important not to create too much "noise", it is equally important to make sure that the logs provide enough information to identify the course of the event or the source of the error. Every software engineer has encountered a message along the lines of "A fatal error has occurred", and knows how much more difficult debugging can get, when there is nothing to narrow down the potential error cause. If an event is important enough to log, you should strive to provide enough information about it with the assumption that the log might be read and analyzed by a different team member.

When logging, include the event description, event trigger, and other relevant bits of information, such as user ID, document name, and so on. Also include the source of the event (name of the function, class, and so on).

The following two additional attributes can make the logs easier to analyze:

- **Adding timestamps**: When adding timestamps, put the timestamp in the beginning of the log line, in the most verbose format possible.

- **Adding unique identifiers**: Using unique identifiers can further help direct your analysis to a particular transaction and event sequence. It is useful to log transaction IDs, user IDs, and so on.

By default, the function logs include a unique invocation ID **Globally Unique Identifier (GUID)**, traceable through a single function execution. This GUID is especially useful in the asynchronous and parallelized serverless environment for being able to trace the logs to a specific function execution.

You can access the invocation ID in your function code by adding an execution context parameter to the function signature as follows:

```
... TraceWriter log, ExecutionContext executionContext)
```

You can then access the invocation ID by accessing `executionContext.InvocationId`:

```
log.Info($"Randomized text score function returned a score of
{score}. RequestUri={req.RequestUri}, RequestUri={req.RequestUri},
invocation ID={executionContext.InvocationId}");
```

In the **Monitor** tab, you will then see the following logs:

```
2017-05-29T01:57:25.223 Function started (Id=bcb493a9-f316-4372-
83df-090369390ee9)
2017-05-29T01:57:25.722 Randomized text score function returned a
score of 0.426169512991872. RequestUri=https://textevaluation.
azurewebsites.net/api/ScoreText? name=Api Hub Table, invocation
ID=bcb493a9-f316-4372-83df-090369390ee9
2017-05-29T01:57:25.722 Function completed (Success, Id=bcb493a9-
f316-4372-83df-090369390ee9, Duration=491ms)
```

When running locally, the log output includes even more details, such as the following:

```
[5/29/2017 1:59:07 AM] Executing HTTP request: {
[5/29/2017 1:59:07 AM] "requestId": "a554fab7-b2b4-4df1-acd9-
84f19686b551",
[5/29/2017 1:59:07 AM] "method": "GET",
[5/29/2017 1:59:07 AM] "uri": "/api/ScoreText"
[5/29/2017 1:59:07 AM] }
[5/29/2017 1:59:07 AM] Executing 'Functions.ScoreText'
(Reason='This function was programmatically called via the host
APIs.', Id=31c445a9-e717-40cb-89e9-4396fe34e76f)
[5/29/2017 1:59:07 AM] Function started (Id=31c445a9-e717-40cb-
89e9-4396fe34e76f)
[5/29/2017 1:59:08 AM] Randomized text score function returned a
score of 0.261883611447124. RequestUri=http://localhost:7071/
api/ScoreText?name=Local Environment!, invocation ID=31c445a9-
e717-40cb-89e9-4396fe34e76f
[5/29/2017 1:59:08 AM] Function completed (Success, Id=31c445a9-
e717-40cb-89e9-4396fe34e76f, Duration=452ms)
[5/29/2017 1:59:08 AM] Executed 'Functions.ScoreText' (Succeeded,
Id=31c445a9-e717-40cb-89e9-4396fe34e76f)
[5/29/2017 1:59:08 AM] Executed HTTP request: {
[5/29/2017 1:59:08 AM] "requestId": "a554fab7-b2b4-4df1-acd9-
84f19686b551",
[5/29/2017 1:59:08 AM] "method": "GET",
[5/29/2017 1:59:08 AM] "uri": "/api/ScoreText",
[5/29/2017 1:59:08 AM] "authorizationLevel": "Anonymous"
[5/29/2017 1:59:08 AM] }
[5/29/2017 1:59:08 AM] Response details: {
[5/29/2017 1:59:08 AM] "requestId": "a554fab7-b2b4-4df1-acd9-
84f19686b551",
[5/29/2017 1:59:08 AM] "status": "OK"
[5/29/2017 1:59:08 AM] }
```

Logging in a readable format

The logs should be readable, preferably, by both humans and machines.

To make the logs human readable, avoid complex encoding of events or errors (for higher programming languages, there is really no reason for numeric encoding of errors).

To make the logs machine readable, consider logging the events in the JSON format rather than clear text. For instance, instead of logging:

```
Scored tweet: Loving the serverless compute :-), user: DivineOps,
sentiment score: 0.8760291
```

As we did in `Chapter 6`, *Integrating Azure Functions with Cognitive Services API* consider logging like this:

```
Scored tweet: {'username':'DivineOps', 'tweetText':'Loving the
serverless compute :-)', 'sentimentScore': '0.8760291'}
```

Logging at the proper level

Categorizing events at the right logging level makes them a lot easier to find and analyze. When the logging levels are set correctly, you can limit your error search to the Error logs only, the normal operations analysis to the Info logs only, and so on.

WebJobs TraceWriter provides the following (fairly standard) logging levels:

- Verbose
- Info
- Warning
- Error

Logging during normal operation

Even though many development teams choose to only use the "Error" level logs, it is a great idea to log during normal application operation. "Info" level logs are extremely useful for the analysis of application performance and usage. Timestamped logs can be used for application profiling. Gathering Info logs statistics can bring unexpected insights into how your application is most commonly used, and help identify the required scale and potential bottlenecks.

Debugging the functions locally

The precompiled functions that run locally in Visual Studio 2017 provide the exact same debugging experience as any other .NET application including breakpoints, local variables, call stack, and more. The Visual Studio 2017 function tools also bring full IntelliSense and the ability to unit test the functions.

When running C# script-based functions, or other script language based functions online, the debugging experience may vary. Still, with C# script-based functions, it is possible to attach a Visual Studio debugger to a function deployed online.

In this section, we will focus on working with class-library-based precompiled functions in Visual Studio.

As mentioned in the introduction to this chapter, debugging, typically, starts with execution testing, which involves triggering the function under particular conditions. With Azure Functions, the execution testing approach is highly dependent on the function trigger type. Some functions are very easy to trigger locally, while others require more effort to trigger. In some cases, the trigger itself may be cloud-based (such as the Storage Blob trigger, Storage Queue trigger, or the Service Bus Queue trigger), but the function listening on the event can still be run and debugged locally.

Debugging functions with Visual Studio

When running the functions locally, you get the rich Visual Studio debugging experience, which allows you to set breakpoints, and use the **Step In/Step Out/Step Over** buttons or keyboard shortcuts to navigate the code. You can inspect the local variables using the **Locals** or **Watch** tabs or the **Immediate** window. You can also inspect the function's **Call Stack** as needed:

In this book, we will not elaborate on the debug tooling any further, as it is already familiar to most .NET developers. A detailed walkthrough of the Visual Studio debugger can be found here `https://msdn.microsoft.com/en-us/library/y740d9d3.aspx`.

Triggering the functions

Given that the debugging experience is very much like what you are already used to in .NET development, the next challenge is to be able to trigger the function. Some functions, like a timer-triggered function are, easy to trigger, while others--functions that listen on a particular event, especially, a cloud-based event, are harder to trigger. For this reason, to perform execution testing, we will sometimes need to write additional code that is responsible for either creating or simulating the particular event the function is listening for.

As mentioned earlier, along with the expected success scenario, it is important to simulate common errors like incorrect input or inaccessible third-party API, and make sure that the function handles errors gracefully.

Let us elaborate on the function debugging approaches based on each type of trigger that we have discussed in the previous chapters.

HTTP-triggered function

HTTP-triggered functions can be tested and debugged locally without the need for an internet connection. As long as the WebJobs connection strings in the `local.settings.json` file are set to an empty string, your function can be run locally on a local WebJobs job host on your computer, and it will not require any cloud-based components to function correctly:

```
"AzureWebJobsStorage": "",
"AzureWebJobsDashboard": "",
```

You also have the option of running this function on the WebJobs job host based on your Azure environment. To do that, you need to point the `AzureWebJobsStorage` connection string to the Azure storage account that you have created for your Azure Functions App. All types of function triggers other than HTTP require a valid connection to an Azure storage account.

In the previous chapters, we used two types of HTTP-triggered functions--the regular HTTP `Request/Response` function and a Webhook triggered function. In both cases, the function is triggered by making an HTTP request to a function endpoint URL. When running the function locally, the URLs will be formed based on localhost, port `7071`, and the function name. The function URL will be displayed in Functions Core Tools when the job host starts, as can be seen in the following screenshot:

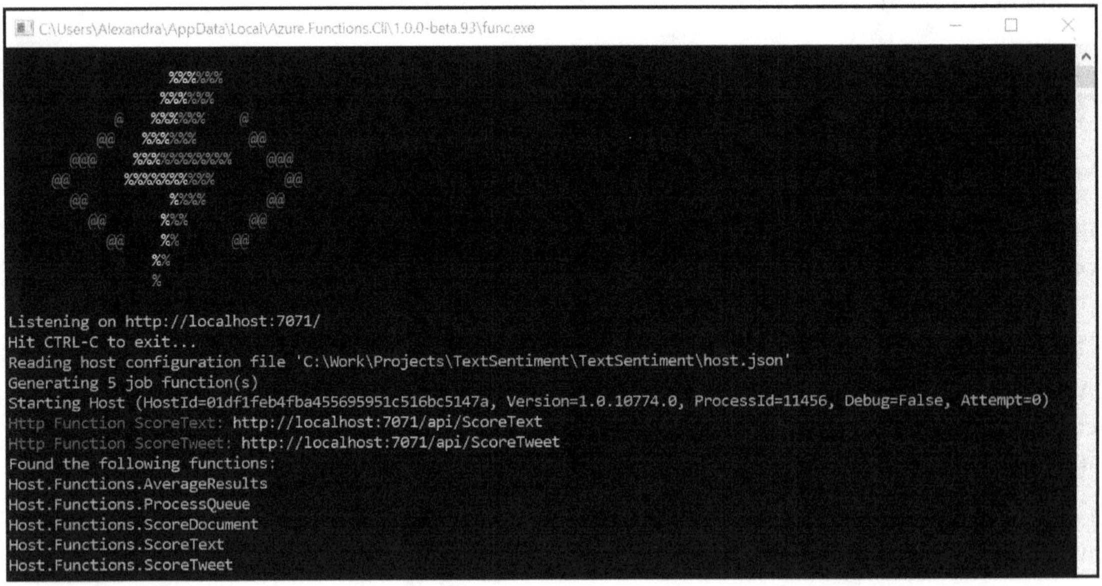

As we've seen earlier, we can easily trigger an HTTP GET request by browsing to the function URL in our browser, and submitting the function parameters in the query string.

To test other types of HTTP requests, such as the HTTP POST method, locally, you can use a third-party tool like Postman, Fiddler, or Paw. You can also trigger the function using Function Core Tools, which will be described in the next section.

In the following, we will provide a local testing example using the Postman tool. Postman can be installed as a Chrome plugin or as a standalone application.

Let's take a look at the following steps to explore the use of the Postman tool:

1. To install Postman in Chrome or on the OS, visit `https://www.getpostman.com/`.
2. After installing Postman, open the application. In the **New Tab** tab that opens, enter the `ScoreTweet` function URL in the **Enter request URL** text box. In the drop-down menu, switch the type of HTTP request from GET to POST:

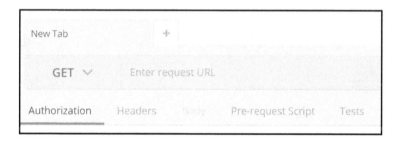

3. Since our function **Authentication level** is set to **Anonymous**, no authentication headers are required.
4. Switch to the **Body** tab, and switch the type of content to **raw**.
5. Paste the following JSON representation of a tweet in the **Body** tab as follows:

```
{
    "TweetText": "Loving the serverless compute :-)",
    "TweetId": "841105860118138880",
    "CreatedAt": "Mon Mar 13 01:57:18 +0000 2017",
    "CreatedAtIso": "2017-03-13T01:57:18.000Z",
    "RetweetCount": 0,
    "TweetedBy": "DivineOps",
    "MediaUrls": [],
    "TweetLanguageCode": "en",
    "TweetInReplyToUserId": "",
    "Favorited": false,
    "UserMentions": [],
    "OriginalTweet": null,
```

```
"UserDetails": {
        "FullName": "Sasha Rosenbaum",
        "Location": "Chicago, IL",
        "Id": 444131405,
        "UserName": "DivineOps",
        "FollowersCount": 659,
        "Description": "",
        "StatusesCount": 959,
        "FriendsCount": 771,
        "FavouritesCount": 753,
        "ProfileImageUrl": ""
    }
}
```

6. Make sure the Function App is running locally in Visual Studio.

7. In Postman, click on **Send**. You will get a response with a 200 OK status:

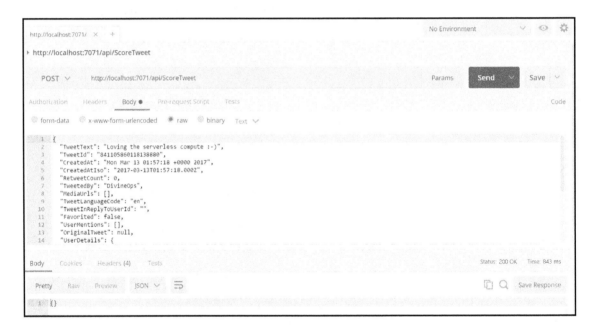

8. Repeating a similar process with the `ScoreText` function, we can submit an HTTP `GET` request (notice the `name` parameter in the function URL), and get the expected score result in the response (as we haven't changed this function since the beginning, it still returns a random double score between `0` and `1`):

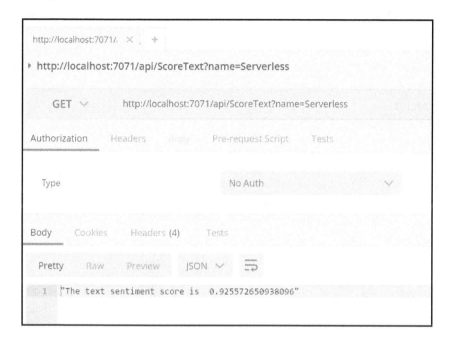

9. Note that you can continue using Postman when debugging the function after publishing them to your Azure environment by simply changing the base URL of your requests to the online endpoint to `https://<YourAppName>.azurewebsites.net/api/<FunctionName>`.

10. In Postman, you can save the previous HTTP requests you made, making it easy to re-trigger the same functions in your next debugging session.

Triggering functions using Functions Core tools

You can trigger function executions from Functions Core tools. To do so, execute the following steps:

1. If you do not have Functions Core tools installed globally, you can install them by following the directions here, `https://github.com/Azure/azure-functions-cli`. Note that you may first need to install npm.
2. Once the tools are installed, open a PowerShell window (or a CMD window)
3. Navigate to the `\bin\Debug\net461` directory under your Functions project's directory.
4. Invoke the function directly by running the following command:

   ```
   func run <YourFunctionName>
   ```

5. You can also provide a number of parameters to this command, including providing inline content using the `-c` option. For instance, for a standard `HttpTrigger` function, the request body could be provided in the following way:

   ```
   func run MyHttpTrigger -c '{\"name\": \"Trigger\"}'
   ```

To learn more about this command, visit `https://docs.microsoft.com/en-us/azure/azure-functions/functions-run-local#passing-test-data-to-a-function`.

Blob Storage triggered function

Unlike the HTTP-triggered function, this function requires an integration with Azure Storage, which is entirely cloud-based. The function can be run and debugged locally, but it requires the WebJobs job host to be based in Azure. To make sure that the job host is based in Azure, we need to set the `AzureWebJobsStorage` setting to our Azure Function App storage account connection string, as discussed in previous chapters.

We cannot debug a Blob Storage triggered function without an internet connection. We can, however, debug the function locally without using the Azure Portal to interact with the storage account. To connect to the storage account from the local computer, we need an application called Azure Storage Explorer. You can download the Azure Storage Explorer application from `http://storageexplorer.com/`.

Let's demonstrate the usage of Azure Storage Explorer on the `ScoreDocument` function by performing the following steps:

1. Install the Azure Storage Explorer application.
2. Open the Storage Explorer application. From the main menu, select the **Add an Azure Account** option, and in the drop-down list, keep the value as **Azure**:

3. Click on **Sign in** and sign in with your Azure account.
4. Browse to the subscription you are working with.
5. Navigate to **Storage Accounts** -> `textscoredocuments` -> **Blob Containers** -> `documents` container, that we are watching in the `ScoreDocument` function implemented in Chapter 4, *Configuring Endpoints, Triggers, Bindings, and Scheduling*.
6. Make sure the Function App is running locally in Visual Studio, and the `ScoreDocument` function is enabled locally (you may also want to disable the `ScoreDocument` function in your Azure environment, so that the local and Azure deployment won't compete for the same trigger).

7. In the **Blob Containers** tab in Storage Explorer application, click on **Upload Files...**, and upload a new text file as shown in the following screenshot:

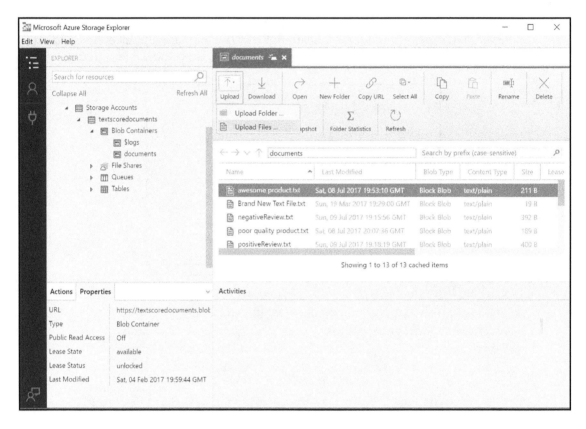

8. The local `ScoreDocument` function will be triggered, and you will see the expected text score output in Functions Core Tools window.

Triggering a function using custom code

As mentioned earlier, some functions can be relatively hard to trigger. In certain cases, when the function input can be easily simulated (such as simulating a queue message), the function can be triggered from Function Core Tools, as described earlier. In some cases, simulating an event that triggers a function requires custom code, or an integration tool such as Storage Explorer.

For certain trigger types, such as Storage Blobs and Queues, or Service Bus Queues and Topics, you may choose to create the "real" event to trigger the function. This is especially true if you want to test the full integrated flow.

Both Azure Storage and Service Bus provide C# SDKs as well as REST APIs, making them easy to code against. The custom code used to generate the required events can be written as part of any type of application, including a unit test project. In this chapter, we will explore the possibility of creating Azure Functions to trigger and test other functions.

Triggering a function using functions

Among other things, timer-triggered functions can be used to generate the needed conditions for another function's execution. In `Chapter 5`, *Integrations and Dependencies*, we worked with Azure Logic Apps to trigger the execution of functions dependent on external services, such as Azure Service Bus. Azure Logic Apps are a convenient tool for testing functions in the cloud, but they cannot be run locally. A timer-triggered function can be used for the same purpose in a local environment.

 It would be a better practice to separate the test functions into a different project. At the time of writing, however, you cannot run two function projects side-by-side on the same machine, since they are hard-wired to take the same port.

Triggering the Service Bus queue function locally

To demonstrate the last statement in the preceding section, let us use a timer-triggered function to test the `ProcessQueue` function that we created in `Chapter 5`, *Integrations and Dependencies*, which is triggered by a Service Bus queue message.

As mentioned, a Service Bus message can be simulated in other ways, including using triggering from the Function Core Tools. The following process, however, allows us to execute the actual "real" event flow, rather than debugging with a dummy message.

Creating an access policy for the Service Bus Queue

To write messages to the Service Bus Queue, we first need to create an appropriate access policy. In this case, we will create a policy with only the **Send** permission, which is the minimal required permission to send a new message to the Service Bus Queue.

Let's create an access policy for the Service Bus queue by performing the following steps:

1. To create a new policy, in Azure Portal, navigate to the **Service Bus** -> `TextSentimentSb` -> **Shared Access Policies** -> **Add**.
2. Enter the following required settings:
   - **Policy name**: Here, name the policy as `SendPolicy`
   - **Claim**: Select the **Send** option here
3. After the policy is created, copy the **PRIMARY KEY** connection string, as shown in the following screenshot:

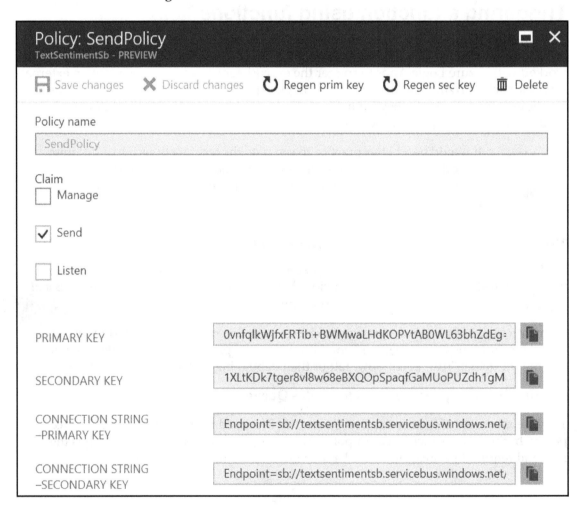

Creating the test function

Let's create the `test` function by performing the following steps:

1. To create a new timer-triggered function, in Visual Studio, right-click on the project, and navigate to **Add -> New Item -> Azure Function**.

2. Fill in the following required settings:
   - **Trigger:** `TimerTrigger` – `C#`
   - **Name:** `TestProcessQueue`
   - **Schedule:** `0 * * * * *`

   This schedule will trigger the `TestProcessQueue` function every minute.

3. Now we can add the code to generate a dummy e-mail message and drop it into the Service Bus `emailqueue`. To do so, open the `TestProcessQueue.cs` file, and replace the code with the following (for testing purposes we are adding a simple string message):

```csharp
using System;
using Microsoft.Azure.WebJobs;
using Microsoft.Azure.WebJobs.Host;
using Microsoft.ServiceBus.Messaging;

namespace TextEvaluation
{
 public static class TestProcessQueue
  {
    [FunctionName("TestProcessQueue")]
    public static void Run(
    [TimerTrigger("0 * * * * *")]TimerInfo myTimer,
    [ServiceBus("emailqueue",
    AccessRights.Send, Connection = "serviceBusSend")]
    ICollector<string>outputSbEmailQueue, TraceWriter log)
  {
    // Create dummy email message
    var dummyEmail = $"Dummy email string for Service Bus " +
        $"email queue created at: {DateTime.Now}";

    log.Info(dummyEmail);
    // Add the message to Service Bus email queue
    outputSbEmailQueue.Add(dummyEmail);
  }
 }
}
```

Notice that we've added the `ServiceBus` output parameter to the function's signature. This will generate the correct output binding for Service Bus in the `function.json` file.

4. Add the new Service Bus connection string to the application settings of the project. Open the `local.settings.json` file, and create a new `serviceBusSend` setting with the relevant access key, as shown in the following code snippet:

```
"serviceBusSend": "Endpoint=sb://textsentimentsb.servicebus
.windows.net/;SharedAccessKeyName=SendPolicy;SharedAccessKey=
<Your Access Key>",
```

5. Add a breakpoint in the `TestProcessQueue.cs` file to see when the function gets triggered.
6. In the `ProcessQueue.cs` file, add a breakpoint at line 10.
7. Run the Function App locally.

If you get an error `"Can't figure out which ctor to call"` when executing the `TestProcessQueue` function, check if the queue name setting in the Service Bus binding is correct (that is, `queueName` and not just `queue`). Upgrading to the latest version of Functions SDK should fix the issue.

8. When the breakpoint in the `ProcessQueue.cs` file fires, in the **Output** pane, switch the tab to **Locals** to see that the function was triggered by the dummy e-mail message we sent from `TestProcessQueue` function, as shown in the following screenshot:

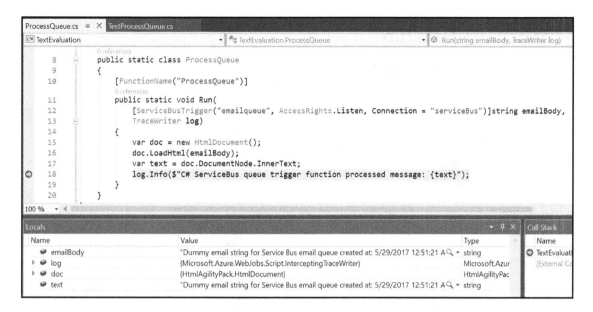

9. You can now execute the full `ProcessQueue` function flow by sending a message to the Service Bus messaging tier on demand.

10. You can also trigger the `TestProcessQueue` function using Function Core Tools rather than waiting for the timer trigger to fire. To do so, open a PowerShell window, and navigate to the `\bin\Debug\net461` directory under your project's directory. Execute the following command:

`func run TestProcessQueue`

You may choose to disable the `TestProcessQueue` function when not in use, by adding the `"Disable"` setting on the function trigger attribute.

Handling errors

The exception handling process in a .NET-based Function App is similar to any other .NET application. Best practices for handling exceptions in .NET can be found at the following two links:

- **MSDN**: https://msdn.microsoft.com/en-us/library/seyhszts%28v=vs. 110%29.aspx
- **Code project**: https://www.codeproject.com/Articles/9538/Exception-Handling-Best-Practices-inNET

We will not elaborate on best practices further in this book.

Let us, instead, outline the error handling in Functions Core tools local environment for two cases--handled and unhandled exceptions.

To demonstrate exception handling, let us create another timer-triggered function called `ErrorFunction`. To do so, follow the same steps as in the previous section on creating the `test` function, and move on to the following steps:

1. When the function is created, open the `ErrorFunction.cs` file, and paste the following code. As you can see, the following code generates an unhandled exception:

```
using System;
using Microsoft.Azure.WebJobs;
using Microsoft.Azure.WebJobs.Host;

namespace TextEvaluation
{
 public static class ErrorFunction
 {
   [FunctionName("ErrorFunction")]
   public static void Run(
   [TimerTrigger("0 * * * * *")]TimerInfo myTimer, TraceWriter
   log)
   {
      // Throw unhandled exception
      throw new Exception("This is a unhandled exception",
        new Exception("This is an inner exception"));

   }
  }
 }
```

2. Run the function locally. The function will auto-break, and generate the unhandled exception dialogue, which should be familiar to you if you have developed .NET applications before. You can click on **View Details** in the dialogue to see more data, including the inner exception, as shown in the following screenshot:

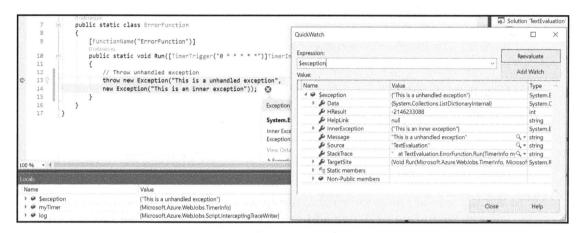

3. If you click on **Continue** to continue running the function, you will also see the error output logged in Functions Core Tools.

> Notice that the error message, including the inner exception message, is being logged here. Also note the log line on function completion indicates failure -- Function completed (Failure, Id=af7309c4-6b63-4ec2-b21a-8fdf5d9d58a2, Duration=13954ms).

> The unhandled exception is being logged automatically (since we did not, and could not, call the log method explicitly). This log output can be very useful when running into unexpected issues.

4. To demonstrate a handled exception, let's change the function code to the following. Here, we will wrap the exception within the try...catch block, and will log the exception message after it's caught. Note that we will log to Error level:

```
using System;
public static void Run(TimerInfo myTimer, TraceWriter log)
{
try
{
    // Throw a handled exception
```

```
    throw new Exception("This is a handled exception",
      new Exception("This is an inner exception"));
}
catch (Exception ex)
{
    log.Error($"Caught an exception: {ex.ToString()}");
}
}
```

Note that the function now completes successfully, and the log output only includes what we chose to log.

Note that it is best to log `exception.ToString()` (rather than `exception.Message`) to make sure that we are not missing any relevant information.

When the error occurs, we can choose to report it to the function's triggering component, or retry the operation.

5. We also should report the error to our function's monitoring tools, and possibly alert an administrator. When adding such alerts, however, make sure that there is no chance that your administrator's e-mail will be flooded by thousands of error messages when the function scales out.

Remote debugging in the cloud

The remote debugging of a Function App can be helpful if the function experiences an issue only after deployment. To debug the function in Azure, you can attach the debugger to the Function App. This will allow you to step through the deployed function in Visual Studio.

To perform remote debugging, execute the following steps:

1. First, we need to change two settings in Visual Studio to enable remote debugging. In Visual Studio, navigate to **Tools -> Options -> Debugging,** and then deselect the **Enable Just My Code** and **Require source files to exactly match the original version** options as shown in the following screenshot:

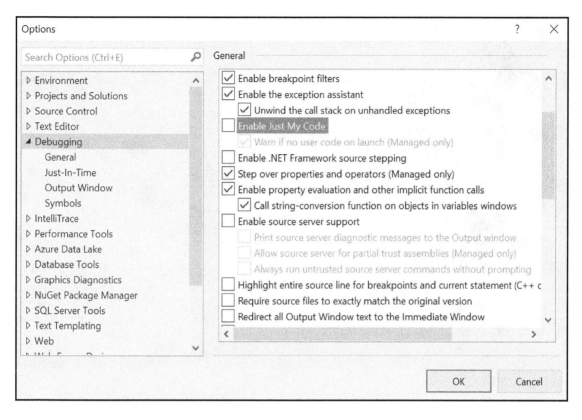

2. In Visual Studio, navigate to **View** -> **Cloud Explorer.**

3. Navigate to your subscription -> **App Services** -> TextEvaluation.

4. Right-click on the service and choose **Attach Debugger**.

5. After the debug symbols load, you will be able to set up breakpoints and step through the function. To hit a breakpoint, you will need to trigger the function execution in Azure.

6. You can step into method implementations, and inspect the local variables with the **Locals**, **Watch**, or **Immediate** windows, as shown in the following screenshot:

```
17
18        //Call shared code to score the tweet text
19        var score = await ScoreText.ScoreTextSentiment(tweetText);
20        // Create new score entity as JObject
21        var tweetScore = new JObject {
22              new JProperty("Username", user),
23              new JProperty("TweetText", tweetText),
24              new JProperty("TextSentimentScore", score)
25        };
```

100%

Locals		
Name	Value	Type
▷ 🔵 req	{Method: POST, RequestUri: 'https://textsentiment.azurewebsites.net/api/ScoreTweet?co	System.N
▷ 🔵 outputTable	{Microsoft.Azure.ApiHub.Table.Internal.Table<Newtonsoft.Json.Linq.JObject>}	Microsof
▷ 🔵 log	{Microsoft.Azure.WebJobs.Script.InterceptingTraceWriter}	Microsof
🔵 jsonContent	"{\r\n \"TweetText\": \"Loving the serverless compute :-)\",\r\n \"TweetId\": \"8411 🔍 ▾	string
▷ 🔵 data	{{ "TweetText": "Loving the serverless compute :-)", "TweetId": "841105860118138880"	object {N
🔵 tweetText	"Loving the serverless compute :-)" 🔍 ▾	object {sl
🔵 user	"DivineOps" 🔍 ▾	object {sl

The remote debugging experience is similar to the local experience, although in some cases, the network connection latency may cause issues for the debugger. Despite latency issues, remote debugging can prove useful when issues arise only after deployment.

Summary

In this chapter, we discussed the process of debugging the serverless functions. We discussed both the local, and the online debugging process, and how to enable cloud-triggered functions to be debugged locally. We also covered the basics of the debugging, logging, and error handling processes.

In the next chapter, we will discuss how to verify the correctness of the code implemented with Azure serverless compute. We will cover best practices, and elaborate on Unit, Integration, and Performance testing of Azure serverless compute.

8
Testing Your Azure Functions

In the previous chapter, we discussed how to debug a .NET based serverless compute application locally and in the cloud. In this chapter, we will continue to testing of the serverless compute.

During the course of this chapter, the reader will learn about the following topics:

- Best practices of software testing
- Testing the Azure serverless compute
- Unit testing
- Integration testing
- Performance testing

We will cover how to approach function testing, and show examples of some common test cases.

The importance of testing

Testing is a crucial part of the application life cycle, and it differs greatly from debugging. Although debugging certainly involves execution testing, the debugging activity is aimed at locating and correcting code defects, while testing is aimed at demonstrating application correctness. The testing process involves proving that the software requirements are implementable in practice, and that they have been implemented according to the specification. Certain testing approaches, such as correctness proofs and peer reviews, don't even require code execution.

In the modern world, most software development teams aim to create a continuous integration and/or continuous delivery (CI/CD) framework. Automated testing is a prerequisite of any type of CI/CD framework, as you have to verify the application correctness prior to pushing the code changes to production.

Testability has been one of the challenges of serverless compute since its arrival. Luckily for us, the new release of C# based precompiled functions fully supports the traditional Unit testing frameworks and features.

Software testing

Software testing is the process of evaluating the quality of a software product.

Most software products are complex, and can be looked at from a number of different perspectives. While it is required that the software product executes correctly, this is not sufficient for it to be considered a quality product. Drawbacks such as slow speed of execution or poor usability can prevent a perfectly correct application from being successfully delivered to its consumers. Thus, it is important for the testing procedures to cover more than just code correctness.

There are more testing types and approaches than this book can attempt to cover, and the number of tests that can be written and executed is practically infinite. As you will see from reading the next few pages, software testing can be more of an art than a science. Even the best testing approaches have major flaws, and 100% correctness verification is, actually, impossible. This is due to the fact that even the simplest of programs have complex decision trees, and anticipating all inputs is infeasible. Additionally, software design requirements tend to change rapidly during both development and maintenance, making the tester chase a moving target.

Perhaps, it would be useful to admit that perfection is mathematically unattainable, since we have finite time to test for infinite possibilities. The software testing problem is, indeed, a subset of the Halting Problem, which is undecidable (to learn more about the Halting problem, please visit `https://en.wikipedia.org/wiki/Halting_problem`).

Admitting defeat, however, is scary to do in a world where our lives frequently depend on systems run by software. It is a good start to acknowledge that software testing is, by no means, easy, and invest time into learning and implementing good quality tests, or hire a good **quality assurance** (**QA**) professional. At the very minimum, we should test the most critical use cases, and ensure that no failures are catastrophic.

It is, perhaps, incorrect to say that any tests are better than no tests. Having false confidence in an incorrect code can actually be counter-productive. Testing best practices honed by decades of software development can help us maximize the utility of our tests.

Let us start with a number of the following useful definitions:

Black-box testing: This examines the functionality without any knowledge of the internal implementation, approaching the software from the end user perspective, and treating it as a "black box".

White-box testing: This tests the internal implementation and execution of the program, and not just its functionality.

Code coverage: This is the degree to which the source code or program is executed when a test suite runs. Code coverage tools, typically, aim to reach a state in which every statement in the program is executed at least once.

Code coverage is a useful metric, but can be taken to an unuseful extreme if the development team focuses solely on achieving full code coverage, and forgoes other important quality criteria. In addition, code coverage can be misleading, as the program may perform correctly on the range of inputs used in testing, but not all possible inputs.

Test-Driven Development (TDD): This approach to software development became popular with the rise of the Agile methodology. In this approach, the tests are written before the program code. The software requirements are turned into test cases, and automated (initially failing) tests are added to the test suite. After that, new code that allows passing these tests is added to the application, and refactored to meet the coding standards.

TDD tends to improve code modularity, code coverage, and creates a regression test suite that can be leveraged months or years later during any upgrade or maintenance activity. The main drawbacks are that creating and maintaining the test suite is time consuming, and that since tests are mostly created by the same person who writes the code, the tests may share "blind spots" with the code.

Automated testing: This is the process in which automated tools that are separate from the code itself are used to run a predefined test suite.

Automated testing has many advantages over manual testing. Unlike humans, programs are very good at consistently executing long and boring repetitive procedures, which makes automated testing significantly more reliable than manual testing. Automated testing is also crucial for building a continuous integration and delivery (CI/CD) pipeline, because without good quality automated tests, a CI/CD pipeline would simply push code defects into production.

Still, it is important to mention the drawbacks of automated testing, such as the time investment into developing a quality test-suite, and the need to update all tests with any changes to requirements. Another disadvantage is the possibility of a false confidence when automated tests pass, but some defects are left uncovered.

Use case: This, in software development, is a list of sequential steps executed by an "actor" on a system to achieve a goal. The actor can be an end user, or an external system. For instance, when interacting with a retail application, the series of steps that the consumer performs to find the desired product, add the product to the shopping cart, provide payment method details and a shipping address, and to complete the purchase may be considered as one of the typical use cases of the system. These steps may be "recorded" and reproduced in a QA environment as part of the system testing procedures.

Test case: This is a set of inputs, execution conditions, and expected results defined for a particular objective, such as verifying compliance with a requirement or executing a certain program path.

Software assessment perspectives

A software product can be evaluated from multiple standpoints.

We can look at the product from the perspective of a business analyst, an architect, a developer, a QA engineer, a customer (who commissioned the product), and an end user (who might be different from the customer). Each of these roles may wish to pursue a different software assessment goal when developing a test suite.

The developer and QA engineer may wish to assess whether or not all or parts of the code perform the functions they were designed to do, and perform them in a reasonable amount of time. The customer, architect, and business analyst may wish to assess whether or not the product meets the agreed-upon requirements. The end user, who may be unaware of the specific design requirements, may wish to assess the software from a usability perspective.

Let us summarize the key software assessment goals, and the types of testing that help evaluate software quality from each specific standpoint.

Code correctness

Code correctness refers to a software performing in accordance with the specification. Code correctness can to be assessed in the following ways:

- The software meets the design requirements
- The software responds correctly to both valid and invalid inputs
- The software can be successfully installed and run on the hardware and OS with the intended configuration (and not only in the development environment)

Many types of testing can be used to verify code correctness. Let us mention three key types.

Unit testing

Unit testing verifies the functionality of a specific section of code. In object-oriented programming, a unit often refers to the entire class, although it could also refer to each particular method. Unit testing aims to eliminate the development defects before the code is promoted to QA.

While unit testing is useful to detect code defects, it's primary aim is not debugging. Unit tests, usually, help improve the code quality by forcing certain coding standards. They also significantly improve regression testing by making it easy to verify that the new code did not introduce defects to existing features.

In unit testing, each test case is independent of others. Unit testing tools, typically, use method stubs and mock objects to isolate one module from another for testing purposes. These can be defined as follows:

- **Method stubs**: These simulate "real" application methods by having the same signature, accepting the same inputs, and returning a predefined set of outputs. Method stubs allow the tester to test for both success and failure cases by generating specific outputs.
- **Mock objects**: These simulate the behavior of "real" objects in controlled ways. Mock objects allow the tester to simulate object states that are otherwise difficult to reproduce.

Unit testing is a white-box type of testing, where the tests work closely with the application source code.

Integration testing

Integration testing is any type of testing that tests the integration between different system components. Integration testing can test different types of combinations, and can be performed as either white-box or black-box testing. Integration testing aims to uncover defects that arise during interactions between the different system modules.

System testing

System testing verifies that the entire integrated system works correctly. System testing tests both the software and the hardware operation, and often executes full use cases involving the entire system.

Some of the types of testing discussed later in this section, such as usability testing and load testing, also fall under the system testing umbrella. System testing is, by design, a black-box type of testing.

Performance

Even if the code is 100% correct, the usability of the system depends on its performance. If the system is too slow or inefficient, consumers will abandon it unless they are forced to use it. Such a monopoly is rare in the world of commercial software.

To illustrate this point, we can provide some statistics based on consumer-facing web applications. For modern web applications, some polls show that 47% of the consumers expect the page to load in under 2 seconds, and abandon the site if it takes more than 3 seconds to load. As technology improves, user expectations only get higher.

The following chart illustrates the web page abandonment rate as a function of the page load time.

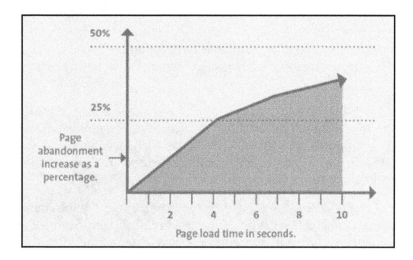

The following two metrics need to be assessed to verify the system's performance:

- The software performs its functions in acceptable time
- The software consumes an acceptable amount of resources

Let's review two key types of testing that can be used to verify performance.

Performance testing

As the name suggests, performance testing verifies that the system can perform effectively under a workload. It assesses whether the system is efficient, and returns expected results in an acceptable amount of time. In certain types of software, such as real-time systems, the time constraints may be very strict.

Performance testing may measure the system's response time, network speed and bandwidth. It may also measure the CPU, memory and disk IO consumption of the underlying infrastructure. If the system is not scalable, performance testing may assess if it is capable of performing sufficiently under the maximum expected load. If the system is scalable, performance testing may measure that the system scales efficiently, and also that it consumes resources in a cost-effective manner without generating unacceptable costs.

Load testing

Load, or stress, testing is a type of performance testing that aims to verify that the system can operate under a particular load, such as heavy usage traffic or large quantities of processed data.

Load testing is a black-box testing, and usually, entire system testing. For web applications, a common pattern for creating load tests is to record a user session on the website, and create a test that replays the user actions. The test can then be enhanced with additional steps, or parametrized, and it can be run by multiple external threads simultaneously, simulating heavy load on the system.

With the power of cloud, it has become easy to temporarily acquire the compute power needed to generate a peak load. We will discuss the built-in Visual Studio Team Services features that allow load testing with temporarily provisioned cloud infrastructure towards the end of this chapter.

Usability

Software usability testing is done from an end-user perspective to assess if the product is user friendly, pleasant, and easy to use. Usability testing aims to assert the following:

- The software can be learned in an acceptable amount of time by the intended end user
- The software can be used efficiently by the intended end user

For instance, if a web application requires frequent full-page reloads which take a second or two, its usability may suffer even if the code performs correctly.

Unlike a few decades ago, nowadays, the users can, and will, abandon a software product just because it is slightly inconvenient, or has an unpleasant design. Because of that, there has been a lot more emphasis on **user experience** (**UX**) design in recent years. UX design aims to improve the usability of the software, for instance, by making it interactive--able to load the new data requested by the user without a full-page reload, or responsive--able to scale to fit different desktop and mobile device dimensions. UX design also addresses the look and feel of the application by developing pleasant color schemes, shapes, and sizes of the elements on the screen.

In serverless compute per se, you are unlikely to encounter any UX design considerations beyond providing good documentation and meaningful success and error responses to your API consumers, and hence, this book will not discuss usability testing in more detail. It is, however, important to remember that usability of your web and mobile front-ends can "make or break" your entire application.

Testing the functions

In the following sections, we will cover the functions testing. We will focus, primarily, on **Unit** and **Integration** testing. These tests can be run locally on the development machine, or run automatically by continuous integration tools.

Unit testing

When developing unit tests, C# developers, typically, leverage one of the unit testing frameworks, such as **NUnit**, **XUnit**, or **MSTest**. Testing frameworks make it easy to perform common tasks such as creating new tests, running groups of tests, and reviewing the test run summary.

This book will leverage MSTest, which is fully integrated with Visual Studio.

Unit testing approach

A common approach to writing tests can be called AAA, which stands for Arrange -> Act -> Assert. With this approach, each test case is structured as follows:

- **Arrange**: This section of the test initializes the objects, variables, and mocks, and sets the data passed to the unit under test
- **Act**: This section invokes the unit under test with the arranged parameters
- **Assert**: This section verifies that the unit under test behaved as expected

To learn more about Arrange/Act/Assert pattern, please visit `https://msdn.microsoft.com/en-us/library/hh694602.aspx#Write your tests`

Naming convention

It is recommended that you choose a consistent naming convention for your tests, as it makes the results a lot easier to analyze. There are a number of approaches used for unit test naming. We will choose a popular naming convention described at `http://osherove.com/blog/2005/4/3/naming-standards-for-unit-tests.html`. Generally, the naming convention suggests that the unit test name should be comprised of the following:

[UnitOfWork_StateUnderTest_ExpectedBehavior]

Let's explore all the parts of the naming structure:

- `UnitOfWork`: This is the unit under test, such as a class or method.
- `StateUnderTest`: This is the requirement being tested. For instance, a description of the specific "type" of input parameters provided in this particular test case, such as "empty string".
- `ExpectedBehavior`: This refers to the expected outcome of the test case, such as "exception thrown" or "returns integer".

This naming convention allows us to define the test case and the expected outcome very clearly in the test name. This can help us write the test, and, more importantly, quickly identify which use cases pass and fail, and which use cases still haven't been covered. Hence, following the naming convention can save us a lot of valuable time.

Unit test best practices

While unit testing best practices are somewhat subjective, there are a number of the following standards most engineers agree upon:

- Test only one code unit at a time
- Mock out all the external components and dependencies
- Make each test independent of the others
- Avoid situations where tests must run in a specific order, or are otherwise interdependent
- Have one, and only one test to verify each behavior. It is counter-productive to have multiple test failures indicate the same defect.
- Only make one logical assertion per test. The assertion should, specifically, verify the expected behavior under test, not any additional observations about the code behavior
- Name unit tests clearly and consistently

- Avoid unnecessary preconditions
- Make sure the "state under test" is defined in the arrange section, and any assumptions are made as clear as possible
- Consequently, also avoid shared test setup (although this may be required in certain cases)

In some cases, you may discover that a particular code unit is more difficult to test than usual. This, arguably, indicates a "code smell". TDD helps avoid situations like this by forcing developers to start with the tests. Certain coding best practices, such as using dependency injection, help make the code more testable as well.

What to cover

It is difficult to determine all the recommended test cases for a unit. One approach aims to cover every single execution path. Another is to test for success, failure, and known edge cases, with most of the tests focusing on failure and edge cases.

A unit is expected to perform successfully when its inputs are valid, and its dependencies perform successfully. A single test can often be sufficient to test the unit behavior under the success conditions.

A unit is expected to fail (gracefully) when its inputs are invalid, or its dependencies are failing. Multiple failures can occur separately or in combination, and thus, multiple test cases may be required.

An **edge case** is a situation that occurs at an extreme (maximum or minimum) value of the parameter. Edge cases are likely to cause errors, and thus, it is recommended to test for boundary conditions.

With regard to inputs, given a valid input range, it is wise to test the behavior of the unit on the following:

- The minimum and maximum value in range
- Below minimum and above maximum values of the range
- A value within a valid range

In addition, testing for null inputs and date ranges may require special attention.

With regard to dependencies (such as external libraries, services, and APIs), different possible failures may be simulated to verify the unit's response.

Mocking frameworks

As mentioned earlier, in the context of software testing, mocking refers to creating simple objects to simulate the behavior of "real" objects. When the unit under test has dependencies on other modules, it is very useful to create mocks of these modules. Doing so allows you to isolate the behavior of the unit under test. It also allows you to simulate multiple conditions that may be difficult to replicate in real life. Mocking makes it easy to test success, failure, and edge case conditions by simulating different inputs or outputs returned by the mock object.

You can mock interfaces and classes by defining your own classes that derive from them, but this can get cumbersome and time consuming. There are multiple free C# mocking frameworks aimed at streamlining the mocking process. Those frameworks allow you to mock interfaces and define the mock behavior in just a few lines of code. Most of these frameworks can be installed as NuGet packages. Among them are Fake It Easy, Rhino Mocks, and Moq.

This book will leverage the Moq framework. Moq documentation can be found at the following link:

```
https://github.com/Moq/moq4/wiki/Quickstart
```

Dependency injection

In software engineering, **dependency injection** is a technique, whereby, one object supplies the dependencies of another object. In dependency injection, a dependency (a service) is passed to the dependent object (a client), so that the service becomes a part of the client state. Dependency injection is one of the forms of the technique called inversion of control. There are multiple types of dependency injection.

It is easiest to illustrate dependency injection with an example. Let us demonstrate the type called **constructor injection**.

A class without dependency injection may look like the following code snippet:

```
public class Client
{
 public void SendMessage()
 {
    // instantiate the specific implementation of the service
    IService service = new Service();
    // use the service
    service.SendMessage();
 }
}
```

Notice that the specific implementation of the IService interface in this case is completely up to the Client class, and is not influenced by the code that instantiates the Client class.

The same code, using constructor dependency injection, may look like the following code snippet:

```
public class Client
{
  private IService _service;
  public Client(IService service)
  {
    _service = service;
  }
  public void SendMessage()
  {
    // use the service implementation supplied by DI
    _service.SendMessage();
  }
}
```

Notice that the specific implementation of the IService interface is provided to the Client class at the time of its instantiation.

It is easy to see that dependency injection has made the preceding code more testable by allowing the code instantiating the Client class to provide different IService implementations. In production code, we will provide the "real" IService implementation when creating the Client, while in test code we can provide a mock.

It is also possible to provide a default implementation of the IService interface inside the Client class by making the parameter optional. This approach (which we've used in the EvaluateText class) removes the responsibility of the instantiating class to know the details of the implementation of the Client class, while still improving testability.

As of now, the Azure Functions do not allow for adding dependency injections beyond the input and output bindings (parameters) of the function. Thus, if the function has an external dependency on an additional service or API, it is best to encapsulate the dependency in a separate class, which can be unit tested more extensively than a function.

To learn more, and to review the different types of dependency injection, please visit https://en.wikipedia.org/wiki/Dependency_injection.

Creating a test project

Let's take a look at the following steps to create a test project:

1. Open the TextEvaluation project in Visual Studio
2. To create a test project, and autogenerate tests for a class, you can right-click on the class name, and choose **Create Unit Tests**. The following dialog will open, allowing you to choose the target test project and the naming approach:

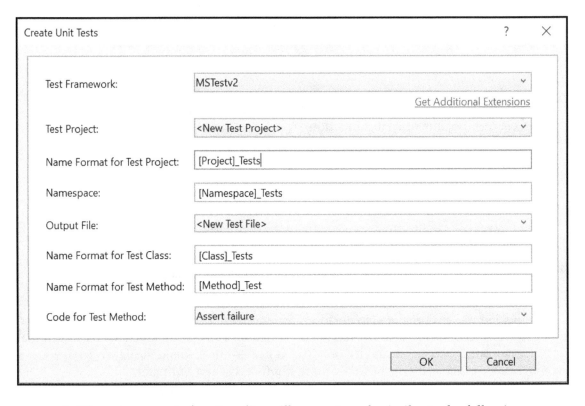

3. The auto generate functionality will generate code similar to the following:

```
using System;
using Microsoft.VisualStudio.TestTools.UnitTesting;
using TextEvaluation;
namespace TextEvaluation_Tests
```

```
{
    [TestClass()]
    public class AverageResults_Tests
    {
        [TestMethod()]
        public void Run_Test()
        {
            Assert.Fail();
        }
    }
}
```

4. We will now want to change the test name to follow the descriptive name convention, and add more test methods to cover the different test cases.

Creating a unit test

To get started with a unit test, we can get started with a success scenario of the simplest function we have. To do so, we will use the ProcessQueue function. If you remember, we left the ProcessQueue function with a very simple implementation, which, technically, does nothing but log the event of processing the queue message. This lack of external dependencies will make it easy for us to show the simplest possible unit test.

As a reminder, the last version of the ProcessQueue function looked similar to this (only the log message format below was changed):

```
[FunctionName("ProcessQueue")]
public static void Run(
[ServiceBusTrigger("emailqueue", AccessRights.Listen, Connection =
"serviceBus")]string emailBody,
TraceWriter log)
{
    var doc = new HtmlDocument();
    doc.LoadHtml(emailBody);
    var text = doc.DocumentNode.InnerText;
    log.Info($"{{'messageContent': {text}}}");
}
```

Now we can add a unit test for the function. In the **Arrange** section, we will initialize the parameters required to call the function. The ProcessQueue function expects to receive two parameters: a string message from a Service Bus trigger, and a TraceWriter log.

The `TraceWriter` log is an abstract class that is implemented by a `TraceMonitor` class in the `Microsoft.Azure.WebJobs.Extensions` library, thus, we can pass an instance of the `TraceMonitor` class to the function. To use `TraceMonitor`, we first need to install the `Microsoft.Azure.WebJobs.Extensions` NuGet package on the `TextEvaluation_Tests` project.

The test code will be as follows:

```
using Microsoft.VisualStudio.TestTools.UnitTesting;
using TextEvaluation;
using Microsoft.Azure.WebJobs.Extensions;
[TestMethod()]
    public void ProcessQueueRun_InputString_LoggedInput()
    {
        /////////////////////////////////////////////
        // Arrange
        /////////////////////////////////////////////
        var log = new TraceMonitor();
        var emailBody = "Test Service Bus message";
        /////////////////////////////////////////////
        // Act
        /////////////////////////////////////////////
        ProcessQueue.Run(emailBody, log);
        /////////////////////////////////////////////
        // Assert
        /////////////////////////////////////////////
    }
```

Unfortunately, this type of test provides us with a near-zero value. Our **Assert** section is completely empty, and all that we are able to establish is that the function can be successfully triggered, and raises no exceptions. This is still useful for debugging purposes, and for a minimal sanity check, but if we are going to use this test as a part of an automated test suite, and rely on its results as an indicator that the function code is production ready, we need to be able to verify that the function worked as expected.

Note that the lack of "assertable" outcomes is partially due to the fact that the existing function code does not perform any significant action. As it is, the only goal of the `ProcessQueue` function is to log the receipt of the message. Thus, correct logging is the outcome that needs to be asserted.

To assert that the logging is being performed as expected, we can mock the `TraceWriter` class using the Moq framework.

Instead of a `TraceWriter` class, you can also use an `Microsoft.Extensions.Logging.ILogger` interface in Azure Functions. To do so, you can pass the `ILogger` log parameter to the function, and an `ILogger` instance will be provided. Using `ILogger` may provide more flexibility in certain cases.

To use the Moq framework, we will need to install the Moq Nuget package on the test project.

We can then use Moq to mock the `TraceWriter` class, and set up the `Trace` method, including the method's callback. In the callback, we can add the produced log messages to a locally defined list of strings so that we are able to assess which log messages were produced.

Note that, if you have experience with Rhino Mocks, you may find the syntax of passing `log.Object` to the function a little confusing. That is because, in Moq, the defined mock is actually a wrapper class. Overall, because of this, Moq actually tends to be less verbose, and thus, somewhat cleaner.

To learn more about Moq, please visit `https://github.com/Moq/moq4/wiki/Quickstart`.

The ProcessQueue function - input string, and logged output

```
using Microsoft.VisualStudio.TestTools.UnitTesting;
using TextEvaluation;
using Microsoft.Azure.WebJobs.Host;
using Moq;
using System.Collections.Generic;
using System.Diagnostics;
using System.Linq;
namespace TextEvaluation_Tests
{
[TestClass()]
public class ProcessQueue_Tests
{
[TestMethod()]
public void ProcessQueueRun_InputString_LoggedInput()
{
    /////////////////////////////////////////
    // Arrange
    /////////////////////////////////////////
    var emailBody = "Test Service Bus message";
    var expectedLogMessage = $"{{'messageContent': {emailBody}}}";
    var logMessages = new List<string>();
    // set up the log mock
```

```
        var log = new Mock<TraceWriter>(TraceLevel.Error);
        log.Setup(l => l.Trace(It.IsAny<TraceEvent>()))
          .Callback((TraceEvent t) => logMessages.Add(t.Message));
        ////////////////////////////////////////////
        // Act
        ////////////////////////////////////////////
        ProcessQueue.Run(emailBody, log.Object);
        ////////////////////////////////////////////
        // Assert
        ////////////////////////////////////////////
        Assert.AreEqual(expectedLogMessage, logMessages.First());
    }
  }
}
```

Getting more granular

In the preceding case, the function is the smallest testable unit. However, in many cases, even the simplest functions will rely on a functionality defined in another class, or supplied by external APIs. The more complex the function gets, the more external components it relies on, the more likely it is that a full function test will be an Integration test rather than a Unit test.

Even if we do not choose to encapsulate the calls to external APIs in a separate unit, the dependencies themselves dictate the fact that we are moving further towards Integration tests. This fact can be seen clearly when we write tests, as we will notice a long list of things that need to be mocked, or relied upon. You will see an example of this in the *Integration testing* section covering a test of the ScoreTweet function.

Given the preceding, implementing parts of the function's functionality in a separate class actually has a number of advantages. Creating separate classes allows for true separation of concerns, decoupling the code from the concrete implementation, and using dependency injection for improved testability. With this, the common classes such as, in our case, EvaluateText.cs and StoreOutput.cs, become the subjects of true unit tests.

Asynchronous tests

Since serverless compute is mostly asynchronous, we need to write asynchronous tests. This may present a challenge in certain unit testing frameworks. In the latest MSTest, all that is required is to define the test method type to be public async Task. Then we can use the await modifier to await a function or another asynchronous method.

Unit test examples

To demonstrate an example of unit test methods, we will cover a couple of possible test cases for the `EvaluateText` class.

As you remember from previous chapters, `EvaluateText` uses dependency injection of the `HttpMessageHandler` class. The dependency injection will allow us to mock the `HttpClient` class, and isolate the `EvaluateText` methods from the dependency on Text Analytics API.

Since the `HttpClient` class does not derive from an interface, we are, instead, mocking the `HttpMessageHandler` class. Supplying `HttpMessageHandler` as a parameter to the `HttpClient` constructor allows us to mock the `SendAsync` method, which is then used in the implementation of the `PostAsync` method of the `HttpClient` class.

Some of the discussion on how one can approach mocking of the `HttpClient` class can be viewed in the epic thread here at `https://github.com/dotnet/corefx/issues/1624`.

Take a look at the `EvaluateText` dependency injection part in the following code snippet:

```
public class EvaluateText
{
    private readonly HttpClient _client;

    // Constructor
    public EvaluateText(HttpMessageHandler messageHandler = null)
    {
      if (messageHandler == null)
      {
         _client = new HttpClient();
      }
      else
      {
         _client = new HttpClient(messageHandler);
      }

    // Methods implementation...
}
```

Unit test examples

In the following unit test, we are looking at a use case in which a valid input text string is submitted to the `ScoreTextSentiment` method, and the Text Analytics API returns a valid output with a double text sentiment score. The `ScoreTextSentiment` method is then expected to correctly parse the API output, and return the expected double score.

To arrange the test case, we create an expected score, and a valid input string. We then mock `HttpMessageHandler`, and set up the `SendAsync` method to return `HttpStatusCode.OK (200)`, and a correctly formatted JSON output with the expected text sentiment score. Notice that the `inputText` string, in itself, bears no significance as long as it is a valid string (so that it does not cause any side effects).

Note that the syntax of the Moq `Setup` method differs from the usual here, since we are accessing a protected rather than a public method. The syntax requires adding a using `Moq.Protected;` statement. The syntax examples for protected methods can be found under "miscellaneous" at `https://github.com/Moq/moq4/wiki/Quickstart`.

In the "act" section, we create a new instance of the `EvaluateText` class, inject the dependency on the mocked instance of `HttpMessageHandler`, and then execute the `ScoreTextSentiment` method.

In the "assert" section, we validate that the method indeed returned the expected text sentiment score.

Take a look at the following test implementation:

```
[TestMethod()]
public async Task EvaluateText_ApiReturnsScore_ReturnsTheScore()
{
    ///////////////////////////////////////////
    // Arrange
    ///////////////////////////////////////////
    const double EPSILON = 0.0000000001;
    var expectedScore = 0.500000000000001;
    var inputText = "dummy text";
    // mock messageHandler
    var messageHandler = new Mock<HttpMessageHandler>();
    messageHandler.Protected()
      .Setup<Task<HttpResponseMessage>>("SendAsync",
      ItExpr.IsAny<HttpRequestMessage>(),
      ItExpr.IsAny<CancellationToken>())
      .Returns(Task<HttpResponseMessage>
      .Factory.StartNew(() =>
    {
        return new HttpResponseMessage(HttpStatusCode.OK)
        {
            Content = new StringContent(
            "{\"documents\":[{ \"score\": "
            + expectedScore + "," +
            "\"id\":\"0\" }], \"errors\":[]}")
        };
    }));
```

```
/////////////////////////////////////////
// Act
/////////////////////////////////////////
var evalText = new EvaluateText(messageHandler.Object);
var score = await evalText.ScoreTextSentiment(inputText);
/////////////////////////////////////////
// Assert
/////////////////////////////////////////
Assert.AreEqual(expectedScore, score, EPSILON);
}
```

Run the test to verify that the `ScoreTextSentiment` method in `EvaluateText` does, indeed, return the expected score that was returned by the mocked API response.

The EvaluateText class - API failure and method failure

In the following test case, we arrange to test for the external API failure.

When a server error is returned from the Text Analytics API, our `EvaluateText` implementation presently fails with an exception, since the HTTP response content is not a valid JSON. The MSTest framework allows us to expect the exception using the `ExpectedException` attribute, and also to specify whether a specific exception type or any of the derived types are considered valid.

In the "arrange" section of the test, we will create a valid input string, and set up the `SendAsync` method in the `HttpMessageHandler` mockup class to return `HttpStatusCode.InternalServerError`.

In the "act" section, we will execute the `ScoreTextSentiment` method using the new `HttpMessageHandler` mockup.

No "assert" section is required, as the expected outcome is defined by the `ExpectedException` attribute. The test method will fail unless the `ScoreTextSentiment` method throws one of the exceptions derived from `System.Exception`.

Throwing an exception in case of an API error is currently the valid, expected code behavior that we aim to assert. You may want to improve the `CallTextSentimentApi` method code in `EvaluateText` class to handle the Text Analytics API errors in a more graceful manner. Getting more visibility into what your code actually does in particular use cases is the great advantage of developing a unit test suite.

Take a look at the following test method implementation:

```
[TestMethod()]
[ExpectedException(typeof(System.Exception), AllowDerivedTypes =
true)]
public async Task EvaluateText_ApiReturnsError_ExceptionThrown()
{
  //////////////////////////////////////////////
  // Arrange
  //////////////////////////////////////////////
  var inputText = "dummy text";
  var messageHandler = new Mock<HttpMessageHandler>();
  messageHandler.Protected()
    .Setup<Task<HttpResponseMessage>>("SendAsync",
    ItExpr.IsAny<HttpRequestMessage>(),
    ItExpr.IsAny<CancellationToken>())
    .Returns(Task<HttpResponseMessage>
    .Factory.StartNew(() =>
    {
      return new HttpResponseMessage(
        HttpStatusCode.InternalServerError);
    }));
  //////////////////////////////////////////////
  // Act
  //////////////////////////////////////////////
  var evalText = new EvaluateText(messageHandler.Object);
  var score = await evalText.ScoreTextSentiment(inputText);

  //////////////////////////////////////////////
  // Assert
  //////////////////////////////////////////////
  //Expects exception
}
```

Run the test to validate that the `ScoreTextSentiment` method in `EvaluateText` does, indeed, throw an exception in case a server error is returned by the mocked API response.

Integration testing

As discussed earlier, Integration testing is testing that demonstrates integration between one or more system components. In many cases, an Azure Function testing will fall under integration rather than unit testing. In this case, we are talking about white-box testing with the tests still defined in the unit test project, and structured very similarly to unit tests. The main difference is the simultaneous invocation of multiple dependencies, and, in some cases, the inability to completely isolate the function from external dependencies.

Let us demonstrate an Integration test with an example of a `ScoreTweet` function. In this test case, we will use a valid tweet as an input, and mock the `outputTable` parameter. The mock will allow us to return a single existing entity when `ListEntitiesAsync` is called, and make sure that `UpdateEntityAsync` is subsequently called with the new score we got.

The ScoreTweet function - updating an entity

Since the method code is quite lengthy, we will explain it in the following sections.

Using statements and test class and method definitions are in the following first code snippet:

```
using Microsoft.VisualStudio.TestTools.UnitTesting;
using TextEvaluation;
using Microsoft.Azure.ApiHub;
using Moq;
using Newtonsoft.Json.Linq;
using System.Net.Http;
using System.Collections.Generic;
using System.Threading;
using System.Threading.Tasks;
using System.Diagnostics;
using Microsoft.Azure.WebJobs.Host;
namespace TextEvaluation_Tests
  {
    [TestClass()]
    public class ScoreTweet_Tests
    {
      [TestMethod()]
      public async Task ScoreTweet_ExistingTweet_UpdatedEntity()
      {
```

The "arrange" section of the test will consist of multiple mocks. First, we will mock up the logs using the `TraceWriter` mock. In this case, we are expecting two log messages, which are produced by a correct function execution in a specific sequence.

The first part of the "arrange" test section is in the following code snippet:

```
/////////////////////////////////////////
// Arrange
/////////////////////////////////////////
// Setup Logs
var logMessages = new List<string>();
var log = new Mock<TraceWriter>(TraceLevel.Error);
log.Setup(l => l.Trace(It.IsAny<TraceEvent>()))
  .Callback((TraceEvent t) => logMessages.Add(t.Message));
```

```
var tweetText = "Loving the serverless compute :-)";
var user = "DivineOps";
var score = 0.949561040962202;
var expectedLogMessages = new List<string>()
{
  "Updating existing row in output table",
  $"Scored tweet: {tweetText}, user: {user}, " +
  $"sentiment score: {score}"
};
```

Next, we mock the output table using the Moq framework. To do so, we set up the table itself, and create a list of entities to be returned from the ListEntitiesAsync method. This list contains a single entity of an existing tweet, and hence, the decision tree path invoked in the StoreOutput.StoreOutputSQL method by the test code, is the case of a single existing entity that should be updated.

The second part of the "arrange" test section is in the following code snippet:

```
// Mock outputTable
var outputTable = new Mock<ITable<JObject>>();
var entity = new JObject {
  new JProperty("ID", "0"),
  new JProperty("Username", user),
  new JProperty("TweetText", tweetText),
  new JProperty("TextSentimentScore", score)
};
var entities = new SegmentedResult<JObject>();
entities.Items = new List<JObject>() { entity };

// Setup the ListEntitiesAsync method
// To return a list with a single entity defined above
outputTable.Setup(t => t.ListEntitiesAsync(
  It.IsAny<Query>(),
  It.IsAny<ContinuationToken>(),
  It.IsAny<CancellationToken>())
  .ReturnsAsync(entities);
```

Lastly, we need to mock up HttpRequestMessage, which triggers the function. In this case, it is sufficient to only initialize the message Content, as the query parameters are not parsed, and the HTTP response is not expected.

The third part of the "arrange" test section is in the following code snippet:

```
// HTTP request
var req = new HttpRequestMessage()
{
 Content = new StringContent(
   "{\"TweetText\": \""+ tweetText +"\", " +
   "\"UserDetails\": {\"UserName\": \""+ user +"\"}}")
};
```

Notice that in this case, we cannot control the implementation of `HttpClient`, as it is inaccessible to us. By design, all the function's input and output bindings are passed as function parameters, and hence, can be mocked and injected. This excludes, however, any additional implementation dependencies of the function (in our case, the dependency on the Text Analytics API).

Given the preceding, all possible tests in `ScoreTweet_Tests` will have an implicit dependency on a call to the Text Analytics API. Since the `HttpClient` class cannot be mocked, a real call will be executed, and the test result will be dependent on the API response. This is not ideal. The situation will be improved if/when Azure Functions allow for dependency injection of additional parameters.

 An external API can be mocked by providing a URL pointing to a dummy API that returns preconfigured responses. A dummy API can be implemented from scratch, or mocked using third party tools like mockable.io or SoapUI. This is a great alternative if calling a Production API in Dev/Test environments is not an option for operational or cost reasons.

In the meantime, since a "real" call to the Text Analytics API is executed, the `TextEvaluation_Tests` project needs to have access to the application settings used to call the API. To add these settings, find the `app.config` file in the test project tree. Open the file, and add the following `<appSettings>` block with the same values used in the `TextEvaluation` project's `local.settings.json` file:

```
<configuration>
 <appSettings>
    <add key="textSentimentApiUrl" value="https://westus.
    api.cognitive.microsoft.com/text/analytics/v2.0/sentiment"/>
    <add key="textSentimentApiKey" value="YourApiKey"/>
 </appSettings>
 ...
</configuration>
```

Coming back to the test code, the "act" section of the test contains a single line of code with a call to the function's `Run` method:

```
//////////////////////////////////////////
// Act
//////////////////////////////////////////
await ScoreTweet.Run(req, outputTable.Object, log.Object);
```

In the "assert" section of the test, we will assert that the expected log messages were produced in the correct order, and that the `UpdateEntityAsync` method on the `outputTable` mockup was called once.

If we wanted to comply strictly with a "one assert per test" approach, we could separate the assertion of the correct logs being produced from the assertion that the update entity code path was executed, however, both are technically aimed to assert the same behavior:

```
//////////////////////////////////////////
// Assert
//////////////////////////////////////////
// Compare all log messages
CollectionAssert.AreEqual(expectedLogMessages, logMessages);
// Verify that Update entity was called
outputTable.Verify(t => t.UpdateEntityAsync(It.IsAny<string>(),
    It.IsAny<JObject>(), It.IsAny<CancellationToken>()),
    Times.Once());
```

Performance testing

As discussed earlier, performance testing is, typically, a black-box testing aimed at estimating the system's performance under a particular workload.

In the previous chapter, we discussed multiple ways to trigger the functions, both locally, and in the cloud. These methods can be used to trigger the function's execution with particular inputs with the aim of measuring the function's performance.

The function's performance under load can be measured with a tool such as Application Insights, which will be discussed in `Chapter 11`, *Monitoring Your Application's Health*.

Load testing

Load testing **HTTP-triggered** functions can be set up by creating Web tests using either the Visual Studio IDE or VSTS online workspace.

Such testing can be set up using a URL-based test that calls the function URL from specified geo-locations with appropriate parameters, and measure the function's performance. The load testing setup with VSTS will be covered in detail in the next chapter after setting up the VSTS account and continuous delivery pipeline.

Load testing of **non-HTTP triggered** functions involves triggering Unit Tests from Load Tests. This process will not be covered in this book. To learn how to create a Load Test project in Visual Studio, and to run Unit Tests from it, please visit `https://msdn.microsoft.com/en-us/library/ff355993.aspx?f=255MSPPError=-2147217396#`.

Note that installation of load-testing tools requires a Visual Studio Enterprise edition.

Summary

In this chapter, we walked in detail through testing best practices, and covered the process of testing Azure Functions, focusing primarily on Unit and Integration testing using the MSTest framework.

In the next chapter, we will walk through one more of the critical steps in the modern application life cycle, that is, the ability to deploy the code from source control, and construct a continuous delivery pipeline.

9
Configuring Continuous Delivery

In this chapter, we will discuss the importance of using version control for our software development projects, and the benefits of creating a continuous integration and delivery (CI/CD) pipeline.

We will walk through the following topics in this chapter:

- Best practices and types of version control
- Advantages of continuous delivery
- Configuring source control for a Function App project
- Building a CI/CD pipeline for serverless functions with VSTS
- Load testing with VSTS

Version Control System

Version Control System (VCS), also known as source control, is a system that records changes to sets of files, and maintains a history of all the past file versions. A VCS can be used for any type of files, but it is commonly used to track changes in software development projects.

By this point in the book, you may have already checked your project into source control. In fact, you may have done so as soon as you had a working version of your very first function. Being accustomed to using source control creates an automatic desire to commit any meaningful changes, and for a good reason. Using a VCS may seem so obvious that I have questioned whether this book should even cover the source control benefits. There are, however, some scary survey statistics out there claiming that less than 50% of all software projects are in any type of VCS.

I prefer not to make authoritative statements about software development, but I will make this one:

If you are not using source control for your development projects, you should start now.

It is free, it is easy to learn, and it is going to save you so much grief! The importance of keeping track of all changes increases exponentially with every additional member of your team, but even single-developer projects need a VCS. The ability to keep version history, and go back to a code file from 3 hours, 3 days, or 3 months ago for a working code example is truly priceless. More on that in a moment.

There are two main types of version control systems today: **distributed** and **centralized**. While there are advantages and disadvantages to both, the software development community now largely agrees that distributed VCS are superior.

Centralized VCS

A centralized VCS, such as **SVN** (**Apache Subversion**) or **Team Foundation Server** (**TFS**), maintains a central copy of your project, which is the authoritative source of truth. Every developer can check out a copy of the main repository, and later pull any updates that have been made to it. The developer can also make changes to their local copy, and then commit them to the central copy of the project, so that they become available to other developers.

If a number of developers made changes to the same files since the last commit, the changes will need to be merged. The merges typically happen locally, and any merge conflicts need to be resolved before the code can be committed to the central repository.

 If you are just getting started with source control, and think that merges are painful, please consider that the only other alternative is to simply override other people's changes with your latest version. The consequences of such an override are unpredictable, and often very difficult to diagnose.

Distributed VCS

In a distributed VCS, such as Git or Mercurial, there is no concept of a central copy. When a developer clones a remote repository, they get a full copy including all the metadata and history of the project to their machine. Distributed VCS do not preclude you from keeping a central, authoritative copy of your project, rather, they allow you to have fully functional local copies as well.

What does this mean in practice?

The main difference is that the distributed VCS breaks the centralized commit into two separate actions, which are as follows:

- **Commit**: This records the changeset on the local repository
- **Push**: This pushes one or more local commits to the remote repository

This creates a number of advantages, which are listed as follows:

- The actions performed on the local repository, such as commits or reverts, are much faster
- A developer can commit work to the source control without an internet connection
- It is easier to fork open source projects, since you get the full copy of the project with its history when you clone a repository
- It is easier to use source control for small personal projects, since you can create a full-blown local repository without the need for the overhead of self-hosting or paying someone to host your centralized VCS
- A developer can commit multiple changesets locally, without impacting the team

Being able to commit multiple changes before pushing them to the central repository allows the developer to have all the advantages of the source control, such as version history and the ability to revert changes on much smaller units of work.

To illustrate, imagine the following situation:

- The central authoritative copy of your team's project is plugged into a continuous integration pipeline that runs an extensive test suite
- You are working on a feature that requires major changes to three different parts of the system before the automated tests can pass

In this scenario, if you are using a centralized VCS, you will be forced to hold off on committing your changes until all of the modifications across the entire project are fully complete and ready to pass the tests. Alternatively, you would need to create a separate branch for the changes.

In the same scenario, if you are using a distributed VCS, you will be able to commit each of the three smaller changesets locally, and then push them to the central repository when all of the changes are complete and pass all the CI tests. Thus the flow becomes easier, and any of the smaller changesets can be reverted to the last local commit, rather than needing to go back to the last major version in the central repository.

One disadvantage of a distributed VCS is that it creates a full copy of the repository, which could conceivably get large, on the local machine. This is, typically, not an issue, because code files are lightweight text files, and the changes are (typically) stored as diffs, and not full-file copies.

While speaking of distributed VCS, it is perhaps worth noting that Git and GitHub are not synonymous. Git is a distributed VCS that can be used to create and maintain your repository, both locally and remotely. GitHub is a web-based hosting service for Git repositories. GitHub has become the default hosting service for open source projects, because it lets you host publicly accessible repositories for free. This means that as long as you are willing to share your code with other people, you do not need to pay for hosting. You can also pay GitHub for private hosting services, which would only allow authorized users to access your repositories.

One of the biggest benefits of Git is that the VCS tools themselves are free, and since the VCS is distributed, you can easily create and maintain a local repository on your machine (which can be backed up periodically), so, getting source control for small personal development projects is a no-brainer. (If you're wondering why you need source control for small personal projects, just remember the last time you made a breaking change and it took you three excruciating hours just to get things "unscrewed").

Note that this book does not aim to be a "how-to" guide of any particular VCS. To learn more about how to use Git, please visit `https://git-scm.com/book/en/v1/Getting-Started`. For TFS, please visit `https://www.visualstudio.com/en-us/docs/tfvc/overview`.

Common practices

There are a number of approaches commonly used by all VCS, regardless of the type which are as follows:

Branching: This, in VCS, is the duplication of the repository so that changes can happen in parallel on both of the branches (imagine the branches on a tree). Branches are useful for experimenting with the code without impacting the main "trunk"/master branch. Once the changes are complete, and if they are successful, they can be merged back into the master branch.

Branching happens to be a divisive topic, with some CI/CD experts avoiding branches altogether, and others recommending to create a branch for every single feature under development (an approach called **feature branching**). To gain some insight into the discussion, you can read this blog article by Martin Fowler at `https://martinfowler.com/bliki/FeatureBranch.html`.

Ignore list: This is a file in the repository that lists specific names or name patterns of project files that are intentionally untracked. Examples of name patterns include "everything with a `.user` extension", or "everything under the `bin` folder".

For instance, it is usually recommended to ignore binary files. These files, typically, cannot be "diff"-ed, and hence, would be committed fully each time compilation happens, generating a lot of unnecessary volume in VCS. They also provide no useful insight into the code changes.

You can learn how to add file name patterns to the Git ignore list at `https://git-scm.com/docs/gitignore`.

Committing best practices

Most of the committing and pushing best practices are self-evident. One practice that might not be obvious is the importance of writing good commit messages. Descriptive commit messages can really help, especially after three months, when you are trying to figure out what prompted you to make a certain change, or in three years, when you inherit a repository from someone you cannot get in touch with.

The commonly stated best practices to adopt when committing code changes are as follows:

- Writing descriptive commit messages
- Committing often
- Committing related changes together
- Committing when a "unit of work" is done
- Testing the code before committing
- Running the full local test suite before pushing the commits to the central repository

Database versioning

Databases that have a schema should be versioned as well. Versioning the database, usually, starts with generating scripts that create the current database schema, and then creating upgrade scripts for every subsequent version. There are tools that can create such scripts automatically, based on your current database and your database changes. For SQL, you can consider RedGate, or SSDT tools in Visual Studio (`https://msdn.microsoft.com/en-us/library/aa833194(v=vs.100).aspx`) for this task.

Continuous Integration and delivery

Continuous Integration (CI) is a practice of merging all of the developers' working copies into a shared source control "mainline" frequently, perhaps several times a day.

In the past, some development teams would work on segregated code branches for weeks or even months, implementing somewhat separate features. This created a situation where the project versions grew out of sync, and merging the changes became a very time consuming and painful process of trying to reconcile the versions. This process was referred to as "integration hell". The main purpose of CI is to eliminate these integration issues.

CI is a prerequisite of continuous delivery, and using both is commonly referred to as the CI/CD approach.

Continuous Delivery (CD) is the practice of producing software in short cycles, ensuring that the software can be reliably released at any time. Unlike continuous deployment, CD doesn't aim to push every code change to production, but aims to ensure that it *can* be pushed.

In the past, most companies' software release cycles took a significant period of time, ranging from months to years. The new release version was worked on in a separate branch and a separate environment, with production "hotfixes" being deployed to the production version in parallel. This created another reason for the "integration hell", because releasing a software update almost always introduced unforeseen issues and uncovered incompatibilities. It also created a situation in which the new version design could completely "miss the target" and be rejected by the consumers.

CD aims to release the changes to production at much more frequent intervals, such as weeks or days, and eliminate integration hell by making sure that every change can be merged into the production branch.

CD, typically, involves building a deployment pipeline similar to the following (image source -`https://en.wikipedia.org/wiki/Continuous_delivery`):

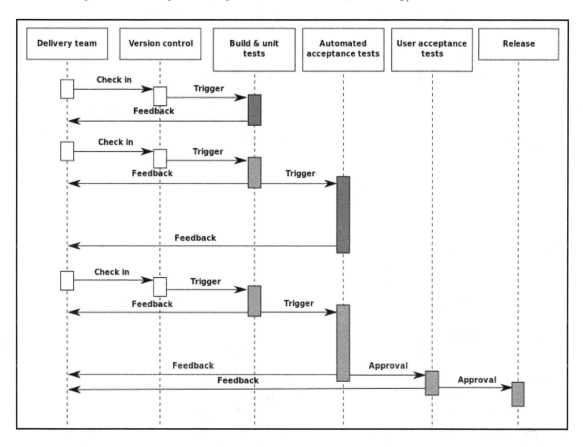

As illustrated by the preceding diagram, high-quality automated testing is crucial to the success of continuous delivery. Without an effective test-suite, we simply create a situation where every code change is pushed down the line to the last defense--user acceptance tests, or even straight to the end users. Thus, CD only works when every change can be validated by good quality regression tests.

CI/CD practice introduces numerous advantages, such as improved product quality and reliability, improved productivity and short time to market. Thus, the approach has been adopted widely in the last decade.

Continuous delivery is somewhat of a holy grail of software development. While the benefits are clear, a true CD conforming to all best practices is difficult to implement right away. This is why most development teams start by gradually adopting strategies that bring them closer to the ideal CD state.

One of the most significant restrictions of CD is the need for "**feature toggles**", or the ability to hide incomplete changes in the production environment. If, for instance, you are working on developing a large feature which requires weeks of work and collaboration between multiple people on the team, and CD best practices dictate that you need to push every change into the production branch, you will have to develop a way to "turn off"/hide the changes from the end user until they are fully ready. This is usually done by using a toggle to disable the new feature during runtime.

Feature toggles are convenient, and make it easy to turn updates on and off for subsets of users, and roll them out if and when you are ready. At the same time, implementing feature toggles can get complex.

That is why some development teams use somewhat "relaxed" versions of CD, such as maintaining a separate staging branch that can be promoted into production when the code is ready. The idea of this approach is that the environment branches get strictly promoted upwards: Dev -> Test -> Staging -> Production, that the Staging gets promoted into Production frequently, and that there are no hotfixes on the Production branch that can cause integration issues. Thus, the team gets the benefits of avoiding "integration hell" without being required to push every single code change to the Production branch.

Another best practice of continuous delivery that can get complex is the ability to roll the code back to *any* reasonably recent version. This approach creates a challenge with any significant (especially, relational) database changes, as the old version of the code needs to still perform correctly on the new database, and vice versa. To illustrate, if you have split the field "Full Name" in the database to "First Name" and "Last Name", you will have to keep writing to both the new and the old fields, so that the previous version of the code remains compatible with the new schema and can work with the data that was added after the change. When using a relational database, you will also need to maintain the "downgrade" scripts for the database.

Again, many software development teams start with a relaxed version of this practice, where they aim to be able to roll back at least one version. This approach yields a lot of benefits (any defects, or changes disliked by the end users can be reverted and fixed immediately) while not being as time consuming. The database downgrade script challenge can also be addressed by making additive non-breaking changes (most database changes tend to be additive naturally as the software evolves), and indeed maintaining the code that writes to the "retired" columns and tables for a while.

In Azure PaaS, the single version rollback is supported natively by the platform by using deployment slots. A deployment slot, essentially, provides a copy of the Production environment into which the code can be deployed. The slot can then be promoted to Production with zero downtime by making a DNS swap. If defects are discovered, the Production slot can be swapped back to serve the end users, while the development team works on code fixes.

Version control for functions

Most serverless compute-supporting vendors started the offer by providing a purely online development experience. Version control is one of the main reasons that this development experience was not welcomed by most developers. Having a local project allows you to create a source control repository, and check in your changes as you develop new features.

In this chapter, we will use **Visual Studio Team Services** (**VSTS**) as our repository hosting provider, and Git as our version control system. We will also use VSTS to build a CI/CD pipeline.

Configuring VSTS

VSTS is a cloud-based project management tool, which can serve as an extension of Visual Studio. VSTS allows developer teams to manage all aspects of the application life cycle, from project management to source control, to code build, and release. Many of the VSTS features are free for up to five users.

VSTS supports two version control systems: TFS and Git. Given the previously discussed advantages of distributed VCS, we will use Git.

To sign up for VSTS, and create your first repository, execute the following steps:

1. To sign up for VSTS, you can use either your personal Microsoft account, or use the organizational account provided by your company. To sign up for VSTS using your Microsoft account, go to the VSTS site, `https://go.microsoft.com/fwlink/?LinkId=307137clcid=0x409`, and sign in with the same Microsoft account that owns your Azure subscription.
2. Once you are logged in, you will get to choose the name of your VSTS account, and the type of source control for your first project.

3. Choose a memorable name for your VSTS account. The URL `https://YourVstsAccount.visualstudio.com` will become your team's VSTS website where you will host any future repositories:

4. Choose **Git** as the version control system.
5. Click on **Change details** to configure the project details.
6. Enter the project name, the type of project organization , and the site location (only some Azure regions are available for VSTS hosting).

   The options for work organization are Agile, Scrum, and CMMI. These options pertain to how the project management board is organized, which will not be covered here:

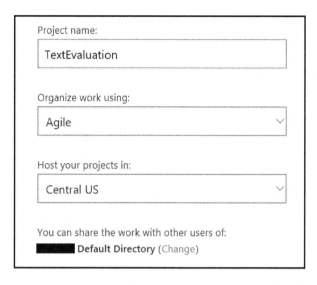

7. If you have other people in your Azure Active Directory tenant, you will be able to share the repository with them. If you click on the **Change** button, you will be able to choose one of the Azure Active Directory tenants you have access to.

8. Click on **Continue**.

9. This will create a new VSTS site, `https://YourVstsAccount.visualstudio.com`. It will also create a new VSTS project named `TextEvaluation`, and a new Git repository named `TextEvaluation`.

10. Copy the new repository URL. It will be constructed similar to the following:

```
https://YourVstsAccount.visualstudio.com/_git/TextEvaluation
```

Configuring the repository

Note that you can manage the new repository using Git commands from the command line/PowerShell if you have Git tools installed on your machine, or from Visual Studio. The process that follows outlines adding the repository using Visual Studio.

To add the existing code in our `TextEvaluation` functions project to the new source control repository we've created in VSTS, execute the following steps:

1. In the bottom-right corner of the Visual Studio IDE, click on **Add to Source Control -> Git**, as seen in the following screenshot:

2. In **Team Explorer**, select **Push to Remote Repository**, and then click on **Publish Git Repo**, as shown in the following screenshot:

3. Enter the new repository URL.
4. Click on **Publish**.
5. This will configure the local repository, and add the new online repository we've created as a remote origin.
6. Browse to the local `TextEvaluation` project folder. If hidden files are visible on your machine, you will now see a `.git` hidden folder, a `.gitattributes` file, and a `.gitignore` file.
7. To review the Git ignore list, in Visual Studio, switch to the **Team Explorer** view, as shown in the following screenshot:

8. Click on **Settings -> Repository Settings -> Ignore and Attributes Files -> Edit Ignore file**.

9. The Git ignore file will open in Visual Studio, and you will notice that the `bin` and `debug` folders, test folders, NuGet package folders, user settings files, publishing profiles, and many other types of local compilation and configuration files have been automatically added to the ignore list. This is very useful, since we do not need to construct the ignore list from scratch.

> The repository we created in VSTS is private to our Azure Active Directory tenant, and hence, we can commit the application config files.
>
> When using a public repository host such as GitHub, it is crucial to exclude the config files which contain sensitive information such as passwords or account keys. If you wish to exclude the config files, add them to the Git ignore list prior to the first commit.
>
> For the sake of clarity on what the excluded configuration settings should look like, you can add a config template with sample values to the repository instead of the real config file.

10. If you've made any changes to the Git ignore list, in **Team Explorer**, click on **Changes**, add a commit comment, and click on **Commit All**:

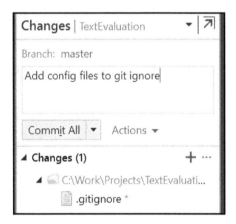

 If you are new to Git, remember that commit and push are separate actions, and committing the changes commits them to the local Git repository clone on your machine.

11. To push the local repository content to the remote origin (central repository in VSTS), navigate to **Synchronization** -> **Outgoing Commits** -> **Push**, as shown in the following screenshot:

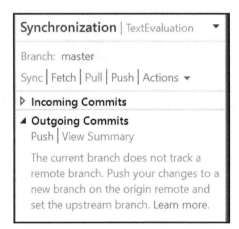

12. The push will create a master branch on the remote origin, and push the code to that branch. You can now see all the project files in VSTS, as seen in the following screenshot:

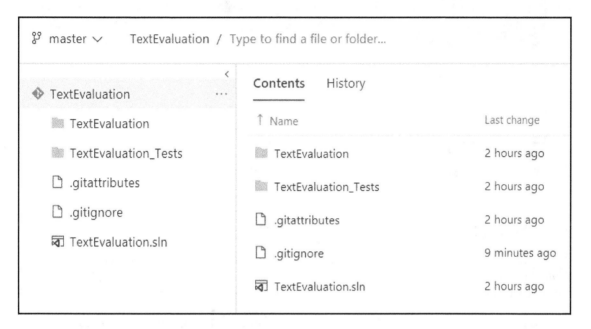

As noted before, all of the aforementioned actions can be performed using Git commands from the command line/PowerShell. It is usually best to stick to one method of managing the repository (either command line or Visual Studio) to avoid confusion.

Linking the Azure subscription to VSTS

To enable integration between VSTS and your Azure subscription, we need to first link your **Team Services accounts** to the right subscription.

To do so, navigate to Azure **Portal** -> **Browse** -> **Team Services Accounts** -> `Your Account` -> **Link**:

This will allow us to easily access to the VSTS projects from Azure services and vice versa.

Continuous delivery for functions

Now that our `TextEvaluation` project source code is in source control, we can configure a CI/CD pipeline to build, test, and release (publish) our code to our Azure Function App with every commit. We will use VSTS as our continuous delivery tool.

Before we configure the CI/CD pipeline, let us configure a staging deployment slot.

Deployment slots

As briefly mentioned before, deployment slots are an Azure PaaS feature which allows for a zero-downtime swap between your application environments. A deployment slot is, essentially, a replica of your production environment, which can be swapped with production by a DNS change handled by the Azure platform.

This feature is commonly used by developers to deploy production-ready code to a staging slot for final testing. If the staging deployment passes the tests, it can be promoted to production. Furthermore, if any issues are reported after deployment to production, the slots can be swapped back (since your former production environment is still available in the staging slot) with no downtime. This allows you to revert back a version, and work on any needed code fixes without impacting your users. (More than two slots per application are available in regular App Service, so that more than one version can be maintained.)

Deployment slots have existed for years in App Service (Web, API, and Mobile Apps), and are currently in preview for Azure Functions. A feature that is currently not available for functions, but will be enabled down the line, is A/B testing, also called "testing in production". With testing in production, you can redirect a percentage of the traffic to your staging slot to test the latest changes on a small portion of end users.

To create a new deployment slot in your Function App, execute the following steps:

1. To turn on the preview deployment slots feature, go to your **Function App -> Settings**.
2. Click on **On** in the setting shown in the following screenshot. Note that this action is irreversible, and also resets your function keys:

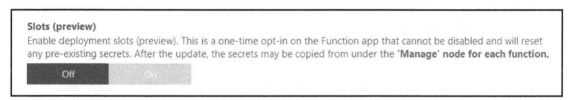

3. You will now see a new drop-down menu, **Slots (preview)**, appear in the Function App.
4. Click on the plus sign next to **Slots (preview)** to add a new deployment slot as shown in the following screenshot:

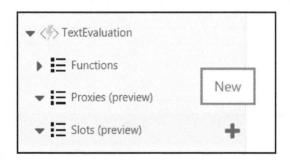

5. To create the deployment slot, enter the slot name and click on **Create**:

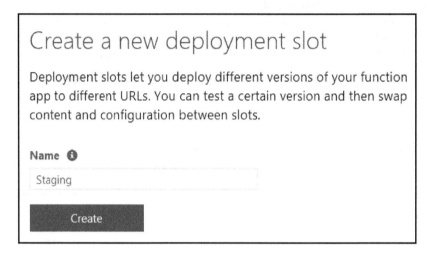

6. You will now see a `Staging` slot appear in the list. From the environment settings standpoint, the staging slot is essentially a replica of your production slot. Clicking on the slot will allow you to see the slot overview, settings, and platform features in the same way you would for your original Function App.

7. The deployment slot Function App endpoints can be accessed on a separate URL, constructed as `https://[YourAppName]-[SlotName].azurewebsites.net`. In our case, the URL is `https://textevaluation-staging.azurewebsites.net`:

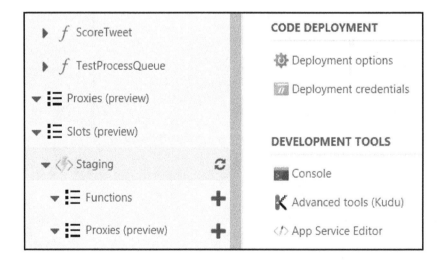

Configuring the VSTS build process

Now that the code is in source control, and the staging slot is available for deployment, we are ready to set up the continuous delivery pipeline. First we will configure the application Build process.

 In the future, you should be able to configure the Build and Release process directly from the functions portal, by configuring the Continuous Delivery feature. Doing so will generate the appropriate templates in VSTS.

To create a new build for the Function App, execute the following steps:

1. Browse to your VSTS website, `https://[YourVstsAccount].visualstudio.com`.

2. Navigate to **Builds** -> **New**, and select the **ASP.NET Core (.NET Framework)** template, as shown in the following screenshot. This template has the correct steps to build the Function App project:

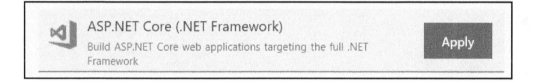

3. After you click on apply, the build steps (**Tasks**) shown in the following screenshot will be automatically configured for you:

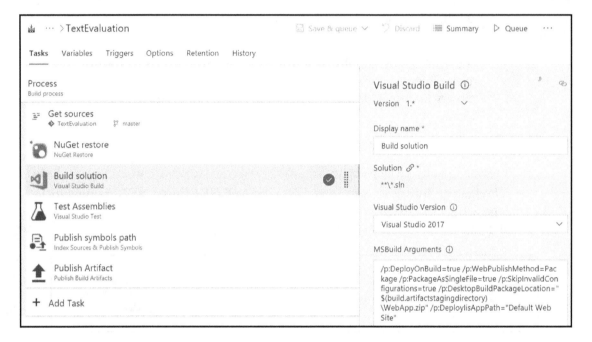

Note that the build automatically configures the testing steps as well, running any tests that are already defined in the solution.

4. To make sure that the build is triggered automatically when new code changes are checked in, navigate to the build's **Triggers** tab. Enable the continuous integration trigger to start the build whenever code is pushed into the master branch:

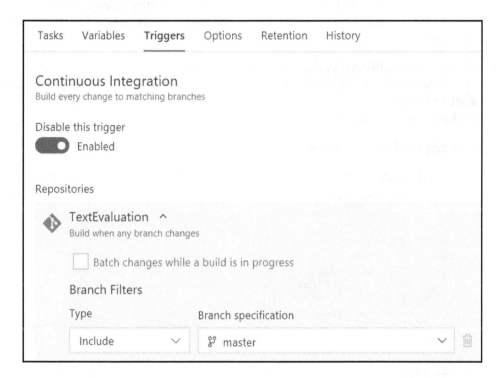

5. Navigate to the build's **Options** tab, and make sure that the **Hosted VS2017** type of agent is selected (this is the agent compatible with Functions):

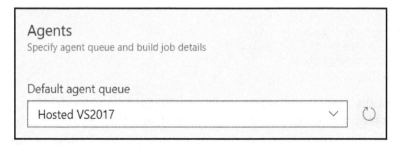

Configuring the NuGet restore task

NuGet restore pulls the packages referenced in the solution from one or more NuGet feed. The `https://www.nuget.org` feed is configured as a source by default, but additional custom feeds can be added. In our Function App, we are currently using an additional custom NuGet feed - Azure App Service feed, to get Azure Functions and WebJobs pre-release packages.

In Visual Studio, the additional package source gets configured automatically when installing the functions tools. In VSTS, we will need to provide the additional configuration to the NuGet restore step by supplying a `NuGet.Config` file which specifies both the default and the custom NuGet feeds we use.

To do so, execute the following steps:

1. Add a file named `NuGet.Config` to the main project folder on your machine.
2. Add the following code to the file:

```xml
<?xml version="1.0" encoding="utf-8"?>
<configuration>
 <packageSources>
 <add key="nuget.org"
     value="https://api.nuget.org/v3/index.json"
     protocolVersion="3" />
 <add key="App Service"
     value="http://www.myget.org/F/azure-appservice/api/v2" />
</packageSources>
<disabledPackageSources>
<add key="Microsoft and .NET" value="true" />
</disabledPackageSources>
<packageRestore>
    <add key="enabled" value="True" />
    <add key="automatic" value="True" />
</packageRestore>
<bindingRedirects>
    <add key="skip" value="False" />
</bindingRedirects>
</configuration>
```

3. Check the file into the online repository (in the Visual Studio IDE, go to **Team Explorer** and click on **Changes** -> **Commit**, and then **Sync** -> **Push**).
4. Now that the file is in source control, modify the NuGet restore Build step to use it by clicking on the **NuGet restore** task and selecting **Feeds to use** -> **Feeds in my NuGet.config** -> Browse, then choose the config file from source control:

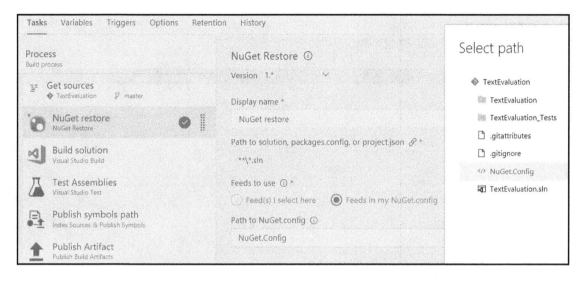

5. Click on **Save and Queue** to verify that the build completes successfully, or commit and push a change to the repository to trigger the build.

6. You will see the build get scheduled and then start, as shown in the following screenshot:

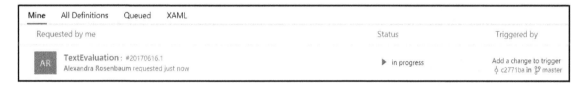

Note: You may see a warning that the build only partially succeeded, and see the following error during the Publish Symbols Path step:

> *Indexed source information could not be retrieved from* '...\TextEvaluation.pdb'.
> *Symbol indexes could not be retrieved.*

You can fix the problem by updating your project's debug configuration in Visual Studio. To do so, perform the following steps:

1. In Visual Studio, right-click on the TextEvaluation project and click on **Properties**.
2. Open the **Build** tab.
3. Select **Release** for **Configuration** (or All Configurations).

4. Click on **Advanced**, and change the output debugging information to **pdb-only**, as shown in the following screenshot:

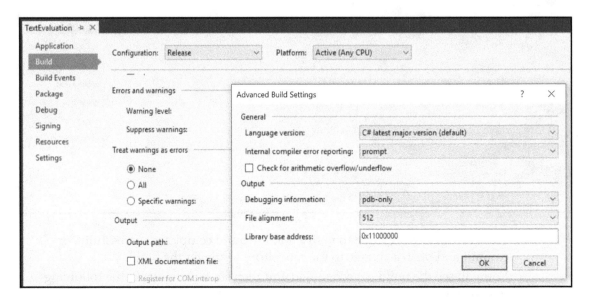

This will make sure that the VSTS Build process successfully indexes the symbols in the PDB file.

E-mail notifications

By default, VSTS will email you a notification for each finished build and its status.

You can configure which notifications are on in the main **VSTS configuration** -> **Notifications**, as shown in the following screenshot:

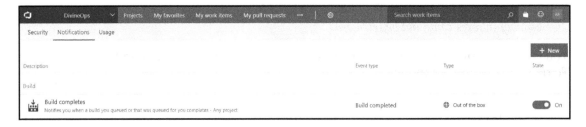

Configuring Release

After your build is configured and runs successfully, we can configure the release which will deploy the compiled application into the Azure Function App.

To do so, execute the following steps:

1. In VSTS, navigate to **Releases -> Create release definition**:

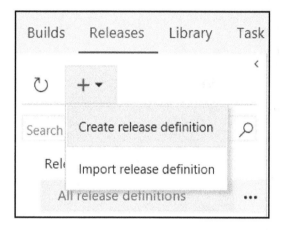

2. From the menu that opens up, choose the **Azure App Service Deployment** template.
3. In the next dialog, select **Build** as the source of the deployment artifact, and choose the `TextEvaluation` project and repository.

4. Check the **Continuous deployment (create release and deploy whenever a build completes)** checkbox to deploy the package whenever the build completes successfully, as shown in this screenshot:

5. Click on **OK**.
6. After the template has been generated, configure the subscription name and App Service name.
7. Check the **Deploy to slot** checkbox, and select your **Resource group** and the **Staging** slot.
8. Leave the package folder at default:

9. In the **Artifacts** tab, the `TextEvaluation` build will be automatically configured as the artifact source, as shown in the following screenshot:

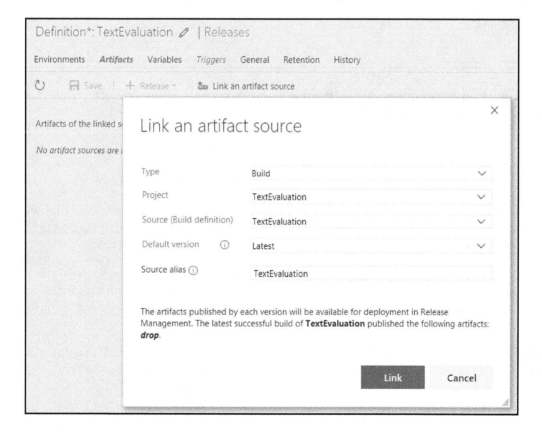

10. Under **Triggers**, the release trigger will be set to deploy automatically when the new build artifact is available. You can also set the trigger branch to master to be more specific:

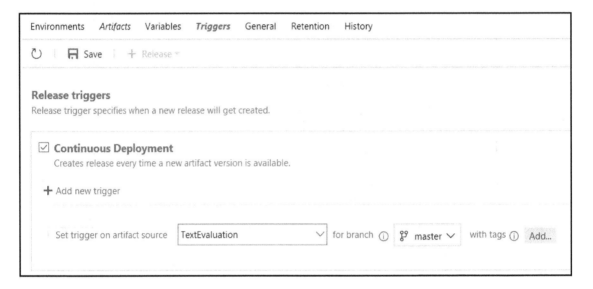

11. Commit and push a code change in the `TextEvaluation` project to trigger a build and release process.
12. Verify that both build and release get triggered and run successfully, and that the code is pushed into the **Staging** slot of the `TextEvaluation` Function App.

Your new CI/CD pipeline just delivered a code change into the Staging slot!

You may have noticed in the preceding steps that the VSTS configuration states that we are configuring continuous deployment, rather than continuous delivery. That is, we are deploying the latest code changes every time a push to the repository is made.

That is correct, however, we are pushing the code into the Staging, rather than Production, deployment slot. Using the Staging slot is what makes this process a continuous delivery, allowing for additional steps, such as user acceptance testing, before the code is promoted to Production.

The promotion of Staging to Production can easily be automated as well. However, many teams prefer to have a human make the final decision on pushing the code to Production.

Once you are finished with user acceptance testing, you can swap the Staging slot up into Production by naviaging to the Function app **Overview -> Swap**:

Congratulations!

You just built a full CI/CD pipeline for your serverless compute!

Load testing with VSTS

To test HTTP-triggered functions, you can use the VSTS Web tests. These tests will allow you to estimate your response time and response latency from multiple locations on the globe, and identify if your function can perform well under increasing load.

 Creating load tests for non-HTTP-triggered functions involves triggering Unit Tests from load tests. We will not cover the process here. To learn how to create a Load Test project in Visual Studio, and run Unit Tests from it, please visit `https://msdn.microsoft.com/en-us/library/ ff355993.aspx?f=255MSPPError=-2147217396#`. This type of testing requires Visual Studio Enterprise edition.

There are multiple ways to design a VSTS Web test, including recording a use case execution in your browser, configuring the steps of the test using Visual Studio, or configuring a URL test from the VSTS workspace. Since triggering functions does not involve multiple steps in the UI, the URL test is the easiest way to create a new load test for a function.

 Load testing is priced separately, since it uses additional cloud compute resources. The pricing also includes a free grant. To learn more about load test pricing, please visit `https://azure.microsoft.com/en-us/pricing/ details/visual-studio-team-services`.

In this example, we will create a simple load test for the ScoreText function. To create the load test, execute the following steps:

1. Go to your VSTS site -> **Test** -> **Load test** -> **New** -> **URL based test**.
2. Set the **HTTP method** to GET.
3. Add the staging slot URL of the ScoreText function.
4. In the **QueryString Parameters**, add the name parameter with a value of your choice.

    Here you can also select different HTTP methods, such as POST, and add the request **Body** if required. If your function is authenticated with an API Key, you can add the key as a header:

5. Click on Test **Settings**, and configure the run duration, the load pattern, the number of concurrent users, the browser mix, and the location from which the test is run, as shown in the following screenshot. If your application will be accessed from multiple geo-locations, you can create a test for each location to assess the latency in remote locations:

Load test*: ScoreText load test | Runs

Web Scenarios   **Settings**

🖫 Save   ⏵ Run test   ⭳ Import .HAR file

Run duration (minutes)	1
Load pattern	Constant ⌄
Max v-users	10
Warmup duration (seconds)	0
Browser mix	IE - 40%, Chrome - 60% ⌄

Select the load agents

⦿ Use automatically provisioned agents

     Geo-location   North Central US (Illinois) ⌄

6. Save the settings.
7. Click on **Run Test**.

8. After the test completes, you will see the summary of the function's performance. This will show the average response time, requests per second, and failed requests, as shown in the following screenshot:

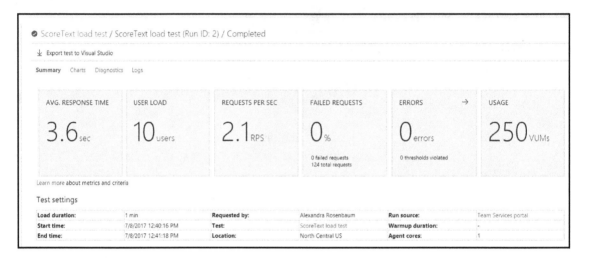

9. You can also see the performance and throughput over time by clicking on the **Charts** tab.

You now have a simple web-based load test that can help you evaluate the performance of your HTTP-based function!

To learn more about the load test metrics, and about load testing Web applications, please visit `https://www.visualstudio.com/en-us/docs/test/performance-testing/getting-started/get-started-simple-cloud-load-test`.

Automating Function App deployment

As mentioned in Chapter 2, *Getting Started with the Azure Environment*, every resource in Azure can be defined as an Azure Resource Manager JSON template, and also deployed using such a template. This allows for automated deployment of infrastructure and networking components. In case of Azure Functions, the entire Function App can be deployed as a template.

The process of defining a Function App as a template and deploying it to Azure is outlined here at https://docs.microsoft.com/en-us/azure/azure-functions/functions-infrastructure-as-code.

Summary

In this chapter, we reviewed the benefits of using source control, and the benefits of continuous integration and delivery approaches in software development.

We have created a VSTS account, and configured a source control repository for our Function App project using a Git repository on a VSTS server.

Then, we went through the step-by-step configuration process of a continuous integration and delivery (CI/CD) pipeline for our Function App using VSTS. We set up an automated Build, Test, and Release process that deploys the application into the Azure Function App staging deployment slot every time new code changes are checked in into source control.

We have also created a Web-based load test for an HTTP-based function using VSTS.

In the next chapter, we will focus on application monitoring.

10
Securing Your Application

In this chapter, we will discuss the different aspects of securing an application deployed using serverless computing. We will discuss the shared responsibility model between the client and the cloud provider, and outline the security controls provided by the Azure platform. We will walk through a step-by-step guidance for the following aspects:

- Connecting a Function App to a private network
- Deploying a Function App on a private network, without internet access
- Protecting the Function App with a network firewall
- Configuring function authorization with API keys
- Configuring Function App authentication with Azure Active Directory and Facebook identity providers
- Handling data encryption in transit and at rest
- Managing administrative access to the application

Unlike the previous chapters, the examples in this chapter are not presented in the context of the text sentiment analysis application. This is because the different approaches to securing the application are sometimes mutually exclusive. Thus, we will demonstrate each security feature on new Function App deployment.

Securing the application

There are many different levels to application security. When running in a traditional data center, you are responsible for the entire security stack, top to bottom. When running in the public cloud, you move towards a shared responsibility model with your cloud vendor, where part of the security controls are handled by the vendor.

The different layers of security can be viewed as the following list:

- Physical
- Host infrastructure
- Networking
- Application level:
  - Authentication and authorization
  - Code quality
  - Data encryption:
    - Encryption in transit
    - Encryption at rest
    - Managing keys and secrets
- Administrative access

The level of responsibility of the cloud provider versus the client depends on the hosting model you are using--IaaS, PaaS, or SaaS. IaaS requires the highest involvement on the client's part, and SaaS requires the least. This chapter will review security controls in the context of serverless computing, which is a part of the PaaS family.

Physical security

Physical security pertains to the management of data center buildings and facilities, physical servers, and networking devices. Physical security includes protection from unauthorized access to the facility. It also involves ensuring uninterrupted service by securing a reliable power supply, air and cooling regulation, and physical device management.

The public cloud providers accept full responsibility for ensuring the physical security of their data centers.

This provides one of the main advantages of moving the infrastructure to the public cloud.

Since physical security is handled by the platform, we will not discuss it further in this chapter. The details of physical security implementation in Azure are not disclosed publicly, however, some information can be acquired from Azure compliance reports. The reports can be found on the Azure Trust Center website `https://azure.microsoft.com/en-us/support/trust-center`.

Host infrastructure

Host infrastructure security pertains to the configuration, management, and security of compute (virtual machines, containers, and so on) and storage. This includes access permissions management of the servers, as well as applying optimal configuration at the OS level, and keeping up to date with security patching. In the IaaS model, the shared responsibility of the client starts at securing the host infrastructure.

With the PaaS model, including serverless compute, the cloud provider accepts full responsibility of securing the host infrastructure.

This provides another significant advantage of moving to the public cloud, particularly, to the PaaS services and serverless compute.

Since host infrastructure security is handled by the platform, we will not discuss it further in this chapter. Once again, certain details on it can be acquired from Azure compliance reports, which can be found on the Azure Trust Center website `https://azure.microsoft.com/en-us/support/trust-center`.

Networking security

Networking security pertains to the configuration, management, and security of virtual networks, load balancers, DNS servers, and the network security devices.

Part of the networking security controls, such as DDOS protection, is handled by the cloud provider. In IaaS model, the client shares the responsibility for deploying and securing the networking components.

Azure serverless compute can be deployed in two different modes: in a "public" environment, with the networking components fully handled by the platform, and in a "private" environment, where the networking components are partially handled by the client.

In this chapter, we will discuss the different deployment modes in detail. In the following sections, we will review the network security options in the following order:

- Overview of networking concepts
- Giving a Function App access to a private network

- Deploying a Function App on a private network, where the application has a publicly reachable IP
- Deploying a Function App on a private network, where the application has a private IP

Integrating functions with a private network

There are the following three different ways to integrate Azure serverless compute with a private network:

1. Deployment into a public App Service connected to a private network.
2. Deployment into ASE with a public Function App endpoint.
3. Deployment into ASE with a private Function App endpoint.

All three options require the Function App to be deployed into an App Service plan rather than a Consumption plan.

App Service

The Regular Azure App Service is a multi-tenant PaaS environment, that is inexpensive because of the economy of scale, but offers the client little to no control over the underlying infrastructure.

When deployed into an App Service plan, the Azure Function App can be integrated with a private network using a point-to-site VPN connection. This way, resources within the private network become reachable from the Function App, and vice versa.

App Service Environment (ASE)

ASE is a dedicated and isolated environment for Azure App Service. It offers the client more control over the infrastructure and networking underlying the App Service. It is also significantly more expensive than the multi-tenant App Service. When deployed into an ASE, the Function App is deployed on a private address space.

The ASE can be configured to either have a public or a private IP for the Function App endpoint. In both modes, the Function App can have a network firewall restricting traffic to it. When assigned a private IP, the Function App can be completely isolated from the internet, and only reachable on an internal network.

Networking concepts

Before we proceed with an explanation of the different Function App deployment methods, we need to define a number of networking concepts. If you are familiar with networking in general, and Azure networking components in particular, feel free to proceed to the Azure *App Service* section.

The definitions of key networking concepts follow:

Private IP address space is an IP address space of IPv4 addresses defined by the RFC 1918 document. Addresses in this private space are not allocated to any particular organization, any organization may use them. The packets addressed to and from these IPs cannot be transmitted over the public internet.

The private IP addresses are commonly used for **Local Area Networks (LANs)** in homes and corporate offices. An additional **network address translation** (**NAT**) device is then deployed on the LAN network perimeter to allow communication between the LAN and the internet. The NAT device acts as an agent translating IP address destinations between the public and the private network.

Private IP address spaces are often seen as an additional security measure, since they are not directly routable from the internet. To learn more, please visit `https://en.wikipedia.org/wiki/Private_network`.

IP address spaces are commonly defined by **CIDR notation**, a representation of a leading IP address followed by /X, where the X is the count of leading 1 bits in the routing mask (meaning that the smaller the X, the larger is the number of available addresses). To learn more, please visit `https://en.wikipedia.org/wiki/Classless_Inter-Domain_Routing#CIDR_notation`.

The private IP spaces defined by RFC 1918 are as follows:

CIDR Notation	Number of addresses
10.0.0.0/8	16,777,216
172.16.0.0/12	1,048,576
192.168.0.0/16	65,536

It is common to separate the private network into smaller chunks, defining address spaces of 65,000 addresses or less. As you can see from the preceding table, each CIDR provides a different order of magnitude. The /8 network can be broken into 256 separate /16 networks, and /12 can be broken into 16 of them.

Network planning in the IPv4 world can be a complicated exercise, as the LAN addresses can freely overlap, as long as the LANs are not connected to each other. Once the LANs are connected (for instance, when two different companies merge their IT environments), conflicting static IPs can create an issue.

Virtual Network (**VNet**) is a representation of your private network in Azure. VNets can be defined using any of the private IP address spaces mentioned in the preceding RFC 1918 table. By default, Azure VNets are completely isolated from one another, any on-premises private networks and the public internet.

VNets can be connected to one another and to on-premise networks in a number of different ways (VNet peering, VPN, Express Route connections). For a VNet to be successfully linked to another network, their address spaces must not overlap.

VNets can be segmented into multiple subnets, or smaller sub-address spaces in the VNet address space. It is common to subnet a network for zoning purposes (DMZ, web, application, database zones, and so on). In Azure, subnets within a single VNet are, by default, routable from one another.

In addition to their private IPs, the Azure resources (VMs or PaaS services) in a VNet can also be assigned public IP addresses routable from the internet.

To learn more about virtual networks, please visit `https://docs.microsoft.com/en-us/azure/virtual-network/virtual-networks-overview`.

Network Security Group (NSG) is a network firewall that contains a list of inbound and outbound rules, which allow or deny traffic to or from resources connected to an Azure VNet.

NSG can be associated to individual VMs or entire subnets. When an NSG is associated to a subnet, the rules apply to all the resources in the subnet.

NSGs have two sets of rules, inbound and outbound. Each rule is defined by a 5-tuple, (plus the rule priority). The rule attributes are as follows:

- Priority
- Source IP
- Source port
- Destination IP
- Destination port
- Protocol

The rules are applied in the order of priority, with the last default rule in the NSG being a "Deny All" rule. In both inbound and outbound rules, the "Deny All" rule is meant to stop all traffic that wasn't specifically allowed by any of the rules with higher priority ("catching" all traffic from unknown sources). The rules allow for the wildcard "*" value. A wildcard means "any", as in any port, any protocol and so on. Rules also allow for predefined tags such as **INTERNET** and **VIRTUAL NETWORK**, meaning all the addresses coming from the internet or the current VNet, respectively.

An example of the Deny All rule is as follows:

Name	Priority	Source IP	Source port	Destination IP	Destination port	Protocol
DenyAllInBound	65500	*	*	*	*	*

The rules' application to the network traffic can be illustrated by the following diagram:

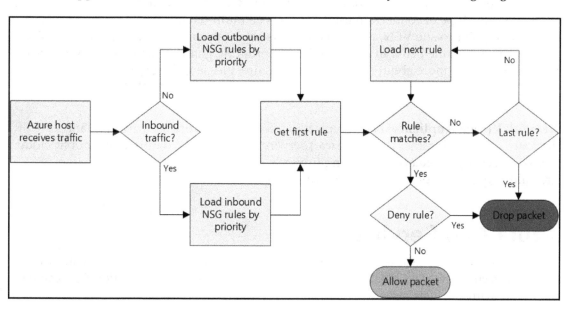

To learn more about NSGs, please visit https://docs.microsoft.com/en-us/azure/virtual-network/virtual-networks-nsg.

VPN connection: VPN, or the Virtual Private Network connection allows you to create a secure connection from one private network to another, going over the public internet. VPN creates an encrypted connection, or a "tunnel" between two networks, and allows devices connected to both the networks to securely communicate with one another. There are two common types of a VPN connection: site-to-site and point-to-site. A site-to-site VPN is, typically, used to connect two LANs with one another. To learn more about VPN, please visit https://en.wikipedia.org/wiki/Virtual_private_network.

A **VPN gateway** is a networking device used to establish a VPN tunnel between two private networks over the internet. There are different device types and routing types that can be established by the gateway. To learn more about the VPN gateway in Azure, please visit https://docs.microsoft.com/en-us/azure/vpn-gateway/vpn-gateway-about-vpngateways.

Point-to-Site VPN: A point-to-site or "P2S" VPN connection is a connection intended to create links from individual computers into a private network. P2S VPNs are most commonly used for connecting from a private computer into a secure network location. P2S VPN is also the type of connection used to connect a multi-tenant App Service to a private network. In point-to-site VPN, private computers establish communication with the VPN gateway device on the LAN. In Azure, a dynamic routing gateway is required to establish a P2S VPN. To learn more about the P2S VPN in Azure, please visit https://docs.microsoft.com/en-us/azure/vpn-gateway/vpn-gateway-howto-point-to-site-classic-azure-portal.

Network Virtual Appliance: **NVA,** typically, refers to a network security appliance deployed on virtual (rather than physical) servers because of the nature of the public cloud. Network security appliances, including firewalls, IPS, IDS, WAF, or next generation firewalls help protect private networks from unwanted traffic.

Azure App Service

When deployed using a Consumption plan, no integration of Azure Functions with private networks is currently possible. In an App Service plan, however, the Function App can be integrated with a private network.

Integrating the Function App with a private VNet allows the Function App to connect to backend resources, such as application servers or databases, on a private IP (or DNS name) without the need to expose the backend endpoints to the internet. If the VNet is connected to a private network on-premise, you will also be able to browse from the Function App to the on-premise network on a private IP range.

To deploy a function into an App Service plan, execute the following steps:

1. Browse to the **Azure Portal** -> **New** -> **Function App** -> **Create**.
2. Fill in the required parameters -- **App name**, **Subscription**, **Resource Group**, and **Storage**.
3. In **Hosting Plan**, select **App Service Plan**.
4. Click into the **App Service plan/Location** blade, and select **Create New**.
5. Choose the name and geographic location for your plan.
6. In **Pricing tier**, choose the **Standard S1** tier. The **Standard S1** is the minimum required tier for networking integration.
7. Click on **Create**:

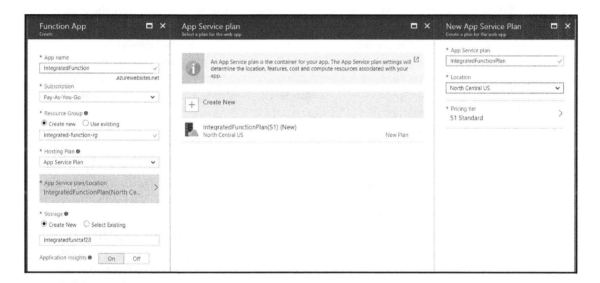

VNet integration

Once the Function App is deployed, you can configure the network integration.

There are a number of requirements that a VNet and App Service need to fulfil to be available for the integration, and they are as follows:

- The VNet needs to be in the same subscription as your Function App
- The VNet must have a point-to-site VPN enabled with a dynamic routing gateway (P2S VPN does not work with a static routing gateway)
- The App Service plan needs to be, at least, on the Standard S1 tier

Typically, when you configure a function integration with a VNet, you will integrate with an existing VNet which already has some resources deployed into it. It is possible, however, to deploy a new VNet from the Function App networking blade. In the following example, we will deploy a new VNet for the integration.

To get more details on App Service networking integration, including integrating with an existing VNet, please visit https://docs.microsoft.com/en-us/azure/vpn-gateway/vpn-gateway-howto-point-to-site-resource-manager-portal.

To deploy a new VNet, and integrate it with the Function App, execute the following steps:

1. Browse to your Function App and click on **Platform features** -> **Networking** -> **VNet integration** -> **Setup**.
2. Fill in the required parameters--VNet name, first subnet name, and the required IP ranges. The parameter values are outlined as follows:
   - **Virtual Network Address Block**: This is the IP address space for the entire virtual network. In the example that follows, we choose **10.0.0.0/16**, which gives us over 65,000 addresses (please refer to the *Networking concepts* section in the beginning of this chapter for explanation of CIDR notation).
   - **Subnet Address Block**: This is the IP address space for the first subnet on the VNet, where we can deploy resources that need to be connected to our Function App, such as databases or application servers. In the following example, we choose **Subnet Name** as **default** and the range of **Subnet Address Block** as **10.0.1.0/24**, which gives us 255 addresses on the subnet.
   - **Gateway Subnet Address Block**: As discussed earlier, a VPN Gateway is required to set up a point-to-site VPN connection. The VPN gateway requires a specific subnet named Gateway Subnet. In the following example, we choose the range of **10.0.254.0/24** (one of the last IP blocks of this size in our VNet) for deploying the Gateway (it is recommended to allocate at least /27, meaning 32 addresses, to the Gateway Subnet).
   - **Point-to-Site Address Block**: When clients connect to the VNet through the P2S VPN, their IP addresses will be allocated from this address range. Hence, this range should not overlap with any existing or future subnets on the VNet, and can be from a separate private block than the VNet to ensure no future overlap. In our example, we choose **176.16.0.0/24**, which, gives us 255 addresses for potential P2S connections.

The filled form is shown in the following screenshot:

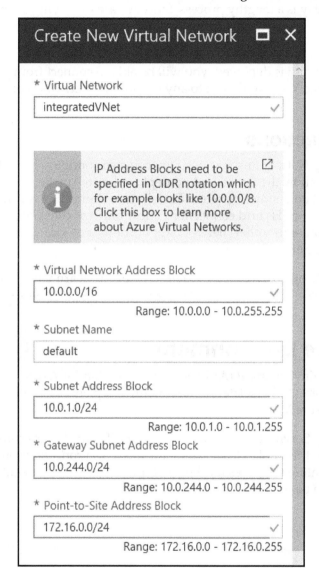

3. Once you have configured all the required parameters, click on **Create**, and wait
   for the VNet creation to be completed.

While deploying new VNets and subnets is very quick, deploying a VPN Gateway is a lengthy process. Since we are deploying a new VPN Gateway, the whole process may take up to an hour.

Once the virtual network is deployed, you will be able to connect from your Function App to the resources on the VNet, and even to any on-premise networks connected to this VNet.

Hybrid connections

Under Function App Networking features, you can also configure hybrid connections. Hybrid connections allow the Function App deployed into App Service to connect to an application endpoint on another network. Each hybrid connection is configured with a single TCP host and port. Hybrid connections allow only for connections from your App Service to an on-premise (or other) network applications, not vice versa. These connections are configured using Service Bus Relays.

We will not elaborate on the hybrid connections setup. To learn more, please visit `https://docs.microsoft.com/en-us/azure/app-service/app-service-hybrid-connections`.

App Service Environment

Azure **App Service Environment** (**ASE**) is a premium plan for Azure App Service, which provides dedicated and fully isolated infrastructure. App Service Environment is always deployed into an Azure VNet.

Important note: App Service Environments incur significant charges compared to the other services described in this book. Please take these costs into consideration when deploying ASE. Please check online resources for the most up-to-date pricing details. The current pricing structure can be reviewed in the following screenshot:

Pricing details

Monthly App Service Environment Fee	1000.00 USD/mo ❶
Isolated Worker - I1 Tier	279.74 USD/mo ❶
Isolated Worker - I2 Tier	559.49 USD/mo ❶
Isolated Worker - I3 Tier	1118.98 USD/mo ❶

There are two concurrent meters associated with the App Service Environment.

❶ **Monthly App Service Environment Fee**
Each App Service Environment incurs a monthly fee that covers the Front Ends, File Servers, and other infrastructure required to support up to 100 App Service plan instances. This monthly charge accrues independently of any App Service plans deployed and is prorated by the hour.

❶ **Hourly Cost**
App Service plans deployed into an App Service Environment are charged per hour based on the instance count and instance type(s) selected.

ASE deployment modes

You can deploy ASE in the following two modes:

1. **Public facing**: The applications in the ASE have a public facing IP address
2. **Private facing**: The applications in the ASE have a private IP address

The underlying infrastructure is deployed on a private IP range in an Azure VNet in both cases. The main difference between the two is whether the applications deployed into the ASE have a public IP address which is reachable from the internet, or a private IP address which is reachable only from within the private network.

To learn more about App Service Environment and the two deployment modes, please visit `https://docs.microsoft.com/en-us/azure/app-service-web/app-service-app-service-environment-intro.`

Public App Service Environment

In this section, we will create a new public facing App Service Environment using the default settings for the VNet.

Note that creating the VNet during the ASE deployment will configure a default address range for the VNet and a subnet name for the ASE:

- **VNet address range: 192.168.250.0/23**
- **Subnet Name: default**
- **Subnet Address Range: 192.168.250.0/24**

If you need to create an App Service Environment on a different private network than this one, you will need to first create the VNet, and then deploy ASE into it. Note that ASE must reside in its own subnet with a range of at least eight addresses. Note that you cannot change the address range of the subnet after ASE is deployed, so the recommended address range should be much larger to account for potential future scaling out.

To create a new public facing ASE (using the defaut VNet configuration), perform the following steps:

1. Browse to **Azure Portal -> New -> App Service Environment -> Create**.
2. Fill in the required parameters: **Name**, **Subscription**, and **Resource Group**.
3. Click into the **Virtual Network** blade to configure the new VNet.
4. Fill in the VNet name and location.
5. To create an externally facing ASE with a public IP address, choose **External** under **VIP Type**, and **1** in the **Number of IP Addresses** parameter:

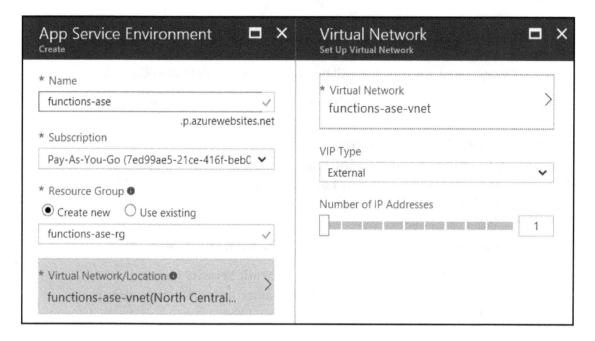

6. Once all the required settings are configured, click on **Create**.

It can take over an hour for the ASE to get deployed.

After the ASE is deployed, to create a new Function App hosted in the new ASE, perform the following steps:

1. In the **Azure Portal**, navigate to **New -> Function App**.
2. Enter the Function App name, subscription, resource group, and storage account.
3. In **Hosting Plan**, choose **App Service Plan**, and click on **Create New**.
4. Choose the name for the plan.
5. In **Location**, instead of choosing a data center location, choose the **functions-ase** environment.
6. In **Pricing Tier**, choose **L1** isolated.
7. Click on **OK**, then on **Create**.

8. Once the Function App is deployed, go to the application, and create a new C# HTTP-triggered function with anonymous authorization level.

Once created, the function will be available on this default URL:

```
https://[FunctionAppName].[AseName].p.azurewebsites.net/api/[FunctionName]
```

Adding a Network Security Group

As mentioned earlier, **Network Security Groups (NSGs)** are network firewalls protecting Azure VMs and subnets. Since the new Function App we've deployed on ASE is deployed on a private subnet, we can now protect it with an NSG. NSG will allow us to restrict unwanted traffic to the application.

To create a new network security group, execute the following steps:

1. Navigate to **Azure Portal** -> **New** -> **Network Security Group**.
2. Fill in the required parameters: **Name**, **Subscription**, **Resource group**, and **Location:**

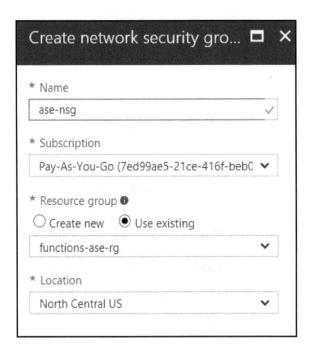

3. To take effect, the network security needs to be associated with the subnet. To associate the NSG we've created with the ASE subnet, from the NSG overview, navigate to **Subnets** -> **Associate**.

4. In VNet, choose **functions-ase-vnet**.

5. In subnet, choose the **default** subnet, or the subnet that your ASE is deployed to:

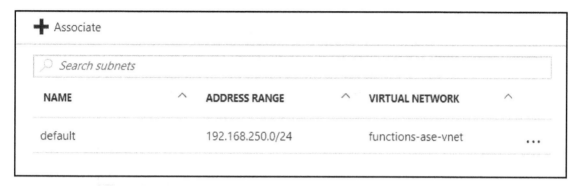

6. Now the inbound and outbound traffic to the ASE subnet is controlled by the network security group.

7. When the network security group is deployed, a number of traffic rules are configured by default. To see the configured inbound traffic rules, and to add/remove rules, go to **NSG settings** -> **Inbound security rules**, and press on the **Default rules** button. As you can see in the following screenshot, the default rules allow all VNet inbound traffic, but deny all traffic from the internet:

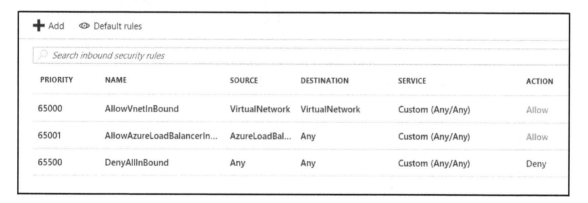

8. Since the traffic from the internet is now restricted, you will not be able to browse to your function's endpoint from a public IP. To validate that the rule is working, try browsing to the function's URL. You will get a response similar to the following:

You can still browse to the function from inside the VNet or from any network connected to the VNet. To validate this in our test environment, you could deploy a VM into a separate subnet on the same VNet, and browse to the function's URL from that VM. We will walk through such a VM deployment next, in the Private ASE deployment section.

If you require your application to be accessible from the intranet only, you can leave the NSG closed to all external traffic. If you do require access from the "outside" world, you can allow traffic from additional locations. To do that, you can add a new rule to the NSG's inbound traffic rules, identifying the traffic by a CIDR block or a particular IP. You can also configure the expected traffic's protocol and port, or specify **any** in the protocol and the "*" wildcard for the port.

In the next example, we will add a specific rule to allow the traffic from your personal computer's public IP on HTTPS (TCP protocol, port 443) with a priority of 100.

To add a new rule, execute the following steps:

1. Browse to the NSG and click on **Inbound Security Rules**.
2. Click on **Add**.
3. Fill in the rule name.
4. Fill in the rule priority between 100 and 4096. The priority must be different then to any existing rules. The rules execute in order of priority, from lowest to highest.

5. Find out your personal computer's public IP address by browsing to `https://www.whatismyip.com`.

6. In **Source**, choose **CIDR block**.

7. In **Source IP address range** paste your computer's public IP.

8. In **Service**, choose **HTTPS** (this will set the protocol to TCP and the port range to `443`).

9. In **Action**, choose **Allow**:

10. Click on **Create**.
11. Once the rule is added to the NSG, browse to your function's endpoint from your public IP once more. The function's URL will be accessible again.

 The NSG also has default outbound traffic rules associated with it, and you can configure additional outbound traffic rules in **Settings** -> **Outbound security rules**.

Adding an NVA

A custom network virtual appliance, such as a network Firewall or a WAF, can be deployed in addition to, or instead of, an NSG. Deploying an NVA requires setting up custom traffic routes to re-route all the inbound and outbound traffic through the particular appliance. Deploying an NVA is beyond the scope of this chapter. To learn more regarding NVA deployment in Azure networks, please visit https://docs.microsoft.com/en-us/azure/architecture/reference-architectures/dmz/secure-vnet-dmz.

Private App Service Environment

Deploying a Function App in an ASE with a private IP allows the Function App to be completely isolated from the public internet, and to be routable from within the private network only. When deploying the ASE, you will create a private domain, which will be routable only from within the VNet and private networks connected to it.

Private App Service Environment is also referred to as ILB ASE, where ILB stands for Internal load balancer.

To deploy, and be able to browse to, a Function App on a private ASE, you will need to go through all the configuration processes listed as follows:

1. Deploying the ILB ASE on a private VNet.
2. Deploying the Function App into the ILB ASE.
3. Deploying a VM into the same private VNet.
4. Configuring a certificate for the internal domain of the ASE.
5. Configuring DNS for the internal domain of the ASE.

Only after completing all of these steps you will be able to access the Function App on the private network.

The details of each process are outlined next.

Deploying the ILB ASE

The private ASE deployment is very similar to the public ASE deployment. You can follow the guide from the previous section with one difference. In the first deployment step, in the VIP type, choose **Internal** instead of **External**, and choose a name for your private domain.

It is a good idea to pick a domain name that will not conflict with any public facing domains (otherwise you will experience issues with traffic routing). In our example, we will use **internal-functions-ase.net** as our private domain name, as shown in the following screenshot:

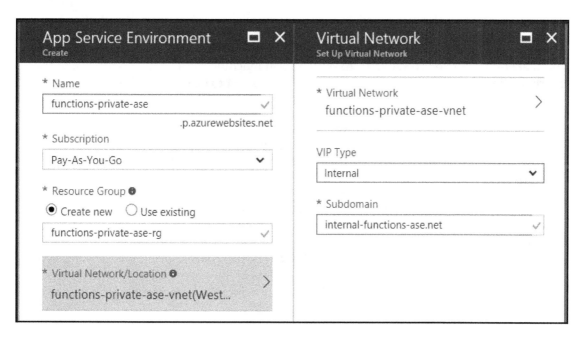

Click on **Create**.

 It may take over an hour for the new App Service Environment to deploy.

Deploying the Function App into the ILB ASE

Once the App Service environment is deployed, to deploy a new Function App into it, perform the following steps:

1. In the **Azure Portal**, click on **New -> Function App**.
2. Enter the function app name, subscription, resource group, and storage account.
3. In **Hosting Plan**, choose **App Service Plan**, and click on **Create New**.
4. Choose the name for the plan.
5. In **Location**, instead of choosing a data center location, choose the **functions-private-ase** App Service Environment.
6. In **Pricing tier**, choose **L1** isolated.
7. Click on **OK**, then on **Create**.

Deploying a VM on the same private VNet

The Internal domain deployed to the ASE is not accessible from the public internet, hence you will not be able to browse to it from your local machine right away. To browse to the internal domain (and hence the Function App), you need to be connected to the private VNet it is in.

If you try to browse to the Function App you've created from the Functions Portal on your local machine, you will receive an error: "We are unable to access your function keys. If the error persists, please contact support." This is because the Azure Portal is unable to reach your private domain.

We can browse to the new Function App from any Azure-based or on-premise servers that are deployed on a private network connected to **functions-ase-vnet**. The servers could be located on the same VNet, or connected to the VNet via VNet peering, VPN, or Express Route connection. You could browse to the Function App from your local computer, if you established a VPN connection to the VNet the ASE is in. Please review the *Networking concepts* section in the beginning of this chapter to get more information on private network connections.

One of the easiest ways to connect to the new Function App is to deploy a VM on the same VNet. Using this option, we will deploy a new Azure Virtual Machine to **functions-ase-vnet**. The VM needs to be deployed on a separate subnet within the VNet, not on the same subnet as ASE (it is a requirement that the ASE must reside on its own subnet).

The virtual machine type and size that you deploy are up to you. Azure offers a large variety of virtual machine sizes, and any size VM will work in this case. You can choose from two disk types - SSD or HDD. Either will work in this case. You can also choose to enable a feature called managed disk, which improves the resiliency of the VM. Enabling the feature is not required in this case.

This book does not aim to offer advice on virtual machine deployment. In the following section, we will deploy an example virtual machine. Feel free to choose the exact same settings we are using in the example, or modify them according to your preferences. To learn more about Azure Windows VMs, please visit the following link:

`https://docs.microsoft.com/en-us/azure/virtual-machines/windows/`

To deploy the VM, perform the following steps:

1. In **Azure Portal**, click on **Virtual Networks** -> `[Your VNet Name]` -> **Subnets** -> **Add Subnet.**

2. Add the subnet name, and accept the default **Address range (CIDR block)**, as shown in the following screenshot:

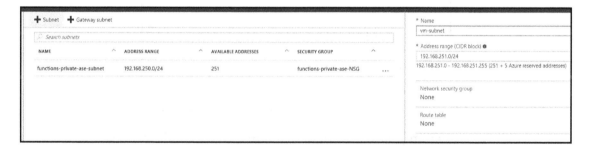

3. Click on **OK.**

4. Browse back to **Azure Portal** | **New** | **Compute** | **Windows Server 2016 Datacenter**.

5. In **Basic** settings, fill in **Name**, **VM disk type**, **User name**, and **Password**. Make sure that the username is not "admin" (admin is a restricted username on Windows VMs) and that the password complies with password strength requirements. An example is shown in the following screenshot:

6. Choose the appropriate subscription, resource group, and location.
7. If you have an existing Windows Server license, you may choose to apply it to save the license costs.
8. Click on **OK**.
9. In **Size, select D1_V2** (or a different VM size that will allow you to have adequate performance for an adequate price)
10. In **Settings**, choose to use managed disk or not, depending on your preference.
11. In **Virtual Network**, select **functions-ase-vnet**.
12. In **Subnet**, select **vm-subnet**.

13. Leave the other settings as defaults, as shown in the following screenshot:

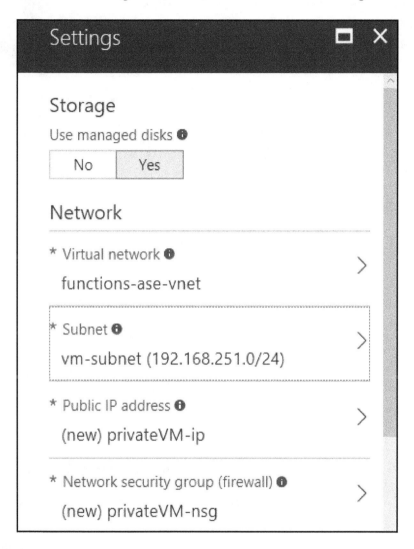

14. Click on **OK**.
15. Review the confirmation summary, and click on **Create**.
16. Once the VM has been deployed, browse to **Virtual Machines** | <Your VM Name> | **Overview.**

17. Click on **Connect** as shown in the following screenshot:

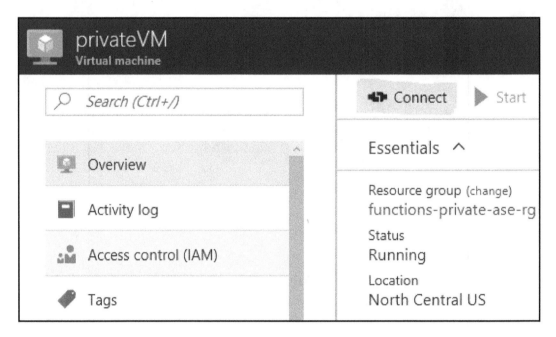

18. Download and open the RDP link.
19. In credentials, choose **use a different account**, and enter the username and password you selected when creating the VM.
20. You will be connected to the VM via RDP.

Creating the ILB certificate

Once the ASE is deployed, we will need to add a certificate covering both the default private domain (***.internal-functions-ase.net** in our case), and the **scm** subdomain (***.scm.internal-functions-ase.net** in our case), which is needed for the App Service management tools.

In production, the certificates should be signed by a recognized **Certificate Authority (CA)**. While doing testing, you can create a self-signed certificate. To create a self-signed certificate using PowerShell, execute the following steps:

1. On the VM we just created, create a directory called `C:\certs`.
2. On the VM, open Windows PowerShell as administrator (right-click and click on **Run as administrator**).

3. In the PowerShell window, enter the commands that are provided in the following example code. (Use your private domain name and a password of your choice. Set the password to a non-trivial string that you will remember):

```
# Create a secure password
$pwd = ConvertTo-SecureString -String "verysecurepassword" -
Force -AsPlainText

# Create private domain certificate
$cert = New-SelfSignedCertificate -certstorelocation
"cert:\localmachine\my" -dnsname
*.internal-functions-ase.net, *.scm.internal-functions-ase.net

# Get the certificate path
$path = "cert:\localMachine\my\" + $cert.thumbprint
# Export the private domain certificate
Export-PfxCertificate -cert $path -FilePath
"c:\certs\defaultCert.pfx" -Password $pwd
```

4. From the VM, browse to Azure portal, navigate to your ILB ASE environment, and click on **ILB Certificate**.
5. Click on **Set ILB Certificate**.
6. Click on **Upload** and browse to your VM C:\certs directory where we saved the certificate.
7. Click on **OK** and enter the certificate password to upload the certificate, as shown in the following screenshot:

8. It may take a little while for the certificate to get installed on the ASE.

Configuring DNS for the internal domain

In most deployments in Azure, the platform takes care of configuring the DNS. However, when deploying an ILB ASE, the platform has no access to your private environment, and hence you must configure the DNS for the internal domain yourself.

You can configure a custom DNS server for the entire VNet, which is the way to go in a production environment. For test purposes, it is easiest to configure the DNS entries in the hosts file on the VM itself.

To configure the DNS entries in the hosts file, execute the following steps:

1. Browse to **Azure Portal** -> **ASE** -> `<Your ASE Environment>` -> **IP Addresses**.
2. Note the Internal load balancer IP, and the internal domain name you have configured, as shown in the following screenshot:

IP addresses

These IP addresses are used by this App Service Environment. Learn more

Domain/subdomain name:	internal-functions-ase.net
Internal Load Balancer IP address	192.168.250.9
Outbound IP address	65.52.209.41
Management IP address	65.52.209.41

3. On the VM, browse to the `C:\Windows\System32\drivers\etc` directory.
4. Run Notepad as an administrator, and open the hosts file.
5. After the current file content, add mappings from your ILB IP to the subdomain your Function App is on, and to the **scm** subdomain. (Note that you cannot use a wildcard in the hosts file, you must list the specific subdomain).

Given that my ILB IP is `192.168.250.9`, my internal ASE domain is `internal-functions-ase.net`, and my Function App name is `privateFun`, the lines in the hosts file look like the following code snippet:

```
192.168.250.9    privatefun.internal-functions-ase.net
192.168.250.9    privatefun.scm.internal-functions-ase.net
```

Access the Function App

Now that you have completed all the configuration steps, you can browse from the VM to the Function App.

To verify that you have connectivity, complete the following steps:

1. From the VM, browse to the Function App
   URL, `https://privatefun.internal-functions-ase.net/`. You may get a
   certificate error because the certificate is self-signed. After you accept the
   certificate, you should see the default home page stating that the application is up
   and running:

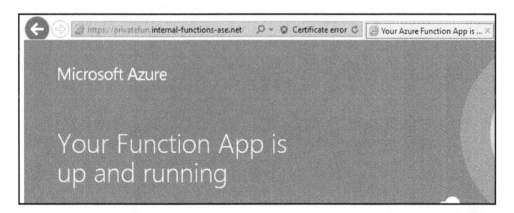

2. From the VM, browse to **Azure Portal** -> **Function App** -> `<Your ILB Function App>`.

3. Verify that you can create a new function:

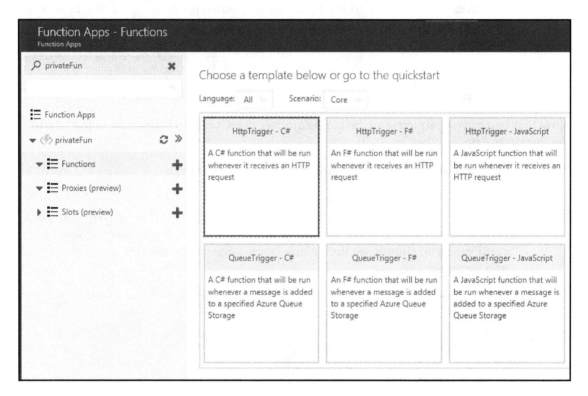

4. Click on **View Certificate** and follow the wizard to install it on the VM. After a few minutes, you will be able to browse to the Function App successfully.

 If the certificate wasn't created on the VM itself, you may get a message prompting you to accept the certificate.

Now you are able to deploy Azure Functions on a private domain, routable only from within your private network!

Application-level security

In serverless computing, application-level security is where the developer should focus the majority of their efforts, as most of the other layers can be provided by the platform. Regardless of how secure the Azure platform is, if the application code exposes sensitive information, or is vulnerable to attacks, the platform-level security will not help.

Authorization and authentication

To secure access to your Azure Functions' endpoints to only allowed users, you can use authentication and/or authorization.

Authentication is the process of verifying who you are. **Authorization** is the process of verifying what you have access to. Authentication and authorization can be used in combination, or separately.

Out-of-the-box, Azure supports both authentication and authorization for HTTP-triggered functions. Additional or alternative authentication and authorization procedures can be implemented in the function's code.

An HTTP-triggered function can be deployed in one of the following modes:

1. **Anonymous**: No authentication or authorization is required to access the function endpoint.
2. **API key authorization**: API key authorization provides a way to authorize access to a particular function or the entire Function App by the presence of an API key on the request.

3. **User-based authentication**: The access to the Function App can be secured by requiring user authentication using one of the available identity providers.

Anonymous mode

Anonymous mode is the configuration we have used so far throughout the book.

Anonymous functions do not require any authentication to be accessed. Anyone with access to the function URL can execute the call. For a public PaaS service, this means that anyone on the internet could access the function. For a private ASE this means anyone inside the private network perimeter.

There is certainly use for publicly accessible functions, although in most use cases, the serverless compute would not be directly exposed to the application user (since FaaS is more likely to handle the logic tier of the application rather than the presentation tier). Unless the function public exposure is intentional, some type of authentication or authorization must be used. Authentication will help secure the application, and prevent a potential intruder from accessing or contaminating the application data. Authentication will also prevent cost inflation in case of a DDoS attack or a similar malicious attempt.

API key authorization

In the API key mode, the function is authorized with an API key. This mode is chosen by default when deploying new functions.

HTTP trigger

When using the API key mode, the key can be passed as a query string variable or an HTTP header.

To be secure, the API key authorization must be used in combination with transport layer encryption (TLS, formerly, SSL), to prevent the API key from being passed over HTTP in clear text, and possibly being stolen during a man-in-the-middle attack (`https://www.owasp.org/index.php/Man-in-the-middle_attack`).

There are two ways to pass the API key to the function:

- In a query string parameter
- In the HTTP request header

If using a query string parameter to pass the API key, the request made to the function will look like the following:

```
https://<AppName>.azurewebsites.net/api/<FunctionName>?code=<ApiKey>
```

Note that it is best practice *not* to pass API keys in the query string even if the connection is encrypted (for more information on best practices, visit the OWASP site `https://www.owasp.org/index.php/REST_Security_Cheat_Sheet`).

When using an HTTP header option to pass the API key, the header name is **x-functions-key**. The functions **Tests** pane, or a tool like Postman (discussed in `Chapter 7`, *Debugging Your Azure Functions*) can be used to test an HTTP GET/POST request with the **x-functions-key** header, as shown in the screenshot:

In Azure functions, there are different types of API keys that can be configured for a function:

- A **function** key is a key specific to a particular function.
- A **host** key is shared by all functions in the Function App.
- A **master** key is the default host key, which cannot be revoked (but can be renewed if needed). Only the master key (named _master) can be used if the **Admin** authorization mode is chosen. The master key also provides administrative access to the runtime APIs.

When creating a new HTTP triggered function in the Functions Portal, you can select either **Function** or **Admin** under **Authorization level** drop-down menu:

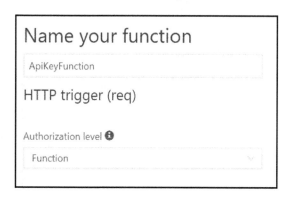

In the **Function** mode, you can make requests with either **function** or **host** keys. The **Admin** mode specifically requires the **master** key.

You can manage both **function** and **host** keys from the function's management panel. To access them, browse to your **Functions App** -> <Function Name> -> **Manage** -> **Keys**.

As you can see in the following screenshot, you can view, copy, renew, and revoke both types of keys from the management panel:

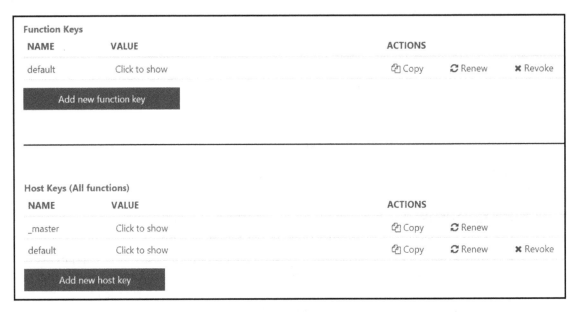

From Visual Studio, the authorization level of the function can be changed by configuring it in the function's signature attribute. For instance, changing the value of the `AuthorizationLevel` setting from `AuthorizationLevel.Anonymous` to `AuthorizationLevel.Function` will set the authorization level to `function`. It will also create the following settings in the `function.json`:

```json
"bindings": [
    {
        "authLevel": "function",
        "name": "req",
        "type": "httpTrigger",
        "direction": "in"
    },
```

Webhook trigger functions

Webhook-triggered functions are also authorized by an API key, and the authorization is set to the API key mode automatically.

Unless explicitly configured otherwise, the function key named **default** will be expected. For a generic JSON webhook, the key is passed in the "code" query string parameter similar to an HTTP-triggered function.

If you wish to send a different key, you will need to add a new key in the management panel by clicking on **Add new function key**. If you leave the key text box empty, and hit on **Save**, a new random string key will be generated for you:

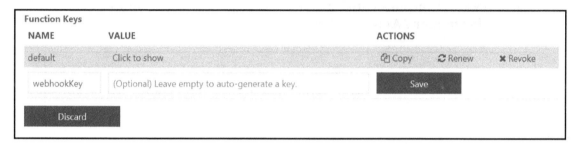

Then you can send the key name in either the query-string parameter called `clientid`

(like in the following example URL: `https://<AppName>.azurewebsites.net/api/<FunctionName>?clientid=<keyname>`) or in an HTTP-header parameter called `x-functions-clientid`.

 By default, there are two keys named **default** in the management panel: the function-level default key and the host-level default key. When two keys have the same name, the function key takes precedence.

User-based authentication

When working with HTTP-triggered functions, you can configure user-based authentication for the function. This is a built-in option of Azure App Service, which allows you to easily configure multiple identity providers to authenticate your users. For a general overview of the feature, please visit `https://docs.microsoft.com/en-us/azure/app-service/app-service-authentication-overview`.

When user authentication is configured, you can leave the function `authLevel` at anonymous, as the HTTP request will need to be authenticated before the URL can be accessed. If you do, however, need to secure access to the resources on a function-by-function basis, you can use the function API keys in combination with user-based authentication.

In the following section, we will give examples of configuring authentication using two different identity providers, **Azure Active Directory** and **Facebook.**

To set up user-based authentication with **Azure Active Directory,** execute the following steps:

1. Browse to **Functions Portal** -> `<Function App Name>` -> **Platform features** -> **Authentication / Authorization**:

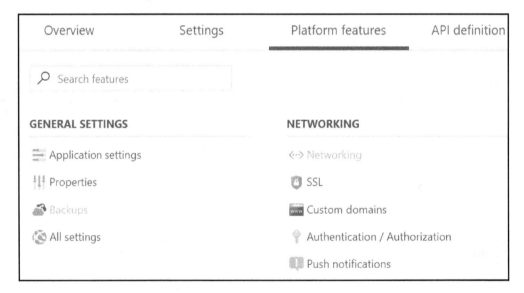

2. Turn the **App Service Authentication** on.
3. You will see a list of different authentication providers:

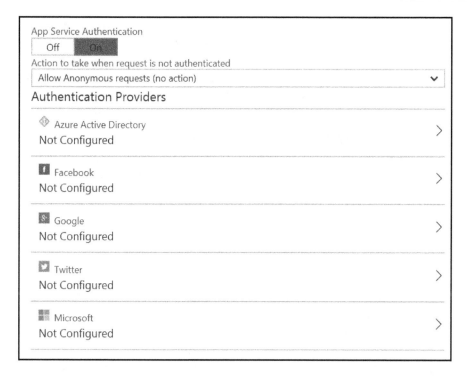

4. Switch the **Action to take when request is not authenticated** drop-down menu from **Allow Anonymous requests (no action)** to **Azure Active Directory**.

5. Click on **Azure Active Directory** identity provider to configure the settings.

6. We will cover the next steps of configuring **Azure Active Directory** as the identity provider in detail in the next section.

Configuring Azure Active Directory

Azure Active Directory (**AAD**) is a cloud-based multi-tenant directory, which is an **Identity as a Service** (**IDaaS**) solution. AAD can be used as your main identity provider. It also provides tooling for integration with on-premise Windows AD, the ability to federate with multiple other directories, and SSO into thousands of third-party applications, such as Dropbox, Chef, Wordpress, and so on. For more information about AAD, please visit `https://docs.microsoft.com/en-us/azure/active-directory/active-directory-whatis/`.

Every Azure tenant is actually an AAD tenant. If you have signed up for an Azure account using a Microsoft Account, a new AAD tenant was created for you with a default domain of `<emailAbbreviation>.onmicrosoft.com` (you can add a custom domain name for your AAD tenant by going to **Azure Portal** -> **Azure Active Directory** -> **Domain Names** -> **Add domain name**). If your Azure account is owned by an organization, it is integrated with the organizational domain. Thus, your Azure subscription always has a default AAD tenant.

You can also set up a new AAD tenant if you need a separate identity provider for an application. This AAD tenant can be assigned a different domain, and have a different configuration than the default tenant of your Azure account/subscription. To learn more about creating a new tenant, please visit `https://docs.microsoft.com/en-us/rest/api/datacatalog/create-an-azure-active-directory-tenant`.

When you choose AAD as your identity provider in Azure functions, you are offered the following two ways to set up the integration:

- **In Express** management mode, the Function App will automatically be integrated with the default AAD tenant of the current Azure subscription. This is the mode we will use in this chapter.
- In **Advanced** mode, you can manually enter the client ID and client secret of an AAD application created in another AAD tenant. This setup is not complex, but requires some familiarity with Azure AD features. This book does not aim to provide a deep dive into Azure AD configuration. To learn more about Azure AD, please visit `https://docs.microsoft.com/en-us/azure/active-directory/develop/active-directory-developers-guide`.

To configure AAD authentication using the **Express** mode, execute the following steps:

1. In **Managament mode**, choose **Express**.
2. Your Azure tenant AAD will be chosen as **Current Active Directory**.
3. In second **Management mode**, choose **Create New AD App**.
4. In **Create App**, fill in the AD App name.

5. Leave the **Grant Graph Permissions** and the **Grant Common Data Services Permissions** as **Off**, as shown in the following screenshot:

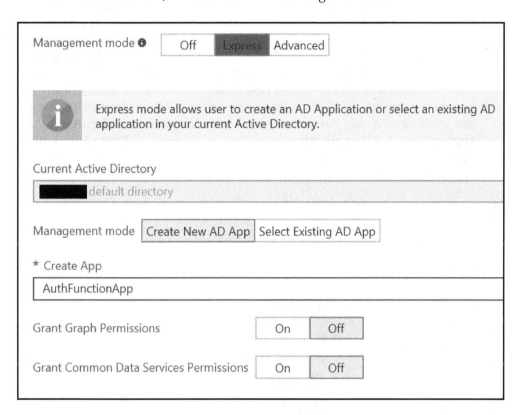

6. Click on **OK**.

Explanation of the selected options:

- When you select the **Create New AD App** option, a new AAD application is automatically created for the Function App. Creating an AAD application allows you to register your Function App in your AAD tenant, so that the user identities known to your AAD tenant can be used in the Function App authentication. The AAD application allows you to configure the specific access policy required by your Function App. In this case, a new AAD application is automatically created and configured for us. If you wish to change the AAD application settings, you can navigate to **Azure Portal -> Azure Active Directory -> Enterprise applications -> All applications ->** AuthFunctionApp **-> Properties.** You will see the following configuration menu, allowing you to review and change the AAD application settings:

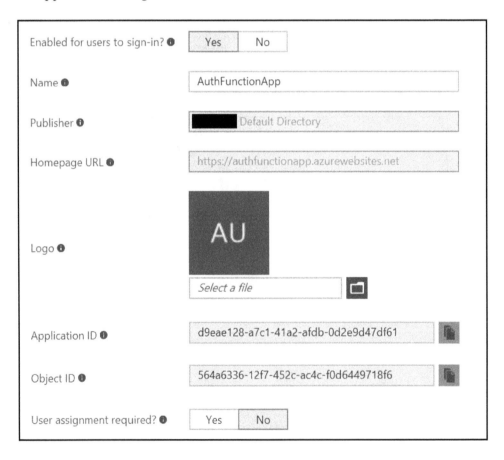

To learn more about AAD applications, please visit: `https://docs.`
`microsoft.com/en-us/azure/active-directory/develop/active-`
`directory-integrating-applications`

- The **Grant Graph Permissions** option would grant the Function App permission to access Microsoft Graph API (to learn more, visit `https://developer.`
`microsoft.com/en-us/graph/docs/concepts/overview`).
- The **Grant Common Data Services Permissions** option would grant the Function App permission to access the Azure Service Management API as a signed-in user.

Note that after the AAD application has been created, you can update its configuration by browsing to your **Function App -> Platform features -> Authentication/Authorization -> Azure Active Directory**. From here, you can assign or revoke application permissions by clicking on the **Manage Permissions** button as shown in the following screenshot:

Signing into your Function App with AAD

After we have configured AAD as our Function App identity provider, the Function App users will be required to authenticate before gaining access to function URLs. Users can sign in using their AAD credentials. You can sign into the application using your Azure account, since it is defined in your Azure AAD tenant. If you are using an organizational account, other people in your organization (in your AAD tenant) will be able to sign in as well. If you are using a Microsoft account, you can still add additional users to your AAD tenant.

To test the sign-in process, browse to one of the HTTP-triggered functions' URLs. Every time you browse to any of the functions' URLs, you will be required to authenticate with your AAD credentials.

When signing in for the first time, you will also be required to allow the `AuthFunctionApp` AAD application to access your profile in AAD:

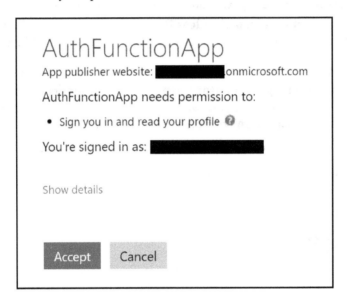

After you have confirmed the permissions, you will be signed in using the `AuthFunctionApp` AAD application. This permits you to access all the functions in the Function App until your token expires.

AAD branding

When providing access to external users, it is important to consider the branding of your login page. If the login page looks unfamiliar or suspicious, users are likely to deny the application permissions, and you are likely to receive many support requests on the subject. AAD provides an ability to add an application logo, choose the application name, and customize the login page. To learn more, please visit the following link:

```
https://docs.microsoft.com/en-us/azure/active-directory/active-directory-add-
company-branding
```

Third-party identity providers

In addition to authentication with Azure AD, Azure Functions provide a built-in integration with a number of third-party identity providers such as Google and Twitter. This allows your users to seamlessly sign up and start using your application using one of their existing social media identities.

When authenticating with a third-party provider, you will need to start by configuring an authentication "application" for your Function App with the identity provider. In some cases, you will first need to sign up for a "developer" program with the provider, which is, typically, free. Each provider has their own process of creating and configuring an authentication application. Similar to the process in AAD, the provider's users can then choose to grant or deny your new application permissions to access their data.

We will explore the third-party identity providers with an example of Facebook.

To create an authentication application in Facebook, perform the following steps:

1. Browse to `https://developers.facebook.com`.
2. Click on **My Apps -> Add a new app.**
3. Choose an application name and a contact email.
4. Click on **OK**.
5. After the new Facebook authentication application is created, on the new application page, click on the **Settings** button to configure the required settings.
6. At the bottom of the **Basic Settings** page, click on the **Add Platform** button, and choose **Website**.
7. In **Site URL**, paste the base URL of your Function App (the default or custom domain).
8. In **App Domains** near the top of the page, add the same base URL. Configuring the application domain is required for your Facebook application to allow requests to the function's URL.

9. To configure the integration with your Function App, you will need your Facebook authentication application's **App ID** and **App Secret**. You can find **App ID** and **App Secret** on the application settings page, as shown in the screenshot:

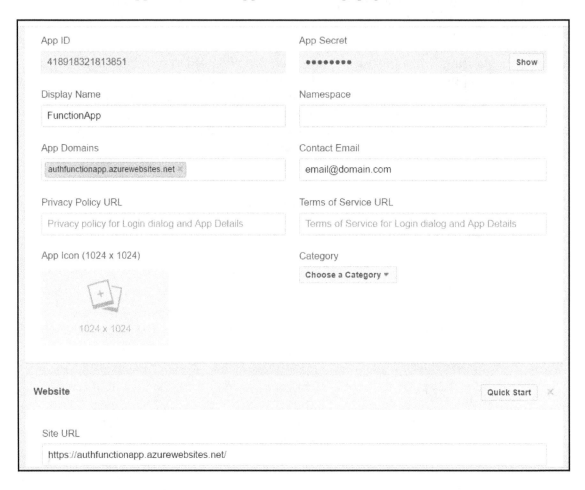

10. To configure Facebook as an identity provider for your Function App, browse to **Azure Portal** -> `Your Function App` -> **Platform features** -> **Authentication/Authorization** -> **App Service Authentication**.

11. Select **Facebook** from the list of identity providers.

12. Paste the **App ID** and **App Secret** of your Facebook authentication application.

13. You can then choose the scope of permissions that the Function App will be allowed to use. When first browsing to your Function App, users will need to be prompted by Facebook to give your application the permissions you required.

14. Take a look at the Facebook provider setup example in the following screenshot:

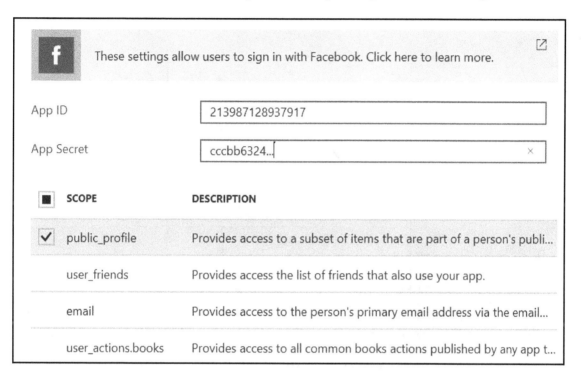

15. Click on **OK**, then click on **save** to confirm the changes.

16. It will take few moments for the changes to become active.

17. Browse to the function's URL to test the sign-in process.

18. When signing in for the first time, you will receive a message similar to the AAD confirmation message, which allows you to grant or deny the new Facebook application the required permissions you have configured in the Functions Portal:

As with Azure AD, the branding of your application is important. As you can see in the preceding screenshot, the default application does not necessarily provide the user with enough context to feel comfortable with proceeding. You can configure the branding, legal, and security settings for your application in your Facebook application settings page.

Code quality

Returning back to other aspects of application level security, it is important to mention code quality. Poor code quality can provide a potential attacker with an ability to stress the system, or exploit the system's vulnerabilities by such means as SQL injection or cross-site scripting. One of the trusted sources for code quality security standards is **Open Web Application Security Project (OWASP)**.

To learn more about assessing code quality using the OWASP standards, please visit `https://www.owasp.org/index.php/Source_Code_Analysis_Tools`.

Managing keys and secrets

Keys, certificates, and secrets used in your application should never be stored in config files in clear text, or committed to source control. Whenever possible, a secure key storage should be used to manage the keys. Azure provides a hardware security module (HSM) "as a service", called Azure Key Vault. Key vault provides a way to encrypt and manage the keys in a secure fashion, and allows developers to "bring their own keys". To learn more about Azure Key Vault, please visit `https://docs.microsoft.com/en-us/azure/key-vault/key-vault-whatis`.

At the time of this writing, configuring Azure Functions integration with Key Vault is a manual process. A more streamlined integration for securing function keys will be added in the future.

Data encryption at rest

Data encryption at rest ensures that if an adversary obtains access to your data, they will not be able to take advantage of it. While the physical access to Azure data centers is only granted on the need-to-access basis, and even deleted data is securely destroyed using procedures required by the highest industry compliance standards, it is recommended to encrypt your application data at rest whenever possible.

Azure offers a number of built-in encryption features for the data storage services used in our application. Take a look at the following list:

- **Storage service encryption (SSE)**: This encrypts data in Blob and File storage using Microsoft-owned keys. You can easily enable SSE by going to `<Your storage account>` -> **Encryption** -> **Enabled**. To learn more, please visit `https://docs.microsoft.com/en-us/azure/storage/storage-service-encryption`.
- **Transparent Data Encryption (TDE) for Azure SQL Database**: This encrypts the entire SQL database at rest. TDE can be easily enabled by going to `<Your SQL Database>` -> **transparent data encryption** -> **On**, and is now enabled by default on new Azure SQL databases. To learn more, please visit `https://docs.microsoft.com/en-us/sql/relational-databases/security/encryption/transparent-data-encryption-with-azure-sql-database`.

- Azure SQL Database also supports a new encryption technology, called **Always Encrypted**, which allows for data encryption at rest, in transit and in use, so that sensitive data never appears in plain text in the database. To learn more, please visit `https://docs.microsoft.com/en-us/azure/sql-database/sql-database-always-encrypted`.
- Azure SQL Database also supports **Dynamic Data Masking** to further protect sensitive information from non-privileged users. To learn more, please visit `https://docs.microsoft.com/en-us/azure/sql-database/sql-database-dynamic-data-masking-get-started`.

Data encryption in transit

Data in transit is data being sent over a network connection. Data encryption in transit is required to prevent a "man-in-the-middle attack", when an intruder is able to gain information from "listening" to the network traffic being transmitted in clear text. Protocols such as HTTP and Telnet send data in clear text, while protocols such as HTTPS and SSH encrypt the data in transit.

To enable HTTPS, you need to create a public-key certificate, signed by a trusted **Certificate Authority (CA)**, to confirm that the certificate holder is indeed the owner of the domain that presents it. The newer protocol most commonly used today to encrypt HTTP traffic is TLS, however, the certificates are still commonly referred to as SSL certificates. To read more about TLS encryption, please visit `https://en.wikipedia.org/wiki/Transport_Layer_Security`.

Function endpoints on the default domain, `*.azurewebsites.net`, are encrypted by default by using a wildcard certificate assigned to the domain. However, when you assign a custom domain to your application, you need to provide an SSL certificate to enable your application to use HTTPS.

Configuring a custom domain

As you know, when a new Azure Function App is created, it is assigned a default public (sub)domain name of `<FunctionAppName>.azurewebsites.net`. While there is nothing wrong with continuing to use the default domain, most application developers prefer to have a custom domain of their choosing assigned to the application production environment. Custom domains help with application branding and discoverability. Having a custom domain also helps establish a trust relationship with your users, as browsing to a familiar domain secured by an SSL certificate allows the users to know that they are, indeed, working with you, and not an impersonator.

You can assign a custom domain name to your Function App (not every particular function in the application). (If one of the functions requires a separate domain name, it should be deployed as a separate Function App).

The new custom domain name can be purchased from a domain registrar such as GoDaddy, or purchased directly from Azure DNS. To learn more about purchasing the domain from Azure, please visit `https://docs.microsoft.com/en-us/azure/app-service-web/custom-dns-web-site-buydomains-web-app`.

For instance, for our text sentiment application, we may choose the domain name `textsentiment.com` (as long as it hasn't been purchased by someone else), and purchase it from a registrar.

After you have purchased the domain name, you will need to set up a DNS record telling your domain registrar which public IP your Azure application resolves on.

Domain Name Servers (**DNS**) are essentially internet "phonebooks" or "maps" which tell the internet where each public domain name should be routed. Internet domain name resolution is supported by a wide network of DNS servers, including DNS root servers that maintain an authoritative record of what IP each domain name should resolve to (this is why attacks on DNS servers, especially, root servers, can result in wide internet outages). For your application to become reachable on the new domain name, a DNS server needs to be updated with a DNS record, and these changes need to be advertised and propagated across the DNS server network, so that your domain name can become resolvable from any computer on the world wide web. This process may take up to 24 hours.

You can set up the DNS record with your own domain registrar (Azure DNS, GoDaddy) or a free DNS service provider such as Cloudflare. Cloudflare (and other similar providers) allows you to set up DNS records for a number of domains using its name servers for free. To learn more, please visit `https://www.cloudflare.com`.

When setting up the DNS record, you can use one of the two options:

- Using an **A-record**. An A-record allows you to map your custom domain, such as `textsentiment.com`, to your application's public IP. You Function App's public IP can be found in its domain settings.
- Using a **CNAME**. A CNAME allows you to map your custom domain name, such as `textsentiment.com` to your Azure domain name, `<FunctionAppName>.azurewebsites.net`.

In both cases, after your DNS record is created, the domain name `textsentiment.com` will start resolving to your Azure Function App.

Different registrars and DNS providers have slightly different processes for setting up the DNS records, and thus creating a new DNS record is beyond the scope of this chapter. To review the process of setting up a custom domain in more detail, including setting up an A-record or a CNAME, please visit the link `https://docs.microsoft.com/en-us/azure/app-service-web/web-sites-custom-domain-name`, or the documentation pages of your DNS provider of choice.

After your domain has been successfully mapped, and the DNS changes have been propagated, you can add the new domain to your Function App. To do so, execute the following steps:

1. Browse to **Functions Portal** -> `<YourFunctionApp>` -> **Platform features** -> **Custom Domains**.
2. Click on **Custom Domains** -> **Add hostname**:

3. Add the new domain you have acquired.
4. Click on **Validate**:

5. Azure will verify that the DNS record mapping this domain to your Function App exists.
6. If the mapping is verified successfully, your Function App will now become reachable on the custom domain. The default `azurewebsites` subdomain will remain reachable.

 Remember, the DNS record may take up to 24 hours to propagate, so you won't be able to successfully validate the domain with Azure immediately after setting it up.

Configuring SSL

As you have noticed, the default Azure Function App subdomain, `YourFunctionApp.azurewebsites.net`, is secured with an SSL certificate. After you assign a custom domain to your Function App, you will need to configure an SSL certificate to secure that domain as well.

The easiest way to obtain the certificate is to purchase it directly from Azure. To learn more on how to purchase the certificate from Azure, please visit `https://docs.microsoft.com/en-us/azure/app-service-web/web-sites-purchase-ssl-web-site`.

You can also obtain the certificate from a different trusted **Certificate Authority** (**CA**). Each CA will have their own process for purchasing SSL certificates.

After you have acquired an SSL certificate for your custom domain, you can configure the certificate in your Function App. To do so, execute the following steps:

1. To associate the certificate with your Function App, browse to `<Your Function App>` -> **Platform features** -> **SSL**, and select to import the certificate if you have acquired it from Azure, or upload the certificate if you have acquired it from another CA:

2. After the certificate has been imported, in SSL bindings, click on **Add binding**, and select the domain name to secure, the certificate to assign, and the SSL type -- **Server Name Indication** (**SNI**) or **IP based**.
3. After the binding is added, you will be able to browse to your Function App endpoint on your custom domain using HTTPS.

For more details on certificate assignment, please visit `https://docs.microsoft.com/en-us/azure/app-service-web/web-sites-purchase-ssl-web-site`.

Configuring CORS

When you configure a web or mobile client-side scripts such as JavaScript to execute HTTP requests against a back-end service (such as an HTTP-triggered function), you often run into same origin restrictions. Most user agents (browsers or mobile browsers) apply same-origin restrictions to client-side scripts. Same-origin is defined as having the same hostname, protocol, and port as the code which originated the request. The same-origin policy is applied for security reasons to prevent the execution of malicious scripts, for instance, scripts trying to gain access to the user's sensitive data by using session cookies from the previous sessions which were stored by the browser. To read more about the same-origin policy, please visit `https://en.wikipedia.org/wiki/Same-origin_policy`.

With the rise of **Single Page Applications** (**SPAs**), AJAX, and interactive UX that relies highly on client-side scripts, it became more and more common for web pages to request data from separate domains. These requests can be as simple as loading CSS stylesheets and images. These can also be user-authenticated AJAX requests that perform the full range of HTTP requests to load new data and submit transactions without needing to reload the entire web page. AJAX requests became very popular among web developers, because they significantly improve the user experience.

If the frontend side of your application includes JavaScript code making HTTP requests to an Azure Functions backend, you will need to configure CORS on the Function App.

CORS, which stands for Cross-Origin Resource Sharing, is a mechanism which allows the browser to determine whether it is safe to allow the script to make a cross-origin request.

You can list all the specific domains that are allowed to access the backend application, or a wildcard "*" value to signify that all origins are allowed. A wildcard "*" value does not allow the request to supply credentials or pass cookies. Using a wildcard means allowing all origins to access your backend, and should be treated with caution. To read more about how CORS works, please visit `https://en.wikipedia.org/wiki/Cross-origin_resource_sharing`.

To enable CORS for your Azure Function App, execute the following steps:

1. Browse to the **Functions Portal** -> `<Your App Name>` -> **Platform features** -> **CORS**.
2. Add any origins that need access to your Function App.
3. Click on **Save**.

4. The allowed origins will be enabled for the entire Function App (not just a particular function).

5. As you can see in the screenshot, certain Functions management and monitoring origins are allowed by default:

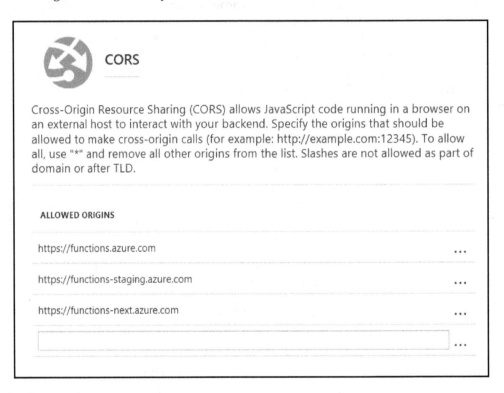

Administrative access

Part of any security conversation is configuring developer and administrator access to the application itself. In the next section, we will discuss how to configure administrative access to our Azure resources.

Role-based access control

The Azure Portal allows for **Role-based access control** (**RBAC**). RBAC allows for granular access to the Azure resources.

Azure RBAC accepts the following two types of accounts:

- Azure Active Directory accounts. Using AAD, you can grant access to users or groups from the default AAD tenant of your subscription.
- Microsoft accounts. When using Microsoft accounts, you can grant access to any email that has been set up as a Microsoft account.

 If your environment is fully automated, and your application is deployed by a CI/CD pipeline, you may consider limiting administrator access to the application to the bear minimum, to prevent configuration drift.

You can configure user access through PowerShell, CLI, REST API, or the Azure Portal. To configure RBAC for your Function App using the portal, browse to **Functions Portal ->** `<Your Application Name>` **-> Platform features -> Access Control (IAM)**.

Here you can add and remove access for any AAD users and groups. You can assign different roles to different users, allowing for different types of access to resources. The core roles are the following:

- **Owner:** Has full permissions over Azure resources
- **Contributor:** Can create and manage Azure resources, but cannot grant and revoke user access
- **Reader:** Has read-only access to the Azure resources

There are also a number of roles that allow access to particular types of resources. Moreover, you can add new custom roles that have the specific permissions you require. To read about Azure RBAC in more detail, please visit `https://docs.microsoft.com/en-us/ azure/active-directory/role-based-access-control-what-is`.

By default, the **Subscription admins** group (which you are a part of if you are an administrator on the Azure subscription) is given access to every new resource, and hence, also the Function App.

To configure access for a new user, perform the following steps:

1. Browse to your **Function App -> Platform features**.
2. Click on **Access Control (IAM).**
3. Here you can see and search the list of users that already have access to the application.

4. To add access for a new user, click on the **Add** button in the top panel, as seen in the following screenshot:

5. To add the user, type in the user email. You can also add access for an entire AAD group by selecting the group name.
6. Select the appropriate user role:

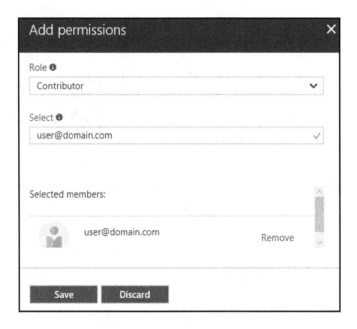

7. Click on **Save**.
8. The user will now be granted the chosen permissions to the selected Azure resource or group of resources.

Instead of access to specific resources, access can also be granted to the entire resource group or subscription. To do so, you can click on the **Resource Group** -> **Access Control (IAM)** and follow the same preceding steps listed. Resource Group and Subscription permissions are inherited by the resources in them.

Resource locks

Azure resources can be locked down to prevent changes or deletions. Locks can be added on any Azure resource such as storage accounts, databases, Function Apps, and so on. The locks can help prevent accidental changes to your application.

The locks are of the following two types:

- **Delete** type. This will prevent the Azure resource from being deleted.
- **ReadOnly** type. This will prevent any changes to the Azure resource, meaning specifically, changes from the Azure management standpoint. For instance, if a storage account is locked, you won't be able to enable **Storage Service Encryption (SSE)** on the account, but you will be able to upload new documents to the storage account.

Locks are not meant to secure the resources against Azure administrators, but mainly to prevent accidental changes. If a change needs to be performed on a locked resource, an administrator will first need to remove the lock.

To add a resource lock to the Function App, perform the following steps:

1. Navigate to your **Function App** -> **Platform features** -> **Locks**.
2. Click on **Add**.
3. Fill in the lock name.
4. Choose the lock type.
5. Click on **OK**:

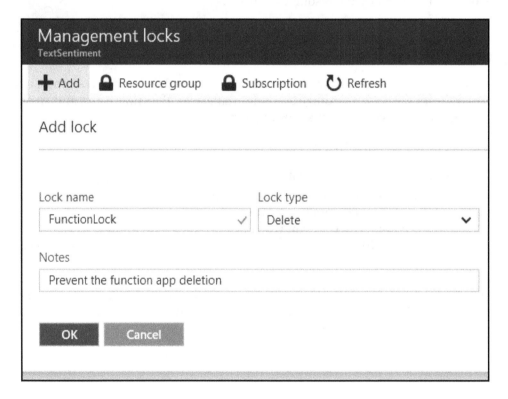

6. Our Function App is now protected against deletion. If a user, or even administrator, tries to delete the application, they will receive an error stating that the lock has to be deleted first.

Summary

In this chapter, we reviewed the different layers of application security as it pertains to serverless computing.

First, we have covered networking security, and the three different options for integration of Azure Functions with a private network based in Azure or even on-premise. We have discussed securing the application access with Network Security Groups -- Azure network firewalls.

We reviewed authentication, authorization, and key management of Azure Functions in detail, and provided steps for configuring different authentication and authorization types. We have provided a step-by-step guide for configuring the Function App authentication using Azure Active Directory and Facebook as identity providers.

We also reviewed the options available for data encryption in transit and at rest, configuring a custom domain and SSL certificate for the Function App, and setting up CORS.

Lastly, we have looked at identity and access from two standpoints: one of securing user access to the application, and the other of securing administrative access to the Azure resources.

In the next chapter, we will focus on monitoring our serverless compute-based application.

11
Monitoring Your Application

In this chapter, we will cover how to monitor the performance and availability of our serverless compute application, focusing primarily on working with the Application Insights service.

We will focus on the following topics:

- Understanding application monitoring goals and best practices
- Using the Functions Monitoring tab
- Using the Application Insights monitoring service
- Configuring Application Insights dashboards and alerts to gain an insight into Functions' performance and health

Application performance management

Application performance management (**APM**) refers to the monitoring and management of performance and availability of software applications. APM helps ensure optimal performance of the system and its availability, and helps the development teams identify and resolve any issues.

As today's software applications are complex, comprised of numerous parts, and expected to be operational nearly 100% of the time, application monitoring requires more and more sophisticated tools.

Application monitoring focuses on the following two main goals:

- **Detect and diagnose**: Monitoring helps detect, triage, and diagnose issues

- **Measure and learn**: Monitoring helps gain insight into application performance, learn, and improve the application

Let's dive deeper into each part and the best approach to handle it.

Detect

The first key goal of application monitoring is to detect application failures. Ideally, your monitoring will be able to achieve the following things:

- **Identify most issues**: Your monitoring tools should be able to report much more than a binary "up" or "down" state. Ideally, all failures, even things that are invisible to the end user, should be reported, although not all of them should generate alerts.
- **Identify issues as early as possible**: You would want to know about any issues as early as possible, ideally before the end user. For instance, if you are running out of connections in your database connection pool, detecting it early will allow you to scale out or free up resources before your users start getting timeouts.
- **Generate no false alarms**: If you routinely wake up your team in the middle of the night with false positive "site is down" alerts, sooner or later they will start ignoring the alert, and even the real failures will be ignored. Good monitoring tools have thresholds to allow for transient failures. For instance, an alert rule can be "alert an administrator if the site didn't respond to four consecutive health probes".
- **Have a good signal-to-noise ratio**: Monitoring tools can easily overflow with information that provides little value, which is especially problematic when it masks the reports that require immediate action. To improve the signal-to-noise ratio, consider the following steps:
    - **Create event hierarchy**: When looking at your monitoring tools, you should be able to detect the criticality level of the event that is being reported. While a silent exception (an exception that does not prevent the system from operating correctly) should still be reported so that it can be fixed, it should not be reported with the same criticality level as an error that is affecting your end users.

- **Group similar events:** Even critical errors will become noise if they are reported hundreds of times a second. A good monitoring tool should group similar events and report them in batches to prevent administrators from drowning in a sea of alerts.
- **Allow report customization**: Deciding which report information is most valuable depends not only on the system, but also on the audience. A developer might be interested in application exceptions, while an operations person might be interested in the memory utilization of your servers (and yes, it still matters in the serverless compute world). The monitoring tool should allow each party to see the information they choose.

Diagnose

Detecting errors allows you to respond swiftly and fix issues before they have any significant impact. However, detecting is only half the story. To be able to effectively troubleshoot the issue, you need to be able to correctly diagnose what is causing it. As discussed in Chapter 8, *Testing Your Azure Functions* in the section on logging, there is nothing worse (from the troubleshooting standpoint) than getting a message along the lines of "A critical error has occurred".

The errors your report must provide enough context (meaningful messages, stack traces, and so on) to investigate where the error occurred and what could potentially be causing it. Good monitoring tools help in diagnosing the problem by allowing live data analysis. The ability to filter and group data by different metrics can be of huge help in identifying what causes the issue.

The typical response process is as follows:

1. Detect
   - This involves getting informed about an issue

2. Triage
   - Is the issue on a critical path?
   - How many users are affected?
   - How often does the issue occur?

3. Diagnose
   - When does the issue happen?
     - Is it correlated with a code change or a database change, resource contention, external dependency, and so on?

- Are the occurrences correlated by location, server instance, user type, use case, and so on?
- Where does the issue occur?
- What is causing the issue?

Ideally, the monitoring tool should help you through all of the steps of this journey.

Measuring and learning

Apart from detecting and resolving issues, application monitoring allows you to continuously improve your application. Gathering performance metrics enables you to identify your application's normal behavior, potential bottlenecks, and areas of improvement. It allows you to identify the most prominent use cases and learn how typical end users interact with your application.

This allows you to be proactive and smooth the rough edges before significant issues arise. This also allows you to learn more about your end users and adapt to their behavior and needs. Most successful SaaS applications today are built around continuously monitoring and seeking to improve the end user experience.

Ideally, the monitoring tool should make it easy to gain new insights from your data by allowing you to gather and analyze historical data, construct different viewpoints, and report custom metrics.

Monitoring tools

Typical monitoring tools include the following three key capabilities:

- The ability to retain and search logs
- The ability to visualize metrics through charts
- The ability to set up alerts

Let us briefly discuss each capability.

Collecting logs

Just as debugging started with print statements, monitoring systems started with log collection. Most monitoring systems allow you to collect, aggregate, and search logs from different parts of your system. Logs may also be the source of part or most of your application's telemetry data.

Creating charts

Charts are key to measuring your application performance and spotting anomalies quickly. The visual representation of data allows you to identify performance baselines, get a sense of how abnormal any particular spike is, and zoom in on a problematic time range.

Most monitoring tools today allow you to create custom charts and dashboards based on your application's telemetry, so that you can get the most valuable insight in the most readable form.

Setting up alerts

Alerts allow you to send a warning to your administrators about an issue occurring in the application, using one or more notification channels. Alerts allow your team to react before the consequences get dire, potentially even before the end users notice the issue.

Alerts are typically set based on metrics thresholds (such as "the CPU is over 80%" or "the server response time is over 2 seconds") or event occurrences (such as "an exception of type X has occurred").

Avoiding alert fatigue

Alerts are key in any monitoring system, however, it is crucial to get the alerts "right". Sending warnings too often causes alert fatigue, and like in "the boy who cried wolf" story, your administrators will soon start to ignore real problems along with the white noise.

To avoid alert fatigue, it is helpful to be able to set up thresholds not only on event/metric values, but also on the minimal period of time (for instance, "the CPU is over 80% for longer than 10 minutes") or count (for instance, "the number of 408 HTTP responses in the last 5 minutes is greater than 10"), after which human involvement is considered necessary.

In addition, good monitoring tools can aggregate events that spike suddenly, by sending out only one alert with an aggregated failure count (compare this with a 1,000 emails triggered by the same type of error flooding your inbox).

Alerting on actionable items

Alerts should signify events that you can do something about. It is important to remember to alert only on actionable items. This is especially meaningful when administrators are paged outside of work hours. Certain performance metrics are very important in order to understand and improve your system, but they are not immediately actionable.

Some alerts are informational and need to be acted upon in the short term (for instance, "the file storage will be full in a month") or even in the long term (for instance, "70% of users leave the site before purchasing"). These alerts should be labeled appropriately and raised via non-invasive channels, such as email.

Other alerts are critical, but cannot be fixed by the person on call. Even if the alert is critical, unless the person on call can immediately start the response chain, there is no sense in waking them up in the middle of the night. Imagine a system administrator being awake all night waiting for the morning to get in touch with the business owner or the development team who can authorize or implement the change needed to fix the issue.

Lastly, if the action required by the alert can be automated, then rather than alerting a human, the alert should trigger the automation.

Functions monitoring tools

Azure Functions come with two "built-in" monitoring options - the **Monitor** tab, and integration with Application Insights.

The **Monitor** tab is a built-in, free feature that focuses primarily on log collection. In the **Monitor** tab you can see and investigate your latest function invocations, gather information about invocation duration and success rate, and explore logs and exception details.

Application Insights is an Azure APM service that can monitor both cloud-based and on-premises applications. Application Insights offers a wide range of analytics tools and can monitor many different types of applications across different platforms (web applications, container-based applications, mobile applications, desktop applications, and so on) and technology stacks. Azure Functions provide a built-in integration with Application Insights, which enables monitoring, reporting, and alerting using a rich set of capabilities.

In addition to insight into your function code, Application Insights offer insight into the underlying infrastructure performance by reporting details of the infrastructure resources consumed by the functions. This makes it easier to identify performance constraints and bottlenecks, and, to an extent, "puts servers back into serverless compute".

You can also integrate with third-party monitoring tools to monitor and analyze your functions by reporting telemetry in your function's code. This approach, however, will not allow you to monitor the underlying infrastructure.

Functions Monitor tab

The Monitor tab is the function's built-in monitoring feature that allows you to explore recent invocation details and logs.

The **Monitor** tab is very useful during development, but is unlikely to be sufficient for the needs of a production application. In production, especially for functions that scale dynamically and may have thousands of invocations per second, the ability to aggregate data and identify trends is crucial, and thus Application Insights are the recommended monitoring tool.

To see the monitoring of one of your functions, navigate to your **Function App -> Function Name -> Monitor**.

Here, you will see all the recent invocations of your function along with the success and failure rates. Clicking on a specific invocation will allow you to explore the invocation parameters and logs. You can also see the duration of each function invocation:

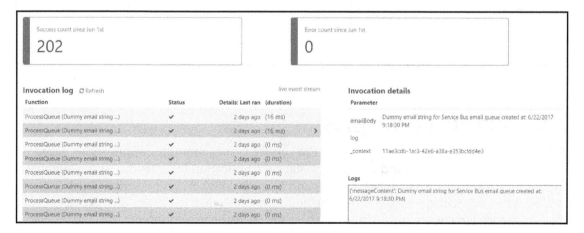

If your function fails, you can investigate the failure in the **Monitor** tab. To simulate failure, we can throw an unhandled (rather than handled) exception in `ErrorFunction` using the following code:

```
[FunctionName("ErrorFunction")]
public static void Run([TimerTrigger("* * * * * *")]
TimerInfo myTimer, TraceWriter log)
{
  // Throw unhandled exception
  throw new Exception("This is a unhandled exception",
    new Exception("This is an inner exception"));
}
```

In the following screenshot of the **Monitor** tab, note that the exception details were logged and it is possible to explore a full stack trace even though logging wasn't explicitly invoked:

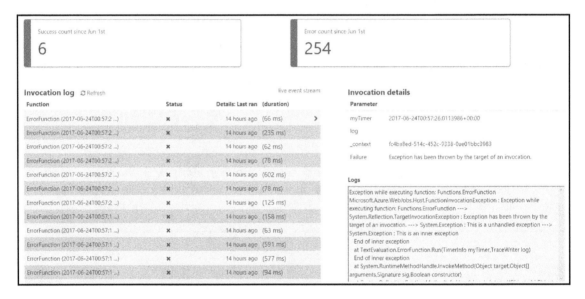

Application Insights

Application Insights is a cross-platform APM service that can monitor applications based on a wide variety of platforms and technology stacks. Application Insights can pull telemetry from your backend code (such as C#, Java, and Node.js code), frontend scripts (such as JavaScript and Angular code), and hosting environments (such as Azure Web Apps, Docker, Azure Functions, and Virtual Machine OS performance counters).

Application Insights monitors a wide variety of metrics. In addition to the built-in metrics, you can add your own custom events and metrics. Application Insights reporting comes with minimal overhead. Tracking calls are non-blocking and are batched and sent in a separate thread.

To enable reporting to Application Insights, you typically need to install a small instrumentation package into your application, and you can instrument both your backend and frontend code to report to the Application Insights.

Azure Functions come with a built-in integration to Application Insights, which means that your Azure Function App is already instrumented, and all you need to do to enable reporting is to provide an Instrumentation Key for an Application Insights resource.

To learn more about Application Insights, please visit `https://docs.microsoft.com/en-us/azure/application-insights/app-insights-overview`.

Monitoring functions with Application Insights

To enable monitoring of your Azure Functions App with Application Insights, you need to provide the application with an instrumentation key of an Application Insights resource.

If you are creating a new Function App, you can simply enable the integration by turning Application Insights on during deployment. This will add the **Application Insights** instrumentation key to the Function app's App Settings:

If you want to enable the integration for an existing Function App, you can do so by creating a new Application Insights resource and adding its instrumentation key to your application.

To do so, execute the following steps:

1. Navigate to **Azure Portal -> Application Insights -> Add**.
2. Fill in the **Application Insights** resource name (by default, **Application Insights** generate resources with the same name as your application. You can stick to this pattern, or add a suffix like AI to make it easy to identify that you are looking at an **Application Insights** resource).

3. Choose **General** as the application type.
4. Select the appropriate subscription, resource group, and a location closest to you (Application Insights can only be deployed in certain Azure regions).

5. An example of a filled form is shown in the following screenshot:

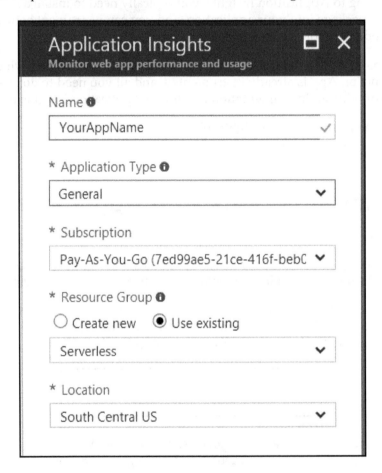

6. After the **Application Insights** resource is deployed, browse to its properties, and copy the instrumentation key, as shown in the following screenshot:

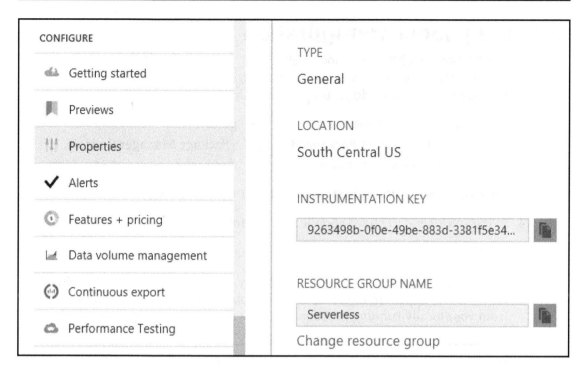

7. Navigate to your **Function App** -> **Platform Features** -> **App Settings**.
8. Add a new setting with the name of `APPINSIGHTS_INSTRUMENTATIONKEY`, and the value of the instrumentation key you copied.
9. Click on **Save**.

Once the setting is saved, your Function App will start reporting telemetry to the Application Insights resource. No code modification is needed.

Setting up local configuration

To enable Application Insights during local debugging, we need to install the Application Insights `NuGet` library in the `TextEvaluation` project, and add the same instrumentation key to the local configuration. To do so, execute the following steps:

1. In Visual Studio, open the `TextEvaluation` project.
2. Click on **Tools** -> **NuGet Package Manager** -> **Package Manager Console.**
3. Run the following command:

   ```
   Install-Package Microsoft.ApplicationInsights -Pre
   ```

4. In the `local.settings.json` file, add the following new setting:

   ```
   "APPINSIGHTS_INSTRUMENTATIONKEY": "<YourInstrumentationKey>"
   ```

5. Now when you run the Function App locally in Visual Studio, your development machine will appear in the server list in Application Insights and report telemetry from your locally running functions, as shown in the following screenshot:

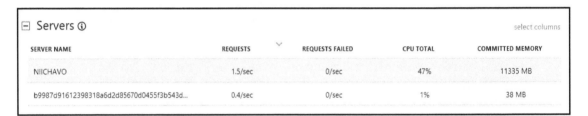

Note that you may choose to report the local development environment telemetry to a separate Application Insights resource, so that it doesn't skew the average performance metrics of your Azure deployment.

Staging slot reporting

By default, the metrics from the Function App staging deployment slot are being reported to the same Application Insights resource as production. This can generate confusion when trying to identify errors created by new code changes pushed to staging only. It is is recommended to separate the reporting of the staging slot metrics into a separate Application Insights resource.

To do so, in Azure Portal, execute the following steps:

1. Navigate to **Application Insights -> Add**.
2. Enter a new resource name.
3. Set the application type to **General**, and enter your subscription, resource group, and location.
4. Once the resource is deployed, go to **Properties** and copy the instrumentation key.
5. Go to your **Function App -> Slots -> Staging -> Platform features -> App Setting**.
6. Replace **APPINSIGHTS_INSTRUMENTATIONKEY** with the instrumentation key you just copied.
7. Check the **Slot setting** checkbox next to the key, as shown in the following screenshot:

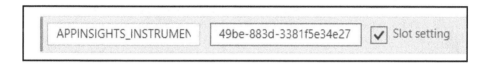

8. Click on **Save**.

You will now see the staging slot performance and exceptions reported separately from production. This is going to help us identify any new errors and issues generated by code changes pushed to staging separately from production issues.

Application Insights dashboards

Since Application Insights service is designed for a 360° view of the entire application, it includes a vast variety of metrics available for tracking. Some of these metrics, such as page view counts, page load time, or the type of browsers that your end users work with are naturally useful in a web application, but not relevant in a serverless compute environment.

When implementing monitoring for the entire system, you can utilize the same Instrumentation Key to report the performance of the web front end of your application (such as TextScoresDashboard web app) to the same Application Insights resource. To learn how to instrument a web application with Application Insights, please visit https://docs.microsoft.com/en-us/azure/application-insights/app-insights-asp-net. In this chapter, we will not cover the instrumentation of a web application, but rather focus on tracking performance of serverless functions.

From the serverless compute standpoint, there are a number of built-in Application Insights dashboards that are immediately useful in monitoring the functions' performance. All dashboards can be customized as needed, and new dashboards can be added to track useful metrics and to customize alerts. In the following sections, we will overview some of the dashboards and built-in capabilities of Application Insights.

At large, Application Insights offer the following two ways to look at the telemetry coming from your application:

- **Live Stream**: This focuses on displaying the on-going live data with minimal latency and does not store or aggregate information. Because there is no data storage, Live Stream is free.
- **Metrics**: The various Metrics dashboards aggregate values over a period of time. The aggregation type (sum, average, min%, and so on) and the time granularity (including the period of time that is reported and the intervals over which the metrics are aggregated) can be configured for each dashboard. Historical data is retained for 90 days. You can also export the telemetry to retain it for longer periods of time.

Let us give a more detailed overview of the preceding features.

Live Stream

The Live Stream dashboard streams live application data with 1 second latency and does not store historical information. Live Stream allows you to have an ongoing insight into your application's performance and is especially useful when deploying new features.

The Live Stream data is streamed on demand (only when you open the Live Stream dashboard) and there is no charge for it.

By default, the following metrics (displayed in the following screenshot) are collected:

- Incoming request rate and duration
- Incoming request failure rate
- Outgoing request (dependency calls) rate and duration
- Outgoing request failure rate
- Committed memory
- Process CPU
- Exception rate
- Application exceptions (in the **Sample Telemetry** tab)

- The number of active servers that are allocated to the functions:

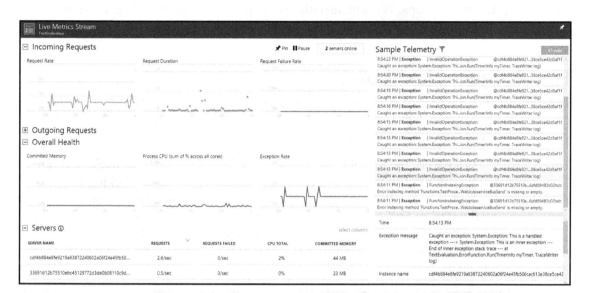

You can filter out the metrics related only to a particular server instance by clicking on the server name (bottom-left corner of the preceding screenshot).

You can also choose to pause the live stream by clicking on the **Pause** button (top of the preceding screenshot). You can then restart it by clicking on **Go Live**.

At the time of writing, Outgoing Requests related metrics are not working for Function Apps. These metrics will become available shortly.

To learn more about the Live Stream dashboard, please visit `https://docs.microsoft.com/en-us/azure/application-insights/app-insights-live-stream`.

Metrics dashboards

All of the Metrics dashboards collect the telemetry reported by your application and retain it for 90 days. Metrics dashboards aggregate data and display it over a certain time range with a certain time granularity.

Metrics dashboards include many preconfigured dashboards, and also the Metrics Explorer where you can add custom dashboards of your own. All Metrics dashboards are highly configurable and can be modified to suit your specific needs.

In the following section, we will overview a number of dashboards that are very useful in monitoring Azure Functions. We will also discuss some of the dashboard configuration options with the example of the performance dashboard.

Performance dashboard

The performance dashboard is, by default, configured to track the server response time, grouped by operation name. The metrics are aggregated (averaged by default), and each point on the chart represents 30 minutes of data.

This dashboard is a part of the Metrics dashboards and retains historical data for 90 days. Consequently, you can modify the time range that is displayed by either clicking on the **Time range** button above the chart and entering the desired start and end time values, or by dragging the start or end pointers below the chart. You can also choose the time granularity over which the data is displayed. The available choices depend on the overall displayed time range. Choosing the performance dashboard **Time range** is shown in the following screenshot:

Dashboard customization

Clicking on the **Edit** button in the top-right corner of the chart will allow you to see which metrics are tracked and customize the chart to reflect additional metrics, as shown in the following screenshot:

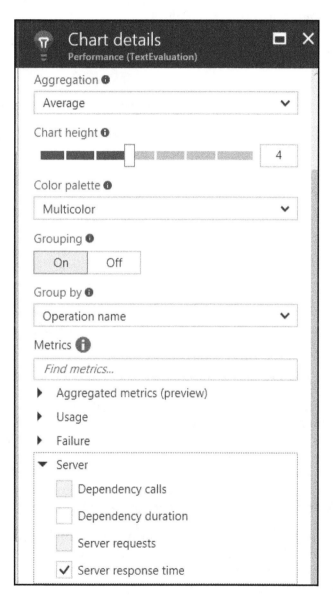

You can select a number of different metrics to display on a single chart. Some metrics become unavailable once others are selected due to incompatibility of data type, aggregation type, or units.

You can also configure the visual aspects of the chart, such as chart type (line, area, bar), color scheme, height, and *y*-axis `min/max` values.

In addition, you can filter the metrics by one of the data properties. In the following screenshot, we choose to look at the metrics of a particular server instance allocated to our Function App:

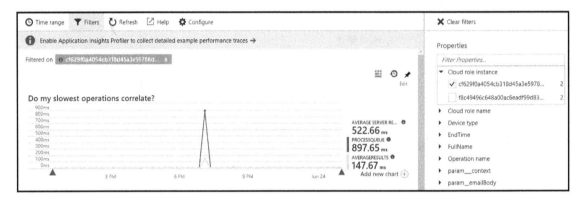

To learn more about different dashboard customization options, visit `https://docs.` `microsoft.com/en-us/azure/application-insights/app-insights-metrics-explorer`.

Servers dashboard

As we know, serverless compute does not actually run without servers. Depending on your Function App's hosting plan (Consumption plan or App Service plan) and resource requirements, zero or more virtual servers will be provisioned for running your Functions App at any given moment. Under the App Service plan, you can choose the number of instances you wish to use for your functions (or choose to scale automatically to the maximum cost-effective number of instances), and under the Consumption Plan, the servers will be allocated dynamically when your function workload increases.

The **Servers** dashboard in the Application Insights resource provides an insight into how many servers are currently utilized by your application, and a comprehensive view of resource utilization per server. This is useful for identifying resource contentions and bottlenecks, or potential scaling issues.

The following chart shows an out-of-the box **Servers** dashboard with the Function App scaled scaled to three server instances. The dashboard shows useful resource consumption metrics such as CPU, and can be filtered to a particular server by clicking on the server instance name:

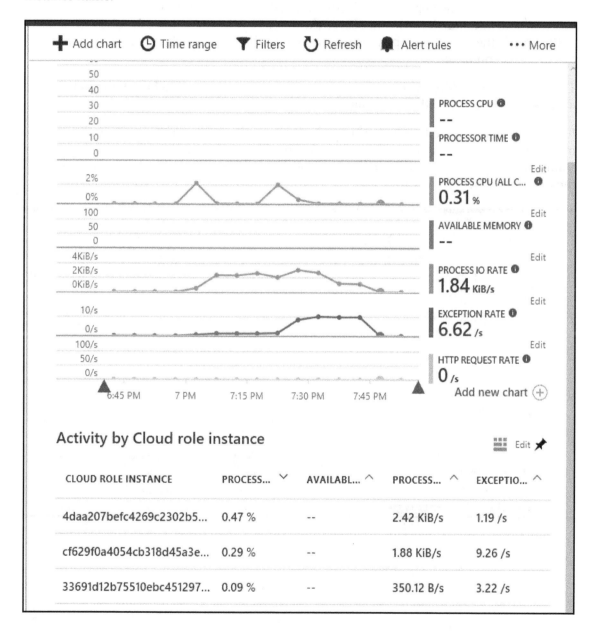

Failures dashboard

The **Failures** dashboard is preconfigured to track exceptions and failed requests. By default, it tracks the total server requests, the failed requests, and the failed requests by operation name. It also tracks the dependency failure rate (which is not currently reported for functions). In addition, it tracks the server exceptions by the exception's problem ID, which in this case is the exception type plus its origin. Like the other dashboards, these charts and tables are customizable.

To demonstrate working with the **Failures** dashboard, let's configure **ErrorFunction** to run every second and watch the reporting.

In the last version of the **ErrorFunction** code, we were throwing a handled exception. This means that the exceptions are actually handled by the function, and the function itself completes successfully. Hence, we see no failed requests, but a lot of server exceptions in the Failures dashboard report:

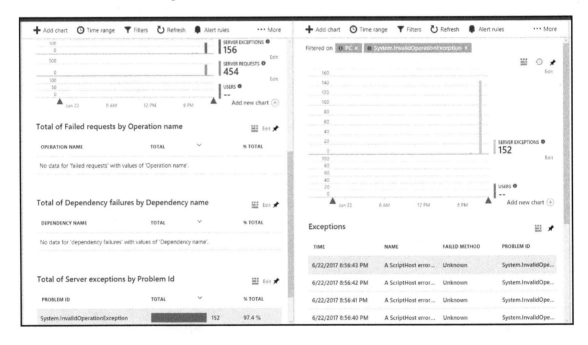

We can explore further details about each exception, including the call stack and trace by clicking on the specific exception type and occurrence:

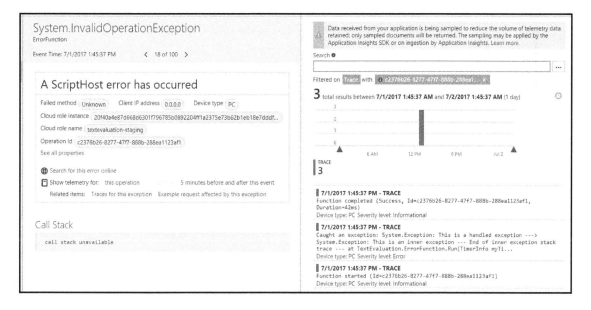

To see the reporting of a failed request, we can switch the **ErrorFunction** code from throwing a handled exception to throwing an unhandled exception. Now, we will see all the **ErrorFunction** executions as failed requests:

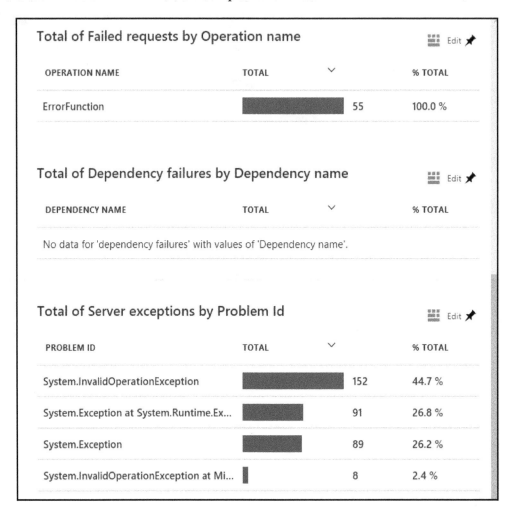

Metrics Explorer

The **Metrics Explorer** tab allows you to add and configure any additional charts and tables you wish to deploy. As mentioned previously, you can add/remove custom charts in other tabs as well.

To create a new chart in Metrics Explorer, perform the following steps:

1. Click on **Add Chart.**
2. Configure the display settings of the new chart.
3. Chose the metrics you wish to display. All of the metrics reported by the Function App will be available in the metrics list, as shown in the following screenshot:

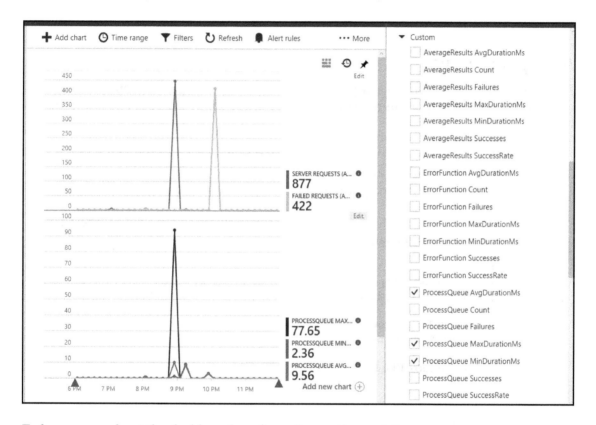

To learn more about the dashboard configuration options, visit `https://docs.microsoft.com/en-us/azure/application-insights/app-insights-metrics-explorer`.

Custom telemetry

Application Insights allow you to monitor custom events by sending application-specific telemetry to the Application Insights API. This allows you to extend the default telemetry collected by Application Insights with properties and metrics specific to your application.

To learn more about how to configure and send custom metrics, visit `https://docs.microsoft.com/en-us/azure/application-insights/app-insights-api-custom-events-metrics`.

Analytics view

Application Insights analytics allow you to write custom queries against your data to gain new insights into your application performance. To explore the Analytics view, perform the following steps:

1. Browse to the Application Insights **Overview** tab.
2. Click on the **Analytics** button.
3. To demonstrate the analytics functionality, run the following query.

   This query will plot the average execution duration grouped by operation name (function name) for the last hour:

   ```
   requests
   | where timestamp > ago(1h)
   | summarize avg(duration) by operation_Name, bin(timestamp,
   1ms)
   | extend local_hour = (timestamp - 6h)
   | render timechart
   ```

4. The plot will look like the following:

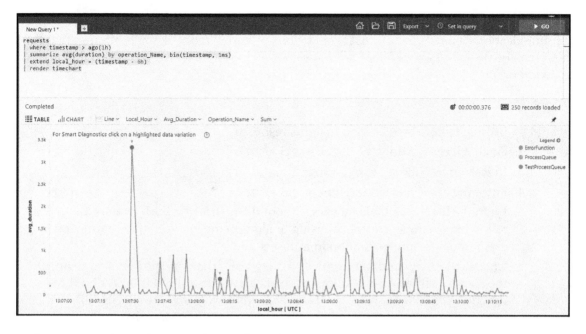

To learn more about the capabilities of Application Insights Analytics, visit `https://docs.microsoft.com/en-us/azure/application-insights/app-insights-analytics`.

To explore the Analytics query language reference, visit `https://docs.microsoft.com/en-us/azure/application-insights/app-insights-analytics-reference`.

Setting up alerts

Application Insights allows you to configure custom alerts based on metric values or activity log events.

When an alert is triggered, you can choose to perform one or more of the following actions:

- Email administrators
- Email a custom email list
- Trigger a Webhook call
- Call an Azure Automation runbook.

Triggering a Webhook allows you to integrate with other monitoring systems and communication channels (many chat applications provide Webhook integration so that the alerts can be posted to your IT chat room) or trigger an automated set of actions that needs to execute.

To set up an alert in the portal, execute the following steps:

1. Browse to your Application Insights resource.
2. Go to **Alerts -> Add**.
3. In **Resource**, choose `TextEvaluation`.
4. Enter the name and description of the alert.
5. From the list of available metrics, choose the metric you wish to alert on. In the following example, we are choosing to alert on the `ProcessQueue` function's execution maximum duration in milliseconds.
6. Choose the alert condition (greater than, greater than or equal to, and so on) and the alert threshold. In the following example, the threshold is exceeded if the function takes longer than 1,000 milliseconds to run, and we can also see a visualization of past performance that helps us estimate how likely the threshold is to be exceeded.
7. Choose the period of time after which the alert is triggered. In the following example, we choose a period of 5 minutes, which means that the `ProcessQueue` function maximum duration needs to consistently exceed 1,000 milliseconds for 5 minutes after the rule was first satisfied before the alert is triggered. This allows us to avoid firing alerts due to transient issues caused, for instance, by temporary blips in network connectivity. As discussed earlier, alerts should only be fired when human involvement is necessary. Reasonable thresholds help achieve this goal.
8. Choose the action of the alert--email owners, contributors, and readers.
9. An example of a filled out form is shown in the following screenshot:

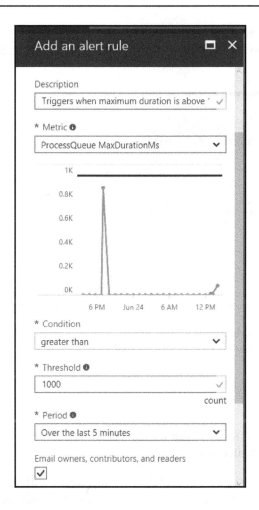

10. Click on **OK.**

You will now be alerted if the `ProcessQueue` function execution duration exceeds 1,000 milliseconds.

Smart Detection

Application Insights also enables "Smart Detection" alerts. Smart Detection automatically warns you about potential performance issues in your application. It uses machine learning to analyze the telemetry sent by your application and identifies abnormal patterns, such as increased failure rate or rising server response time.

The smart detection is turned on automatically and requires no configuration, however, you can choose the alert action for each type of problem in Smart Detection settings, as shown in the following screenshot:

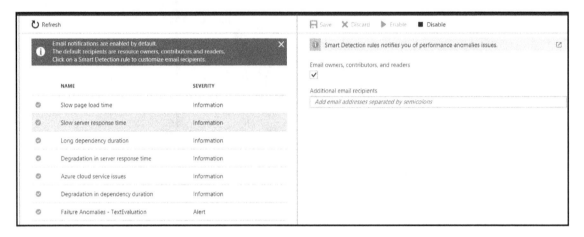

To learn more about smart detection, visit `https://docs.microsoft.com/en-us/azure/application-insights/app-insights-proactive-diagnostics`.

Summary

In this chapter, we learned how to monitor the Azure serverless compute performance and application health using Azure native tools.

We have described how to set up the Functions integration with Application Insights monitoring service. We saw an overview of Application Insights features that are most relevant to serverless compute, and learned how to configure visual dashboards. We walked through configuring the service to monitor the function's performance, identify and investigate bottlenecks and failures, and set up alerts to notify administrators in case human intervention is needed.

In the next chapter, we will learn how to design applications relying on serverless compute for high availability, disaster recovery, and scale.

12
Designing for High Availability, Disaster Recovery, and Scale

In this chapter, we will cover the following three aspects of designing modern reliable systems:

- Designing the application for High Availability
- Implementing a Disaster Recovery plan
- Designing services to scale

We will discuss availability and business continuity at design level, both for the Azure Functions and other services used in the application.

High Availability

In information technology, **High Availability (HA)** is a characteristic that aims to ensure continuous uptime of the system for a desirably long period of time. Availability of the system is usually expressed as a percentage of uptime in a given year.

High Availability differs greatly from **Disaster Recovery** (**DR**), although the two are typically discussed together in the context of ensuring the system's uptime.

For commercial systems, the system's availability is typically backed by an uptime SLA. An **SLA** (short for **service-level agreement**) is defined as an official commitment that exists between the service provider and the customer. SLAs typically refer to a percentage of uptime that is financially backed by the provider, meaning that if the system experienced a longer downtime than what is permitted by the SLA, the customer would receive a monetary refund. There may be a significant difference between an actual system uptime, and its committed SLA (where the actual uptime could be higher or lower), as the SLA only refers to the percentage of uptime that the service provider is comfortable backing financially.

Most SLAs are expressed as monthly commitments, meaning that the client would receive a refund based on the downtime in a given month (not the aggregated downtime for the entire year).

The uptime SLAs are typically expressed as a percent of availability out of a 100%, and are also referred to as a "class of nines". The following table is a useful translation of percent availability into minutes of downtime. For instance, when committing to a four nines SLA, the service provider can only allow for 4.38 minutes of downtime a month:

Availability %	Downtime per year	Downtime per month
99.9% ("three nines")	8.76 hours	43.8 minutes
99.95% ("three and a half nines")	4.38 hours	21.56 minutes
99.99% ("four nines")	52.56 minutes	4.38 minutes
99.995% ("four and a half nines")	26.28 minutes	2.16 minutes
99.999% ("five nines")	5.26 minutes	25.9 seconds
99.9999% ("six nines")	31.5 seconds	2.59 seconds

When you create a commercial application, you are most likely to both provide an SLA to your customers, and rely on the SLAs of third-party services utilized by the application. When working with serverless computing and other cloud services, you rely heavily on the SLAs provided by the public cloud vendors.

Service downtime

The definition of downtime is also important when discussing High Availability and SLAs. For most modern information technology services, **downtime** is defined by the number of minutes for which the service is unavailable. There are, however, some vendors who exclude **planned downtime**, typically caused by a planned system maintenance or upgrade, from the calculation of service availability. This can have a significant impact on the reported percentage of the uptime of the service. When purchasing a service, you should pay close attention to the definition of uptime/downtime in the SLA. In today's global, internet-based, 24/7 technology world, there are no longer time windows during which an interruption of service can be considered completely non-disruptive.

Azure services SLAs

The financially backed SLA for most Azure cloud services is 99.95% (meaning 21.56 minutes of possible downtime a month), including planned downtime. The actual uptime of most Azure services is significantly higher. In most cases, the uptime is over five nines (less than 25.9 seconds of downtime a month!).

Azure Functions are backed by a 99.95% SLA.

The uptime SLA is structured in the following manner:

Monthly uptime percentage	Service Credit
< 99.95%	10%
< 99%	25%

Here, Service Credit is the percentage of the monthly service fee credited to the customer upon claim approval, and the monthly uptime is calculated using the following formula:

$$\text{Monthly Uptime \%} = \frac{(\text{Maximum Available Minutes} - \text{Downtime})}{\text{Maximum Available Minutes}} * 100$$

The maximum available minutes are a sum of minutes when an application was deployed and expected to run across all applications in a given Azure subscription (note that the uptime calculation is not per application). The downtime is a sum of all the minutes during which an application was unavailable across all applications in a given subscription. Visit https://azure.microsoft.com/en-us/support/legal/sla/app-service/v1_4/ for the precise definitions of maximum available minutes, downtime, and so on.

What this means to you as a customer is that if, on average, your Azure Functions based applications in a subscription experience more than 21.56 minutes of downtime a month, Microsoft will refund part of your monthly bill. More importantly, though, this means that as a service provider, Microsoft is confident that across all of the customer applications deployed in Azure Functions, the average downtime will not exceed 0.05% a month. Otherwise the company would be facing not just financial consequences, but also very negative publicity.

What is covered by the SLA

A tremendously important implication of an SLA such as this one is that you are no longer responsible for ensuring a particular service redundancy. (**Redundancy** is the deployment of functional capabilities that would be unnecessary in a fault-free environment). Azure platform is taking full responsibility of ensuring the service's availability during planned maintenance or unplanned failure of the underlying infrastructure, be it at the hardware, network, or operating system level.

This is important because ensuring service redundancy is both difficult and costly.

To illustrate this point, consider a comparison to a traditional data center. To achieve a similar uptime SLA for our application in a traditional data center, we would need to run at least two VMs on two different physical servers (otherwise a hardware failure would take down both), manage synchronous application replication, and add a load balancer which could automatically fail over to a replica in case the primary VM was unavailable. Then, we would also need to ensure the high availability of the load balancer itself, and the reliability of the networking infrastructure. All of this would get quite costly, even for a very simple application. All of this is included in the monthly cost of a Function App, and you only pay for the compute power you use.

What is not covered by the SLA

When talking about a SLA, it is important to note that the SLA does not cover the following situations:

- The SLA will not cover Disaster Recovery situations, meaning that the SLA does not apply in the case of a natural disaster, war, or a similar major event. We will discuss disaster recovery in more detail in the next section of this chapter.
- The SLA will not cover application-level failure, meaning issues with the deployed code or deviations from the officially advised service configuration.
- Lastly, and most importantly, the SLA will not cover integration between different system components.

The last point gives us a segue to the next topic.

Fault tolerance

Fault tolerance is the property that enables a system to continue operating properly in the event of a failure of some of its components. A fault-tolerant design enables a system to continue its intended operation (possibly at a reduced level), rather than failing completely, when some part of the system fails. To learn more about fault tolerance, please visit `https:/` `/en.wikipedia.org/wiki/Fault_tolerance`.

In complex systems, which is nearly any software application nowadays, it is insufficient to ensure an uptime of each separate service within the application. Rather, we must ensure a fault-tolerant communication between these services as well.

Let's take another look at the full application architecture in the following diagram and discuss the components individually and together:

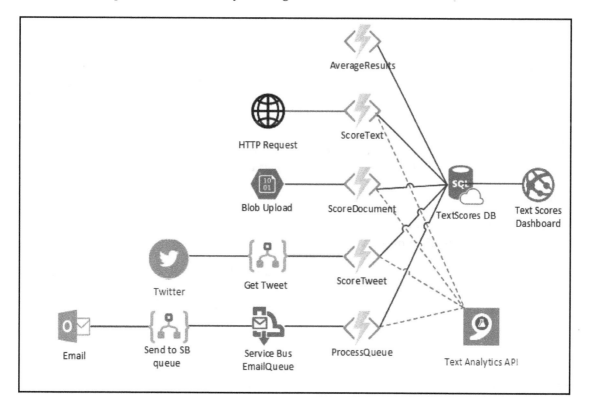

The email input, Twitter feed input, Blob file upload, and the HTTP request are all external inputs to the system and do not affect the uptime of the system (although errors in external inputs must be both assumed and handled gracefully). The rest of the components are integral to the system.

First, let's list the SLAs of each component in the following table:

Component	SLA	Minutes of downtime/month
SQL Database	99.99%	4.38
Functions	99.95%	21.56
Web Apps	99.95%	21.56
Logic Apps	99.95%	21.56
Service Bus	99.9%	43.8
Blob Storage	99.9%	43.8
Text Analytics API	99.9%	43.8

There are different approaches to calculating the overall system availability, some of them involving downtime probability estimates, which can get rather complex. The simplest possible approach to calculating the system availability is by multiplying the availability of each of its components. This approach is rather pessimistic, as it assumes that each component will go down at a different time and that the entire system will go down whenever a single component goes down (the chain is only as strong as the weakest of its links). This gives us an estimate of the worst-case scenario:

Worst Case Availability = (99.95%)^3 * (99.9%)^3 * 99.99% = 99.554%

Maximum downtime a month = max uptime - max uptime * SLA = 31*24*60*(1 - 0.99554) ≈ 205 minutes = 3 hours 25 minutes

This estimate sounds high, but remember that we are talking about the absolute worst case scenario, where each one of the system's components experiences maximum downtime at different times and the entire system comes to a halt because of a fault in each individual component.

Now, let's apply the design principles that help implement fault tolerance to make sure that we stay way above this pessimistic estimate. The good news is that many of the reliability principles are already built into the services we are using.

Elimination of single points of failure

This aspect of the system planning is, in our case, entirely handled by the platform. Each particular service used in the system has built-in local redundancy and automated failover, which is the only way to backup the high-uptime SLA provided by the services.

Transient fault handling

Transient faults are temporary conditions that cause a failure, such as a momentary loss of network connectivity or a service timeout due to overload. Distributed systems composed of multiple services interacting over network are much more prone to transient faults than monolith applications.

Transient faults are, in most cases, self-correcting, and thus a subsequent retry of the failed operation is likely to succeed. The main challenge with retries, however, is that there is no easy way to distinguish between a transient and non-transient fault, and thus in the case of a non-transient fault, indefinite retries must be prevented.

The following practices help address transient fault handling when implemented in concert:

1. Setting operation and/or network timeouts.
2. The Retry pattern.
3. The Circuit Breaker pattern.
4. Message Queuing (applicable in certain cases).

Let us discuss each pattern in more detail in the following sections.

Setting timeouts

Setting a timeout on a call to an external service or thread is an important part of handling transient faults. Reasonable timeouts help prevent blocking the current thread and prevent the failure from spreading across the system in case a response is never returned.

The Retry pattern

The **Retry pattern** enables the system to retry an operation that failed if the failure was likely caused by a transient failure.

The Retry pattern should only be implemented for operations that are likely to succeed when re-attempted and we should always check if the tools and frameworks used by the service already implement this pattern. When implementing the pattern, it is important to consider the following two variables:

- **Retry interval**: This is the period of time the system waits for before re-attempting the failed operation. Retry intervals can be immediate, regular, incremental, or exponential, depending on the length of time the system waits before each subsequent call.
- **Retry count**: This is the number of times the system re-attempts the failed operation before abandoning the retries. Two things to consider when choosing a retry count are the aggregated latency of the operation if performing the maximum number of retry attempts and of course, avoiding infinite retries.

To read more about the Retry pattern considerations and transient fault handling, visit the following link:

```
https://docs.microsoft.com/en-us/azure/architecture/best-practices/transient-faults
```

The Circuit Breaker pattern

The **Circuit Breaker** pattern prevents the system from repeatedly trying to execute an operation that is likely to fail. Implementing the Circuit Breaker pattern in concert with the Retry pattern helps prevent infinite retries.

When the Circuit Breaker is implemented, the system stops the retry attempts after a defined number of retries. The number of retries can depend on the type of operation or the type of failure encountered. For instance, the system may retry the call three times in case of a 408 request timeout HTTP error code and zero times in case of a 401 *unauthorized* HTTP error code.

To read more about the Circuit Breaker pattern and possible implementation approaches, visit the following link:

```
https://docs.microsoft.com/en-us/azure/architecture/patterns/circuit-breaker
```

Message Queuing

Message Queuing is an exchange of data between the sender and receiver processes. Message queues provide an asynchronous communication protocol in which the sender and receiver are not mandated to be available at the same time, which is also called **temporal decoupling**. The sender process messages are placed into the queue until the receiver is able to retrieve them.

Message queues enhance the system's ability to operate asynchronously and decouple the sender and receiver services from one another. They also allow the sender and receiver services to scale independently and allow for workload buffering, adding a persistent storage component for messages that have not yet been processed. Queues can also be used to improve the user experience by allowing the UI to quickly put a message into a queue and return a response, while the backend services are handling the longer tasks required to process the user request. In comparison to shared memory, queues eliminate the possibility memory corruption by the receiver process and also introduce inherent ordering (typically FIFO) of the requests.

Additionally, queues allow for implementation of the retry logic on the receiver, rather than the sender, side, which can be beneficial for the system operation and user experience.

We can consider, for instance, the Blob file upload part of the text sentiment application. If the processing by the Blob triggered function upon upload was handled without a queue, the responsibility for re-uploading the file in case of an error (even an error caused by a transient fault) would fall on the user. Since Azure Storage adds a message to a queue to signify that a new Blob has been uploaded, the message/Blob processing can be retried by the WebJobs SDK without the need to re-upload. We will cover the retries process in more detail in the next section.

It is important to note that Message Queuing is not always appropriate. Queues are inherently asynchronous and have strict limitations on the message size. The main disadvantage of queuing is that it introduces additional complexity into the system.

The Retry pattern in Azure Functions

In the serverless compute part of our application, there are following three areas where a transient fault can be experienced:

- Input triggers
- Calls to external services
- Writes to data stores

Let us discuss each in more detail.

The Retry logic for input triggers

Azure Functions (or, more precisely, the underlying WebJobs SDK) implement the Retry/Circuit Breaker patterns for triggers that may experience transient faults.

For a Blob-trigger processing failure, a retry policy is implemented by the `WebJobs` SDK. Upon a new Blob upload, a message is added to a queue and dequeued by the Blob-trigger function. If a Blob-trigger function fails, the message is returned to the queue, and the processing is retried. The default retry count is 5, and can be configured by changing a `MaxDequeueCount` setting. After the maximum number of attempts, a message is added to the `webjobs-blobtrigger-poison` queue. For more information on Blob-trigger retries, visit `https://docs.microsoft.com/en-us/azure/app-service-web/websites-dotnet-webjobs-sdk-storage-blobs-how-to#a-idpoisona-how-to-handle-poison-blobs`.

The process works similarly for most of the functions trigger types. Timer trigger, Http trigger and EventHub trigger do not execute a retry if a function fails.

For a Service Bus-triggered function, the Retry policy is implemented by the combination of rules on the WebJobs SDK and the Service Bus side. The SDK gets the new Service Bus message in the **PeekLock mode** and then calls the **Complete** method if the processing was successful, or the **Abandon** method if the processing failed. The lock is automatically renewed if the lock timeout is exceeded .

If the message is abandoned, it returns to the Service Bus queue. The subsequent processing of abandoned the message is dependent on the settings of the queue. If the message exceeds its **time to live** or fails to be processed after the maximum number of delivery attempts, it will be moved by to the Service Bus' dead letter queue.

The maximum delivery count and the message time to live for a Service Bus queue can be set by navigating to **Azure Portal -> Service Bus ->** `<Service Bus Name>` **->** `<Queue Name>` **-> Properties -> Maximum Delivery Count**, as shown in the following screenshot:

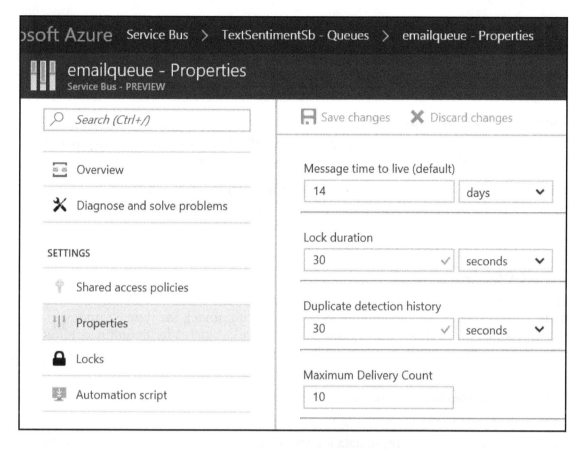

Messages from the dead letter queue can be processed separately. To learn more about the dead letter queue, visit `https://docs.microsoft.com/en-us/azure/service-bus-messaging/service-bus-dead-letter-queues`.

The Retry logic for external calls

Our text sentiment analysis application relies on a single external service, the Text Analytics API. When calling the API, we must implement both Retry and Circuit Breaker patterns, as the call can experience a transient fault (such as a momentary network connectivity loss) and a non-transient fault (an issue with the Text Analytics API endpoint). In this case, the Retry logic implementation is not handled by the platform, and must be implemented in the function's code.

You can write custom code to implement the Retry/Circuit Breaker logic. You can also leverage a `NuGet` library, such as Polly, that makes it easier to configure the Retry policy depending on your desired timeout, max retry count, and so on. To learn more about Polly, visit `https://github.com/App-vNext/Polly`.

The Retry logic in Logic Apps

Since our application leverages Logic Apps along with Functions, it is useful to provide information on Retry logic implementation in Logic Apps as well.

In a Logic App, you can define a Retry policy with a retry interval and count. Find more information at `https://docs.microsoft.com/en-us/azure/logic-apps/logic-apps-workflow-actions-triggers`.

Fault containment

Many failures at a single system component can cause a domino effect, taking down major parts of the system. Preventing this effect is crucial to improving the system's uptime. Remember that the relatively low uptime SLA we have calculated for the entire application was caused by the assumption that a single failing component can disrupt normal operation for the entire system.

The two main approaches to fault containment revolve around input validation and error handling.

Input validation checks the input data for correctness, meaningfulness, and security. Input validation can include data type validation, data range validation, and cross-reference validation (for example, comparison with a known lookup table).

Error handling prevents bubbling of errors into upstream components and introducing errors into the current component's output. Errors can be handled by proactive error checking, or by exception handling. When using exception handling, the exception "breaks" the normal flow of the program and executes an exception handler.

For the context of this book, it is sufficient to mention three good practices in error handling:

- The error effect on the upstream and downstream components should be minimized

- The effect of the error on user experience should be minimized (gracefully reporting the error) or avoided (successfully retrying the operation on a redundant component)
- The error must be reported to the application's monitoring tools

Fault detection

While fault containment might partially or even completely mask failures from the system's user, the system itself must always be aware of the failures.

Both transient and non-transient faults must be detected and reported to the system's monitoring tools. A high number of transient faults on a certain system component may indicate overload and the need to increase capacity. Non-transient, repeatable failures indicate a code or configuration defect that needs to be corrected. Even when a failure is caused by a service external to the system, it is still better to adjust the system's behavior to prevent the error, instead of repeatedly swallowing exceptions. Fault detection is necessary to identify and correct the system defects and improve performance.

Fault correction also requires fault isolation or identifying which of the system components is failing. We discussed the importance of reporting the exception context, which helps isolate the offending component in `Chapter 7`, *Debugging Your Azure Functions*, in *Logging* section.

Prevention of human errors

In both High Availability and Disaster Recovery, a significant percentage of the issues in software systems are caused by a human error. This does not refer to incorrect input or unexpected usage of the system, but rather the mistakes made in system code, setup, or configuration.

The human error horror stories account for much of IT folklore, and include incidents such as the following:

- Unintentionally deleting entire data stores holding business critical data
- Deploying test configuration to production systems
- Causing a vast hardware or network outage with a typo
- Making the entire company domain unusable by failing to renew an SSL certificate.

These errors usually occur during an introduction of a change (such as new version deployment) into the system. They can also be a result of attempting to apply a change to a different part of the system, or a different system altogether. For instance, bash commands using wildcard characters or recursive bash commands can easily have a broader effect than intended by the user. As an example of such an overly ambitious command, try searching for `sudo rm -rf /`.

The prevention mechanism for human errors caused by typos and unintended scripts lies in limiting user permissions and locking down the critical components of the system (in Azure, as discussed in `Chapter 10`, *Securing Your Application*, this can be done by setting Read-Only or Delete locks on a resource to prevent accidental changes or deletions).

Automation is another approach that helps prevent human errors during code deployment or changes to the system. Automating the deployment from source control and building a CI/CD pipeline that includes automated tests can prevent a lot of defects from being deployed into the Production environment.

The advantage of automation is that the process can be tested and corrected prior to execution and that the Production execution will inevitably include all the implemented steps. That is in contrast with the incredibly error-prone process of an IT team manually following a long deployment checklist, often during off hours.

It is worth noting that in certain cases, automation itself can introduce issues. For instance, running an outdated version of an automation script or, running a Dev automation script on a Production environment can have unpredictable results if the scripts do not implement a fail-safe mechanism.

Disaster Recovery

In information technology, **Disaster Recovery (DR)** is a set of policies and procedures aimed at protecting a system from a natural or human-induced disaster. The term Disaster can refer to any major event that may disrupt operations of an entire data center. Disaster Recovery aims to continue (or quickly resume) the system operation in case of a negative event.

Hence, Disaster Recovery planning can be addressed in the following two ways or a combination of the two:

- **Resilience**: This involves planning for uninterrupted service of the critical business functions, for instance through redundancy
- **Recovery**: This involves planning to recover and restore the business functions that fail

When planning for Disaster Recovery, the following two objectives must be defined first, typically by the business owner of the system:

- **Recovery Point Objective (RPO)**: This is the maximum period of time in which the system's data might be lost due to a major incident
- **Recovery Time Objective (RTO)**: This is the targeted duration of time within which the system's operation must be restored after a major incident

In simple terms, the RPO represents how much data you are okay with losing, and the RTO represents how long it should take you to restore the system operation back to normal. RPO and RTO directly affect the planning of the DR site. For instance, an RPO of 15 minutes means that the data replication must be near real-time. An RTO of 30 minutes means that the failover process must be highly automated.

Both RPO and RTO are objectives and, require significant planning and failover testing to be executed. In reality, organizations often have low RPO and RTO objectives, but during an actual incident, due to lack of proper planning or unforeseen circumstances, these objectives might not be met.

The lower the RPO and RTO, the higher will be the cost of Disaster Recovery plan, and the lower the costs of actual recovery from a disaster. A decade ago, the expectation for most systems was that it was sufficient to restore them from the daily tape backup. This implies the RPO of over 24 hours, as the shipping of tapes offsite typically takes place at a certain time of the day. Assuming, for instance, that the daily backup is taken at midnight and the tapes are shipped offsite at 7 AM, and assuming also that the incident was bad enough to make the new tapes made on the following day unusable, the worst case potential time interval for data loss is 31 hours, rather than 24.

Nowadays, the expectations of users of even non-critical systems are a lot higher than that. While loss of access to social media or video streaming websites is not life threatening, both types of services would be subject to tremendous amounts of bad publicity and very high user turnover if their websites were down for even a single hour.

What is a disaster?

When thinking of a disastrous event, we usually think of an earthquake, flood, hurricane, war, or act of terrorism. Statistically, though, most DR situations are caused by mundane events. Up to 43% are caused by power failure and up to 13% are caused by a human error.

Studies also show that even though DR may be expensive, every $1 spent on business continuity measures saves around $4 in recovery costs.

While High Availability aims at continuous operation in case of minor incidents, such as a single server malfunction or a storage rack failure, Disaster Recovery involves protection against major events. Hence, while High Availability is typically achieved by synchronous replication and component redundancy, Disaster Recovery must involve different types of measures, because a major incident can be assumed to take down an entire local data center.

Thus, when protecting against a major disaster, the system components are typically replicated to another location miles away. Different DR recommendations may advise on anywhere from 30 miles to 300 miles distance between the primary and DR locations. Among other things, the distance depends on the kind of disasters your primary and secondary data center site may be subject to, since you want to avoid the situation in which the same hurricane or power outage takes down both locations. The distance can also depend on the size of the country your system is located in, as some countries are relatively small and some data must remain within the country's borders.

Disaster Recovery planning in Azure

As described in the previous section, High Availability of PaaS offerings is handled by the Azure platform. Disaster Recovery, on the other hand, is up to the developer. For critical production deployments, you should ensure geo-replication of the system to another region.

When deploying services in the Azure cloud, you need to pick a location to which the service will be deployed. While the specific locations of Azure data centers are not publicly disclosed for security reasons, you know the geographic region of the data center, and can choose the location closest to your users.

For DR purposes, Azure Cloud has paired regions. Paired regions are, whenever possible, separated by 300 miles, to lower the probability of a natural disaster affecting both. At the same time, the paired regions are connected by dark fiber, to make the network latency as low as possible. Planned updates are rolled out to paired regions at different times, and in case of a broad outage, a recovery of one out of each pair will be prioritized. Except for Brazil South, paired regions are always within the same geographic and national borders. To read more about paired regions or review the pairs list, visit `https://docs.microsoft.com/en-us/azure/best-practices-availability-paired-regions`.

You can choose to put your DR site anywhere, but it is recommended to select paired regions as your production/DR regions.

When taking into account that distances between the production and DR data centers can be as high as 300 miles, synchronous replication of data becomes impractical due to network latency. The next best option is to duplicate the stateless components of your application (such as Functions and Web Apps) and asynchronously replicate the data stores (such as SQL Azure database, Blob Storage, or CosmosDB).

DR site type

Traditionally, DR sites come in the following three flavors:

- A **cold** DR site means having a ready-to-go data center facility with little to no existing hardware and no ready-to-go application or data backups. When deploying services in the public cloud, this definition nearly loses meaning as there is always a ready-to-go data center facility where your application could be re-provisioned.
- A **warm** DR site has the required hardware and network already provisioned, albeit usually in smaller capacity than the production site. A warm DR site also has ready-to-go backups of the application and data, although the backups may be several days old. A warm DR site was defined back in the day when typical application backups where written to tape and physically shipped to a secondary location (this form of backup is still in practice today in many organizations).
- A **hot** DR site is a duplicate of the production environment at full or near full capacity, with near real-time synchronization of application and data. In traditional IT, hot DR sites are very expensive, as they essentially double the cost of the production infrastructure and also require highly efficient data replication.

Even if you have a hot DR site up and running, your Disaster Recovery is only as good as your failover process. **Failover** is the process of switching to a redundant standby system upon failure in the main system (production deployment). **Failback** is the process of restoring the system from the standby to main production deployment. In complex systems, both failover and failback can become extremely complicated and require multiple sequential steps to succeed. For that reason, most failover procedures are highly automated.

The failover procedure should be tested several times a year, to make sure that the process is still up to date and fully functional. A typical testing procedure involves bringing the DR site up and running automated and smoke testing against the DR site. This is done while keeping the production user traffic pointed at the main production deployment.

Implementing a hot DR site

With Azure PaaS services, the duplication of the stateless application components in reduced capacity is simple and cheap, and most services can subsequently be scaled in minutes to meet the production performance needs. Furthermore, if you have an automated and consistent deployment process, the services can be brought up from scratch in a consistent and very fast manner. Thus, if your RTO allows for a few minutes of downtime, you might be able to meet it even with a warm DR site.

Most importantly, the asynchronous geo-replication of data is typically a feature built into the data store, which you can enable with a couple of clicks or script commands. All of the preceding makes the hot DR site implementation very straightforward and also incredibly cost effective compared to traditional warm and hot DR sites. For critical applications, the cost of potential downtime far outweighs the cost of synchronizing your data stores to a secondary region.

DR in Functions

To deploy a hot DR site for Azure Functions, we need to enable geo-replication of the Function App to multiple Azure regions. To enable geo-replication of the application, we will need to deploy the same Function App in multiple regions and then use an Azure Traffic Manager to load balance the traffic between the regions.

Azure Traffic Manager is a DNS resolver that will route the traffic to the most appropriate endpoint based on the routing method you select. To learn more about Azure Traffic Manager, please visit the following link:

`https://docs.microsoft.com/en-us/azure/traffic-manager/traffic-manager-overview`

Currently, you can only use Traffic Manager with Functions deployed under the App Service hosting plan.

Traffic Manager offers a number of routing methods, most notably the Priority and Performance routing methods:

- With the **Priority** routing method, you can choose a primary and backup endpoints for your service. This allows you to configure a warm DR site to fail over to in case your primary site is unavailable.
- With the **Performance** routing method, you can add multiple service endpoints, and the users will be routed to the closest endpoint. This allows you to configure a hot DR site to handle parts of your traffic.

To learn more about Traffic Manager routing methods, please visit `https://docs.microsoft.com/en-us/azure/traffic-manager/traffic-manager-routing-methods`.

In the following example, we will use the Performance routing method since our aim is to configure a hot DR site.

To deploy Traffic Manager for an Azure Function App, execute the following steps:

1. Create two or more Function Apps using *App Service hosting plan* in multiple geographical regions. The process of deploying a Function App into an App Service plan is described in `Chapter 10`, *Securing Your Application*, in the Azure App Service section

2. Deploy the same Function App project to all of the regions. To do so, you can set up a continuous delivery pipeline as described in `Chapter 9`, *Configuring Continuous Delivery* to simultaneously deploy the project artifacts to all of the required regions.

3. In **Azure Portal**, click on **Create New | Traffic Manager profile**.

4. Choose a name for Traffic Manager profile, and select the appropriate **Subscription** and **Resource group**.

5. In **Routing method**, choose **Performance**, as shown in the following screenshot:

6. Click on **Create**.
7. Once the Traffic Manager profile is deployed, browse to **Endpoints** and click **Add**.
8. In **Type**, choose **Azure endpoint**.
9. Add a name for the endpoint. It is a good convention to specify the Function App name and the geographical location of the Function App in the name of the endpoint.
10. In **Target resource type** choose **App Service**.
11. In **Target resource** browse and select the name of your Function App in the appropriate geographical location, as displayed in the following screenshot:

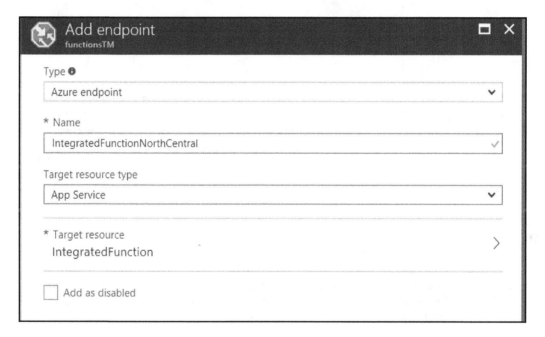

12. Click **Create**.

13. Repeat the process to add all other Function App locations that you wish to distribute the traffic to.

14. Browse to **Endpoints** to see the list of all endpoints loadbalanced by the Traffic Manager profile, and their status, as shown in the following screenshot:

The traffic to your Function App is now load balanced between multiple geographical regions, and if one of the regions becomes unavailable, the traffic will be served by the other regions.

Web Apps

Similar to Functions, to implement DR, a web application can be deployed to multiple regions, with Azure Traffic Manager configured to route the traffic to the appropriate regions. The deployment steps are identical to the Functions load balancing with Traffic Manager that were described in the previous section.

Logic Apps

Logic Apps can be deployed in multiple regions to achieve redundancy in either active, or passive (disabled) mode. For HTTP-triggered Logic Apps, the backend service and region can be abstracted away by using the API Management Gateway integration. To learn more, visit https://blogs.msdn.microsoft.com/mvpawardprogram/2017/02/21/protecting-azure-logic-apps/.

Azure Service Bus

Service Bus allows for Queue/Topic partitioning. Service Bus partitioning allows for higher throughput, by partitioning the messages across multiple message brokers and messaging stores.

Partitioning is enabled by default and is advised for high availability as, without partitioning, Service Bus uses a single messaging store and could thus be more prone to temporary outages.

In DR scenarios, to allow failover between data centers, you can use paired namespaces, where the paired backlog queue is deployed in a different data center. To learn more, visit `https://docs.microsoft.com/en-us/azure/service-bus-messaging/service-bus-outages-disasters` and `https://docs.microsoft.com/en-us/azure/service-bus-messaging/service-bus-paired-namespaces`.

Azure Storage

Azure Storage comes with a number of replication options. We will mention the following three:

- **LRS - locally redundant storage**: This is the minimal replication type, which provides three storage replicas in the same region. This handles the storage high availability.
- **GRS - geo redundant storage**: This type provides three replicas in the same region, and additional three replicas in a secondary region. This handles disaster recovery.
- **RA-GRS - read-access geo redundant storage**: This type is similar to GRS, with the secondary replicas available for read access. This handles disaster recovery, and allows additional usage of the replicas during normal operation.

For Storage disaster recovery planning, either GRS or RA-GRS replication should be chosen. The replication mode of the storage is configured at the time of storage account deployment. To read more about storage redundancy, visit `https://docs.microsoft.com/en-us/azure/storage/storage-redundancy`.

Azure SQL Database

Azure SQL Database allows you to easily deploy up to four read-only replicas of your database in different regions. Completed transactions are asynchronously replicated to read-only replicas. The secondary databases are available for querying at all times and can be failed over to in case of a disaster. Active geo-replication provides an RPO of under five seconds (which is an amazing RPO for a data store).

To configure geo-replication of SQL Database, execute the following steps:

1. Navigate to **Azure Portal** -> **SQL Databases** -> <Database Name> -> **Geo-Replication**.
2. Choose a target region (an Azure paired region will be recommended) as shown in the following screenshot:

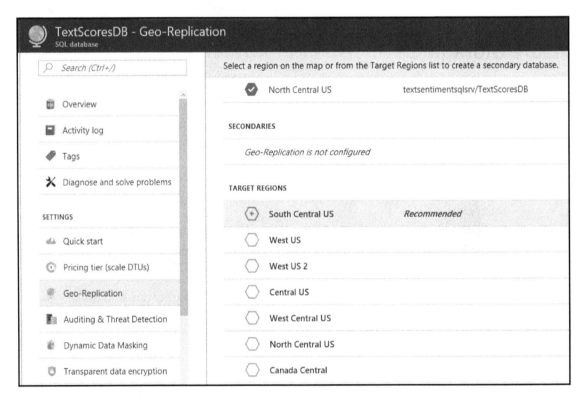

3. Configure the target server (similar to the new SQL server deployment process described in Chapter 3, *Setting Up the Development Environment*).
4. Click on **OK**.

5. The database will be replicated to the selected region. The first replication may take some time to complete, depending on the database size. After that, all changes to your primary database will be replicated to the secondary region.

To learn more about SQL Database Geo-Replication, visit `https://docs.microsoft.com/en-us/azure/sql-database/sql-database-geo-replication-overview`.

Note that other Azure PaaS data stores provide excellent geo-replication capabilities as well. If you are using Azure Cosmos DB, please visit the following link to review its disaster recovery capabilities at `https://docs.microsoft.com/en-us/azure/cosmos-db/regional-failover`.

The Text Analytics API

Even though you provide a location when deploying a cognitive services API endpoint, this location is only used for metadata storage. The Text Analytics API is a service external to our application and its availability in case of a major incident is governed by Microsoft and backed by the uptime SLA.

Scaling the application

Prior to the arrival of the public cloud, scaling applications to meet potential user demand required significant planning and upfront investments. A possibility of high load meant the need to provision spare hardware capacity to handle the maximum load well in advance of the event. Certain businesses, such as retail companies, which experience high load only during holidays, had to maintain large amounts of unused spare infrastructure during the entire year. Other businesses, such as utilities, which may experience high load due to unpredictable weather conditions, had to anticipate the maximum required capacity and run on over-provisioned infrastructure. Despite the very high cost of over-provisioned infrastructure, dynamic scaling was rarely implemented, as it required each organization to re-invent the wheel and required high collaboration between segregated teams, such as infrastructure and development. The level of automation required to enable dynamic scaling seemed too difficult and costly to implement for any given organization. Even today, in many organizations, allocating a new virtual machine still requires weeks of processing, and purchasing and installing new physical servers can take months.

With the arrival of fully internet-based software businesses requiring high scale, the implementation of dynamic scaling across aggregated infrastructure suddenly became the only way to cost-effectively meet demand. Dynamic computing power allocation became a core capability, and the software-defined data center has emerged. With the public cloud, any developer can take advantage of the dynamic scaling capabilities offered by the provider for most of the PaaS services. Even in the IaaS world, public cloud offers built-in scaling capabilities (such as auto-scaling of VM Scale Sets) and the ability to automate scaling on demand.

When discussing the ease with which our application's services can be scaled in the cloud, it is useful to keep the perspective of how difficult this can be in traditional IT.

Scaling serverless compute

As discussed earlier, the Azure serverless compute comes in two flavours--two different hosting plans, which directly affect the type of built-in dynamic scaling. Depending on the use case, one of the plans may be a better fit for your application's scaling needs.

Consumption plan

When deploying Azure Functions under the Consumption hosting plan, the scaling is handled automatically by the platform. The compute power is dynamically allocated when the functions are triggered, scaled out if the load increases, and scaled in if the load decreases. The Consumption plan dynamically allocates CPU and memory resources by adding processing instances. Each instance is allocated up to 1.5 GB of memory.

The Consumption plan is ideal for short running functions that experience load fluctuation and may need to be scaled out quickly to process intermittent high load. Due to dynamic resource allocation, the Consumption plan tends to be significantly cheaper than the App Service plan. The cost structure will be discussed in detail in Chapter 13, *Designing Cost-Effective Services*.

Function Apps deployed under the Consumption plan have the following two limitations:

- **Limited execution time**: By default, the execution time limit is five minutes, and can be increased to 10 minutes.
- **Relatively slow startup time after the function goes idle**: This happens because new compute resources need to be re-allocated to the Function App. For most functions, the cold start time is only a few seconds (specifically for Blob-triggered functions the cold start time may be up to 10 minutes).

These limitations may force the developer to choose the App Service plan for certain Function Apps.

An external "ping" mechanism or a timer trigger can be added to prevent the Function App from going idle, although this approach is not recommended. For long or continuously running functions it is best to leverage the App Service plan.

No developer action is required to handle scaling under the Consumption plan. Your Function App will be scaled by the platform to meet demand.

App Service plan

Under the App Service hosting plan, the auto-scaling is available, although it is not as dynamic. As will be discussed in `Chapter 13`, *Designing Cost Effective Services*, the App Service allocates dedicated VMs to your App Service when you are running in the **Basic**, **Standard**, or **Premium** tier.

The App Service plan is good for long running functions, as there is no limit on the function execution time. It is also good for functions that require fast start-up time after a period of inactivity, since the App Service plan has at least one dedicated instance always allocated to the Function App. You can also enable the **Always On** setting on the App Service to prevent the instance from going idle.

App Service plan is also required for integration with private networks, as discussed in `Chapter 10`, *Securing Your Application*.

The App Service plan can be scaled both up (to a higher tier with more powerful VMs) and out (to a higher number of VM instances). The auto-scaling is done by scaling out (or scaling in) of the number of instances in the App Service plan. Auto-scaling can be configured either based on metrics or based on schedule. Enabling auto-scaling requires the Basic tier or higher.

App Service auto-scaling allows for pretty granular rule configuration. To configure the auto-scaling for a Function App deployed under the App Service hosting plan, perform the following steps:

1. Navigate to **Azure Portal** -> **App Service** -> `<App Service Name>` -> **Scale out** (App Service plan).
2. Click on **Scale by schedule and performance rules**.
3. Click on **a scale out rule**.

4. In the following example, we will set up a rule to increase the instance count by three if the application memory percent utilization has exceeded 80% for more than 15 minutes. A number of different metrics, such as CPU percentage, HTTP queue length, or Disk queue length, can be chosen as load indicators.

5. The time aggregation setting configures how the data is combined over the duration.

6. The cool down setting configures how long the platform should wait for the system to "settle in" into the new operation mode before applying the scaling rule again.

7. An example of the filled out form is shown in the following screenshot:

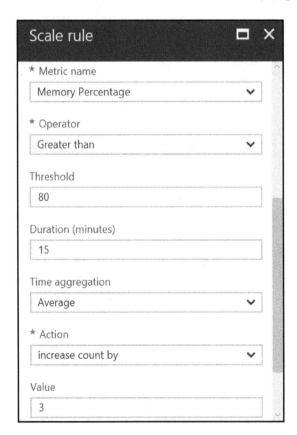

A similar rule can be configured to scale in when the load decreases.

Alternatively, if your application faces a predictable load fluctuation, you can choose to scale based on schedule, a recurring event (for example scaling up on weekends) or on a particular date. An example of setting up the scaling based on a particular date is shown in the following screenshot:

To learn more about App Service scaling, visit the following link:

```
https://docs.microsoft.com/en-us/azure/monitoring-and-diagnostics/insights-
how-to-scale?toc=%2fazure%2fapp-service-web%2ftoc.json
```

Scaling other application components

Let us provide a brief overview of scaling capabilities of other services used in our text sentiment application.

Web Apps

Web Apps are a part of the Azure App Service, and hence they have exactly the same scaling capabilities as the App Service plan of Azure Functions, which we outlined in the previous section.

Azure SQL Database

Azure SQL Database comes in a number of pricing/performance tiers--**Basic**, **Standard**, **Premium**, and **Premium** RS (with each further tier broken down into levels).

Each tier has a certain maximum size and available number of **Database Transaction Units (DTUs)**, which are a blended measure of CPU, memory, and IO. For a more detailed explanation of DTUs, visit `https://docs.microsoft.com/en-us/azure/sql-database/sql-database-what-is-a-dtu`.

SQL Database tiers currently range from 2 GB to 4 TB of maximum size and from 5 to 4,000 DTUs. To learn more about the different available sizes, DTUs and other performance metrics of each database tier, visit `https://docs.microsoft.com/en-us/azure/sql-database/sql-database-service-tiers`.

The SQL Database is not scaled automatically between tiers by the platform. The database can be scaled in the portal or using PowerShell, the C# SDK, or the REST API. A PowerShell script can be scheduled to run at certain intervals to monitor the database performance metrics and scale the database to the next available performance tier when required. The following link provides an example of such a script:

`https://docs.microsoft.com/en-us/azure/sql-database/scripts/sql-database-monitor-and-scale-database-powershell`

Azure Service Bus

Service bus comes in three pricing tiers: Basic, Standard, and Premium. You can switch between Basic and Standard tiers by user action and the Premium tier has to be chosen at the time of deployment.

Even the Basic tier can handle millions of operations, however, when expecting high or time dense loads, Standard or Premium tier should be chosen and partitioning should be enabled.

Azure Storage

Azure Blob Storage accounts can currently grow up to 500 TB of storage in a single account and this limit will be increased in the future.

If additional capacity is required, the application may need to utilize multiple storage accounts or, use an alternative data store, such as Azure Data Lake. To learn more about Azure Data Lake, please visit `https://docs.microsoft.com/en-us/azure/data-lake-store/data-lake-store-overview`.

Logic Apps

Logic Apps are scaled dynamically by the platform, and they can handle billions of actions. The service availability at scale is backed by an uptime SLA.

Text Analytics API

Text Analytics API is a service external to our application and its availability at scale is governed by Microsoft and backed by an uptime SLA.

Load testing

While it may not be your responsibility to handle scaling of some of the PaaS services used in the application, it is your responsibility to verify that your application will perform adequately under maximum expected load. As described in `Chapter 8`, *Testing Your Azure Functions*, load testing is a major component of ensuring the reliability and adequate performance of your application.

Before deploying to production, it is recommended to run a load test simulating the maximum expected load on your entire system.

Summary

During the course of this chapter, we discussed the three major design considerations of building a reliable application: the application's High Availability, Disaster Recovery readiness, and the ability to scale on demand and be prepared to handle high or fluctuating load.

We have reviewed the implementation of HA, DR, and scaling in Azure serverless computing, and provided brief references to their implementation in the other services used in our text sentiment application.

In the next and final chapter of this book, we will analyze the cost of the text sentiment application and learn how to choose the most cost-effective tier for each application component based on the expected load.

13
Designing Cost-Effective Services

In this chapter, we will discuss the pricing of the Azure services used in building the text sentiment analysis application, and how to estimate the pricing based on the expected load. We will cover different service tiers of various services and discuss how to choose the appropriate service tier. In this chapter, we will do the following:

- Walking through the two pricing models available for Azure Functions
- An overview of the cost structure of the Azure services used in building the text sentiment analysis application
- Discussing how to select the most appropriate service tier based on expected load
- Estimating the total monthly pricing of the application as a function of user traffic load

Pay for what you use

In the fairly recent past, going from an idea to execution of building a software application was a costly and time-consuming business. As a first step, you needed to acquire physical servers and a proper facility to install them. Then, you had to purchase operating system licenses, and licenses for third-party software products. To provide high availability, you needed to install redundant servers, and purchase expensive network appliances. You also had to secure, patch, and maintain this hardware. To protect the application against major outages (which could be caused by an event as simple as an electricity service interruption), you had to duplicate the same hardware and software installations in a secondary location. Additionally, you had to purchase a public IP address, and pay an internet provider for the network bandwidth. And if your application's user base grew, scaling it out meant a lot of additional expenses and required months of planning.

You can see how even for a simple web application, the upfront capital investment required was cost prohibitive for most people and sometimes even organizations. The cost was high enough to prevent most potential entrepreneurs from giving their idea a try.

Luckily, this is not the world we live in anymore. When it comes to web and mobile applications, the financial barrier of entry has been reduced to near zero. By renting servers and outsourcing IT operations to public cloud providers, we are able to take advantage of the economy of scale like never before.

With serverless computing, as well as most PaaS services in the cloud, the pricing model is to pay only for what you use. These services often also offer a free tier sufficient for initial development and testing. This enables anyone with a good idea, technical acumen, and some free time to deploy an application. New applications can be made available to potential customers within, literally, minutes.

While incomparable to the costs of managing infrastructure, the cost of compute is non-negligible. Serverless compute offers, perhaps, the most direct correlation between the load and the price. While most PaaS services are billed on per node per minute model (with a node typically representing a VM instance), most vendors charge for serverless compute on per execution basis.

This is great news if your application is small or if your traffic ebbs and flows, but it might not be the best thing if you are consistently getting a lot of traffic. Luckily, Azure Functions offer more than one pricing model--the Consumption plan and the App Service plan. Each model is suitable for different types of workloads.

Azure Functions pricing

Azure Functions are available in the following two different pricing models:

- **Consumption plan**: This plan is allocated and scaled dynamically and priced per function execution.
- **App Service plan**: This plan is priced on per node per hour basis, and thus offers predictable pricing. This plan offers auto-scaling options, but isn't as dynamic as the Consumption plan.

In most cases, the Consumption plan will be significantly cheaper than the App Service plan. However, when dealing with continuously running functions, it is usually cheaper to run under the App Service plan. In addition to that, as discussed in previous chapters, certain features (such as no function execution time limit, no cold startup latency, and ability to integrate with private networks), are only available under the App Service plan.

For all of the services used in our text sentiment analysis application, the pricing model is to pay for what you use. Hence, the total cost of each service will depend on the user traffic load. In this chapter, we will calculate each service pricing as a function of the total number of user requests. To demonstrate how the pricing changes when the load increases, we will calculate the total service cost in the following three cases.

Number of user requests are as follows:

- 1,000 requests a day
- 10,000 requests a day
- 100,000 requests a day

 The specific prices quoted in this chapter may change in the future. It is best to confirm the most recent pricing information online, or with your organization's service representative.

Consumption plan

As mentioned earlier, the Consumption plan is priced based on the number of function executions and the execution time/consumed resources. This plan dynamically allocates resources based on the load.

Function's resource consumption is measured in gigabyte seconds, or GB-s, calculated by multiplying the average memory size (in GB) consumed by the function, by the time (in seconds) the function takes to execute. The maximum allowed memory per function is 1,536 MB. To learn more, please visit `https://azure.microsoft.com/en-us/pricing/details/functions/`.

The Consumption plan comes with a free grant of 1 M executions and 400,000 GB-s. The free grant is per Azure subscription (combined over all Function Apps in the subscription):

Meter	Price	Free Grant/Month
Execution time	$0.000016/GB-s	400,000 GB-s
Total executions	$0.20 per million executions	1 million executions

The Consumption plan pricing based on load

On average, the functions across our application consumed about 0.002 GB-s of memory per execution. This low memory consumption would fall within the free memory grant even over millions of executions. For the sake of the example, let's assume that our functions used 100 times more memory, 0.2 GB-s memory per execution.

Both 1,000 and 10,000 requests a day will fall within the free grant range, so we will start the calculation at 10,000 requests a day.

Price as a function of load:

10,000 requests a day

- Monthly: 10,000 * 31 = 310,000 executions
- Memory: 310,000 * 0.2 GB-s = 62,000 GB-s
- Pricing: falls within the free grant

100,000 requests a day

- Monthly: 100,000 * 31 = 3,100,000 executions.
- (3,100,000 - 1,000,000 executions) * $0.2 = $0.42
- Memory: 3,100,000 * 0.2 GB-s = 620,000 GB-s
- (620,000 - 400,000 GB-s) * $0.000016 = $3.52
- Pricing: $3.94/Month

App Service plan

The App Service plan lets you pre-allocate resources and makes your costs predictable. While auto-scaling is possible with App Service plan, it does not scale directly based on the request number, but rather based on metrics such as CPU or memory utilization. The App Service plan also has some instance allocation limits based on the pricing tier.

The pricing of the App Service is based on the tier and the number of instances. The Standard tier is recommended for most production applications, and we will, for simplicity, stick to Standard tier in the following estimate. (Note that Free, Shared, Basic and Premium tiers are also available. To view the features available in each tier, visit `https://azure.microsoft.com/en-us/pricing/details/app-service/plans`.

The summary of the Standard tier pricing is as follows:

Tier	Cores	RAM	Storage	Price/Month
S1 standard	1	1.75 GB	50 GB	~$74.40
S2 standard	2	3.50 GB	50 GB	~$148.80
S3 standard	4	7 GB	50 GB	~$297.60

Note that even with a single "instance," the high availability of the service is handled by the platform on all the tiers from Basic and up. The high availability is covered by a 99.95% SLA.

Also note that the prices are charged based on hourly use, so if the service only ran for a number of hours in a given month (for instance, if the number of instances was scaled up for a brief period of time), the total monthly price will reflect that.

For detailed information on the App Service pricing, visit `https://azure.microsoft.com/en-us/pricing/details/app-service/`.

The App Service plan pricing based on load

In the case of the App Service, the amount of compute power that we need depends on the load distribution. For instance, if all the load on our functions came during a single hour, the service would need to scale out to a large number of instances during that hour. It is best to run a load test on your application to determine the load distribution and the resource consumption of the application. We can, however, simplify the calculation by making some reasonable assumptions.

For 100,000 user requests a day, if we assume an even spread of traffic load around the clock, the load amounts to 100,000/(24*60*60) = 1.16 requests a second, which can be easily handled by a single instance (remember that the platform handles high availability even for a single instance). On the other hand, if the entire expected traffic load was likely to come within a few minutes, it would be easier and cheaper to deploy the application under the Consumption plan.

For the sake of the calculation, let's assume a somewhat even distribution of load, which would allow us to support 10,000 of user requests a day using a single instance of the Standard S1 tier, and 100,000 user requests a day using a single instance of the Standard S2 tier.

Price as a function of load:

> **1,000 or 10,000 requests a day**
>
>> Recommended tier: Standard S1, one instance
>>
>> Pricing: ~$75/Month
>
> **100,000 requests a day**
>
>> Recommended tier: Standard S2, one instance
>>
>> Pricing: ~$150/Month

The pricing difference with the Consumption plan seems striking, however, taking into account the additional features available in the App Service plan, it is required in certain cases.

The App Service plan will also be cheaper than the Consumption plan when deploying continuously running functions.

The overall application cost

It is unlikely for serverless compute, to be used as a completely standalone service to implement the entire functionality needed by an application. Hence, it is important to consider the pricing of other services used in conjunction with Azure Functions.

Even in our little text sentiment analysis application, there are quite a few different services involved. To gain a full picture of the application pricing, we need to price estimate those services as well.

Take a look at the following text sentiment analysis application architecture diagram and consider all the services used in the application:

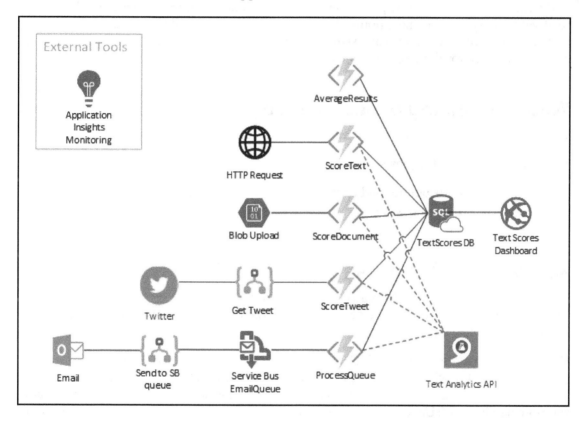

In this section, we will give a short overview of the pricing of services in the preceding diagram and calculate the overall application cost based on the total number of user requests.

Just as we did earlier, please note that the specific prices quoted in this chapter may change in the future. It is best to confirm the most recent pricing information online, or by contacting your organization's service representative.

Web Apps

Used in building the Web dashboard in `Chapter 3`, *Setting up the Development Environment*, and onward, Azure Web Apps are a part of App Service offering, and as such, are priced in the exact same manner explained earlier for the App Service plan.

In the case of a simple Web Apps, however, it is more likely that the load is spread relatively evenly over business hours and that a single request will not require a lot of memory resources. Hence, we can assume that a single instance of the Standard S1 tier will be sufficient even for the 100,000 requests a day.

Web App pricing based on load

Web App pricing can also be based on the load, as follows:

1,000, 10,000 or 100,000 requests a day:

- Recommended tier: Standard S1, one instance
- Pricing: ~$75

Azure SQL Database

Azure SQL Database is a PaaS database service and is priced per database per service tier. The performance tier is determined by **Database Transaction Units** (**DTUs**) and the maximum available size.

DTUs are a blended measure of CPU, memory, and IO. To get more details on the performance and specifics of each SQL Azure service tier, visit `https://docs.microsoft.com/en-us/azure/sql-database/sql-database-service-tiers#understanding-dtus`, and for more details on DTUs, visit `https://docs.microsoft.com/en-us/azure/sql-database/sql-database-what-is-a-dtu`.

The available service tiers are Basic, Standard, and Premium. Scaling between tiers requires a user action.

The Basic tier is best suited for development and test workloads, the Standard tier is suited for production applications, and the Premium tier is suited for IO-intensive workloads. The Premium RS tier is suited for IO intensive workloads for which lower SLA is acceptable (and comes with a significantly decreased price tag as compared to Premium).

Let's take a look at the brief tier summary in the following table:

Service tier	DTUs	Max storage	Price/Month
Basic	5	2 GB	~$5
Standard S0-S3	10 - 100	250 GB	~$15 - $150
Premium P1-P15	125 - 4,000	500 GB - 4 TB	~$465 - $16,000
Premium RS S1-S6	125 - 1,000	500 GB	~$116 - $930

Note that the pricing of the database is also charged on hourly basis, so if the database was scaled up or down after a period of time, the total price will reflect it.

The 99.99% SLA covers Basic, Standard, and Premium tiers (not Premium RS).

For more detailed and up-to-date information, visit `https://azure.microsoft.com/en-us/pricing/details/sql-database/`.

Azure SQL Database pricing based on load

To estimate the monthly and yearly growth of the database size, let's assume that a single user request generates the data growth of approximately 10 KB.

> If you want to calculate the approximate database size for your typical data, you can run the `sp_spaceused 'Tablename'` query on your SQL database to estimate the average row size of each SQL table.

Keep in mind that you do not have to reserve the highest needed tier for the whole year, as you can perform a zero-downtime scale up in minutes. If the database gets large over time, you could also explore archival storage for older transactions to save costs.

Price as a function of load:

1,000 requests a day

- Monthly growth: 1,000 * 31 * 10 KB = 310 MB, Yearly growth 3.72 GB
- Recommended tier: Standard S1
- Pricing: ~$15 a month

10,000 requests a day

- Monthly growth: 10,000 * 31 * 10 KB = 3.1 GB. Yearly growth 37.2 GB
- Recommended tier: up to Standard S1
- Pricing: ~$15 a month

100,000 requests a day

- Monthly growth - 100,000 * 31 * 10 KB= 31 GB. Yearly growth 372 GB
- Recommended tier: up to Premium P1

 For simplicity, we chose the Premium P1 pricing as a monthly cost. However, the database could be provisioned at a lower tier, and gradually scaled up as needed. This would lower the total monthly cost.

- Pricing: up to ~$465 a month

Azure Blob Storage

The pricing of Azure Blob Storage depends on the storage tier (hot or cool, where cool is intended for archival data only) and the redundancy option. The redundancy options were discussed in `Chapter 12`, *Designing for High Availability, Disaster Recovery, and Scale*. For a production application, it is recommended to use the hot **Geo-Redundant Storage** (**GRS**) tier, which provides inherent support for both HA and DR requirements.

For the hot GRS tier, the price of the data storage is as follows:

First 50 TB/Month	$0.0368/GB
Next 450 TB/Month	$0.0354/GB
Over 500 TB/Month	$0.0339/GB

The price of access operations is as follows:

Price per 10,000 operations	GRS-hot
Put Blob/block, list, and create container	$0.1
All other operations (except delete, which is free)	$0.004
Data retrieval and data write	0

Geo-replication data transfer/GB	$0.02

Storage is covered by 99.9% SLA.

For more detailed information and the most up-to-date pricing, visit `https://azure.microsoft.com/en-us/pricing/details/storage/blobs/`.

Azure Blob Storage pricing based on load

As you may have noticed, storage is very cheap compared to other services, so instead of extrapolating growth over time, we can simply do our calculations based on the maximum expected size. Dealing with text files, it is unlikely that we will ever exceed even a 100 GB of storage.

In terms of access operations, it is important to note that when uploading block Blobs larger than 32 MB, the API will break them down into 32 MB blocks, and each block will count as a separate transaction. This is, again, unlikely to happen in the case of uploading text files, which tend to be smaller than 32 MB. Hence, we can count each upload as a single transaction. The price of 10,000 upload transactions is $0.1.

Let's estimate the highest, 100,000 request a day use case, and assume that 100 GB of storage is already in use. This will give us an estimate of the "ceiling" on our monthly storage cost.

Price as a function of load:

100,000 requests a day

- Storage: 100 GB * $0.0368 = $3.68
- Geo-Replication: 100 GB* $0.02 = $2
- Upload transactions (per 10,000): 10 * $0.1 = $1
- Pricing: $6.68/Month

Azure Logic Apps

Azure Logic Apps are billed per action execution. An **action** is defined as any of the steps of the workflow. The pricing is ladder based, meaning that the price per action gets lower as the volume of actions increases.

Take a look at the following Logic Apps pricing summary:

Actions Executed/Month	Price Per Execution
First 250,000 actions	$0.0008/action
250,000 to 1 M actions	$0.0004/action
1 M to 50 M actions	$0.00015/action
50 M to 100 M actions	$0.00009/action
Over 100 M actions	$0.000054/action

Logic Apps are covered by a 99.9% SLA.

For Enterprise Agreement customers, certain amounts of Logic App actions are included in App Service pricing.

For more detailed and up-to-date pricing information, visit `https://azure.microsoft.com/en-us/pricing/details/logic-apps/`.

Azure Logic App pricing based on load

Both of the Logic Apps we have used in the text sentiment analysis application consisted of only two steps -- the trigger, and the following action. Hence, we will do the calculation for a 2-action Logic App.

Price as a function of load:

1,000 requests a day

- Monthly: 1,000 * 31 * 2 actions = 62,000 actions priced at $0.0008 an action
- Pricing: ~$50/month

10,000 requests a day

This time, we jump a step on the pricing ladder after 250,000 actions, hence we have the following:

- Monthly: 10,000 * 31 * 2 actions = 620,000 actions = 250,000 actions * $0.0008 + 370,000 actions * $0.0004 = $148.08
- Pricing: ~$150/month

100,000 requests a day

This time, we jump a step on the pricing ladder after 250,000 actions, and after 750,000 actions, and hence we have the following:

- Monthly: 100,000 * 31 * 2 actions = 6,200,000 actions = 250,000 actions * $0.0008 + 750,000 actions * $0.0004 + 5,200,000 actions * $0.00015 = $780.04
- Pricing: ~$780/month

Azure Service Bus

Azure Service Bus is offered in three service tiers, with different features available in each tier. The pricing is per tier per operation, where an operation is any API call to the Service Bus service.

- The **Basic tier** is priced at $0.05 per million operations.
- The **Standard tier** supports more features than the Basic tier. Standard tier has a basic charge of $10 a month, plus a "ladder" structure of price per million of operations.
- The **Premium tier** has dedicated CPU and Memory resources. Since the resources are dedicated, the Premium tier is priced at $22.26 per compute container per day.

For the purposes of our calculation, we will stick to Basic tier pricing.

All service tiers are covered by a 99.9% SLA.

For more detailed and up-to-date pricing information, visit `https://azure.microsoft.com/en-us/pricing/details/service-bus/`.

Azure Service Bus pricing based on load

Each user request in our case counts as two operations, a send and a receive of the Service Bus message. The pricing of the Basic tier is $0.05 per million operations. Since both 1,000 and 10,000 requests a day generate less than a million operations, we will start the calculation at 10,000 requests a day.

Price as a function of load:

10,000 requests a day

- Monthly: 10,000 * 31 * 2 = 620,000 operations (less than 1 million operations)
- Pricing: $0.05

100,000 requests a day

- Monthly: 100,000 * 31 * 2 operations= 6,200,000 operations
- Pricing: $0.35

The Text Analytics API

The Text Analytics API is priced based on tier, each tier allowing a certain number of transactions a month. At the time of this writing, there is a preview discount of 50% on the API pricing.

Service tier	Maximum transactions	Price/Month	Overage rate per 1,000 transactions
Free	5,000	$0	N/A
Standard S1	100,000	$150	$1.5
Standard S2	500,000	$500	$1
Standard S3	2,500,000	$1,250	$0.5
Standard S4	10,000,000	$2,500	$0.25

Text Analytics API pricing based on load

The Text Analytics API pricing can also be based on the load, as follows:

1000 requests a day

- Monthly: 1000 * 31 = 31,000 transactions.
- Recommended tier: Standard S1
- Pricing: $150

10,000 requests a day

- Monthly: 10,000 * 31 = 310,000 transactions.
- Recommended tier: Standard S2
- Pricing: $500

100,000 requests a day

- Monthly: 100,000 * 31 = 3,100,000 transactions.
- Recommended tier: Standard S4
- Pricing: $2,500

Network bandwidth

The **ingress** (incoming) network traffic into Azure is always free however, a small charge applies to the **egress** (outgoing) network traffic. In the application developed in this book, all of the data transfers are inbound, and fall under the free ingress traffic.

For some applications, however, especially those that involve downloading large files from the cloud (such as large video files download), the aggregated egress charges may become significant. To review the structure and pricing of the egress bandwidth, visit `https://azure.microsoft.com/en-us/pricing/details/bandwidth/`.

For our text sentiment analysis application, thus, the network bandwidth will be free of charge.

Application Insights

Application Insights come in the following two pricing models:

- **Basic**. This model is priced based on the amount of data produced by the application
- **Enterprise**. This model pricing is priced per "node" (an instance of the deployed application)

The following calculations are made under the basic pricing model.

Under the basic pricing model, 1 GB of data per month is included for free and each additional GB of data is priced at $2.30. Data retention for 90 days is free and data export is priced at 50 cents per GB after the first GB. In addition, multi-step web tests are priced at $10 per test per month.

We can explore the data usage of the `TextEvaluation` application by going to the Application Insights resource and clicking on the **Data Volume Management** tab. Based on prior usage of the application, we can estimate that Application Insights collected roughly 0.5 GB data per 10,000 function executions (of course, the amount of data will be highly dependent on your application).

Note that exceptions generate a larger data volume. The preceding data estimate assumes 10,000 successful executions.

Application Insights pricing based on load

Price as a function of load:

1000 requests a day

- 1000 * 31 = 31,000 executions = 3.1 * 0.5 GB = ~1.55 GB
- Pricing: $1.26

10,000 requests a day

- 10,000 * 31 = 31 * 0.5 GB = ~15.5 GB
- Pricing: $33

100,000 requests a day

- 100,000 * 31 = 310 * 0.5 GB = 155 GB
- Pricing: $354

Note that if your application generates a lot of data, you can limit the cost of Application Insights by setting a daily volume cap. You can set the data cap by navigating to **Application Insights -> Features and Pricing -> Daily Cap**.

For more details and up-to-date information on pricing, visit `https://azure.microsoft.com/en-us/pricing/details/application-insights/`.

Visual Studio Team Services

Visual Studio Team Services (**VSTS**) is free for small teams (under five users), but may charge additional usage prices for features such as the Build and Release pipeline and cloud-based load testing.

This chapter will assume that the continuous delivery needs of our serverless application fit within the VSTS free grants.

To review VSTS pricing in detail, visit `https://azure.microsoft.com/en-us/pricing/details/visual-studio-team-services/`.

Calculating the overall applications costs

Any calculations we make here are theoretical and the best way to learn the real behavior and the scale needs of your application is through performing load testing and by monitoring and analyzing production. For the initial budgeting purposes, however, we need to make assumptions that will allow us to estimate the ballpark costs.

First, let's take a look at each one of the services used in our application, looking at pricing as a function of load perspective. This gives us an overall sense of what each component of the application will cost and a sense of whether or not it is cost-effective in an overall architecture. For instance, if the Logic App becomes the costliest component of the application, maybe it is best to move its functionality into Azure Functions and pay the price of custom code development once, rather than paying a higher price for convenience on every execution.

Note that we are not providing a sum total, because the price of the entire application is not a straightforward sum of the prices of all services. We will calculate the application price estimate next.

The prices have been rounded up to the nearest dollar.

Take a look at the price summary table:

Requests/day	1,000	10,000	100,000
App Service plan	$75	$75	$150
Consumption plan	$0	$0	$4
Web App	$75	$75	$75
SQL Database	$15	$15	$465
Blob Storage	$7	$7	$7
Logic App	$0	$150	$780
Service Bus	$1	$1	$1
The Text Analytics API	$150	$500	$2,500
Bandwidth	$0	$0	$0
Application Insights	$1	$33	$354

Estimating the total application pricing depends on the load distribution between components. For instance, if each of the four functions we've built gets equal load and each stores the results in the database, the database will get a four times the function load.

To show an example calculation, let's assume a certain load on each end point (we are removing the `ScoreText` and `AverageResults` functions from the application since they were introduced mostly for example purposes).

We will pick the Consumption plan for Functions, as it is significantly cheaper and suits our needs. We are also providing only the final prices here, as the calculations would be the same as in previous examples.

Take a look at the following diagram, representing a potential production deployment of our text sentiment analysis application:

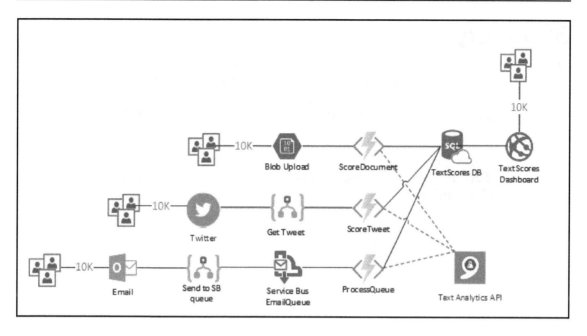

Monthly cost estimate:

- Functions: 30,000 requests = $12
- SQL Database: 30,000 requests = $15
- Text Analytics API: 30,000 requests = $1250
- Logic Apps: 20,000 requests = $300
- Service Bus: 10,000 requests = $1
- Blob Storage: 10,000 requests = $7
- Web App: 10,000 requests = $75
- Application Insights 40,000 requests = $44 *

The total monthly cost of the application is $1,704, of which, notably, only $12 are going to the serverless compute.

* Application Insights are getting the total of 40,000 requests, assuming that both the Functions and the Web Apps are logging telemetry to the Application Insights resource.

Summary

In this final chapter, we discussed the pricing of Azure Functions and learned how to estimate the cost of serverless computing in Azure. We also reviewed the pricing of the other PaaS services used in the `TextEvaluation` application as a function of expected user traffic load. Finally, we have estimated the total expected price of the application's deployment.

In the book's appendixes, we will discuss Azure C# script-based functions and the comparison of Azure Functions to other types of Azure "compute-as-a-service" offers, such as Azure WebJobs and Azure Batch.

C# Script-Based Functions

In this appendix, we will discuss C# script-based functions. The C# script-based functions are still available in Functions Portal, albeit they are not as popular as precompiled functions. If you are working with C# script-based functions, you will need to consider the slight differences in implementation in comparison to precompiled functions, or any traditional .NET application.

In this appendix, we will cover the implementation of the following tasks in C# script-based functions:

- Using NuGet libraries
- Sharing code between functions

C# script-based functions

C# script-based functions are functions based on the `.csx` files, which can be deployed in the Functions Portal, but not using Visual Studio. The `.csx` files allow for writing C# script code. C# script allows you to define methods that aren't inside a class. At compilation time, the code is compiled into an overarching class. To learn more about C# script-based functions, please visit `https://docs.microsoft.com/en-us/azure/azure-functions/functions-reference-csharp`.

If you are working with C# script-based functions, you will notice a few differences from the precompiled functions.

C# script-based functions do not have attributes in the function's signature. All of the required bindings are defined directly in the `function.json` file.

As an example, we can look at our first `HelloWorld` function that we have created in `Chapter 2`, *Getting Started with the Azure Environment*. This was an HTTP-triggered C# script-based function. The function's signature in the `run.csx` file looked like the following:

```
using System.Net;
public static async Task<HttpResponseMessage>
Run(HttpRequestMessage req, TraceWriter log)
```

And the `function.json` looked like the following:

```json
{
    "bindings": [
    {
      "authLevel": "anonymous",
      "name": "req",
      "type": "httpTrigger",
      "direction": "in"
    },
    {
      "name": "return",
      "type": "http",
      "direction": "out"
    }
    ],
    "disabled": false
}
```

The two main differences between C# script-based functions and precompiled functions come into play when working on the following tasks:

- Using NuGet libraries
- Sharing code between functions

Let us review the implementation details specific to C# script-based functions.

Using NuGet libraries

Most .NET developers make heavy use of the NuGet packages repository to leverage libraries implemented by Microsoft and third-party providers. The process of adding dependencies on external libraries in C# script-based functions is different from a traditional .NET application.

There are the following two ways to reference an external assembly in a C# script-based function:

- Using an #r directive
- Adding a reference in the project.json file

Let us explore both options in more detail.

Option 1 - the #r directive

To reference **framework assemblies** and a number of other commonly used assemblies, you can use the #r AssemblyName directive.

For instance, a Newtonsoft.Json library that we have used in the ScoreTweet function is one of the common libraries that can be referenced with an #r directive. If we were to deploy ScoreTweet as a C# script-based function, we would need to add the following line before the function code:

```
#r "Newtonsoft.Json"
```

The full function code using the #r directive will be provided in the *Sharing code between functions* section later in this chapter.

When using a **privately developed assembly**, you may add the assembly to your function's bin directory, and then reference it by using the full file name, like the following:

```
#r "MyAssembly.dll"
```

Certain assemblies, such as System or System.Linq, are **automatically imported** into the C# script-based functions, and do not require a #r directive. To see the full list of framework assemblies available in script-based functions, visit https://docs.microsoft.com/en-us/azure/azure-functions/fun ctions-reference-csharp.

Option 2 - the project.json file

To add other NuGet packages to the Function App, we need to reference them in the project.json file. Let us show a step-by-step example of how to configure such a reference.

Let us create a script-based version of our `ProcessQueue` function, and add a reference to the NuGet library called `HtmlAgilityPack`. To do so, execute the following steps:

1. Browse to your Function App.
2. Click on **Functions** -> **Add** -> **ServiceBusQueueTrigger - C#**.
3. Choose `ProcessQueueScript` in the new function's name, and choose the same Service Bus connection and queue that we've used in `Chapter 5`, *Integrations and Dependencies*.

4. Paste the following code into the function's `run.csx` file:

```
using System;
using System.Threading.Tasks;
using HtmlAgilityPack;
public static async Task Run(string emailBody, TraceWriter log)
{
    var doc = new HtmlDocument();
    doc.LoadHtml(emailBody);
    var text = doc.DocumentNode.InnerText;
    log.Info($"Message: {text}");
}
```

5. Create a new `project.json` file on your computer and paste the following code into it:

```
{
    "frameworks": {
      "net46": {
        "dependencies": {
          "HtmlAgilityPack": "1.4.9.5"
        }
      }
    }
}
```

6. Browse to the `ProcessQueueScript` function -> **View Files** -> **Add**. The `project.json` file should be created in the `ProcessQueueScript` function folder, at the same level as `run.csx`.
7. Run the function.
8. The Functions Runtime will restore the `HtmlAgilityPack` NuGet package.

You will now be able to use the `HtmlAgilityPack` NuGet library in the function code.

Sharing code between functions

In a C# script-based Function App, adding a new file to one of the functions will not make it available to other functions in the application.

To share code between functions, we will need to do the following two things:

- Create a folder named Shared at the root level of a Function App, and add shared code files to this folder. The WebJobs SDK (that Azure Functions are based on) watches for any code changes in the Shared folder and makes sure that the changes are picked up by the functions.
- Create #load directives to the specific location of the shared files in each function that references the shared code.

 You can add other folders to the function's watch list by modifying the watchDirectories setting of the WebJobs host here at https://github. com/Azure/azure-webjobs-sdk-script/wiki/host.json.

To show an example of the process, we will create a C# script-based version of the ScoreTweet function.

To share code between C# script-based functions in the same Function App, execute the following steps:

1. Browse to Azure Portal.
2. In your Function App, click on **Functions** -> **New** -> **Generic Webhook - C#**.
3. Name the function ScoreTweetScript.
4. Browse to **Functions portal** -> **Platform features** -> **Development Tools** -> **App Service Editor**. A Visual Studio Online editor will open.
5. At the WWWROOT level, click on **New** folder.
6. Name the folder Shared. The folder must be created at the same root level as the host.json file.
7. Add a new file named EvaluateText.csx in the Shared folder.
8. Add the following code to the EvaluateText.csx file (this is the same code we have used in precompiled functions in Chapter 5, *Integrations and Dependencies*):

```
using System;
public class EvaluateText
{
    public double ScoreTextSentiment(string text)
```

```
    {
        // Generate random text score between 0 and 1
        double score = new Random().NextDouble();
        return score;
    }
}
```

9. To reference the code in the `ScoreTweetScript` function, we will need to add a `#load` directive specifying the file location inside the `Shared` folder. Modify the `run.csx` file of the `ScoreTweetScript` function to look like the following:

```
#r "Newtonsoft.Json"
#load "..\Shared\EvaluateText.csx"
using System;
using System.Net;
using Newtonsoft.Json;
using System.Threading.Tasks;

public static async Task Run
(HttpRequestMessage req, TraceWriter log)
{
    string jsonContent = await req.Content.ReadAsStringAsync();
    dynamic data = JsonConvert.DeserializeObject(jsonContent);
    var tweetText = data.TweetText.ToString();
    var user = data.UserDetails.UserName.ToString();

    //Call shared code to score the tweet text
    var score = new EvaluateText().ScoreTextSentiment(tweetText);
    log.Info($"Scored tweet: {tweetText}, " +
        $"user: {user}, sentiment score: {score}");
}
```

Now you can share the code in `EvaluateText.csx` with any other functions added to the same Function App.

Summary

In this appendix, we have reviewed C# script-based functions, and discussed the two main implementation differences between script-based and precompiled functions.

In the next appendix, we will review the alternative Azure compute on-demand options, and how they compare to Azure Functions.

B

Azure Compute On-Demand Options

In this appendix, we will discuss additional Azure services that provide compute on-demand capabilities. We will briefly outline each service's main features and its comparison to Azure Functions. We will also review the workloads that are best suited for each service. We will provide this overview for the following services:

- Azure WebJobs
- Azure Logic Apps
- Azure Batch
- Azure PaaS Cloud Services (Worker Roles)

Compute on-demand

In addition to Azure Functions, Azure offers a number of other "compute on-demand" options, which allow you to run your compute operations without the need to manage the infrastructure. Depending on the exact definition of serverless compute that you prefer, some or all of the services that we will discuss in this appendix can also be considered serverless.

In the following sections, we will provide a high-level overview of the Azure services offering compute on-demand, their key differences from Azure Functions, and what types of workloads are best suited for each service.

Azure WebJobs

Azure WebJobs are a part of Azure App Service, and run in the same compute "container" as your Web App, at no additional cost. WebJobs are intended to run background tasks for your Azure Web, API, or Mobile apps without the need to provision infrastructure.

The WebJobs SDK provides built-in integrations with commonly used services such as Azure Storage or Azure Service Bus, and it is extensible. WebJobs can be deployed to an Azure Web App without an actual Web frontend. With this approach, WebJobs can be used to run any scheduled or continuously executing background jobs.

WebJobs can run programs (`.exe`, `.cmd`, `.jar`, and more) or scripts (`.ps1`, `.sh`, `.js`, and more). A typical job is implemented as a console application or a script.

WebJobs can be triggered in the following three ways:

- **On-demand**: This type of job can be triggered from the Azure Portal.
- **Continuously**: This type of job will execute continuously, but it can be started or stopped from the Azure Portal.
- **On schedule**: This type of job will execute on a schedule governed by a CRON expression. The schedule is defined in the `settings.job` file placed in the root of your WebJob ZIP file.

WebJobs can scale to run on every instance used by your Web App, or can be configured to run on a single instance only. WebJobs can be configured to auto-scale with the Web App, but they do not scale as dynamically as Azure Functions under the Consumption Plan.

Although WebJobs can implement much of the functionality similar to Azure Functions, they are not aimed at executing externally triggered, dynamically scalable compute on-demand. Rather, WebJobs are aimed at executing background tasks tied to a particular web application, such as queue processing or sending emails.

To learn more about Azure WebJobs, visit `https://docs.microsoft.com/en-us/azure/app-service-web/websites-webjobs-resources`.

Azure Logic Apps

You are already familiar with Azure Logic Apps since we have previously used them in `Chapter 5`, *Integrations and Dependencies*.

Similar to Azure Functions, Logic Apps are triggered by external events and scale dynamically to meet demand. Unlike Functions, however, Logic Apps focus on allowing you to construct the execution flow from pre-defined building blocks. With hundreds of existing triggers and action steps, Logic Apps are an amazing tool for execution of common workflows.

The main difference between Functions and Logic Apps is the ability to write custom code to implement your execution flow.

The following table provides a quick outline of feature comparison:

_	Logic Apps	Functions
Custom code and triggers	No custom code, triggers, or action steps*	Based on custom code
Developer experience	Not required	Required
Code maintenance	Not required	Required
Private network deployment	Not possible	Possible
Dedicated resources deployment	Not possible	Possible (with the App Service Plan)
Time to market	Ultra-fast	Very fast
Pricing per execution	Higher	Lower (the Consumption Plan)

* Some code customization is actually possible, however, this is not the intended usage.

The choice between Logic Apps and Functions is not an either/or, and both services can be used in tandem in your application to fulfill different types of needs.

Azure Batch

Azure Batch is a compute on-demand service best suited for running intrinsically parallel, **high-performance computing (HPC)** workloads.

Intrinsically parallel workloads are the workloads that can easily split into multiple tasks performed simultaneously on many servers. Common examples include financial risk modelling, image processing, or genetic sequence analysis.

These workloads typically require very long processing times or large amounts of compute power. Hence, they can benefit tremendously from HPC, where parallel processing by multiple servers is used to run the application more efficiently and quickly.

With Azure Batch, you define the compute resources you need to execute your compute workloads without the need to provision, configure, and manage the infrastructure and networking. With Batch, you need to specify the OS, the node (instance) size, the target number of nodes to run on, and the scaling policy.

As you can see, Functions and Batch stand on the opposite ends of the compute on-demand continuum. Functions are suited for fast-paced, externally triggered, dynamically scaling operations, and Batch is suited for long-running, compute-heavy, and complex tasks.

As with other services, Functions and Batch can work in tandem in the same application, serving different compute needs.

To learn more about Azure Batch, visit `https://docs.microsoft.com/en-us/azure/batch/batch-technical-overview`.

Azure PaaS Cloud Services

Azure PaaS Cloud Services are a part of the older Azure Service Manager API. Cloud services were the first Azure PaaS Service released by Microsoft.

PaaS Cloud Services consist of Web Roles, which are designed to host Web applications in IIS, and Worker Roles, which are designed for running the backend processing jobs.

Like with any PaaS offering, you do not need to manage the infrastructure or ensure high availability. You can configure the instance size and the number of instances you need deployed, and the platform will handle the provisioning.

Unlike the App Service, PaaS Cloud Services offer you limited admin access to the VMs and allow you to install custom software by running startup scripts. The underlying infrastructure, however, isn't persistent, and a particular role instance could be re-provisioned at any time. This means that installing additional software on the underlying VMs manually will not be persisted, and also that running very long startup scripts will impact your application performance if a new instance is provisioned. Still, this allows for implementation of certain scenarios that require admin VM access in a PaaS environment.

PaaS Worker Roles can be deployed without any accompanying Web Roles, and can be utilized to run background jobs. Worker Roles essentially run a continuous polling job that checks for external events, such as messages being dropped in a queue. When a new message is received, it is picked up and processed by one of the instances of the Worker Role. If there are no new messages, the thread sleeps for a defined period of time. The job triggering and message dequeuing processes are handled in your application code. Using a worker role is very similar to running a background job on a VM, with only the instance provisioning being taken care of by the platform.

Although Azure PaaS Cloud Services are still available and aren't retiring any time soon, it is recommended to deploy new workloads on one of the newer platform services. To learn more about PaaS Cloud Services, visit `https://docs.microsoft.com/en-us/azure/cloud-services/cloud-services-choose-me`.

Summary

In this appendix, we gave a brief overview of additional Azure services that provide compute on-demand capabilities, and discussed the different workload types that are best suited for each one.

This concludes the serverless compute in .NET with Azure book.

Thank you for dedicating the time to reading this book!

Enjoy the world of serverless compute!

Index

Hands-On Neural Networks with Keras

Design and create neural networks using deep learning and artificial intelligence principles

Niloy Purkait

BIRMINGHAM - MUMBAI

Hands-On Neural Networks with Keras

Commissioning Editor: Sunith Shetty
Acquisition Editor: Devika Battike
Content Development Editor: Unnati Guha
Technical Editor: Sayli Nikalje
Copy Editor: Safis Editing
Project Coordinator: Manthan Patel
Proofreader: Safis Editing
Indexer: Rekha Nair
Graphics: Jisha Chirayil
Production Coordinator: Jyoti Chauhan

First published: March 2019

Production reference: 1300319

Published by Packt Publishing Ltd.
Livery Place
35 Livery Street
Birmingham
B3 2PB, UK.

ISBN 978-1-78953-608-9

www.packtpub.com

`mapt.io`

Mapt is an online digital library that gives you full access to over 5,000 books and videos, as well as industry leading tools to help you plan your personal development and advance your career. For more information, please visit our website.

Why subscribe?

- Spend less time learning and more time coding with practical eBooks and Videos from over 4,000 industry professionals

- Improve your learning with Skill Plans built especially for you

- Get a free eBook or video every month

- Mapt is fully searchable

- Copy and paste, print, and bookmark content

Packt.com

Did you know that Packt offers eBook versions of every book published, with PDF and ePub files available? You can upgrade to the eBook version at `www.packt.com` and as a print book customer, you are entitled to a discount on the eBook copy. Get in touch with us at `customercare@packtpub.com` for more details.

At `www.packt.com`, you can also read a collection of free technical articles, sign up for a range of free newsletters, and receive exclusive discounts and offers on Packt books and eBooks.

Contributors

About the author

Niloy Purkait is a technology and strategy consultant by profession. He currently resides in the Netherlands, where he offers his consulting services to local and international companies alike. He specializes in integrated solutions involving artificial intelligence, and takes pride in navigating his clients through dynamic and disruptive business environments.

He has a masters in Strategic Management from Tilburg University, and a full specialization in data science from Michigan University. He has advanced industry grade certifications from IBM, in subjects like signal processing, cloud computing, machine and deep learning. He is also perusing advanced academic degrees in several related fields, and is a self-proclaimed lifelong learner.

I would like to thank the academic researchers, software developers, and the open source community at large for making this work possible and my friends and family who supported me over many tireless nights of research. Also my parents, Hir and Rupa for their love, encouragement, and willingness to read nonsensical drafts. Thanks Cleo, for your patience and loving support in dealing with a geeky and passionate technology enthusiast.

About the reviewer

Mayur Ravindra Narkhede has a good blend of experience in data science and the industrial domain. He is a researcher with a B.Tech in computer science and an M.Tech in computer science and engineering, with a specialization in artificial intelligence.

A data scientist whose core experience lies in building automated end-to-end solutions, he is proficient at applying technology, artificial intelligence, machine learning, data mining, and design-thinking to help identify and achieve avenues for business growth.

He has worked on multiple advanced solutions, including ones to do with machine learning and predictive model development for the oil and gas industry, financial services, road traffic and transport, and life sciences; and big data platforms for asset-intensive industries.

Packt is searching for authors like you

If you're interested in becoming an author for Packt, please visit authors.packtpub.com and apply today. We have worked with thousands of developers and tech professionals, just like you, to help them share their insight with the global tech community. You can make a general application, apply for a specific hot topic that we are recruiting an author for, or submit your own idea.

Table of Contents

Section 2: Advanced Neural Network Architectures

Chapter 4: Convolutional Neural Networks

Preface

A neural network is a mathematical function that is used to solve a wide range of problems in different areas of **Artificial Intelligence** (**AI**) and deep learning. *Hands-On Neural Networks with Keras* will start by giving you an understanding of the core concepts of neural networks. You will delve into combining different neural network models and work with real-world use cases, to better understand the value of predictive modelling and function approximation. Moving ahead, you will become well versed with an assortment of the most prominent architectures. These include, but are not limited to, **Convolutional Neural Networks** (**CNNs**), **recurrent neural networks** (**RNNs**), **Long Short-Term Memory** (**LSTM**) networks, **autoencoders**, and **Generative Adversarial Networks** (**GANs**) using real-world training datasets.

We will explore the fundamental ideas and implementational details behind cognitive tasks like computer vision and **natural language processing** (**NLP**), using state of the art neural network architectures. We will learn how to combine these tasks to design more powerful inference systems that can drastically improve productivity in various personal and commercial settings. The book takes a theoretical and technical perspective required to develop an intuitive understanding of the inner workings of neural nets. It will address various common use cases, ranging from supervised, unsupervised, an self-supervised learning tasks. Throughout the course of this book, you will learn to use a variety of network architectures, including CNNs for image recognition, LSTMs for natural language processing, Q-networks for reinforcement learning, and many more. We will dive into these specific architectures and then implement each of them in a hands-on manner, using industry-grade frameworks.

By the end of this book, you will be highly familiar with all prominent deep learning models, and frameworks, as well as all the options you have to initiate a successful transition to applying deep learning to real-world scenarios, embedding AI as the core fabric of your organization.

Who this book is for

This book is for **machine learning** (**ML**) practitioners, deep learning researchers, and AI enthusiasts who are looking to become well versed with different neural network architectures using Keras. A working knowledge of the Python programming language is mandatory.

What this book covers

Chapter 1, *Overview of Neural Networks*, describes how to think intuitively about the fundamental nature, structure, and different forms of data. You will learn how to deal with basic data types, advanced data structures (image, video, audio, text, sensor, and multimedia data), and learn the underlying abstractions of extracting information from these varying data structures.

Chapter 2, *A Deeper Dive into Neural Networks*, takes an in-depth look at the mathematical background of neural networks. Then, you will explore how being a Keras user can make you more productive and outperform the competition, by means of rapid development cycles that iteratively improve your machine learning project outcomes.

Chapter 3, *Signal Processing - Data Analysis with Neural Networks*, covers how to become familiarized with the necessary types of transformations and normalizations essential to make neural networks work well with complete hands-on examples.

Chapter 4, *Convolutional Neural Networks*, provides an overview of different types of convolutional and pooling layers that may be used in neural networks used to process sensory input from images on your laptop to databases and real-time **Internet of Things (IoT)** applications. You will then gain information about processing pipelines associated with CNNs, and experiment with the latest object detection APIs and models available.

Chapter 5, *Recurrent Neural Networks*, focuses deeper on the theory behind different types of recurrent networks and what it means to be a Turing-complete algorithm.

Chapter 6, *Long Short-Term Memory Networks*, helps you to explore in detail a specific type of RNN known as LSTM networks, and understand yet another neural network architecture that was inspired by our own biology.

Chapter 7, *Reinforcement Learning with Deep Q-Networks*, begins with explaining the underlying architectures of reinforcement learning networks in detail and explains how to implement core and extended layers in Keras for desired outcomes

Chapter 8, *Autoencoders*, provides in-depth knowledge and ideas regarding the functioning of autoencoder neural networks.

Chapter 9, *Generative Networks*, addresses the use case of synthetic data generation and manipulation, commonly achieved through generative models like variational autoencoders and GANs.

`Chapter 10`, *Contemplating Present and Future Developments*, covers the topics of learning and transferring representations using neural networks. It also includes an overview of potential future developments to look out for in the field of AI, including paradigms like quantum computing.

To get the most out of this book

Having some prior knowledge of Python will be beneficial.

Download the example code files

You can download the example code files for this book from your account at `www.packt.com`. If you purchased this book elsewhere, you can visit `www.packt.com/support` and register to have the files emailed directly to you.

You can download the code files by following these steps:

1. Log in or register at `www.packt.com`.
2. Select the **SUPPORT** tab.
3. Click on **Code Downloads & Errata**.
4. Enter the name of the book in the **Search** box and follow the onscreen instructions.

Once the file is downloaded, please make sure that you unzip or extract the folder using the latest version of:

- WinRAR/7-Zip for Windows
- Zipeg/iZip/UnRarX for Mac
- 7-Zip/PeaZip for Linux

The code bundle for the book is also hosted on GitHub at `https://github.com/PacktPublishing/Hands-On-Neural-Networks-with-Keras`. In case there's an update to the code, it will be updated on the existing GitHub repository.

We also have other code bundles from our rich catalog of books and videos available at `https://github.com/PacktPublishing/`. Check them out!

Download the color images

We also provide a PDF file that has color images of the screenshots/diagrams used in this book. You can download it here: `https://www.packtpub.com/sites/default/files/downloads/9781789536089_ColorImages.pdf`.

Conventions used

There are a number of text conventions used throughout this book.

`CodeInText`: Indicates code words in text, database table names, folder names, filenames, file extensions, pathnames, dummy URLs, user input, and Twitter handles. Here is an example: "This refers to the type of data that's stored in the tensor, and can be checked by calling the `type()` method on a tensor of interest."

A block of code is set as follows:

```
import numpy as np
import keras
from keras.datasets import mnist
from keras.utils import np_utils
```

When we wish to draw your attention to a particular part of a code block, the relevant lines or items are set in bold:

```
keras.utils.print_summary(model, line_length=None, positions=None,
                          print_fn=None)
```

Any command-line input or output is written as follows:

```
! pip install keras-vis
```

Bold: Indicates a new term, an important word, or words that you see on screen.

Warnings or important notes appear like this.

Tips and tricks appear like this.

Get in touch

Feedback from our readers is always welcome.

General feedback: If you have questions about any aspect of this book, mention the book title in the subject of your message and email us at customercare@packtpub.com.

Errata: Although we have taken every care to ensure the accuracy of our content, mistakes do happen. If you have found a mistake in this book, we would be grateful if you would report this to us. Please visit www.packt.com/submit-errata, selecting your book, clicking on the Errata Submission Form link, and entering the details.

Piracy: If you come across any illegal copies of our works in any form on the internet, we would be grateful if you would provide us with the location address or website name. Please contact us at copyright@packt.com with a link to the material.

If you are interested in becoming an author: If there is a topic that you have expertise in, and you are interested in either writing or contributing to a book, please visit authors.packtpub.com.

Reviews

Please leave a review. Once you have read and used this book, why not leave a review on the site that you purchased it from? Potential readers can then see and use your unbiased opinion to make purchase decisions, we at Packt can understand what you think about our products, and our authors can see your feedback on their book. Thank you!

For more information about Packt, please visit packt.com.

Section 1: Fundamentals of Neural Networks

This section familiarizes the reader with the basics of operating neural networks, how to select appropriate data, normalize features, and execute a data processing pipeline from scratch. Readers will learn how to pair ideal hyperparameters with appropriate activation, loss functions, and optimizers. Once completed, readers will have experienced working with real-world data to architect and test deep learning models on the most prominent frameworks.

This section comprises the following chapters:

- Chapter 1, *Overview of Neural Networks*
- Chapter 2, *Deeper Dive into Neural Networks*
- Chapter 3, *Signal Processing – Data Analysis with Neural Networks*

Overview of Neural Networks

1

Greetings to you, fellow sentient being; welcome to our exciting journey. The journey itself is to understand the concepts and inner workings behind an elusively powerful computing paradigm: the **artificial neural network** (**ANN**). While this notion has been around for almost half a century, the ideas accredited to its birth (such as *what an agent is*, or *how an agent may learn from its surroundings*), date back to Aristotelian times, and perhaps even to the dawn of civilization itself. Unfortunately, people in the time of Aristotle were not blessed with the ubiquity of big data, or the speeds of **Graphical Processing Unit** (**GPU**)-accelerated and massively parallelized computing, which today open up some very promising avenues for us. We now live in an era where the majority of our species has access to the building blocks and tools required to assemble artificially-intelligent systems. While covering the entire developmental timeline that brings us here today is slightly beyond the scope of this book, we will attempt to briefly summarize some pivotal concepts and ideas that will help us think intuitively about our problem here.

In this chapter, we will cover the following topics:

- Defining our goal
- Knowing our tools
- Understanding neural networks
- Observing the brain
- Information modeling and functional representations
- Some fundamental refreshers in data science

Defining our goal

Essentially, our task here is to conceive a mechanism that is capable of dealing with any data that it is introduced to. In doing so, we want this mechanism to detect any underlying patterns present in our data, in order to leverage it for our own benefit. Succeeding at this task means that we will be able to translate any form of raw data into knowledge, in the form of actionable business insights, burden-alleviating services, or life-saving medicines. Hence, what we actually want is to construct a mechanism that is capable of universally approximating any possible function that could represent our data; the elixir of knowledge, if you will. Do step back and imagine such a world for a moment; a world where the deadliest diseases may be cured in minutes. A world where all are fed, and all may choose to pursue the pinnacle of human achievement in any discipline without fear of persecution, harassment, or poverty. Too much of a promise? Perhaps. Achieving this utopia will take a bit more than designing efficient computer systems. It will require us to evolve our moral perspective in parallel, reconsider our place on this planet as individuals, as a species, and as a whole. But you will be surprised by how much computers can help us get there.

It's important here to understand that it is not just any kind of computer system that we are talking about. This is something very different from what our computing forefathers, such as Babbage and Turing, dealt with. This is not a simple Turing machine or difference engine (although many, if not all, of the concepts we will review in our journey relate directly back to those enlightened minds and their inventions). Hence, our goal will be to cover the pivotal academic contributions, practical experimentation, and implementation insights that followed from centuries, if not decades, of scientific research behind the fundamental concept of generating intelligence; a concept that is arguably most innate to us humans, yet so scarcely understood.

Knowing our tools

We will mainly be working with the two most popular deep learning frameworks that exist, and are freely available to the public at large. This does not mean that we will completely limit our implementations and exercises to these two platforms. It may well occur that we experiment with other prominent deep learning frameworks and backends. We will, however, try to use either TensorFlow or Keras, due to their widespread popularity, large support community, and flexibility in interfacing with other prominent backend and frontend frameworks (such as Theano, Caffe, or Node.js, respectively). We will now provide a little background information on Keras and TensorFlow:

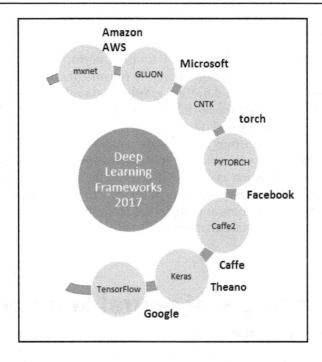

Keras

Many have named Keras the *lingua franca* of deep learning, due to its user friendliness, modularity, and extendibility. Keras is a high-level application programming interface for neural networks, and focuses on enabling fast experimentation. It is written in Python and is capable of running on top of backends such as TensorFlow or Keras. Keras was initially developed as part of the research effort of the ONEIROS (Open-ended Neuro-Electronic Intelligent Robot Operating System) project. Its name is a reference to the Greek word, *Κέρας*, which literally translates to *horn*. The word eludes to a play on words dating back to ancient Greek literature, referring to the horn of Amalthea (also known as **Cornucopia**), an eternal symbol of abundance.

Some functionalities of Keras include the following:

- Easy and fast prototyping
- Supports implementation of several of the latest neural network architectures, as well as pretrained models and exercise datasets
- Executes impeccably on CPUs and GPUs

TensorFlow

TensorFlow is an open source software library for high-performance numerical computation using a data representation known as **tensors**. It allows people like me and you to implement something called **dataflow graphs**. A dataflow graph is essentially a structure that describes how data moves through a network, or a series of processing neurons. Every neuron in the network represents a mathematical operation, and each connection (or *edge*) between neurons is a multidimensional data array, or *tensor*. In this manner, TensorFlow provides a flexible API that allows easy deployment of computation across a variety of platforms (such as CPUs, GPUs, and their very own **Tensor Processing Units** (**TPUs**)), and from desktops, to clusters of servers, to mobile and edge devices. Originally developed by researchers and engineers from the Google Brain team, it provides an excellent programmatic interface that supports neural network design and deep learning.

The fundamentals of neural learning

We begin our journey with an attempt to gain a fundamental understanding of the concept of learning. Moreover, what we are really interested in is how such a rich and complex phenomenon as learning has been implemented on what many call the most advanced computer known to humankind. As we will observe, scientists seem to continuously find inspiration from the inner workings of our own biological neural networks. If nature has indeed figured out a way to leverage loosely connected signals from the outside world and patch them together as a continuous flow of responsive and adaptive awareness (something most humans will concur with), we would indeed like to know exactly what tricks and treats it may have used to do so. Yet, before we can move on to such topics, we must establish a baseline to understand why the notion of neural networks are far different from most modern **machine learning** (**ML**) techniques.

What is a neural network?

It is extremely hard to draw a parallel between neural networks and any other existing algorithmic mannerism for problem-solving that we have thus far. Linear regression, for example, simply deals with calculating a line of best fit with respect to the mean of squared errors from plotted observation points. Similarly, centroid clustering just recursively separates data by calculating ideal distances between similar points iteratively until it reaches an asymptotic configuration.

Neural networks, on the other hand, are not that easily explicable, and there are many reasons for this. One way of looking at this is that a neural network is an algorithm that itself is composed of different algorithms, performing smaller local calculations as data propagates through it. This definition of neural networks presented here is, of course, not complete. We will iteratively improve it throughout this book, as we go over more complex notions and neural network architectures. Yet, for now, we may well begin with a layman's definition: a neural network is a mechanism that automatically learns associations between the inputs you feed it (such as images) and the outputs you are interested in (that is, whether an image has a dog, a cat, or an attack helicopter).

So, now we have a rudimentary idea of what a neural network is—a mechanism that takes inputs and learns associations to predict some outputs. This versatile mechanism is, of course, not limited to being fed images only. Indeed, such networks are equally capable of taking inputs such as some text or recorded audio, and guessing whether it is looking at Shakespeare's *Hamlet*, or listening to *Billie Jean*, respectively. But how could such a mechanism compensate for the variety of data, in both form and size, while still producing relevant results? To understand this, many academics find it useful to examine how nature can solve this problem. In fact, the millions of years of evolution that occurred on our planet, through genetic mutations and environmental conditions, has produced something quite similar. Better yet, nature has even equipped each of us with a version of this universal function approximator, right between our two ears! We speak, of course, of the human brain.

Observing the brain

Before we briefly delve into this notorious comparison, it is important for us to clarify here that it is indeed just a comparison, and not a parallel. We do not propose that neural networks work exactly in the manner that our brains do, as this would not only anger quite a few neuroscientists, but also does no justice to the engineering marvel represented by the anatomy of the mammalian brain. This comparison, however, helps us to better understand the workflow by which we may design systems that are capable of picking up relevant patterns from data. The versatility of the human brain, be it in making musical orchestras, art masterpieces, or pioneering scientific machinery such as the Large Hydron Collider, shows how the same architecture is capable of learning and applying highly complex and specialized knowledge to great feats. It turns out that nature is a pretty smart cookie, and hence we can learn a lot of valuable lessons by just observing how it has gone about implementing something so novel as a learning agent.

Building a biological brain

Quarks build up atoms, atoms build up molecules, and molecules grouped together may, once in a while, build up chemically excitable biomechanical units. We call these units **cells**; the fundamental building blocks of all biological life forms. Now, cells themselves come in exuberant variety, but one specific type of them is of interest to us here. It is a specific class of cells, known as **nerve cells**, or **neurons**. Why? Well, it turns out that if you take about 10^{11} neurons and set them up in a specific, complementary configuration, you get an organ that is capable of discovering fire, agriculture, and space travel. To realize how these bundles of neurons learn, however, we must first comprehend how one single neuron works. As you will see, it is the repetitive architecture in our brain, composed of these very same neurons, that gives rise to the grander phenomenon that we (pompously) call intelligence.

The physiology of a neuron

A neuron is simply an electrically excitable cell that receives, processes, and transmits information through electrical and chemical signals. Dendrites extend from the neuron cell body and receive messages from other neurons. When we say that neurons *receive* or *send* messages, what we actually mean is that they transmit electrical impulses along their axons. Lastly, neurons are *excitable*. In other words, the right impulse supplied to a neuron will produce electrical events, known as **action potentials**. When a neuron reaches its action potential (or *spikes*), it releases a neurotransmitter, which is a chemical that travels a tiny distance across a synapse before reaching other neurons. Any time a neuron spikes, neurotransmitters are released from hundreds of its synapses, reaching the dendrites of other neurons that themselves may or may not spike, depending on the nature of the impulse. This is the very mannerism that allows these vast networks of neurons to communicate, compute, and work together to solve complex tasks that we humans face daily:

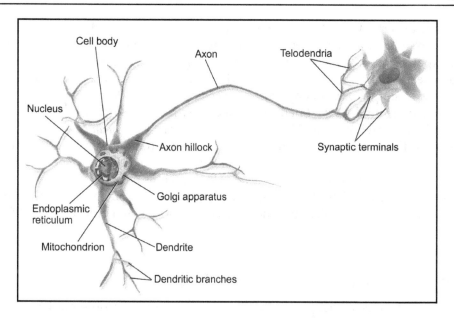

So, all a neuron really does is take in some electric input, undergo some sort of processing, and then *fire* if the outcome is positive, or remain inactive if the outcome of that processing is negative. What do we mean here by whether an outcome is *positive*? To understand this, it is useful to have a little parenthesis on how information and knowledge is represented in our own brains.

Representing information

Consider a task where you have to correctly classify images of dogs, cats, and attack helicopters. One way of thinking about a neuronal learning system is that we dedicate several neurons to represent the various features that exist in the three respective classes. In other words, let's say that we have employed three expert neurons for our classification task here. Each one of these neurons is an expert in the domain of what a dog, cat, and an attack helicopter looks like.

How are they experts? Well, for now, we can think that each of our domain expert neurons are supported by their own cabinet of employees and support staff, all diligently working for these experts, collecting and representing different breeds of dogs, cats, and attack helicopters, respectively. But we don't deal with their support staff for the time being. At the moment, we simply present any image to each of our three domain experts. If the picture is of a dog, our *dog expert* neuron immediately recognizes the creature and fires, almost as if it were saying, *Hello, I believe this is a dog. Trust me, I'm an expert*. Similarly, when we present our three experts a picture of a cat, our cat neuron will signal to us that they have detected a cat in our image by firing. While this is not exactly how each neuron represents real-world objects, such as cats and dogs, it helps us gain a functional understanding of neuron-based learning systems. Hopefully, you have enough information now to be introduced to the biological neuron's less sophisticated brother, the artificial neuron, next.

The mysteries of neural encoding

In reality, many neuroscientists argue that this idea of a unified representative neuron, such as our *cat expert* neuron, doesn't really exist in our brain. They note how such a mechanism will require our brain to have thousands of neurons dedicated only to specific faces we have known, such as our grandmother, the baker around the corner, or Donald Trump. Instead, they postulate a more distributed representation architecture. This distributed theory states that a specific stimulus, such as the picture of a cat, is represented by (and will trigger) a unique pattern of firing neurons, widely distributed in the brain. In other words, a cat will be represented by perhaps (a wild guess) 100 different neurons, each dedicated to identifying specific cat-like features from the image (such as its ears, tail, eyes, and general body shape). The intuition here is that some of these cat neurons may be recombined with other neurons to represent other images that have elements of *cat* within. The picture of a jaguar, or the cartoon cat *Garfield*, for example, could be reconstructed using a subset of the very same cat neurons, in conjunction with some other neurons that have learned attributes that are more specific to the size of jaguars, or Garfield's famous orange and black stripes, perhaps.

Distributed representation and learning

In some curious medical cases, patients with physical trauma to the head have not only failed to associate with their loved ones when confronted with them, but even claimed that these very loved ones were impostors just disguised as their loved ones! While a bizarre occurrence, such situations may shed more light onto the exact mechanisms of neural learning. Clearly, the patient recognizes this person, as some neurons encoding the visual patterns corresponding to the features of their loved ones (such as face and clothes) are fired. However, since they interestingly report this disassociation with these same loved ones despite being able to recognize them, it must mean that all the neurons that would normally fire upon coming across this loved one (including the neurons encoding the emotional representations our patient may have for this person) did not fire at the moment when our patient met their significant acquaintance.

These sorts of distributed representations may well allow our brain the versatility in extrapolating patterns from very little data, as we observe ourselves capable of doing. Modern neural networks, for example, still require you to provide it with hundreds (if not thousands) of images before it can reliably predict whether it is looking at a bus or a toaster. My three year-old niece, on the other hand, is able to parallel this accuracy with about three to five pictures of buses and toasters each. Even more fascinating is the fact that the neural networks running on your computer can, at times, take gigawatts of energy to perform computations. My niece only needs 12 watts. She will get what she needs from a few biscuits, or perhaps a small piece of a cake that she carefully sneaks away from the kitchen.

The fundamentals of data science

Let's get acquainted with some basic terminologies and concepts of data science. We will get into some theory and then move on to understand some complex terms such as entropy and dimensionality.

Information theory

Before a deeper dive into various network architectures and some hands-on examples, it would be a pity if we did not elaborate a little on the pivotal notion of gaining information through processing real-world signals. We speak of the science of quantifying the amount of information present in a signal, also referred to as information theory. While we don't wish to provide a deep mathematical overview on this notion, it is useful to know some background on learning from a probabilistic perspective.

Intuitively, learning that an unlikely event has occurred is more informative than learning that an expected event has occurred. If I were to tell you that you can *buy food at all supermarkets today*, I won't be met with gasps of surprise. Why? Well, I haven't really told you something beyond your expectations. Conversely, if I told you that you *cannot* buy food at all supermarkets today, perhaps due to some general strike, well, then you would be surprised. You would be surprised because an unlikely piece of information has been presented (in our case, this is the word *not*, appearing in the configuration previously presented). Such intuitive knowledge is what we attempt to codify, in the field of information theory. Other similar notions include the following:

- An event with a lower likelihood of occurrence should have lower information content
- An event with a higher likelihood of occurrence should have higher information content
- An event with a guaranteed occurrence should have no information content
- An event with an independent likelihood of occurrence should have additive information content

Mathematically, we can actually satisfy all of these conditions by using the simple equation modeling the self-information of an event (*x*), as follows:

$$l(x) = -\log_e P(x)$$

l(x) is denoted in the *nat* unit, quantifying the amount of information gained by observing an event of probability, *1/e*. Although the preceding equation is nice and neat, it only allows us to deal with a single outcome; this is not too helpful in modeling the dependent complexities of the real world. What if we wanted to quantify the amount of uncertainty in an entire probability distribution of events? Then, we employ another measure, known as **Shannon entropy**, as shown in the following equation:

$$H(p(x)) - E_{x \sim p}\left[I(x)\right] = \int_x p(x)I(x)dx = -\int_x p(x)\log(p(x))dx$$

Entropy

Let's say you're a soldier stuck behind enemy lines. Your goal is to let your allies know what kind of enemies are coming their way. Sometimes, the enemy may send tanks, but more often, they send patrols of people. Now, the only way you can signal your friends is by using a radio with simple binary signals. You need to figure out the best way to communicate with your allies, so as to not waste your precious time and get discovered by the enemy. How do you do this? Well, first you map out many sequences of binary bits, each specific sequence corresponding to a specific type of enemy (such as patrols or tanks). With a little knowledge of the environment, you already know that patrols are much more frequent than tanks. It stands to reason then, that you probably will be using the binary signal for *patrol* much more often than the one for *tank*. Hence, you will allocate fewer binary bits to communicate the presence of an incoming patrol, as you know you will be sending that signal more often than others. What you're doing is exploiting your knowledge about the distribution over types of enemies to reduce the number of bits that you need to send on average. In fact, if you have access to the overall underlining distribution of incoming patrols and tanks, then you could theoretically use the smallest number of bits to communicate most efficiently with the friendlies on the other side. We do this by using the optimal number of bits at each transmission. The number of bits to represent a signal is known as the entropy of this data, and can be formulated with the following equation:

$$H(y) = \sum_i y_i \log \frac{1}{y_i} = -\sum_i y_i \log y_i$$

Here, $H(y)$ denotes a function that refers to the optimal number of bits to represent an event with the probability distribution, y. y_i simply refers to the probability of another event, i. So, supposing that seeing an enemy patrol is 256 times more likely to happen than seeing an enemy tank, we would model the number of bits to use to encode the presence of an enemy patrol, as follows:

Patrol bits = log(1/256pTank)

> *= log(1/pTank) + log(1/(2^8))*
>
> *= Tank bits - 8*

Cross entropy

Cross entropy is yet another mathematical notion, allowing us to compare two distinct probability distributions, denoted by *p* and *q*. In fact, as you will see later, we often employ entropy-based loss function in neural networks when dealing with categorical features. Essentially, the cross entropy between two probability distributions (https://en. wikipedia.org/wiki/Probability_distribution), *(p, q)*, over the same underlying set of events, measures the average number of pieces of information needed to identify an event picked at random from a set, under a condition; the condition being that the coding scheme used is optimized for a predicted probability distribution, rather than the *true* distribution. We will revisit this notion in later chapters to clarify and implement our understandings:

$$H(p, q) = E_p \left[-\log(q) \right] = - \int_x p(x). \log(q(x)) dx$$

The nature of data processing

Earlier, we discussed how neurons may electrically propagate information and communicate with other neurons using chemical reactions. These same neurons help us determine what a *cat* or *dog* look like. But these neurons never actually see the full image of a cat. All they deal with is chemical and electric impulses. These networks of neurons can carry out their task only because of other sensory preprocessing organs, such as our eyes and optic nerve, that have prepared the data in an appropriate format for our neurons to be able to interpret. Our eyes take in the electromagnetic radiation (or light) that represents the image of a cat, and convert it into efficient representations thereof, communicated through electrical impulses. Hence, a prime difference between artificial and biological neurons relates to the medium of their intercommunication. As we saw, biological neurons use chemicals and electrical impulses as a means of communication. Similarly, artificial neurons rely on the universal language of mathematics to represent patterns from data. In fact, there exists a whole discipline surrounding the concept of representing real-world phenomena mathematically for the purpose of knowledge extraction. This discipline, as many of you are familiar with, is known as **data science**.

From data science to ML

Pick up any book on data science; there is a fair chance that you will come across an elaborate explanation, involving the intersection of fields such as statistics and computer science, as well as some domain knowledge. As you flip through the pages rapidly, you will notice some nice visualizations, graphs, bar charts—the works. You will be introduced to statistical models, significance tests, data structures, and algorithms, each providing impressive results for some demonstrative use case. This is not data science. These are indeed the very tools you will be using as a successful data scientist. However, the essence of what data science is can be summarized in a much simpler manner: *data science is the scientific domain that deals with generating actionable knowledge from raw data. This is done by iteratively observing a real-world problem, quantifying the overall phenomena in different dimensions, or features, and predicting future outcomes that permit desired ends to be achieved. ML is just the discipline of teaching machines data science.*

While some computer scientists may appreciate this recursive definition, some of you may ponder what is meant by *quantifying a phenomenon*. Well, you see, most observations in the real world, be it the amount of food you eat, the kind of programs you watch, or the colors you like on your clothes, can be all defined as (approximate) functions of some other quasi-dependent features. For example, the amount of food you will eat in any given day can be defined as a function of other things, such as how much you ate in your previous meal, your general inclination to certain types of food, or even the amount of physical exertion you get.

Similarly, the kind of programs you like to watch may be approximated by features such as your personality traits, interests, and the amount of free time in your schedule. Reductively speaking, we work with quantifying and representing differences between observations (for example, the viewing habits between people), to deduce a functional predictive rule that machines may work with.

We induce these rules by defining the possible outcomes that we are trying to predict (that is, whether a given person likes comedies or thrillers) as a function of input features (that is, how this person ranks on the Big Five personality test) that we collect when observing a phenomenon at large (such as personalities and the viewing habits of a population):

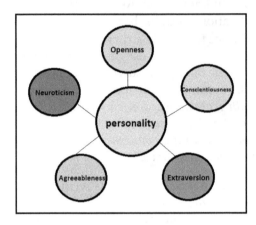

If you have selected the right set of features, you will be able to derive a function that is able to reliably predict the output classes that you are interested in (in our case, this is viewer preferences). What do I mean by the right features? Well, it stands to reason that viewing habits have more to do with a person's personality traits than their travel habits. Predicting whether someone is inclined towards horror movies as a function of, say, their eye color and real-time GPS coordinates, will be quite useless, as they are not informative to what we are trying to predict. Hence, we always choose relevant features (through domain knowledge or significance tests) to reductively represent a real-world phenomenon. Then, we simply use this representation to predict the future outcomes that we are interested in. This representation itself is what we call a predictive model.

Modeling data in high-dimensional spaces

As you saw, we can represent real-world observations by redefining them as a function of different features. The speed of an object, for example, is a function of the distance it traveled over a given time. Similarly, the color of a pixel on your TV screen is actually a function of the red, green, and blue intensity values that make up that pixel. These elements are what data scientists call features or dimensions of your data. When we have dimensions that are labeled, we deal with a supervised learning task, as we can check the learning of our model with respect to what is truly the case. When we have unlabeled dimensions, we calculate the distances between our observation points to find similar groups in our data. This is known as **unsupervised ML**. Hence, in this manner, we can start building a model of a real-world phenomenon, by simply representing it using informative features.

The curse of dimensionality

The natural question that follows is: how exactly do we build a model? Long story short, the features that we choose to collect while observing an outcome can all be plotted on a high-dimensional space. While this may sound complicated, it is just an extension of the Cartesian coordinate system that you may be familiar with from high school mathematics. Let's recall how to represent a single point on a graph, using the Cartesian coordinate system. For this task, we require two values, x and y. This is an example of a two-dimensional feature space, with the x and y axis each being a dimension in the representational space. Add a z axis, and we get a three-dimensional feature space. Essentially, we define ML problems in an n-dimensional feature space, where n refers to the number of features that we have on the phenomenon we are trying to predict. In our previous case of predicting viewer preference, if we solely use the Big Five personality test scores as input features, we will essentially have a five-dimensional feature space, where each dimension corresponds to a person's score on one of the five personality dimensions. In fact, modern ML problems can range from 100 to 100,000 dimensions (and sometimes even more). Since the number of possible configurations of features increases exponentially with respect to increases in the number of different features, it becomes quite hard, even for computers, to conceive and compute in such proportions. This problem in ML is generally referred to as the *curse of dimensionality*.

Algorithmic computation and predictive models

Once we have a high-dimensional representation of relevant data, we can commence the task of deriving a predictive function. We do this by using algorithms, which are essentially a set of preprogrammed recursive instructions that categorize and divide our high-dimensional data representation in a certain manner. These algorithms (these are most commonly clustering, classification, and regression) recursively separate our data points (that is, personality rankings per person) on the feature space into smaller groups where the data points are comparatively more alike. In this manner, we use algorithms to iteratively segment our high-dimensional feature space into smaller regions, which will eventually correspond to our output classes (ideally). Hence, we can reliably predict the output class of any future data points simply by placing them on our high-dimensional feature space and comparing them to the regions corresponding to our model's predicted output classes. Congratulations, we have a predictive model!

Matching a model to use cases

Every time we choose to define an observation as a function of some features, we open up a Pandora's box of semi-causally linked features, where each feature itself could be redefined (or quantified) as a function of other features. In doing so, we might want to take a step back, and consider what exactly we are trying to represent. Is our model capturing relevant patterns? Can we rely on our data? Will our resources, be it algorithms or computational firepower, suffice for learning from the data we have?

Recall our earlier scenario of predicting the quantity of food an individual is likely to consume in each meal. The features that we discussed, such as their physical exertion, could be redefined as a function of their metabolic and hormonal activity. Similarly, dietary preferences could be redefined as a function of their gut bacteria and stool composition. Each of these redefinitions adds new features to our model, bringing with them additional complexity.

Perhaps we can even achieve a greater accuracy in predicting exactly how much takeout you should order. Would this be worth the effort of getting a stomach biopsy every day? Or installing a state-of-the-art electron microscope in your toilet? Most of you will agree: no, it would not be. How did we come to this consensus? Simply by assessing our use case of dietary prediction and selecting features that are relevant *enough* to predict what we want to predict, in a fashion that is reliable and proportional to our situation. A complex model supplemented by high-quality hardware (such as toilet sensors) is unnecessary and unrealistic for the use case of dietary prediction. You could as easily achieve a functional predictive model based on easily obtainable features, such as purchase history and prior preferences.

The essence of this story is that you may define any observable phenomenon as a function of other phenomenon in a recursive manner, but a clever data scientist will know when to stop by picking appropriate features that reasonably fit your use case; are readily observable and verifiable; and robustly deal with all relevant situations. All we need is to approximate a function that reliably predicts the output classes for our data points. Inducting a too complex or simplistic representation of our phenomenon will naturally lead to the demise of our ML project.

Functional representations

Before we march forth in our journey to understand, build, and master neural networks, we must at least refresh our perception of some fundamental ML concepts. For example, it is important to understand that you are never modeling a phenomenon completely. You are only *functionally* representing a part of it. This helps you think about data intuitively, forming but a small piece in the large puzzle, represented by a general phenomenon that you are trying to understand. This also helps you realize that times change. The importance of features, as well as surrounding environments, are both subject to such change, eroding the predictive power of your model. Such intuition is naturally built with practice and domain knowledge.

In the following section, we will briefly refresh our memory with some classic pitfalls of ML use cases, with a few simple scenario-driven examples. This is important to do as we will notice these same problems reappear when we undertake our main journey of understanding and applying neural networks to various use cases.

The pitfalls of ML

Consider the problem of predicting the weather forecast. We will begin constructing our predictive model by doing some feature selection. With some domain knowledge, we initially identify the feature *air pressure* as a relevant predictor. We will record different *Pa* values (Pascals, a measure of air pressure) over different days on the island of Hawaii, where we live. Some of these days turn out to be sunny, and others rainy.

Unbalanced class priors

After several sunny days, your predictive model tells you that there is a very high chance of the following day also being sunny, yet it rains. Why? This is simply because your model has not seen enough instances of both prediction classes (sunny and rainy days) to accurately assess the chance of there being rain. In this case, it is said to have unbalanced class priors, which misrepresent the overall weather pattern. According to your model, there are only sunny days because it has only seen sunny days as of yet.

Underfitting

You have collected about two months worth of air pressure data, and balanced the number of observations in each of your output classes. Your prediction accuracy has steadily increased, but starts tapering off at a suboptimal level (let's say 61%). Suddenly, your model's accuracy starts dropping again, as it gets colder and colder outside. Here, we face the problem of underfitting, as our simplistic model is unable to capture the underlying pattern of our data, caused by the seasonal coming of winter. There are a few simple remedies to this situation. Most prominently, we may simply improve our model by adding more predictive features, such as the outside temperature. Doing so, we observe after a few days of data collection that once again, our accuracy climbs up, as the additional feature adds more information to our model, increasing its predictive power. In other cases of underfitting, we may well have chosen to select a more computationally-intensive predictive model, add more data and engineer better features, or reduce any mathematical constraints (such as the lambda hyperparameter for regularization) on the model.

Overfitting

After collecting about a few years of data, you confidently boast that you have developed a robust predictive model with 96% accuracy to your farmer friend. Your friend says, *Well, great news, can I have it?* You, being an altruist and philanthropist, immediately agree and send him the code. A day later the same friend calls back from his home in Guangdong province in China, angry that your model did not work and has ruined his crop harvest. What happened here? This was simply a case of overfitting our model to the tropical climate of Hawaii, which does not generalize well outside of this sample. Our model did not see enough variations that actually exist in the possible values of pressure and temperatures, with the corresponding labels of *sunny* and *rainy*, to sufficiently be able to predict the weather on another continent. In fact, since our model only saw Hawaiian temperatures and air pressures, it memorized trivial patterns in the data (for example, there are never two rainy days in a row) and uses these patterns as rules for making a prediction, instead of picking up on more informative trends. One simple remedy here is, of course, to gather more weather data in China, and fine-tune your prediction model to the local weather dynamics. In other similar situations involving overfitting, you may attempt to select a simpler model, denoise the data by removing outliers and errors, and center it with respect to mean values.

Bad data

After explaining to your dear friend from China (henceforth referred to as Chan) the miscalculation that just occurred, you instruct him to set up sensors and start collecting local air pressure and temperature to construct a labeled dataset of sunny and rainy days, just like you did in Hawaii. Chan diligently places sensors on his roof and in his fields. Unfortunately, Chan's roof is made of a reinforced metal alloy with a high thermal conductivity, which erratically inflates the reading from both the pressure and temperature sensors from the roof in an inconsistent and unreliable manner. This corrupted data, when fed to our predictive model, will naturally produce suboptimal results, as the learned line is perturbed by noisy and misrepresentative data. A clear remedy would be to replace the sensors, or simply discard the faulty sensor readings.

Irrelevant features and labels

Eventually, using enough data from Hawaii, China, and some other places in the world, we notice a clear and globally generalizable pattern, which we can use to predict the weather. So, everybody is happy, until one day, your prediction model tells you it is going to be a bright sunny day, and a tornado comes knocking on your door. What happened? Where did we go wrong? Well, it turns out that when it comes to tornadoes, our two-featured binary classification model does not incorporate enough information about our problem (this being the dynamics of tornadoes) to allow us to approximate a function that reliably predicts this specifically devastating outcome. So far, our model did not even try to predict tornadoes, and we only collected data for sunny and rainy days.

A climatologist here might say, *Well, then start collecting data on altitude, humidity, wind speed, and direction, and add some labeled instanced of tornadoes to your data*, and, indeed, this would help us fend off future tornadoes. That is, until an earthquake hits the continental shelf and causes a tsunami. This illustrative example shows how whatever model you choose to use, you need to keep tracking relevant features, and have enough data per each prediction class (such as whether it is sunny, rainy, tornado-ey, and so on) to achieve good predictive accuracy. Having a good prediction model simply means that you have discovered a mechanism that is capable of using the data you have collected so far, to induct a set of predictive rules that are seemingly being obeyed.

Summary

In this chapter, we gained a functional overview of biological neural networks, with a small and brief preview covering concepts such as neural learning and distributed representations. We also refreshed our memory on some classic data science dilemmas that are equally relevant for neural networks as they are for other ML techniques. In the following chapter, we will finally dive into the much-anticipated learning mechanism loosely inspired by our biological neural networks, as we explore the basic architecture of an ANN. We amicably describe ANNs in such a manner because, despite aiming to work as effectively as their biological counterparts, they are not quite there yet. In the next chapter, you will go over the main implementation considerations involved in designing ANNs and progressively discover the complexity that such an endeavour entails.

Further reading

- **Symbolic versus connectionist learning**: http://www.cogsci.rpi.edu/~rsun/sun.encyc01.pdf
- **History of artificial intelligence**: http://sitn.hms.harvard.edu/flash/2017/history-artificial-intelligence/
- **History of the human brain**: http://www.mybrain.co.uk/public/learn_history4.php

A Deeper Dive into Neural Networks

2

In this chapter, we will encounter more in-depth details of neural networks. We will start from building a perceptron. Moving on, we will learn about activation functions. And we will also be training our first perceptron.

In this chapter, we will cover the following topics:

- From the biological to the artificial neuron – the perceptron
- Building a perceptron
- Learning through errors
- Training a perceptron
- Backpropagation
- Scaling the perceptron
- A single layered network

From the biological to the artificial neuron – the perceptron

Now that we have briefly familiarized ourselves with some insights on the nature of data processing, it's about time we see how the artificial cousins of our own biological neurons work themselves. We start with a creation of Frank Rosenblatt, dating back to the 1950s. He called this invention of his the **Perceptron** (`http://citeseerx.ist.psu.edu/viewdoc/download?doi=10.1.1.335.3398rep=rep1type=pdf`). Essentially, you can think of the perceptron as a single neuron in an **artificial neural network (ANN)**. Understanding how a single perceptron propagates information forward will serve as an excellent stepping stone to understanding the more state-of-the-art networks that we will face in later chapters:

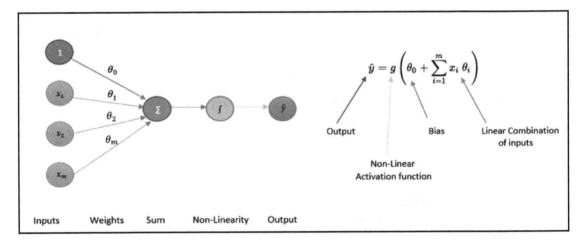

Building a perceptron

For now, we will define a perceptron using six specific mathematical representations that demonstrate its learning mechanism. These representations are the inputs, weights, bias term, summation, and the activation function. The output will be functionally elaborate upon here under.

Input

Remember how a biological neuron takes in electrical impulses from its dendrites? Well, the perceptron behaves in a similar fashion, yet it prefers to ingest numbers in lieu of electricity. Essentially, it takes in feature inputs, as shown in the preceding diagram. This particular perceptron only has three input channels, these being x_1, x_2, and x_3. These feature inputs (x_1, x_2, and x_3) can be any independent variable that you choose to represent your observation by. Simply speaking, if we want to predict whether it will be sunny or rainy on any given day, we can record independent variables such as temperature and air pressure per day, along with the appropriate output class of that day (whether the day itself was sunny or rainy). We will then feed these independent variables that we have, one day at a time, as input features into our perceptron model.

Weights

So, we know how data flows into our simple neuron, but how do we transform this data into actionable knowledge? How do we build a model that takes these input features, and represents them in a manner that helps us predict the weather on any given day?

Giving us two features that we can use as input in our model, for the binary classification task of determining *rainy* or *sunny* days.

Well, the first step will be to pair up each input feature with a respective weight. You can think of this weight as the relative importance this specific input feature has with respect to the output class that we are trying to predict. In other words, the weight for our input feature temperature should ideally reflect exactly how much this input feature is related to the output classes. These weights are randomly initialized at first, and are learned as our models see more and more data. Our hope here in doing this is that after enough iterations through our data, these weights will be nudged in the right direction, and learn the ideal configuration of temperature and pressure values that correspond to rainy and sunny days. We actually know, from domain knowledge, that temperature is highly correlated to weather, and hence will expect our model to, ideally, learn heavier weights for this feature, as data propagates through it. This can be somewhat comparable to the myelin sheath that covers axons in a biological neuron. If a specific neuron fires frequently, its myelin sheath is said to thicken, which insulates the axon, and allows the neuron to communicate faster next time.

Summation

So, now we have our input features flowing into our perceptron, with each input feature paired up with a randomly initialized weight. The next step is fairly easy. First, we represent all three of our features and their weights as two different 3 x 1 matrices. We want to use these two matrices to represent the combined effect of our input features and their weights. As you will recall from high school mathematics, you cannot actually multiply two 3 x 1 matrices together. So, we have to perform a little mathematical trick to reductively represent our two matrices as one value. We simply transpose our feature matrix, as follows:

$$x = \begin{bmatrix} x_1 \\ x_2 \\ x_3 \\ . \\ . \\ . \\ x_n \end{bmatrix} \qquad x^T = \begin{bmatrix} x_1 & x_2 & x_3 & ... x_n \end{bmatrix}$$

We can use this new transposed feature matrix (of dimension 3 x 1) and multiply it with the weight matrix (of dimension 1 x 3). When we perform a matrix-by-matrix multiplication, the result we obtain is referred to as the **dot product** of these two matrices. In our case, we compute the dot product of our transposed feature matrix and our weights matrix. Doing so, we are able to reduce our two matrices to one single scalar value, which represents the collective influence of all of our input features and their respective weights. Now, we will see how we can use this collective representation and gauge it against a certain threshold to assess the quality of this representation. In other words, we will use a function to assess whether this scalar representation encodes a useful pattern to remember. A useful pattern will ideally be one that helps our model distinguish between the different classes in our data, and thereby output correct predictions.

Introducing non-linearity

So now, we know how data enters a perceptron unit, and how associated weights are paired up with each input feature. We also know how to represent our input features, and their respective weights, as n x 1 matrices, where n is the number of input features. Lastly, we saw how we can transpose our feature matrix to be able to compute its dot product with the matrix containing its weights. This operation left us with one single scalar value. So, what's next? This is not a bad time to take a step back and ponder over what we are trying to achieve, as this will help us to understand the idea behind why we want to employ something like an activation function.

Well, you see, real-word data is often non-linear. What we mean by this is that whenever we attempt to model an observation as a function of different inputs, this function itself cannot be represented linearly, or on a straight line.

If all patterns in data only constituted straight lines, we would probably not be discussing neural networks at all. Techniques such as **Support Vector Machines** (**SVMs**) or even linear regression already excel at this task:

Modeling sunny and rainy days with temperature, for example, will produce a non-linear curve. In effect, this just means that we cannot possibly separate our decision boundary using a straight line. In other words, on some days, it may rain despite high temperatures, and on other days, it may remain sunny despite low temperatures.

This is because temperature is not linearly related to the weather. The weather outcome on any given day is very likely to be a complex function, involving interactive variables such as wind speed, air pressure, and more. So, on any given day, a temperature of 13 degrees could mean a sunny day in Berlin, Germany, but a rainy day in London, UK:

There are some cases, of course, where a phenomenon may be linearly represented. In physics, for example, the relationship between the mass of an object and its volume can be linearly defined, as shown in the following screenshots:

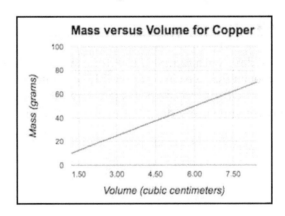

This is an example of a non-linear function:

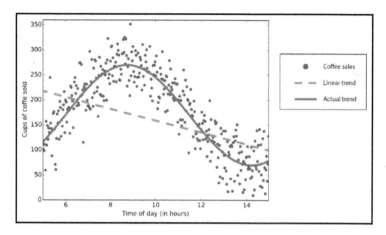

A linear function	A non-linear function
$Y = mx + b$	$Y = mx^2 + b$

Here, m is the slope of the line, x is any point (an input or an x-value) on the line, and b is where the line crosses the y axis.

Unfortunately, linearity is often not guaranteed with real-world data, as we model observations using multiple features, each of which could have a varied and disproportional contribution towards determining our output classes. In fact, our world is extremely non-linear, and hence, to capture this non-linearity in our perceptron model, we need it to incorporate non-linear functions that are capable of representing such phenomena. By doing so, we increase the capacity of our neuron to model more complex patterns that actually exist in the real world, and draw decision boundaries that would not be possible, were we to only use linear functions. These types of functions, used to model non-linear relationships in our data, are known as **activation functions**.

Activation functions

Well, basically what we have done so far is represent our different input features and their weights in a lower dimension, as a scalar representation. We can use this reduced representation and pass it through a simple non-linear function that tells us whether our representation is above or below a certain threshold value. Similar to the weights we initialized before, this threshold value can be thought of as a learnable parameter of our perceptron model.

In other words, we want our perceptron to figure out the ideal combinations of weights and a threshold, allowing it to reliably match our inputs to the correct output class. Hence, we compare our reduced feature representation with a threshold value, and then activate our perceptron unit if we are above this threshold value, or do nothing otherwise. This very function that compares our reduced feature value against a threshold, is known as an **activation function**:

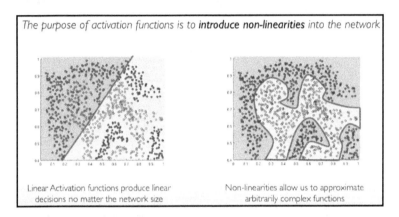

The purpose of activation functions is to **introduce non-linearities** into the network

Linear Activation functions produce linear decisions no matter the network size

Non-linearities allow us to approximate arbitrarily complex functions

These non-linear functions come in different forms, and will be explored in further detail in subsequent chapters. For now, we present two different activation functions; the **heavy set step** and the **logistic sigmoid** activation functions. The perceptron unit that we previously showed you was originally implemented with such a heavy step function, leading to binary outputs of 1 (active) or 0 (inactive). Using the step function in our perceptron unit, we observe that a value above the curve will lead to activation (1), whereas a value below or on the curve will not lead to the activation unit firing (0). This process may be summarized in an algebraic manner as well.

The following screenshot shows the heavy step function:

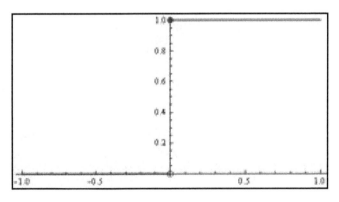

The output threshold formula is as follows:

$$\text{output} = \begin{cases} 0 & \text{if } \sum_j w_j x_j \leq \text{threshold} \\ 1 & \text{if } \sum_j w_j x_j > \text{threshold} \end{cases}$$

In essence, a step function is not really a non-linear function, as it can be rewritten as two finite linear combinations. Hence, this piece-wise constant function is not very flexible in modeling real-world data, which is often more probabilistic than binary. The logistic sigmoid, on the other hand, is indeed a non-linear function, and may model data with more flexibility. This function is known for **squishing** its input to an output value between 0 and 1, which makes it a popular function for representing probabilities, and is a commonly employed activation function for neurons in modern neural networks:

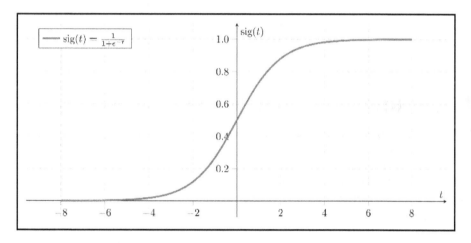

Each type of activation function comes with its own set of advantages and disadvantages that we will also delve into in later chapters. For now, you can intuitively think about the choice of different activation functions as a consideration based on your specific type of data. In other words, we ideally try to experiment and pick a function that best captures the underlining trends that may be present in your data.

Hence, we will employ such activation functions to threshold the incoming inputs of a neuron. Inputs are consequentially transformed and gauged against this activation threshold, in turn causing a neuron to fire, or abstain therefrom. In the following illustration, we can visualize the decision boundary produced by an activation function.

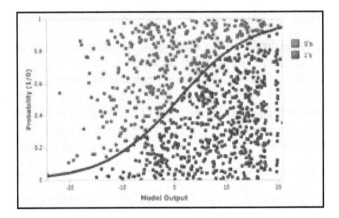

Understanding the role of the bias term

So, now we have a good idea of how data enters our perceptron; it is paired up with weights and reduced through a dot product, only to be compared to an activation threshold. Many of you may ask at this point, *what if we wanted our threshold to adapt to different patterns in data?* In other words, what if the boundaries of the activation function were not ideal to separately identify the specific patterns we want our model to learn? We need to be able to play with the form of our activation curve, so as to guarantee some flexibility in the sort of patterns each neuron may locally capture.

And how exactly will we shape our activation function? Well, one way to do this is by introducing a **bias term** into our model. This is depicted by the arrow leaving the first input node (marked with the number '1') in the following diagram:

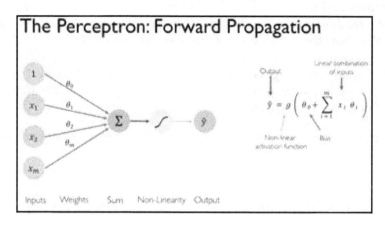

Representatively, we can think of this bias as the weight of a **fictional** input. This fictional input is said to be always present, allowing our activation unit to fire at will, without requiring any input features to be explicitly present (as shown in the green circle previously). The motivation behind this term is to be able to manipulate the shape of our activation function, which in turn impacts the learning of our model. We want our shape to flexibly fit different patterns in our data. The weight of the bias term is updated in the same manner as all the other weights are. What makes it different is that it is not disturbed by its input neuron, which simply always holds a constant value (as shown previously).

So, how do we actually influence our activation threshold using this bias term? Well, lets consider a simplified example. Suppose we have some outputs generated by a stepped activation function, which produces either a '0'or a '1'for every output, like so:

$$output = \begin{cases} 0 \ if \sum_j w_j x_j \leq threshold \\ 1 \ if \sum_j w_j x_j > threshold \end{cases}$$

We can then rewrite this formula to include the bias term, as follows:

$$output = \begin{cases} 0 \ if \sum_i w_i x_i + bias < 0 \\ 1 \ if \sum_i w_i x_i + bias \geq 0 \end{cases}$$

In other words, we are using yet another mathematical trick and redefining the threshold value as the negative of our bias term (*Threshold = -(bias)*). This bias term is randomly initialized at the beginning of our training session, and is iteratively updated as the model sees more examples, and learns from these examples. Hence, it is important to understand that although we randomly initialize model parameters, such as the weights and biases, our hope is to actually show the model enough input examples and their corresponding output classes. In doing so, we want our model to learn from its errors, searching for the ideal parametric combinations of weights and bias corresponding to the correct output classes. Do note that when we initialize different weights, what we are actually doing is modifying the steepness of our activation function.

The following graph shows how different weights impact the steepness of a sigmoid activation function:

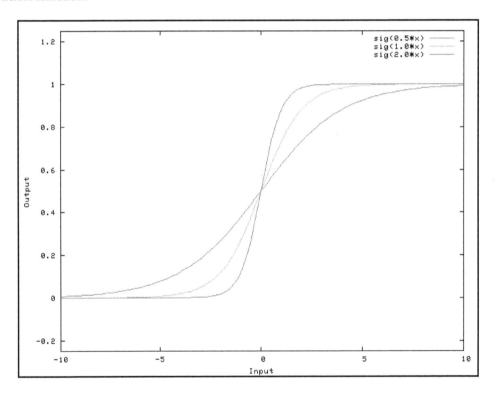

We essentially hope that by tinkering with the steepness of our activation function, we are able to ideally capture a certain underlying pattern in our data. Similarly, when we initialize different bias terms, what we are actually trying to do is shift the activation function in an optimal manner (to the left or to the right), so as to trigger activation corresponding to specific configurations of input and output features.

The following graph shows how different bias terms impact the position of a sigmoid activation function:

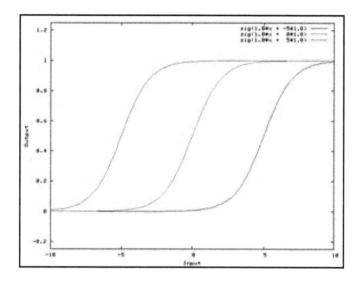

Output

In our simple perceptron model, we denote the actual output class as y, and the predicted output classes as $\hat{y}$. The output classes simply refer to the different classes in our data that we are trying to predict. To elaborate, we use the input features (x_n), such as temperature (x_1) and air pressure (x_2) on a given day, to predict whether that specific day is a sunny or rainy one ($\hat{y}$). We can then compare our model's predictions with the actual output class of that day, denoting whether that day was indeed rainy or sunny. We can denote this simple comparison as ($\hat{y} - y$), which allows us to observe by how much our perceptron missed the mark, on average. But more on that later. For now, we can represent our entire prediction model using all that we have learned so far, in a mathematical manner:

$$\hat{y} = g(\theta_0 + X^T\theta)$$

$$\text{where: } X = \begin{bmatrix} x_1 \\ \vdots \\ x_m \end{bmatrix} \text{ and } \theta = \begin{bmatrix} \theta_1 \\ \vdots \\ \theta_m \end{bmatrix}$$

The following diagram displays an example of the preceding formula:

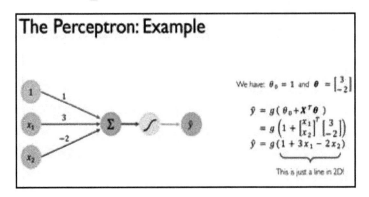

If we graphically plot our prediction line ($\hat{y}$) shown precedingly, we will get to visualize the decision boundary separating our entire feature space into two subspaces. In essence, plotting a prediction line simply gives us an idea of what the model has learned, or how the model chooses to separate the hyperplane containing all our data points into the various output classes that interest us. Actually, by plotting out this line, we are able to visualize how well our model does by simply placing observations of sunny and rainy days on this feature space, and then checking whether our decision boundary ideally separates the output classes, as follows:

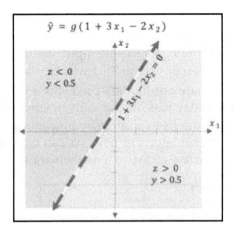

Learning through errors

All we essentially do to our input data is compute a dot product, add a bias term, pass it through a non-linear equation, and then compare our prediction to the real output value, taking a step in the direction of the actual output. This is the general architecture of an artificial neuron. You will soon see how this structure, configured repetitively, gives rise to some of the more complex neural networks around.

Exactly how we converge to ideal parametric values by taking a step in the right direction is through a method known as the **backward propagation of errors**, or **backpropagation** for short. But to propagate errors backwards, we need a metric to assess how well we are doing with respect to our goal. We define this metric as a loss, and calculate it using a loss function. This function attempts to incorporate the residual difference between what our model thinks it sees, and the actual ground reality. Mathematically speaking, this is shown as $(y - \hat{y})$. It is important to understand here that the loss values can actually be defined as a function of our model parameters. Thus, tweaking these parameters permits us to reduce our loss and get our predictions closer to actual output values. You will see exactly what we mean by this when we review the full training process of our perceptron.

The mean squared error loss function

A prominently used loss function is the **mean squared error** (**MSE**) function, represented algebraically in the following formula. As you will notice, this function, at its core, simply compares the actual model output (y) with the predicted model output ($\hat{y}$). This function is particularly helpful for us to asses our predictive power, as this function models the loss quadratically. That is to say, if our model performs poorly, and our predicted and actual output values become more and more divergent, the loss increases by an exponent of two, allowing us to penalize higher errors more severely:

$$\frac{1}{n} \sum (y_i - \hat{y}_i)^2$$

The average MSE between output values y_i, and predicted values $\hat{y}_i$.

We will revisit this notion to understand how we reduce the difference between what our model predicts versus the actual output using various types of loss functions. For now, it suffices to know that our model's loss may be minimized through a process known as **gradient descent**. As we will soon see, gradient descent is simply grounded in calculus and implemented through backpropagation-based algorithms. The process of mathematically reducing the difference between predicted and actual output, by tuning the parameters of a network, is actually what makes the network learn. This tuning occurs as we train our model, by showing it new examples of inputs and associated outputs.

Training a perceptron

So far, we have a clear grasp of how data actually propagates through our perceptron. We also briefly saw how the errors of our model can be propagated backwards. We use a loss function to compute a loss value at each training iteration. This loss value tells us how far our model's predictions lie from the actual ground truth. But what then?

Quantifying loss

Since the loss value gives us an indication of the difference between our predicted and actual outputs, it stands to reason that if our loss value is high, then there is a big difference between our model's predictions and the actual output. Conversely, a low loss value indicates that our model is closing the distance between the predicted and actual output. Ideally, we want our loss to converge to zero, which means that there is in effect not much difference between what our model thinks it sees, and what it is actually shown. We make our loss converge to zero by simply using another mathematical trick, grounded in calculus. How, you ask?

Loss as a function of model weights

Well, remember when we said that we can also think of our loss value as a *function* of the model parameters? Consider this. Our loss value tells us how far our model is from the actual prediction. This same loss can also be redefined as a function of our model's weight (θ). Recall that these weights are what actually lead to our model's prediction at each training iteration. Thinking about this intuitively, we want to be able to change our model weights with respect to the loss, so as to reduce our prediction errors as much as possible.

More mathematically put, we want to minimize our loss function so as to iteratively update the weights for our model, and ideally converge to the best possible weights. These will be the best weights in the sense that they will best be able to represent features that are predictive of our output classes. This process is known as **loss optimization**, and can be mathematically illustrated as follows:

$$\boldsymbol{\theta}^* = \underset{\theta}{\operatorname{argmin}} \frac{1}{n} \sum_{i=1}^{n} \mathcal{L}\big(f\big(x^{(i)}; \boldsymbol{\theta}\big), y^{(i)}\big)$$

$$\boldsymbol{\theta}^* = \underset{\theta}{\operatorname{argmin}} J(\boldsymbol{\theta})$$

Gradient descent

Note that we represent our ideal model weights (θ^*) as the minima of our loss function over the entire training set. In other words, for all the feature inputs and labeled outputs we show our model, we want it to find a place in our feature space where the overall difference between the actual (y) and predicted ($\hat{y}$) values are the smallest. The feature space we refer to is all the different possible combinations of weights that the model may initialize. For the sake of having a simplified representation of our loss function, we denote it as $J(\theta)$. We can now iteratively solve for the minimum of our loss function, $J(\theta)$, and descend the hyperplane to converge to a global minimum. This process is what we call **gradient descent**:

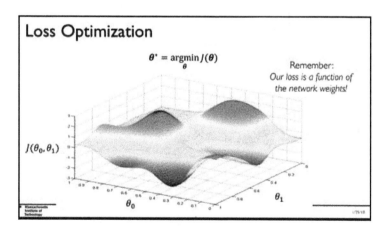

Backpropagation

For the more mathematically oriented, you must be wondering how exactly we descend our gradient iteratively. Well, as you know, we start by initializing random weights to our model, feed in some data, compute dot products, and pass it through our activation function along with our bias to get a predicted output. We use this predicted output and the actual output to estimate the errors in our model's representations, using the loss function. Now here comes the calculus. What we can do now is differentiate our loss function, $J(\theta)$, with respect to the weights of our model (θ). This process essentially lets us compare how changes in our model's weights affect the changes in our model's loss. The result of this differentiation gives us the gradient of our $J(\theta)$ function at the current model weight (θ) along with the direction of the highest ascent. By highest ascent, we meant the direction in which the difference between prediction and output values seem higher. Hence, we simply take a step in the opposite direction, and descend the gradient of our loss function, $J(\theta)$, with respect to our model weights (θ). We present an algorithmic representation of this concept, in form of pseudo-code, as follows:

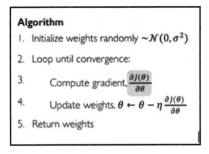

Algorithm

1. Initialize weights randomly $\sim \mathcal{N}(0, \sigma^2)$

2. Loop until convergence:

3.   Compute gradient, $\dfrac{\partial J(\theta)}{\partial \theta}$

4.   Update weights, $\theta \leftarrow \theta - \eta \dfrac{\partial J(\theta)}{\partial \theta}$

5. Return weights

The following graph is a visualization of the gradient descent algorithm:

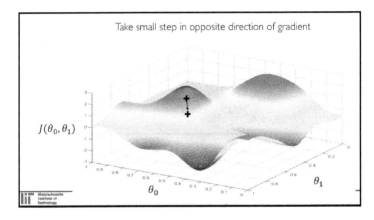

As we see, the gradient descent algorithm allows us to take steps down the loss hyperplane, until our model converges to some optimal parameters. At this point, the difference between our model's predictions and reality will be quite negligible, and we can consider our model trained!:

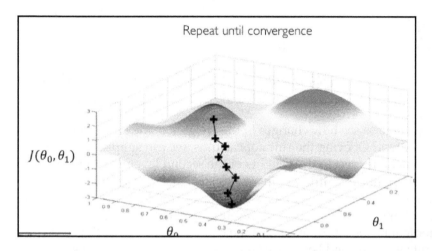

Thus, we compute the changes in our network weights with respect to the changes of the values generated by the loss function (i.e. the gradients of the network weights). Then, we proportionally update the network weights, in the opposite direction of the computed gradients, so as to adjust for the errors.

Computing the gradient

Now that we are familiar with the backpropagation algorithm as well as the notion of gradient decscent, we can address more technical questions. Questions like, *how do we actually compute this gradient?* As you know, our model does not have the liberty of visualizing the loss landscape, and picking out a nice path of descent. In fact, our model cannot tell what is up, or what is down. All it knows, and will ever know, is numbers. However, as it turns out, numbers can tell a lot!

Let's reconsider our simple perceptron model to see how we can backpropagate its errors by computing the gradient of our loss function, $J(\theta)$, iteratively:

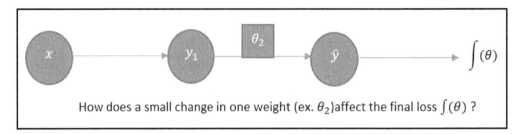

How does a small change in one weight (ex. θ_2)affect the final loss $\int (\theta)$?

What if we wanted to see how changes in the weights of the second layer impact the changes in our loss? Obeying the rules of calculus, we can simply differentiate our loss function, $J(\theta)$, with respect to the weights of the second layer (θ_2). Mathematically, we can actually represent this in a different manner as well. Using the chain rule, we can show how changes in our loss with respect to the second layer weights are actually a product of two different gradients themselves. One represents the changes in our losses with respect to the model's prediction, and the other shows the changes in our model's prediction with respect to the weights in the second layer. This may be represented as follows:

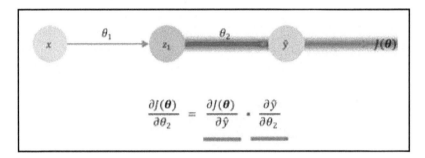

$$\frac{\partial J(\theta)}{\partial \theta_2} = \frac{\partial J(\theta)}{\partial \hat{y}} \cdot \frac{\partial \hat{y}}{\partial \theta_2}$$

As if this wasn't complicated enough, we can even take this recursion further. Let's say that instead of modeling the impact of the changing weights of the second layer (θ_2), we wanted to propagate all the way back and see how our loss changes with respect to the weights of our first layer. We then simply redefine this equation using the chain rule, as we did earlier. Again, we are interested in the change in our model's loss with respect to the model weights for our first layer, (θ_1). We define this using the product of three different gradients; the changes in our loss with respect to output, changes in our output with respect to our hidden layer value, and finally, the changes in our hidden layer value with respect to our first layer weights. We can summarize this as follows:

$$\frac{\partial J(\theta)}{\partial \theta_1} = \frac{\partial J(\theta)}{\partial \hat{y}} \cdot \frac{\partial \hat{y}}{\partial z_1} \cdot \frac{\partial z_1}{\partial \theta_1}$$

And so, this is how we use the loss function, and backpropagate the errors by computing the gradient of our loss function with respect to every single weight in our model. Doing so, we are able to adjust the course of our model in the right direction, being the direction of the highest descent, as we saw before. We do this for our entire dataset, denoted as an epoch. And what about the size of our step? Well, that is determined by the learning rate we set.

The learning rate

While somewhat intuitive, the learning rate of a model simply determines how fast it can learn. Mathematically put, the learning rate determines the exact size of the step we take at each iteration, as we descend the loss landscape to converge to ideal weights. Setting the right learning rate for your problem can be challanging, specially when the loss landscape is complex and full of surprises, as can be seen in the illustration here:

"Visualizing the loss landscape of neural nets". Dec 2017.

This is quite an important notion. If we set a learning rate too small, then naturally, our model learns less than it potentially could per any given training iteration. Even worse with low learning rates is when our model gets stuck in a local minimum, thinking that it has reached a global minimum. Conversely, a high learning rate could, on the other hand, deter our model from capturing patterns of predictive value.

If our steps are too large, we may simply keep overshooting over any global minima present in our feature space of weights, and hence, never converge on our ideal model weights.

One solution to this problem is to set an adaptive learning rate, responsive to the specific loss landscape it may encounter during training. We will explore various implementations of adaptive learning rates (such as Momentum, Adadelta, Adagrad, RMSProp, and more) in subsequent chapters:

$$\theta \leftarrow \theta - \eta \frac{\partial J(\theta)}{\partial \theta}$$

How can we set the learning rate?

Scaling the perceptron

So, we have seen so far how a single neuron may learn to represent a pattern, as it is trained. Now, let's say we want to leverage the learning mechanism of an additional neuron, in parallel. With two perceptron units in our model, each unit may learn to represent a different pattern in our data. Hence, if we wanted to scale the previous perceptron just a little bit by adding another neuron, we may get a structure with two fully connected layers of neurons, as shown in the following diagram:

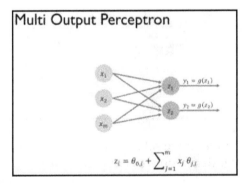

Multi Output Perceptron

$$z_i = \theta_{0,i} + \sum_{j=1}^{m} x_j \, \theta_{j,i}$$

Note here that the feature weights, as well as the additional fictional input we will have per neuron to represent our bias, have both disappeared. To simplify our representation, we have instead denoted both the scalar dot product, and our bias term, as a single symbol.

We choose to represent this mathematical function as the letter z. The value of z is then fed to the activation function, just as we previously did, thus $y = g(z)$. As you can see in the preceding diagram, our input features connect to two different neurons, each of which may adjust its weights and biases to learn a specific and distinct representation from the data it is fed. These representations are then used to predict our output classes, and updated as we train our model.

A single layered network

Right, now we have seen how to leverage two versions of our perception unit, in parallel, enabling each individual unit to learn a different underlying pattern that is possibly present in the data we feed it. We naturally want to connect these neurons to output neurons, which fire to indicate the presence of a specific output class. In our sunny-rainy day classification example, we have two output classes (sunny or rainy), hence a predictive network tasked to solve this problem will have two output neurons. These neurons will be supported by the learning of neurons from the previous layer, and ideally will represent features that are informative for predicting either a rainy or a sunny day. Mathematically speaking, all that is simply happening here is the forward propagation of our transformed input features, followed by the backward propagation of the errors in our prediction. One way of thinking about this is to visualize each node in the following diagram as the holder of a specific number. Similarly, each arrow can be seen as picking up a number from a node, performing a weighted computation on it, and carrying it forward to the next layer of nodes:

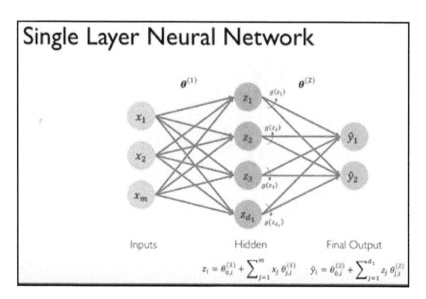

Now, we have a neural network with one hidden layer. We call this a hidden layer as the state of this layer is not directly enforced, as opposed to the input and output layers. Their representations are not hardcoded by the designer of the network. Rather, they are inferred by the network, as data propagates through it.

As we saw, the input layer holds our input values. The set of arrows connecting the input layer to the hidden layer simply compute the bias adjusted dot product (z), of our input features (x) and their respective weights (θ_1). The (z) values then reside in the hidden layer neurons, until we apply our non-linear function, $g(x)$, to these values. After this, the arrows leading away from the hidden layer compute the dot product of $g(z)$ and the weights corresponding to *the* hidden layer, (θ_2), before carrying the result forward to the two output neurons, $\hat{y}_1$ and $\hat{y}_2$. Notice that with each layer comes a respective weights matrix, which is iteratively updated by differentiating our loss function with respect to the weight matrices from the previous training iteration. Hence, we train a neural network by descending the gradient of our loss function relative to our model weights, converging to a global minimum.

Experimenting with TensorFlow playground

Let's see how different neurons can actually capture different patterns in our data using a dummy example. Suppose that we have two output classes in our data, as plotted in the following diagram. The task of our neural network is to learn the decision boundaries separating our two output classes. Plotting this two-dimensional dataset, we get something similar to the following diagram, where we see several decision boundaries that classify the different possible outputs:

We will employ a phenomenal open-source tool to visualize our model's learnings, known as TensorFlow playground. This tool simply allows to simulate a neural network with some synthetic data, and lets us actually *see* what patterns our neurons are picking up on. It lets you tinker with all the concepts we have overviewed so far, including different types and forms of input features, activation functions, learning rate, and many more. We highly encourage you to experiment with the different synthetic datasets they provide, play with the input features and progressively add neurons, as well as hidden layers to see how this affects learning. Do also experiment with different activation functions to see how your model can capture various complex patterns from data. Seeing, is indeed believing! (Or more scientifically put, nullius in verba). As we can see in our diagram below, both neurons in the hidden layer are actually capturing different curvatures in our feature space, learning a specific pattern in the data. You can visualize the weights of our model by observing the thickness of the lines connecting the layers. You can also visualize the output of each neuron (the shaded blue and white areas shown within the neurons) to see what underlining pattern that specific neuron is capturing in our data. This representation, as you will see by experimenting on the playground, is iteratively updated and converges to an ideal value, given the form and type of the data, activation functions, and learning rates used:

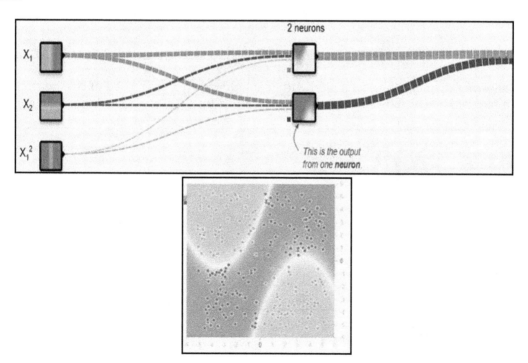

A model with one hidden layer, two neurons, and the sigmoid activation function, trained for 1,000 epochs

Capturing patterns heirarchically

We previously saw how a specific model configuration with two neurons, each equipped with a sigmoid activation function, manages to capture two different curvatures in our feature space, which is then combined to plot our decision boundary, represented by the aforementioned output. However, this is just one possible configuration, leading to one possible decision boundary.

The following diagram shows a model with two hidden layers with the sigmoid activation function, trained for 1,000 epochs:

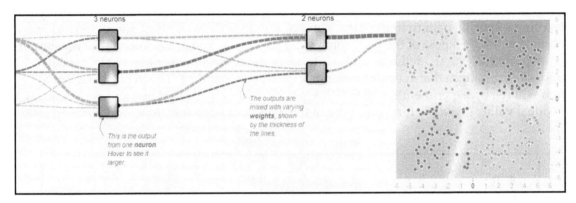

The following diagram shows a model with one hidden layer, composed of two neurons, with a rectified linear unit activation function, trained for 1,000 epochs, on the same dataset:

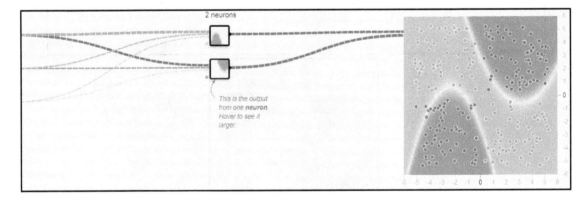

The following diagram shows a model with one hidden layer, composed of three neurons, with a rectified linear unit activation function, again on the same dataset:

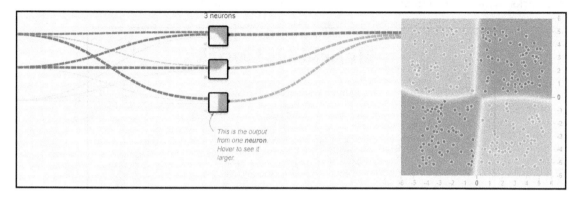

Note that by using different activation functions, and manipulating the number of hidden layers and their neurons, we can achieve very different decision boundaries. It is up to us to asses which of them is ideally predictive, and is suitable for our use case. Mostly, this is done through experimentation, although domain knowledge about the data you are modelling may go a long way.

Steps ahead

Congratulations! In just a few pages, we have already come a long way. Now you know how neural networks learn, and have an idea of the higher-level mathematical constructs that permit it to learn from data. We saw how a single neuron, namely the perceptron, is configured. We saw how this neural unit transforms its input features as data propagates forward through it. We also understood the notion of representing non-linearity through activation functions, and how multiple neurons may be organized in a layer, allowing each individual neuron in the layer to represent different patterns from our data. These learned patterns are updated at each training iteration, for each neuron. We know now that this is done by computing the loss between our predictions and actual output values, and adjusting the weights of each neuron in the model, until we find an ideal configuration.

In fact, modern neural networks employ various types of neurons, configured in diverse ways, for different predictive tasks. While the underlining learning architecture of neural networks always remains the same, the specific configuration of neurons, in terms of their number, inter-connectivity, activation functions used, etc. are elements which define the different types of neural network architectures you may come across. For the time being, we leave you with a comprehensive illustration generously provided by the Asimov institute.

In the following diagram, you can see some prominent types of neurons, or *cells*, along with their configurations that form some of the most commonly used state of the art neural networks, which you will also throughout the course of this book:

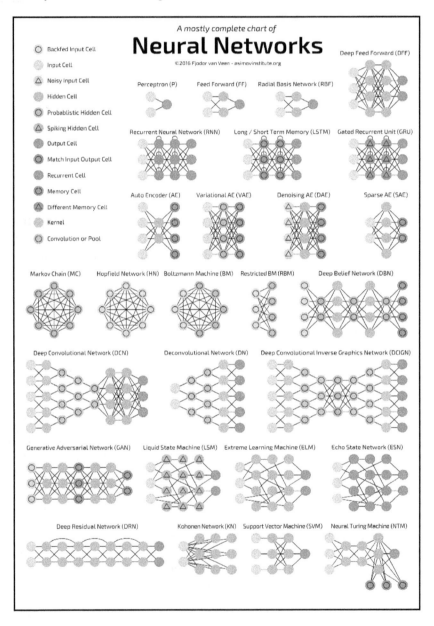

Summary

Now that we have achieved a comprehensive understanding of neural learning systems, we can start getting our hands dirty. We will soon implement our first neural network, test it out for a classic classification task, and practically face many of the concepts we have covered here. In doing so, we will cover a detailed overview of the exact nature of loss optimization, and the evaluation metrics of neural networks.

3
Signal Processing - Data Analysis with Neural Networks

Having acquired substantial knowledge on neural networks, we are now ready to perform our first operation using them. We will start with processing signals, and see how a neural network is fed data. You will be mesmerized at how increasing the levels and complexity of neurons can actually make a problem look simple. We will then look at how language can be processed. We will make several predictions using datasets.

In this chapter, we will cover the following topics:

- Processing signals
- Images as numbers
- Feeding a neural network
- Examples of tensors
- Building a model
- Compiling the model

- Implementing weight regularization in Keras
- Weight regularization experiments
- Implementing dropout regularization in Keras
- Language processing
- The internet movie reviews dataset
- Plotting a single training instance
- One-hot encoding
- Vectorizing features
- Vectorizing labels
- Building a network
- Callbacks
- Accessing model predictions
- Feature-wise normalization
- Cross validation with the scikit-learn API

Processing signals

There may only be four fundamental forces in our universe, but they are all signals. By signal, we mean any kind of feature representations we may have of a real-world phenomenon. Our visual world, for example, is full of signals that indicate motion, color, and shapes. These are very dynamic signals, and it is a miracle that biology is able to process these stimuli so accurately, even if we do say so ourselves. Of course, in the grander scheme of things, realizing that nature has had hundreds of millions of years to perfect this recipe may humble us, if only a little. For now, we can admire the marvel that is the human visual cortex, which is equipped with 140 million densely interconnected neurons. In fact, an entire series of layers (V1 – V5) exist through which information propagates as we engage in progressively more complex image processing tasks. The eye itself, using rods and cones to detect different patterns of light intensity and colors, does an excellent job of piecing together electromagnetic radiation and converting it into electrical impulses through photo transduction.

When we look at an image, our visual cortex is actually interpreting the specific configuration of electromagnetic signals that the eye is converting into electrical signals and feeding it. When we listen to music, our eardrum, or myringa, simply converts and amplifies a successive pattern of vibrational signals so that our auditory cortex may process it. Indeed, it appears that the neural mechanisms in the brain are extremely efficient at abstracting and representing patterns that are present in different real-world signals. In fact, neuroscientists have even found that some mammalian brains have the capacity to be rewired in a manner that permits different cortices to process types of data that they were originally never intended to encounter. Most notably, scientists found that rewiring the auditory cortex of ferrets allowed these creatures to process visual signals from the auditory regions of the brain, allowing them to *see* using very different neurons that they previously employed for the task of audition. Many scientists cite such studies to put forth the case that the brain may be using a master algorithm, which is capable of handling any form of data, and turning it into efficient representations of the world around it.

As intriguing as this is, it naturally raises a thousand more questions about neural learning than it answers, and we sadly do not have the scope to address all of them in this book. Suffice it to say, whatever algorithm—or sets of algorithms—that lets our brain achieve such efficient representations of the world around us, are naturally of great interest to neurologists, deep learning engineers, and the rest of the scientific community alike.

Representational learning

As we saw earlier with our perceptron experiments on the TensorFlow Playground, sets of artificial neurons seem to be capable of learning fairly simple patterns. This is nothing remotely close to the sort of complex representations we humans can perform and wish to predict. However, we can see that, even in their nascent simplicity, these networks seem to be able to adapt to the sort of data we provide them with, at times even outperforming other statistical predictive models. So, what's going on here that is so different than previous approaches to teach machines to do things for us?

It can be very useful to teach a computer what skin cancer looks like, simply by showing it the vast number of medically relevant features that we may have. Indeed, this is what our approach has been toward machines thus far. We would hand-engineer features so that our machines could easily digest them and generate relevant predictions. But why stop there? Why not just show the computer what skin cancer actually *looks* like? Why not show it millions of images and let *it* figure out what is relevant? Indeed, that's exactly what we try to do when we speak of deep learning. As opposed to traditional **Machine Learning (ML)** algorithms, where we represent the data in an explicitly processed representation for the machine to learn, we take a different approach with neural networks. Here, what we actually wish to achieve is for the network to learn these representations on its own.

As shown in the following diagram, a network achieves this by learning simple representations and using them to define more and more complex representations in successive layers, until the ultimate layer learns to represent output classes accurately:

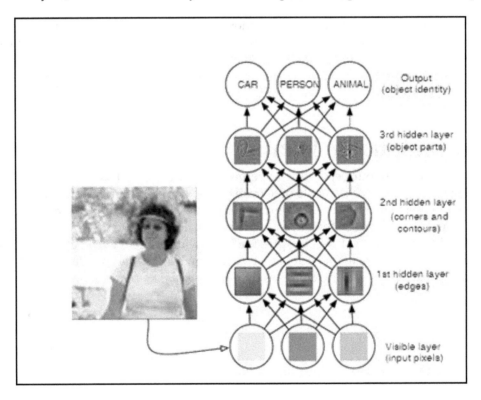

This approach, as it turns out, can be quite useful for teaching your computer to detect complex movement patterns and facial expressions, just as we humans do. Say you want it to accept packages on your behalf when you're away, or perhaps detect any potential robbers trying to break in to your house. Similarly, what if we wanted our computer to schedule our appointments, find potentially lucrative stocks on the market, and keep us up to date according to what we find interesting? Doing so involves processing complex image, video, audio, text, and time-series data, all of which come in complex dimensional representations, and cannot be modeled by just a few neurons. So, how do we work with the neural learning system, akin to what we saw in the last chapter? How do we make neural networks learn the complex and hierarchical patterns in eyes, faces, and other real-world objects? Well, the obvious answer is that we make them bigger. But, as we will see, this brings in complexities of its own. Long story short, the more learnable parameters you put in a network, the higher the chance that it will memorize some random patterns, and hence will not generalize well. Ideally, you want a configuration of neurons that perfectly fits the learning job at hand, but this is almost impossible to determine a priori without performing experiments.

Avoiding random memorization

Another answer can be to manipulate not only the overall number of neurons, but also the degree of interconnectivity among those neurons. We can do this through techniques such as *dropout regularization* and *weighted parameter*, as we will see soon enough. So far, we have already seen the various computations that can be performed through each neuron as data propagates through a network. We also saw how the brain leverages hundreds of millions of densely interconnected neurons to get the job done. But, naturally, we can't just scale up our networks by arbitrarily adding more and more neurons. Long story short, simulating a neural structure close to the brain is likely to require thousands of **petaflops** (a unit of computing speed equal to one thousand million million (10^{15}) floating-point operations per second) of computing power. Maybe this will be possible in the near future, with the aforementioned paradigm of massively parallelized computing, along with other advances in software and hardware technologies. For now, though, we have to think of clever ways to train our network so that it can find the most efficient representations without wasting precious computational resources.

Representing signals with numbers

In this chapter, we will see how we can layer sequences of neurons to progressively represent more and more complex patterns. We will also see how concepts such as regularization and batched learning are essential in getting the most out of a training session. We will learn to process different types of real-world data in the form of images, texts, and time-series dependent information.

Images as numbers

For tasks such as these, we need deep networks with multiple hidden layers if we are hoping to learn any representative features for our output classes. We also need a nice dataset to practice our understanding and familiarize ourselves with the tools we will be using to design our intelligent systems. Hence, we come to our first hands-on neural network task as we introduce ourselves to the concepts of computer vision, image processing, and hierarchical representation learning. Our task at hand is to teach computers to read numbers not as 0 and 1s, as they already do, but more in the manner of how we would read digits that are composed by our own kin. We are speaking of handwritten digits, and for this task, we will be using the iconic MNIST dataset, the true *hello world* of deep learning datasets. For our first example, there are good theoretical and practical reasons behind our choice.

From a theoretical perspective, we need to understand how we can use layer neurons to progressively learn more complex patterns, like our own brain does. Since our brain has had about 2,000 to 2,500 years worth of training data, it has gotten quite good at identifying complex symbols such as handwritten digits. In fact, we normally perceive this as an absolutely effortless task, since we learn how to distinguish between such symbols from as early as preschool. But this is actually quite a daunting task. Consider the vast variations in how each of these digits may be written by different humans, and yet our brains are still able to classify these digits, as if it were much ado about nothing:

While exhaustively coding explicit rules would drive any programmer insane, as we look at the preceding image, our own brain intuitively notice some patterns in the data. For example, it picks up on how both **2** and **3** have a half-loop at the top of them, and how **1, 4**, and **7** have a straight downward line. It also perceives how a **4** is actually one downward line, one semi-downward line, and another horizontal line in between the others. Due to this, we are able to easily break down a complex pattern into smaller patterns. This is specifically easy to do with handwritten digits, as we just saw. Therefore, our task will be to see how we can construct a deep neural network and hope for each of our neurons to capture simple patterns from our data, such as line segments, and then progressively construct more complex patterns in deeper layers using the simple patterns we learned in the previous layers. We will do this to learn about the accurate combinations of representations that correspond to our output classes.

Practically speaking, the MNIST dataset has been studied for about two decades by many pioneers in the field of deep learning. We have gained a good wealth of knowledge out of this dataset, making it ideal for exploring concepts such as layer representations, regularization, and overfitting, among others. As soon as we understand how to train and test a neural network, we can repurpose it for more exciting tasks.

Feeding a neural network

Essentially, all of the data that enters and propagates through the network is represented by a mathematical structure known as a **tensor**. This applies to audio data, images, video, and any other data we can think of, to feed our data-hungry network. In mathematics (https://en.wikipedia.org/wiki/Mathematics), a tensor is defined as an abstract and arbitrary geometric (https://en.wikipedia.org/wiki/Geometry) entity that maps aggregations of vectors in a multi-linear (https://en.wikipedia.org/wiki/Linear_map) manner to a resulting tensor. In fact, vectors and scalars are considered simpler forms of tensors. In Python, tensors are defined with three specific properties, as follows:

- **Rank**: Specifically, this denotes the number axes. A matrix is said to have the rank 2, as it represents a two-dimensional tensor. In Python libraries, this is often indicated as `ndim`.
- **Shape**: The shape of a tensor can be checked by calling the shape property on a NumPy *n*-dimensional array (which is how a tensor is represented in Python). This will return a tuple of integers, indicating the number of dimensions a tensor has along each axis.

- **Content**: This refers to the type of data that's stored in the tensor, and can be checked by calling the `type()` method on a tensor of interest. This will return data types such as float32, uint8, float64, and so on, except for string values, which are first converted into vector representations before being represented as a tensor.

The following is a tensor graph. Don't worry about the complex diagram—we will look at what it means later:

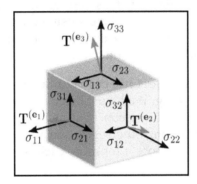

Examples of tensors

The illustration we previously saw was that of a three dimensional tensor, yet tensors can appear in many forms. In the following section, we will overview some tensors of different ranks, starting with a tensor of rank zero:

- **Scalar**: Values simply denote a single numeric value on its own. This can also be described as a tensor of dimension 0. An example of this is processing a single grayscale pixel of an image through a network.
- **Vector**: A bunch of scalars or an array of numbers is called a **vector**, or a tensor of rank 1. A 1D tensor is said to have exactly one axis. An example of this is processing a single flattened image.
- **Matrix**: An array of vectors is a matrix, or 2D tensor. A matrix has two axes (often referred to as rows and columns). You can visually interpret a matrix as a rectangular grid of numbers. An example of this is processing a single grayscale image.
- **Three-dimensional tensor**: By packing several matrices into a new array, you get a 3D tensor, which is visually interpretable as a cube of numbers. An example of this is processing a dataset of grayscale images.

- **Four-dimensional tensor**: By packing 3D tensors in an array, you can create a 4D tensor, and so on. An example of this is processing a dataset of colored images.
- **Five-dimensional tensor**: These are created by packing 4D tensors in an array. An example of this is processing a dataset of videos.

Dimensionality of data

So, consider the tensor of a shape (400, 600, 3). This is a common input shape that refers to a three-dimensional tensor that's used to represent a color image of 400 x 600 pixels. Since the MNIST dataset uses binary grayscale pixel values, we only deal with matrices of 28 x 28 pixels when representing an image. Here, each image is a tensor of dimension two, and the whole dataset can be represented by a tensor of dimension three. In a color image, each pixel value actually has three numbers, representing the amount of red, green, and blue light intensity represented by that pixel. Hence, with colored images, the two-dimensional matrices that are used to represent an image now scale up to three-dimensional tensors. Such a tensor is denoted by a tuple of $(x, y, 3)$, where x and y represent the pixel dimensions of the image. Hence, a dataset of color images can be represented by a four-dimensional tensor, as we will see in later examples. For now, it is useful to know that we can use NumPy n-dimensional arrays to represent, reshape, manipulate, and store tensors in Python.

Making some imports

So, let's get started, shall we? We will perform some simple experiments by leveraging all the concepts we have learned about in the previous chapters, and perhaps also encounter some new ones while on the job. We will use Keras, as well as the TensorFlow API, allowing us to also explore the eager execution paradigm. Our first task will be to implement a simple version of the multi-layered perceptron. This version is known as the **feedforward neural network**, and is a basic architecture that we can use to further explore some simple image classification examples. Obeying customary deep learning tradition, we will begin our first classification task by using the MNIST dataset for handwritten digits. This dataset has 70,000 grayscale images of digits between 0 and 9. The large size of this dataset is ideal, as machines require about 5,000 images per class to be able to come close to human-level performance at visual recognition tasks. The following code imports the libraries we will be using:

```
import numpy as np
import keras
from keras.datasets import mnist
from keras.utils import np_utils
```

Keras's sequential API

As you may well know, each Python library often comes with a core data abstraction that defines the data structure that the library is able to manipulate to perform computations. NumPy has its arrays, while pandas has its DataFrames. The core data structure of Keras is a model, which is essentially a manner to organize layers of interconnected neurons. We will start with the simplest type of model: the sequential model (`https://keras.io/getting-started/sequential-model-guide/`). This is available as a linear stack of layers through the sequential API. More complex architectures also allow us to review the functional API, which is used to build custom layers. We will cover these later. The following code imports the sequential model, as well as some of the layers we will be using to build our first network:

```
from keras.models import Sequential
from keras.layers import Flatten, Dense, Dropout
from keras.layers.core import Activation
from keras import backend as K
```

Loading the data

Now, let's load in the data and split it up. Thankfully, MNIST is one of the core datasets that's already implemented in Keras, allowing a nice one-liner import, which also lets us split up our data in training and test sets. Of course, real-world data is not that easy to port and split up. A lot of useful tools exist for this purpose in `Keras.utils`, which we will cover briefly later, but also encourage you to explore. Alternatively, other **ML** libraries such as scikit-learn come with some handy tools (such as `train_test_split`, `MinMaxScaler`, and `normalizer`, to name a few methods), which, as their names indicate, let you split up, scale, and normalize your data as often required to optimize neural network training. Let's import and load the datasets, as follows:

```
from keras.datasets import mnist
(x_train, y_train),(x_test, y_test)= fashion_mnist.load_data()
```

Checking the dimensions

Next, we need to check out what our data looks like. We will do this by checking its type, then shape, and finally by plotting our individual observations using `matplotlib.pyplot`, like so:

```
type(x_train[0]),x_train.shape,y_train.shape
```

You will get the following result:

```
(numpy.ndarray, (60000, 28, 28), (60000,))
```

Plotting the points:

```
import matplotlib.-pyplot as plt
%matplotlib inline
plt.show(x_train[0], cmap= plt.cm.binary)
<matplotlib.image.AxesImage at 0x24b7f0fa3c8>
```

This will plot a figure similar to what's shown in the following screenshot:

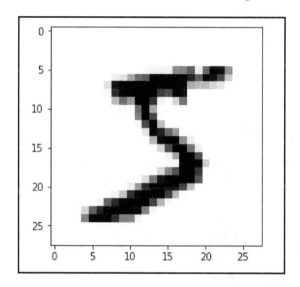

As we can see, our training set has 60,000 images, with each image represented by a 28 x 28 matrix. When we represent our whole dataset, we are just representing a tensor of three dimensions (60,000 x 28 x 28). Now, let's rescale our pixel values, which usually lie between 0 and 225. Rescaling these values to values between 0 and 1 makes it a lot easier for our network to perform computations and learn predictive features. We encourage you to carry out experiments with and without normalization so that you can assess the difference in predictive power:

```
x_train=keras.utils.normalize(x_train, axis=1)
x_test=keras.utils.normalize(x_test, axis=1)
plt.imshow(x_train[0], cmap=plt.cm.binary)
```

The preceding code generates the following output:

```
<matplotlib.image.AxesImage at 0x24b00003e48>
```

The following plot is acquired:

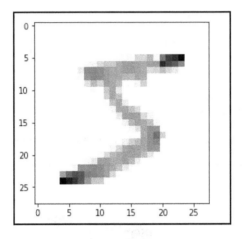

Building a model

Now we can move on and build our predictive model. But before jumping into the interesting code, we must know the theory that surrounds a few important things.

Introducting Keras layers

The core building blocks of a neural network model in Keras is its layers. Layers are basically data-processing filters that *contort* the data they are fed into more useful representations. As we will see, prominent architectures of neural networks mostly vary in the manner in which layers are designed, and the interconnection of neurons among them. The inventor of Keras, Francois Chollet, describes this architecture as performing a *progressive distillation* on our data. Let's see how this works:

```
#Simple Feedforward Neural Network
model = Sequential()

#feeds in the image composed of 28 X 28 a pixel matrix as one sequence
 of 784
model.add(Flatten(input_shape=(28,28)))
model.add(Dense(24, activation='relu'))
model.add(Dense(8, activation='relu'))
model.add(Dense(10, activation='softmax'))
```

We define our model by initializing an instance of a blank model with no layers. Then, we add our first layer, which always expects an input dimension corresponding to the size of the data you want it to ingest. In our case, we want the model to ingest sets of 28 x 28 pixels, as we defined previously. The extra comma we added refers to how many examples the network will see at a time, as we will soon see. We also call the `Flatten()` method on our input matrix. All this does is convert each 28 x 28 image matrix into a single vector of 784-pixel values, each corresponding to its own input neuron.

We continue adding the layers until we get to our output layer, which has a number of output neurons corresponding to the number of our output classes—in this case, the 10 digits between 0 and 9. Do note that only the input layer needs to specify an input dimension of data entering it, as the progressive hidden layers are able to perform automatic shape inference (and only the first, because the following layers can do automatic shape inference).

Initializing weights

We also have the option to initialize the neurons on each layer with specific weights. This is not a prerequisite, as they will be automatically initialized with small random numbers if not specified otherwise. Weight initialization practices are actually a whole separate sub-field of study in neural networks. It is prominently noted that the careful initialization of the network can significantly speed up the learning process.

You can use the `kernel_initializer` and `bais_initializer` parameters to set both the weights and biases of each layer, respectively. Remember that these very weights will represent the knowledge that's acquired by our network, which is why ideal initializations can significantly boost its learning:

```
#feeds in the image composed of 28✕28 as one sequence of 784
model.add(Flatten(input_shape=(28,28)))
model.add(Dense(64, activation='relu',
        kernel_initializer='glorot_uniform',
        bias_initializer='zeros'))
model.add(Dense(18, activation='relu'))
model.add(Dense(10, activation='softmax'))
```

A comprehensive review of the different parameter values is beyond the scope of this chapter. We may encounter some use cases where tweaking these parameters is beneficial later on (refer to chapter optimization). Some values for the `kernel_initializer` parameter include the following:

- `glorot_uniform`: The weights are drawn from samples of uniform distributions between `-limit` and `limit`. Here, the term `limit` is defined as `sqrt(6 / (fan_in + fan_out))`. The term `fan_in` simply denotes the number of input units in the weight tensor, while `fan_out` is the number of output units in the weight tensor.
- `random_uniform`: The weights are randomly initialized with small uniform values ranging between -0.05 and 0.05.
- `random_normal`: The weights are initialized for obeying a Gaussian distribution[1], with a mean of 0 and a standard deviation of 0.05.
- `zero`: The layer weights are initialized at zero.

Keras activations

At the moment, our network is composed of a flattened input layer, followed by a sequence of two dense layers, which are fully connected layers of neurons. The first two layers employ a **Rectified Linear Unit (ReLU)** activation function, which plots out a bit differently than the sigmoid we saw in Chapter 2, *A Deeper Dive into Neural Networks*. In the following diagram, you can see how some of the different activation functions that are provided by Keras plot out. Remember, picking between them requires an intuitive understanding of the possible decision boundaries that may help with or hinder the partitioning your feature space. Using the appropriate activation function in conjunction with ideally initialized biases can be of paramount importance in some scenarios, but trivial in others. It is always advisable to experiment, leaving no stone unturned:

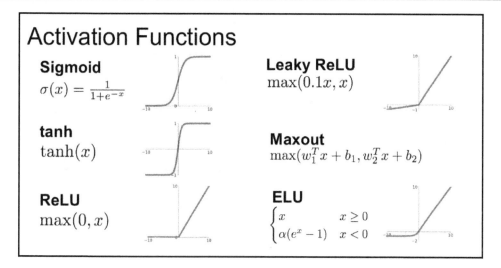

The fourth (and last) layer in our model is a 10-way Softmax layer. In our case, this means it will return an array of ten probability scores, all of which will add up to 1. Each score will be the probability that the current digit image belongs to one of our output classes. Hence, for any given input, a layer with the Softmax activation computes and returns the class probability of that input, with respect to each of our output classes.

Summarizing your model visually

Going back to our model, let's summarize the output of what we are about to train. You can do this in Keras by using the `summary()` method on the model, which is actually a shortcut for the longer `utility` function (and hence harder to remember), which is as follows:

```
keras.utils.print_summary(model, line_length=None, positions=None,
                          print_fn=None)
```

Using this, you can actually visualize the shapes of the individual layers of the neural network, as well as the parameters in each layer:

```
model.summary()
```

The preceding code generates the following output:

```
Layer (type) Output Shape Param #
=================================================================
flatten_2 (Flatten) (None, 784) 0
_____
dense_4 (Dense) (None, 1024) 803840
_____
dense_5 (Dense) (None, 28) 28700
_____
dense_6 (Dense) (None, 10) 290
=================================================================
Total params: 832,830
Trainable params: 832,830
Non-trainable params: 0
_____
```

As you can see, contrary to the perceptron we saw in Chapter 2, *A Deeper Dive into Neural Networks*, this extremely simple model already has 51, 600 trainable parameters that are capable of scaling its learning almost exponentially compared to its ancestor.

Compiling the model

Next, we will compile our Keras model. Compilation basically refers to the manner in which your neural network will learn. It lets you have hands-on control of implementing the learning process, which is done by using the compile method that's called on our model object. The method takes at least three arguments:

```
model.compile(optimizer='resprop', #'sgd'
              loss='sparse_categorical_crossentropy',
              metrics=['accuracy'])
```

Here, we describe the following functions:

- **A `loss` function**: This simply measures our performance on the training data, compared to the true output labels. Due to this, the `loss` function can be used as an indication of our model's errors. As we saw earlier, this metric is actually a function that determines how far our model's predictions are from the actual labels of the output classes. We saw the **Mean Squared Error (MSE)** `loss` function in `Chapter 2`, *A Deeper Dive into Neural Networks*, of which many variations exist. These `loss` functions are implemented in Keras, depending on the nature of our **ML** task. For example, if you wish to perform a binary classification (two output neurons representing two output classes), you are better off choosing binary cross-entropy. For more than two categories, you may try categorical cross-entropy, or sparse categorical cross-entropy. The former is used when your output labels are one-hot encoded, whereas the latter is used when your output classes are numerical categorical variables. For regression problems, we often advise the MSE `loss` function. When dealing with sequence data, as we will later, then **Connectionist Temporal Classification (CTC)** is deemed a more appropriate type of `loss` function. Other flavors of loss may differ in the manner they measure the distance between predictions and actual output labels (for example, `cosine_proximity` uses a cosine measure of distance), or the choice of probability distribution to model the predicted values (for example, the **Poisson loss function** is perhaps better if you are dealing with count data).

- **An `optimizer`**: An intuitive way to think of an optimizer is that it tells the network how to get to a global minimum loss. This includes the goal you want to optimize, as well as the size of the step it will take in the direction of your goal. Technically, the optimizer is often described as the mechanism that's employed by the network to self-update, which is does by using the data it is fed and the `loss` function. Optimization algorithms are used to update weights and biases that are the internal parameters of a model in the process of error reduction. There are actually two distinct types of optimization functions: functions with constant learning rates (such as **Stochastic Gradient Decent (SGD)**) and functions with adaptive learning rates (such as Adagrad, Adadelta, RMSprop, and Adam). The latter of the two are known for implementing heuristic-based and pre-parameterized learning rate methods. Consequentially, using adaptive learning rates can lead to less work in tuning the hyperparameters of your model.

- `metrics`: This simply denotes the evaluation benchmark we monitor during training and testing. Accuracy is most commonly used, but you may design and implement a custom metric through Keras, if you so choose. The main functional difference between the loss and accuracy score that's shown by the metric is that the accuracy measure is not involved in the training process at all, whereas loss is used directly in the training process by our optimizer to backpropagate the errors.

Fitting the model

The `fit` parameter initiates the training session, and hence should be thought of as synonymous to training our model. It takes your training features, their corresponding training labels, the number of times the model sees your data, and the number of learning examples your model sees per training iteration as training measures, respectively:

```
model.fit(x_train, y_train, epochs=5, batch_size = 2) #other arguments
                        validation split=0.33, batch_size=10
```

You can also have additional arguments to shuffle your data, create validation splits, or give custom weights to output classes. Shuffling training data before each epoch can be useful, especially to ensure that your model does not learn any random non-predictive sequences in our data, and hence simply overfit the training set. To shuffle your data, you have to set the Boolean value of the shuffle argument to **True**. Finally, custom weights can be particularly useful if you have underrepresented classes in your dataset. Setting a higher weight is equivalent to telling your model, *Hey, you, pay more attention to these examples here*. To set custom weights, you have to provide the `class_weight` argument with a dictionary that maps class indices to custom weights corresponding to your output classes, in order of the indices that are provided.

The following is an overview of the key architectural decisions you will face when compiling a model. These decisions relate to the training process you instruct your model to undergo:

- `epochs`: This argument must be defined as an integer value, corresponding to the number of times your model will iterate through the entire dataset. Technically, the model is not trained for a number of iterations given by epochs, but merely until the epoch of index epochs is reached. You want to set this parameter *just right*, depending on the nature of complexity you want your model to represent. Setting it too low will lead to simplistic representations that are used for inference, whereas setting it too high will make your model overfit on your training data.

- `batch_size`: The `batch_size` defines the number of samples that will be propagated through the network per training iteration. Intuitively, this can be thought of as the number of examples the network sees at a time while learning. Mathematically, this is simply the number of training instances the network will see before updating the model weights. So far, we have been updating our model weights at each training example (with a `batch_size` of 1), but this can quickly become a computational and memory management burden. This becomes especially cumbersome in instances where your dataset is too big to even load into memory. Setting a `batch_size` helps prevent this. Neural networks also train faster in mini-batches. In fact, batch size even has an impact on the accuracy of our gradient estimate during the backpropagation process, as shown in the following diagram. The same network is trained using three different batch sizes. Stochastic denotes random, or a batch size of one. As you can see, the direction of the stochastic and mini-batch gradients (green) fluctuates much more in comparison to the steady direction of the larger full-batch gradient (blue):

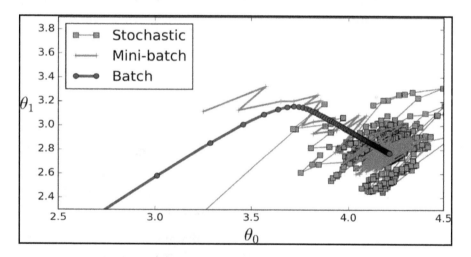

- The **number of iterations** (which don't need to be explicitly defined) simply denotes the number of passes, where each pass contains the number of training examples denoted by the `batch_size`. To be clear, by one pass, we mean a forward filtering of data through our layers, as well as the backpropagation of errors. Suppose that we set our batch size to 32. One iteration encompasses our model by viewing 32 training examples, then updating its weights accordingly. In a dataset of 64 examples with a batch size of 32, it will take only two iterations for your model to cycle through it.

Now that we have called the `fit` method on our training samples to initiate the learning process, we will observe the output, which simply displays the estimated training time, loss (in errors), and accuracy per epoch on our training data:

```
Epoch 1/5
60000/60000 [==========] - 12s 192us/step - loss: 0.3596 - acc: 0.9177
Epoch 2/5
60000/60000 [==========] - 10s 172us/step - loss: 0.1822 - acc: 0.9664
Epoch 3/5
60000/60000 [==========] - 10s 173us/step - loss: 0.1505 - acc: 0.9759
Epoch 4/5
60000/60000 [==========] - 11s 177us/step - loss: 0.1369 - acc:
                          0.97841s - loss:
Epoch 5/5
60000/60000 [==========] - 11s 175us/step - loss: 0.1245 - acc: 0.9822
```

In only five full runs through our data, we achieve an accuracy of 0.96 (96.01%) during training. Now, we must verify whether our model is truly learning what we want it to learn by testing it on our secluded test set, which our model hasn't seen so far:

```
model.evaluation(x_test, y_test)

10000/10000 [==============================] - 1s 98us/step
[0.1425468367099762, 0.9759]
```

Evaluating model performance

Whenever we evaluate a network, we are actually interested in our accuracy of classifying images in the test set. This remains true for any ML model, as our accuracy on the training set is not a reliable indicator of our model's generalizability.

In our case, the test set accuracy is 95.78%, which is marginally lower than our training set accuracy of 96%. This is a classic case of overfitting, where our model seems to have captured irrelevant noise in our data to predict the training images. Since that inherent noise is different on our randomly selected test set, our network couldn't rely on the useless representations it had previously picked up on, and so performed poorly during testing. As we will see throughout this book, when testing neural networks, it is important to ensure that it has learnt correct and efficient representations of our data. In other words, we need to ensure that our network is not overfitting on our training data.

By the way, you can always visualize your predictions on the test set by printing out the label with the highest probability value for the given test subject and plotting the said test subject using Matplotlib. Here, we are printing out the label with maximum probability for test subject 110. Our model thinks it is an 8. By plotting the subject, we see that our model is right in this case:

```
predictions= load_model.predict([x_test])

#predict use the inference graph generated in the model to predict class
labels on our test set
#print maximum value for prediction of x_test subject no. 110)

import numpy as np
print(np.argmax(predictions[110]))
---------------------------------------------
8
---------------------------------------------
plt.imshow(x_test[110]))
<matplotlib.image.AxesImage at 0x174dd374240>
```

The preceding code generates the following output:

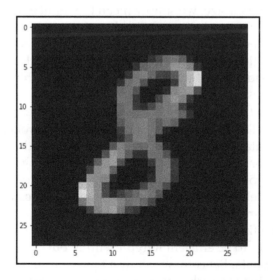

Once satisfied, you can save and load your model for later use, as follows:

```
model.save('mnist_nn.model')
load_model=kera.models.load_model('mnist_nn.model')
```

Regularization

So, what can you do to prevent a model from learning misleading or irrelevant patterns from the training data? Well, with neural networks, the best solution is to almost always get more training data. A model that's trained on more data will indeed allow your model to have better out-of-set predictivity. Of course, getting more data is not always that simple, or even possible. When this is the case, you have several other techniques at your disposal to achieve similar effects. One of them is to constrain your model in terms of the amount of information that it may store. As we saw in the *behind enemy lines* example in `Chapter 1,` *Overview of Neural Networks*, it is useful to find the most efficient representations of information, or representations with the lowest entropy. Similarly, if we can only afford our model the ability to memorize a small number of patterns, we are actually forcing it to find the most efficient representations that generalize better on other data that our model may encounter later on. This process of improving model generalizability through reducing overfitting is known as **regularization**, and will be go over it in more detail before we use it in practice.

Adjusting network size

When we speak of a network's size, we simply mean the number of trainable parameters within the network. These parameters are defined by the number of layers in the network, as well as the number of neurons per each layer. Essentially, a network's size is a measure of its complexity. We mentioned how having too large a network size can be counterproductive and lead to overfitting. An intuitive way to think about this is that we should favor simpler representations over complex ones, as long as they achieve the same ends—sort of a *lex parsimoniae*, if you will. The engineers who design such learning systems are indeed deep thinkers. The intuition here is that you could probably have various representations of your data, depending on your network's depth and number of neurons per layer, but we will favor simpler configurations and only progressively scale a network if required, to prevent it from using any extra learning capacity to memorize randomness. However, letting our model have too few parameters may well cause it to underfit, leaving it oblivious to the underlying trends we are trying to capture in our data. Through experimentation, you can find a network size that fits just right, depending on your use case. We force our network to be efficient in representing our data, allowing it to generalize better out of our training data. Beneath, we show a few experiments that are performed while varying the size of the network. This lets us compare how our loss on the validation set differs per epoch. As we will see, larger models are quicker to diverge away from the minimum loss values, and they will start to overfit on our training data almost instantly:

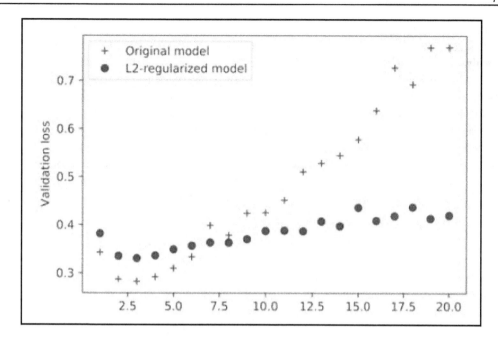

Size experiments

Now we will perform some short experiments by varying the size of our network and gauging our performance. We will train six simple neural networks on Keras, each progressively larger than the other, to observe how these separate networks learn to classify handwritten digits. We will also present some of the results from the experiments. All of these models were trained with a constant batch size (`batch_size=100`), the `adam` optimizer, and `sparse_categorical_crossentropy` as a `loss` function, for the purpose of this experiment.

The following fitting graph shows how increasing our neural network's complexity (in terms of size) impacts our performance on the training and test sets of our data. Note that we are always aiming for a model that minimizes the difference between training and test accuracy/loss, as this indicates the minimum amount of overfitting. Intuitively, this simply shows us how much our networks learning benefits if we allocate it more neurons. By observing the increase in accuracy on the test set, we can see that adding more neurons does help our network to better classify images that it has never encountered before. This can be noticed until the *sweet spot*, which is where the training and test values are the closest to each other. Eventually, however, increases in complexity will lead to diminishing returns. In our case, our model seems to overfit the least at a dropout rate around 0.5, after which the accuracy of the training and test sets start to diverge:

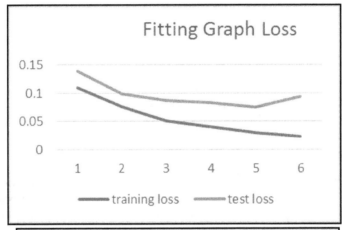

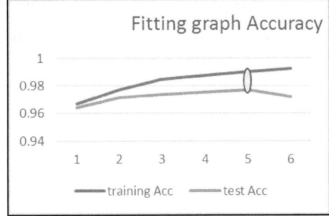

To replicate these results by increasing the size of our network, we can tweak both the breadth (number of neurons per layer) and the depth of the network (number of layers in network). Adding depth to your network is done in Keras by adding layers to your initialized model by using `model.add()`. The `add` method takes the type of layer (for example, `Dense()`), as an argument. The `Dense` function takes the number of neurons to be initialized in that specific layer, along with the activation function to be employed for said layer, as arguments. The following is an example of this:

```
model.add(Dense(512, activation='softmax'))
```

Regularizing the weights

Another way to make sure that your network doesn't pick up on irrelevant features is through regularizing the weights of our model. This simply allows us to put a constraint on the complexity of the network by limiting its layer weights to only take small values. All this does is make the distribution of layer weights more regular. How do we do this? By simply adding a cost to the `loss` function of our network. This cost actually represents a penalization for neurons that have larger weights. Conventionally, we implement this cost in three ways, namely L1, L2, and elastic net regularization:

- **L1 regularization**: We add a cost that is proportional to the absolute value of our weighted coefficients.
- **L2 regularization**: We add a cost that is proportional to the square of the value of the weighted coefficients. This is also known as **weight decay**, as the weights exponentially decay to zero if no other update is scheduled.
- **Elastic net regularization**: This regularization method allows us to capture the complexity of our model by using a combination of both L1 and L2 regularization.

Using dropout layers

Finally, adding dropout neurons to layers is a technique that's widely used to regularize neural networks and prevent them from overfitting. Here, we, quite literally, drop out some neurons from our model at random. Why? Well, this results in a two-fold utility. Firstly, the contributions these neurons had for the activations of neurons further down our network are randomly ignored during a forward pass of data through our network. Also, any weight adjustments during the process of backpropagation are not applied to the neuron. While seemingly bizarre, there is good intuition behind this. Intuitively, neuron weights are adjusted at each backward pass to specialize a specific feature in your training data. But specialization breeds dependence. What often ends up happening is the surrounding neurons start relying on the specialization of a certain neuron in the vicinity, instead of doing some representational work themselves. This dependence pattern is often denoted as complex co-adaptation, a term that was coined by **Artificial Intelligence** (**AI**) researchers. One among them was Geoffrey Hinton, who was the original co-author of the backpropagation paper and is prominently referred to as the godfather of deep learning. Hinton playfully describes this behavior of complex coadaptation as *conspiracies* between neurons, stating that he was inspired by a fraud prevention system at his bank. This bank continuously rotated its employees so that whenever Hinton paid the bank a visit, he would always encounter a different person behind the desk.

Thinking about dropout intuitively

For those of you who are familiar with Leonardo Dicaprio's movie *Catch me if you can*, you'll recall how Leonardo charmed the bank workers by asking them on dates and buying them treats, only so he could defraud the bank by cashing in his fake airline checks. In fact, due to the frequent fraternization of the employees and DiCaprio's character, the bank workers were paying more attention to irrelevant features such as DiCaprio's charm. What they should have actually been paying attention was the fact that DiCaprio was cashing out his monthly salary checks more than three times each month. Needless to say, businesses don't usually behave so generously. Dropping out some neurons is synonymous to rotating them to ensure that none of them get lazy and let a sleazy Leonardo defraud your network.

When we apply a dropout to a layer, we simply drop some of the outputs it would have otherwise given. Suppose a layer produces the vector [3, 5, 7, 8, 1] as an output for a given input. Adding a dropout rate of (0.4) to this layer would simply convert this output to [0, 5, 7, 0, 1]. All we did was initialize 40% of the scalars in our vector as zero.

Dropout only occurs during training. During testing, layers with dropouts have their outputs scaled down by the factor of the dropout rate that was previously used. This is actually done to adjust for the fact that more neurons are active during testing than training, as a result of the dropout mechanism.

Implementing weight regularization in Keras

So far, we have visited the theories behind three specific ways that allow us to improve our model's generalizability on unseen data. Primarily, we can vary our network size to ensure it has no extra learning capacity. We can also penalize inefficient representations by initializing weighted parameters. Finally, we can add dropout layers to prevent our network from getting lazy. As we noted previously, seeing is believing.

Now, let's implement our understanding using the MNIST dataset and some Keras code. As we saw previously, to change the network size, you are simply required to change the number of neurons per layer. This can be done in Keras during the process of adding layers, like so:

```
import keras.regularizers
model=Sequential()
model.add(Flatten(input_shape=(28, 28)))
model.add(Dense(1024, kernel_regularizer=
                    regularizers.l2(0.0001),activation ='relu'))
model.add(Dense(28, kernel_regularizer=regularizers.l2(0.0001),
         activation='relu'))
model.add(Dense(10, activation='softmax'))
```

Weight regularization experiments

Simply put, regularizers let us apply penalties to layer parameters during optimization. These penalties are incorporated in to the `loss` function that the network optimizes. In Keras, we regularize the weights of a layer by passing a `kernel_regularizer` instance to a layer:

```
import keras.regularizers
model=Sequential()
model.add(Flatten(input_shape=(28,28)))
model.add(Dense(1024, kernel_regularizer=regularizers.l2(0.0001),
        activation='relu'))
model.add(Dense(10, activation='softmax'))
```

As we mentioned previously, we add L2 regularization to both our layers, each with an alpha value of (0.0001). The alpha value of a regularizer simply refers to the transformation that's being applied to each coefficient in the weight matrix of the layer, before it is added to the total loss of our network. In essence, the alpha value is used to multiply each coefficient in our weight matrix with it (in our case, 0.0001). The different regularizers in Keras can be found in `keras.regularizers`. The following diagram shows how regularization impacts validation loss per epoch on two models that are the same size. One observes that our regularized model is much less prone to overfitting, since the validation loss does not significantly increase as a function of time. On the model without regularization, we can clearly see that this is not the case, and after about seven epochs, the model starts overfitting, and so performs worse on the validation set:

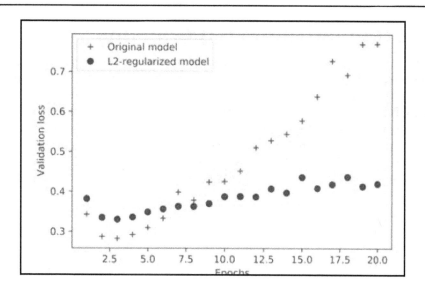

Implementing dropout regularization in Keras

In Keras, adding a dropout layer is also very simple. All you are required to do is use the `model.add()` parameter again, and then specify a dropout layer (instead of the dense layer that we've been using so far) to be added. The `Dropout` parameter in Keras takes a float value that refers to the fraction of neurons whose predictions will be dropped. A very low dropout rate might not provide the robustness we are looking for, while a high dropout rate simply means we have a network prone to amnesia, incapable of remembering any useful representations. Once again, we strive for a dropout value that is just right; conventionally, the dropout rate is set between 0.2 and 0.4:

```
#Simple feed forward neural network
model=Sequential()

#feeds in the image composed of 28 X 28 a pixel matrix as one sequence of
784
model.add(Flatten(input_shape=(28,28)))
model.add(Dense(1024, activation='relu'))
model.add(Dropout(0.3)
model.add(Dense(28, activation='relu'))
model.add(Dense(10, activation='softmax'))
```

Dropout regularization experiments

The following are two experiments that we performed using a network of the same size, with different dropout rates, to observe the differences in performance. We started with a dropout rate of 0.1, and progressively scaled to 0.6 to see how this affected our performance in recognizing handwritten digits. As we can see in the following diagram, scaling our dropout rate seems to reduce overfitting, as the model's superficial accuracy on the training set progressively drops. We can see that both our training and test accuracy converges near the dropout rate of 0.5, after which they exhibit divergent behavior. This simply tells us that the network seems to overfit the least when a dropout layer of rate 0.5 is added:

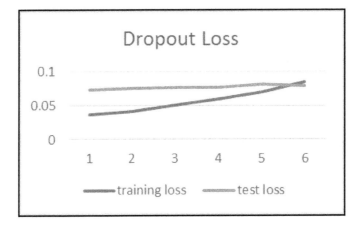

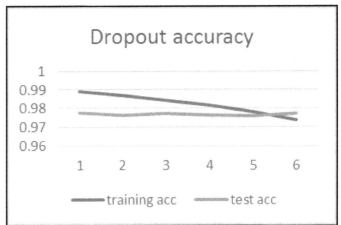

Complexity and time

Now, you have seen some of the most prominent tricks in our repertoire to reduce overfitting through regularization. In essence, regularization is just a manner of controlling the complexity of our network. Complexity control is not just useful to restrict your network from memorizing randomness; it also brings more direct benefits. Inherently, more complex networks are computationally expensive. They will take longer to train, and hence consume more of your resources. While this makes an insignificant difference when dealing with the task at hand, this difference is still quite noticeable. In the following diagram is a time complexity chart. This is a useful way of visualizing training time as a function of network complexity. We can see that an increase in our network's complexity seems to have a quasi-exponential effect on the increase in average time taken per training iteration:

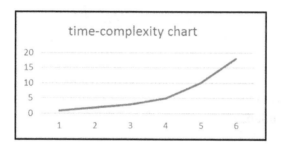

A summary of MNIST

So far in our journey, you were introduced to the fundamental learning mechanisms and processes that govern a neural network's functionality. You learned that neural networks need tensor representations of input data to be able to process it for predictive use cases. You also learned how different types of data that are found in our world, such as images, videos, text, and so on, can be represented as tensors of n-dimensions. Furthermore, you saw how to implement a sequential model in Keras, which essentially lets you build sequential layers of interconnected neurons. You used this model structure to construct a simple feedforward neural network for the task of classifying handwritten digits with the MNIST dataset. In doing so, you learned about the key architectural decisions to consider at each stage of model development.

During model construction, the main decisions pertain to defining the correct input size of your data, choosing a relevant activation function per layer, and defining the number of output neurons in your last layer, according to the number of output classes in your data. During the compilation process, you got to choose the optimization technique, `loss` function, and a metric to monitor your training progress. Then, you initiated the training session of your newly minted model by using the `.fit()` parameter, and passing the model the final two architectural decisions to be made before initiating the training procedure. These decisions pertained to the batch size of your data to be seen at a time, and the total number of epochs to train the model for.

Finally, you saw how to test your predictions, and learned about the pivotal concept of regularization. We concluded this classification task by experimenting with regularization techniques to modify our model's size, layer weights, and add dropout layers, which in turn helped us improve the generalizability of our model to unseen data. Lastly, we saw that increasing model complexity is unfavourable unless explicitly required due to the nature of our task:

- **Exercise x**: Initialize different weighted parameters and see how this affects model performance
- **Exercise y**: Initialize different weights per layer and see how this affects model performance

Language processing

So far, we have seen how we can train a simple feedforward neural network on Keras for an image classification task. We also saw how we can mathematically represent image data as a high-dimensional geometric shape, namely a tensor. We saw that a higher-order tensor is simply composed of tensors of a smaller order. Pixels group up to represent an image, which in turn group up to represent an entire dataset. Essentially, whenever we want to employ the learning mechanism of neural networks, we have a way to represent our training data as a tensor. But what about language? How can we represent human thought, with all of its intricacies, as we do through language? You guessed it—we will use numbers once again. We will simply translate our texts, which are composed of sentences, which themselves are composed of words, into the universal language of mathematics. This is done through a process known as **vectorization**, which we will explore first-hand during our task of classifying the sentiment of movie reviews by using the **internet movie database (IMDB)** dataset.

Sentiment analysis

As our computing power improved over the years, we started applying computational techniques to domains that were previously frequented only by linguists and qualitative academics. It turns out that tasks that were initially considered too time-consuming to pursue became ideal for computers to optimize as processors increased in potency. This led to an explosion of computer-assisted text analysis, not only in academia, but also in the industry. Tasks such as computer-assisted sentiment analysis can be specifically beneficial for various use cases. This can be used if you're a company trying to track your online customer reviews, or an employer wanting to do some identity management on social media platforms. In fact, even political campaigns increasingly consult services that monitor public sentiments and conduct opinion mining on a large variety of political topics. This helps politicians prepare their campaign points and understand the general aura of opinions that are held by people. While such use of technology can be quite controversial, it can vastly help organizations understand their flaws in products, services, and marketing strategies, while catering to their audience in a more relevant manner.

The internet movie reviews dataset

The simplest form of sentiment analysis task deals with categorizing whether a piece of text represents a positive or negative opinion. This is often referred to as a *polar* or *binary sentiment classification task*, where 0 refers to a negative sentiment and 1 refers to a positive sentiment. We can, of course, have more complex sentiment models (perhaps using the big-five personality metrics we saw in Chapter 1, *Overview of Neural Networks*), but for the time being, we will concentrate on this simple yet conceptually loaded binary example. The example in question refers to classifying movie reviews from the Internet Movie Database or IMDB.

The IMDB dataset consists of 50,000 binary reviews, which are evenly split into positive and negative opinions. Each review consists of a list of integers, where each integer represents a word in that review. Once again, the guardians of Keras have thoughtfully included this dataset for practice, and hence can be found in Keras under keras.datasets. We encourage you to enjoy this importing data using Keras, as we won't be doing so in future exercises (nor will you be able to do it in the real world):

```
import keras
from keras.datasets import imdb
(x_train,y_train), (x_test,y_test)=imdb.load_data(num_words=12000)
```

Loading the dataset

As we did previously, we load our dataset by defining our training instances and labels, as well as our test instances and labels. We are able to use the `load_data` parameter on `imdb` to load in our pre-processed data into a 50/50 train–test split. We can also indicate the number of most frequently occurring words we want to keep in our dataset. This helps us control the inherent complexity of our task as we work with review vectors of reasonable sizes. It is safe to assume that rare words occurring in reviews would have to do more with the specific subject matter of a given movie, and so they have little influence on the *sentiment* of that review in question. Due to this, we will limit the number of words to 12,000.

Checking the shape and type

You can check the number of reviews per split by checking the `.shape` parameter of `x_train`, which is essentially a NumPy array of *n*-dimensions:

```
x_train.shape, x_test.shape, type(x_train)
((25000,), (25000,), numpy.ndarray)
```

Plotting a single training instance

As we can see, there are 25,000 training and test samples. We can also plot out an individual training sample to see how we can represent a single review. Here, we can see that each review simply contains a list of integers, where each integer corresponds to a word in a dictionary:

```
x_train[1]

[1,
 194,
 1153,
 194,
 8255,
 78,
 228,
 5,
 6,
 1463,
 4369,
 5012,
 134,
```

```
26,
4,
715,
8,
118,
1634,
14,
394,
20,
13,
119,
954,
```

Decoding the reviews

If you're curious (which we are), we can of course map out the exact words that these numbers correspond to so that we can read what the review actually says. To do this, we must back up our labels. While this step is not essential, it is useful if we want to visually verify our network's predictions later on:

```
#backup labels, so we can verify our networks prediction after
vectorization
xtrain = x_train
xtest = x_test
```

Then, we need to recover the words corresponding to the integers representing a review, which we saw earlier. The dictionary of words that were used to encode these reviews is included with the IMDB dataset. We will simply recover them as the word_index variable and reverse their order of storage. This basically allows us to map each integer index to its corresponding word:

```
word_index =imdb.get_word_index()
reverse_word_index = dict([[(value, key) for (key, value) in
word_index.items()])
```

The following function takes two arguments. The first one (n) denotes an integer referring to the nth review in a set. The second argument defines whether the nth review is taken from our training or test data. Then, it simply returns the string version of the review we specify.

This allows us to read out what a reviewer actually wrote. As we can see, in our function, we are required to adjust the position of indices, which are offset by three positions. This is simply how the designers of the IMDB dataset chose to implement their coding scheme, and so this is not of practical relevance for other tasks. The offset of the three positions in question occurs because positions 0, 1, and 2 are occupied by indices for padding, denoting the start of a sequence, and denoting unknown values, respectively:

```
def decode_review(n, split= 'train'):
if split=='train':
    decoded_review=' '.join([reverse_word_index.get(i-3,'?')for i in
                    ctrain[n]])
elif split=='test':
    decoded_review=' '.join([reverse_word_index.get(i-3,'?')for i in
                    xtest[n]])
return decoded_review
```

Using this function, we can decode review number five from our training set, as shown in the following code. It turns out that this is a negative review, as denoted by its training label, and inferred by its content. Note that the question marks are simply an indication of unknown values. Unknown values can occur inherently in the review (due to the use of emojis, for example) or due to the restrictions we have imposed (that is, if a word is not in the top 12,000 most frequent words that were used in the corpus, as stated earlier):

```
print('Training label:',y_train[5])
decode_review(5, split='train'),
Training label: 0.0
```

Preparing the data

Well then, what are we waiting for? We have a series of numbers representing each movie review, with their corresponding label, indicating (1) for positive or (0) for negative. This sounds like a classic structured dataset, so why not start feeding it to a network? Well, it's not that simple. Earlier, we mentioned that neural networks have a very specific diet. They are almost exclusively *Tensor-vores*, and so feeding them a list of integers won't do us much good. Instead, we must represent our dataset as a tensor of n-dimensions before we attempt to pass it on to our network for training. At the moment, you will notice that each of our movie reviews is represented by a separate list of integers. Naturally, each of these lists are of different sizes, as some reviews are smaller than others. Our network, on the other hand, requires the input features to be of the same size. Hence, we have to find a way to *pad* our reviews so that each of them represents a vector of the same length.

One-hot encoding

Since we know that the maximum number of unique words in our entire corpus is 12,000, we can assume that the longest possible review can only be 12,000 in length. Hence, we can make each review a vector of length 12,000, containing binary values. How does this work? Suppose we have a review of two words: *bad* and *movie*. A list containing these words in our dataset may look like [6, 49]. Instead, we can represent this same review as a 12,000-dimensional vector populated with 0s, except for the indices of 6 and 49, which would instead be 1s. What you're essentially doing is creating 12,000 dummy features to represent each review. Each of these dummy features represents the presence or absence of any of the 12,000 words in a given review. This approach is also known as **one-hot encoding**. It is commonly used to encode features and categorical labels alike in various deep learning scenarios.

Vectorizing features

The following function will take our training data of 25,000 lists of integers, where each list is a review. In return, it spits out one-hot encoded vectors for each of the integer lists it received from our training set. Then, we simply redefine our training and test features by using this function to transform our integer lists into a 2D tensor of one-hot encoded review vectors:

```
import numpy as np
def vectorize_features(features):

#Define the number of total words in our corpus
#make an empty 2D tensor of shape (25000, 12000)
dimension=12000
review_vectors=np.zeros((len(features), dimension))

#interate over each review
#set the indices of our empty tensor to 1s
for location, feature in enumerate(features):
    review_vectors[location, feature]=1
return review_vectors

x_train = vectorize_features(x_train)
x_test = vectorize_features(x_test)
```

You can see the result of our transformations by checking the type and shape of our training features and labels. You can also check what one individual vector looks like, as shown in the following code. We can see that each of our reviews is now a vector of length 12000:

```
type(x_train),x_train.shape, y_train.shape
(numpy.ndarray, (25000, 12000), (25000,))

x_train[0].shape, x_train[0]
((12000,), array([0., 1., 1., ..., 0., 0., 0.]), 12000)
```

Vectorizing labels

We can also vectorize our training labels, which simply helps our network handle our data better. You can think of vectorization as an efficient way to represent information to computers. Just like humans are not very good at performing computations using Roman numerals, computers are notoriously worse off when dealing with unvectorized data. In the following code, we are transforming our labels into NumPy arrays that contain 32-bit floating-point arithmetic values of either 0.0 or 1.0:

```
y_train= np.asarray(y_train).astype('float32')
y_test = np.asarray(y_test).astype('float32')
```

Finally, we have our tensor, ready to be consumed by a neural network. This 2D tensor is essentially 25,000 stacked vectors, each with its own label. All that is left to do is build our network.

Building a network

The first architectural constraints that you must consider while building a network with dense layers are its the depth and width. Then, you need to define an input layer with the appropriate shape, and successively choose from different activation functions to use per layer.

As we did for our MNIST example, we simply import the sequential model and the dense layer structure. Then we proceed by initializing an empty sequential model and progressively add hidden layers until we reach the output layer. Do note that our input layer always requires a specific input shape, which for us corresponds to the 12,000 - dimensional one-hot encoded vectors that we will be feeding it. In our current model, the output layer only has one neuron, which will ideally fire if the sentiment in a given review is positive; otherwise, it won't. We will choose **Rectified Linear Unit (ReLU)** activation functions for our hidden layers and a sigmoid activation function for the ultimate layer. Recall that the sigmoid activation function simply squished probability values between 0 and 1, making it quite ideal for our binary classification task. The ReLU activation function simply helps us zero out negative values, and hence can be considered a good default to begin with in many deep learning tasks. In summary, we have chosen a model with three densely interconnected hidden layers, containing 18, 12, and 4 neurons, respectively, as well as an output layer with 1 neuron:

```
from keras.models import sequential
from keras.layers import Dense
model=Sequential()
model.add(Dense(6, activation='relu', input_shape=(12000)))
model.add(Dense(6, activation='relu'))
model.add(Dense(1, activation='sigmoid'))
```

Compiling the model

Now we can compile our freshly built model, as is deep learning tradition. Recall that in the compilation process, the two key architectural decisions are the choice of the `loss` function, as well as the optimizer. The `loss` function simply helps us measure how far our model is from the actual labels at each iteration, whereas the optimizer determines how we converge to the ideal predictive weights for our model. In `Chapter 10`, *Contemplating Present and Future Developments*, we will review advanced optimizers and their relevance in various data processing tasks. For now, we will show how you can manually adjust the learning rate of an optimizer.

We have chosen a very small learning rate of 0.001 on the **Root Mean Square (RMS)** prop for demonstrative purposes. Recall that the size of the learning rate simply determines the size of the step we want out network to take in the direction of the correct output at each training iteration. As we mentioned previously, a big step can cause our network to *walk over* the global minima in the loss hyperspace, whereas a small learning rate can cause your model to take ages to converge to a minimum loss value:

```
from keras import optimizers
model.compile(optimizer=optimizers.RMSprop(1r=0.001),
```

```
loss='binary_crossentropy',
metrics=['accuracy'])
```

Fitting the model

In our previous MNIST example, we went over the least number of architectural decisions to get our code running. This lets us cover a deep learning workflow quite quickly, but at the expense of efficiency. You will recall that we simply used the `fit` parameter on our model and passed it our training features and labels, along with two integers denoting the epochs to train the model for, and the batch size per training iteration. The former simply defines how many times our data runs through the model, while the latter defines how many learning examples our model will see at a time before updating its weights. These are the two paramount architectural considerations that must be defined and adapted to the case at hand. However, there are several other useful arguments that the `fit` parameter may take.

Validation data

You may be wondering why we train our model blindly for an arbitrary number of iterations and then test it on our holdout data. Wouldn't it be more efficient to gauge our model to some unseen data after each epoch, just to see how well we are doing? This way, we are able to assess exactly when our model starts to overfit, and hence end the training session and save some expensive hours of computing. We could show our model the test set after each epoch, without updating its weights, purely to see how well it does on our test data after that epoch. Since we do not update our model weights at each test run, we don't risk our model overfitting on the test data. This allows us to get a genuine understanding of how generalizable our model is *during* the training process, and not after. To test your model on a validation split, you can simply pass the validation features and labels as a parameter, as you did with your training data, to the `fit` parameter.

In our case, we have simply used the test features and labels as our validation data. In a rigorous deep learning scenario with high stakes, you may well choose to have separate test and validation sets, where one is used for validation during training, and the other is reserved for later assessments before you deploy your model to production. This is shown in the following code:

```
network_metadata=model.fit(x_train, y_train,
                           validation_data=(x_test, y_test),
                           epochs=20,
                           batch_size=100)
```

Now, when you execute the preceding cell, you will see the training session initiate. Moreover, at the end of each training epoch, you will see that our model takes a brief pause to compute the accuracy and loss on the validation set, which is then displayed. Then, without updating its weights after this validation pass, the model proceeds to the next epoch for another training round. The preceding model will run for 20 epochs, where each epoch will iterate over our 25,000 *training* examples in batches of 100, updating the model weights after each batch. Note that in our case, the model weights are updated 250 times per epoch, or 5,000 times during the preceding training session of 20 epochs. So, now we can better assess when our model starts to memorize random features of our training set, but how do we actually interrupt the training session at this point? Well, you may have noticed that instead of just executing `model.fit()`, we defined it as `network_metadata`. As it happens, the `fit()` parameter actually returns a history object containing the relevant training statistics of our model, which we are interested in recovering. This history object is recorded by something called a **callback** in Keras.

Callbacks

A `callback` is basically a Keras library function that can interact with our model during the training session to check on its internal state and save relevant training statistics for later scrutiny. While quite a few callback functions exist in `keras.callbacks`, we will introduce a few that are crucial. For those of you who are more technically oriented, Keras even lets you construct custom callbacks. To use a callback, you simply pass it to the `fit` parameter using the keyword argument `callbacks`. Note that the history callback is automatically applied to every Keras model, and so it does not need to be specified as long as you define the fitting process as a variable. This lets you recover the associated history object.

Importantly, if you initiated a training session previously in your Jupyter Notebook, then calling the `fit()` parameter on the model will continue training the same model. Instead, you want to reinitialize a blank model, before proceeding with another training run. This can be done by simply rerunning the cells where you previously defined and compiled your sequential model. Then, you may proceed by implementing a callback by passing it to the `fit()` parameter by using the `callbacks` keyword argument, as follows:

```
early_stopping= keras.callbacks.EarlyStopping(monitor='loss')
network_metadata=model.fit(x_train, y_train, validation_data=(x_test,
                        y_test), epochs=20, batch_size=100,
                        callbacks=[early_stopping])
```

Early stopping and history callbacks

In the preceding cell, we used a callback known as **early stopping**. This callback allows us to monitor a specific training metric. Our choices are between our accuracy or loss on the training set or on the validation set, which are all stored in a dictionary pertaining to our model's history:

```
history_dict = network_metadata.history
history_dict.keys()
dict_keys(['val_loss','val_acc','loss','acc'])
```

Choosing a metric to monitor

The ideal choice is always *validation loss* or *validation accuracy*, as these metrics best represent the out of set predictability of our model. This is simply due to the fact that we only update our model weights during a training pass, and not a validation pass. Choosing our *training accuracy* or *loss* as a metric (as in the following code) is suboptimal in the sense that you are benchmarking your model by its own definition of a benchmark. To put this in a different way, your model might keep reducing its loss and increasing in accuracy, but it is doing so by rote memorization—not because it is learning general predictive rules as we want it to. As we can see in the following code, by monitoring our *training* loss, our model continues to decrease loss on the training set, even though the loss on the validation set actually starts increasing shortly after the very first epoch:

```
import matplotlib.pyplot as plt

acc=history_dict['acc']
loss_values=history_dict['loss']
val_loss_values=history_dict['loss']
val_loss_values=history_dict['val_loss']

epochs = range(1, len(acc) + 1)
plt.plot(epochs, loss_values,'r',label='Training loss')
plt.plot(epochs, val_loss_valuesm, 'rD', label-'Validation loss')
plt.title('Training and validation loss')plt.xlabel('Epochs')
plt.xlabel('Epochs')
plt.ylabel('Loss')
plt.legend()
plt.show()
```

The preceding code generates the following output:

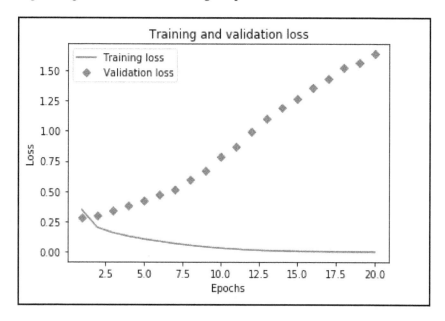

We used Matplotlib to plot out the preceding graph. Similarly, you can clear out the previous loss graph and plot out a new accuracy graph of our training session, as shown in the following code. If we had used validation accuracy as a metric to track our early stopping callback, our training session would have ended after the *first* epoch, as *this* is the point in time where our model appears to be the most generalizable to unseen data:

```
plt.clf()
acc_values=history_dict['acc']
val_acc_values=history_dict['val_acct']
plt.plot(epochs, history_dict.get('acc'),'g',label='Training acc')
plt.plot(epochs, history_dict.get('val_acc'),'gD',label='Validation acc')
plt.title('Training and validation accuracy')
plt.xlabel('Epochs')
plt.ylabel('Loss')
plt.legend()
plt.show()
```

The preceding code generates the following output:

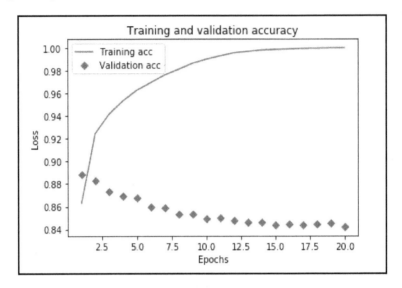

Accessing model predictions

In the MNIST example, we used the *Softmax* activation function as our last layer. You may recall that the layer generated an array of 10 probability scores, adding up to 1 for a given input. Each of those 10 scores referred to the likelihood of the image being presented to our network corresponding to one of the output classes (that is, it is 90% sure it sees a 1, and 10% sure it sees a 7, for example). This approach made sense for a classification task with 10 categories. In our sentiment analysis problem, we chose a sigmoid activation function, because we are dealing with binary categories. Using the sigmoid here simply forces our network to output a prediction between 0 and 1 for any given instance of data. Hence, a value closer to 1 means that our network believes that the given piece of information is more likely to be a positive review, whereas a value closer to zero states our network's conviction of having found a negative review. To view our model's predictions, we simply define a variable called predictions by using the predict() parameter on our trained model and passing it our test set. Now we can check our network predictions on a given example from this set, as follows:

```
predictions=model.predict([x_test])
predictions[5]
```

In this case, it appears that our network is quite confident that review 5 from our test set is a positive review. Not only can we check whether this is indeed the case by checking the label stored in y_test[5], we can also decode the review itself due to the decoder function we built earlier. Let's put our network's prediction to the test by decoding review 5 and checking its label:

```
y_test[5], decode_review(5, split='test')
```

It turns out our network is right. This is an example of a complex linguistic pattern that requires a higher-level understanding of linguistic syntax, real-world entities, relational logic, and the propensity for humans to blabber aimlessly. Yet, with only 12 neurons, our network has seemingly understood the underlying sentiment that's encoded in this piece of information. It makes a prediction with a high degree of certainty (99.99%), despite the presence of words such as *disgusting*, which are very likely to appear in negative reviews.

Probing the predictions

Let's examine another review. To probe our predictions, we will make a few functions that will help us visualize our results better. Such a gauging function can also be used if you want to restrict your model's predictions to instances where it is most certain:

```
def gauge_predictions(n):
if (predictions[n]<=0.4) and (y_test[n]==0):
    print('Network correctly predicts that review %d is negative' %(n))
elif (predictions[n] <=0.7) and (y_test[n]==1);
elif (predictions[n]>-0.7) and (y_test[n]==0):
else:
    print('Network is not so sure. Review mp. %d has a probability score of
%(n),
            predictions[n])
def verify_predictions(n):
    return gauge_predictions(n), predictions[n], decode_review(n,
split='test')
```

We will make two functions to help us better visualize our network's errors, while also limiting our predictive accuracy to upper and lower bounds. We will use the first function to arbitrarily define good predictions as instances where the network has a probability score above 0.7, and bad instances where the score is below 0.4, for a *positive review*. We simply reverse this scheme for the negative reviews (a good prediction score for a *negative review* is below 0.4 and a bad one is above 0.7). We also leave a middle ground between 40 and 70%, labeled as uncertain predictions so that we can better understand the reason behind its accurate and inaccurate guesses. The second function is designed for simplicity, taking an integer value that refers to the *n*th review you want to probe and verify as input, and returning an assessment of what the network thinks, the actual probability score, as well as what the review in question reads. Let's use these newly forged functions to probe yet another review:

```
verify-predictions(22)
network falsely predicts that review 22 is negative
```

As we can see, our network seems to be quite sure that review 22 from our test set is negative. It has generated a probability score of 0.169. You could also interpret this score as that our network believed with 16.9% confidence that this review is positive, and so it must be negative (since these are the only two classes we used to train our network). It turns out that our network got this one wrong. Reading the review, you will notice that the reviewer actually expresses their appreciation for what they deemed to be an undervalued movie. Note that the tone is quite ambiguous at the beginning, with words like *silly* and *fall flat*. However, contextual valence shifters later on in the sentence allow our biological neural networks to determine that the review actually expresses a positive sentiment. Sadly, our artificial network does not seem to have caught up with this particular pattern. Let's continue our exploratory analysis using yet another example:

```
verify_predictions(19999)
Network is not so sure. Review no. 19999 has a probability score of
[0.5916141]
```

Here, we can see that our network is not too sure about the review, even though it has actually guessed the correct sentiment in the review, with a probability score of 0.59, which is closer to 1 (positive) than 0 (negative). To us, this review clearly appears positive—even a bit promotionally pushy. It is intuitively unclear why our network is not certain of the sentiment. Later in this book, we will learn how to visualize word embeddings using our network layers. For now, let's continue our probing with one last example:

```
verify_predictions(4)
Network correctly predicts that review 4 is positive
```

This time, our network gets it right again. In fact, our network is 99.9% sure that this is a positive review. While reading the review, you'll notice that it has actually done a decent job, as the review contains words like *boring*, *average*, and suggestive language such as *mouth shut*, which could all easily be present in other negative reviews, potentially misleading our network. As we can see, we conclude this probing session by providing a short function that you can play around with by randomly checking your network's predictions for a given number of reviews. We then print out our network's predictions for two randomly chosen reviews from our test set:

```
from random import randint
def random_predict(n_reviews):
for i in range(n_reviews):
print(verify_predictions(randint(0, 24000)))
random_predict(2)
Network correctly predicts that review 20092 is positive
```

Summary of IMDB

Now you should have a better idea of how to go about processing natural language texts and dialogues through a simple feedforward neural network. In this subsection of our journey, you learned how to execute a binary sentiment classification task using a feedforward neural network. In doing so, you learned how to pad and vectorize your natural language data, preparing it for processing with neural networks. You also went over the key architectural changes that are involved in binary classification, such as using an output neuron and the sigmoid activation function on the last layer of our network. You also saw how you can leverage a validation split in your data to get an idea of how your model performs on unseen data after each training epoch. Moreover, you learned how to indirectly interact with your model during the training process by using Keras callbacks. Callbacks can be useful for a variety of use cases, ranging from saving your model at a certain checkpoint or terminating the training session when a desired metric has reached a certain point. We can use the history callback to visualize training statistics, and we can use the early stopping callback to designate a moment to terminate the current training session. Finally, you saw how you can probe your network's predictions per review to better understand what kind of mistakes it makes:

- **Exercise**: Improve performance with regularization, as we did in the MNIST example.

Predicting continuous variables

So far, we have performed two classification tasks using neural networks. For our first task, we classified handwritten digits. For our second task, we classified sentiments in movie reviews. But what if we wanted to predict a continuous value instead of a categorical value? What if we wanted to predict how likely an event may occur, or the future price of a given object? For such a task, examples such as predicting prices in a given market may come to mind. Hence, we will conclude this chapter by coding another simple feedforward network by using the Boston Housing Prices dataset.

This dataset resembles most real-world datasets that data scientists and machine learning practitioners would come across. You are given 13 features that refer to a specific geographical area located in Boston. With these features, the task at hand is to predict the median price of houses. The features themselves include various indicators ranging from residential and industrial activity, level of toxic chemicals in the air, property tax, access to education, and other socio-economic indicators that are associated with location. The data was collected during the mid-1970s, and seems to have brought along some bias from the time. You will notice that some features seem very nuanced and perhaps even inappropriate. Features such as feature number 12 can be very controversial to use in machine learning projects. You must always consider the higher-level implications when using a certain source or type of data. It is your duty as a machine learning practitioner to ensure that your model does not introduce or reinforce any sort of societal bias, or contribute in any way to disparities and discomfort for people. Remember, we are in the business of using technology to alleviate human burden, not add to it.

Boston Housing Prices dataset

As we mentioned in the previous section, this dataset contains 13 training features that are represented on an observed geographical region.

Loading the data

The dependent variable that we are interested in predicting is the housing price per location, which is denoted as a continuous variable that denotes house prices in thousands of dollars.

Hence, each of our observations can be represented as a vector of dimension 13, with a corresponding scalar label. In the following code, we are plotting out the second observation in our training set, along with its corresponding label:

```
import keras
from keras.datasets import boston_housing.load_data()
(x_train, y_train),(x_test,y_test)=boston_housing.load_data()
x_train[1], y_train[1]
```

Exploring the data

This dataset is a much smaller dataset in comparison to the ones we've dealt with so far. We can only see 404 training observations and 102 test observations:

```
print(type(x_train),'training data:',x_train.shape,'test
data:',x_test.shape)
<class 'numpy.ndarray'>training data:(403, 13) test data: (102, 13)
```

We will also generate a dictionary containing the description of our features so that we can understand what each of them actually encodes:

```
column_names=['CRIM','ZN','INDUS','CHAS','NOX','RM','AGE','DIS','RAD','TAX'
,'PTRATIO','B','LST
  AT']

key= ['Per capita crime rate.',
    'The proportion of residential land zoned for lots over 25,000
    square feet.',
    'The proportion of non-retail business acres per town.',
    'Charles River dummy variable (=1 if tract bounds river; 0
    otherwise).',
    'Nitric oxides concentration (parts per 10 million).',
    'The average number of rooms per dwelling.',
    'The porportion of owner-occupied units built before 1940.',
    'Weighted distances to five Boston employment centers.',
    'Index of accessibility to radial highways.',
    'Full-value property tax rate per $10,000.',
    'Pupil-Teacher ratio by town.',
    '1000*(Bk-0.63)**2 where Bk is the proportion of Black people by
    town.',
    'Percentage lower status of the population.'}
```

Now let's create a pandas `DataFrame` and have a look at the first five observations in our training set. We will simply pass out the training data, along with the previously defined column names, as arguments to the pandas `DataFrame` constructor. Then, we will use the `.head()` parameter on our newly forged `.DataFrame` object to get a nice display, as follows:

```python
import pandas as pd
df= pd.DataFrame(x_train, columns=column_names)
df.head()
```

Feature-wise normalization

We can see that each feature in our observation seems to be on a different scale. Some values range in the hundreds, while others are between 1 and 12, or even binary. While neural networks may still ingest unscaled features, it almost exclusively prefers to deal with features on the same scale. In practice, a network can learn from heterogeneously scaled features, but it may take much longer to do so without any guarantee of finding an ideal minimum on the loss landscape. To allow our network to learn in an improved way for this dataset, we must homogenize our data through the process of feature-wise normalization. We can achieve this by subtracting the feature-specific mean and dividing it by the feature-specific standard deviation for each feature in our dataset. Note that in live-deployed models (for the stock exchange, for example), such a scaling measure is impractical, as the means and standard deviation values may keep on changing, depending on new, incoming data. In such scenarios, other normalization and standardization techniques (such as log normalization, for example) are better to use:

```python
mean=x_train.mean(axis=0)
std=x_train.std(axis=0)
x_train=(x_train-mean)/std
x_test=(x_test-mean)/std
print(x_train[0]) #First Training sample, normalized
```

Building the model

The main architectural difference in this regression model, as opposed to the previous classification models we built, is to do with the way we construct the last layer of this network. Recall that in a classic scalar regression problem, such as the one at hand, we aim to predict a continuous variable. To implement this, we avoid using an activation function in our last layer, and use only one output neuron.

The reason we forego an activation function is because we do not want to constrain the range that the output values of this layer may take. Since we are implementing a purely linear layer, our network is able to learn to predict a scalar continuous value, just as we want it to:

```
from keras.layers import Dense, Dropout
from keras.models import Sequential
model= Sequential()
model.add(Dense(26, activation='relu',input_shape=(13,)))
model.add(Dense(26, activation='relu'))
model.add(Dense(12, activation='relu'))
model.add(Dense(1))
```

Compiling the model

The main architectural difference during compilation here is to do with the `loss` function and metric we choose to implement. We will use the MSE `loss` function to penalize higher prediction errors, while monitoring our model's training progress with the **Mean Absolute Error** (**MAE**) metric:

```
from keras import optimizers
model.compile(optimizer= opimizers.RMSprop(lr=0.001),
              loss-'mse',
              metrics=['mae'])
model.summary()
```

Layer (type)	Output Shape	Param #
dense_1 (Dense)	(None, 6)	72006
dense_2 (Dense)	(None, 6)	42
dense_3 (Dense)	(None, 1)	7

```
Total params: 72,055
Trainable params: 72,055
Non-trainable params: 0
```

As we saw previously, the MSE function measures the average of the squares of our network's prediction errors. Simply put, we are simply measuring the average squared difference between the estimated and actual house price labels. The squared term emphasizes the spread of our prediction errors by penalizing the errors that are further away from the mean. This approach is especially helpful with regression tasks where small error values still have a significant impact on predictive accuracy.

In our case, our housing price labels range between 5 and 50, measured in thousands of dollars. Hence, an absolute error of 1 actually means a difference of $1,000 in prediction. Thus, taking using an absolute error-based `loss` function might not give the best feedback mechanism to the network.

On the other hand, the choice of MAE as a metric is ideal to measure our training progress itself. Visualizing squared errors, as it turns out, is not very intuitive to us humans. It is better to simply see the absolute errors in our models' predictions, as it is visually more informative. Our choice of metric has no actual impact on the training mechanism of the model—it is simply providing us with a feedback statistic to visualize how good or bad our model is doing during the training session. The MAE metric itself is essentially a measure of difference between two continuous variables.

Plotting training and test errors

In the following graph, we can see that the average error is about 2.5 (or $2,500 dollars). While this may be a small variance when predicting the prices on houses that cost $50,000, it starts to matter if the house itself costs $5,000:

```
1   import matplotlib.pyplot as plt
2
3   import numpy as np
4
5   def plot_history(history):
6       plt.figure()
7       plt.xlabel('Epoch')
8       plt.ylabel('Mean Abs Error [1000$]')
9       plt.plot(history.epoch, np.array(history.history['mean_absolute_error']),
10              label='Train Loss')
11      plt.plot(history.epoch, np.array(history.history['val_mean_absolute_error']),
12              label = 'Val loss')
13      plt.legend()
14      plt.ylim([0, 15])
15
16  plot_history(network_metadata)
```

Finally, let's predict some housing prices using data from the test set. We will use a scatter plot to plot the predictions and actual labels of our test set. In the following graph, we can see a line of best fit, along with the data points. Our model seems to capture the general trend in our data, despite having some outlandish predictions for some points:

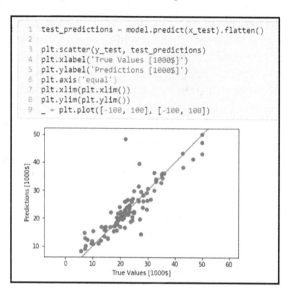

Moreover, we can plot a histogram that shows the distribution of our prediction errors. It appears that our model seems to do pretty well on most counts, but has some trouble predicting certain values, while overshooting and undershooting for a small number of observations, as shown in the following diagram:

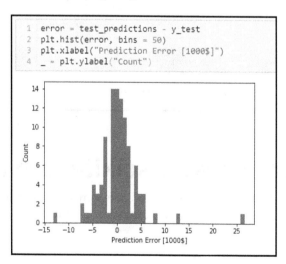

Validating your approach using k-fold validation

We noted earlier how our dataset is significantly smaller than the ones we previously dealt with. This leads to several complications while training and testing. Primarily, splitting the data into training and test samples, as we did, left us with only 100 validation samples. This is hardly enough for us to assuredly deploy our model, even if we wanted to. Furthermore, our test scores may change a lot depending on which segment of the data ended up in the test set. Hence, to reduce our reliance on any particular segment of our data for testing our model, we adopted a common machine learning approach known as **k-fold cross validation**. Essentially, we split our data into *n* number of smaller partitions and used the same number of neural networks to train on each of those smaller partitions of our data. Hence, a k-fold cross validation with five folds will split up our entire training data of 506 samples into five splits of 101 samples (and one with 102). Then, we use five different neural networks, each of which trains on four splits out of the five data splits and tests itself on the remaining split of data. Then, we simply average the predictions from our five models to generate a single estimation:

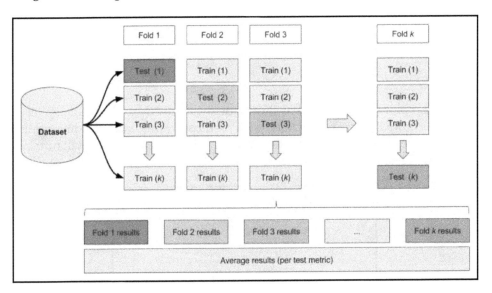

Cross validation with scikit-learn API

The advantage of cross validation over repeated random sub-sampling is that all of the observations are used for both training and validation, and each observation is used for validation exactly once.

The following code shows you how to implement a five-fold cross validation in Keras, where we use the entire dataset (training and testing together) and print out the averaged predictions of a network on each of the cross validation runs. As we can see, this is achieved by training the model on four random splits and testing it on the remaining split, per each cross validation run. We use the scikit-learn API wrapper provided by Keras and leverage the Keras regressor, along with sklearn's standard scaler, k-fold cross-validator creator, and score evaluator:

```
import numpy as np
import pandas as pd

from keras.models import Sequential
from keras.layers import Dense
from keras.wrappers.scikit_learn import KerasRegressor


from sklearn.model_selection import cross_val_score
from sklearn.model_selection import KFold

from sklearn.preprocessing import StandardScaler
from sklearn.pipeline import Pipeline

from keras.datasets import boston_housing
(x_train,y_train),(x_test,y_test) = boston_housing.load_data()

x_train.shape, x_test.shape
```

```
------------------------------------------------------------
((404, 13), (102, 13))
------------------------------------------------------------
```

```
import numpy as np

x_train = np.concatenate((x_train,x_test), axis=0)
y_train = np.concatenate((y_train,y_test), axis=0)

x_train.shape, y_train.shape
```

```
------------------------------------------------------------
((506, 13), (506,))
------------------------------------------------------------
```

You will notice that we constructed a function named `baseline_model()` to build our network. This is a useful way of constructing networks in many scenarios, but here it helps us feed the model object to the `KerasRegressor` function that we are using from the scikit-learn API wrapper that Keras provides. As many of you may well be aware, scikit-learn has been the go-to Python library for ML, with all sorts of pre-processing, scaling, normalizing, and algorithmic implementations. The Keras creators have implemented a scikit-learn wrapper to enable a certain degree of cross functionality between these libraries:

```
def baseline_model():
    model = Sequential()
    model.add(Dense(13, input_dim=13, kernel_initializer='normal',
            activation='relu'))
    model.add(Dense(1, kernel_initializer='normal'))
    model.compile(loss='mean_squared_error', optimizer='adam')
    return model
```

We will take advantage of this cross functionality to perform our k-fold cross validation, as we did previously. Firstly, we will initialize a random number generator with a constant random seed. This simply gives us consistency in initializing our model weights, helping us to ensure that we can compare future models consistently:

```
#set seed for reproducability
seed = 7
numpy.random.seed(seed)

# Add a data Scaler and the keras regressor containing our model function
to a list of estimators

estimators = []
estimators.append(('standardize', StandardScaler()))
estimators.append(('mlp', KerasRegressor(build_fn=baseline_model,
                    epochs=100, batch_size=5, verbose=0)))
#add our estimator list to a Sklearn pipeline

pipeline = Pipeline(estimators)

#initialize instance of k-fold validation from sklearn api

kfold = KFold(n_splits=5, random_state=seed)

#pass pipeline instance, training data and labels, and k-fold
crossvalidator instance to evaluate score

results = cross_val_score(pipeline, x_train, y_train, cv=kfold)

#The results variable contains the mean squared errors for each of our
 5 cross validation runs.
```

```
print("Average MSE of all 5 runs: %.2f, with standard dev: (%.2f)" %
     (-1*(results.mean()), results.std()))
```

```
-----------------------------------------------------------
Model Type: <function larger_model at 0x000001454959CB70>
MSE per fold:
[-11.07775911 -12.70752338 -17.85225084 -14.55760158 -17.3656806 ]
Average MSE of all 5 runs: 14.71, with standard dev: (2.61)
```

We will create a list of estimators to pass to the sklearn transformation pipeline, which is useful to scale and process our data in sequence. To scale our values this time, we simply use the StandardScaler() preprocessing function from sklearn and append it to our list. We also append the Keras wrapper object to the same list. This Keras wrapper object is actually a regression estimator called KerasRegressor, and takes the model function we created, along with the desired number of batch size and training epochs as arguments. **Verbose** simply means how much feedback you want to see during the training process. By setting it to 0, we ask our model to train silently.

 Note that these are the same parameters that you would otherwise pass along to the .fit() function of the model, as we did earlier to initiate our training sessions.

Running the preceding code gives us an estimate of the average performance of our network for the five cross-validation runs we executed. The results variable stores the MSE scores of our network for each run of the cross validator. We then print out the mean and standard deviation (average variance) of MSEs over all five runs. Notice that we multiplied our mean value by -1. This is simply an implementational issue, as the unified scoring API of scikit-learn always maximizes a given score. However, in our case, we are trying to minimize our MSE. Hence, scores that need to be minimized are negated so that the unified scoring API can work correctly. The score that is returned is the negative version of the actual MSE.

Summary

In this chapter, we saw how we can perform a regression task with neural networks. This involved some simple architectural changes to our previous classification models, pertaining to model construction (one output layer with no activation function) and the choice of `loss` function (MSE). We also tracked the MAE as a metric, since squared errors are not very intuitive to visualize. Finally, we plotted out our model's predictions versus the actual prediction labels using a scatter plot to better visualize how well the network did. We also used a histogram to understand the distribution of prediction errors in our model.

Finally, we introduced the methodology of k-fold cross validation, which is preferred over explicit train test splits of our data, in cases where we deal with very few data observations. What we did instead of splitting our data into a training and test split was split it into a *k* number of smaller partitions. Then, we generated a single estimate of predictions by using the same number of models as our data subsets. Each of these models were trained on a *k*-1 number of data partitions and tested on the remaining one data partition, after which their prediction scores were averaged. Doing so prevents our reliance on any particular split of our data for testing, and hence we get a more generalizable prediction estimate.

In the next chapter, we will learn about **Convolutional Neural Networks** (**CNNs**). We will implement CNNs and detect objects using them. We will also solve some image recognition problems.

Exercises

- Implement three different functions, each returning a network varying in size (depth and width). Use each of these functions and perform a k-fold cross validation. Assess which size fits best.
- Experiment with MAE and MSE `loss` functions, and note the difference during training.
- Experiment with different `loss` functions and note the differences during training.
- Experiment with different regularization techniques and note the differences during training.

Section 2: Advanced Neural Network Architectures

2

This section familiarizes the reader with different types of convolutional and pooling layers that may be used in neural networks to process sensory input, from images on your laptop, to databases and real-time IoT applications. Readers will learn about using pretrained models, such as LeNet, and partial convolutional networks for image and video reconstruction on Keras, gain insights into how to deploy models using REST APIs, and then embed them in Raspberry computing devices for custom use cases, such as photography, surveillance, and inventory management.

Readers will be exposed to the underlying architectures of reinforcement learning networks in detail and learn how to implement core and extended layers in Keras for desired outcomes.

Then, they will dive deeper into the theory behind different types of recurrent networks and what it means to be a Turing-complete algorithm, examine specific consequences of backpropagation through time, including the issues of vanishing gradients, and obtain a comprehensive understanding of how temporal information is captured in such models.

Readers will then explore a specific type of **recurrent neural network** (**RNN**) in detail, known as **Long Short-Term Memory** (**LSTM**), and become familiar with yet another neural network architecture that was inspired by our own biology.

This section comprises the following chapters:

- Chapter 4, *Convolutional Neural Networks*
- Chapter 5, *Recurrent Neural Networks*
- Chapter 6, *Long-Short Term Memory Networks*
- Chapter 7, *Reinforcement Learning with Deep Q-Networks*

4
Convolutional Neural Networks

In the last chapter, we saw how to perform several signal-processing tasks while leveraging the predictive power of feedforward neural networks. This foundational architecture allowed us to introduce many of the basic features that comprise the learning mechanisms of **Artificial Neural Networks (ANNs)**.

In this chapter, we dive deeper to explore another type of ANN, namely the **Convolutional Neural Network (CNN)**, famous for its adeptness at visual tasks such as image recognition, object detection, and semantic segmentation, to name a few. Indeed, the inspiration for these particular architectures also refers back to our own biology. Soon, we will go over the experiments and discoveries of the human race that led to the inspiration for these complex systems that perform so well. The latest iterations of this idea can be traced back to the ImageNet classification challenge, where AlexNet was able to outperform the state-of-the-art computer vision systems of the time at image classification tasks on supermassive datasets. However, the idea behind CNNs, as we will soon see, was a product of multidisciplinary scientific research, backed by millions of years of trail runs.

In this chapter, we will cover the following topics:

- Why CNNs?
- The birth of vision
- Understanding biological vision
- The birth of the modern CNN
- Designing a CNN
- Dense versus convolutional layer
- The convolution operation
- Preserving the spatial structure of an image
- Feature extraction using filters

Why CNNs?

CNNs are very similar to ordinary neural networks. As we have seen in the previous chapter, neural networks are made up of neurons that have learnable weights and biases. Each neuron still computes the weighted sum of its inputs using dot products, adds a bias term, and passes it through a nonlinear equation. The network will show just one differentiable score function that will be, from raw images at one end to the class scores at other end.

And they will also have a loss function such as the softmax, or SVM on the last layer. Moreover, all the techniques that we learned ti develop neural networks will be applicable.

But then what's different with ConvNets you may ask. So the main point to note is that the ConvNet architecture explicitly assumes that the inputs that are received are all images, this assumption actually helps us to encode other properties of the architecture itself. Doing so permits the network to be more efficient from an implementation perspective, vastly reducing the number of parameters required in the network. We call a network *convolutional* because of the convolutional layers it has, in addition to other types of layers. Soon, we will explore how these special layers, along with a few other mathematical operations, can help computers visually comprehend the world around us.

Hence, this specific architecture of neural networks excels at a variety of visual-processing tasks, ranging from object detection, face recognition, video classification, semantic segmentation, image captioning, human pose estimation, and many, many more. These networks allow an array of computer vision tasks to be performed effectively, some critical for the advancement of our species (such as medical diagnoses), and others bordering on entertainment (superimposing a certain artistic style on a given image). Before we dive deep into its conception and contemporary implementation, it is quite useful to understand the broader scope of what we are trying to replicate, by taking a quick tour of how vision, something so complex, yet so innate to us humans, actually came about.

The birth of vision

The following is an epic tale, an epic tale that took place nearly 540 million years ago.

Around this time, on the pale blue cosmic dot that would later become known as Earth, life was quite tranquil and hassle-free. Back then, almost all of our ancestors were water dwellers, who would just float about in the serenity of the oceans, munching on sources of food only if they were to float by them. Yes, this was quite different than the predatory, stressful, and stimulating world of today.

Suddenly, something quite curious occurred. In a comparatively short period of time that followed, there was an explosion in the number and variety of animal species present on our planet. In only a span of about 20 million years that came after, the kind of creatures you could find on our watery earth drastically changed. They changed from the occasional single-celled organisms you would encounter, organized in loosely connected colonies, to complex multi-cellular organisms, popping up in every creek and corner.

Biologists remained baffled for a very long time, debating what caused this *big bang* of evolutionary acceleration. What we had actually discovered was the birth of the biological visual system. Studying the fossil records of the organisms from that time, zoologists were able to present decisive proof, connecting this explosion of species with the first appearance of photo-receptive cells. These cells allowed organisms to sense and respond to light, triggering an evolutionary arms race that eventually led to the sophisticated mammalian visual cortex that you are likely using right now to interpret this piece of text. Indeed, the gift of sight made life much more dynamic and proactive, as now organisms were able to sense and respond to their environments.

Today, vision is one of the main sensory systems in nearly all organisms, intelligent or not. In fact, we humans use almost half of our neuronal capacity for visual processing, making it the biggest sensory system we employ to orient ourselves, recognize people and objects, and go about our daily lives. As it turns out, vision is a very important component of cognitive systems, biological or otherwise. Hence, it is quite reasonable to go about examining the development and implementation of visual systems created by nature. After all, there's no point reinventing the wheel.

Understanding biological vision

Our next insight into biological visual systems comes from a series of experiments conducted by scientists from Harvard University, back in the late 1950s. Nobel laureates David Hubel and Torstein Wiesel showed the world the inner workings of the mammalian visual cortex, by mapping the action of receptor cells along with the visual pathway of a cat, from the retina to the visual cortex. These scientists used electrophysiology to understand exactly how our sensory organs intake, process, and interpret electromagnetic radiation, to generate the reality we see around us. This allowed them to better appreciate the flow of stimuli and related responses that occur at the level of individual neurons:

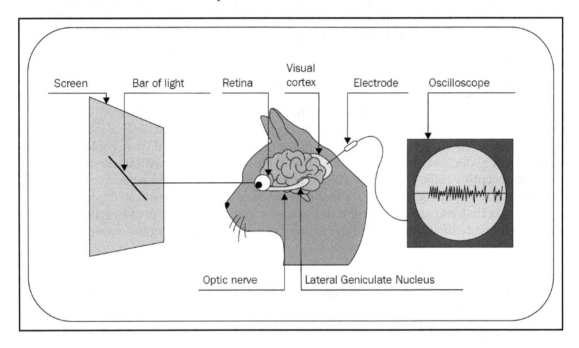

The following screenshot describes how cells respond to light:

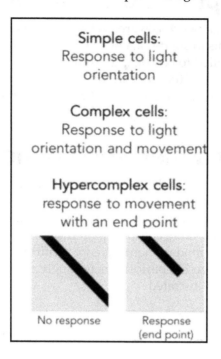

Thanks to their experiments in the field of neuroscience, we are able to share with you several key elements of their research that directly affected the scientific understanding of visual signal processing, leading to a cascade of academic contributions that brings us to this date. These elements enlighten the mechanism of visual information processing leveraged by our own brain, inspiring the design of the CNN, a cornerstone of modern visual intelligence systems.

Conceptualizing spatial invariance

The first of these notions comes from the concept of **spatial invariance**. The researchers noticed that the cat's neural activations to particular patterns would be consistent, regardless of the exact location of the patterns on the screen. Intuitively, the same set of neurons were noted to fire for a given pattern (that is, a line segment), even if the pattern appeared at the top or the bottom of the screen. This showed that the neurons' activations were spatially invariant, meaning that their activations were not dependent on the spatial location of the given patterns.

Defining receptive fields of neurons

Secondly, they also noted that neurons were *in charge* of responding to specific regions of a given input. They named this property of a neuron as its **receptive field**. In other words, certain neurons only responded to certain regions of a given input, whereas others responded to different regions of the same input. The receptive field of a neuron simply denotes the span of input to which a neuron is likely to respond.

Implementing a hierarchy of neurons

Finally, the researchers were able to demonstrate that a hierarchy of neurons exists in the visual cortex. They showed that lower-level cells are tasked to detect simple visual patterns, such as line segments. The output from these neurons is used in subsequent layers of neurons to construct more and more complex patterns, forming the objects and people we see and interact with. Indeed, modern neuroscience confirms that the structure of the visual cortex is hierarchically organized to perform increasingly complex inferences using the output of previous layers, as illustrated:

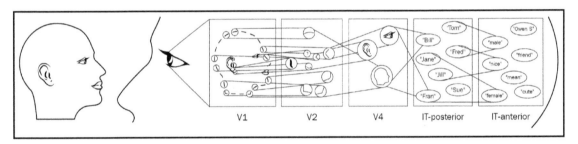

The preceding diagram means that recognizing a friend involves detecting the line segments making up their face (**V1**), using those segments to build shapes and edges (**V2**), using those shapes and edges to form complex shapes such as eyes and noses (**V3**), and then leveraging previous knowledge to infer who out of your friends does this current bundle of eyes and nose resemble the most (**IT-posterior**). Based upon that reasoning, even higher-level activations pertaining to notions of that friend's personality, attractiveness, and so on, may emerge (**IT-anterior**).

The birth of the modern CNN

It wasn't until the 1980s that Heubel and Wiesel's findings were repurposed in the field of computer science. The *Neurocognitron* (Fukushima, 1980: `https://www.rctn.org/bruno/public/papers/Fukushima1980.pdf`) leveraged the concept of simple and complex cells by sandwiching layers of one after the other. This ancestor of the modern neural network used the aforementioned alternating layers to sequentially include modifiable parameters (or simple cells), while using pooling layers (or complex cells) to make the network invariant to minor altercations from the simple cells. While intuitive, this architecture was still not powerful enough to capture the intricate complexities present in visual signals.

One of the major breakthroughs followed in 1998, when famed AI researchers, Yan Lecun and Yoshua Bengio, were able to train a CNN, leveraging gradient-based weight updates, to perform document recognition. This network did an excellent job of recognizing digits of zip codes. Similar networks were quickly adopted by organizations such as the US postal service, to automate the tedious task of sorting mail (nope, not the electronic kind). While the results were impressive enough for commercial interest in narrow segments, these networks were still not able to handle more challenging and complex data, such as faces, cars, and other real-world objects. However, the collective work of these researchers and many others led to the modern incarnation of the larger and deeper CNNs, first appearing at the ImageNet classification challenge. These networks have now come to dominate the realm of computer vision, making their appearance in today's most sophisticated artificial visual intelligence systems. These networks are now used for tasks such as medical image diagnosis, detecting celestial objects in outer space, and making computers play old-school Atari games, to name a few.

Designing a CNN

Now, armed with the intuition of biological vision, we understand how neurons must be organized hierarchically, to detect simple patterns and use these to progressively build more complex patterns corresponding to real-world objects. We also know that we must implement a mechanism for spatial invariance to allow neurons to deal with similar inputs occurring at different spatial locations of a given image. Finally, we are aware that implementing a receptive field for each neuron is useful to achieve a topographical mapping of neurons to spatial locations in the real world, so that nearby neurons may represent nearby regions in the field of vision.

Dense versus convolutional layer

You will recall from the previous chapter that we used a feedforward neural network, composed of fully connected dense layers of neurons, to perform the task of handwritten digit recognition. While constructing our network, we were forced to flatten our input pixels of 28 x 28 into a vector of 784 pixels, for each image. Doing so caused us to lose any spatially relevant information that our network could leverage for classifying the digits it was shown. We simply showed it a 784-dimensional vector for each image in our dataset and expected it to recognize digits thereafter. While this approach was sufficient to attain a considerable accuracy in classifying simple handwritten digits from the nice and clean MNIST dataset, it quickly becomes impractical in more complex data that we may want to deal with, involving a multitude of local patterns of different spatial orientations.

We would ideally like to preserve spatial information and reuse neurons for the detection of similar patterns occurring in different spatial regions. This would allow our convolutional networks to be more efficient. Through reusing its neurons to recognize specific patterns in our data irrespective of their location, CNNs are advantageous to use in visual tasks. A densely connected network, on the other hand, would be forced to learn a pattern again, if it were to appear in another location of the image. Given the natural spatial hierarchies that exist in visual data, using convolution layers is an ideal way to detect minute local patterns and use them to progressively build more complex ones.

The following screenshot illustrates the hierarchical nature of visual data:

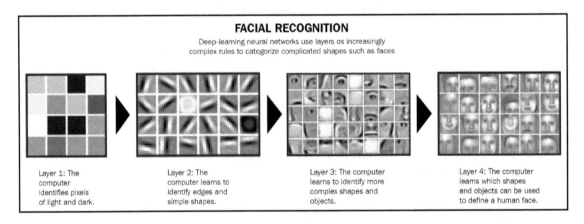

FACIAL RECOGNITION
Deep-learning neural networks use layers os increasingly complex rules to categorize complicated shapes such as faces

Layer 1: The computer identifies pixels of light and dark.

Layer 2: The computer learns to identify edges and simple shapes.

Layer 3: The computer learns to identify more complex shapes and objects.

Layer 4: The computer learns which shapes and objects can be used to define a human face.

Another problem we mentioned with dense layers is to do with their weakness in capturing local patterns from data. The dense layer is well known for capturing global patterns involving all pixels in images. As the findings of Hubel and Wiesel suggest, however, we want to limit the receptive field of our neurons to local patterns present in the data and use those patterns to progressively form more complex ones. This would allow our network to deal with very different forms of visual data, each with different types of local patterns enclosed. To overcome these problems, among others, the core component of CNN was developed, known as the **convolution operation**.

The convolution operation

The word *convolvere* comes from Latin and translates to *convolve* or *roll together*. From a mathematical perspective, you may define a convolution as the calculus-based integral denoting the amount by which two given functions overlap, as one of the two is slid across the other. In other words, performing the convolution operation on two functions (*f* and *g*) will produce a third function that expresses how the shape of one is modified by the other. The term *convolution* refers to both the result function and the computation process, with roots in the mathematical subfield of signal processing, as we can here in this diagram:

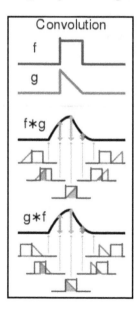

So, how can we leverage this operation to our advantage?

Preserving the spatial structure of an image

Firstly, we will use the inherent spatial structure of an image by simply feeding it as an *n*-dimensional tensor into our neural network. This means that the network will receive each pixel in its original matrix position, and not reduced to a position inside a single vector, as we did before. In the case of the MNIST example, a convolutional network would receive as input a 28 x 28 x 1 tensor, representing each image. Here, 28 x 28 represents a two-dimensional grid upon which the pixels are arranged to form the handwritten digits, whereas 1 at the end denotes the color channels of the image (that is, the number of pixel values per pixel, in a given image). As we know, a colored dataset may have image dimensions such as 28 x 28 x 3, where 3 denotes the different red, green, and blue values that form the color of an individual pixel. Since we only deal with single grayscale values per pixel in the MNIST dataset, the color channel is denoted as 1. Hence, it is important to understand that an image enters our network as a three-dimensional tensor, preserving the spatial structure of our image data:

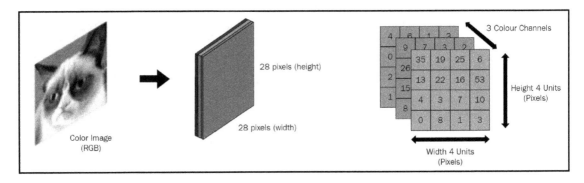

Receptive field

Now we can leverage the properties of additional spatial information, inherent to the image, in the architecture of our network. In other words, we are now ready to perform a convolution operation. This simply means that we will use a smaller segment of space and slide it over our input image as a filter to detect local patterns. The intuition here is to connect patches of our input data space to corresponding neurons in the hidden layers. Doing so allows the neuron to only observe a local area of the image at each convolution, thereby limiting its receptive field. Limiting a neuron's receptive field is useful for two main reasons. Since we reason that nearby pixels are more likely to be related to each other in an image, limiting the receptive field of neurons in our network makes these neurons better able to distinguish local variances between pixels in a given image. Moreover, this practice also allows us to drastically reduce the number of learnable parameters (or weights) in our network. In this manner, we use a **filter**, which is essentially a matrix of weights and apply it iteratively over the input space starting from the top-left corner of an image. We move a stride to the right at each convolution, by centering our filter on top of each pixel, in our input space. Once having convolved over the image segment corresponding to the top rows of pixels, we repeat the operation from the left side of the image once again, this time, for the rows underneath. This is how we slide the filter across our entire input image, extracting local features at each convolution by computing the dot products of our input area and the so-called **filters**.

The diagram here depicts the initial step of a convolution operation. Progressively, the three-dimensional blue rectangle shown here will be slid across segments (in red) of the entire image, giving the convolution operation its name. The rectangle itself, is known as a filter, or a **convolutional kernel**:

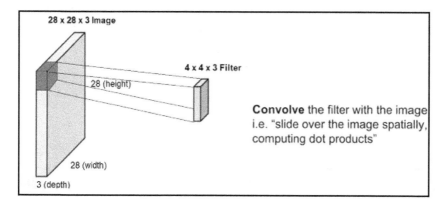

Feature extraction using filters

Each filter can be essentially thought of as an arrangement of neurons, similar in spirit to the ones we encountered in `Chapter 3`, *Signal Processing - Data Analysis with Neural Networks*. Here, the filter's neurons are initialized with random weights and progressively updated using the backpropagation algorithm during training. The filter itself is in charge of detecting a particular type of pattern, ranging from line segments to curves and more complex shapes. As a filter passes over an area of the input image, the filter weights are multiplied (element-wise) with the pixel values at that location, generating a single output vector. Then, we simply reduce this vector to a scalar value using a summation operation, exactly as we did for our feedforward neural network previously. These scalar values are generated at each new position the filter is moved to, spanning the entire input image. The values are stored in something referred to as the **activation map** (also known as a **feature map** or a **response map**) for a given filter. The activation map itself is conventionally smaller in dimension than the input image, and it embodies a new representation of the input image, while accentuating certain patterns within.

The weights of the filters themselves can be thought of as the learnable parameters of a convolutional layer and are updated to capture patterns relevant to the task at hand, while the network trains:

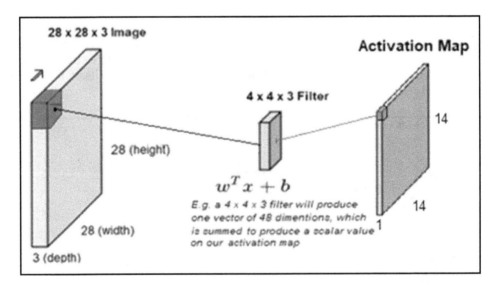

Backpropagation of errors in CNNs

As our network trains to find ideal filter weights, we hope that the activation map of a given filter is able to capture the most informative visual patterns that may exist in our data. Essentially, these activation maps are generated using matrix-wise multiplication. These activation maps are fed into the subsequent layer as inputs, and thus information propagates forward, up until the final layers of our model, which perform the classification. At this point, our `loss` function assesses the difference in the network's predictions versus the actual output, and backpropagates the prediction errors to adjust the networks weights, for each layer.

This is basically how a ConvNet is trained, on a very high level. The convolution operation consists of iteratively computing the dot product of a transposed filter matrix (holding the weights of our convolutional filter) with the corresponding input space of pixels to extract generalizable features from the training examples. These feature maps (or activation maps) are then first fed into pooling layers to reduce their dimensionality, and subsequently fed into fully connected layers to determine which combination of filters best represent a given output class. As the model weights are updated during a backward pass, new activation maps are generated at the next forward pass, which ideally encode more representative features of our data. Here, we present a brief visual summary of the ConvNet architecture:

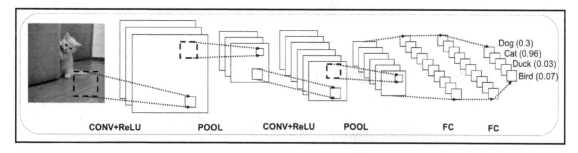

It follows the following steps:

1. Learns features in input image through convolution
2. Introduce non-linearity through activation function(real-world data is non-linear)
3. Reduce dimensionality and preserve spatial invariance with pooling

Using multiple filters

Since filters are pattern-specific (that is, each filter excels at picking up a certain type of pattern), we require more than just one filter to pick up all the different types of patterns that may exist in our image. This means that we may use multiple filters for a given convolutional layer in our network, allowing us to extract multiple distinct local features for a given region of input space. These local features, stored in the activation map of that specific filter, may be passed on to subsequent layers to build more complex patterns. Progressive convolutional layers will use different filters to convolve over the input activation map from the previous layer, again extracting and transforming the input map into a three-dimensional tensor output corresponding to the activation maps for each filter used. The new activation maps will again be three-dimensional tensors and can be similarly passed on the subsequent layers. Recall that when an image enters our network, it does so as a three-dimensional tensor with (width, height, and depth) corresponding to the input image dimensions (where depth is denoted by the pixel channels). In our output tensor, on the other hand, the depth axis denotes the number of filters used in the previous convolutional layer, where each filter produces its own activation map. In essence, this is how data propagates forward in a CNN, entering as an image and exiting as a three-dimensional activation map, being progressively transformed by various filters as the data propagates through deeper layers. The exact nature of transformations will become clearer soon, when we will build a ConvNet. We'll discuss theory a little bit more, and then we will be ready to proceed.

Stride of a convolution

The following diagram depicts the convolution operation that you have now familiarized yourself with, in two dimensions (for simplicity). It shows a 4 x 4 filter (red box) being slid across a larger image (14 x 14), taking a step of two pixels at a time:

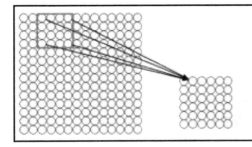

- Filter of size 4x4 : 16 different weights
- Apply this same filter to 4x4 patches in input
- Shift by 2 pixels for next patch

This "patchy" operation is **convolution**

The number of pixels by which a filter shifts at each iteration is known as its **stride**. At each stride, a dot product is computed using the pixel matrix from the corresponding input region, as well as the filter weights. These dot products are stored as a scalar value in the activation map for that filter (shown as a 6 x 6 square as follows). Hence, the activation map denotes a reduced representation of the layer inputs, and essentially is a matrix composed of the summed-up dot products we get by convolving our filter over segments of the input data. On a higher level, the activation map represents the activation of neurons for specific patterns that the respective filter is detecting. Longer strides of these filters will lead to less detailed sampling of the corresponding input regions, whereas shorter strides will allow individual pixels to be sampled more often, permitting a higher definition activation map.

What are features?

While the overall mechanism of collecting features with different types of filters may be clear, you may well be wondering what a feature actually looks like and how we go about extracting them from a filter.

Let's consider a simple example to clarify our understanding. Suppose you wished to detect the letter X from a bunch of grayscale images of letters. How would a CNN go about doing this? Well, let's first consider the image of an X. As shown as follows, we can think of the pixels with positive values form the lines of an X, whereas pixels with a negative value simply represent blank space in our image, as shown in this diagram:

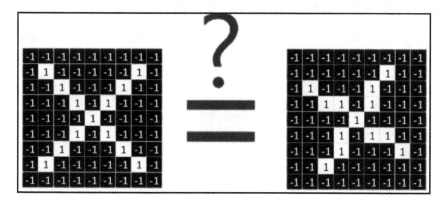

But then comes the problem of positional variance: What if the X appears slightly rotated or distorted in any other way? In the real world, the letter X comes in many sizes, shapes, and so on. How can we break up the image of an X using smaller filters that capture its underlying patterns? Well, here's one way:

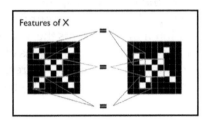

As you may have noticed, we can actually break down the image into smaller segments, where each segment (denoted by the green, orange, and purple boxes) represents recurring patterns within the image. In our case, we are able to use two diagonally oriented filters and one intersecting filter and slide each of them across our image to pick up on the line segments that form an X. Essentially, you may think of each filter as a pattern detector of sorts. As these different filters convolve over our input image, we are left with activation maps that start to resemble long horizontal lines and crosses, which the network learns to combine to recognize the letter X.

Visualizing feature extraction with filters

Let's consider another example, to solidify our understanding of how filters detect patterns. Consider this depiction of the number 7, taken from the MNIST dataset. We use this 28 x 28 pixelated image to show how filters actually pick up on different patterns:

Intuitively, we notice that this 7 is composed of two horizontal lines, as well as a slanted vertical line. We essentially need to initialize our filters with values that can pick up on these separate patterns. Next, we observe some 3 x 3 filter matrices that a ConvNet would typically learn for the task at hand:

-1 -1 -1	0 0 0	-1 1 0	0 1 -1
1 1 1	1 1 1	-1 1 0	0 1 -1
0 0 0	-1 -1 -1	-1 1 0	0 1 -1

While not very intuitive to visualize, these filters are actually sophisticated edge detectors. To see how they work, let's picture each 0 in our filter weights as the color grey, whereas each value of 1 takes the color white, leaving -1 with the color black. As these filters convolve over an input image, element-wise multiplications are performed using the filter values and the pixels underneath. The product of this operation is yet another matrix, known as an **activation map**, representing particular features picked up by their respective filters, for a given input image. Now let's see the effects of executing a convolution operation over the input image of a 7, using each of these four filters, to exactly understand what kind of patterns they individually pick up on. The following illustration plots out the activation map for each filter in the convolutional layer, once it is shown the image of a 7:

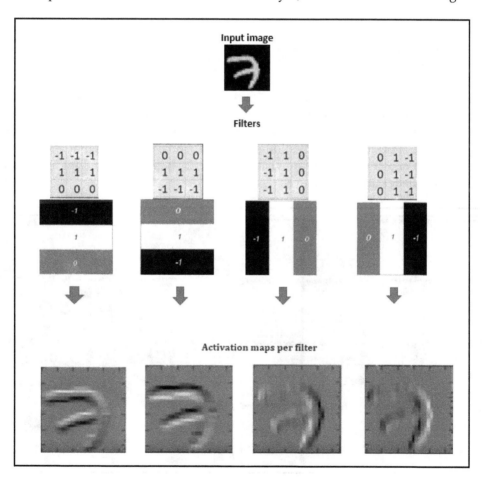

We observe that each filter is able to pick up on a specific pattern in the input image by simply computing the dot product summation of pixel values and filter weights at each spatial location. The patterns picked up can be denoted by the white regions in the aforementioned activation maps. We see that the first two filters adeptly pick up on upper and lower horizontal lines in the image of the 7, respectively. We also notice how the latter two filters pick up on the inner and outer vertical lines that form the body of the digit 7, respectively. While these are still examples of fairly simple pattern detections, progressive layers in ConvNets tend to be able to pick up on much more informative structures, by differentiating colors and shapes, which are essentially patterns of numbers, to our network.

Looking at complex filters

The following image shows the top nine activation maps per grid, associated with specific inputs, for the second layer of a ConvNet. On the left, you can think of the mini-grids as activations of individual neurons, for given inputs. The corresponding colored grids on the right relate to the inputs these neurons were shown. What we are visualizing here is the kind of input that *maximizes* the activation of these neurons. We notice that already some pretty-clear circle detector neurons are visible (grid 2, 2), being activated for inputs such as the top of lamp shades and animal eyes:

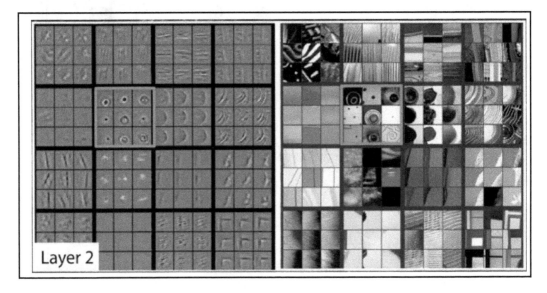

Similarly, we notice some square-like pattern detectors (grid 4, 4) that seem to activate for images containing door and window frames. As we progressively visualize activation maps for deeper layers in CNNs, we observe even more complex geometric patterns being picked up, representing faces of dogs (grid 1, 1), bird legs (grid 2, 4), and so on:

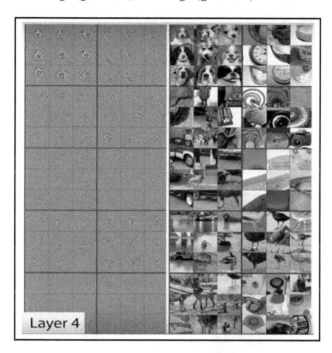

Summarizing the convolution operation

All that we are doing here is applying a set of weights (that is, a filter) to local input spaces for feature extraction. We do this iteratively, moving our filter across the input space in fixed steps, known as a **stride**. Moreover, the use of different filters allows us to capture different patterns from a given input. Finally, since the filters convolve over the entire image, we are able to spatially share parameters for a given filter. This allows us to use the *same* filter to detect similar patterns in different locations of the image, relating to the concept of spatial invariance discussed earlier. However, these activation maps that a convolutional layer outputs are essentially abstract high-dimensional representations. We need to implement a mechanism to reduce these representations into more manageable dimensions, before we go ahead and perform classification. This brings us to the **pooling layers**.

Understanding pooling layers

A final consideration when using convolutional layers is to do with the idea of stacking simple cells to detect local patterns and complex cells to downsample representations, as we saw earlier with the cat-brain experiments, and the neocognitron. The convolutional filters we saw behave like simple cells by focusing on specific locations on the input and training neurons to fire, given some stimuli from the local regions of our input image. Complex cells, on the other hand, are required to be less specific to the location of the stimuli. This is where the pooling layer comes in. This technique of pooling intends to reduce the output of CNN layers to more manageable representations. Pooling layers are periodically added between convolutional layers to spatially downsample the outputs of our convolutional layer. All this does is progressively reduce the size of the convolutional layer outputs, thereby leading to more efficient representations, shown as follows:

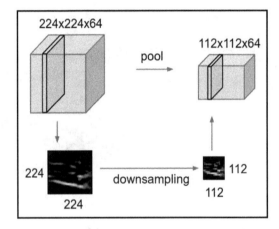

As you can see, the depth of volume is preserved because we have pooled the input volume of size 224 x 224 x 64 with a filter of size 2 and a stride of 2. And this gives an output volume of 112 x 112 x 64.

Types of pooling operations

This similarly reduces the number of learnable parameters required in our network for the same task and prevents our network from overfitting. Finally, pooling is performed for every activation map generated by a given layer (that is, every slice of depth of the input tensor) and resizes its input spatially using its own filters. It is very common to see pooling layers with 2 x 2 filters along with a stride of 2, performed on every depth slice. There are many ways to perform this sort of downsampling. Most commonly, this is achieved through a **max pooling** operation, which simply means that we preserve the pixel with the highest value out of all the pixels in the input region under our pooling filter. The following diagram illustrates this max pooling operation on a given slice of our input tensor:

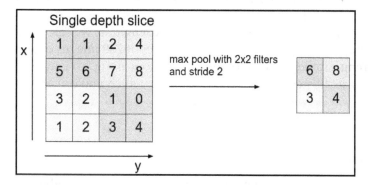

The pooling layer downsamples the activation volume spatially, independently in each depth slice of the input volume. The most common downsampling operation is max, giving rise to max pooling, here shown with a stride of 2. That is, each max is taken over four numbers (the little 2 x 2 square).

You can also downsample by taking the average value of the 2 x 2 squares as shown. This operation is known as **average pooling**. As we will see throughout later chapters, Keras comes with quite a few pooling layers that each perform different types of downsampling operations on the outputs from the previous layer. The choice will largely depend on your specific use case. In the case of image classification, a two-dimensional or three-dimensional max pooling layer is most commonly used. The dimension of the layer simply refers to the type of input it accepts. For example, two-dimensional layers are used to downsample when processing grayscale images, and three-dimensional layers are used in the case of colored images. You can refer to the well-maintained documentation to study it yourself.

Implementing CNNs in Keras

Having achieved a high-level understanding of the key components of a CNN, we may now proceed with actually implementing one ourselves. This will allow us to become familiar with the key architectural considerations when building convolutional networks and get an overview of the implementational details that make these networks perform so well. Soon, we will implement the convolutional layer in Keras, and explore downsampling techniques such as pooling layers to see how we can leverage a combination of convolutional, pooling, and densely connected layers for various image classification tasks.

For this example, we will adopt a simple use case. Let's say we wanted our CNN to detect human emotion, in the form of a smile or a frown. This is a simple binary classification task. How do we proceed? Well, firstly, we will need a labeled dataset of humans smiling and frowning. While there are many ways to go about doing this, we select the **Happy House Dataset** for this purpose. This dataset comes with about 750 images of people, each either smiling or frowning, stored in the h5py files. To follow along, all you need to do is to download the dataset hosted on the Kaggle website, which you can access freely through this link: `https://www.kaggle.com/iarunava/happy-house-dataset`

Probing our data

Let's start by loading in and probing our dataset, to get an idea of what we are dealing with. We make a simple function that reads our h5py files, extracts the training and test data, and places it into the standard NumPy arrays, shown as follows:

```python
import numpy as np
import h5py
import matplotlib.pyplot as plt
# Function to load data
def load_dataset():
# use h5py module and specify file path and mode (read)
all_train_data=h5py.File('C:/Users/npurk/Desktop/Chapter_3_CNN/train_happy.
h5', "r")
all_test_data=h5py.File('C:/Users/npurk/Desktop/Chapter_3_CNN/test_happy.h5
', "r")
# Collect all train and test data from file as numpy arrays
x_train = np.array(all_train_data["train_set_x"][:])
y_train = np.array(all_train_data["train_set_y"][:])
x_test = np.array(all_test_data["test_set_x"][:])
y_test = np.array(all_test_data["test_set_y"][:])
# Reshape data
y_train = y_train.reshape((1, y_train.shape[0]))
y_test = y_test.reshape((1, y_test.shape[0]))
```

```
return x_train, y_train, x_test, y_test
# Load the data
X_train, Y_train, X_test, Y_test = load_dataset()
```

Verifying the data shape

Next, we will print out the shape of our training and test data. In the following code block, we notice that we are dealing with colored images of 64 x 64 pixels. We have 600 of these in our training set and `150` in the test set. We can also have a look at what an image actually looks like, as we did in previous examples using Matplotlib:

```
print(X_train.shape)
print(X_test.shape)
print(Y_train.shape)
print(Y_test.shape)

(600, 64, 64, 3)
(150, 64, 64, 3)
(1, 600)
(1, 150)
# Plot out a single image plt.imshow(X_train[0]) # Print label for image
(smiling = 1, frowning = 0) print ("y = " + str(np.squeeze(Y_train[:, 0])))
y = 0
```

—et voila! Ladies and gentlemen, we have a frowny face:

Normalizing our data

Now, we will prepare our images by rescaling pixel values between 0 and 1. We also transpose our label matrices, as we want them to be oriented as (600, 1), and not (1, 600), referring to our training labels, as shown previously in the training labels. Finally, we print out the shape of our features and labels for both the training and the test set:

```
# Normalize pixels using max channel value, 255 (Rescale data)

X_train = X_train/255.
X_test = X_test/255.

# Transpose labels
Y_train = Y_train.T
Y_test = Y_test.T

# Print stats
print ("Number of training examples : " + str(X_train.shape[0]))
print ("Number of test examples : " + str(X_test.shape[0]))
print ("X_train shape: " + str(X_train.shape))
print ("Y_train shape: " + str(Y_train.shape))
print ("X_test shape: " + str(X_test.shape))
print ("Y_test shape: " + str(Y_test.shape))
-----------------------------------------------------------------
Output:
Number of training examples : 600
Number of test examples : 150
X_train shape: (600, 64, 64, 3)
Y_train shape: (600, 1)
X_test shape: (150, 64, 64, 3)
Y_test shape: (150, 1)
```

Then, we convert our NumPy arrays to floating-point arithmetic values, which our network prefers:

```
#convert to float 32 ndarrays
from keras.utils import to_categorical
X_train = X_train.astype('float32') X_test = X_test.astype('float32')
Y_train = Y_train.astype('float32') Y_test = Y_test.astype('float32')
```

Making some imports

Finally, we get to import the new layers that we will be employing for our emotion classification task. In the bottom section of the block of the previous code, we import a two-dimensional convolutional layer. The dimension of the convolutional layer is a property specific to the task you wish to perform. Since we are dealing with images, a two-dimensional convolutional layer is the best choice. If we were dealing with time-series sensor data (such as biomedical data—for example, EEGs or financial data such as the stock market), then a one-dimensional convolutional layer would be a more appropriate choice. Similarly, we would use three-dimensional convolutional layers if videos were the input data:

```
import keras
from keras.models import Sequential
from keras.layers import Flatten
from keras.layers import Dense
from keras.layers import Activation, Dropout
from keras.optimizers import Adam
from keras.layers import Conv2D
from keras.layers import MaxPooling2D
from keras.layers.normalization import BatchNormalization
```

Similarly, we also imported a two-dimensional max pooling layer, along with a batch-wise normalizer. Batch normalization simply allows us to deal with the changing values of layer outputs, as data propagates through our network.

The problem of 'internal covariate shift' is indeed a well noted phenomena in CNNs as well as other ANN architectures, and refers to the change in the input's statistical distribution after a few training iterations, slowing down the convergence of our model to ideal weights. This problem can be avoided by simply normalizing our data in mini-batches, using a mean and variance reference. While we encourage you to further research the problem of internal covariate shift and the mathematics behind batch normalization, for now it suffices to know that this helps us train our network faster and allows higher learning rates, while making our network weights easier to initialize

Convolutional layer

Two main architectural considerations are associated with the convolutional layer in Keras. The first is to do with the number of filters to employ in the given layer, whereas the second denotes the size of the filters themselves. So, let's see how this is implemented by initializing a blank sequential model and adding our first convolutional layer to it:

```
model=sequential()
#First Convolutional layer
model.add(Conv2D(16,(5,5), padding = 'same', activation = 'relu',
input_shape = (64,64,3)))
model.add(BatchNormalization())
```

Defining the number and size of the filters

As we saw previously, we define the layer by embodying it with 16 filters, each with a height and width of 5 x 5. In actuality, the proper dimensions of our filters are 5 x 5 x 3. However, the depth of all the filters spans the full depth of a given input tensor, and hence never needs to be specified. Since this is the first layer, receiving as input a tensor representation of our training image, the depth of our filters would be 3, for each of the red, green, and blue values per pixel covered.

Padding input tensors

Thinking about the convolution operation intuitively, it becomes apparent that as we slide our filter across an input tensor, what ends up happening is that our filter passes over borders and edges less frequently than it does over other parts of the input tensor. This is simply because each pixel that is not located at the edge of an input may be resampled by the filter multiple times, as it strides across an image. This leaves our output representations with uneven samplings of borders and edges from our input, referred to as **the border effect**.

We can avoid this by simply padding our input tensor with zeros, shown as follows:

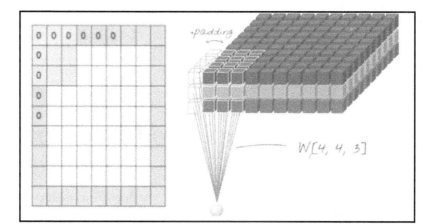

In this manner, the pixels that would normally appear at the edge of our input tensor now appear later on, allowing an even sampling to be performed on all pixels within the input. We specify in our first convolutional layer that we want to preserve the input length and width of our inputs, so as to ensure the output tensor has the same spatial dimensions with respect to its length and width. This is done by defining the padding parameter of the layer as same. The depth of a convolutional layer output, as previously stated, is denoted by the number of filters we choose to use. In our case, this would be 16, denoting the 16 activation maps produced as each of our 16 filters convolve over the input space. Finally, we define the input shape as the dimensions of any single input image. For us, this corresponds to the 64 x 64 x 3 coloured pixels that we have in our dataset, shown again as follows:

```
model = Sequential()
#First Convolutional layer
model.add(Conv2D(16,(5,5), padding = 'same', activation = 'relu',
input_shape = (64,64,3)))
model.add(BatchNormalization())
```

Max Pooling layer

The activation maps from our first convolutional layer are normalized and fed into the max pooling layer below. Similar to the convolution operation, pooling is applied one input region at a time. For the case of max pooling, we simply take the largest value in our grid of pixels, which represents the strongest correlating pixels to each feature, and combine these max values to form a lower dimensional representation of the input image. In this manner, we preserve more important values and discard the remaining values in a given grid of the respective activation map.

This downsampling operation does naturally cause a certain degree of information loss, yet drastically reduces the amount of storage space required in networks, giving it a considerable efficiency boost:

```
#First Pooling layer
model.add(MaxPooling2D(pool_size = (2,2)))
model.add(Dropout(0.1))
```

Leveraging a fully connected layer for classification

Then, we simply add a few more layers of convolution, batch normalization, and dropouts, progressively building our network until we reach the final layers. Just like in the MNIST example, we will leverage densely connected layers to implement the classification mechanism in our network. Before we can do this, we must flatten our input from the previous layer (16 x 16 x 32) to a 1D vector of dimension (8,192). We do this because dense layer-based classifiers prefer to receive 1D vectors, unlike the output from our previous layer. We proceed by adding two densely connected layers, the first one with 128 neurons (an arbitrary choice) and the second one with just one neuron, since we are dealing with a binary classification problem. If everything goes according to plan, this one neuron will be supported by its cabinet of neurons from the previous layers and learn to fire when it sees a certain output class (for example, smiling faces) and abstain from this when presented with images from the other class (for example, frowning faces). Note that we again use a sigmoid activation function for our last layer, which computes the class probability per given input image:

```
#Second Convolutional layer
model.add(Conv2D(32, (5,5), padding = 'same', activation = 'relu'))
model.add(BatchNormalization())
#Second Pooling layer
model.add(MaxPooling2D(pool_size = (2,2)))
#Dropout layer
model.add(Dropout(0.1))
#Flattening layer
model.add(Flatten())
#First densely connected layer
model.add(Dense(128, activation = 'relu'))
#Final output layer
model.add(Dense(1, activation = 'sigmoid'))
```

Summarizing our model

Let's visualize our model to better understand what we just built. You will notice that the number of activation maps (denoted by the depth of subsequent layer outputs) progressively increases throughout the network. On the other hand, the length and width of the activation maps tend to decrease, from (64 x 64) to (16 x 16), by the time the dropout layer is reached. These two patterns are conventional in most, if not all, modern iterations of CNNs.

The reason behind the variance in input and output dimensions between layers can depend on how you have chosen to address *the border effects* we discussed earlier, or what *stride* you have implemented for the filters in your convolutional layer. Smaller strides will lead to higher dimensions, whereas larger strides will lead to lower dimensions. This is simply to do with the number of locations you are computing dot products at, while storing the result in an activation map. Larger filter strides (or steps) will reach the end of an image earlier, having computed fewer dot product values over the same input space of a smaller filter stride. The strides of a convolutional layer may be set by defining the strides parameter, with an integer or tuple/list of single integers for the given layer. The integer value(s) will refer to the length of the stride at each convolution operation:

```
model.summary()
```

Following will be the summary:

```
1  model.summary()

Layer (type)                     Output Shape            Param #
===================================================================
conv2d_29 (Conv2D)               (None, 64, 64, 16)      1216

batch_normalization_29 (Batc     (None, 64, 64, 16)      64

max_pooling2d_29 (MaxPooling     (None, 32, 32, 16)      0

dropout_29 (Dropout)             (None, 32, 32, 16)      0

conv2d_30 (Conv2D)               (None, 32, 32, 32)      12832

batch_normalization_30 (Batc     (None, 32, 32, 32)      128

max_pooling2d_30 (MaxPooling     (None, 16, 16, 32)      0

dropout_30 (Dropout)             (None, 16, 16, 32)      0

flatten_15 (Flatten)             (None, 8192)            0

dense_29 (Dense)                 (None, 128)             1048704

dense_30 (Dense)                 (None, 1)               129
===================================================================
Total params: 1,063,073
Trainable params: 1,062,977
Non-trainable params: 96
```

As we noted earlier, you will notice that both the convolutional and the max pooling layers generate a three-dimensional tensor with dimensions corresponding to the output height, output width, and output depth. The depth of the layer outputs are essentially activation maps for each filter initialized. We implemented our first convolutional layer with 16 filters, and the second layer with 32 filters, hence the respective layers will produce that many numbers of activation maps, as seen previously.

Compiling the model

At the moment, we have covered all the key architectural decisions involved in designing a ConvNet and are now ready to compile the network we have been building. We choose the `adam` optimizer, and the `binary_crossentropy` loss function, as we previously did for the binary sentiment analysis task from the previous chapter. Similarly, we also import the `EarlyStopping` callback to monitor our loss on the validation set, to get an idea of how well our model is doing on unseen data, at each epoch:

```
1  model.compile(optimizer = 'adam',
2                loss = 'binary_crossentropy',
3                metrics = ['accuracy'])
```

```
1  from keras.callbacks import EarlyStopping
2
3  early_stopping = keras.callbacks.EarlyStopping(monitor='val_loss')
```

```
1  model.fit(X_train, Y_train, validation_data=(X_test, Y_test),
2            epochs=20,
3            batch_size=50,
4            callbacks=[early_stopping])
```

```
Train on 600 samples, validate on 150 samples
Epoch 1/20
600/600 [==============================] - 24s 40ms/step - loss: 1.1793 - acc: 0.5583 - val_loss: 0.5761 - val_acc: 0.6267
Epoch 2/20
600/600 [==============================] - 21s 35ms/step - loss: 0.5251 - acc: 0.7850 - val_loss: 0.4851 - val_acc: 0.7600
Epoch 3/20
600/600 [==============================] - 20s 34ms/step - loss: 0.3586 - acc: 0.8400 - val_loss: 0.3339 - val_acc: 0.8667
Epoch 4/20
600/600 [==============================] - 20s 34ms/step - loss: 0.2379 - acc: 0.9117 - val_loss: 0.2766 - val_acc: 0.8800
Epoch 5/20
600/600 [==============================] - 20s 34ms/step - loss: 0.1905 - acc: 0.9267 - val_loss: 0.1928 - val_acc: 0.9400
Epoch 6/20
600/600 [==============================] - 20s 34ms/step - loss: 0.1688 - acc: 0.9250 - val_loss: 0.1650 - val_acc: 0.9600
Epoch 7/20
600/600 [==============================] - 20s 34ms/step - loss: 0.1287 - acc: 0.9533 - val_loss: 0.1554 - val_acc: 0.9400
Epoch 8/20
600/600 [==============================] - 21s 35ms/step - loss: 0.0968 - acc: 0.9600 - val_loss: 0.2802 - val_acc: 0.8800

<keras.callbacks.History at 0x2baa51ba7b8>
```

Checking model accuracy

As we saw previously, we achieved a test accuracy of 88% at the last epoch of our training session. Let's have a look at what this really means, by interpreting the precision and recall scores of our classifier:

```
1  # Predict the test set results
2  Y_pred = model.predict_classes(X_test)
```

```
1  from sklearn.metrics import accuracy_score, confusion_matrix, recall_score, precision_score, f1_score
2
3
4  print ("test accuracy: %s" %accuracy_score(Y_test, Y_pred))
5  print ("precision: %s"  %precision_score(Y_test, Y_pred))
6  print ("recall: %s" %recall_score(Y_test, Y_pred))
7  print ("f1 score: %s"  %f1_score(Y_test, Y_pred))
8
9
```

```
test accuracy: 0.88
precision: 0.9852941176470589
recall: 0.7976190476190477
f1 score: 0.8815789473684211
```

As we noticed previously, the ratio of correctly predicted positive observations to the total number of positive observations in our test set (otherwise known as the **precision score**) is pretty high at 0.98. The recall score is a bit lower and denotes the number of correctly predicted results divided by the number of results that should have been returned. Finally, the F-measure simply combines both the precision and recall scores as a harmonic mean.

To supplement our understanding, we plot out a confusion matrix of our classifier on the test set, as shown as follows. This is essentially an error matrix that lets us visualize how our model performed. The x axis denotes the predicted classes of our classifier, whereas the y axis denotes the actual classes of our test examples. As we see, our classifier falsely detects about 17 images where it thinks that the person is smiling, whereas they are in fact frowning (also known as a **false positive**).

On the other hand, our classifier only makes one mistake in classifying a smiling face as a frowning face (also known as a **false negative**). Thinking of false positives and negatives helps us evaluate the utility of our classifier in real-world scenarios and lets us perform a cost benefit analysis of deploying such a system. In our case, this would not be necessary, given the subject matter of our classification task; however, other scenarios (such as skin cancer detection, for example) will require careful consideration and evaluation before using such learning systems:

```
1  import seaborn as sns
2
3  cm = confusion_matrix(Y_test,Y_pred)
4  sns.heatmap(cm,annot=True)
```

<matplotlib.axes._subplots.AxesSubplot at 0x2bb0ed3a1d0>

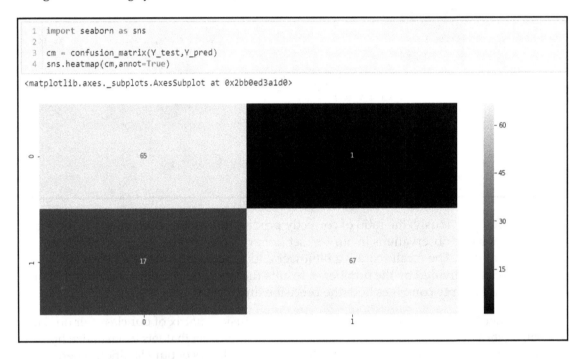

Whenever you are satisfied with your models' accuracy, you may save a model shown as follows. Note that this not only constitutes best practice, as it gives you well-documented records of your previous attempts, steps taken, and results achieved, but is also useful if you want to further probe the model, by peering into its intermediate layers to see what it has actually learned, as we will momentarily do:

```
1  model.save('C:/Users/npurk/Desktop/Chapter_3_CNN/smile_detector.h5py')
2  model = keras.models.load_model('C:/Users/npurk/Desktop/Chapter_3_CNN/smile_detector.h5py')
```

The problem with detecting smiles

We must note at this point, that the problem of external validity (that is, the generalizability of our model) persists with a dataset like the smile detector. Given the restricted manner in which data has been collected, it would be unreasonable to expect our CNN to generalize well on other data. Firstly, the network is trained with low resolution input images. Moreover, it has only seen images of one smiling or frowning person in the same location each time. Feeding this network an image of, say, the managerial board of FIFA will not cause it to detect smiles however large and present they may be. We would need to readapt our approach. One way can be through applying the same transformations to the input image as done for the training data, by segmenting and resizing the input image per face. A better approach would be to gather more varied data and augment the training set by rotating and contorting the training examples, as we will see in later chapters. The key here is to include people smiling at different poses and orientations, with different lighting conditions, in your dataset, to truly capture all useful visual representations of a smile. If it is too expensive to collect more data, generating synthetic images (using the Keras image generator) can also be a viable option. The quality of your data can drastically improve the performance of your network. For now, we will explore some techniques to inform ourselves of the inner workings of a CNN.

Inside the black box

It is one thing to train a **smile detector** from a narrow dataset of similar images. Not only can you directly verify your predictions, but each false prediction doesn't exactly cost you a fortune. Now, if you were using a similar system to monitor behavioral responses of psychiatric patients (as a hypothetical example), you would probably want to ensure a high accuracy by ensuring that your model really understands what a smile means and is not picking up some irrelevant pattern in your training set. In the context of high-risk industries such as healthcare or energy, any misunderstandings can have disastrous consequences ranging from the loss of lives to the loss of resources. Hence, we want to be able to ensure that our deployed model has indeed picked up on truly predictive trends in the data and has not memorized some random features with no out-of-set predictivity. This has happened throughout the history of the use of neural networks. In the following section, we have selected a few tales from neural network folklore to illustrate these dilemmas.

Neural network fails

Once upon a time, the US Army had gotten the idea of using neural networks for automated detection of camouflaged enemy tanks. Researchers were commissioned to design and train a neural network to detect camouflaged tank images, from aerial photography of enemy locations. The researchers simply fine-tuned the model weights to reflect the correct output labels for each training example, and then tested the model on their secluded test examples. Luckily (or so it appeared), their network was able to classify all test images adequately, confirming to the researchers that their task had ended. Yet, soon enough, the researchers heard back from angry Pentagon officials claiming that the network they had handed over did no better than random chance at classifying camo-tanks. Confused, the researchers probed their training data and compared it to what the Pentagon had tested the network with. They discovered that the photos of camouflaged tanks used for training the network were all taken on cloudy days, whereas the negatives (photos without camo-tanks) were all taken on sunny days. The consequence of this was that their network had only learned to distinguish the weather (through brightness of the pixels) rather than approaching the intended classification task at hand:

It is quite often that neural networks, after a deluge of training iterations, achieve super-human accuracy on their training sets. For instance, one researcher observed such a phenomenon when they attempted to train a network to classify different types of land and sea mammals. Having achieved a great performance, the researchers tried to dig in further in order to decode any classification rules we humans might still ignore for this task. It turned out that a large part of what their sophisticated network had learned to do was with the presence or absence of blue pixels in an image, which naturally do not occur often on pictures with land mammals.

The last in our short selection of neural network failure tales is the case of the self-driving car that self-drove off a bridge. Confused automation engineers attempted to probe the trained network to understand what went wrong. To their surprise, they discovered something very curious. Instead of detecting the road on the street to follow, the network was, for some reason, relying on the continuous patches of green grass separating the road from the sidewalk for its orientation. When encountering the bridge, this patch of green grass disappeared, causing the network to behave in the seemingly unpredictable way it did.

Visualizing ConvNet learnings

These stories motivate our need to ensure that our models do not overfit on random noise, but actually capture representatively predictive features. We know how predictive inaccuracies can be introduced through careless data considerations, the inherent nature of your task, or inherent randomness in modeling. The conventionally popularized narrative on neural networks often includes terms such as **black box** to describe its learning mechanism. While understanding what individual neurons have learned may not be intuitive for all sorts of neural nets, this is hardly true for CNNs. Interestingly, ConvNets allow us to, literally, visualize their learned features. As we saw earlier, we can visualize neural activations for given input images. But we can do even more. In fact, there are a multitude of methods that have been developed in recent years to probe a CNN, to better understand what it has learned. While we do not have the time to cover all of these, we will be able to cover the most practically useful ones.

Visualizing neural activations of intermediate layers

Firstly, we can visualize how progressive layers in our CNN transform the inputs they are fed, by looking at their activation maps. Recall that these are simply the reduced representations of the inputs that the network propagates through its architecture as it sees data. Visualizing the intermediate layers (convolutional or pooling) gives us an idea of the activation of neurons in our network at each stage as the input is broken down by the various learned filters. Since each two-dimensional activation map stores features extracted by a given filter, we must visualize these maps as two-dimensional images, where each image corresponds to a learned feature. This method is often referred to as visualizing intermediate activations.

To be able to extract the learned features of our network, we will have to make some minor architectural tweaks to our model. This brings us to Keras's functional API. Recall that, previously, we were defining a sequential model using Keras's sequential API, which essentially let us sequentially stack layers of neurons to perform our classification tasks. These models ingested input tensors of images or word representations and spat out class probabilities assigned to each input. Now we will use the functional API, which allows building multi-output models, directed acyclic graphs, and even models with shared layers. We will use this API to peer into the depths of our convolutional network.

Predictions on an input image

First and foremost, we prepare an image (although you may use several) to be ingested by our multi-output model, so we are able to see the intermediate layer activations that occur as this image propagates through our new model. We take a random image from our test set for this purpose and prepare it as a four-dimensional tensor (with batch size 1, since we are only feeding our network a single image):

```
1  input_image = X_test[8]
2  input_image = np.expand_dims(input_image, axis=0)
3  print(input_image.shape)

(1, 64, 64, 3)
```

Next, we initialize a multi-output model to make a prediction on our input image. The purpose of this is to capture the intermediate activations, per each layer of our network, so we can visually plot out the activation maps generated by different filters. This helps us understand which features our model has actually learned.

Introducing Keras's functional API

How exactly will we do this? Well we start by importing the Model class from the functional API. This lets us define a new model. The key difference in our new model is that this one is capable of giving us back multiple outputs, pertaining to the outputs of intermediate layers. This is achieved by using the layer outputs from a trained CNN (such as our smile detector) and feed it into this new multi-output model. Essentially, our multi-output model will take an input image and return filter-wise activations for each of the eight layers in our smile detector model that we previously trained.

You can also limit the number of layers to visualize through the list slicing notation used on `model.layers`, shown as follows:

```
1  #retrive a blank multi-output model from the functional API
2  from keras.models import Model
3
4  #retrieve layer outputs for layers in previously trained sequential model
5  layer_outputs_smile_detector = [layer.output for layer in model.layers[:]]
6
7  #define multi-output model that takes input image tensors and outputs intermediate layer activations
8  multioutput_model = Model(inputs=model.input, outputs=layer_outputs)
9
10 #Generate activation tensors of intermediate layers
11 activations = multioutput_model.predict(input_image)
```

The last line of the preceding code defines the activations variable, by making our multi-output model perform inference on the input image we fed it. This operation returns the multiple outputs corresponding to each layer of our CNN, now stored as a set of NumPy arrays:

```
1  print('number of layers:', len(activations))
2  print('Datatype:', type(activations[0]))
3  print('1st layer output shape:', activations[0].shape)
4  print('4th layer output shape:', activations[3].shape)
5  print('8th layer output shape:', activations[7].shape)

number of layers: 8
Datatype: <class 'numpy.ndarray'>
1st layer output shape: (1, 64, 64, 16)
4th layer output shape: (1, 32, 32, 16)
8th layer output shape: (1, 16, 16, 32)
```

As you see, the activations variable stores a list of 8 NumPy *n*-dimensional arrays. Each of these 8 arrays represents a tensor output of a particular layer in our smile detector CNN. Each layer output represents the activations from the multiple filters used. Hence, we observe multiple activation maps per layer. These activation maps are essentially two-dimensional tensors that encode different features from the input image.

Verifying the number of channels per layer

We saw that each layer has a depth that denoted the number of activation maps. These are also referred to as channels, where each channel contains an activation map, with a height and width of (*n* x *n*). Our first layer, for example, has 16 different maps of size 64 x 64. Similarly, the fourth layer has 16 activation maps of size 32 x 32. The eighth layer has 32 activation maps, each of size 16 x 16. Each of these activation maps was generated by a specific filter from its respective layer, and are passed forward to subsequent layers to encode higher-level features. This will concur with our smile detector model's architectural build, which we can always verify, as shown here:

```
1  model.summary()

Layer (type)                    Output Shape           Param #
=================================================================
conv2d_29 (Conv2D)              (None, 64, 64, 16)     1216

batch_normalization_29 (Batc    (None, 64, 64, 16)     64

max_pooling2d_29 (MaxPooling    (None, 32, 32, 16)     0

dropout_29 (Dropout)            (None, 32, 32, 16)     0

conv2d_30 (Conv2D)              (None, 32, 32, 32)     12832

batch_normalization_30 (Batc    (None, 32, 32, 32)     128

max_pooling2d_30 (MaxPooling    (None, 16, 16, 32)     0

dropout_30 (Dropout)            (None, 16, 16, 32)     0

flatten_15 (Flatten)            (None, 8192)           0

dense_29 (Dense)                (None, 128)            1048704

dense_30 (Dense)                (None, 1)              129
=================================================================
Total params: 1,063,073
Trainable params: 1,062,977
Non-trainable params: 96
```

Visualizing activation maps

Now the fun part! We will plot out the activation maps for different filters in a given layer. Let's start with the first layer. We can plot each of the 16 activation maps out, as shown here:

While we will not show all 16 of these activation maps, here are a few interesting ones we found:

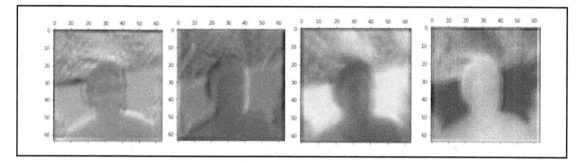

As we can clearly see, each filter has captured distinct features from the input image, relating to the horizontal and vertical edges of the face, as well as the background of the image. As you visualize deeper activation maps of deeper layers, you will note that the activations become increasingly abstract in nature and less interpretable to the human eye. These activations are said to be encoding higher-level notions pertaining to a face's location and the eyes and ears within. You will also notice that the more and more activation maps remain blank the deeper you probe into the network. This means that fewer filters were activated in the deeper layers because the input image did not have the patterns corresponding to the ones encoded by the filters. This is quite common, as we would expect activation patterns to increasingly relate to the class of the image shown as it propagates through deeper layers of the network.

Understanding saliency

We saw earlier that the intermediate layers of our ConvNet seemed to encode some pretty clear detectors of face edges. It is harder to distinguish, however, whether our network understands what a smile actually is. You will notice in our smiling faces dataset that all pictures have been taken on the same background at the same approximate angle from the camera. Moreover, you will notice that the individuals in our dataset tend to smile as they lift their head up high and clear, yet mostly tilt their head downward while frowning. That's a lot of opportunity for our network to overfit on some irrelevant pattern. Hence, how do we actually know that our network understands that a smile has more to do with the movement of a person's lips than it has to do with the angle at which someone's face is tilted? As we saw in our neural network fails, it can happen quite often that the network picks up on irrelevant patterns. In this part of our experiments, we will visualize the **saliency maps** for the given network inputs.

First introduced in a paper by the visual geometry group at Oxford University, the idea behind saliency maps is to simply compute the gradient of a desired output category with respect to changes in the input image. Put differently, we are trying to determine how a small change in the pixel values of our image affects our network's beliefs on what it is seeing for a given image:

$$\frac{\partial output}{\partial input}$$

Intuitively, let's suppose that we have trained a convolutional network on images of various animals: giraffes, leopards, dogs, cats, and many more. Then, to test what it has learned, we show it the image of a leopard and ask it, *Where do you think the leopard is in this image?* Technically speaking, we are ranking the pixels of our input image, based on the influence each of them has on the **class probability score** that our network spits out for this image. Then, we can simply visualize the pixels that had the greatest influence in classifying a given image, as these would be the pixels where positive changes lead to increasing our network's class probability score, or confidence, that the given image pertains to a certain class.

Visualizing saliency maps with ResNet50

To keep things interesting, we will conclude our smile detector experiments and actually use a pre-trained, very deep CNN to demonstrate our leopard example. We also use the Keras `vis`, which is a great higher-level toolkit to visualize and debug CNNs built on Keras. You can install this package using the `pip` package manager:

```
1  from keras.applications import ResNet50
2  from vis.utils import utils
3  from keras import activations
4
5  # Hide warnings on Jupyter Notebook
6  import warnings
7  warnings.filterwarnings('ignore')
8
9  # Build the ResNet50 network with ImageNet weights
10 model = ResNet50(weights='imagenet', include_top=True)
11
12 # Utility to search for layer index by name.
13 # Alternatively we can specify this as -1 since it corresponds to the last layer.
14 layer_idx = utils.find_layer_idx(model, 'fc1000')
15
16 # Swap softmax with linear
17 model.layers[layer_idx].activation = activations.linear
18 model = utils.apply_modifications(model)
```

Here, we import the ResNet50 CNN architecture with pretrained weights for the ImageNet dataset. We encourage you to explore other models stored in Keras as well, accessible through `keras.applications`. We also switch out the Softmax activation for the linear activation function in the last layer of this network using `utils.apply_modifications`, which rebuilds the network graph to help us visualize the saliency of maps better.

ResNet50 was first introduced as the ILSVRC competition and won first place in 2015. It does very well at avoiding the accuracy degradation problem associated with very deep neural networks. It was trained on about a thousand output classes from the ImageNet dataset. It is considered a high-performing, state-of-the-art CNN architecture, made available for free by its creators. While it uses some interesting mechanics, known as **residual blocks**, we will refrain from commenting further on its architecture till later chapters. For now, let's see how we can use the pretrained weights of this model to visualize the saliency maps of a few leopard pictures.

Loading pictures from a local directory

If you would like to follow along, simply google some nice leopard pictures and store them in a local directory. You can use the image loader from the `utils` module in Keras `vis` to resize your images to the target size that the ResNet50 model accepts (that is, images of 224 x 224 pixels):

```
1   from vis.utils import utils
2   from matplotlib import pyplot as plt
3   %matplotlib inline
4   plt.rcParams['figure.figsize'] = (14, 10)
5
6   img1 = utils.load_img('C:/Users/npurk/Pictures/Saved Pictures/leo_1.jpg', target_size=(224, 224))
7   img2 = utils.load_img('C:/Users/npurk/Pictures/Saved Pictures/leo_2.jpg', target_size=(224, 224))
8   img3 = utils.load_img('C:/Users/npurk/Pictures/Saved Pictures/leo_3.jpg', target_size=(224, 224))
9   img4 = utils.load_img('C:/Users/npurk/Pictures/Saved Pictures/leo_4.jpg', target_size=(224, 224))
10  img5 = utils.load_img('C:/Users/npurk/Pictures/Saved Pictures/leo_5.jpg', target_size=(224, 224))
11  img6 = utils.load_img('C:/Users/npurk/Pictures/Saved Pictures/leo_6.jpg', target_size=(224, 224))
12
13  f, ax = plt.subplots(nrows=2, ncols=3)
14  ax[0, 0].imshow(img1)
15  ax[0, 1].imshow(img2)
16  ax[0, 2].imshow(img3)
17  ax[1, 0].imshow(img4)
18  ax[1, 1].imshow(img5)
19  ax[1, 2].imshow(img6)
```

Since we wish to make the experiment considerably arduous for our network, we purposefully selected pictures of camouflaged leopards to see how well this network does at detecting some of nature's most intricate attempts to hide these predatory creatures from the sight of prey, such as ourselves:

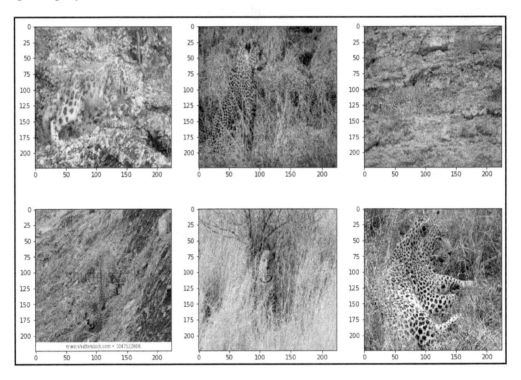

Using Keras's visualization module

Even our biological neural networks implemented throughout our visual cortex seem to have some difficulty finding the leopard in each image, at first glance. Let's see how well its artificial counterpart does at this the task. In the following segment of code, we import the saliency visualizer object from the `keras-vis` module, as well as a utils tool that lets us search for layers by name. Note that this module does not come with the standard Keras install. However, it can be easily installed using the `pip` package manager on Python. You can even execute the install through your Jupyter environment:

```
! pip install keras-vis
```

Searching through layers

Next, we perform a utility search to define our last densely connected layer in the model. We want this layer as it outputs the class probability scores per output category, which we need to be able to visualize the saliency on the input image. The names of the layer can be found in the summary of the model (model.summary()). We will pass four specific arguments to the visualize_salency() function:

```
1  from vis.visualization import visualize_saliency
2  from vis.utils import utils
3
4
5  leopards = [img1,img2,img3,img4,img5,img6]
6  # Utility to search for layer index by name.
7  # Alternatively we can specify this as -1 since it corresponds to the last layer.
8  layer_idx = utils.find_layer_idx(model, 'fc1000')
9
10  gradients=[]
11  for i, img in enumerate(leopards):
12      # 288 is the imagenet index corresponding to `Leopard, panthera pardus`
13      grads = visualize_saliency(model, layer_idx, filter_indices=288, seed_input=cougars[i])
14      gradients.append(grads)
```

This will return the gradients of our output with respect to our input, which intuitively inform us what pixels have the largest effect on our model's prediction. The gradient variable stores six 224 x 224 images (corresponding to the input size for the ResNet50 architecture), one for each of the six input images of leopards. As we noted, these images are generated by the visualize_salency function, which takes four arguments as input:

- A seed input image to perform prediction on (seed_input)
- A Keras CNN model (model)
- An identifier for the model's output layer (layer_idx)
- The index of the output class we want to visualize (filter_indices)

The index reference we use here (288) refers to the index of the label *leopard* on the ImageNet dataset. Recall that earlier we imported pretrained layer weights for the currently initialized model. These weights were achieved by training the ResNet50 model on the ImageNet dataset. If you're curious about the different output classes, you can find them along with their respective indices, here: https://gist.github.com/yrevar/942d3a0ac09ec9e5eb3a.

Visualizing the saliency maps for the first three images, we can actually see that the network is paying attention to the locations where we find the leopard in the image—perfect! This is indeed what we want to see, as it denotes that our network really understands (roughly) where the leopard is located in our image, despite our best attempts at showing it noisy images of camouflaged leopards:

```
1  f, ax = plt.subplots(2, 3)
2  ax[0,0].imshow(leopards[0])
3  ax[0,1].imshow(leopards[1])
4  ax[0,2].imshow(leopards[2])
5  ax[1,0].imshow(gradients[0], cmap='Spectral')
6  ax[1,1].imshow(gradients[1], cmap='Spectral')
7  ax[1,2].imshow(gradients[2], cmap='Spectral')
```

<matplotlib.image.AxesImage at 0x1df4ba81208>

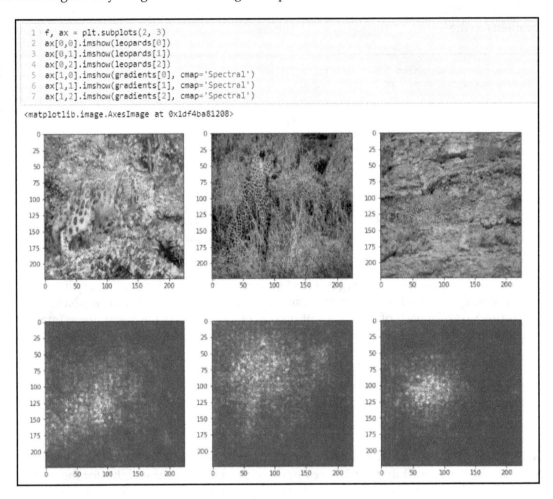

Exercise

- Probe all the layers in the network. What do you notice?

Gradient weighted class activation mapping

Another nifty gradient-based method is the **gradient weighted class activation map** (**Grad-CAM**). This is useful specifically if you have input images with entities belonging to several output classes and you want to visualize which areas in the input picture your network associates most with a specific output class. This technique leverages the class-specific gradient information flowing into the final convolutional layer of a CNN to produce a coarse localization map of the important regions in the image. In other words, we feed our network an input image and take the output activation map of a convolution layer by weighing every channel of the output (that is, the activation maps) by the gradient of the output class with respect to the channel. This allows us to better utilize the spatial information corresponding to what our network pays most attention to, represented in the last convolutional layer of the network. We can take these gradient weighted activation maps and overlay them on top of the input image to get an idea of which parts of our input the network associates highly with a given output class (that is, leopard).

Visualizing class activations with Keras-vis

For this purpose, we use the `visualize_cam` function, which essentially generates a Grad-CAM that maximizes the layer activations for a given input, for a specified output class.

The `visualize_cam` function takes the same four arguments we saw earlier, plus an additional one. We pass it the arguments corresponding to a Keras model, a **seed input** image, a **filter index** corresponding to our output class (ImageNet index for leopard), as well as two model layers. One of these layers remains the fully connected dense output player, whereas the other layer refers to the final convolutional layer in the ResNet50 model. The method essentially leverages these two reference points to generate the gradient weighted class activation maps, as shown:

```
1   import matplotlib.cm as cm
2   from vis.visualization import visualize_cam, overlay
3   from keras import activations
4
5   # Find the fully connected output layer
6   layer_idx = utils.find_layer_idx(model, 'fc1000')
7   #Find the penultimate convolutional layer
8   final_conv_layer = utils.find_layer_idx(model, 'res5c_branch2c')
9
10  plt.figure()
11  f, ax = plt.subplots(1, 2)
12
13
14  for i, img in enumerate([img3, img6]):
15
16      grads = visualize_cam(model,                               #ResNet50 model on ImageNet weights
17                  seed_input=img,                                 #Image with leopard
18                  filter_indices=288,                             #Filter Index for leopard in imagenet dataset
19                  layer_idx=layer_idx,                            #Last fully connected layer
20                  penultimate_layer_idx=final_conv_layer) #Penultimate convolutional layer
21
22      # overlay the heatmap on top of the original image.
23      jet_heatmap = np.uint8(cm.jet(grads)[..., :3] * 255)
24      ax[i].imshow(overlay(jet_heatmap, img))
```

`<Figure size 1008x720 with 0 Axes>`

As we see, the network correctly identifies the leopards in both images. Moreover, we notice that the network relies on the leopard's black-dotted patterns for identification of its class. It stands to reason that the network uses this pattern to identify a leopard, as this is pretty distinctive of its class. We can see the network's attention through the heatmap, which focuses mostly on the clear dotted regions of the leopard's body and not necessarily the leopard's face, as we might do ourselves if confronted with one. Perhaps millions of years of biological evolution have adapted the layer weights in the fusiform gyrus region of our brain to distinctively pick up on faces, as this was a pattern of consequence for our survival:

- **Paper on Grad-CAM**: https://arxiv.org/pdf/1610.02391.pdf

Using the pretrained model for prediction

By the way, you may actually run an inference on a given image using the ResNet50 architecture on pretrained ImageNet weights, as we have initialized here. You can do this by first preprocessing the desired image on which you want to run inference into the appropriate four-dimensional tensor format, as shown here. The same of course applies for any dataset of images you may have, as long as they are resized to the appropriate format:

```
1
2  from keras.preprocessing.image import img_to_array
3  # convert the image pixels to a 4-D numpy array
4  img_predict = img_to_array(img1)
5  img_predict = np.expand_dims(img_predict, axis=0)
6  img_predict.shape
7

(1, 224, 224, 3)
```

```
1  yhat = model.predict(img_predict)
2
3  from keras.applications.resnet50 import decode_predictions
4  # convert the probabilities to class labels
5  predictions = decode_predictions(yhat, top=1000)
6  # retrieve the most likely result, e.g. highest probability
7  label = predictions[0][0]
8  labels = predictions[0][:]
9  # print the classification
10 print('%s (%.2f%%)' % (label[1], label[2]*100))

snow_leopard (1080.04%)
```

The preceding code reshapes one of our leopard images into a 4D tensor by expanding its dimension along the 0 axis, then feeds the tensor to our initialized ResNet50 model to get a class probability prediction. We then proceed to decode the prediction class into a human-readable output. For fun, we also defined the `labels` variable, which includes all the possible labels our network predicted for this image, in descending order of probability. Let's see which other labels our network attributes to our input image:

```
1  labels[:5]
```
```
[('n02128757', 'snow_leopard', 10.800396),
 ('n02130308', 'cheetah', 9.888457),
 ('n02100735', 'English_setter', 8.046139),
 ('n02128385', 'leopard', 7.3484097),
 ('n02110341', 'dalmatian', 6.5762362)]
```

Visualizing maximal activations per output class

In the final method, we simply visualize the overall activations associated with a particular output class, without explicitly passing our model an input image. This method can be very intuitive, while being quite aesthetically pleasing. For the purpose of our last experiment, we import yet another pretrained model, **the VGG16 network**. This network is another deep architecture based on the model that won the ImageNet classification challenge in 2014. Similar to our last example, we switch out the Softmax activation of our last layer with a linear one:

```
1  from keras.applications import VGG16
2  from vis.utils import utils
3  from keras import activations
4
5  # Build the VGG16 network with ImageNet weights
6  model = VGG16(weights='imagenet', include_top=True)
7
8  # Utility to search for layer index by name.
9  # Alternatively we can specify this as -1 since it corresponds to the last layer.
10  layer_idx = utils.find_layer_idx(model, 'predictions')
11
12  # Swap softmax with linear
13  model.layers[layer_idx].activation = activations.linear
14  model = utils.apply_modifications(model)
```

Then, we simply import the activation visualizer object from the visualization module implemented in `keras-vis`. We plot out the overall activations for the leopard class, by passing the `visualize_activation` function our model, the output layer, and the index corresponding to our output class, leopard. As we see here, the network has actually captured the general shape of leopards at different orientations and locations in the image. Some appear zoomed-in, others are far less distinct, yet cat-like ears and the dotted-black pattern are quite distinguishable throughout the image—neat, right? Let's have a look at the following screenshot:

```
1  from vis.visualization import visualize_activation
2
3  from matplotlib import pyplot as plt
4  %matplotlib inline
5  plt.rcParams['figure.figsize'] = (18, 6)
6
7  # 20 is the imagenet category for 'ouzel'
8  img = visualize_activation(model, layer_idx, filter_indices=[288])
9  plt.imshow(img)
```

```
<matplotlib.image.AxesImage at 0x1c381974f60>
```

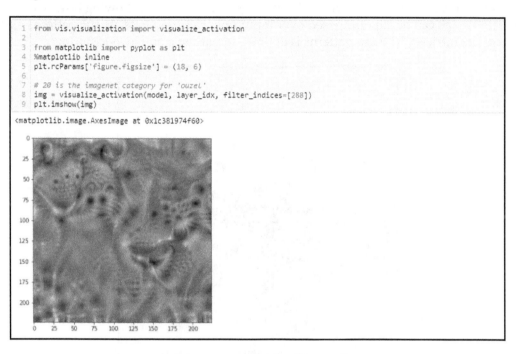

Converging a model

Next, you can make the model converge on this output class to visualize what the model thinks is a leopard (or another output class) after many iterations of convergence. You can define how long you want your model to converge through the `max_iter` argument, as shown here:

```
1  img = visualize_activation(model, layer_idx, filter_indices=288, max_iter=500, verbose=True)
```

Using multiple filter indices to hallucinate

You can also play around by passing the `filter_indices` parameter different indices corresponding to different output classes from the ImageNet dataset. You could also pass it a list of two integers, corresponding to two different output classes. This basically lets your neural network *imagine* visual combinations of two separate output classes by simultaneously visualizing the activations pertaining to both output classes. These can at times turn out to be very interesting, so let both your imaginations run wild! It is noteworthy that Google's DeepDream leverages similar concepts, showing how overexcited activation maps can be superimposed over input images to generate artistic patterns and images. The intricacy of these patterns is at times remarkable and awe-inspiring:

Picture of the author of this book, taken in front of the haunted mansion in Disneyland, Paris. The image has been processed using the open source DeepDream generator, which we encourage you to play around with, not just to marvel at its beauty. It can also generate quite handy gifts for artistic relatives, around the holiday season.

Problems with CNNs

Many may claim that the hierarchically nested pattern recognition technique leveraged by CNNs very much resembles the functioning of our own visual cortex. This may be true at a certain level. However, the visual cortex implements a much more complex architecture and makes it run efficiently on about 10 watts of energy. Our visual cortex also does not easily get fooled by images where face-like features appear, (although this phenomenon occurs often enough to have secured its proper term in modern neuroscience. **Pareidolia** is a term associated with the human mind interpreting signals in a manner to generate higher-level concepts, where none actually exists. Scientists have shown how this phenomenon is related to the earlier activation of neurons located in the fusiform gyrus area of the visual cortex, responsible for several visual recognition and classification tasks. In cases of pareidolia, these neurons *jump the gun,* as it were, and cause us to detect faces or hear sounds, even when this is really not the case. The famous picture of the Martian surface illustrates this point, as most of us can clearly make out the outlines and features of a face, whereas all the picture actually contains is a pile of red dust:

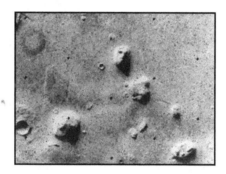

Image Courtesy NASA/JPL-Caltech

Neural network pareidolia

This problem is naturally not unique to our biological brains. In fact, despite the excellent functioning of CNNs for many visual tasks, this problem of neural network pareidolia is one that computer vision researchers are always trying to solve. As we noted, CNNs learn to classify images through learning an assortment of filters that pick up useful features, capable of breaking down the input image in a probabilistic manner. However, the features learned by these filters do not represent all the information present in a given image. The orientation of these features, with respect to one another, matters just as much! The presence of two eyes, lips, and a nose does not inherently constitute the essence of a face. Rather, it's the spatial arrangement of these elements within an image that makes the face in question:

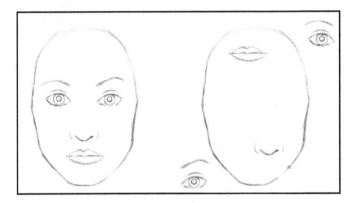

Summary

In this chapter, firstly, we used convolutional layers that are capable of decomposing a given visual input space into hierarchically nested probabilistic activations of convolution filters that subsequently connect to dense neurons that perform classification. The filters in these convolutional layers learn weights corresponding to useful representations that may be queried in a probabilistic manner to map the set of input features present in a dataset to the respective output classes. Furthermore, we saw how we can dive deep into our convolution network to understand what it has learned. We saw four specific ways to do this: intermediate activation-based, saliency-based, gradient weighted class activations, and activation maximization visualizations. Each gives a unique intuition into which patterns are picked up by the different layers of our network. We visualized these patterns for given images, as well as for entire output classes, to intuitively understand which elements of our network pays attention while performing inference.

Finally, although we reviewed a lot of neuroscience-based inspirations that led to the development of the CNN architecture, modern CNNs in no way compete with the intricate mechanisms implemented throughout the mammalian visual cortex. In fact, many of the structural design of the layers in the visual cortex do not even remotely resemble what we have designed here so far. For instance, the layers of the visual cortex are themselves structured into subsequent cortical columns, containing neurons with supposedly non-overlapping receptive fields, the purpose of which is unbeknown to modern neuroscience. Even our retina performs a deluge of sensory preprocessing through the use of rod cells (receptive to low-intensity light), cone cells (receptive to high-intensity light), and ipRGC cells (receptive to time-dependent stimuli) before sending the visual signals in the form of electrical impulses to the lateral geniculate nucleus at the base of the thalamus, otherwise known as the relay center for visual signals. It is from here that the signals begin their journey, propagating back and forth through the six densely interconnected (and not convolutional) layers of the visual cortex, as we go about our lives. In essence, human vision is quite sequential and dynamic, much different than the artificial implementation of it. In summation, while we are far from endowing visual intelligence to machines in the manner biology has done to us, CNNs represent the pinnacle of modern achievements in computer vision, making it a venerably adaptable architecture for countless machine vision tasks.

Here, we conclude our chapter on the exploration of CNNs. We will revisit more complex architectures in later chapters and experiment with data augmentation techniques and more complex computer vision tasks. In the next chapter, we will explore another neural network architecture known as RNN, which is especially useful for capturing and modeling sequential information such as time variant data, common in many fields ranging from industrial engineering to natural language dialogue generation.

5
Recurrent Neural Networks

In the previous chapter, we marveled over the visual cortex and leveraged some insights from the way it processes visual signals to inform the architecture of **Convolutional Neural Networks** (**CNNs**), which form the base of many state-of-the-art computer vision systems. However, we do not understand the world around us with vision alone. Sound, for one, also plays a very important role. More specifically, we humans love to communicate and express intricate thoughts and ideas through sequences of symbolic reductions and abstract representations. Our built-in hardware allows us to interpret vocalizations or demarcations thereof, composing the base of human thought and collective understandings, upon which more complex representations (such as human languages, for instance) may be composed. In essence, these sequences of symbols are reduced representations of the world around us, through our own lenses, which we use to navigate our surroundings and effectively express ourselves. It stands to reason that we would want machines to understand this manner of processing sequential information, as it could help us to resolve many problems we face with such sequential tasks in the real world. But what kind of problems?

Following are the topics that will be covered in this chapter:

- Modeling sequences
- Summarizing different types of sequence processing tasks
- Predicting an output per time step
- Backpropagation through time
- Exploding and vanishing gradients
- GRUs
- Building character-level language models in keras
- Statistics of character modeling
- The purpose of controlling stochastically
- Testing different RNN models
- Building a SimpleRNN
- Building GRUs
- On processing reality sequentially

- Bi-directional layer in Keras
- Visualizing output values

Modeling sequences

Perhaps you want to get the right translation for your order in a restaurant while visiting a foreign country. Maybe you want your car to perform a sequence of movements automatically so that it is able to park by itself. Or maybe you want to understand how different sequences of adenine, guanine, thymine, and cytosine molecules in the human genome lead to differences in biological processes occurring in the human body. What's the commonality between these examples? Well, these are all sequence modeling tasks. In such tasks, the training examples (being vectors of words, a set of car movements generated by on-board controls, or configuration of *A*, *G*, *T*, and *C* molecules) are essentially multiple time-dependent data points of a possibly varied length.

Sentences, for example, are composed of words, and the spatial configuration of these words allude not only to what has been said, but also to what is yet to come. Try and fill in the following blank:

Don't judge a book by its ___.

How did you know that the next word would be *cover*? You simply look at the words and their relative positions and performed some sort of Bayesian inference, leveraging the sentences you have previously seen and their apparent similarity to the example at hand. In essence, you used your internal model of the English language to predict the most probable word to follow. Here, *language model* simply refers to the probability of a particular configuration of words occurring together in a given sequence. Such models are the fundamental components of modern speech recognition and machine translation systems, and simply rely on modeling the likelihood of sequences of words.

Using RNNs for sequential modeling

The field of natural language understanding is a common area where **recurrent neural networks** (**RNNs**) tend to excel. You may imagine tasks such as recognizing named entities and classifying the predominant sentiment in a given piece of text. However, as we mentioned, RNNs are applicable to a broad spectrum of tasks that involve modeling time-dependent sequences of data. Generating music is also a sequence modeling task as we tend to distinguish music from a cacophony by modeling the sequence of notes that are played in a given tempo.

RNN architectures are even applicable for some visual intelligence tasks, such as video activity recognition. Recognizing whether a person is cooking, running, or robbing a bank in a given video is essentially modeling sequences of human movements and matching them to specific classes. In fact, RNNs have been deployed for some very interesting use cases, including generating text in Shakespearean style, creating realistic (but incorrect) algebraic papers, and even producing source code for the Linux operating system with proper formatting.

So, what makes these networks so versatile at performing these seemingly diverse tasks? Well, before we answer this, let's refresh our memory on some of the difficulties we faced using neural nets so far:

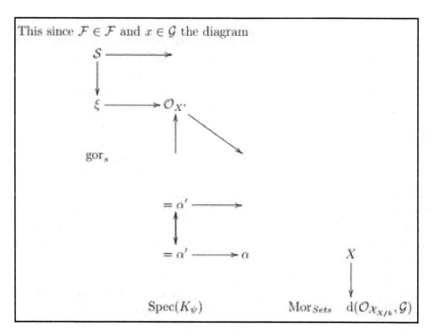

Fake algebraic geometry, generated by RNN, courtesy of Andrej Karpathy

Which means:

is a limit. Then $\mathcal{G}$ is a finite type and assume S is a flat and $\mathcal{F}$ and $\mathcal{G}$ is a finite type f_*. This is of finite type diagrams, and
- the composition of $\mathcal{G}$ is a regular sequence,
- $\mathcal{O}_{X'}$ is a sheaf of rings.

What's the catch?

A problem with all of the networks we have built so far is that they only accepted inputs and outputs of fixed sizes for given training examples. We have always had to specify our input shape, defining the dimensions of the tensor entering our network, which in turn returns a fixed size output in terms of a class probability score, for example. Moreover, the hidden layers in our networks each had their own weights and activations, which behaved somewhat independently of each other, without identifying relationships between successive input values. This holds true for both the feedforward and the CNNs that we have familiarized ourselves with in previous chapters. For each network we built, we used non-sequential training vectors, which would propagate through a constant number of layers and produce a single output.

While we did see some multi-output models to visualize the intermediate layers of CNNs, we never really modified our architecture to operate over a sequence of vectors. This basically prohibited us from sharing any time-dependent information that may affect the likelihood of our predictions. Discarding time-dependent information has got us by so far for the tasks we dealt with. In the case of image classification, the fact that your neural network saw the image of a cat at the last iteration does not really help it classify the current image it is viewing because the class probabilities of these two instances are not temporally related. However, this approach already caused us some trouble for the use case of sentiment analysis. Recall in Chapter 3, *Signal Processing - Data Analysis with Neural Networks*, that we classified movie reviews by treating each review as a bag of undirected words (that is, not in their sequential order). This approach entailed transforming each review into a fixed-length vector that's defined by the size of our vocabulary (that is, the number of unique words in the corpus, which we had chosen to be 12,000 words). While useful, this is certainly not the most efficient or scalable form of representing information, as a sentence of any given length must be represented by a 12,000-dimensional vector. The simple feedforward network we trained (attaining an accuracy just above 88 %) incorrectly classified the sentiment of one of the reviews, which has been reproduced here:

```
1  verify_predictions(22)

Network falsely predicts that review 22 is negative

(None,
 array([0.16930683], dtype=float32),
 "? how managed to avoid attention remains a mystery a potent mix of comedy and crime this one takes chances where tarantino pl
ays it safe with the hollywood formula the risks don't always pay off one character in one sequence comes off ? silly and falls
flat in the lead role thomas jane gives a wonderful and complex performance and two brief appearances by mickey rourke hint at
the high potential of this much under and mis used actor here's a director one should keep one's eye on")
```

Our network seemed to have gotten confused due to the (unnecessarily) complex sentence with several long-term dependencies and contextual valence shifters. In retrospect, we noted unclear double negatives referring to various entities such as the director, actor, and the movie itself; yet we were able to make out that the overall sentiment of the review was clearly positive. Why? Simply because we are able to track concepts that are relevant to the general sentiment of the review, as we read it word for word. In our minds, we are able to assess how each new word of the review we see affects the general meaning of the statement we have read so far. In this manner, we adjust our sentiment score for a review as we read along and come across new information (such as adjectives or negations) that may affect this score at a given time step.

Just like in CNNs, we want our network to be able to use representations that have been learned on a certain segment of the input, which are then usable later on in other segments and examples. In other words, we need to be able to share the weights of our network from previous time steps to connect bits of information as we sequentially go over our input review. This is pretty much what RNNs allow us to do. These layers leverage the additional information that's encoded in successive events, which it does by looping over a sequence of input values. Depending on the architectural implementation, RNNs can save relevant information in its memory (also referred to as its state) and use this information to perform predictions at subsequent time steps.

This mechanism is notably different from the networks we saw earlier, which processed each training iteration independently and did not maintain any state between predictions. There are several different implementations of recurrent neural networks, ranging from **Gated Recurrent Units (GRUs)**, stateful and stateless **Long Short-Term Memory (LSTM)** networks, bi-directional units, and many more. As we will soon discover, each of these architectures help to address a certain type of problem, building on the shortcomings of each other:

Advantages	Drawbacks
• Possibility of processing input of any length • Model size not increasing with size of input • Computation takes into account historical information • Weights are shared across time	• Computation being slow • Difficulty of accessing information from a long time ago • Cannot consider any future input for the current state

Basic RNN architecture

Now, let's have a look at how the RNN architecture differentiates itself from the other networks that we have seen so far by unrolling it through time. Let's consider a new time series problem: speech recognition. This task can be performed by computers to identify the flow of words during a segment of human speech. This can be used to transcribe the speech itself, translate it, or use it as input for instructions, similar to the manner in which we instruct each other. Such applications form the base of systems such as Siri or Alexa and perhaps more complex and cognitive virtual assistants of the future. So, how can an RNN decode the sequence of decomposed vibrations that are recorded by the microphone on your computer into a string variable corresponding to the input speech?

Let's consider a simplified theoretical example. Imagine that our training data maps a sequence of human vocalizations to a set of human-readable words. In other words, you show your network an audio clip and it spits out a transcript of whatever was said within. We task an RNN to go over a segment of speech by treating it as sequences of vectors (representing sound bytes). The network can then try to predict what words of the English language these sound bytes may represent at each time step:

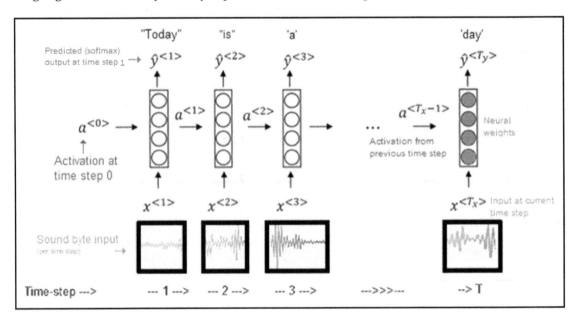

Consider the set of vectors that represent the sound byte for the words *today is a nice day*. A recurrent layer will unfold this sequence in several time steps. In the first time step, it will take the vector representing vocalization for the first word in the sequence as input (that is, *today*), compute a dot product with the layer weights, and pass the product through a non-linear activation function (commonly tanh for RNNs) to output a prediction. This prediction corresponds to a word that the network thinks it has heard. At the second time step, the recurrent layer receives the next sound byte (that is, for the word *is*) in the sequence, along with the activation values from the first time step. Both of these values are then squashed through the activation function to produce a prediction for the current time step. This basically allows the layer to leverage information from the previous time steps to inform the prediction at the current time step. This process is repeated as the recurrent layer receives each vocalization in a given sequence, along with the activation values from previous vocalizations. The layer may compute a Softmax probability score for each word in our dictionary, picking the one with the highest value as output for the given layer. This word corresponds to what our network thinks it has heard at this time.

Temporarily shared weights

Why is it useful to temporally connect activations? Well, as we pointed out earlier, each word affects the probability distribution of the next word to come. If our sentence began with the word *Yesterday*, it is much more likely to be followed by the word *was*, than the word *is*, reflecting the use of the past tense. Such syntactic information can be passed along through recurrent layers to inform the predictions of the network at each step by using what the network has output in previous time steps. As our network trains on given segments of speech, it will adjust its layer weights to minimize the difference between what it predicts and the true value of each output by (hopefully) learning such grammatical and syntactic rules, among other things. Importantly, the recurrent layer's weights are temporally shared, allowing activations from previous time steps to have influence over predictions of subsequent time steps. Doing so, we no longer treat each prediction in isolation, but as a function of the network's activations at previous time steps, along with some input at the current time step.

The actual workflow of speech recognition models may be a bit more complex than what we described previously, which involves data normalization techniques such as the Fourier transformation, which lets us decompose audio signals into their constituent frequencies. In essence, we always try to normalize our input data with the goal to better represent data to our neural networks, as this helps it to converge faster to encode useful predictive rules. The key take-away from this example is that recurrent layers can leverage earlier temporal information to inform its predictions at the current time step. As we progress through this chapter, we will see how these architectures can be adopted for modeling different lengths of sequence input and output data.

Sequence modeling variations in RNNs

The speech recognition example consists of modeling a synchronized many-to-many sequence, where we predicted many sets of vocalizations to many words that correspond to these vocalizations. We can use a similar architecture for the task of video captioning, where we would want to sequentially label each frame of the video with the dominant object within. This is yet another synchronized many-to-many sequence, as we output a prediction at each time step that corresponds to the input frame of the video.

Encoding many-to-many representations

We can also have a semi-synchronized many-to-many sequence in the case of machine translation. This use case is semi-synchronized, as we do not immediately output a prediction at each time step. Instead, we use the encoder section of our RNN to capture the entire phrase so that it can be translated before we proceed and actually translate it. This lets us find better representations of the input data in the output language, instead of just translating each word at a time. The latter approach is not very robust and often leads to inaccurate translations. In the following example, an RNN translates the French phrase *C'est pas mal!* into the equivalent term in English, *It's nice!*, which is a much more accurate translation than the literal, *It's not bad!*. Hence, RNNs can help us to decipher the peculiar rules that are applied to complementing a person in the French language. This may help avoid quite a few misunderstandings:

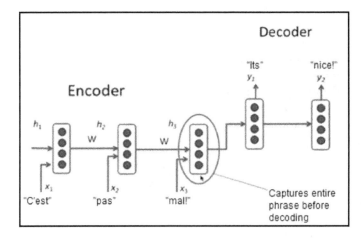

Many-to-one

Similarly, you can also have a many-to-one architecture to address tasks such as attributing many sequences of words forming a sentence to one corresponding sentiment score. This is just like what we had to do in our previous exercise with the IMDb dataset. Last time, our approach involved representing each review as an undirected bag-of-words. With RNNs, we can approach this problem by modeling a review as a directed sequence of individual words, in their correct order, hence leveraging the spatial information from the arrangement of words to inform our sentiment score. Here is a simplified example of a many-to-one RNN architecture for sentiment classification:

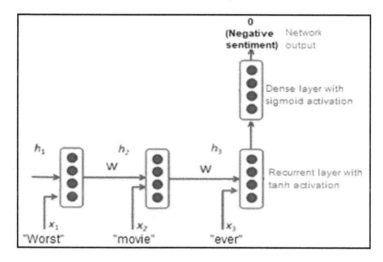

One-to-many

Finally, different variations of sequential tasks may demand different architectures. Another commonly used architecture is the one-to-many RNN model, which we would use for the use case of music generation or image captioning. For music generation, we essentially feed our network one input note, make it predict the next note in the sequence, and then leverage its very own prediction as input for the next time step:

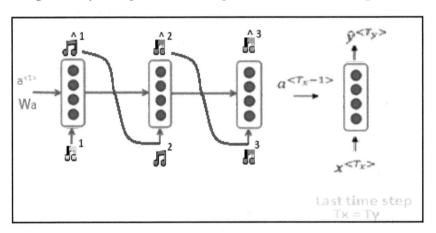

One-to-many for image captioning

Another novel example of a one-to-many architecture is what is commonly used for the task of image captioning. This is when we show our network an image and ask it to describe what is going on with a small caption. To do this, we essentially feed our network one image at a time to output many words corresponding to what is going on in the image. Commonly, you may stack a recurrent layer on top of a CNN that has already been trained on some entities (objects, animals, people, and so on). Doing so, you could use the recurrent layer to intake the output values of the convolutional network all together, and sequentially go over the image to output meaningful words corresponding to a description of the input image. This is a more complex setup that we will elaborate on in later chapters. For now, it is useful to know that LSTM networks (shown as follows) are a type of RNN that's inspired by semantic and episodic divisions of the human memory structure and will be the prime topic of discussion in Chapter 6, *Long-Short Term Memory Networks*. In the following diagram, we can see how the network is able to pick up on the fact that there are several giraffes standing about, leveraging the output it receives from the CNN.

Summarizing different types of sequence processing tasks

Now, we have familiarized ourselves with the basic idea of what a recurrent layer does and have gone over some specific examples of use cases (from speech recognition, machine translation, and image captioning) where variations of such time-dependent models may be used. The following diagram provides a visual summary of some of the sequential tasks we discussed, along with the type of RNN that's suited for the job:

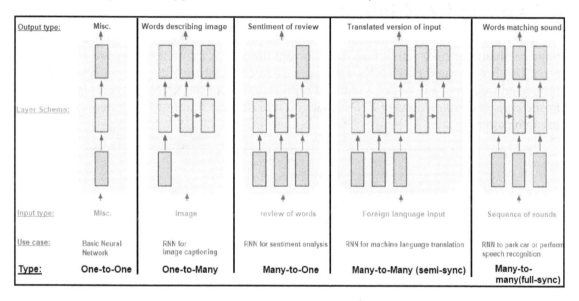

Next, we will dive deeper into the governing equations, as well as the learning mechanism behind RNNs.

How do RNNs learn?

As we saw previously, for virtually all neural nets, you can break down the learning mechanism into two separate parts. The forward propagation equations govern the rules that allow data to propagate forward in our neural network, all of the way to the network predictions. The backpropagation of errors are defined by equations (such as the loss function and the optimizer), which allow our model's prediction errors to move backward through our model's layers, adjusting the weights on each layer toward the correct prediction values.

This is essentially the same for RNNs, yet with a few architectural variations to account for time-dependent information flows. To do this, RNNs can leverage an internal state, or *memory*, to encode useful time-dependent representations. First, let's have a look at the forward pass of data in a recurrent layer. A recurrent layer basically combines the input vector that's entering the layer with a state vector to produce a new output vector at each time step. Soon, we will see how iteratively updating these state vectors can be leveraged to preserve temporally relevant information in a given sequence.

A generic RNN layer

The following diagram hopefully familiarizes this process. On the left, the gray arrow in the diagram illustrates how activations from current time steps are sent forward to future time steps. This holds true for all RNNs, forming a distinct signature of their architecture. On the right-hand side, you will notice a reduced representation of the RNN unit. This is one of the most common demarcations of RNNs that you will find in countless computer science research papers:

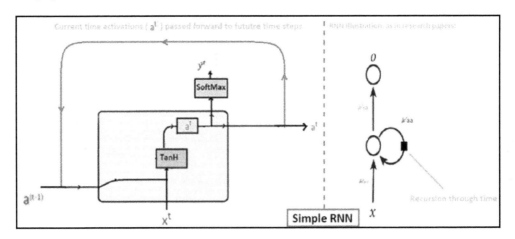

To sequence, or not to sequence?

The RNN layer essentially processes its input values in a time-dependent and sequential manner. It employs a state (or memory), which allows us to address sequence modeling tasks in a novel way. However, there are quite a few examples where approaching non-sequential data in a sequential manner has allowed us to address standard use cases in more efficient ways. Take the example of the research conducted by DeepMind on steering the attention of a network on images.

Instead of simply applying a computation-heavy CNN for image classification, DeepMind researchers showed how RNNs that have been trained through reinforcement learning can be used to perform the same function and achieve even better accuracy at more complex tasks such as classifying cluttered images, along with other dynamic visual control problems. One of the main architectural take backs from their work was that their RNN effectively extracted information from images or videos by adaptively selecting sequence or regions to process at a high resolution, thereby reducing the redundant computational complexity of processing an entire image at a high resolution. This is pretty neat, as we don't necessarily need to process all of the parts of an image to perform classification. Most of what we need is usually centered around a local area of the image in question: `https://deepmind.com/research/publications/recurrent-models-visual-attention/`.

Forward propagation

So, how does information actually flow through this-here RNN architecture? Let's use a demonstrative example to introduce the forward pass operations in RNNs. Imagine the simple task of predicting the next word in a phrase. Suppose our phrase is: *to be or not to be.* As the words enter the network, we can break down the computations that are performed at each time step into two conceptual categories. In the following diagram, you can visualize each arrow as performing a computation (or dot product operation) on a given set of values:

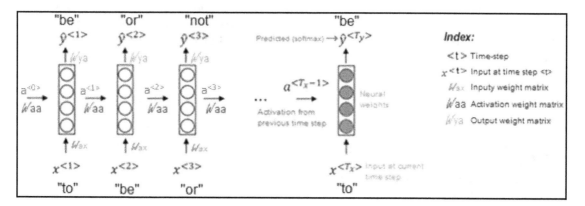

We can see that, in a recurrent cell, computations occur both vertically and horizontally as data propagates through it. It is important to remember that all parameters (or weight matrices) of the layer are temporally shared, meaning that the same parameters are used for computations at every time step. At the first time step, our layer will use these sets of parameters to compute two output values. One of these is the layer's activation value at the current time step, whereas the other represents the predicted value at the current time step. Let's start with the first one.

Computing activations per time step

The following equation denotes the activation of a recurrent layer at time, *t*. The term *g* denotes the non-linear activation function that's chosen for the recurrent layer, which is conventionally a tanh function. Inside the brackets, we find two matrix-level multiplications being performed and then being added up along with a bias term (*ba*):

$$at = g \, [\, (W^{ax} \, x \, x^t \,) + (Waa \, x \, a(t\text{-}1)) + ba \,]$$

The term (W^{ax}) governs the transformation of our input vector, x, at time, *t*, as it enters the recurrent layer. This matrix of weights is temporally shared, meaning that we use the same weight matrix at each time step. Then, we get to the term (*Waa*), which refers to the temporally shared weight matrix governing the activations from the previous time step. At the first time step, (*Waa*) is randomly initialized with very small values (or zeros), since we don't actually have any activation weights to compute with just yet. The same holds for the value (*a<0>*), which is also initialized as a zeroed vector. Hence, at time step one, we our equation will look something like this:

$$a1 = tanH \, [\, (W^{ax} \, x \, x1 \,) + (Waa \, x \, a(0)) + ba \,]$$

Simplifying the activation equation

We can further simplify this equation by stacking the two weight matrices (Wax and Waa) horizontally into a single matrix (W_a) that defines all of the weights (or the state) of a recurrent layer. We will also vertically stack the two vectors representing the activations from the previous time step (*a(t-1)*) and the input at the current time (x t) to form a new matrix that we denote as [*a(t-1)*, x t] . This lets us simplify our previous activation, as follows:

$$at = tanH \, [\, (W^{ax} \, x \, x \, t \,) + (Waa \, x \, a(t\text{-}1)) + ba \,] \; or \; at = tanH \, (W^a \, [\, a(t\text{-}1), \, x \, t \,] + ba \,)$$

Conceptually, since the height of the two matrices ($W^{ax, Waa}$) remains constant, we are able to stack them horizontally in the manner we did. The same goes for the length of the input (x t) and activation vector ($a(t-1)$), which also remains constant as data propagates through an RNN. Now, the computation step can be denoted as the weight matrix (W_a) is multiplied both with the activation from the previous time step, as well as with the input from the current time step, after which a bias term is added and the whole term is passed through a non-linear activation function. We can visualize this process unfolding through time with the new weight matrix, as shown in the following diagram:

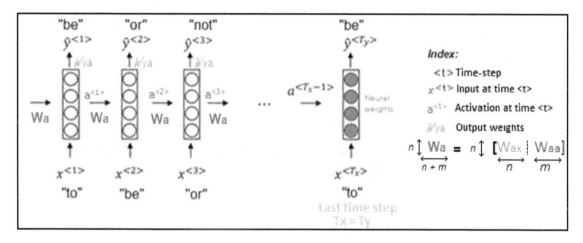

In essence, the use of the temporally shared weight parameters (such as *Wa* and *Wya*) allows us to leverage information from earlier on in the sequence to inform predictions at later time- teps. Now, you know how activations are iteratively computed for each time step as data flows through a recurrent layer.

Predicting an output per time step

Next, we will look at the equation that leverages the activation value that we just calculated to produce a prediction ($\hat{y}$) at the given time step (t). This is represented like so:

$$\hat{y}^t = g\,[\,(Way \; x \; at) + by\,]$$

This tells us is that our layer's prediction at a time step is determined by computing a dot product of yet another temporally shared output matrix of weights, along with the activation output (*at*) we just computed using the earlier equation.

Due to the sharing of the weight parameters, information from previous time steps is preserved and passed through the recurrent layer to inform the current prediction. For example, the prediction at time step three leverages information from the previous time steps, as shown by the green arrow here:

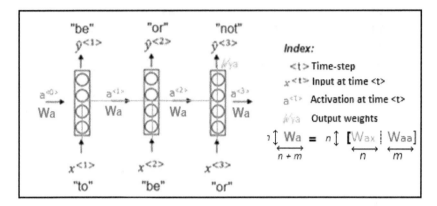

To formalize these computations, we mathematically show the relation between the predicted output at the third time step with respect to the activations at previous time steps, as follows:

- $\hat{y}^3$ = sigmoid [(Way x a3) + by]

Where a(3) is define by the following:

- a3 = sigmoid (Wa [a(2), x3] + ba)

Where a(2) is defined by the following:

- a2 = sigmoid (Wa [a(1), x2] + ba)

Where a(1) is defined by the following:

- a1 = sigmoid (Wa [a(0), x1] + ba)

Finally, a(0) is commonly initialized as a vector of zeros. The main concept to understand here is that the RNN layer recursively processes a sequence through many time steps before passing the activations forward. Now, you are completely familiar with all the equations that govern the forward propagation of information in RNNs at a high level. This method, while powerful at modeling many temporal sequences, does have its limitations.

The problem of unidirectional information flow

A primary limitation is that we are only able to inform our prediction at current time steps with activation values from previous time steps, but not from future time steps. Why would we want to do this? Well, consider the problem of named entity recognition, where we may employ a synchronized many-to-many RNN to predict whether each word in our sentence is a named entity (such as the name of a person, a place, a product, and so on). We may run into some problems, such as the following:

- The Spartan marched forward, despite the obstacles thrown at him.
- The Spartan lifestyle that these people face is unimaginable to many.

As we can see, by looking as the first two words only, we ourselves would not be able to tell whether the word Spartan refers to a noun (and hence is a named entity) or refers to an adjective. It is only later on, when we read the rest of the sentence, that we are able to attribute the correct label on the word. Similarly, our network will not be able to accurately predict that the word Spartan in the first sentence is a named entity unless we let it leverage activation values from future time steps. Since RNNs can learn sequential grammar rules from an annotated dataset, it will be able to learn the fact that named entities are often followed by verbs (such as marched) rather than nouns (such as lifestyle), and hence will be able to accurately predict that the word *Spartan* refers to a named entity on the first sentence only. This becomes possible with a specific type of RNN known as a bi-directional RNN, which we will look at later on in this chapter. It is also noteworthy that an annotated dataset with part of speech tags (tags referring to whether a word is a noun, adjective, and so on) will greatly increase your network's ability to learn useful sequential representations, like we want it to do here. We can visualize the first part of both our sentences, annotated with part of speech tags, as follows:

- The Spartan marched...à:

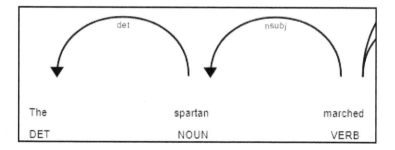

- The Spartan lifestyle... à:

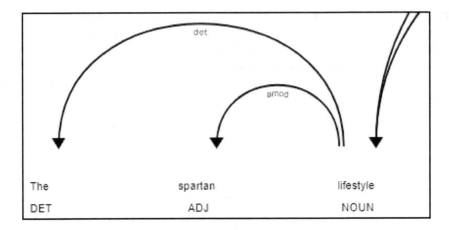

The sequences of words that precede this provide us with more information on the current word than the words that come before it. We will soon see how bi-directional RNNs may leverage information from future time steps as well as past time steps to compute predictions at the present time.

The problems of long-term dependencies

Another common problem we face with simple recurrent layers is their weakness in modeling long-term sequence dependencies. To clarify what we mean by this, consider the following examples, which we feed to an RNN word by word to predict the next words to come:

- The monkey had enjoyed eating bananas for a while and was eager to have more,
- The monkeys had enjoyed eating bananas for a while and were eager to have more.

To predict the word at the 11th time step each sequence, the network must remember whether the subject of the sentence (monkey), seen at time-step 2, is a singular or plural entity. However, as the model trains and the errors are backpropagated through time, the weights for the time steps that are closer to the current time step are affected to a larger extent than the weights of earlier time steps. Mathematically speaking, this is the problem of vanishing gradients, which is associated with extremely small values of the chain rule-based partial derivatives of our loss function. The weights in our recurrent layer, which are normally updated in proportion to these partial derivatives at each time step, are not *nudged* enough in the right direction, prohibiting our network to learn any further. In this manner, the model is unable to update the layer weights to reflect long-term grammatical dependencies from earlier time steps, like the one reflected in our example. This is an especially cumbersome problem, since it significantly affects the backpropagation of errors in recurrent layers. Soon, we will see how to partially address this problem with more complex architectures such as the GRU and the LSTM networks. First, let's understand the process of backpropagation in RNNs, which gives birth to this problem.

You may well have wondered how exactly an RNN backpropagates its errors to adjust the temporarily shared weights of the layer as it goes over a sequence of inputs. This process is even described by an interesting name. Unlike other neural networks we have come across, RNNS are known to perform backpropagation through time.

Backpropagation through time

Essentially, we are backpropagating our errors through several time steps, reflecting the length of a sequence. As we know, the first thing we need to have to be able to backpropagate our errors is a loss function. We can use any variation of the cross-entropy loss, depending on whether we are performing a binary task per sequence (that is, entity or not, per word à binary cross-entropy) or a categorical one (that is, the next word out of the category of words in our vocabulary à categorical cross entropy). The loss function here computes the cross-entropy loss between a predicted output $(\hat{y})$ and actual value (y), at time step, t:

$$Loss^t(\hat{y}^t, y^t) = [-y^t \times log(\hat{y}^t)] - [(1-\hat{y}) \times log(1 - \hat{y}^t)]$$

This function essentially lets us perform an element-wise loss computation of each predicted and actual output, at each time step for our recurrent layer. Hence, we generate a loss value at each prediction the network makes, for each word (or sequence) it sees. We can then sum up each individual loss value to define the overall loss of our recurrent layer, operating over *ty* number of time steps. Hence, the overall loss of our network can be denoted as follows:

$$Loss(\hat{y}, y) = \sum_{t=1}^{ty} Loss^t(\hat{y}^t, y^t)$$

Using this denotation of the overall loss of our network, we can differentiate it with respect to the layer weights at each time step to compute the model's errors. We can visualize this process by referring back to our recurrent layer diagram. The arrows demarcate the backpropagation of errors through time.

Visualizing backpropagation through time

Here, we backpropagate the errors in our model with respect to the layer weights at each time step and adjust the weight matrices, *Way* and *Wa*, as the model trains. We are still essentially computing the gradient of the loss function with respect to all of the network parameters, and proportionally nudging both the weight matrices in the opposite direction for each time step in our sequence:

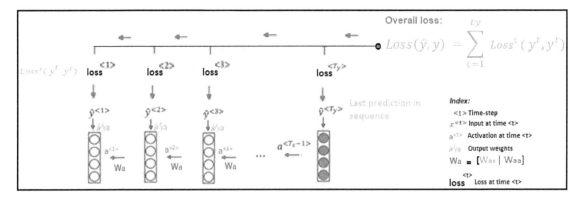

Now, we know how RNNs overate over a sequence of vectors and leverage time-dependent contingencies to inform predictions at each step.

Exploding and vanishing gradients

Backpropagating the model's errors in a deep neural network, however, comes with its own complexities. This holds equally true for RNNs, facing their own versions of the vanishing and exploding gradient problem. As we discussed earlier, the activation of neurons in a given time step is dependent on the following equation:

$$at = tanH [(W^{ax} x^x t) + (Waa \; x \; a(t-1)) + ba]$$

We saw how *Wax* and *Waa* are two separate weight matrices that the RNN layers share through time. These matrices are multiplied to the input matrix at current time, and the activation from the previous time step, respectively. The dot products are then summed up, along with a bias term, and passed through a tanh activation function to compute the activation of neurons at current time (*t*). We then used this activation matrix to compute the predicted output at current time ($\hat{y}^t$), before passing the activation forward to the next time step:

$$\hat{y}^t = softmax [(Way \; x \; at) + by]$$

Hence, the weight matrices (*Wax*, *Waa*, and *Way*) represent the trainable parameters of a given layer. During backpropagation through time, we first compute the product of gradients, which represent the changes in the layer weights of each time step with respect to the changes in the predicted and actual output. Then, we use these products to update the respective layer weights in the opposite direction of the change. However, when backpropagating across multiple time steps, these products may become infinitesimally small (hence not shifting the layer weights significantly), or gargantuanly big (hence overshooting from ideal weights). This is mainly true for the activation matrix (*Waa*). It represents the memory of our RNN layer since it encodes time-dependent information from previous time steps. Let's clarify this notion with a conceptual example to see how updating the activation matrix at earlier time steps becomes increasingly hard when dealing with long sequences. Suppose you wanted to calculate the gradient of your loss at time step three with respect to your layer weights, for example.

Thinking on the gradient level

The activation matrix at a given time step is a function of the activation matrix from the previous time step. Hence, we are forced to recursively define the loss at time step three as a product of the sub-gradients of layer weights from previous time steps:

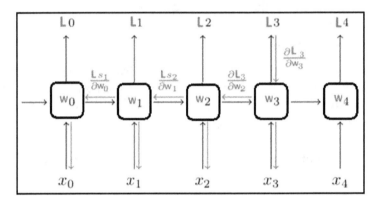

Here, (L) represents the loss, (W) represents the weight matrices of a time step, and the x values are the inputs at a given time steps. Mathematically, this is equivalent to the following:

$$
\frac{\partial L_3}{\partial W} = \frac{\partial L_3}{\partial y_3} \cdot \frac{\partial y_3}{\partial h_2} \cdot \frac{\partial h_2}{\partial W}
$$

$$
= \sum_{t=0}^{2} \frac{\partial L_3}{\partial y_3} \cdot \frac{\partial y_3}{\partial h_2} \cdot \frac{\partial h_2}{\partial h_t} \cdot \frac{\partial h_t}{\partial W}
$$

$$
= \sum_{t=0}^{2} \frac{\partial L_3}{\partial y_3} \cdot \frac{\partial y_3}{\partial h_2} \cdot \left(\prod_{j=t+1}^{2} \frac{\partial h_j}{\partial h_{j-1}} \right) \cdot \frac{\partial h_t}{\partial W}
$$

The derivatives of these functions are stored in a Jacobean matrix, representing point-wise derivations of the weight and loss vectors. Mathematically, the derivatives of these functions are bound by an absolute value of 1. However, small derivative values (close to 0), over several time-steps of matrix-wise multiplications, degrade exponentially, almost vanishing, which in turn prohibits the model from converging. The same holds true for large values (larger than 1) in the activation matrix, where the gradients will become increasingly large until they are attributed a NaN value (not a number), abruptly terminating the training process. How can we address these problems?

You can find more information on vanishing gradients at: `http://www.wildml.com/2015/10/recurrent-neural-networks-tutorial-part-3-backpropagation-through-time-and-vanishing-gradients/`.

Preventing exploding gradients through clipping

In the case of exploding gradients, the problem is much more evident. Your model simply stops training, returning a value error of NaN, corresponding to the exploded gradient values. A simple solution to this is to clip your gradients by defining an arbitrary upper bound or threshold value to prevent the gradients from getting too big. Keras lets us implement this with ease as you can define this threshold by manually initiating an optimizer and passing it a `clipvalue` or `clipnorm` argument, as shown here:

```
from keras import optimizers

# All parameter gradients will be clipped to
# a maximum norm of 1.
sgd = optimizers.SGD(lr=0.01, clipnorm=1.)


from keras import optimizers

# All parameter gradients will be clipped to
# a maximum value of 0.5 and
# a minimum value of -0.5.
sgd = optimizers.SGD(lr=0.01, clipvalue=0.5)
```

You can then pass the `optimizers` variable to your model when compiling it. This idea of clipping gradients is extensively discussed, along with other problems that are associated with training RNNs, in the paper titled: *On the difficulty of training recurrent neural networks*, which is available at `http://proceedings.mlr.press/v28/pascanu13.pdf`.

Preventing vanishing gradients with memory

In the case of vanishing gradients, our network stops learning anything new as the weights are insignificantly nudged at each update. The problem is particularly cumbersome for the case of RNNs, as they attempt to model long sequences over potentially many time steps, and so the model has a very hard time backpropagating the errors to nudge the layer weights of earlier time steps. We saw how this can affect language modeling tasks such as learning grammar rules and entity-based dependencies (with the monkey example). Thankfully, several solutions have been devised to address this problem. Some have ventured along the lines of careful initialization of the activation matrix, *Waa*, using a ReLU activation function to pre-train the layer weights in an unsupervised manner. More commonly, however, others have addressed this problem by designing more sophisticated architectures that are capable of storing long-term information based on its statistical relevance to current events in the sequence. This is essentially the base intuition behind more complex RNN variations such as the **Gated Recurrent Units (GRUs)** and **Long Short-Term Memory (LSTM)** networks. Let's see how GRUs address the problem of long-term dependencies.

GRUs

The GRU can be considered the younger sibling of the LSTM, which we will look at Chapter 6, *Long-Short Term Memory Networks*. In essence, both leverage similar concepts to modeling long-term dependencies, such as remembering whether the subject of the sentence is plural, when generating following sequences. Soon, we will see how memory cells and flow gates can be used to address the vanishing gradient problem, while better modeling long term dependencies in sequence data. The underlying difference between GRUs and LSTMs is in the computational complexity they represent. Simply put, LSTMs are more complex architectures that, while computationally expensive and time-consuming to train, perform very well at breaking down the training data into meaningful and generalizable representations. GRUs, on the other hand, while computationally less intensive, are limited in their representational abilities compared to LSTM. However, not all tasks require heavyset 10-layer LSTMs (like the ones used by Siri, Cortana, Alexia, and so on). As we will soon see, character-level language modeling can be achieved with quite simple architectures to begin with, producing increasingly interesting results with relatively lightweight models such as GRUs. The following diagram shows the basic architectural difference between the SimpleRNN we have been discussing so far and the GRU.

The memory cell

Again, we have two input values entering the unit, namely the sequence input at the current time and the layer activations from the preceding time step. One of the main differences in the GRU is the addition of a memory cell (c), which lets us store some relevant information at a given time step to inform later predictions. In practice, this changes how we calculate the activations at a given time step (c^t, which here is the same as a^t) in GRUs:

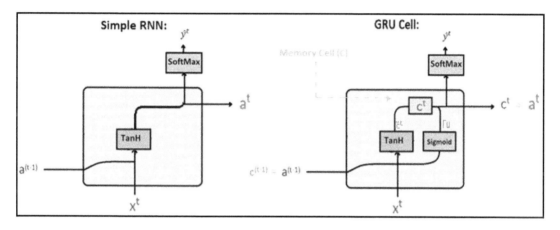

Going back to the monkey example, a word-level GRU model has the potential to better represent the fact that there are several entities in the second sentence that's given here, and hence will remember to use the word **were** instead of **was** to complete the sequence:

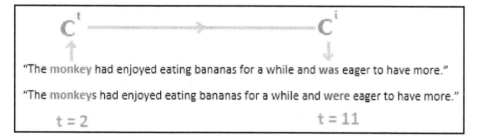

How does this memory cell actually work? Well, the value of (c^t) stores the activation values (a^t) at a given time step (time step 2) and is passed forward to subsequent time steps if deemed relevant to the sequence at hand. Once the relevance of this activation is lost (that is, a new dependency has been detected in the sequence), the memory cell can be updated with a new value of (c^t), reflecting time-dependent information that may be more relevant:

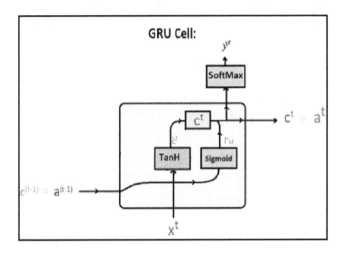

A closer look at the GRU cell

Representing the memory cell

When processing our example sentences, a word-level RNN model may store the activations at time step 2 (for the words *monkey* and *monkeys*), and save it until time step 11, where it is used to predict the output words *was* and *were*, respectively. At each time step, a contender value ($c^{\sim t}$) is generated, which attempts to replace the value of the memory cell, (c^t). However, as long as (c^t) remains statistically relevant to the sequence, it is conserved, only to be discarded later on for more relevant representation. Let's see how this is mathematically implemented, starting with the contender value, ($c^{\sim t}$). To implement this parameter, we will initialize a new weight matrix, (Wc). Then, we will compute the dot product of (Wc) with the previous activation (c^{t-1}) and the input at the current time (x t) and pass the resulting vector through a non-linear activation function such as tanh. This operation is strikingly similar to the standard forward propagation operation we saw previously.

Updating the memory value

Mathematically, we can represent this computation as follows:

$$c^{\cdot t} = tanh\ (\ Wc\ [\ c^{t\text{-}1},\ ^{\times}\ t\ ] + bc)$$

More importantly, the GRU also implements a gate denoted by the Greek alphabet gamma (Γu), which basically computes a dot product of inputs and previous activations through yet another non-linear function:

$$\Gamma u = sigmoid\ (\ Wu\ [\ c^{t\text{-}1},\ ^{\times}\ t\ ] + bu)$$

The purpose of this gate is to determine whether we should update our current value (c^{t}) with a candidate value ($c^{\cdot t}$). The value of the gate (Γu) can be thought of as a binary value. In practice, we know that the sigmoid activation function is known for squishing values between zero and one. In fact, the vast majority of input values entering a sigmoid activation function will come out as either zero or one, hence it is practical to think of the gamma variable as a binary value that decides whether to replace (c^{t}) with ($c^{\cdot t}$) or not at every time step:

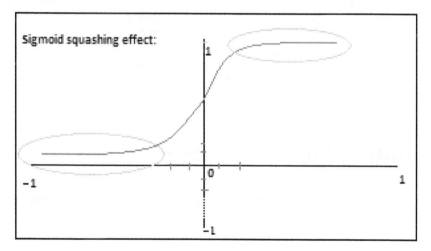

Mathematics of the update equation

Let's see how this would work out in practice. We will use our earlier example once more, which has been extended here to theoretically demonstrate when a world-level GRU model may work:

The monkey had enjoyed eating bananas for a while and was eager to have more. The bananas themselves were the best one could find on this side of the island...

As a GRU layer goes over this sequence, it may store the activation values at the second time step as (c^t), detecting the presence of a singular entity (that is, *monkey*). It will carry forward this representation until it reaches a new concept in the sequence (*The bananas*), at which point the update gate (Γu) will allow the new candidate activation value (c-t) to replace the old value in the memory cell (c), reflecting the new plural entity, *bananas*. Mathematically, we can tie all of this up by defining how the activation value (ct) is calculated in a GRU:

$$ct = (\Gamma u \times c\text{-}t) + [(1\text{-} \Gamma u) \times ct\text{-}1]$$

As we can see here, the activation values at a given time step are defined by a sum of two terms. The first term reflects the product of the gate value and the candidate value. The second term denotes the inverse of the gate value, multiplied by the activation from the previous time step. Intuitively, the first term simply controls whether to let the update term be included in the equation by being either one or zero. The second term controls the potential neutralization of the activation of the previous time step (ct-1). Let's have a look at how these two terms work together to decide whether or not an update is performed at a given time step.

Implementing the no-update scenario

In the case where the value (Γu) is zero, the first term reduces to zero altogether, removing the effect of (c-t), while the second term simply takes the activation value from the previous time step:

```
If Γu = 0:
ct = ( 0 x c-t ) + ((1 - 0) x ct-1 )
   = 0 + ct-1
Therefore, ct = ct-1
```

In this scenario, no update is performed, and the previous activations (ct) are preserved and passed forward to the next time step.

Implementing the update scenario

On the other hand, if the gate holds a 1, the equation allows c-t to become the new value of ct, since the second term reduces to zero ((1-1) x ct-1). This is what allows us to effectively perform an update to our memory cell, hence conserving useful time-dependent representations. The update scenario can be denoted mathematically like so:

```
If Γu = 1:
ct = ( 1 x c~t ) + ((1 - 1) x ct-1 )
   = c~t+ (0 x ct-1)
Therefore, ct = c~t
```

Preserving relevance between time steps

The nature of the two terms that are used to perform our memory update helps us to preserve relevant information across multiple time steps. Hence, this implementation potentially provides a solution to the vanishing gradient issue by modeling long-term dependencies with the use of a memory cell. You may wonder, however, how exactly does the GRU assess the relevance of an activation? The update gate simply allows the replacement of the activation vector (c^t) with the new candidate ($c^{\sim t}$), but how do we know how relevant the previous activation (c^{t-1}) is to the current time step? Well, earlier, we presented a simplified equation for governing the GRU unit. A last addition to its implementation is the relevance gate (Γr), which helps us to do exactly what it suggests. Hence, we calculate the candidate value ($c^{\sim t}$) using this relevance gate (Γr) to incorporate the relevance of activation values from the previous time step (c^{t-1}) to the current one (c^t). This helps us to assess how relevant the activations from the previous time steps are to the current input sequence at hand and is implemented in a very familiar way, as shown in the following diagram:

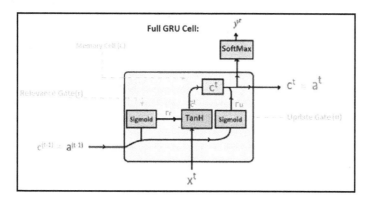

Formalizing the relevance gate

The following equations show the full spectrum of the GRU equations, including the relevance gate term, which is now included in the computation we performed earlier to get the contender memory value, (c-t):

- **Earlier:** $c\text{-}t = tanh\ (\ Wc\ [\ ct\text{-}1,\ ^x\ t\ ] + bc)$

- **Now:** $c\text{-}t = tanh\ (\ Wc\ [\ \Gamma r\ ,\ ct\text{-}1,\ ^x\ t\ ] + bc)$

- **Where:** $\Gamma r = sigmoid\ (\ Wr\ [\ ct\text{-}1,\ ^x\ t\ ] + br)$

Not surprisingly, (Γr) is computed by initializing yet another weight matrix (Wr) and computing its dot product with past activations (c^{t-1}) and current inputs (^{x} t) before summing them through a sigmoid activation function. The equation that's computing the current activation (c^t) remains the same, except for the (c^{-t}) term within it, which is now incorporating the relevance gate (Γr) in its calculation:

$$ct = (\ \Gamma u\ x\ c\text{-}t\ ) + [\ (\ 1\text{-}\ \Gamma u\ )\ x\ ct\text{-}1\ ]$$

The predicted output at a given time step is calculated in the same manner as it was for the SimpleRNN layer. The only difference is that the term (a^t) is replaced by the term (c^t), which denotes the activations of neurons in a GRU layer at time step (t):

$$\hat{y}^t = softmax\ [\ (Wcy\ x\ ct) + by\ ]$$

Practically speaking, both terms (a^t and c^t) can be thought of as synonymous in the case of GRUs, but we will later see architectures where this no longer applies, such as in LSTMs. For the time being, we have covered the basic equations that govern the forward propagation of data in a GRU unit. You've seen how we can compute the activations and the output values at each time step and use different gates (such as the update and relevance gates) to control the flow of information, allowing us to assess and store long-term dependencies. What we saw here is a very common implementation that addresses the vanishing gradients problem. However, it is but one of potentially many more. Researchers have found this particular formulaic implementation to be a successful way to gauge relevance and model sequential dependencies for an array of different problems since their introduction in 2014 by Kyunghyun Cho et al.

Building character-level language models in Keras

Now, we have a good command over the basic learning mechanism of different types of RNNs, both simple and complex. We also know a bit about different sequence processing use cases, as well as different RNN architectures that permit us to model these sequences. Let's combine all of this knowledge and put it to use. Next up, we will test these different models on a hands-on task and see how each of them do.

We will explore the simple use case of building a character level language model, much like the autocorrect model almost everybody is familiar with, which is implemented on word processor applications for almost all devices. A key difference will be that we will train our RNN to derive a language model from Shakespeare's Hamlet. Hence, our network will take a sequence of characters from Shakespeare's *Hamlet* as input and iteratively compute the probability distribution of the next character to come in the sequence. Let's make some imports and load in the necessary packages:

```
from __future__ import print_function
import sys
import numpy as np
import re
import random
import pickle

from nltk.corpus import gutenberg

from keras.models import Sequential
from keras.layers import Dense, Bidirectional, Dropout
from keras.layers import SimpleRNN, GRU, BatchNormalization

from keras.callbacks import LambdaCallback
from keras.callbacks import ModelCheckpoint
from keras.utils.data_utils import get_file
from keras.utils.data_utils import get_file
```

Loading in Shakespeare's Hamlet

We will use the **Natural Language Toolkit** (**NLTK**) package in Python to import and preprocess the play, which can be found in the `gutenberg` corpus:

```
from nltk.corpus import gutenberg
hamlet = gutenberg.words('shakespeare-hamlet.txt')
text =''
for word in hamlet:             # For each word
text+=str(word).lower()         # Convert to lower case and add to string
variable
text+= ' '                      # Add space
print('Corpus length, Hamlet only:', len(text))

----------------------------------------------------------------
Output:
Corpus length, Hamlet only: 166765
```

The string variable (`text`) contains the entire sequence of characters that make up the play Hamlet. We will now break it up into shorter sequences that we can feed to our recurrent network at successive time steps. To forge the input sequences, we will define an arbitrary length of characters that the network sees at each time step. We will sample these characters from the text string by iteratively sliding over them and collecting sequences of characters (denoting our training features), along with the next character of the given sequence (as our training labels). Naturally, taking samples over longer sequences allows the network to compute more accurate probability distributions, hence reflecting contextual information on the character to follow. As a result, however, this is also computationally more intensive, both for training the model and to generate predictions during testing.

Each of our input sequences (x) will correspond to 40 characters, and one output character (y1) that corresponds to the next character in the sequence. We can create this data structure of 11 characters per row by using the range function to span by segments characters of our entire string (text) at a time, and saving them in a list, as shown here. We can see that we have broken up the entire play into about 55, 575 sequences of characters.

Building a dictionary of characters

Now, we will proceed and create a vocabulary, or dictionary of characters, for mapping each character to a specific integer. This is a necessary step for us to be able to represent these integers as vectors, which we can sequentially feed into our network at each time step. We will create two versions of our dictionary: one with characters mapped to indices, and the other with indices mapped to characters.

This is just for the sake of practicality, as we will need both lists for reference:

```
characters = sorted(list(set(text)))
print('Total characters:', len(characters))
char_indices = dict((l, i) for i, l in enumerate(characters))
indices_char = dict((i, l) for i, l in enumerate(characters))
```

Output:
Total characters= 65

You can always check how large your vocabulary is by checking the length of the mapping dictionary. In our case, it appears that we have 66 unique characters that make up the sequences forming the play Hamlet.

Preparing training sequences of characters

After constructing our dictionary of characters, we will break up the text making up Hamlet into a set of sequences that can be fed to our network, with a corresponding output character for each sequence:

```
'''
Break text into :
Features   -    Character-level sequences of fixed length
Labels     -    The next character in sequence
'''
training_sequences = []          # Empty list to collect each sequence

next_chars = []                  # Empty list to collect next character in
sequence

seq_len, stride = 35, 1    # Define lenth of each input sequence & stride
to move before sampling next sequence

for i in range(0, len(text) - seq_len, stride):    # Loop over text with
window of 35 characters, moving 1 stride at a time

training_sequences.append(text[i: i + seq_len]) # Append sequences to
traning_sequences

next_chars.append(text[i + seq_len])             # Append following
character in sequence to next_chars
```

We created two lists and looped over our text string to append a sequence of 40 characters at a time. One list holds the training sequences, while the other holds the next character to come, following the 40 characters of the sequence. We have implemented an arbitrary sequence length of 40, but you are free to experiment with it. Keep in mind that setting too small a sequence will not allow you network to look far back enough to inform predictions, whereas setting to big a sequence may give your network a hard time converging, as it won't be able to find the most efficient representations. Just like the story of Goldilocks and the three bears, you will aim for a sequence length that is *just right*, as informed by experiments and/or domain knowledge.

Printing out example sequences

Similarly, we also arbitrarily choose to stride through our text file with a window of one character at a time. This simply means that we can potentially sample each character multiple times, just like how our convolutional filter progressively sampled an entire image by striding through it in fixed steps:

```
# Print out sequences and labels to verify

print('Number of sequences:', len(training_sequences))
print('First sequences:', training_sequences[:1])
print('Next characters in sequence:', next_chars[:1])
print('Second sequences:', training_sequences[1:2])
print('Next characters in sequence:', next_chars[1:2])
```

Output

```
Number of sequences: 166730
First sequences: ['[ the tragedie of hamlet by william']
Next characters in sequence: [' ']
Second sequences: [' the tragedie of hamlet by william ']
Next characters in sequence: ['s']
```

The difference here is that we embed this sequentially in the training data itself, instead of letting a layer perform the striding operation while training. This is an easier (and more logical) approach with text data, which can be easily manipulated to produce the sequences of characters, at desired strides, from our entire text of Hamlet. As we can see, each of our lists now stores sequences of strings that are sampled at a stride of three steps, from the original text string. We printed out the first and second sequences and labels of our training data, which demonstrates the sequential nature of its arrangement.

Vectorizing the training data

The next step is one that your already quite familiar with. We will simply vectorize our data by transforming our list of training sequences into a three-dimensional tensor representing one-hot encoded training features, with their corresponding labels (that is, the next word to come in the sequence). The dimensions of the feature matrix can be represented as (*time steps x sequence length x number of characters*). In our case, this amounts to 55,575 sequences, each of a length of 40. Hence, our tensor will be composed of 55,575 matrices, each with 40 vectors of 66 dimensions, stacked on top of each other. Here, each vector represents a single character, in a sequence of 40 characters. It has 66 dimensions, as we have one-hot-encoded each character as a vector of zeros, with 1 in the index position of that character from our dictionary:

```
#Create a Matrix of zeros
# With dimensions : (training sequences, length of each sequence, total
unique characters)
x = np.zeros((len(training_sequences), seq_len, len(characters)),
dtype=np.bool)
y = np.zeros((len(training_sequences), len(characters)), dtype=np.bool)
for index, sequence in enumerate(training_sequences):     #Iterate over
training sequences
for sub_index, chars in enumerate(sequence):              #Iterate over
characters per sequence
x[index, sub_index, char_indices[chars]] = 1       #Update character
position in feature matrix to 1
y[index, char_indices[next_chars[index]]] = 1            #Update character
position in label matrix to 1
print('Data vectorization completed.')
print('Feature vectors shape', x.shape)
print('Label vectors shape', y.shape)

------------------------------------------------------------------------

Data vectorization completed.
Feature vectors shape (166730, 35, 43)
Label vectors shape (166730, 43)
```

Statistics of character modeling

We often distinguish words and numbers as being in different realms. As it happens, they are not so far apart. Everything can be deconstructed using the universal language of mathematics. This is quite a fortunate property of our reality, not just for the pleasure of modeling statistical distributions over sequences of characters. However, since we are on the topic, we will go ahead and define the concept of language models. In essence, language models follow Bayesian logic that relates the probability of posterior events (or tokens to come) as a function of prior occurrences (tokens that came). With such an assumption, we are able to construct a feature space corresponding to the statistical distribution of words over a period of time. The RNNs we will build shortly will each construct a unique feature space of probability distributions. Then, we are able to feed it a sequence of characters and recursively generate the next character to come using the distribution schemes.

Modeling character-level probabilities

In **natural language processing** (**NLP**), the unit of a string is denoted as a token. Depending on how you wish to preprocess your string data, you can have word tokens or character tokens. We will be working with character tokens for the purpose of this example, as our training data is set up to make our network predict a single character at a time. Hence, given a sequence of characters, our network will output a Softmax probability score for each of the characters in our vocabulary of characters. In our case, we initially had 66 total characters in Shakespeare's Hamlet. These included uppercase and lowercase letters, which are quite redundant for the task at hand. Hence, to increase our efficiency and keep track of less Softmax scores, we will reduce our training vocabulary by converting the Hamlet text into lowercase, leaving us with 44 characters. This means that, at each network prediction, it will generate a 44-way Softmax output. We can take the character with the maximum score (that is, do some greedy sampling) and add it to the input sequence, then ask our network what it thinks should come next. RNNs are able to learn the general structure of words in the English language, as well as punctuation and grammar rules, and even have a flair for inventing novel sequences, ranging from cool sounding names to possibly life-saving molecular compounds, depending on what sequence you decide to feed it. In fact, RNNs have been shown to capture the syntax of molecular representations and can be fine-tuned to generate specific molecular targets. This helps researchers considerably in tasks such as drug discovery and is a vivid area of scientific research. For further reading, check out the following link:

https://www.ncbi.nlm.nih.gov/pubmed/29095571

Sampling thresholds

To be able to generate sequences of Shakespeare-like sentences, we need to devise a mannerism to sample our probability distributions. These probability distributions are represented by our model's weights and continuously change at successive time steps during the training process. Sampling these distributions is akin to peeking into the network's idea of Shakespearean text at the end of each training epoch. We are essentially using the probability distributions that have been learned by our model to generate a sequence of characters. Moreover, depending on the sampling strategy we choose, we could potentially introduce some controlled randomness in our generated text to force our model to come up with some novel sequences. This can result in interesting formulations and is quite entertaining in practice.

The purpose of controlling stochasticity

The main concept behind sampling is how you choose control stochasticity (or randomness) in selecting the next character from the probability distributions for possible characters to come. Various applications may ask for different approaches.

Greedy sampling

If you are trying to train an RNN for automatic text completion and correction, you will probably be better off going with a greedy sampling strategy. This simply means that, at each sampling step, you will choose the next character in the sequence based on the character that was attributed the highest probability distribution by our Softmax output. This ensures that your network will output predictions that likely correspond to words you most commonly use. On the other hand, you may want to try a more stratified approach when training an RNN to generate cool names, handwriting in a particular person's style, or even producing undiscovered molecular compounds. In this case, you wouldn't want to choose the most likely characters to come, as this is simply boring. We can instead introduce some controlled randomness (or stochasticity) by picking out the next character in a probabilistic manner, rather than a fixed one.

Stochastic sampling

One approach could be, instead of simply choosing the next character based on the Softmax output values, to reweight the probability distribution of these output values at a given time step. This lets us do things such as assign a proportional probability score for any of the characters of our vocabulary to be chosen next. As an example, suppose a given character has an assigned probability of 0.25 to be the next character in the sequence. We will then choose it one out of four times as the next character. In this manner, we are able to systematically introduce a little randomness, which gives rise to creative and realistic, albeit artificial words and sequences. Playing around by introducing randomness can often be usefully informative in the realm of generative modeling, as we will see in later chapters. For now, we will implement the controlled introduction of randomness in our sampling strategy by introducing a sampling threshold, which lets us redistribute the Softmax prediction probabilities of our model, https://arxiv.org/pdf/1308.0850.pdf:

```python
def sample(softmax_predictions, sample_threshold=1.0):
    softmax_preds = np.asarray(softmax_predictions).astype('float64')
    # Make array of predictions, convert to float
    log_preds = np.log(softmax_preds) / sample_threshold
    # Log normalize and divide by threshold
    exp_preds = np.exp(log_preds)
    # Compute exponents of log normalized terms
    norm_preds = exp_preds / np.sum(exp_preds)
    # Normalize predictions
    prob = np.random.multinomial(1, norm_preds, 1)
    # Draw sample from multinomial distribution

    return np.argmax(prob)
    #Return max value
```

This threshold denotes the entropy of the probability distribution we will be using, to sample a given generation from our model. A higher threshold will correspond to higher entropy distributions, leading to seemingly unreal and less structured sequences. Lower thresholds, on the other hand, will plainly encode English language representations and morphology, generating familiar words and terms.

Testing different RNN models

Now that we have our training data preprocessed and ready in tensor format, we can try a slightly different approach than previous chapters. Normally, we would go ahead and build a single model and then proceed to train it. Instead, we will construct several models, each reflecting a different RNN architecture, and train them successively to see how each of them do at the task of generating character-level sequences. In essence, each of these models will leverage a different learning mechanism and induct its proper language model, based on sequences of characters it sees. Then, we can sample the language models that are learned by each network. In fact, we can even sample our networks in-between training epochs to see how our network is doing at generating Shakespearean phrases at the level of each epoch. Before we continue to build our networks, we must go over some basic strategies to inform our task of language modeling and sampling. Then, we will build some Keras callbacks that let us interact with and sample our model while it trains.

Using custom callbacks to generate text

Next, we will construct a custom Keras callback that will allow us to use the sample function we just constructed to iteratively probe our model at the end of each training epoch. As you will recall, callbacks are a class of functions that allow operations to be performed on our model (such as saving and testing) during the training process. These are very useful functions to visualize how a model performs throughout the training process. Essentially, this function will take a random sequence of characters from the Hamlet text and then generate 400 characters to follow on, starting from the given input. It does this for each of the five sampling thresholds chosen and prints out the generated results at the end of each epoch:

```
def on_epoch_end(epoch, _):
global model, model_name
print('----- Generating text after Epoch: %d' % epoch)
start_index = random.randint(0, len(text) - seq_len - 1)
# Random index position to start sample input sequence
end_index = start_index + seq_len
# End of sequence, corresponding to training sequence length
sampling_range = [0.3, 0.5, 0.7, 1.0, 1.2]
# Sampling entropy threshold
for threshold in sampling_range:print('----- *Sampling Threshold* :',
threshold)
generated = ''
# Empty string to collect sequence
sentence = text[start_index: end_index]
# Random input sequence taken from Hamlet
generated += sentence
```

```
    # Add input sentence to generated
    print('Input sequence to generate from : "' + sentence + '"')
    sys.stdout.write(generated)
    # Print out buffer instead of waiting till the end
    for i in range(400):
    # Generate 400 next characters in the sequence
    x_pred = np.zeros((1, seq_len, len(characters)))
    # Matrix of zeros for input sentence
    for n, char in enumerate(sentence):
    # For character in sentence
    x_pred[0, n, char_indices[char]] = 1.
    # Change index position for character to 1.
    preds = model.predict(x_pred, verbose=0)[0]
    # Make prediction on input vector
    next_index = sample(preds, threshold)
    # Get index position of next character using sample function
    next_char = indices_char[next_index]
    # Get next character using index
    generated += next_char
    # Add generated character to sequence
    sentence = sentence[1:] + next_char
    sys.stdout.write(next_char)
    sys.stdout.flush()
    -------------------------------------------------------------------
```

Output:

print_callback = LambdaCallback(on_epoch_end=on_epoch_end)

Testing multiple models

The last task on our list is to build a helper function that will train, sample, and save a list of RNN models. This function also saves the history objects of the model that we used earlier to plot out the loss and accuracy values per epoch, which can be useful in case you want to explore different models and their relative performances at a later time:

```
def test_models(list, epochs=10):
    global model, model_name
    for network in list:
        print('Initiating compilation...')
        # Initialize model
        model = network()
        # Get model name
        model_name = re.split(' ', str(network))[1]
        #Filepath to save model with name, epoch and loss
        filepath =
"C:/Users/npurk/Desktop/Ch5RNN/all_models/versions/%s_epoch-{epoch:02d}-
```

```
loss-{loss:.4f}.h5"%model_name
        #Checkpoint callback object
        checkpoint = ModelCheckpoint(filepath, monitor='loss', verbose=0,
save_best_only=True, mode='min')
        # Compile model
        model.compile(loss='categorical_crossentropy', optimizer='adam')
        print('Compiled:', str(model_name))
        # Initiate training
        network = model.fit(x, y,
                batch_size=100,
                epochs=epochs,
                callbacks=[print_callback, checkpoint])
        # Print model configuration
        model.summary()
        #Save model history object for later analysis
        with
open('C:/Users/npurk/Desktop/Ch5RNN/all_models/history/%s.pkl'%model_name,
'wb') as file_pi:
            pickle.dump(network.history, file_pi)
```

test_models(all_models, epochs=5)

Now, we can finally proceed to the task of constructing several types of RNNs and training them with the helper function to see how different types of RNNs perform at generating Shakespeare-like texts.

Building a SimpleRNN

The SimpleRNN model in Keras is a basic RNN layer, like the ones we discussed earlier. While it has many parameters, most of them are set with excellent defaults that will get you by for many different use cases. Since we have initialized the RNN layer as the first layer of our model, we must pass it an input shape, corresponding to the length of each sequence (which we chose to be 40 characters earlier) and the number of unique characters in our dataset (which was 44). While this model is computationally compact to run, it gravely suffers from the vanishing gradients problem we spoke of. As a result, it has some trouble modeling long-term dependencies:

```
from keras.models import Sequential
from keras.layers import Dense, Bidirectional, Dropout
from keras.layers import SimpleRNN, GRU, BatchNormalization
from keras.optimizers import RMSprop
'''Fun part: Construct a bunch of functions returning different kinds of
RNNs, from simple to more complex'''
def SimpleRNN_stacked_model():
    model = Sequential()
```

```
    model.add(SimpleRNN(128, input_shape=(seq_len, len(characters)),
return_sequences=True))
    model.add(SimpleRNN(128))
    model.add(Dense(len(characters), activation='softmax'))
    return model
```

Note that this two-layered model has a final dense layer with a number of neurons corresponding to each of the 44 unique characters in our dataset. We equip it with a Softmax activation function, which will output a 44-way probability score at each time step, corresponding to the likelihood of each character to follow. All of the models we build for this experiment will have this final dense layer in common. Finally, all RNNs have the ability to remain stateful. This simply refers to passing on the layer weights for computations on the subsequent sequences of our training data. This feature can be explicitly set in all RNNs, with the `stateful` argument, which takes a Boolean value and can be provided when initializing a layer.

Stacking RNN layers

Why have one, when you can have two? All of the recurrent layers in Keras can return two different types of tensors, depending on what you wish to accomplish. You could either receive a 3D tensor of dimensions as output (`batch_size`, `time_steps`, `output_features`) or simply a 2D one, with dimensions of (`time_steps`, `output_features`). We query the 3D tensor if we want our model to return entire sequences of successive output values on each time step. This is useful if we want to stack an RNN layer on top of another, and then ask the first layer to return all of the activations to the second layer that's stacked. Returning all activations essentially means returning the activation for each specific time step. These values can be subsequently fed into yet another recurrent layer, which aims to encode higher level abstract representations from the same input sequence. The following diagram shows the mathematical consequences of setting the Boolean argument to **True** or **False**:

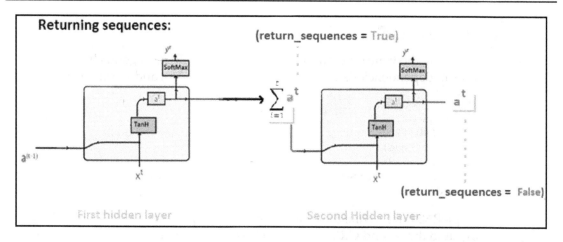

Setting it to true will simply return a tensor with predictions for each time step, instead of the prediction from the last time step only. The stacking of recurrent layers is quite useful. By stacking RNN layers on top on one another, we potentially increase the time-dependent representational value of our network, allowing it to memorize more abstract patterns that are potentially present in our data.

On the other hand, if we want it to only return the output at the last time step for each input sequence, we can ask it to return a 2D tensor. This is necessary when we want to go ahead and actually predict which of the characters from our vocabulary is most likely to be next. We can control this implementation with the `return_sequences` argument, which is passed when we add a recurrent layer. Alternatively, we can set it to false, making our model return the activation values from the last time step only, which can be propagated forward for classification:

```
def SimpleRNN_stacked_model():
    model = Sequential()
    model.add(SimpleRNN(128, input_shape=(seq_len, len(characters)),
return_sequences=True))
    model.add(SimpleRNN(128))
    model.add(Dense(len(characters), activation='softmax'))
    return model
```

 Note that the `return_sequences` argument can only be invoked for the penultimate hidden layers, and not for the hidden layer preceding the densely connected output layer, since the output layer is only tasked with classifying the next sequence to come.

Building GRUs

Excellent at mitigating the vanishing gradients problem, the GRU is a good choice for modeling long-term dependencies such as grammar, punctuation, and word morphology:

```
def GRU_stacked_model():
    model = Sequential()
    model.add(GRU(128, input_shape=(seq_len, len(characters)),
return_sequences=True))
    model.add(GRU(128))
    model.add(Dense(len(characters), activation='softmax'))
    return model
```

Just like the SimpleRNN, we define the dimensions of the input at the first layer and return a 3D tensor output to the second GRU layer, which will help retain more complex time-dependent representations that are present in our training data. We also stack two GRU layers on top of each other to see what the increased representational power of our model produces:

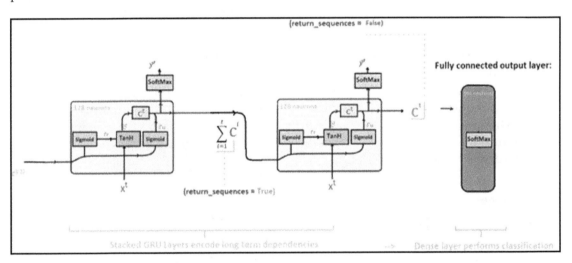

Hopefully, this architecture results in realistic albeit novel sequences of text that even a Shakespeare expert couldn't tell apart from the real deal. Let's visualize the model we built here through the following diagram:

Note that we have also included the line `model.summary()` in our trainer function we built earlier to visually depict the structure of the model after it is fit.

Building bi-directional GRUs

Next in our models to test is yet another GRU unit, but this time with a twist. We nest it within a bi-directional layer, which allows us to feed our model each sequence in both the normal and the reverse order. In this manner, our model is able to *see* what is yet to come, leveraging future sequence data to inform predictions at the current time step. The nature of processing a sequence in a bi-directional manner greatly enhances the extracted representations from our data. In fact, the order of processing a sequence can have a significant effect on the type of representations that are learned after.

On processing reality sequentially

The notion of changing the order of processing a sequence is quite an intriguing one. We humans certainly seem to prefer a certain order of learning things over another. The second sentence that's been reproduced in the following image simply makes no sense to us, even though we know exactly what each individual word within the sentence means. Similarly, many of us have a hard time reciting the letters of the alphabet backward, even though we are extremely familiar with each letter, and compose much more complex concepts with them, such as words, ideas, and even Keras code:

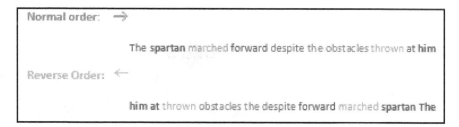

It is very likely that our sequential preferences have to do with the nature of our reality, which is sequential and forward-moving by definition. At the end of the day, the configuration of the 10^{11} neurons in our brain has been engineered by time and natural forces to best encode and represent the deluge of time-dependent sensory signals we come across, every living second of our lives. It stands to reason that our own neural architecture efficiently implements a mechanism that tends to prefer processing signals in a specific order. However, that is not to say that we cannot part ways with a learned order, as many pre-school kids take up the challenge of reciting the alphabet backward and do so quite successfully. Other sequential tasks such as listening to natural language or rhythmic music, however, may be harder to process in reverse order. But don't take my word for it. Try listening to your favorite song in reverse and see whether you still like it as much.

Benefits of re-ordering sequential data

In some manner, it seems that bi-directional networks are able to potentially overcome our own biases in processing information. As you will see, they can learn equally useful representations that we would have otherwise not thought to include to inform and enhance our predictions. It all depends on how important it is to process a given signal, in its sequential order, for the task at hand. In the case of our earlier natural language example, this was quite crucial to determine the **part-of-speech** (**POS**) tag for the word *Spartan*:

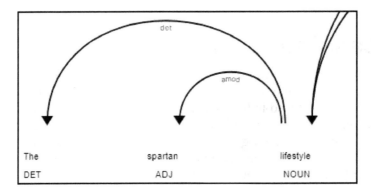

Bi-directional layer in Keras

Therefore, the bi-directional layer in Keras processes a sequence of data in both the normal and reverse sequence, which allows us to pick up on words that come later on in the sequence to inform our prediction at the current time.

Essentially, the bi-directional layer duplicates any layer that's fed to it and uses one copy to process information in the normal sequential order, while the other processes data in the reverse order. Pretty neat, no? We can intuitively visualize what a bi-directional layer actually does by going through a simple example. Suppose you were modeling the two-word sequence **Whats up**, with a bi-directional GRU:

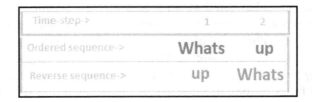

Time-step->	1	2
Ordered sequence->	Whats	up
Reverse sequence->	up	Whats

To do this, you will nest the GRU in a bi-directional layer, which allows Keras to generates two versions of the bi-directional model. In the preceding image, we stacked two bi-directional layers on top of each other before connecting them to a dense output layer, as we did previously:

```
def Bi_directional_GRU():
    model = Sequential()
    model.add(Bidirectional(GRU(128, return_sequences=True),
input_shape=(seq_len, len(characters))))
    model.add(Bidirectional(GRU(128)))
    model.add(Dense(len(characters), activation='softmax'))
    return model
```

The model that processes the sequence in the normal order is shown in red. Similarly, the blue model processes the same sequence in reverse order. Both of these models collaborate at each time step to produce a predicted output, with respect to the current time step. We can see how these two models receive input values and work together to produce the predicted output ($\hat{y}^t$), which corresponds to the two respective time steps of our input:

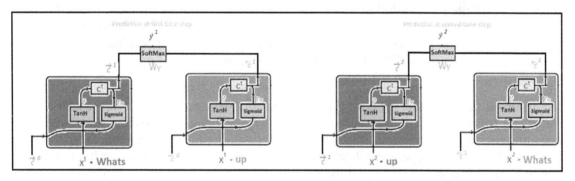

The equations governing the forward propagation of information can be altered slightly to account for data entering our RNN, from both the forward and reverse sequence layers, at each time step. The backward propagation of errors through time is still achieved in the same manner and is done for each orientation of GRU layer (red and blue). In the following formulation, we can see how activations from both the forward and reverse sequence layers are used to compute a predicted output ($\hat{y}^t$) for a given time step (t):

$$\hat{y}^t = g \left(W_y \left[\overrightarrow{a}^t, \overleftarrow{a}^t \right] + b_y \right)$$

The activation and weight matrices here are simply defined by the model nested within the bi-directional layer. As we saw earlier, they will be initialized at the first time step and updated by backpropagating errors through time. Hence, these are the implemented processes that let us generate a bi-directional network, which is an acyclical network where predictions are informed by information flowing both forward and backward, corresponding to the ordering of the sequence. One key disadvantage with implementing the bi-directional layer is that our network needs to see the entire sequence of data before it is able to make a prediction. In use cases such as speech recognition, this becomes problematic, since we must ensure that the target has ceased to speak before we perform our predictions to classify each sound byte as a word. One way to solve this is to keep performing predictions on an input sequence iteratively, and update the previous prediction iteratively as new information flows in.

Implementing recurrent dropout

In earlier chapters, we saw how we can drop out the prediction of a few neurons randomly to better distribute representations over our network and avoid the problem of overfitting. While our current task at hand does not have much of a negative consequence in regards to overfitting, we could not help but briefly introduce the specific case of mitigating overfitting in RNNs. This will help our model better generate novel sequences, instead of copy-pasting segments from the training data.

However, adding a normal dropout layer here just doesn't do the trick. It introduces too much randomness. This often prohibits our model from converging to ideal loss values and encoding useful representations. Instead, we may find a confused model that fails to keep track of relevant time-dependent data. What does seem to work, on the other hand, is the notion of applying the same dropout scheme (or mask) at each time step. This is different from the classic dropout operation, which drops neurons on a random basis for each time step. We can use this recurrent dropout technique to capture regularized representations, since a constant dropout mask is maintained through time. This is one of the most significant techniques that helps to prevent overfitting in recurrent layers and is known as a **recurrent dropout strategy**. Doing so essentially permits our model to representatively encode sequential data without losing valuable information via the randomized dropout process:

```
def larger_GRU():
    model = Sequential()
    model.add(GRU(128, input_shape=(seq_len, len(characters)),
                  dropout=0.2,
                  recurrent_dropout=0.2,
                  return_sequences=True))
    model.add(GRU(128, dropout=0.2,
```

```
                    recurrent_dropout=0.2,
                    return_sequences=True))
    model.add(GRU(128, dropout=0.2,
                    recurrent_dropout=0.2))
    model.add(Dense(128, activation='relu'))
    model.add(Dense(len(characters), activation='softmax'))
    return model
# All defined models
all_models = [SimpleRNN_model,
              SimpleRNN_stacked_model,
              GRU_stacked_model,
              Bi_directional_GRU,
              Bi_directional_GRU,
              larger_GRU]
```

The designers of Keras have kindly implemented two dropout-related arguments that may be passed when constructing a recurrent layer. The `recurrent_dropout` argument accepts a float value that refers to the fraction of neurons upon which the same dropout mask will be applied. You can also specify the fraction of input values entering a recurrent layer to be randomly dropped to control random noise in the data. This can be achieved by passing a float value to the dropout argument (different from `recurrent_dropout`), while defining the RNN layer.

For reference you can read the following papers:

- **A Theoretically Grounded Application of Dropout in Recurrent Neural Networks**: https://arxiv.org/pdf/1512.05287.pdf
- http://mlg.eng.cam.ac.uk/yarin/blog_2248.html

Visualizing output values

For the sake of entertainment, we will display some of the more interesting results from our own training experiments to conclude this chapter. The first screenshot shows the output that's generated by our SimpleRNN model at the end of the first epoch (note that the output prints out the first epoch as epoch 0). This is simply an implementational issue, denoting the first index position in range of *n* epochs. As we can see, even after the very first epoch, the SimpleRNN seems to have picked up on word morphology and generates real English words at low sampling thresholds.

This is just as we expected. Similarly, higher entropy samples (with a threshold of 1.2, for example) produce more stochastic results and generate (from a subjective perspective) interesting sounding words (such as *eresdoin*, *harereus*, and *nimhte*):

```
  1  test_models(all_models, epochs=1)

Initiating compilation...
Compiled: SimpleRNN_model
Epoch 1/1
166730/166730 [==============================] - 33s 199us/step - loss: 2.2307

----- Generating text after Epoch: 0

----- *Sampling Threshold* : 0.3

----- *Input sequence to generate from* : "nd mine more of the same beauty tha"
nd mine more of the same beauty that in the ther and he wert will , and , th me the me the of in the fere , the port ou hame th
e pance , and he fore if in the wing the late , and whe ham . ham . and with me the heme , and , and lith , and me the wort and
my the for . in the peate , and ntte fore the fere , and list , and lord ham . in the ponge , the my lord , and lore , and with
ma that har . of the fere , and , and and , and will

----- *Sampling Threshold* : 0.5

----- *Input sequence to generate from* : "nd mine more of the same beauty tha"
nd mine more of the same beauty thas and in the hinen . wor . in were more , in the lith , gham . not the sering of of her . in
g the galle , and here pall the peaue , ard hat . lowe , and ham . in the senge henat , and hame the harresen . and mente ing t
he wenthin the foll the thend in this ruen the helleere , for . me that ding ous andue the inge in in whe ham . gore the , and
you houd and and , the perte in s and lyour will the o

----- *Sampling Threshold* : 0.7

----- *Input sequence to generate from* : "nd mine more of the same beauty tha"
nd mine more of the same beauty that in the lour inghe ding mist on wire ke by . whe is aun that ine s of hiant hat sheraund qu
einel of s abe shower , thouthes ind . than ' rnne so deuenger for nose so fer ancede the mande not mower ham . or saplee tha ki
ng the e tham . io h mest is phis ne came to the becheno , thit with meme hepere foll the forishis nor wing in shin with that .
ineu . not me hor , and , in thrre tone ming , thet i

----- *Sampling Threshold* : 1.0

----- *Input sequence to generate from* : "nd mine more of the same beauty tha"
nd mine more of the same beauty tham and audy myring , fouge ' ses hi kere thit rnse andes muthieers ched erit my yous afco tor
n tis ine myourille , py lowd stbenen apowee prayet , all , tf feryeakestring ot hey for allwingor this at ganse . (et is myof
ltaeda dod . god iphon so h ctay fither ffothis lenre , nsowhetr shafe it ser the weeles dane , orabughis szall , kndsge llot ?
hea , so fother hamll : th then ther phat , and 'it b

----- *Sampling Threshold* : 1.2

----- *Input sequence to generate from* : "nd mine more of the same beauty tha"
nd mine more of the same beauty thangrdi on welt thees cnoune hel nSawit) hom serusl te hent ay h mereriolr thes ghe : eresdoin
k+e houchie ht sdour sanngrraune ? and bede : ti malrr .ee fred fare wond oy sabcki harereus, s auwurd oy vert yhe yestimeckink
a , and hourd fay - on ' mstseed : at hiubge , eu) . yountonrend , nfares ou hase nowes of thet aptham v nimhte winh' wholes ye
at th gue , onze , avse nownd goar no' cere pusin the

Layer (type)              Output Shape           Param #
=================================================================
simple_rnn_11 (SimpleRNN)  (None, 128)            22016

dense_20 (Dense)           (None, 43)             5547
=================================================================
Total params: 27,563
Trainable params: 27,563
Non-trainable params: 0

Initiating compilation
```

Visualizing the output of heavier GRU models

In the following screenshot, we present the output from our heavier GRU model, which started to produce pretty Shakespeare-sounding strings only after two training epochs. It even throws in Hamlet's name here and there. Note that the loss of your network is not the best assessment metric for the purpose of our illustration. The models that are shown here had a loss of 1.3, which is still pretty far from what we would normally require. You may, of course, keep training your model to produce even more comprehensible bits of Shakespeare. However, comparing the performance of any model with the loss metric is akin to judging apples and oranges in this use case. Intuitively, having reached a loss close to zero simply means that the model has memorized Shakespeare's Hamlet, and won't really generate novel sequences as we want it to do. At the end of the day, you shall remain the best judge of its performance for generative tasks such as this one:

```
----- Generating text after Epoch: 1

----- *Sampling Threshold* : 0.3

----- *Input sequence to generate from* : "n , like sweet bels iangled out of "

n , like sweet bels iangled out of the restion , my lord , and the pard , and the more of the forth , and the parse hamlet , and
the beare , the pray his seene the prease , the sonce , the does , and the mant , and the seene the bodne , i am the man his hau
e his beaue , and dis a passe , the brought , and the growne , and the read , and the seece , and for the father , but the fathe
r , and the does the but his haue so , i part haml

----- *Sampling Threshold* : 0.5

----- *Input sequence to generate from* : "n , like sweet bels iangled out of "
n , like sweet bels iangled out of he purpe , and loce , his most pol . but is the soule , and but the ringed and my frace , or
the clowes , and the forle , and the riplest hamlet : i shall bor ' s to the for his beare , the drowne of resonce , that i pol
. he well he dous it of the clayer . my lord , and the in passion of will his pare his as ham . i makes of deare , and reane for
the fire ic horrow of hing , how she shall heare ,

----- *Sampling Threshold* : 0.7

----- *Input sequence to generate from* : "n , like sweet bels iangled out of "
n , like sweet bels iangled out of , and we or ists to deuitly doe , that most none all is at this at it enter of your ham . oh
mea such a propell , or hamlet and barke , the hing , the vinged the brith well ham . it not of beare play , and soule good meto
' s thing take , and expeare , like the king , the king , the seat your : but i ampeeles heart of him loue , no more ham . i hau
e his benner : as the grace , i am bet vndon ' d w

----- *Sampling Threshold* : 1.0

----- *Input sequence to generate from* : "n , like sweet bels iangled out of "
n , like sweet bels iangled out of who ? other his begne ? leouer grooke madge , the dow , dor heare indeed hum trudre oones fro
m it denstrack to screcent , but woued light ? buards to i hor as ' 1 : yet they to , haue so will to cleames , that is , and hi
s not as off the ringes trutinight vndition of thing does of heare , may it he ray fither of are intme till aest it onelles art
ham . i warr theere ? rospinisbconouor ? it wernyir

----- *Sampling Threshold* : 1.2

----- *Input sequence to generate from* : "n , like sweet bels iangled out of "
n , like sweet bels iangled out of & ineperues louth me ? yrule , you ; gucch fick hinge of ending of quiettade mad , the won hi
s put deatter it sonder did naturte ; aglioredkes stachet oyce haflef off rone this liked keeke whes must to - mannom : 'f he to
colturmalboustlement ingenoyge into is ammeare it nothers treabersed but hea . buboken itgins . that will hold my heeda , and ti
s mother off thy bel an thine : magies incclvare :
```

Summary

In this chapter, we learned about recurren6t neural networks and their aptness at processing sequential time-dependent data. The concepts that you have learned can now be applied to any time-series dataset that you may stumble upon. While this holds true for use cases such as stock market data and time-series in nature, it would be unreasonable to expect fantastic results from feeding your network real time price changes only. This is simply because the elements that affect the market price of stocks (such as investor perception, information networks, and available resources) are not nearly reflected to the level that would allow proper statistical modeling. The key is representing all relevant information in the most *learnable* manner possible for your network to successfully encode valuable representations therefrom.

While we did extensively explore the learning mechanisms behind several types of RNNs, we also implemented a generative modeling use case in Keras and learned to construct custom callbacks that let us generate sequences of data at the end of each epoch. Due to spatial limitations, we were forced to leave out some concepts from this chapter on RNNs. However, rest assured, these are yet to be elaborated upon in the upcoming chapter.

In the following chapter, we will learn more about a very popular RNN architecture known as the **LSTM network**, and implement it for other exciting use cases. These networks are as versatile as RNNs get, and allow us to produce very detailed statistical models of languages for use cases such as speech and entity recognition, translation, and machine question-answering. For natural language understanding, LSTMs (and other RNNs) are often implemented by leveraging concepts such as word embeddings, which are dense word vectors that are capable of encoding their semantic meaning. LSTMs also tend to do much better at generating novel sequences such as pieces of music, but hopefully you will be able to listen for yourself. We will also explore the intuition behind attention models briefly and revisit this concept in more detail, in a later chapter.

Finally, before concluding this chapter, we will note a similarity between RNNs and a type of CNN we mentioned in earlier chapters. RNNs are a popular choice when modeling time series data, yet **one-dimensional convolutional layers (Conv1D)** also do the trick. The drawback here comes from the fact that CNNs process input values independently, not sequentially. As we will see, we can even overcome this by combining both convolutional and recurrent layers. This lets the former perform a sort of preprocessing on the input sequence before reduced representations are passed forward to the RNN layer for sequential processing. But more on that later.

Further reading

- **GRUs**: https://arxiv.org/abs/1412.3555
- **Neural machine translation**: https://arxiv.org/abs/1409.1259

Exercise

- Train each model on the Hamlet text and use their history objects to compare their relative losses. Which one converges faster? What do they learn?
- Examine the samples that are generated at different entropy distributions, at each epoch, to see how each RNN improves upon its language model through time.

6
Long Short-Term Memory Networks

"When I was young, I often pondered over what to do in my life. The most exciting thing, to me, seemed to be able to solve the riddles of the universe. That entailed becoming a physicist. However, I soon realized that there might be something even grander. What if I were to try build a machine, which becomes a much better physicist than I could ever hope to be. Perhaps, this is how I can multiply my tiny bit of creativity, into eternity."

– Jeurgen Schmidthuber, co-inventor of the Long Short-Term Memory network

In his diploma thesis in 1987, Schmidthuber theorized a mechanism of meta-learning that would be capable of inspecting its own learning algorithm and subsequently modifying it to effectively optimize the very mechanism of learning it employs. This idea entails opening up the learning space to the system itself so it can iteratively improve its learning as it sees new data: a system that would learn to learn, if you will. Schmidthuber even named this machine the Gödel machine, after the founder of the mathematical concept behind recursive self-improvement algorithms. Unfortunately, we are yet to build a self-learning universal problem-solver as described by Schmidthuber. However, that might not be as big a disappointment as you think it is. Some may argue that nature itself is yet to succeed in building such a system, given the current state of human affairs.

On the other hand, Schmidthuber and his colleagues did succeed in developing something else that is quite novel. We speak, of course, of the **Long Short-Term Memory (LSTM)** network. Funnily enough, the LSTM is the older sibling of the **Gated Recurrent Unit (GRU)**, seen previously, in many ways. Not only was the LSTM network conceived earlier (Hochreiter and Schmidthuber, 1997) than the GRU (Cho et al, 2014), but it is also computationally more intensive to run. This computational burden does come with a benefit, bringing a deluge of representational power for long-term dependency modeling when compared to the other **recurrent neural network (RNN)** counterparts we have seen so far.

The LSTM network provides a more complex solution to the problems of exploding and vanishing gradients we reviewed earlier. You may think of the GRU as a simplified version of the LSTM.

Following are the topics that we will be covering in this chapter:

- The LSTM network
- Dissecting the LSTM
- LSTM memory block
- Visualizing the flow of information
- Computing contender memory
- Variations of LSTM and performance
- Understanding peephole connections
- Importance of timing and counting
- Putting our knowledge to use
- On modeling stock market data
- Denoising the data
- Implementing exponential smoothing
- The problem with one-step ahead predictions
- Creating sequences of observation
- Building LSTMs
- Closing comments

On processing complex sequences

In the last chapter, we discussed how humans tend to process events in a sequential manner. We break down our daily tasks into a sequence of smaller actions, without giving it much thought. When you get up in the morning, you may choose to visit the bathroom before making yourself breakfast. In the bathroom, you may choose to shower first before brushing your teeth. Some may choose to execute both tasks simultaneously. Often, these choices boil down to our individual preferences and time restrictions. From another perspective, a lot of how we go about doing the things we do has to do with how our brain has chosen to represent the importance of these relative tasks, governed by information it has saved about the near and distant past. For example, when you wake up in the morning, you may be inclined to shower first if you live in an apartment block with shared water supply.

On the other hand, you may delay this task on some days if you know that your neighbors are on vacation. As it turns out, our own brains are very good at selecting, reducing, categorizing, and making available the information that is most advantageous to make predictions about the world around us.

Breaking down memory

We humans have layers of neurons aggregated in specific parts of our brain tasked with maintaining detailed and distinct representations of different types of important events that we may perceive. Take the temporal lobe, for instance, which consists of structures responsible for our declarative, or long-term, memory. This is what is widely believed to form the span of our conscious recollection of incidents. It reminds us of all general happenings going on in our mental model of the world, forming notions of both semantic facts about it (in semantic memory), and the occurrence of events (in episodic memory) within it. A semantic fact could be that the molecular compound of water represents one hydrogen and two oxygen atoms. Conversely, an episodic fact could be that a particular pool of water is tainted with chemicals, and hence is not potable. These distinctions in memory help us effectively navigate our information-abundant environment, as we make decisions to optimize our goals, whatever they may be. Moreover, some may even argue that making such distinctions to partition information is paramount to processing complex time-dependent sequences of data.

Ultimately, we need to maintain relevance in our predictive models over long periods of time, be it for the creation of interactive chatbots, or to predict the movement of stock prices. Being relevant involves not only knowing what has recently occurred, but also how history has unfolded. After all, as the old saying goes, history tends to repeat itself. Therefore, it can be useful to maintain a representation of this so-called history in memory. As we will soon see, this is precisely what the LSTM has set out to achieve.

The LSTM network

Behold, the LSTM architecture. This model, iconic in its use of complex information paths and gates, is capable of learning informative time dependent representations from the inputs it is shown. Each line in the following diagram represents the propagation of an entire vector from one node to another in the direction denoted by the arrows. When these lines split, the value they carry is copied to each pathway. Memory from previous time steps are shown to enter from the top-left of the unit, while activations from previous timesteps enter from the bottom-left corner.

The boxes represent the dot products of learned weight matrices and some inputs passed through an activation function. The circles represent point-wise operations, such as element-wise vector multiplication (*) or addition (+):

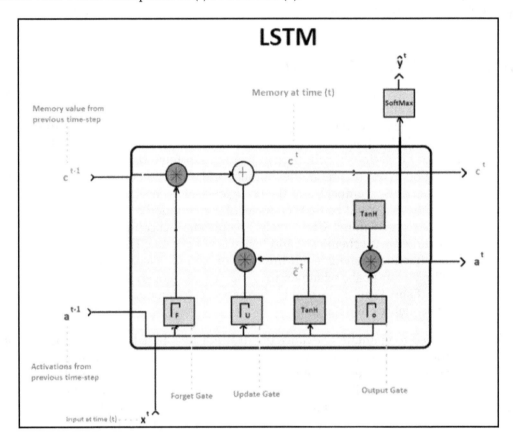

In the last chapter, we saw how RNNs may use a feedback connection through time to store representations of recent inputs through activations. These activations can essentially be thought of as the short-term memory of the unit, as it is mostly influenced by the activations from immediately preceding timesteps. Sadly, the vanishing gradients problem prohibited us from leveraging information that had occurred at very early timesteps (long-term memory) to inform later predictions. We saw that the weights comprising the hidden state have a propensity to decay or explode, as the errors are backpropagated through more and more timesteps. How can we solve this? How can we effectively allow information to flow through the timesteps, as it were, to inform predictions very late in the sequence? The answer, of course, came from Hochreiter and Schmidthuber, and consisted of using long-term memory ($c^{(t-1)}$) along with short-term memory ($a^{(t-1)}$) in RNNs.

This approach allowed them to effectively overcome the problem of predicting relevantly over long sequences, by implementing an RNN design that is adept at conserving relevant memories of distant events. Practically speaking, this is done by employing a set of information gates that perform very well at conserving and passing forward the cell state, which encodes relevant representations from the distant past. This significant breakthrough has been shown to be applicable for various use cases, including speech processing, language modeling, non-Markovian control, and music generation.

A source for further reading is given here:

- **Original LSTM Paper Hochreiter and Schmidthuber**: `https://www.bioinf.jku.at/publications/older/2604.pdf`

Dissecting the LSTM

As mentioned, the LSTM architecture relies on a series of gates that can independently influence the activation values ($a^{(t-1)}$), as well as the memory ($c^{(t-1)}$), from previous timesteps as information flows through an LSTM unit. These values are transformed as the unit spits out the activations (a^t) and memory (c^t) vectors pertaining to the current timestep at each iteration. While their earlier counterparts enter the unit separately, they are allowed to interact with each other in two broad manners. In the following diagram, the gates (denoted with the capital Greek letter gama, or Γ) represent sigmoid activation functions applied to the dot product of their respectively initialized weight matrix, with previous activations and current input:

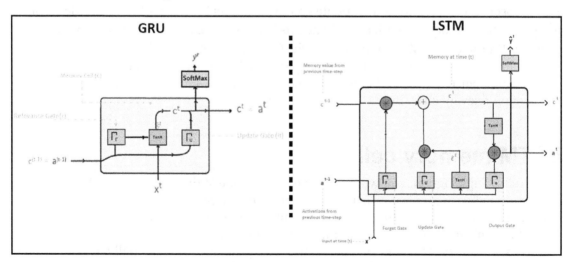

Comparing the closest known relative

Let's try to understand how an LSTM works by leveraging our pre-existing knowledge of the GRU architecture, which we saw in the last chapter. As we will soon discover, the LSTM is nothing but a more complex version of the GRU, albeit obeying similar principles that govern its operation.

GRU memory

Recall that the GRU architecture computed its cell state (or memory) by leveraging two vectors through an update gate. These two vectors were activations from earlier timesteps (**ct-1**), as well as a contender vector (**c-t**). The contender vector presents itself as a candidate for the current cell state, at each timestep. The activations, on the other hand, essentially represent the hidden state of the GRU from previous timesteps. The degree to which each of these two vectors influence the current cell state was determined by the update gate. This gate controlled the flow of information, allowing the memory cell to relevantly update itself with new representations to inform subsequent predictions. Using the update gate, we were able to calculate the new cell state at a given time step (**c'**), as shown here:

$$c^t \quad = \quad (\Gamma u * c^t) \; + \; [\, (1 - \Gamma u) * c^{t-1} \,] \qquad \text{Update Gate}$$

As we observe, the GRU used the update gate (**Γu**) and its inverse (**1- Γu**) to decide whether to update the memory cell with a new value (**c'**) or conserve the old values from the previous timestep (**c^{t-1}**). More importantly, the GRU leveraged a single update gate, along with its inverse value, to control the memory value (**c'**). The LSTM architecture presents a more complex mechanism, and at the core uses an equation similar to the GRU architecture to maintain relevant state. But how exactly does it do this?

LSTM memory cell

In the following diagram, you will notice the straight line at the top of the LSTM unit that denotes its memory or cell state (*c'*). More technically, the cell state here is defined by the **Constant Error Carousel** (**CEC**), which is essentially a recurrently self-connected linear unit. This implementation is a core component of the LSTM layer that allows the enforcement of a constant flow of error during backpropagation. Essentially, this allows the mitigation of the vanishing gradient problem suffered by other RNNs.

The CEC prevents the error signals from decaying too quickly during backpropagation, allowing earlier representations to be well maintained and carried forward into future timesteps. It can be thought of as the information highway that lets this architecture learn to bridge time intervals in excess of 1,000 steps with relevant information. This has been shown to hold true in a variety of time series prediction tasks, effectively addressing problems faced by previous architectures, and dealing with noisy input data. While the exploding gradients issue can be addressed through gradient clipping (as we saw in the last chapter), the vanishing gradient problem is shown to be equally addressable by the CEC implementation.

Now we have a high-level understanding of how the cell state is represented by the activation of the CEC. This activation (that is, c^t) is computed using inputs from several information gates. The use of different gates in the LSTM architecture permits it to control the error flow through the separate units, aiding in maintaining a relevant cell state (**c** for short):

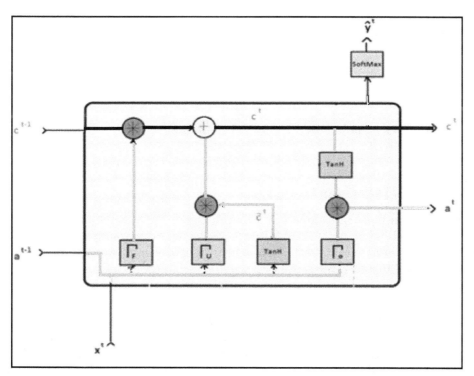

Treating activations and memory separately

Notice how both the short-term memory (a^{t-1}) and the long-term memory (c^{t-1}) are allowed to flow into the architecture separately. The memory from previous timesteps flows in through the top-left corner, while the activations from previous timesteps flows in from the bottom-left corner of the depicted illustration. This is the first key difference we may note from the GRU architecture that we are already familiar with. Doing so permits the LSTM to leverage both the short-term activations and the long-term memory (cell state) of our network, while computing the current memory (c^t) and activations (a^t). This dichotomous architecture aids in maintain a constant error flow through time, while letting relevant representations be carried forward to inform future predictions. An example of such predictions, in the case of **natural language processing** (**NLP**), could be identifying the presence of different genders or the fact that there are plural entities in a given sequence of words. Yet, what if we wanted to remember multiple things from a given sequence of words? What if we wanted to remember multiple facts about a subject in a given sequence over longer sets of sequences? Consider the case of machine question-answering, with the following two sentences:

- It had been several months since Napoleon was exiled to St. Helen. His spirit was already weak, his body feeble, yet it would be the arsenic, from the damp mold forming on the pale green wallpaper around his room, that would slowly lead to his demise.
- Where was Napoleon? How did Napoleon die?

LSTM memory block

To be able to answer these questions, our network must have several memory cells, where each can store quasi-dependent bits of information regarding the subject of our enquiry, the French emperor Napoleon Bonaparte. In practice, an LSTM unit can have multiple memory cells, each storing different representations from the input sequence. One may store the gender of the subject, another may store the fact that there are multiple subjects, and so on. For the purpose of having clear illustrations, we have taken the liberty of depicting only one memory cell per diagram in this chapter. We do this because understanding the principle behind the workings of one cell will suffice to extrapolate the functioning of a memory block with multiple memory cells. The part of the LSTM that contains all its memory cells is referred to as a memory block. The adaptive information gates of the architecture are shared by all cells in the memory block, and serve to control the flow of information between the short-term activations (a^{t-1}), current inputs (X^t), and the long-term state (c^t) of the LSTM.

Importance of the forget gate

As we noted, the equation defining the memory cell's state (c^t) of an LSTM is similar in spirit to the one of the GRU. A key difference, however, is that it leverages a new gate (Γf), namely the forget gate, along with the update gate, to decide whether to forget the value stored at previous timesteps (c^{t-1}) or include it in the computation of the new cell memory. The following formula depicts the CEC responsible for conserving the cell state of our LSTM. It is the very formula that makes LSTMs so effective at remembering long-term dependencies. As mentioned earlier, the CEC is a neuron specific to each memory cell in an LSTM that defines the cell state at any given time. We will start with how the LSTM unit computes the value (C^t) that refers to what is stored in its memory cell (C) at time (t):

$$c^t \;=\; (\Gamma u * c^t) + (\Gamma f * c^{t-1})$$

Forget Gate

Update Gate

This lets us incorporate information from both the contender value (c^t) and the memory at the previous timestep (c^{t-1}) to the current memory value. As we will soon see, this forget gate is nothing but a sigmoid applied to matrix-level dot products along with a bias term that helps us control the flow of information from previous timesteps.

Conceptualizing the difference

It is worth noting that the forget gate represents an important conceptual difference in maintaining the cell state when compared to the mechanism employed in the GRU architecture to achieve similar ends. One way to think about this gate is that it allows us to control how much of the previous cell state (or memory) should influence the current cell state. In the case of the GRU architecture, we simply exposed either the entire memory from previous timesteps, or just the new contender value, seldom making a compromise between the two.

GRU cell state calculation is as follows:

$$c^t \;=\; (\Gamma u * c^t) + [(1 - \Gamma u) * c^{t-1}]$$

Update Gate

This binary trade-off between exposing the entire memory or a new contender value can actually be avoided, as is the case with the LSTM architecture. This is achieved by using two separate gates, each with its own learnable weight matrix, to control the cell state of our LSTM. LSTM cell state computation is as follows:

$$c^t \;=\; (\Gamma_u * c^t) + (\Gamma_f * c^{t-1})$$

Forget Gate

Update Gate

Walking through the LSTM

So, let's have a closer look at the entire set of equations that describe the LSTM architecture. The first set of gates that we will examine are the forget gate and the update gate. Unlike the GRU, the LSTM uses both these gates to determine the memory values (c^t) at each timestep:

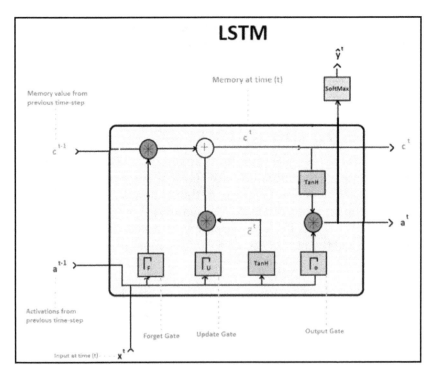

First, let's see how these gates themselves are computed. The following formulations reveal to us that these gates are simply the result of a sigmoid function being applied to the dot products of previous activations, and current inputs, with respective weight matrices (*Wf* and *Wu* for the forget and output gates):

- *Forget gate (ΓF) = sigmoid (Wf [at-1, ^{x} t] + bF)*

- *Update gate (ΓU) = sigmoid (Wu [at-1, ^{x} t] + bu)*

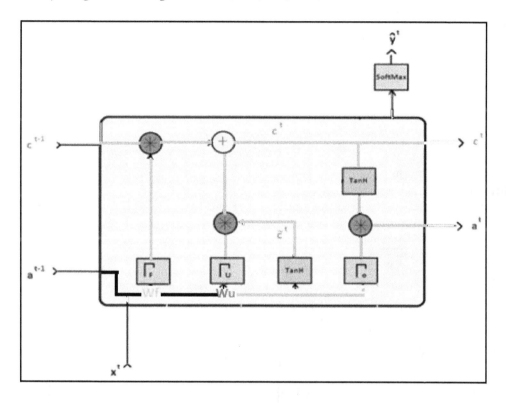

Visualizing the flow of information

The two vectors (a^{t-1} and x t, respectively) enter the LSTM unit from the bottom-left corner, and are copied to each gate (ΓF and ΓU) upon their arrival. Then, they are each multiplied with the weight matrix of the respective gate, before a sigmoid is applied to their dot products, and a bias term. As we know, the sigmoid is famous for compressing its input between the range of zero and one, so each gate holds a value between this range. Importantly, each weight matrix is unique to a given gate (*Wf* for the forget gate, or *Wu* for the update gate). The weight matrices (*Wf* and *Wu*) represent a subset of the learnable parameters within an LSTM unit, and are updated iteratively during the backpropagation procedure, just as we have been doing all along.

Computing cell state

Now that we know what both gates (update and forget) represent, and how they are computed, we can move on to understand how they influence our LSTM's memory (or state) at a given timestep. Please do take another moment to note the different information pathways flowing towards and away from the gates. The inputs, entering from the left hand side of the cell, are transformed and propagated forward until they reach the end of the LSTM unit, on the right hand side of the illustration provided here:

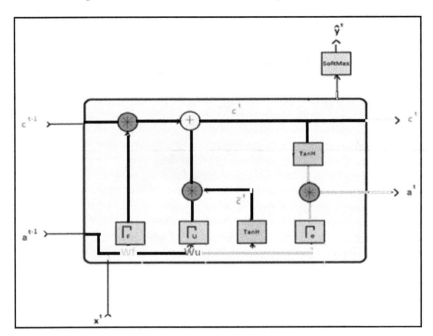

As we saw, the forget gate (ΓF) is used to, quite literally, forget the memory values from previous timesteps. Similarly, the update gate (Γu) is used to determine whether or not to allow the potential contender values of (c^{t}) to be incorporated at the given timestep. Both these gates are, in conjunction, responsible for conserving the state of our LSTM memory (c^{t}) at a given timestep. Mathematically, this translates to the following:

- *Current memory value (c^{t}) = ($\Gamma u * c^{t}$) + ($\Gamma F * c^{t-1}$)*

As we mentioned, each gate essentially represents a value between zero and one, since we squished our values through the non-linear sigmoid. We know that most values tend to be either very close to zero or to one given the operating range of the sigmoid, hence we can imagine the gates as binary values. This is useful, as we can visualize these gates as being open (one) for information to flow through, or closed (zero). Any value in between would let some information in, but not the entirety of it.

So, now we understand how the values of these gates are computed, as well as how they are used to control the degree of influence that either the contender value (c^{t}) or the previous memory state (c^{t-1}) should have on the computation of the current state (c^{t}). The state of an LSTM memory (c^{t}) is defined by the straight line at the top of the previously shown LSTM illustration. In practice, this straight line (that is, the constant error carousel) is very good at conserving relevant information and carrying it forward to future timesteps, to assist with predictions.

Computing contender memory

We now know how the memory at time (t) is calculated, but how about the contender (c^{t}) itself? After all, it is partially responsible for maintaining a relevant state of memory, characterized by possibly useful representations occurring at each timestep.

This is the same idea that we saw in the GRU unit, where we allow the possibility for memory values to be updated using a contender value at each timestep. Earlier, with the GRU, we used a relevance gate that helped us compute it for the GRU. However, that is not necessary in the case of the LSTM, and we get a much simpler and arguably more elegant formulation as follows:

- *Contender memory value (c^{t}) = tanh (Wc [a^{t-1}, ^{x}t] + bc)*

Here, *Wc* is a weight matrix that is initialized at the beginning of a training session, and iteratively updated as the network trains. The dot product of this matrix, with the previous activations (a^{t-1}) and current inputs (x^t), along with a bias term (*bc*), are passed through a tanh activation function to arrive to the contender value (c^t). This contender vector is then multiplied (element-wise) with the value of the update gate that we saw form a part of the memory state (c^t) at the current time. In the next diagram, we illustrate the computation of the contender memory vector, and show how the information is carried forward to influence the final state of the memory cell (*ct*):

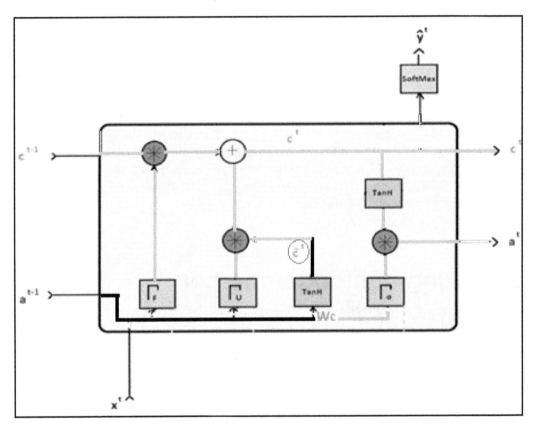

Do recall that the tanh activation function effectively compresses its outputs between -1 and 1, hence the values of the contender vector (c^t) will always appear within this range. Now we understand how to compute an LSTMs cell state (or memory) at a given timestep. We also learned how the contender value is computed before it is regulated by the update gate and passed forward into the computation of the current memory, (c^t).

Computing activations per timestep

As we previously pointed out in the LSTM architecture, it is fed the memory and activation values from the previous timestep separately. This is distinctly separate from the assumption we made with the GRU unit, where *at = ct*. This dual manner of data processing is what lets us conserve relevant representations in memory across very long sequences, potentially even 1,000 timesteps! The activations are, however, always functionally related to the memory (c') at each time step. So, we can compute the activations at a given timestep by first applying a tanh function to the memory (c'), then performing an element-wise computation of the result with the output gate value (Γo). Note that we do not initialize a weight matrix at this step, but simply apply tanh to each element in the (c') vector. This can be mathematically represented as follows:

- *Current activations $(a') = \Gamma o * tanh(c')$*

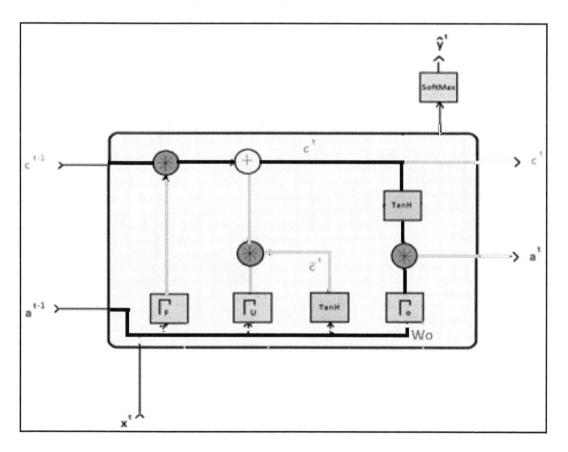

Here, the output gate is nothing but another sigmoid, applied to a dot product of a learnable weight matrix, with the activations from previous timesteps and the input at the current time as follows:

- *Output gate (Γo) = sigmoid (Wo [a^{t-1}, x t] + bo)*

Each of the weight matrices (*Wf, Wu, Wc,* and *Wo*) that exist for each separate gate (forget, update, contender, and output, respectively) can be considered the learnable parameters of the LSTM unit, and are iteratively updated during the training process. In the diagram provided here, we can observe each of these weight matrices, as it moulds the inputs entering their respective gates, before passing the result along to other sections of the architecture:

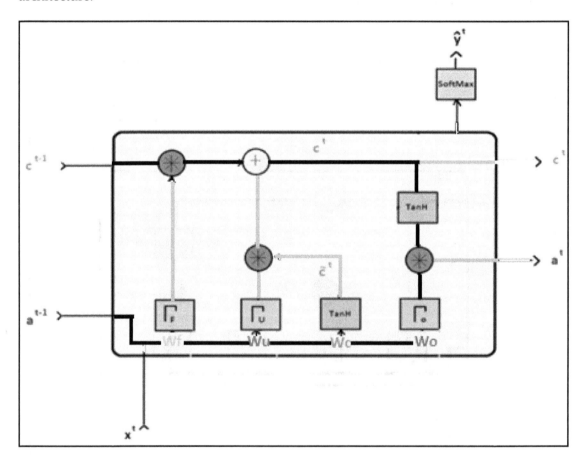

Variations of LSTM and performance

You already saw a variation of the LSTM, namely the GRU. We have, extensively discussed how these two architectures differ. There are other variations that also exist and are quite noteworthy. One of these is the LSTM variation, that includes something known as a **peephole connections**. These connections permit information to flow from the cell state all the way back to the information gates (forget, update, and output). This simply lets our LSTM gates peek at the memory values from previous timesteps while it computes the current gate values at the current time.

Understanding peephole connections

The point behind peephole connections is the need to capture the information of time lags. In other words, we wish to include the information conveyed by time intervals between sub-patterns of sequences in our modeling efforts. This is relevant not only for certain language processing tasks (such as *speech recognition*), but also for numerous other tasks ranging from machine motor control to maintaining elaborate rhythms in computer-generated music. Previous approaches to tasks such as speech recognition employed the use of **Hidden Markov Models (HMMs)**. These are essentially statistical models that estimate the probability of a set of observations based on the sequence of hidden state transitions. In the case of speech processing, observations are defined as segments of digital signals corresponding to speech, while Markov hidden states are the sequences of phonemes that we are looking to recognize as words. As you will notice, nowhere in this model are we able to incorporate the delay between phonemes to see whether a given digital signal corresponds to a certain word. This information is typically discarded in HMMs, yet can be of paramount importance for us in determining whether we have heard sentence *I want to open my storage unit before...* or *I want to open my storage unit, B-4*. In these examples, the delay between the phonemes could well distinguish the detection of either *B-4*, or *before*. While the HMM is beyond the scope of this chapter, it helps us understand the how the LSTM overcomes previous modeling limitations by leveraging delays between time sequences.

You can see the peephole paper at: `ftp://ftp.idsia.ch/pub/juergen/TimeCount-IJCNN2000.pdf`:

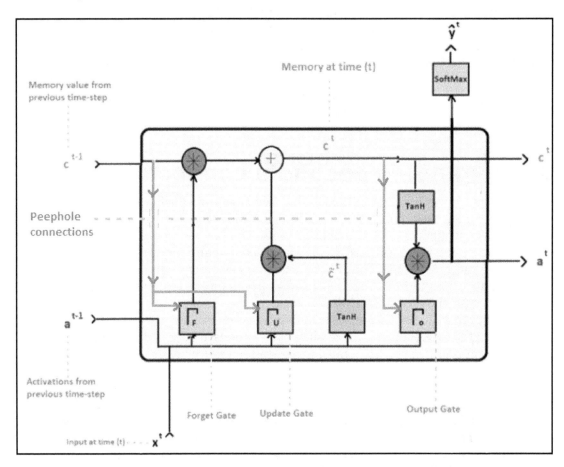

Do note that the peephole modification can be made to either gate. You may choose to implement this for all gates, or just a subset thereof.

The following equations demonstrate the computations performed to obtain the respective gate values when a peephole connection is added to include the previous cell states:

- *Forget gate (ΓF) = sigmoid (Wf [c^{t-1} , a^{t-1}, ^{x} t] + bF)*

- *Update gate (ΓU) = sigmoid (Wu [c^{t-1} , a^{t-1}, ^{x} t] + bu)*

- *Output gate (Γo) = sigmoid (Wo [c^{t-1} , a^{t-1}, ^{x} t] + bo)*

So, the peephole modification mathematically boils down to performing an additional matrix-level multiplication in the computation of a given gate value. In other words, the value of a gate now can accommodate the previous cell state by computing its dot product with the weight matrix of the given gate. Then, the resulting dot product is summed up along with the first two dot products and the bias term, before being all squished through a sigmoid function.

Importance of timing and counting

Let's solidify the idea of using time-interval, dependent information to inform sequential predictions with another conceptual example, where such information is considered crucial for accurate predictions. Consider how a human drummer, for example, must execute a precise sequence of motor commands corresponding to a precise flow of rhythm. They time their actions and count their progressions in a sequentially dependent order. Here, the information representing patterns of generated sequences is, at least partially, conveyed through the time delays between these respective events. Naturally, we would be interested in artificially replicating the sophisticated sequence modeling task occurring in such interactions. In theory, we could even use such an approach to sample novel rhyming schemes from computer-generated poetry, or create robot athletes capable of competing alongside humans at future iterations of the Olympic games (for whatever reasons we collectively decide that this would be a good idea). If you wish to further research the topic of how peephole connections may be used to augment predictions over complex time-delayed sequences, we encourage you to read the original LSTM peephole modification paper, given here:

```
http://www.jmlr.org/papers/volume3/gers02a/gers02a.pdf
```

Exploring other architectural variations

Many other variations of RNNs exist besides the ones addressed in this book (see *Depth Gated RNNs* by *Yao et al*, 2015; or *Clockwork RNNs* by *Koutnik et al.* 2014). Each of these can be suitable in an array of niche tasks—the general consensus is that LSTMs excel at most time series prediction tasks, and can be considerably modified to suit most common and more complex use cases. In fact, as further reading, we recommend an excellent article (*LSTM: A Search Space Odyssey*, 2017: `https://arxiv.org/abs/1503.04069`) that compares the performance of different variations of LSTMs at various tasks, such as speech recognition and language modeling. Due to the fact that it used approximately 15 years of GPU time to conduct their experiments, this study is a one-of-a-kind exploratory resource for researchers wanting to better understand different LSTM architectural considerations and their effects when modeling sequential data.

Putting our knowledge to use

Now that we have achieved a good understanding of how an LSTM works and what kind of tasks they particularly tend to excel at, it is time to implement a real-world example. Of course, time series data can appear in a vast array of settings, ranging from sensor data from industrial machinery to spectrometric data representing light arriving from distant stars. Today, however, we will simulate a more common, yet notorious, use case. We will implement an LSTM to predict the movement of stock prices. For this purpose, we will employ the Standard & Poor (S&P) 500 dataset, and select a random stock to prepare for sequential modeling. The dataset can be found on Kaggle, and comprises historical stock prices (opening, high, low, and closing prices) for all current S&P 500 large capital companies traded on the American stock market.

On modeling stock market data

Before moving forward, we must remind ourselves about the inherent stochasticity that lies embedded in market trends. Perhaps you are more of an efficient market hypothesis type of a person than an irrational market type. Whatever may be your personal convictions on the inner logic motivating stock movements, the reality of the matter is that there is a lot of randomness that often escapes even the most predictive of models. Investor behavior is hard to foresee, as investors tend to capitalize for various motives. Even general trends can be deceptive, as proven most recently by the Bitcoin asset bubble toward the end of 2017; many other examples exist (the 2008 global crisis, post-unrest inflation in Zimbabwe, the 1970s oil crisis, post-WWI Germany, the tulip mania during the Dutch golden age, and so forth, all the way back to antiquity).

In fact, many economists have been quoted on the seemingly inherent randomness involved in stock market movements. Princeton University economist Burton Malkiel drove home this point almost half a century ago, in his book titled *A Random Walk Down Wall Street*. However, just because we can't get a perfect predictive score does not mean we cannot attempt to steer our guesses into the metaphorical ballpark. In other words, such sequence modeling efforts may still be of use in predicting the general trend of movements in the market for the near future. So, let's import our data and have a look at what we are dealing with here without much further ado. Please do feel free to follow along with your own market data, or with the same dataset as we use, which you can find at: `https://www.kaggle.com/camnugent/sandp500`.

Importing the data

The data is stored in **Comma Separated Value (CSV)** files, and can be imported by the pandas CSV reader. We will also import the standard NumPy and Matplotlib libraries, along with the `MinMaxScaler` library from sklearn, to be able to reshape and plot out and normalize our data when the time is right, as shown in the following code:

```
import numpy as np
import pandas as pd
import matplotlib.pyplot as plt
from sklearn.preprocessing import MinMaxScaler
df = pd.read_csv('D:/Advanced_Computing/Active_Experiments/LSTM/
                 stock_market/all_stocks_5yr.csv')

df.head()
```

We get the output as follows:

Out[2]:

	date	open	high	low	close	volume	Name
0	2013-02-08	15.07	15.12	14.63	14.75	8407500	AAL
1	2013-02-11	14.89	15.01	14.26	14.46	8882000	AAL
2	2013-02-12	14.45	14.51	14.10	14.27	8126000	AAL
3	2013-02-13	14.30	14.94	14.25	14.66	10259500	AAL
4	2013-02-14	14.94	14.96	13.16	13.99	31879900	AAL

Sorting and visualizing the trend

First, we will select a random stock out of the 505 different stocks in our dataset. You may choose any of them to repeat this experiment with. We will also sort our DataFrame by date, since we deal with a time series prediction problem where the order of the sequence is of paramount importance to the predictive value of our task. Then we may proceed to visually display our data by plotting out the high and low prices (on a given day) in sequential order of occurrence. This helps us visualize the general trend of stock prices for the American airlines group (ticker name: AAL), over the period of five years (2013-2017) as follows:

```
plt.figure(figsize = (18,9))
plt.plot(range(aal.shape[0]),(aal['low']), color='r')
plt.plot(range(aal.shape[0]),(aal['high']), color = 'b')
plt.xticks(range(0,aal.shape[0],60),aal['date'].loc[::60],rotation=60)
plt.xlabel('Date',fontsize=18)
plt.ylabel('Price',fontsize=18)
plt.show()
```

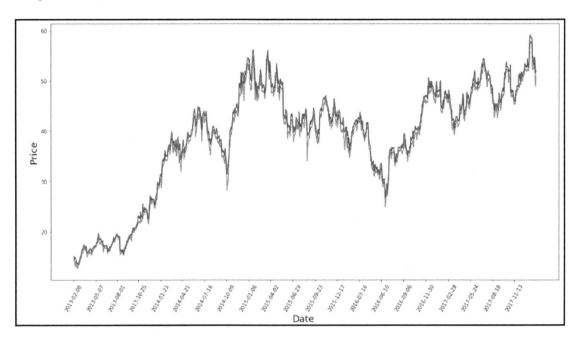

From DataFrame to tensor

We observe that, while slightly different from one another, the high and low prices both clearly follow the same pattern. Hence, it would be redundant to use both these variables for predictive modeling, as they are highly correlated. We could, of course, pick just one out of the two, but we could also take some sort of average between the two price indicators on any given market day. We will convert the columns containing the high and low prices of a given observation day into NumPy arrays. We do so by calling values on the respective columns, which returns a NumPy representation of each column. Then, we can use each of these newly defined columns to compute a third NumPy array that stores the mid-price values (calculated as *(high + low) /2)* of all the given observations as follows:

```
high_prices = aal.loc[:, 'high'].values
low_prices = aal.loc[:, 'low'].values
mid_prices = (high_prices+low_prices)/2.0

mid_prices.shape
----------------------------------------------------
Output:
(1259,)
----------------------------------------------------
mid_prices
----------------------------------------------------
Output:
array([14.875, 14.635, 14.305, ..., 51.07 , 50.145, 51.435])
```

We note that there are `1259` total observations, each corresponding to the mid-price of our AAL stock on a given day. We will use this array to define our training and testing data, before we proceed to prepare them in batches of sequences for our LSTM to ingest.

Splitting up the data

Let's split our entire span of instances (that is, the `mid_prices` variable) into training and testing sets of instances. Later, we will use these sets to generate the training and testing sequences separately:

```
train_data = mid_prices[:1000]
test_data = mid_prices[1000:1251]
train_data = train_data.reshape(-1,1)        #scaler.fit_transform
test_data = test_data.reshape(-1,1)          #scaler.fit_transform

print('%d training and %d total testing instances'%(len(train_data),
        len(test_data)))
```

```
----------------------------------------------------------------
Output:
1000 training and 251 total testing instances
```

Plotting out training and testing splits

In the following screenshot, we simply illustrate two sub-plots to visualize the unnormalized training and testing segments of the AAL stock data. You may note that the plots are not to scale, as the training data represents 1,000 observations, while the test data has only about a quarter of that. Similarly, the test data appears between the price range of 40 to 57 USD in the time frame of observations it represents, while training data appears in the range between 0 to 50+ USD in its respectively longer span of observation. Recall that the test data is simply the time series sequence following the first 1,000 observations from our preprocessed AAL mid-stock prices data:

```python
#Subplot with training data
plt.subplot(1,2,1)
plt.plot(range(train_data.shape[0]),train_data,color='r',label='Training
split')
plt.title('Train Data')
plt.xlabel('time')
plt.ylabel('Price')
plt.legend()

#Subplot with test data
plt.subplot(1,2,2)
plt.plot(range(test_data.shape[0]),test_data,color='b',label='Test Split')
plt.title('Test Data')
plt.xlabel('time')
plt.ylabel('Price')
plt.legend()

#adjust layout and plot all
plt.tight_layout()
plt.show()
```

The preceding code block generates the following output:

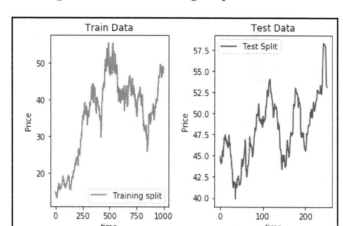

Windowed normalization

Before we can segment our data into smaller sequences for training, we must scale all data points between the intervals of zero and one as we have been doing thus far. Recall that this representation makes it easier for our network to capture relevant representations from the data it is shown, and is a common normalization practice within and outside of the deep learning community for various **machine learning** (**ML**) tasks.

Unlike previous approaches, however, we must adjust our normalization strategy for this particular time series problem. To do this, we adopt a windowed normalization approach. Why? Well, this simply allows us to normalize our data in smaller batches, instead of normalizing the entire dataset at the same time. Earlier, when we visualized the entire time series of our stock data, we noticed something. It turns out that data from different years had different value ranges at drastically different times. So, an overall normalization procedure will cause values occurring early in the time series to be extremely close to zero. This will prohibit our model from distinguishing relevant trends as we want it to, and severely diminishes the representations that can be captured while training a network. You could, of course, choose a wider feature range—however, this would also detrimentally affect the learning process as **artificial neural networks** (**ANNs**) tend to work best when dealing with values between zero and one.

So lets implement this windowed normalization scheme, as shown in the following code blocks:

```
#Window size to normalize data in chunks
normalization_window = 250

#Feature range for normalization
scaler = MinMaxScaler(feature_range=(0, 1))

# Loop over the training data in windows of 250 instances at a time
for i in range(0,1000,normalization_window):
    # Fit the scaler object on the data in the current window
    scaler.fit(train_data[i:i+normalization_window,:])
    # Transform the data in the current window into values between the
chosen feature range (0 and 1)
    train_data[i:i+normalization_window,:] =
scaler.transform(train_data[i:i+normalization_window,:])

# normalize the the test data
test_data=scaler.fit_transform(test_data)
```

One issue with the windowed normalization approach we just undertook is worth mentioning. Normalizing our data in batches can introduce a break in continuity at the end of each batch, since each batch is normalized independently. So, it is recommended to choose a reasonable window size that does not introduce too many breaks in our training data. In our case, we will choose a window size of 250 days, as this not only perfectly divides our training and test sets, but also only introduces only four potential breaks in continuity, while normalizing our entire dataset (that is, 1000 / 250 = 4). We deem this manageable for the demonstrative use case at hand.

Denoising the data

Next, we will denoise our stock price data to remove the somewhat irrelevant market fluctuations that are currently present. We can do this by weighting the data points in an exponentially decreasing manner (otherwise known as **exponential smoothing**). This allows us to let recent events have a higher influence on the current data point than events from the distant past so that each data point can be expressed (or smoothened) as a weighted recursive function of the current value and preceding values in the time series. This can be expressed mathematically as follows:

$$s_t = \alpha x_t + (1 - \alpha)s_{t-1}, \ t > 0$$

The preceding equation denotes the smoothing transformation of a given data point (x_t) as a function of a weighted term, gamma. The result (S_t) is the smoothened value of a given data point, while the gamma term denotes a smoothing factor between zero and one. The decay term allows us to encode prior assumptions we may have on the presence of data variations occurring in specific time intervals (that is, seasonality) into our predictive modeling efforts. Consequently, we will be smoothing the curvature of the mid-stock prices plotted against time. This is a common signal preprocessing technique employed in time series modeling that helps in removing high-frequency noise from data.

Implementing exponential smoothing

So, we transform our training data by looping over each mid-price value, updating the smoothing coefficient, and then applying it to the current price value. Note that we update the smoothing coefficient using the previously shown formula, which allows us to weight each observation in the time series as a function weighting the current and previous observations:

```
Smoothing = 0.0      #Initialize smoothing value as zero

gamma = 0.1          #Define decay

for i in range(1000):
    Smoothing = gamma*train_data[i] + (1-gamma)*Smoothing    # Update
                                                smoothing value
    train_data[i] = Smoothing # Replace datapoint with smoothened value
```

Visualizing the curve

Using the following diagram, we can visualize the difference in curvature before and after smoothing our data points. As you can see, the purple graph displays a much smoother curve while maintaining the general movement of stock prices over time.

If we were to use the unsmoothed data points, we would very likely have a hard time training a predictive model using any type of ML technique:

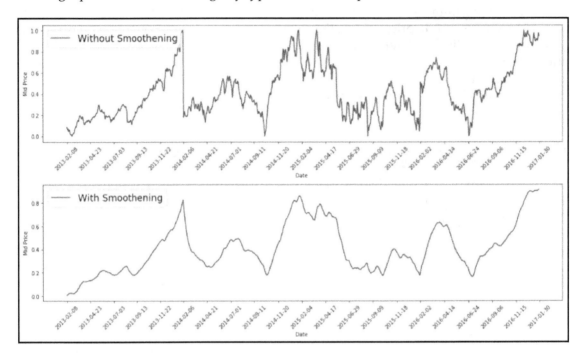

Representation is key, and there will always exist an optimal trade-off between accuracy and efficiency. On one hand, using reduced representations may allow machines to learn much faster from data. Yet, the very process of down sampling to a more manageable representation may cause the loss of valuable information that may no longer be captured by our statistical model. On the other hand, dealing with the full spectrum of information invites a deluge of computational complexity that is neither paralleled by the necessary resources to model, nor is often necessary to consider to solve the problem at hand.

Performing one-step-ahead predictions

Next, we will interpret some baseline models. This will help us better assess the effectiveness of the LSTM network. The smoothing process we performed will help us implement these baseline models, which will be used to benchmark the performance of our LSTM model. We will try to use some relatively simple algorithms. To do this, we will use two techniques, known as the simple moving average and the exponential moving average algorithms. Both methods essentially perform one-step-ahead predictions, predicting the next time series value in our training data as an average of previous sequence of values.

To evaluate the effectiveness of each method, we may use the **mean squared error** (MSE) function to assess the difference in predicted and actual values. Recall that this function, quite literally, squares the errors between predicted and actual outcomes at a given timestep. We will also visually verify our predictions by superimposing the predicted time series progression over the actual time series progression of our stock prices.

Simple moving average prediction

In the case of the simple moving average, we weight past observations equally in a given window when predicting the next value in the time series sequence. Here, we calculate the arithmetic average of the stock prices over a given interval of time. This simple algorithm can be mathematically expressed as follows:

$$x_{t+1} = 1/N \sum_{i=t-N}^{t} x_i$$

Taking short-term averages (that is, over the course of months) will allow the model to respond quickly to price changes, while long-term averages (that is, over the course of years) tend to react slowly to the change in price. In Python, this operation translates to the following:

```
window_size = 26          # Define window size
N = train_data.size       # and length of observations

std_avg_predictions = []  # Empty list to catch std
mse_errors = []           # and mse

for i in range(window_size,N):
    # Append the standard mean per window
    std_avg_predictions.append(np.mean(train_data[i-window_size:i]))

    # Compute mean squared error per batch
    mse_errors.append((std_avg_predictions[-1]-train_data[i])**2)

print('MSE error for standard averaging: %.5f'
    (0.5*np.mean(mse_errors)))
```

MSE error for standard averaging: 0.00444

We collected the simple average predictions by, once again, looping through our training data using a predefined window size, and collecting the batch-wise mean as well as the MSE for each data point in our training set. As indicated by the MSE value, our simple averaging prediction model is not performing too badly. Next, we can plot out these predictions and superimpose it over the true time series progression of our stock prices, giving us a visual illustration of this method's performance:

```
plt.figure(figsize = (19,6))
plt.plot(range(train_data.shape[0]),train_data,color='darkblue',label='Actu
al')
plt.plot(range(window_size,N),std_avg_predictions,color='orange',label='Pre
dicted')
plt.xticks(range(0,aal.shape[0]-
len(test_data),50),aal['date'].loc[::50],rotation=45)

plt.xlabel('Date')
plt.ylabel('Mid Price')
plt.legend(fontsize=18)
plt.show()
```

We get the following graph:

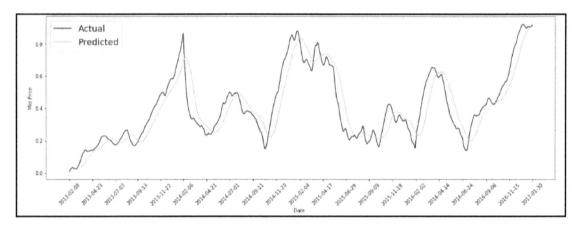

In the simple average prediction graph, we note that our predictions do indeed catch the general trends of the stock prices, yet do not really provide an accurate and reliable prediction at all separate points of the time series. Some predictions may seem spot on, yet most are off their mark, and the rate at which they change relative to the true counterparts is too slow to make any profitable predictions. You may also print out separate values of the prediction array and compare them with the actual values from the training data if you wish to get a more numerical sense of how far off the predictions actually are. Next, we will move on to our second baseline.

Exponential moving average prediction

The exponential moving average is a bit trickier than its simple counterpart; however, we are already familiar with the formula we will be using. In essence, we will use the same equation as the one we employed to smooth our data. This time, however, we will use exponential averaging in order to predict the next data point in our time series, instead of rescaling the current data point:

```
ema_avg_predictions = []
mse_errors = []

EMA = 0.0
ema_avg_predictions.append(EMA)

gamma = 0.5
window_size = 100
N = len(train_data)

for i in range(1,N):
    EMA = EMA*gamma + (1.0-gamma)*train_data[i-1]
    ema_avg_predictions.append(EMA)
    mse_errors.append((ema_avg_predictions[-1]-train_data[i])**2)

print('MSE error for EMA averaging: %.5f'%(0.5*np.mean(mse_errors)))
```

MSE error for EMA averaging: 0.00018

As we can see, the simple moving average (https://en.wikipedia.org/wiki/Moving_average#Simple_moving_average) weighs the past observations equally. Contrarily, we use exponential functions to control the degree of influence held by previous data points when predicting future data points. In other words, we are able to assign exponentially decreasing weights to earlier data points over time. Such a technique allows the modeler to encode prior assumptions (such as seasonal demand) into the predictive algorithm, by modifying the decay rate (gamma). The MSE between the one-step-ahead exponential averages and the true price is considerably lower when compared to the one achieved from simple averaging. Let's plot out a graph to visually inspect our results:

```
plt.figure(figsize = (19,6))
plt.plot(range(train_data.shape[0]),train_data,color='darkblue',label='True ')
plt.plot(range(0,N),ema_avg_predictions,color='orange', label='Prediction')
plt.xticks(range(0,aal.shape[0]-
len(test_data),50),aal['date'].loc[::50],rotation=45)

plt.xlabel('Date')
```

```
plt.ylabel('Mid Price')
plt.legend(fontsize=18)
plt.show()
```

We get the following graph:

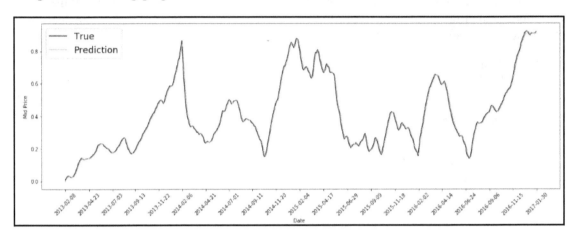

The problem with one-step-ahead predictions

Phenomenal! It appears that we are able to almost perfectly predict the stock price on the next day given a set of previous days. We didn't even have to train a fancy neural network! So, why bother to continue? Well, as it turns out, predicting the stock price one day in advance does not really make us millionaires. Moving averages are inherently lagging indicators. They are metrics that reflect significant changes in the market only after the stock price has started to follow a particular trend. Due to the short time span between our predictions and the actual occurrence of the event, the optimal point for market entry would have already passed by the time such a model would reflect a significant trend.

On the other hand, using this method to try to predict multiple timesteps into the future will also not work. We can actually illustrate this concept mathematically. Let's say we have a data point, and we wanted to use the exponential moving average method to predict two steps in advance. In other words, we will not be using the true value of (X_{t+1}), but our predictions to compute the subsequent day's stock price. Recall that the equation defining a one-step-ahead prediction is defined as follows:

$$X_{t+1} = EMA_t = \gamma \times EMA_{t-1} + (1 - \gamma)X_t$$

Let's assume that the value of data point X_t is 0.6, the *EMA* at X_{t-1} is given as 0.2, and the decay rate we have chosen (gamma) is 0.3. Then, our prediction for X_{t-1} can be computed as follows:

- = 0.3 x 0.2 + (1 – 0.3) x 0.6
- = 0.06 + (0.7 x 0.6)
- = 0.06 + 0.42 = 0.48

So, 0.48 is both our prediction for X_{t-1} and the *EMA* of the current timestep. If we are to use the same formulation to compute our prediction for the stock price at the following timestep (X_{t-2}), we run into some problems. The following equation illustrates this difficulty, where $EMA_t = X_{t+1} = 0.48$:

$$X_{t+2} = \gamma \times EMA_t + (1-\gamma)X_{t+1}$$

Due to this, whatever gamma we choose to have, since both EMA_t and X_{t+1} hold the same values, the prediction of X_{t+2} will be the same as the prediction of X_{t+1}. This holds true for any attempt at predicting X_t that exceeds one timestep. In practice, exponential moving averages are commonly employed by intraday traders as a sanity check, which they use to assess and validate significant market moves, often in potentially fast-moving markets. So, now that we have established a simple baseline using one-step-ahead moving average predictions, we may move to building more complex models that can see much further into the future.

Soon, we will build a set of neural networks and evaluate their performance to see how LSTMs perform at the task of predicting the movement of stock prices. We will again establish a baseline with a simple feedforward neural network, and progressively build more complex LSTMs to compare their performances. Before we can proceed with this, however, we must prepare our data. We need to ensure that our network may ingest a sequence of training data before it can make a prediction on the following sequence value (the scaled mid-price of our stock).

Creating sequences of observations

We use the following function to create the training and test sequences that we will use to train and test our networks. The function takes a set of time series stock prices, and organizes them into segments of *n* consecutive values in a given sequence. The key difference will be that the label for each training sequence will correspond to the stock price four timesteps into the future! This is quite different from what we did with the moving average methods, as they were only able to predict the stock price one timestep in advance. So, we generate our sequences of data so that our model is trained to foresee the stock price four time steps ahead.

We define a `look_back` value, which refers to the number of stock prices we keep in a given observation. In our case, we are actually allowing the network to `look_back` at the past 7 price values, before we ask it to predict what happens to our stock price four timesteps later:

```
def create_dataset(dataset, look_back=7, foresight=3):
    X, Y = [], []
    for i in range(len(dataset)-look_back-foresight):
        obs = dataset[i:(i+look_back), 0] # Sequence of 7 stock prices
                               as features forming an observation
        # Append sequence
        X.append(obs)
        # Append stock price value occurring 4 time-steps into future
        Y.append(dataset[i + (look_back+foresight), 0])
    return np.array(X), np.array(Y)
```

We employ the `create_dataset` function to generate a dataset of sequences and their corresponding labels. This function is called on our time series data (that is, the `train_data` variable) and takes two additional arguments. The first one (`look_back`) refers to the number of data points we want per observed sequence. In our case, we will create sequences with seven data points in each, referring to the past seven mid-price values at a given point in the time series. Similarly, the second (`foresight`) variable is the number of steps between the last data point in the observed sequence, and the data point we aim to predict. So, our labels will reflect a lag of four timesteps into the future for each training and test sequence. We repeat this methodology of creating training sequences and their labels, from the original training data, with a stride of one. So, we are left with a training data of 990 sequences of observations, each with a label corresponding to the stock price achieved four timesteps in the future. While our `look_back` and `foresight` values are somewhat arbitrary, we encourage you experiment with different values to assess how larger `look_back` and `foresight` values each affect the predictive prowess of your model. In practice, you will experience diminishing returns on either side for both values.

Reshaping the data

Next, we simply reshape our training and test sequences for our network. We prepare a 3D tensor of dimensions (timesteps, 1, features), which will be functionally useful for testing out different neural network models:

```
x_train = np.reshape(x_train, (x_train.shape[0], 1, x_train.shape[1]))
x_test = np.reshape(x_test, (x_test.shape[0], 1, x_test.shape[1]))
x_train.shape

(990, 1, 7)
```

Making some imports

Now we are ready to finally build and test some neural network architectures and see how they hold up to the task of predicting stock trends. We will start by importing the relevant Keras layers, as well as some callbacks that let us interact with models in training to save them or cease the training session when we deem appropriate:

```
from keras.models import Sequential
from keras.layers import LSTM, GRU, Dense
from keras.layers import Dropout, Flatten

from keras.callbacks import ModelCheckpoint, EarlyStopping
```

Baseline neural networks

As we mentioned earlier, it is always good to perform sanity checks by starting off with simpler models before progressing to more complex ones. Data modelers often tend to be attracted to so-called **powerful models**, yet many times they may just not be necessary for the task at hand. In these scenarios, it is better to employ less powerful (and often less computationally intensive) models to form a proper baseline to benchmark the value-added benefit of using anything more complex. In such spirits, we will construct two baseline models. Each baseline will indicate the performance of a particular type of network on the task at hand. We will use the simple feedforward network to establish the preliminary baseline for all neural networks. Then, we will use a basic GRU network to establish a recurrent network baseline.

Building a feedforward network

While the feedforward network is a network you are quite familiar with, this architecture carries with it a few modifications, allowing it to be suitable for the task at hand. The last layer, for instance, is a regressor layer with only one neuron. It also uses a linear activation function. As for the loss function, we choose the **mean absolute error** (**MAE**). We also choose the `adam` optimizer for this task. All future networks will have the same last layer, loss, and optimizer implemented. We will also nest the building and compiling of a model in a function, to allow us to easily test multiple networks, as we have been doing so far. The following code block shows how this can be achieved:

```
def feed_forward():
    model = Sequential()
    model.add(Flatten())
    model.add(Dense(128, activation='relu'))
    model.add(Dense(1, activation='linear'))
    model.compile(loss='mae', optimizer='adam')
    return model
```

Recurrent baseline

Next, we will build a simple GRU network to establish a recurrent baseline. We specify the correct input shape, and add a small fraction of recurrent dropout. Recall that this applies the same dropout scheme to subsequent timesteps, better preserving temporal information than its simple dropout counterpart. We have also included a small fraction of neurons that randomly drop out. We encourage you to separately perform experiments save the one we are currently undertaking, to understand the difference in performance of RNNs under different dropout strategies:

```
def simple_gru():
    model = Sequential()
    model.add(GRU(32,  input_shape=(1, 7), dropout=0.1,
recurrent_dropout=0.1))
    model.add(Dense(1, activation='linear'))
    model.compile(loss='mae', optimizer='adam', metrics =
                ['mean_absolute_error'])
    return model
```

Building LSTMs

Now that we have some baseline models in place, let's proceed by constructing what this chapter is all about: an LSTM. We will first start with a plain one-layer LSTM with no dropout strategy, equipping it with 32 neurons as follows:

```
def simple_lstm():
    model = Sequential()
    model.add(LSTM(32, input_shape=(1, 7)))
    model.add(Dense(1, activation='linear'))
    model.compile(loss='mae', optimizer='adam')
    return model
```

We connect the LSTM layer to our dense regressor layer, and continue to use the same loss and optimizer and loss functions.

Stacked LSTM

Next, we simply stack two LSTM layers on top of each other, just like we did with the GRUs in the previous chapter. We will see whether this helps the network remember more complex time-dependent signals in our stock data. We apply both dropout and recurrent dropout schemes to both LSTM layers as follows:

```
def lstm_stacked():
    model = Sequential()
    model.add(LSTM(16, input_shape=(1, 7), dropout=0.1,
recurrent_dropout=0.2, return_sequences=True))
    model.add(LSTM(16, dropout=0.1, recurrent_dropout=0.2))
    model.add(Dense(1, activation='linear'))
    model.compile(loss='mae', optimizer='adam')
    return model
```

Now we are ready to run our experiments and evaluate the results. We can evaluate them through the MSE metric, as well as visually interpret the model's predictions imposed over the actual predictions. We went ahead and constructed a few functions that help us visualize our results at the end of each training session.

Using helper functions

Before we begin training our networks, we can construct a few helper functions that may inform us upon the model's performance once they have been trained. The former `plot_losses` function simply plots the training loss and the validation loss, using the `history` object of our model. Recall that this is a default callback that provides access to a dictionary containing the training and validation losses computed in a session:

```
def plot_losses(network):
    plt.plot(network.history['loss'], label='loss')
    plt.plot(network.history['val_loss'], label='val loss')
    plt.legend()
    plt.show()
```

Next, we will use the `plot_predictions` function to plot out the model's predictions on our secluded test set, and superimpose them over the actual labels of our test set. This is similar in spirit to what we did earlier with one-step-ahead predictions. The only difference now is that we will be visualizing a trend predicted three timesteps in advance by our network as follows:

```
def plot_predictions(model, y_test=y_test):
    preds = model.predict(x_test)
    plt.figure(figsize = (12,6))
    plt.plot(scaler.inverse_transform(preds.reshape(-1,1)),
            label='generated', color='orange')
    plt.plot(scaler.inverse_transform(y_test.reshape(-1,1)),
            label='Actual')
    plt.legend()
    plt.show()
```

Training the model

Finally, we build a training function that will help us initiate the training session for each network, save their model weights at each epoch, and visualize the model performance when the training session has ceased.

This function may take a list of models and execute the described steps on each model. So, get ready to take a brief/extensive stroll (depending on your hardware configuration) after running the following cells of code:

```
def train_network(list, x_train, y_train, epochs=5):
    for net in list:
        network_name = str(net).split(' ')[1]
        filepath = network_name + "_epoch-{epoch:02d}-loss-
                {loss:.4f}-.hdf5"
        print('Training:', network_name)
        checkpoint = ModelCheckpoint(filepath, monitor='loss',
                verbose=0, save_best_only=True, mode='min')
        callbacks_list = [checkpoint]
        model = net()
        network = model.fit(x_train, y_train,
                            validation_data=(x_test, y_test),
                            epochs=epochs,
                            batch_size=64,
                            callbacks=callbacks_list)
        model.summary()
        plot_predictions(model, y_test)
    return network, model

all_networks = [feed_forward, simple_gru, simple_lstm, lstm_stacked]
train_network(all_networks, x_train, y_train, epochs=50)
```

Visualizing results

Finally, we will display the predictions of our model vis-à-vis the actual prices, as shown in the following diagram. Note that although the simple LSTM performs the best (with MAE of 0.0809), it is quite closely matched by the simple feedforward neural network that, by design, has fewer trainable parameters than the LSTM network.

How so? you may wonder. Well, while LSTMs are extremely good at encoding complex time-dependent signals, those signals have to be present in our data in the first place:

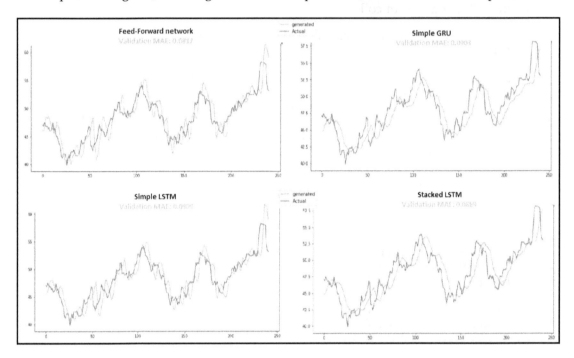

There can be only so much information conveyed through viewing the past seven mid-prices in predicting the future. In our case, it seems that the type of representations our LSTM could conjure for the predictive task was more or less matched by the representations conjured by the feedforward network. There might be a lot of complex signals that the LSTM could model in this context, but they don't seem to be present in our dataset. For instance, we are not, by design, incorporating any information about what happened to the market at time $t+1$ or $t+2$ when predicting the label of x_{t+3}. Moreover, there may exist variables other than past mid-stock prices that would better correlate with the future movement of the stock market. Social media sentiment (on Twitter, read: https://arxiv.org/pdf/1010.3003.pdf), for instance, has been shown to correlate with the movement of stock prices up to seven days in advance! It turns out that the winning emotion was calmness, rather than happiness or neuroticism, which lined up best with market movements up to a week in advance. So, including features that represent other types and sources of information may help increase our LSTM's performance in comparison to the baseline models.

Closing comments

Note that this does not necessarily mean that the movement of all stocks, in all industries, can be better predicted through inclusion of social media data. However, it does illustrate our point that there is some room for heuristic-based feature generation that may allow additional signals to be leveraged for better predictive outcomes. To provide some closing comments on our experiments, we also notice that the simple GRU and the stacked LSTMs both have smoother predictive curves, and are less likely to be swayed by noisy input sequences. They perform remarkably well at conserving the general trend of the stock. The out-of-set accuracy of these models (assessed with the MAE between the predicted and actual value) tells us that they perform slightly worse than the feedforward network and the simple LSTM. However, we may prefer to employ the models with the smoother curve for decision making compared to the noisier predictors, depending on the specific use case.

Summary

In this chapter, we dived deep into the inner workings of the LSTM network. We explored both the concepts and mathematical implementation related to these networks, understanding how information is processed in an LSTM cell and using short-term and long-term memory of events. We also saw why the network gets its name, being adept at conserving relevant cell states over very distant timesteps. While we discussed some variants to the architecture, such as the peephole connection, it is seldom seen in most common LSTM candidate scenarios. Although we executed our demonstrations with a simple time series dataset, we highly encourage you to implement this architecture to tackle other problems that you may already be familiar with (such as the IMDB sentiment classification dataset), and compare results with our earlier efforts.

LSTMs have really been shown to shine at **natural language processing (NLP)** tasks. You could try generating movie scripts with the Wikipedia movies dataset, or even try generating music using the music21 library and some MIDI files with training songs.

Some further coding can be found here:

- **Peephole pseudocode:** https://gist.github.com/EderSantana/
  f07fa7a0371d0e1c4ef1

The theoretical notion behind LSTMs remain quite eliciting—even more so in light of their excellent performance on a variety of sequential and non-sequential tasks. Are we then to crown LSTMs as the ultimate champions, as far as RNNs go? Well, not exactly. One of the next big ideas, bordering the realms of RNNs, comes from the area of attention models, where we, quite literally, try to steer the attention of our neural network while it processes a collection of information. This approach is quite useful in the case of image captioning, as we need to correlate important parts of an image in a given input with must-include words sequenced in a coherent output. We will explore the topic of attention models in further detail in the coming chapters. For interested readers, you may follow up on the task of machine image captioning by reading an excellent paper, titled *Image captioning with semantic attention*, by *Fang et al.* 2016.

In the next chapter, however, we will focus our attention on another part of neural networks and deep learning: reinforcement learning. This is an extremely interesting area of machine learning that deals with how artificial agents must act in a designed environment for them to be able to cumulatively maximize some reward. This approach can be applied to a myriad of use cases, such as teaching machines to perform surgery, generate jokes, or play video games. Having machines capable of leveraging a level of physical or psychological dexterity comparable to (or beyond) that of humans can allow us to build very complex and intelligent systems. Such systems maintain internal states that are relevant to the environment in which the system operates, and are able to update their internal state by studying the consequences of their actions upon the environment while optimizing a specific goal. So, each combination of actions triggers different reward signals that the learning system may leverage for self-improvement.

As we will soon see, designing systems that are allowed to be reinforced through reward signals can lead to very complex behavior, leading machines to perform highly intelligent actions even where humans tend to dominate. The tale of AlphaGo versus Lee Sedol (the once-revered world champion of the ancient Chinese board game Go) comes to mind. As the AlphaGo system beat its human contender five to one in 2016, the event itself was very different to the victory of IBM's Deep Blue over Gary Kasparov (1997). Many who watched the AlphaGo matches against Lee Sedol saw something special in the machine's modus operandi. Some even called it **intuition**.

In the next chapter, we will see how such systems, operating on some fairly straightforward statistical properties of environments and possible actions, can produce beautifully complex outcomes, at times transcending our own expectations.

Exercises

- Examine the time taken for models to converge. Is there a big difference between different models?
- Examine the training and validation losses between the models. What do you notice?
- Experiment with downscaling and upscaling the architecture, note how this affects learning.
- Experiment with different optimizers and loss metrics and note how this affects learning.
- Implement an LSTM on the IMBD dataset for sentiment classification.
- Implement an LSTM on the Wikimovies dataset to build a character/word-level language model and generate artificial movie plots.

7
Reinforcement Learning with Deep Q-Networks

In the last chapter, we saw how recursive loops, information gates, and memory cells can be used to model complex time-dependent signals with neural networks. More specifically, we saw how the **Long Short-Term Memory** (**LSTM**) architecture leverages these mechanics to preserve prediction errors and backpropagate them over increasingly long time steps. This allowed our system to inform predictions using both short-term (that is, from information relating to the immediate environment) and long-term representations (that is, from information pertaining to the environment that was observed long ago).

The beauty of the LSTM lies in the fact that it is able to learn and preserve useful representations over very large periods of time (up to a thousand time steps). By maintaining a constant error flow through the architecture, we can implement a mechanism that allows our network to learn complex cause-and-effect patterns, embedded in the reality we face everyday. Indeed, the problem of educating computers on matters of cause and effect has presented itself to be quite a challenge so far in the field of **Artificial Intelligence** (**AI**). As it happens, real-world environments are heavily populated with sparse and time-delayed rewards, with increasingly complex sets of actions corresponding to these rewards. Modeling optimal behavior in such circumstances involves discovering sufficient information about a given environment, along with the possible set of actions and respective rewards to make relevant predictions. As we know, encoding such complex cause-and-effect relations can be difficult, even for humans. We often succumb to our irrational desires without perusing some pretty beneficial cause and effect relations. Why? Simply put, the actual cause and effect relationship may not correspond to our internal valuation of the situation. We may be acting upon different reward signals, spread out through time, each influencing our aggregate decision.

The degree to which we act upon certain reward signals is highly variant. This is based upon the specific individual and determined by a complex combination of genetic makeup and environmental factors that are faced by a given individual. In some ways, it is embedded in our nature. Some of us are just, inherently, a little more swayed by short-term rewards (such as delicious snacks or entertaining movies) over long-term rewards (such as having a healthy body or using our time efficiently). This isn't so bad, right? Well, not necessarily. Different environments require different balances of short and long-term considerations to be able to succeed. Given the diversity of environments a human may encounter (in individual sense, as well as the broad, species sense), it is not a surprise that we observe such a variety in the interpretation of reward signals among different individuals. On a grand scale, evolution is simply maximizing our chances to survive as many environments that this reality may impress upon us. However, as well will shortly see, this may have consequences for certain individuals (and perhaps some greedy machines) on the minute scale of events.

On reward and gratification

Interestingly, a group of Stanford researchers showed (Marshmallow experiment, in the 1970s, led by psychologist Walter Mischel) how the capability for individuals to delay short term gratification was correlated with more successful outcomes in the long term. Essentially, these researchers called upon children and observed their behavior once they were presented with a set of choices. The children were given two choices that determined how many total marshmallows they could receive during an interaction. They could either choose to cash out one marshmallow on the spot, or cash out two marshmallows if they chose to wait it out for 15 minutes. This experiment gave keen insight into how interpreting reward signals are beneficial or detrimental for performing in a given environment as the subjects who chose two marshmallows turned out to be more successful on average over the span of their lives. It turns out that delaying gratification could be a paramount part of maximizing actions that are more beneficial over the long term. Many have even pointed out how concepts such as religion could be the collective manifestation of delaying short term gratification (that is, do not steal), for favorable, long-term consequences (such as eventually ascending to heaven).

A new way of examining learning

So, it would seem that we develop an internal sense of what actions to take and how this may affect future outcomes. We have mechanisms that enable us to tune these senses through environmental interaction, observing what kind of rewards we get for different actions, over very long periods of time. This appears to be true for humans, as well as most living things that inhabit our planet, including not only fauna but also flora. Even plants are optimizing some sort of energy score throughout the day as they turn their leaves and branches to capture the sunlight that's required for them to live. So, what is this mechanism that permits these organisms to model optimal outcomes? How do these biological systems keep track of the environment and execute timely and precise maneuvers to favorable ends? Well, perhaps a branch of behavioral psychological, known as **reinforcement theory**, may shine some light on this topic.

Proposed by Harvard psychologist B.F. Skinner, this view defines reinforcement as a consequence of an observed interaction between an agent (human, animal, and now, computer program) and its environment. The encoding of information from this interaction may either strengthen or weaken the likelihood of the agent acting in the same way in similar future iterations. In simpler terms, if you walk on hot coals, the pain you feel will act as negative reinforcement, decreasing the likelihood of you choosing to step on hot coals in the future. Conversely, if you rob a bank and get away with it, the thrill and excitement may reinforce this action as a more likely one to consider in the future. In fact, Skinner showed how you can even train the common pigeon to recognize the difference between words of the English language and play games of ping-pong through a simple mechanism of designed reinforcement. He showed how exposing the pigeon to enough reward signals over a period of time was enough to incentivize the pigeon to pick up on the subtle variations between the words it was shown or the movements it was asked to perform. Since picking up on these variations represented the difference between a full and empty stomach for the pigeon, Skinner was able to influence its behavior by incrementally rewarding the pigeon for desirable outcomes. From these experiments, he coined the term *operant conditioning*, relating to breaking down tasks into increments and then rewarding favorable behavior iteratively.

Today, about half a century later, we operationalize these concepts in the realm of **machine learning** (**ML**) to reinforce favorable behavior that a simulated agent is to perform in a given environment. This notion is referred to as reinforcement learning, and can give rise to complex systems that parallel (and perhaps even surpass) our own intellect when performing tasks.

Conditioning machines with reinforcement learning

So far in our journey, we have been dealing with simple regression and classification tasks. We regressed observations against continuous values (that is, when predicting the stock market) and classified features into categorical labels (while conducting sentiment analysis). These are two cornerstone activities pertaining to supervised ML. We showed a specific target label for each observation our network comes across while training. Later on in this book, we will cover some unsupervised learning techniques with neural networks by using **Generative Adversarial Networks** (**GANs**) and autoencoders. Today, however, we employ neural networks to something quite different from these two caveats of learning. This caveat of learning can be named **reinforcement learning**.

Reinforcement learning is noticeably distinct from the aforementioned variations of ML. Here, we do not explicitly label all possible sequences of actions to all possible outcomes in an environment (as in supervised classification)—nor do we try and partition our data based on similarity-based distance measures (as in unsupervised clustering) to segment optimal actions. Rather, we let the machine monitor responses from actions it takes and cumulatively model the maximum possible reward as a function of actions over a period of time. In essence, we deal with goal-oriented algorithms that learn to achieve complex objectives over given time steps. The goal can be to beat the space invaders that are gradually moving down the screen, or for a dog-shaped robot in the real world to move from point A to B.

The credit assignment problem

Just as our parents reinforced our behavior with treats and rewards, so can we reinforce desirable machine actions for given states (or configurations) of our environment. This invokes more of a *trial-and-error* approach to learning, and recent events have shown how such an approach can produce extremely powerful learning systems, opening the door to some very interesting use cases. This considerably distinct yet powerful paradigm of learning does bring some complications of its own into the picture. Consider the credit assignment problem, for instance. That is to say, which of our previous actions are responsible for generating a reward, and to what degree? In an environment with sparse, time delayed rewards, many actions may occur between some action, which later generated the reward in question. It can become very difficult to properly assign due credit to respective actions. In the absence of proper credit assignment, our agent is left clueless while evaluating different strategies to use when trying to accomplish its goal.

The explore-exploit dilemma

Let's assume that our agent even manages to figure out a consistent strategy that delivers rewards. What's next? Should they simply stick to that same strategy, generating the same reward for eternity? Or rather should they keep trying new things all the time? Perhaps, by not exploiting a known strategy, the agent can have a chance at a much bigger reward in the future? This is known as the **explore-exploit dilemma**, referring to the degree to which agents should explore new strategies or exploit known strategies.

At the extreme, we can better appreciate the explore-exploit dilemma by understanding how it can be detrimental to rely on known strategies for immediate reward in the long run. Experiments with rats, for example, have shown that these animals will starve themselves to death if given a mechanism to trigger the release of dopamine (a neurotransmitter that's responsible for regulating our reward system). Clearly, starving was not the right move in the long run, however ecstatic the finale may have been. Yet since the rat exploits a simple strategy that consistently triggers a reward signal, the prospect of long-term rewards (such as staying alive) were not explored. So, how can we compensate for the fact that our environment may present better opportunities later on by foregoing current ones? Somehow, we have to make our agent understand this notion of delayed gratification if we want it to aptly solve complex environments. Soon, we will see how deep reinforcement learning attempts to solve such problems, giving rise to even more complex and powerful systems that some may even call devilishly sharp.

Path to artificial general intelligence

Take the example of the AlphaGo system, which was developed by UK-based start-up DeepMind, which leverages an acute flavor of deep reinforcement learning to inform its predictions. There is good reason behind Google's move to acquire it for a round sum of $500 million, since many claim that DeepMind has made first steps toward something called **Artificial General Intelligence** (**AGI**)—sort of the Holy Grail of AI, if you will. This notion refers to the capability of an artificially intelligent system to perform well on various tasks, instead of the narrow span of application our networks have taken so far. A system that learns through observing its own actions on an environment is similar in spirit (and potentially much faster) to how we humans learn ourselves.

The networks we built in the previous chapters perform well at a narrow classification or regression task, but must be redesigned significantly and retrained to perform on any other task. DeepMind, however, demonstrated how they could train a single network to perform well at several different (albeit narrow) tasks, involving playing several old-school Atari 2600 games. While a bit dated, these games were initially designed to be challenging for humans, making the feat quite a remarkable achievement in the field of AI. In their research (https://deepmind.com/research/dqn/), DeepMind showed how their **Deep Q Networks (DQN)** may be used to make artificial agents play different games just by observing the pixels on the screen without any prior information about the game itself. Their work inspired a new wave of researchers, who set off to train deep learning networks using reinforcement learning-based algorithms, giving birth to deep reinforcement learning. Since then, researchers and entrepreneurs alike have tried leveraging such techniques for a cascade of use cases, including but not limited to making machines move like animals and humans, generating molecular compounds for medicine, and even making bots that can trade on the stock market.

Needless to say, such systems can be much more flexible at modeling real-world events and can be applied to an array of tasks, reducing the resources that are spent on training separate narrow systems. One day, they may even be able to uncover complex and high-dimensional cause and effect relations, leveraging training examples from several domains to encode synergistic representations, which in turn help us to solve more complex problems. Our own discoveries are often inspired by information from various scientific domains. This tends to enhance our understanding of these situations and the complex dynamics that govern them. So, why not let machines do this too? Given the right reward signals for possible actions in a given environment, it may even surpass our own intuitions! Perhaps you can help with this one day. For now, let's start by having a look at how we go about simulating a virtual agent and make it interact with an environment to solve simple problems.

Simulating environments

First things first, we will need a simulated environment. An environment is defined as the *interaction space for a learning agent*. For humans, an environment can be any play you go to in the course of a day. For an artificial agent, this will often be a simulated environment that we have engineered. Why is it simulated? Well, we could ask the agent to learn in real time, like ourselves, but it turns out that this is quite impractical. For one, we would have to design each agent a body and then precisely engineer its actions and the environments that they are to interact with. Moreover, an agent can train much faster in a simulation, without requiring it to be restricted to human time frames. By the time a machine completes a single task in reality, its simulated version could have completed the same task several times over, providing a better opportunity for it to learn from its mistakes.

Next, we will go over the basic terminology that's used to describe a game, which represents an environment where an agent is expected to perform certain tasks to receive rewards and solve the environment.

Understanding states, actions, and rewards

The environment itself can be broken down into a collection of different states, all of which represent the different situations that the agent may find itself in. The agent can navigate through these states by trying out different combinations of actions it is allowed to perform (such as walking left or right and jumping, in respect to a 2D arcade game). The actions that are made by the agent effectively change the state of the environment, making available tools, alternate routes, enemies, or any other goodies the game makers may have hidden to make it more interesting for you. All of these objects and events represent different states that the learning environment may take as the agent navigates through it. A new state is generated by the environment as a result of the agent interacting with it at its previous state, or due to random events occurring in the environment. This is how a game essentially progresses until a terminal state is reached, meaning that the game can go no further (due to a win or a death).

Essentially, we want the agent to pursue timely and favorable actions to solve its environment. These actions must change the environment's state to bring the agent closer toward attaining a given goal (like moving from point A to B or maximizing a score). To be able to do this, we need to design reward signals that occur as a consequence of the agent's interactions with different states of the environment. We can use the notion of reward as feedback that allows our agent to assess the degree of success that's attained by its actions as it optimizes a given goal:

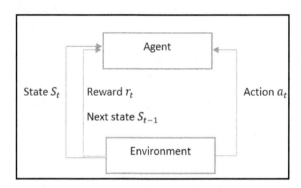

For those of you who are familiar with classic arcade style video games, think of a game of Mario. Mario himself is the agent and is controlled by you. The environment refers to the map that Mario can move about in. The presence of coins and mushrooms represent different states of the game. Once Mario interacts with either of these states, a reward is triggered in the form of points and a new state is born as consequence, which in turn alters Mario's environment accordingly. Mario's goal can be either to move from point A to B (if you're in a hurry to complete the game) or to maximize his score (if you're more interested in unlocking achievements).

A self-driving taxi cab

Next, we will clarify the theoretical understandings we have gathered so far by observing how environments can be solved by artificial agents. We will see how this can be achieved even through randomly sampling actions from an agent's action space (possible actions an agent may perform). This will help us to understand the complexities involved in solving even the simplest of environments, and why we might want to call upon deep reinforcement learning shortly to help us to achieve our goals. The goal we are about to address is creating a self-driving taxi cab in a reduced, simulated environment. While the environment we will deal with is much simpler than the real world, this simulation will serve as an excellent stepping stone into the design architecture of reinforcement learning systems.

To do this, we will be using OpenAI's `gym`, an adequately named module that's used to simulate artificial environments for training machines. You may install the OpenAI gym dependency by using the `pip` package manager. The following command will run on Jupyter Notebooks and initiate the installation of the module:

```
! pip install gym
```

The `gym` module comes with a plethora of pre-installed environments (or test problems), spanning from simple to more complex simulations. The test problem we will be using for the following example comes from the `'TaxiCab-v2'` environment. We will begin our experiments with what is known as the **taxicab simulation**, which simply simulates a grid of roads for a taxi to navigate through so that they can pick up and drop off customers:

```
import numpy as np
import gym
from gym import envs

# This will print allavailable environemnts
# print(envs.registry.all())
```

Understanding the task

The taxi cab simulation was introduced in (Dietterich 2000) to demonstrate problems with applying reinforcement learning in a hierarchical manner. We will, however, use this simulation to solidify our understanding of agents, environments, rewards, and goals, before we continue to simulate and solve more complex problems. For now, the problem we face is relatively simple: pick up passengers and drop them off at a given location. These locations (four in total) are represented by letters. All our agent has to do is travel to these pickup locations, pick up a passenger, then travel to a designated drop-off location where the passenger may disembark. Given a successful disembark, the agent receives +20 points (simulating the money our virtual cabby gets). Each time step our cabby takes before it reaches its destination, is attributed a reward of -1 (intuitively, this is the penalty our cabby incurs for the cost of petrol they must replenish). Lastly, another penalty of -10 exists for pickups and drop-offs that are not scheduled. You could imagine the reason behind penalizing pickups as a taxi company trying to optimize its fleet deployment to cover all areas of the city, requiring our virtual cabby to only pick up assigned passengers. Unscheduled drop-offs, on the other hand, simply reflect disgruntled and baffled customers. Let's have a look at what the taxi cab environment actually looks like.

Rendering the environment

To visualize the environment we just loaded up, we must first initialize it by calling `reset()` on our environment object. Then, we can render the starting frame, corresponding to the position of our taxi (in yellow) and four different pickup locations (denoted by colored letters):

```
# running env.reset() returns the initial state of the environment

print('Initial state of environment:' , env.reset())
env.render()
```

We get the following output:

```
Initial state of environment: 204
+---------+
|R: | : :G|
| : : : : |
| : : : : |
| | : | : |
|Y| : |B: |
+---------+
```

Do note that the preceding screenshot depicts open roads using colons (`:`), and walls that cannot be traversed by the taxi using the symbol (`|`). While the position of these obstacles and routes remain permanent, the letters denoting the pickup points, as well as our yellow taxi, keep changing every time the environment is initialized. We can also notice that resetting the environment generates an integer. This refers to a specific state of the environment (that is, positioning of the taxi and the pickups) that's taken upon initialization.

You can replace the `Taxi-v2` string with other environments in the registry (like `CartPole-v0` or `MountainCar-v0`), and render a few frames to get an idea of what we are dealing with. There's also a few other commands that let you better understand the environment you are dealing with. While the taxi cab environment is simple enough to be simulated using colored symbols, more complex environments may be rendered in a separate window, which opens upon execution.

Referencing observation space

Next, we will try to better understand our environment and action space. All states in the taxi cab environment are denoted by an integer ranging between 0 to 499. We can verify this by printing out the total number of possible states our environment has. Let's have a look at the number of possible different states our environment may take:

```
env.observation_space.n
```

500

Referencing action space

In the taxi cab simulation, our cabby agent is given six distinct actions that it may perform at each time step. We can check the total number of possible actions by checking the environment's action space, as shown here:

```
env.action_space.n
```

6

Our cabby may, at any given time, do one of these six actions. These actions correspond to moving up, down, left, or right; picking someone up; or dropping them off.

Interacting with the environment

To make our agent do something, we can use the step() method on our environment object. The step(i) method takes an integer that refers to one out of the six possible actions that our agent is allowed to take. In this case, these actions were labeled as follows:

- (0) to move down
- (1) to move up
- (2) for a right turn
- (3) for a left turn
- (4) for picking up a passenger
- (5) for dropping the passenger off

Here's how the code is represented:

```
#render current position
env.render()

#move down
env.step(0)

#render new position
env.render()
```

We get the following output:

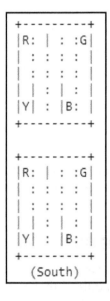

As we can see here, we make our agent take a step downward. Now, we understand how to make our agent do all of the required steps to achieve its goal. In fact, calling `step(i)` on the environment object will return four specific variables, referring to what action (i) did to the environment, from the perspective of the agent. These variables are as follows:

1. `observation`: This is the observed state of the environment. This can be pixel data from game screenshots or another manner of representing the states of the environment to the learning agent.
2. `reward`: This is the compensation for our agent, due to actions taken on a given time step. We use the reward to set goals for our learning agent by simply asking it to maximize the reward it receives in a given environment. Note that the scale of the reward (float) values may differ per experimental setup.

3. `done`: This Boolean (binary) value denotes whether a trial episode has terminated or not. In the case of the taxi-cab simulation, an episode is considered `done` when a passenger has been picked up and dropped off at a given location. For an Atari game, an episode can be defined as the life of the agent, which terminates once you get hit by a space invader.

4. `info`: This dictionary item serves to store information that's used to debug our agents' actions and is usually not used in the learning process itself. It does store valuable information, such as the probabilities affecting the previous change of states, for a given step:

```
# env.step(i) will return four variables
# They are defiend as (in order) the state, reward, done, info
env.step(1)

(204, -1, False, {'prob': 1.0})
```

Solving the environment randomly

Armed with the logic governing OpenAI gym environments, and how to make artificial agents interact therein, we can proceed to implement a random algorithm that allows the agent to (eventually) solve the taxi cab environment. First, we define a fixed state to begin our simulation with. This is helpful if you want to repeat the same experiment (that is, initiate the environment with the same state) while checking how many random steps the agent took in solving the environment each episode. We also define a `counter` variable that simply keeps track of the number of time steps our agent takes as the episode progresses. The reward variable is initialized as `None` and will be updated once the agent takes its first step. Then, we simply initiate a `while` loop that repeatedly samples possible actions that are random from our action space and updates the respective `state`, `reward`, and `done` variables for each sampled action. To randomly sample actions from the environment's action space, we use the `.sample()` method on the `env.action_space` object. Finally, we increment our `counter` and render the environment for visualization:

```
# Overriding current state, used for reproducibility
state = env.env.s = 114

# counter tracks number of moves made
counter = 0

#No reward to begin with
reward = None

dropoffs = 0
```

```
#loop through random actions until successful dropoff (20 points)

while reward != 20:
    state, reward, done, info = env.step(env.action_space.sample())
    counter += 1
    print(counter)
    env.render()

print(counter, dropoffs)
```

We get the following output:

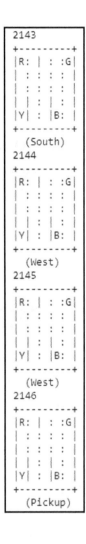

It wasn't until the 2,145[th] attempt that our agent even got to the right passenger in the cab (as indicated by the cab turning green). That's quite long, even if you may not feel the time pass by. Random algorithms are helpful to benchmark our performance when calling upon more complex models as a measure of sanity. But surely we can do better than 6,011 steps (as taken by the agent running on the random algorithm) to solve this simple environment. How? Well, we reward it for being right. To do this, we must first define the notion of reward mathematically.

Trade-off between immediate and future rewards

At first glance, this may appear quite simple. We already saw how the cabby can be incentivized by awarding it +20 points for a correct dropoff, -10 for a false one, and -1 for each time step that it takes to complete the episode. Logically, then, you can calculate the total reward collected by an agent for an episode as the cumulation of all the individual rewards for each time step that's seen by the agent. We can denote this mathematically and represent the total reward in an episode as follows:

$$R = r_1 + r_2 + r_3 + \ldots + r_n$$

Here, n simply denotes the time step of the episode. This seems intuitive enough. We can now ask our agent to maximize the total reward in a given episode. But there's a problem. Just like our own reality, the environment that's faced by our agent may be governed by largely random events. Hence, there may be no guarantee that performing the same action will return the same reward in the similar future states. In fact, as we progress into the future, the rewards may diverge more and more from the corresponding actions that are taken at each state due to the inherent randomness that's present.

Discounting future rewards

So, how can we compensate for this divergence? One way is through discounting future rewards, thereby amplifying the relevance of current rewards over rewards from future time steps. We can achieve this by adding a discount factor to the reward that's generated at each time step while we calculate the total reward in a given episode. The purpose of this discount factor will be to dampen future rewards and amplify current ones. In the short term, we have more certainty of being able to collect rewards by using corresponding state action pairs. This cannot be said in the long run due to the cumulating effects of random events that populate the environment. Hence, to incentivize the agent to focus on relatively certain events, we can modify our earlier formulation for total reward to include this discount factor, like so:

$$R_t = r_t + \gamma r_{t+1} + \gamma^2 r_{t+2} + \ldots + \gamma^{n-t} r_n$$

In our new total reward formulation, γ denotes a discount factor between 0 and 1, and t denotes the present time step. As you may have noticed right away, the exponential decrease of the γ term allows for future rewards to be dampened over current ones. Intuitively, this just means that rewards that are far into the future are taken less into account compared to more contemporary ones while the agent considers its next action. And by how much? Well, that is still up to us. A discount factor nearing zero will produce short sighted strategies, hedonistically favoring immediate rewards over future ones. On the other hand, setting a discount factor too close to one will defeat the purpose of having it in the first place. In practice, a balancing value can be in the range of 0.75-0.9, depending on the degree of stochasticity in the environment. As a rule of thumb, you would want higher gamma (γ) values for more deterministic environments, and lower (γ) values for stochastic environments. We can even simplify the total reward formula that was given prior like so:

$$R_t = r_t + \gamma(r_{t+1} + \gamma(r_{t+2+} \ldots)) = r_t + \gamma R_{t+1}$$

Hence, we formalize the total reward in an episode as the cumulative discounted reward for each time step in the episode. By using the notion of discounted future reward, we can generate strategies for an agent, hence governing its actions. An agent carrying out a beneficial strategy will aim to select actions that maximize the discounted future rewards in a given episode. Now that we have a good idea of how to engineer a reward signal for our agent, it's time to move on and look at an overview of the entire process of learning.

Markov decision process

In reinforcement learning, we are trying to solve the problem of correlating immediate actions with the delayed rewards they return. These rewards are simply sparse, time-delayed labels that are used to control the agent's behavior. So far, we have discussed how an agent may act upon different states of an environment. We also saw how interactions generate various rewards for the agent and unlock new states of the environment. From here, the agent can resume interacting with the environment until the end of an episode. It's about time we mathematically formalize these relations between an agent and environment for the purpose of goal optimization. To do this, we will call upon a framework proposed by Russian mathematician Andrey Markov, now known as the **Markov decision process (MDP)**.

This mathematical framework allows us to model our agent's decision-making process in an environment that is partially stochastic and partially controllable by the agent. This process relies on the Markov assumption, stating that the probability of future states ($st+1$) depends on the current state (st) only. This assumption means that all states and actions leading up to the current state have no influence on the probability of future states. A MDP is defined by the following five variables:

Defined by: $(\mathcal{S}, \mathcal{A}, \mathcal{R}, \mathbb{P}, \gamma)$

$\mathcal{S}$: set of possible states
$\mathcal{A}$: set of possible actions
$\mathcal{R}$: distribution of reward given (state, action) pair
$\mathbb{P}$: transition probability i.e. distribution over next state given (state, action) pair
γ : discount factor

While the first two variables are quite self-explanatory, the third one (**R**) refers to the probability distribution of a reward, given a state-action pair. Here, a state-action pair simply refers to the corresponding action to take for a given state of the environment. Next on the list is the transition probability (**P**), which denotes the probability of the new state given the chosen state-action pair at a time step.

Finally, the discount factor refers to the degree to which we wish to discount future rewards for more immediate ones, which is elaborated on in the following diagram:

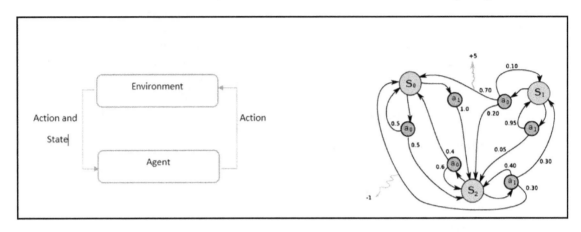

Left: Reinforcement learning problem. Right: Markov decision process

Hence, we can describe interactions between our agent and the environment using the MDP. An MDP is composed of a collection of states and actions, together with rules that dictate the transition from one state to another. We can now mathematically define one episode as a finite sequence of states, actions, and rewards, like so:

$$s_0, a_0, r_1, s_1, a_1, r_2, s_2, \ldots, s_{n-1}, a_{n-1}, r_n, s_n$$

Here, (s_t) and (a_t) denote the state and corresponding action at time t. We can also denote the reward corresponding to this state-action pair as (r_{t+1}). Hence, we begin an episode by sampling an initial state from the environment (s_0). Then, until our goal is completed, we ask our agent to select an action for the corresponding state of the environment it finds itself in. Once the agent executes an action, the environment samples a reward for the action taken by the agent and the next state (s_{t+1}) to follow. The agent then receives both the reward and the next state before repeating the process until it is able to solve the environment. Finally, a terminal state (s_n) is reached at the end of an episode (that is, when our goal is completed, or we deplete our lives in a game). The rules that determine the actions of the agent at each state are collectively known as a **policy**, and are denoted by the Greek symbol (π).

Understanding policy functions

As we can see, the efficiency of our agent to solve an environment depends on what policy it uses to match state-action pairs at each time step. Hence, a function, known as a **policy function** (π), can specify the combination of state-action pairs for each time step the agent comes across. As the simulation runs, the policy is responsible for producing the trajectory, which is composed of game-states; actions that are taken by our agent as a response; and a reward that's generated by the environment, as well as the next state of the game the agent receives. Intuitively, you can think of a policy as a heuristic that generates actions that respond to the generated states of an environment. A policy function itself can be a good or a bad one. If your policy is to shoot first and ask questions later, you may end up shooting a hostage. Hence, all we need to do now is evaluate different policies (that is, the trajectories they produce, including their sequences of states, actions, rewards, and next-states), and pick out the optimal policy (π *) that maximizes the cumulative discounted rewards for a given game. This can be illustrated mathematically as follows:

$$\pi^* = \sum_{t>0} \gamma^t r_t$$

Hence, if we are trying to move from point A to point B, our optimal policy will involve taking an action that allows us to move as close as possible to point B at each time step. Unfortunately, due to the randomness that's present in such environments, we may not speak with such certainty as to claim that our policy absolutely maximizes the sum of discounted rewards. By definition, we cannot account for certain random events like earthquakes, for example, while traveling from point A to B (assuming you're not a seismological expert). Hence, we can also not perfectly account for the rewards that arise as a result of the actions performed due to randomness in an environment. Instead, we can define the optimal policy (π *) as a policy that lets our agent maximize the expected sum of discounted rewards. This can be denoted with a slight modification to the earlier equation, which can be portrayed as follows:

$$\pi^* = \arg\max_{\pi} \mathbb{E}\left[\sum_{t\geq0} \gamma^t r_t | \pi\right]$$

Here, we use the MDP framework and sample the initial state (s₀) from our state probability distribution p(s₀). The actions of our agent (aₜ) are sampled from a policy, given a state. Then, a reward is sampled that corresponds to the utility of the action that's performed at the given state. Finally, the environment samples the next state (sₜ₊₁), from the transition probability distribution of the current state-action pair. Hence, at each time step, we aim to update our optimal policy so that we can maximize the expected sum of discounted rewards. Some of you may wonder at this point, how can we assess the utility of an action, given a state? Well, this is where the value and Q-value functions come in. To evaluate different policy functions, we need to be able to assess the value of different states, as well as the quality of actions corresponding to these states, for a given policy. For this, we need to define two additional functions, known as the value function and the Q-value function.

Assessing the value of a state

First, we need to estimate the value (*V*) of state (*s*) while following a specific policy (π). This tells you the expected cumulative reward at the terminal state of a game while following a policy (π) starting at state (*s*). Why is this useful? Well, imagine that our learning agent's environment is populated by enemies that are continuously chasing the agent. It may have developed a policy dictating it to never stop running during the whole game. In this case, the agent should have enough flexibility to evaluate the value of game states (when it runs up to the edge of a cliff, for example, so as to not run off it and die). We can do this by defining the value function at a given state, *V* π (*s*), as the expected cumulative (discounted) reward that the agent receives from following that policy, starting from the current state:

$$V^{\pi}(s) = \mathbb{E}\left[\sum_{t \geq 0} \gamma^t r_t | s_0 = s, \pi\right]$$

Hence, we are able to use the value function to evaluate how good a state is while following a certain policy. However, this only tells us about the value of a state itself, given a policy. We also want our agent to be able to judge the value of an action in response to a given state. This is what really allows the agent to act dynamically in response to whatever the environment throws at it (be it an enemy or the edge of a cliff). We can operationalize this notion of *goodness* for given state action pairs for a given policy by using the Q-value function.

Assessing the quality of an action

If you walk up to a wall, there are not many actions you can perform. You will likely respond to this state in your environment by choosing the action of turning around, followed by asking yourself why you walked up to a wall in the first place. Similarly, we would like our agent to leverage a sense of goodness for different actions with respect to the states they find themselves in while following a policy. We can achieve this using a Q-Value function. This function simply denotes the expected cumulative reward from taking a specific action, in a specific state, while following a policy. In other words, it denotes the quality of a state-action pairs for a given policy. Mathematically, we can denote the $Q\pi(a, s)$ relation as follows:

$$Q^{\pi}(s,a) = \mathbb{E}\left[\sum_{t \geq 0} \gamma^t r_t | s_0 = s, a_0 = a, \pi\right]$$

The $Q\pi(s, a)$ function allows us to represent the expected cumulative reward from following a policy (π). Intuitively, this function helps us to quantify our total score at the end of a game, given the actions (that is, the different joystick control moves) taken at each state (game screen you observe) of the environment (a game of Mario, for example), while following a policy (move forward while jumping). Using this function, we can then define the best possible expected cumulative reward at the terminal state of a game, given the policy being followed. This can be represented as the maximum expected value that's attainable by the Q-value function and is known as the optimal Q-value function. We can mathematically define this as follows:

$$Q^*(s,a) = \max_{\pi} \mathbb{E}\left[\sum_{t \geq 0} \gamma^t r_t | s_0 = s, a_0 = a, \pi\right]$$

Now, we have a function that quantifies the expected optimal value of state action pairs, given a policy. We can use this function to predict the optimal action to follow, given a game state. However, how do we assess the true label of our prediction? We don't exactly have our game-screens labeled with corresponding target actions to assess how far off the mark our network is. This is where the Bellman equation comes in, which helps us asses the value of a given state action pair as a function of both the current reward generated, as well as the value of the following game state. We can then use this function to compare our network's predictions and back-propagate the error to update the model weights.

Using the Bellman equation

The Bellman equation, which was proposed by American mathematician Richard Bellman, is one of the main workhorse equations powering the chariot of deep Q-learning. It essentially allows us to solve the Markov decision process we formalized earlier. Intuitively, the Bellman equation makes one simple assumption. It states that the maximum future reward for a given action, performed at a state, is the immediate reward plus the maximum future reward for the next state. To draw a parallel to the marshmallow experiments, the maximum possible reward of two marshmallows is attained by the agents through the act of abstaining at the first time step (with a reward of 0 marshmallows) and then collecting (with a reward of two marshmallows) at the second time step.

In other words, given any state-action pair, the quality (Q) of performing an action (a) at the given state (s) is equal to the reward to be received (r) , along with the value of the following state (s') that the agent ends up in. Thus, we can calculate the optimal action for the current state as long as we can estimate the optimal state-action values, $Q^*(s',a')$, for the next time step. As we just saw with the marshmallow example, our agent needs to be able to anticipate the maximum possible reward at a future time (of two marshmallows) to abstain from accepting just one marshmallow at the current time. Using the Bellman equation, we want our agent to take actions that maximize the immediate reward (r), as well as the optimal Q*-value for the next state-action pair to come, $Q^*(s',a')$, dampened by discount factor gamma (y). In more simple terms, we want it to be able to calculate the maximum expected future rewards for actions at the current state. This translates to the following:

$$Q^*(s, a) = \mathbb{E}_{s' \sim \mathcal{E}} \left[r + \gamma \max_{a'} Q^*(s', a') | s, a \right]$$

Now, we know how to mathematically estimate the expected quality of an action at a given state. We also know how to estimate the maximum expected reward of state-action pairs when following a specific policy. From this, we can redefine our optimal policy (π^*) at a given state, (s), as the maximum expected Q-values for actions at given states. This can be shown as follows:

$$\pi^*(s) = max_a Q^*(s, a)$$

Finally, we have all of the pieces of the puzzle to actually try and find an optimal policy (π*) to guide our agent. This policy will allow our agent to maximize the expected discounted rewards (incorporating environmental stochasticity) by choosing ideal actions for each state the environment generates. So, how do we actually go about doing this? A simple, non-deep learning solution is to use a value iteration algorithm to calculate the quality of actions at future time steps (*Qt+1* (*s* , *a*)) as a function of expected current reward (r) and maximum discounted reward at the following state of the game (*γ max a Qt* (*s'* , *a'*)). Mathematically, we can formulate this as follows:

$$Q_{t+1}(s, a) = \mathbb{E}\left[r + \gamma \max_{a'} Q_t(s', a') | s, a\right]$$

Here, we basically update the Bellman equation iteratively until Qt converges to Q*, as *t* increases, ad infinitum. We can actually test out the estimation of the Bellman equation by naively implementing it to solve the taxi cab simulation.

Updating the Bellman equation iteratively

You may recall that a random approach to solving the taxi cab simulation took our agent about 6,000 time steps. Sometimes, out of sheer luck, you may be able to solve it under 2,000 time steps. However, we can further tip the odds in our favor by implementing a version of the Bellman equation. This approach will essentially allow our agent to remember its actions and corresponding rewards per state by using a Q-table. We can implement this Q-table on Python using a NumPy array, with dimensions corresponding to our observation space (the number of different possible states) and action space (the number of different possible actions our agent can make) in the taxi cab environment. Recall that the taxi cab simulation has an environment space of 500 and an action space of six, making our Q-table a matrix of 500 rows and six columns. We can also initialize a reward variable (R) and a value for our discount factor, gamma:

```
#Q-table, functions as agent's memory of state action pairs
Q = np.zeros([env.observation_space.n, env.action_space.n])

#track reward
R = 0

#discount factor
gamma = 0.85

# Track successful dropoffs
dropoffs_done = 0
```

```
#Run for 1000 episodes
for episode in range(1,1001):
    done = False
    #Initialize reward
    R, reward = 0,0
    #Initialize state
    state = env.reset()
    counter=0
    while done != True:
            counter+=1
            #Pick action with highest Q value
            action = np.argmax(Q[state])
            #Stores future state for compairason
            new_state, reward, done, info = env.step(action)
            #Update state action pair using reward and max Q-value for the
new state
            Q[state,action] += gamma * (reward + np.max(Q[new_state]) -
Q[state,action])
            #Update reward
            R += reward
            #Update state
            state = new_state
            #Check how many times agent completes task
            if reward == 20:
                dropoffs_done +=1
    #Print reward every 50 episodes
    if episode % 50 == 0:
        print('Episode {}   Total Reward: {}   Dropoffs done: {}   Time-
Steps taken {}'
                .format(episode,R, dropoffs_done, counter))


Episode 50 Total Reward: -30 Dropoffs done: 19 Time-Steps taken 51
Episode 100 Total Reward: 14 Dropoffs done: 66 Time-Steps taken 7
Episode 150 Total Reward: -5 Dropoffs done: 116 Time-Steps taken 26
Episode 200 Total Reward: 14 Dropoffs done: 166 Time-Steps taken 7
Episode 250 Total Reward: 12 Dropoffs done: 216 Time-Steps taken 9
Episode 300 Total Reward: 5 Dropoffs done: 266 Time-Steps taken 16
```

Then, we simply loop through a thousand episodes. Per episode, we initialize the state of the environment, a counter to keep track of drop-offs that have been performed, and the reward variables (total: R and episode-wise: r). Within our first loop, we nest yet another loop, instructing our agent to pick an action with the highest Q-value, perform the action, and store the future state of the environment, along with the reward that's received. This loop is instructed to run until the episode is considered terminated, as indicated by the Boolean variable done.

Next, we update the state-action pairs in the Q-table, along with the global reward variable (which indicates how well our agent performed overall). The alpha term (α) in the algorithm denotes a learning rate, which helps to control the amount of change between the previous and newly generated Q-value while performing the update of the Q-table. Hence, our algorithm iteratively updates the quality of state action pairs (Q [state, action]) through approximating optimal Q-values for actions at each time step. As this process keeps repeating, our agent eventually converges to optimal state-action pairs, as denoted by Q*.

Finally, we update the state variable, redefining the current state with the new state variable. Then, the loop may begin anew, iteratively updating the Q-values, and ideally converging to optimal state-action pairs that are stored in the Q-table. We print out the overall rewards that are sampled by the environment as a result of our agent's actions every 50 episodes. We can see that our agent eventually converges to the optimal possible reward for the task at hand (that is, the optimal reward considering the traveling costs at each time step, as well as the reward for a correct drop-off), which is somewhere between 9 to 13 points for this task. You will also notice that, by the 50th episode, our agent has performed 19 successful drop-offs in 51 time steps! This approach turns out to perform much better than its stochastic counterpart we implemented before.

Why use neural networks?

As we just saw, a basic value iteration approach can be used to update the Bellman equation and iteratively find ideal state-action pairs to optimally navigate a given environment. This approach actually stores new information at each time step, iteratively making our algorithm more *intelligent*. However, there is a problem with this method as well. It's simply not scalable! The taxi cab environment is simple enough, with 500 states and 6 actions, to be solved by iteratively updating the Q-values, thereby estimating the value of each individual state-action pair. However, more complex simulations, like a video game, may potentially have millions of states and hundreds of actions, which is why computing the quality of each state-action pair becomes computationally unfeasible and logically inefficient. The only option we are left with, in such circumstances, is to try approximating the function $Q(a,s)$ using a network of weighted parameters.

And thus, we venture into the territories of neural networks, which, as we are well aware of by now, make excellent function approximators. The particular flavor of deep reinforcement learning that we will experience shortly is known as deep Q-learning, which naturally gets its name from its task of learning optimal Q-values for given state-action pairs in an environment. More formally, we will use a neural network to approximate the optimal function Q*(s,a) through simulating a sequence of states, actions, and rewards for our agent. By doing this, we can then iteratively update our model weights (theta) in the direction that best matches the optimal state-action pairs for a given environment:

$$Q(s, a; \theta) \approx Q^*(s, a)$$

function parameters (weights)

Performing a forward pass in Q-learning

Now, you understand the intuition behind using a neural network to approximate the optimal function Q*(s,a), finding the best possible actions at given states. It goes without saying that the optimal sequence of actions, for a sequence of states, will generate an optimal sequence of rewards. Hence, our neural network is trying to estimate a function that can map possible actions to states, generating an optimal reward for the overall episode. As you will also recall, the optimal quality function Q*(s,a) that we need to estimate must satisfy the Bellman equation. The Bellman equation simply models maximum possible future reward as the reward at the current time, plus the maximum possible reward, at the immediately following time step:

Current reward   Maximum possible future reward

$$Q^*(s, a) = \mathbb{E}_{s' \sim \varepsilon} \left[r + \gamma \max_{a'} Q^*(s', a') | s, a \right]$$

Optimal quality function   Discount factor

Hence, we need to ensure that the conditions set forth by the Bellman equation are maintained when we aim to predict the optimal Q-value at a given time. To do this, we can define the overall loss function of this model as one that minimizes the error in our Bellman equation and in-play predictions. In other words, at each forward pass, we compute how far the current state-action quality values Q *(s, a ; θ)* are from the ideal ones that have been denoted by the Bellman equation at that time (Y_t). Since the ideal predictions denoted by the Bellman equation are being iteratively updated, we are actually computing our model's loss using a moving target variable (Y_t). This can be formulated mathematically as follows:

Loss, as function of model weights at given time ($θ_t$)   Target   Prediction

$$L_t(\theta_t) = \mathbb{E}_{s,a\sim\rho(\cdot)}\left[(y_t - Q(s,a;\theta_t))^2\right]$$

where $y_t = \mathbb{E}_{s'\sim\varepsilon}\left[r + \gamma \max_{a'} Q(s',a';\theta_{t-1})|s,a\right]$

Target value at time (t)   Current Reward   Max reward at next state   Model weights at (t-1)

Hence, our network will be trained by minimizing a sequence of loss functions, $L_t(θt)$, changing at each time step. Here, the term y_t is the target label for our prediction, at time (*t*), and is continuously updated at each time step. Also note that the term $ρ(s, a)$ simply denotes the internal probability distribution over sequences s and actions taken by our model, also known as its behavior distribution. As you can see, the model weights at the previous time (*t-1*) step are kept frozen when optimizing the loss function at a given time (*t*). While the implementation shown here uses the same network for two separate forward passes, later variations of Q-learning (Mihn et al., 2015) use two separate networks: one to predict the moving target variable satisfying the Bellman equation (named target network), and another to compute the model's predictions at a given time. For now, let's have a look at how the backward pass updates our model weights in deep Q-learning.

Performing a backward pass in Q-Learning

Now, we have a defined loss metric, which computes the error between the optimal Q-function (derived from the Bellman equation) and the current Q-function at a given time. We can then propagate our prediction errors in Q-values, backwards through the model layers, as our network plays about the environment. As we are well aware of by now, this is achieved by taking the gradient of the loss function with respect to model weights, and then updating these weights in the opposite direction of the gradient per learning batch. Hence, we can iteratively update the model weights in the direction of the optimal Q-value function. We can formulate the backpropagation process and illustrate the change in model weights (theta) like so:

$$\nabla_{\theta_i} L_i(\theta_i) = \mathbb{E}_{s,a\sim\rho(\cdot);s'\sim\mathcal{E}} \left[r + \gamma \max_{a'} Q(s',a';\theta_{i-1}) - Q(s,a;\theta_i))\nabla_{\theta_i} Q(s,a;\theta_i) \right]$$

Eventually, as the model has seen enough state action pairs, it will sufficiently backpropagate its errors and learn optimal representations to help it navigate the given environment. In other words, a trained model will have the ideal configuration of layer weights, corresponding to the optimal Q-value function, mapping the agent's actions at given states of the environment.

Long story short, these equations describe the process of estimating an optimal polity (π^*) to solve a given environment. We use a neural network to learn the best Q-values for state action pairs in the given environment, which in turn can be used to calculate trajectories that generate optimal rewards, for our agent (that is, optimal policies). This is how we can use reinforcement learning to train anticipatory and reactive agents operating in a quasi-random simulation with sparse time delayed rewards. Now, we have all of the understanding that's required to go ahead and implement our very own deep reinforcement learning agent.

Replacing iterative updates with deep learning

Before we move on to the implementation, let's clarify what we have learned in regards to deep Q-learning so far. As we saw with the iterative update approach, we can use the transitions (from initial state, action performed, reward generated, and new state sampled, < s, a, r, s' >) to update the Q-table holding the value of these tuples at each time step. However, as we mentioned, this method is not computationally scalable. Instead, we will replace this iterative update performed on the Q-table and try to approximate the optimal Q-value function ($Q^*(s,a)$), using a neural network, like so:

1. Execute a feedforward pass using current state (s) as input, and then predict the Q-values for all of the actions at this state.
2. Execute a feedforward pass using the new state (s') to compute the maximum overall outputs of our network at the next state, that is, *max a' Q(s', a')*.
3. With the maximum overall outputs calculated in step 2, we set the target Q-value for the respective action to *r + γmax a' Q(s', a')*. We also set the target Q-value for all other actions to the same value that's returned by step 1 for each of the unselected action to only compute the prediction error for of the selected action. This effectively neutralizes (sets to zero) the effect of the errors from the predicted actions that were not taken by our agent at each time step.
4. Backpropagate the error to update the model weights

All we did here is build a network that's capable of making predictions on a moving target. This is useful since our model iteratively comes across more information about the physics of the environment as it plays the game. This is reflected by the fact that our target outputs (what actions to perform, at a given state) also keep changing, unlike in supervised learning, where we have fixed outputs that we call labels. Hence, we are actually trying to learn a function $Q^*(s,a)$ *that* can learn the mapping between constantly changing inputs (game states) and outputs (corresponding actions to take).

Through this process, our model develops better intuitions on what actions to perform and gain a better idea of the correct Q-values for state-action pairs as it sees more of the environment. In theory, Q-learning allows us to address the credit assignment problem by correlating rewards to actions that have been taken at previous game states. The errors are backpropagated until our model is able to identify decisive state-action pairs that are responsible for generating a given reward. However, we will soon see that a lot of computational and mathematical tricks are employed to make deep Q-learning systems work as well as they do. Before we dive into these considerations, it may be helpful to further explore the forward and backward passes that occur in a deep Q-network.

Deep Q-learning in Keras

Now that we understand how to train an agent to select optimal state action pairs, let's try to solve a more complex environment than the taxi cab simulation we dealt with previously. Why not implement a learning agent to solve a problem that was originally crafted for humans themselves? Well, thanks to the wonders of the open source movement, that is exactly what we will do. Next on our task list, we will implement the methodologies of Mnih et al. (2013, and 2015) referring to the original DeepMind paper that implemented a Q-learning based agent. The researchers used the same methodology and neural architecture to play seven different Atari games. Notably, the researchers achieved remarkable results for six of the seven different games it was tested on. In three out of these six games, the agent was noted to outperform a human expert. This is why, today, we try and partially replicate these results and train a neural network to play some old-school games like Space Invaders and Ms. Pacman.

This is done by using a **convolutional neural network** (**CNN**), which takes video game screenshots as input and estimates the optimal Q values for actions given states of the game. To follow along, all you need to do is install the reinforcement learning package built on top of Keras, known as `keras-rl`. You will also require the Atari dependency for the OpenAI `gym` module, which we used previously. The Atari dependency is essentially an emulator for the Atari console that will generate our training environments. While the dependency was originally designed to run on the Ubuntu operating system, it has since been ported to be compatible Windows and Mac users alike. You can install both modules for the following experiments using the `pip` package manager.

- You can install the Keras reinforcement learning package with the following command:

  ```
  ! pip install keras-rl
  ```

- You can install the Atari dependency for Windows with the following command:

  ```
  ! pip install --no-index -f https://github.com/Kojoley/atari-
  py/releases atari_py
  ```

- Mnih et al (2015) `https://arxiv.org/pdf/1312.5602v1.pdf`

Making some imports

In the realm of machine intelligence, it has been a long-standing dream to achieve human-level control for tasks like gaming. The complexity involved in automating an agent, operating only on high-dimensional sensory inputs (like audio, images, and so on), has been quite a challenging to accomplish with reinforcement learning. Previous approaches heavily relied on hand-crafted features, combined with linear policy representations that relied too much on the quality of the engineered features, to perform well. Unlike the previous attempts, this technique does not require our agent to have any human-engineered knowledge about the game. It will solely rely on the pixel inputs it receives and encode representations to predict the optimal Q-value for each possible action at each state of the environment it traverses. Pretty cool, no? Let's import the following libraries into our workspace to see how we can proceed with this task:

```
from PIL import Image
import numpy as np
import gym

from keras.models import Sequential
from keras.layers import Dense, Activation, Flatten, Convolution2D, Permute
from keras.optimizers import Adam
import keras.backend as K

from rl.agents.dqn import DQNAgent
from rl.policy import LinearAnnealedPolicy, BoltzmannQPolicy,
EpsGreedyQPolicy
from rl.memory import SequentialMemory
from rl.core import Processor
from rl.callbacks import FileLogger, ModelIntervalCheckpoint
```

Preprocessing techniques

As we mentioned previously, we will be using a CNN to encode representative visual features about each state that's shown to our agent. Our CNN will proceed to regress these higher-level representations against optimal Q-values, corresponding to optimal actions to be taken for each given state. Hence, we must show our network a sequence of inputs, corresponding to a sequence of screenshots you would see, when playing an Atari game.

Were we playing the game of Space Invaders (Atari 2600), these screenshots would look something like this:

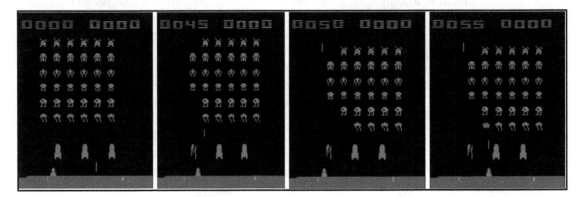

The original Atari 2600 screen frames, which were designed to be aesthetically pleasing to the human palate from the 70s era, exist in the dimensions of 210 x 160 pixels, with a color scheme of 128. While it may be computationally demanding to process these raw frames in sequence, note that there is a lot of opportunity for downsampling our training images from these frames to work with more manageable representations. Indeed, this follows the approach taken by Minh et al. to reduce the input dimensions to a more manageable size. This is achieved by downsampling the original RGB image to a greyscale image with 110 x 84 pixels, before cropping out the extremities of the image where nothing much happens. This leaves us with our final image size of 84 x 84 pixels. This reduction in dimensionality helps our CNN better encode representative visual features, following the theory we covered in Chapter 4, *Convolutional Neural Networks*.

Defining input parameters

Finally, our convolutional network will also receive these cropped images in batches of four at a time. Using these four frames, the neural network will be asked to estimate the optimal Q-values for the given input frame. Hence, we define our input shape, referring to the size of the pre-processed 84 x 84 game screen frames. We also define a window length of 4, which simply refers to the number of images our network sees at a time. For each image, the network will make a scalar prediction for the optimal Q-value, which maximizes the expected future rewards that are attainable by our agent:

```
1  INPUT_SHAPE = (84, 84)
2  WINDOW_LENGTH = 4
```

Making an Atari game state processor

Since our network is only allowed to observe the state of the game through the input images, we must first construct a Python class that lets our **deep-Q learning agent** (DQN) processes the states and the rewards that are generated by the Atari emulator. This class will accept a processor object, which simply refers to the coupling mechanism between an agent and its environment, as implemented in the `keras-rl` library.

We are creating the `AtariProcessor` class as we want to use the same network to perform in different environments, each with different types of states, actions, and rewards. What's the intuition behind this? Well, think of the difference in game screen and possible moves between a Space Invaders game versus a Pacman game. While the defender in the space invaders game can only scroll sideways and fire, Pacman can move up, down, left, and right to respond to the different states of its environment. A custom processor class helps us streamline the training process between different games, without performing too many modifications on the learning agent or on the observed environment. The processor class we will implement will allow us to simplify the processing of different game states and rewards that are generated through the agent acting upon the environment:

```python
class AtariProcessor(Processor):
    def process_observation(self, observation):
        # Assert dimension (height, width, channel)
        assert observation.ndim == 3
        # Retrieve image from array
        img = Image.fromarray(observation)
        # Resize and convert to grayscale
        img = img.resize(INPUT_SHAPE).convert('L')
        # Convert back to array
        processed_observation = np.array(img)
        # Assert input shape
        assert processed_observation.shape == INPUT_SHAPE
        # Save processed observation in experience memory (8bit)
        return processed_observation.astype('uint8')
    def process_state_batch(self, batch):
        #Convert the batches of images to float32 datatype
        processed_batch = batch.astype('float32') / 255.
        return processed_batch
    def process_reward(self, reward):
        return np.clip(reward, -1., 1.) # Clip reward
```

Processing individual states

Our processor class includes three simple functions. The first function (`process_observation`) takes an array representing a simulated game state and converts it into images. The images are then resized, converted back into an array, and returned as a manageable datatype to the experience memory (a concept we will elaborate upon shortly).

Processing states in batch

Next, we have the (`process_state_batch`) function, which processes the images in batch and returns them as a `float32` array. While this step could also be achieved in the first function, the reason we do it separately is to achieve higher computational efficiency. As simple mathematics dictates, storing a `float32` array is four times more memory intensive than storing an 8-bit array. Since we want our observations to be stored in experience memory, we would rather store them in manageable representations. Doing so becomes especially important when processing the millions of states of a given environment.

Processing rewards

Finally, the last function in our class lets us clip the rewards that are generated from the environment by using the (`process_reward`) function. Why do this? Well, let's consider a little bit of background information. While we let our agent train on the real, unmodified game, this change to the reward structure is performed during training only. Instead of letting our agent use the actual score from the game screen, we can fix positive and negative rewards to +1 and -1, respectively. A reward of 0 is not influenced by this clipping operation. Doing so is practically useful as it lets us limit the scale of the derivatives as we backpropagate our network's errors. Moreover, it becomes easier to implement the same agent on a different learning environment since the agent does not have to learn a new scoring scheme for an entirely new type of game.

Limitations of reward clipping

One clear downside of clipping rewards, as noted in the DeepMind paper (Minh et al, 2015), is that this operation prohibits our agent from being able to differentiate rewards of differing magnitude. Such a notion will certainly be relevant for even more complex simulations. Consider a real self-driving car, for instance. The artificial agent in control may need to assess the magnitudes of reward/penalty for dilemmatic actions it may have to take, given a state of the environment. Perhaps the agent faces actions like running over a pedestrian to avoid a more disastrous accident on the road. This limitation, however, does not seem to severely affect our agent's ability to conquer the simpler learning environment that's offered by Atari 2600 games.

Initializing the environment

Next, we simply initialize the space invaders environment using the Atari dependency (separate import not necessary) we added earlier to the available gym environments:

```
env = gym.make('SpaceInvaders-v0')
np.random.seed(123)
env.seed(123)
nb_actions = env.action_space.n
```

We also generate a random seed to consistently initialize the state of the environment so that it has reproduceable experiments. Finally, we define a variable pertaining to the number of actions that can be taken by our agent at any given time.

Building the network

Thinking about our problem intuitively, we are designing a neural network that takes in a sequence of game states that have been sampled from an environment. At each state of the sequence, we want our network to predict the action with the highest Q-value. Hence, the output of our network will refer to Q-values per action, for each possible game state. Hence, we first define a few convolutional layers with an increasing number of filters and decreasing stride-lengths as the layers progress. All of these convolutional layers are implemented with a **Rectified Linear Unit (ReLU)** activation function. Following these, we add a flatten layer to reduce the dimensions of the outputs from our convolutional layers to vector representations.

These representations are then fed to two densely connected layers that perform the regression of game states against Q-values for the actions that are available:

```
input_shape = (WINDOW_LENGTH,) + INPUT_SHAPE
# Build Conv2D model
model = Sequential()
model.add(Permute((2, 3, 1), input_shape=input_shape))
model.add(Convolution2D(32, (8, 8), strides=(4, 4), activation='relu'))
model.add(Convolution2D(64, (4, 4), strides=(2, 2), activation='relu'))
model.add(Convolution2D(64, (3, 3), strides=(1, 1), activation='relu'))
model.add(Flatten())
model.add(Dense(512, activation='relu'))
# Last layer: no. of neurons corresponds to action space
# Linear activation
model.add(Dense(nb_actions, activation='linear'))
print(model.summary())
```

Layer (type)	Output Shape	Param #
permute_2 (Permute)	(None, 84, 84, 4)	0
conv2d_4 (Conv2D)	(None, 20, 20, 32)	8224
conv2d_5 (Conv2D)	(None, 9, 9, 64)	32832
conv2d_6 (Conv2D)	(None, 7, 7, 64)	36928
flatten_2 (Flatten)	(None, 3136)	0
dense_3 (Dense)	(None, 512)	1606144
dense_4 (Dense)	(None, 6)	3078

```
Total params: 1,687,206
Trainable params: 1,687,206
Non-trainable params: 0
```

None

Finally, you will notice that our output layer is a densely connected one, with a number of neurons corresponding to our agent's action space (that is, the number of actions it may perform). This layer also has a linear activation function, just like the regression examples we saw previously. This is because our network is essentially performing a sort of a multivariate regression, where it uses its feature representations to predict the highest Q-value for each action the agent may take at the given input state.

Absence of pooling layers

Another difference you may have noticed from previous CNN examples is the absence of pooling layers. Previously, we used pooling layers to downsample the activation maps produced by each convolutional layer. As you will recall from Chapter 4, *Convolutional Neural Networks*, these pooling layers helped us to implement the notion of spatial invariance to different types of inputs our CNN. However, when implementing a CNN for our particular use case, we may not want to discard information that's specific to the spatial location of representations, as this may actually be an integral part of identifying the correct move for our agent:

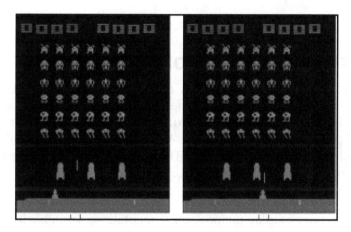

As you can see in the two almost identical images, the location of the projectile, which is fired by the space invaders, significantly alters the game state for our agent. While the agent is far enough to avoid this projectile in the first image, it may meet its doom by making one wrong move (moving to its right) in the second image. Since we would like it to be able to significantly distinguish between these two states, we avoid the use of pooling layers.

Problems with live learning

As we mentioned earlier, our neural network will process a sequence of four frames at a time and regress these inputs to actions with the highest Q-value for each individual state (that is, image) that's sampled from the Atari emulator. However, if we do not shuffle the order in which our network receives each batch of four images, then our network runs into some pretty vexing problems during the learning process.

The reason we do not want our network to learn from consecutive batches of samples is because these sequences are locally correlated. This is a problem since the network parameters, at any given time, will determine the next training examples that are generated by the emulator. Given the Markov assumption, the probability of future game states are dependent on the current game state. Hence, if the current maximizing action dictates our agent to move to the right, then the following training samples in the batch would be dominated by the agent moving right, causing bad and unnecessary feedback loops. Moreover, consecutive training samples are often too similar for the network to effectively learn from them. These issues will likely cause our network's loss to converge to a local (rather than global) minimum during the training process. So, how exactly do we counter this?

Storing experience in replay memory

The answer lies in the idea of forging a replay memory for our network. Essentially, the replay memory can act as a fixed length *experience que* of sorts. It can be used to store the sequential states of the game being played, along with the actions made, reward generated, and the state that's returned to the agent. These experience ques are continuously updated to maintain *n* most recent states of the game. Then, our network will use randomized batches of experience tuples (`state`, `action`, `reward`, and `next state`) that are saved in replay memory to perform gradient decent.

There are different types of replay memory implementations available in `rl.memory`, the `keras-rl` module. We use the `SequentialMemory` object to accomplish our purpose. This takes two parameters, as shown here:

```
memory = SequentialMemory(limit=1000000, window_length=WINDOW_LENGTH)
```

The limit parameter denotes the number of entries to be held in memory. Once the limit is exceeded, newer entries will replace older ones. The `window_length` parameter simply refers to the number of training samples per batch.

Due to the random order of the experience tuple batches, the network is less likely to get entrenched in a local minimum and will eventually converge to find optimal weights, representing the optimal policy for a given environment. Furthermore, using non-sequential batches to perform weight updates means that we achieve higher data efficiency, as the same individual image can be shuffled into different batches, contributing to multiple weight updates. Lastly, these experience tuples can even be collected from human gameplay data, rather than the previous moves that were executed by the network.

Other approaches (Schaul et al., 2016: `https://arxiv.org/abs/1511.05952`) have implemented a prioritized version of experience replay memory by adding an additional data structure that keeps track of the priority of each transition (*state -> action -> reward -> next-state*) in order to replay important transitions more frequently. The intuition behind this is to make the network learn from its best and worst performances more often, rather than instances where not much learning can occur. While these are some clever approaches that help our model converge to relevant representations, we also want it to surprise us from time to time and explore opportunities it hasn't considered yet. This brings us back to, *The explore-exploit dilemma* that we discussed earlier.

Balancing exploration with exploitation

How can we ensure that our agent relies on a good balance of old and new strategies? This problem is made worse through the random initialization of weights for our Q-network. Since the predicted Q-values are a result of these random weights, the model will generate sub-optimal predictions at the initial training epochs, which in turn results in poor Q-value learning. Naturally, we don't want our network to rely too much on strategies it generates at first for given state-action pairs. Just like the dopamine addicted rat, the agent cannot be expected to perform well in the long term if it doesn't explore new strategies and expand its horizons instead of exploiting known strategies. To address this problem, we must implement a mechanism that encourages the agent to try out new actions, ignoring the learned Q-values. Doing so basically allows our learning agent to try out new strategies that may potentially be more beneficial in the long run.

Epsilon-greedy exploration policy

This can be achieved by algorithmically modifying the policy that's used by our learning agent to solve its environment. A common approach to this is using an epsilon-greedy exploration strategy. Here, we define a probability (ε). Then, our agent may ignore the learnt Q-values and try a random action with a probability of ($1 - \varepsilon$). Hence, if the epsilon value is set to 0.5, our network will, on average, ignore actions suggested by its learnt Q-Table and do something random. This is quite an exploratory agent. Conversely, a value of 0.001 for epsilon will make the network more consistently rely on the learned Q-values, picking random actions in only one out of a hundred time steps on average.

A fixed ε value is rarely used as the degree of exploration versus exploitation to implement can differ based on many internal (for example, agents learning rate) and external factors (for example, the degree of randomness versus determinism in a given environment). In the DeepMind paper, the researchers implemented a decaying ε term over time, starting from 1 (that is not relying at all upon the initial random predictions) to 0.1 (relying on predicted Q-values 9 out of 10 times):

```
policy = LinearAnnealedPolicy(EpsGreedyQPolicy(),
                              attr='eps',
                              value_max=1.,
                              value_min=.1,
                              value_test=.05,
                              nb_steps=1000000)
```

Hence, a decaying epsilon ensures that our agent does not rely upon the random predictions at the initial training epochs, only to later on exploit its own predictions more aggressively as the Q-function converges to more consistent predictions.

Initializing the deep Q-learning agent

Now, we have programmatically defined all of the individual components that are necessary to initialize our deep Q-learning agent. For this, we use the imported DQNAgent object from rl.agents.dqn and defined the appropriate parameters, as shown here:

```
#Initialize the atari_processor() class

processor = AtariProcessor()

# Initialize the DQN agent
dqn = DQNAgent(model=model,                  #Compiled neural network model
               nb_actions=nb_actions,        #Action space
               policy=policy,      #Policy chosen (Try Boltzman Q policy)
               memory=memory,      #Replay memory (Try Episode Parameter
                                                  memory)
               processor=processor,          #Atari processor class
#Warmup steps to ignore initially (due to random initial weights)
               nb_steps_warmup=50000,
               gamma=.99,                     #Discount factor
               train_interval=4,              #Training intervals
               delta_clip=1.,                 #Reward clipping
               )
```

The preceding parameters are initialized following the original DeepMind paper. Now, we are ready to finally compile our model and initiate the training process. To compile the model, we can simply call the compile method on our dqn model object:

```
dqn.compile(optimizer=Adam(lr=.00025), metrics=['mae'])
```

The compile method here takes an optimizer and the metric we want to track as arguments. In our case, we choose the Adam optimizer with a low learning rate of 0.00025 and track the **Mean Absolute Error (MAE)** metric, as shown here.

Training the model

Now, we can initiate the training session for our deep Q-learning network. We do this by calling the fit method on our compiled DQN network object. The fit parameter takes the environment being trained on (in our case, the SpaceInvaders-v0) and the number of total game steps (similar to epoch, denoting the total number of game states to sample from the environment) during this training session, as arguments. You may choose to define the optional parameter visualize as True if you wish to visualize how well your agent is doing as it trains. While this is quite fun—even a tad mesmerizing to observe—it significantly affects training speed, and hence is not practical to have as a default:

```
dqn.fit(env, nb_steps=1750000)    #visualize=True

Training for 1750000 steps ...
Interval 1 (0 steps performed)
  2697/10000 [=======>...................] - ETA: 26s - reward: 0.0126
```

Testing the model

We test the model using the following code:

```
dqn.test(env, nb_episodes=10, visualize=True)

Testing for 10 episodes ...
Episode 1: reward: 3.000, steps: 654
Episode 2: reward: 11.000, steps: 807
Episode 3: reward: 8.000, steps: 812
Episode 4: reward: 3.000, steps: 475
Episode 5: reward: 4.000, steps: 625
Episode 6: reward: 9.000, steps: 688
Episode 7: reward: 5.000, steps: 652
Episode 8: reward: 12.000, steps: 826
Episode 9: reward: 2.000, steps: 632
```

```
Episode 10: reward: 3.000, steps: 643

<keras.callbacks.History at 0x24280aadc50>
```

Summarizing the Q-learning algorithm

Congratulations! You have now achieved a detailed understanding behind the concept of deep Q-learning and have applied these concepts to make a simulated agent incrementally learn to solve its environment. The following pseudocode is provided as a refresher to the whole deep Q-learning process we just implemented:

```
initialize replay memory
initialize Q-Value function with random weights
sample initial state from environment
Keep repeating:

        choose an action to perform:
                with probability ε select a random action
                otherwise select action with argmax a Q(s, a')
        execute chosen action
        collect reward and next state
        save experience <s, a, r, s'> in replay memory

        sample random transitions <s, a, r, s'> from replay memory
        compute target variable for each mini-batch transition:

                if s' is terminal state then target = r
                otherwise t = r + γ max a'Q(s', a')
        train the network with loss (target - Q(s,a)`^2)
        s = s'

until done
```

Double Q-learning

Another augmentation to the standard Q-learning model we just built is the idea of Double Q-learning, which was introduced by Hado van Hasselt (2010, and 2015). The intuition behind this is quite simple. Recall that, so far, we were estimating our target values for each state-action pair using the Bellman equation and checking how far off the mark our predictions are at a given state, like so:

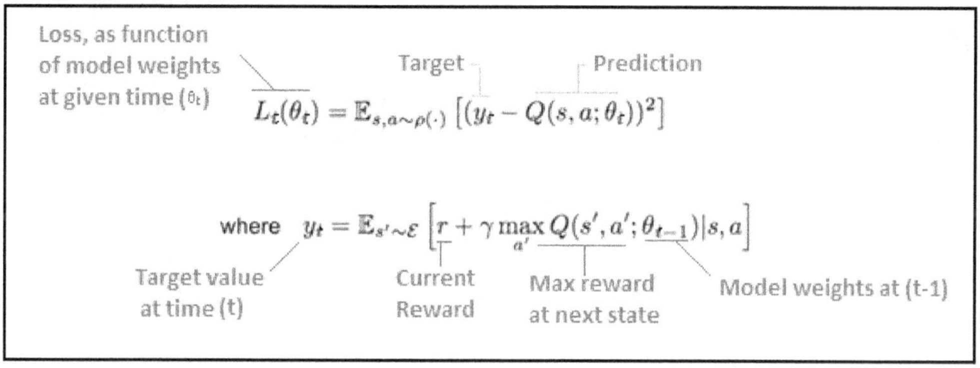

Loss, as function
of model weights
at given time (θ_t)

Target ⌐ ⌐ Prediction

$$L_t(\theta_t) = \mathbb{E}_{s,a \sim \rho(\cdot)}\left[(y_t - Q(s,a;\theta_t))^2\right]$$

where $\quad y_t = \mathbb{E}_{s' \sim \mathcal{E}}\left[r + \gamma \max_{a'} Q(s',a';\theta_{t-1})|s,a\right]$

Target value   Current   Max reward   Model weights at (t-1)
at time (t)   Reward   at next state

However, a problem arises from estimating the maximum expected future reward in this manner. As you may have noticed earlier, the max operator in the target equation (y_t) uses the same Q-values to evaluate a given action as the ones that are used to predict a given action for a sampled state. This introduces a propensity for overestimation of Q-values, eventually even spiraling out of control. To compensate for such possibilities, Van Hasselt et al. (2016) implemented a model that decoupled the selection of actions from the evaluation thereof. This is achieved using two separate neural networks, each parametrized to estimate a subset of the entire equation. The first network is tasked with predicting the actions to take at given states, while a second network is used to generate the targets by which the first network's predictions are evaluated as the loss is computed iteratively. Although the formulation of the loss at each iteration does not change, the target label for a given state can now be represented by the augmented Double DQN equation, as shown here:

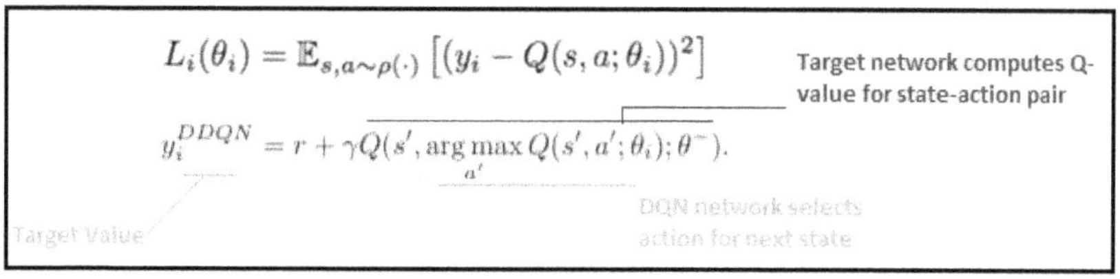

$$L_i(\theta_i) = \mathbb{E}_{s,a \sim \rho(\cdot)}\left[(y_i - Q(s,a;\theta_i))^2\right]$$

Target network computes Q-
value for state-action pair

$$y_i^{DDQN} = r + \gamma Q(s', \arg\max_{a'} Q(s',a';\theta_i);\theta^-).$$

DQN network selects
action for next state

Target Value

As we can see, the target network has its own set of parameters to optimize, (θ-). This decoupling of action selection from evaluation has shown to compensate for the overoptimistic representations that are learned by the naïve DQN. As a consequence, we are able to converge our loss function faster while achieving a more stable learning.

In practice, the target networks weights can also be fixed and slowly/periodically updated to avoid destabilizing the model with bad feedback loops (between the target and prediction). This technique was notably popularized by yet another DeepMind paper (Hunt, Pritzel, Heess et al. , 2016), where the approach was found to stabilize the training process.

 The DeepMind paper by Hunt, Pritzel, Heess et al., *Continuous Control with Deep Reinforcement Learning*, 2016, can be accessed at `https://arxiv.org/pdf/1509.02971.pdf`.

You may implement the Double DQN through the `keras-rl` module by using the same code we used earlier to train our Space Invaders agent, with a slight modification to the part that defines your DQN agent:

```
double_dqn = DQNAgent(model=model,
              nb_actions=nb_actions,
              policy=policy,
              memory=memory,
              processor=processor,
              nb_steps_warmup=50000,
              gamma=.99,
              target_model_update=1e-2,
              train_interval=4,
              delta_clip=1.,
              enable_double_dqn=True,
              )
```

All we simply have to do is define the Boolean value for `enable_double_dqn` to `True`, and we are good to go! Optionally, you may also want to experiment with the number of warm up steps (that is, before the model starts learning) and the frequency with which the target model is updated. We can further refer the following paper:

- **Deep Reinforcement Learning with Double Q-learning**: `https://arxiv.org/pdf/1509.06461.pdf`

Dueling network architecture

The last variation of Q-learning architecture that we shall implement is the Dueling network architecture (https://arxiv.org/abs/1511.06581). As the name might suggest, here, we figuratively make a neural network duel with itself using two separate estimators for the value of a state and the value of a state-action pair. You will recall from earlier in this chapter that we estimated the quality of a state-action pairs using a single stream of convolutional and densely connected layers. However, we can actually split up the Q-value function into a sum of two separate terms. The reason behind this segregated architecture is to allow our model to separately learn states that may or may not be valuable, without having to specifically learn the effect of each action that's performed at each state:

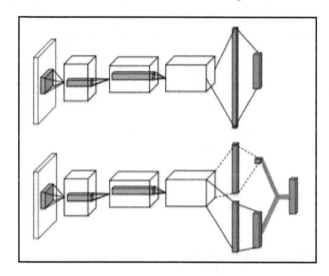

At the top of the preceding diagram, we can see the standard DQN architecture. At the bottom, we can see how the Dueling DQN architecture bifurcates into two separate streams, where the state and state-action values are separately estimated without any extra supervision. Hence, Dueling DQNs use separate estimators (that is, densely connected layers) for both the value of being at a state, $V(s)$, as well as the advantage of performing one action over another, at a given state, $A(s,a)$. These two terms are then combined to predict Q-values for given state-action pair, ensuring that our agent chooses optimal actions in the long run. While the standard Q function, $Q(s,a)$, only allowed us to estimate the value of selecting actions for given states, we can now measure both value of states and relative advantage of actions separately. Doing so can be helpful in situations where performing an action does not alter the environment in a relevant enough manner.

Both the value and the advantage function are given in the following equation:

$$V^*(s) = \max_a Q^*(s, a)$$

$$A^\pi(s, a) = Q^\pi(s, a) - V^\pi(s).$$

DeepMind researchers (Wang et al, 2016) tested such an architecture on an early car racing game (Atari Enduro), where the agent is instructed to drive on a road where obstacles may sometimes occur. Researchers noted how the state value stream learns to pay attention to the road and the on-screen score, whereas the action advantage stream would only learn to pay attention when specific obstacles would appear on the game screen. Naturally, it only becomes important for the agent to perform an action (move left or right) once an obstacle is in its path. Otherwise, moving left or right has no importance to the agent. On the other hand, it is always important for our agent to keep their eyes on the road and at the score, which is done by the state value stream of the network. Hence, in their experiments, the researchers show how this architecture can lead to better policy evaluation, especially when an agent is faced with many actions with similar consequences.

We can implement Dueling DQNs using the `keras-rl` module for the very same Space Invaders problem we viewed earlier. All we need to do is redefine our agent, as shown here:

```
dueling_dqn = DQNAgent(model=model,
            nb_actions=nb_actions,
            policy=policy,
            memory=memory,
            processor=processor,
            nb_steps_warmup=50000,
            gamma=.99,
            target_model_update=10000,
            train_interval=4,
            delta_clip=1.,
            enable_dueling_network=True,
            dueling_type='avg'
            )
```

Here, we simply have to define the Boolean argument `enabble_dueling_network` parameter to `True` and specify a dueling type.

For more information on the network architecture and potential benefits of usage, we encourage you to follow up on the full research paper, *Dueling Network Architectures for Deep Reinforcement Learning*, at `https://arxiv.org/pdf/1511.06581.pdf`.

Exercise

- Implement standard Q-learning with a different policy (Boltzman) on an Atari environment and examine the difference in performance metrics
- Implement a Double DQN on the same problem and compare the difference in performance
- Implement a Dueling DQN for the same problem and compare the difference in performance

Limits of Q-learning

It is truly remarkable how a relatively simple algorithm as such can give rise to complex strategies that such agents can come up with, given enough training time. Notably, researchers (and now, you too) are able to show how expert strategies may be learned through enough interaction with the environment. In the classic game of breakout, for example (included as an environment in the Atari dependency), you are expected to move a plank at the bottom of the screen to bounce a ball back and break some bricks at the top of the screen. After enough hours of training, a DQN agent can even figure out intricate strategies such as getting the ball stuck on the top side of the screen, scoring the maximum amount of points possible:

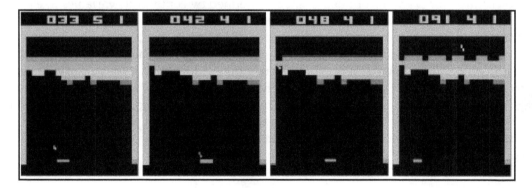

Such intuitive behavior naturally makes you wonder—how far can we take this methodology? What type of environments may we be able to master with this approach, and what are its limits?

Indeed, the power of Q-learning algorithms lies in their ability to solve problems with high-dimensional observation spaces, like images from a game screen. We achieved this using a convolutional architecture, allowing us to correlate state-action pairs with optimal rewards. However, the action spaces that we've concerned ourselves with thus far were mostly discrete and low dimensional. Turning right or left, denotes a discrete action, as opposed to a continuous action, like turning left at an angle. The latter is an example of a continuous action space, as the agent's action of turning to the left depends on the variable denoted by a certain angle, which can take a continuous value. We also did not have that many executable actions to begin with (ranging between 4 and 18 for Atari 2600 games). Other candidate deep reinforcement learning problems, like robotic motion control or optimizing fleet deployment, may require the modeling of very high dimensional and continuous action spaces, where standard DQNs tend to perform poorly. This is simply because DQNs rely on finding actions that maximize the Q-value function, which would require iterative optimization at every step in the case continuous action spaces. Thankfully, other approaches exist for this problem.

Improving Q-learning with policy gradients

In our approach so far, we have been iteratively updating our estimates of Q-values for state-action pairs, from which we inferred the optimal policies. However, this becomes an arduous learning task when dealing with continuous action spaces. In the case of robot motion control, for example, our action space is defined by continuous variables like joint positions and angles of the robot. In such cases, estimating the Q-value function becomes impractical as we can assume that the function itself is extremely complicated. So, instead of learning optimal Q-values for each joint position and angle, at each given state, we can try a different approach. What if we could learn a policy directly, without inferring it from iteratively updating our Q-values for state-action pairs? Recall that a policy is simply a trajectory of states, followed by actions performed, reward generated, and the states being returned to the agent. Hence, we can define a set of parameterized policies (parameterized by the weights (θ) of a neural network), where the value of each policy can be defined by the function given here:

$$J(\theta) = \mathbb{E}\left[\sum_{t \geq 0} \gamma^t r_t | \pi_\theta\right]$$

Here, the value of a policy is represented by the function $J(\theta)$, where theta represents our model weights. On the left-hand side, we can define the value of a given policy with the familiar term we saw before, denoting the expected sum of cumulated future rewards. Our objective under this new setup is to find model weights that return the maximum of the policy value function, $J(\theta)$, corresponding to the best expected future reward for our agent.

Previously, to find the global minimum of a function, we performed an iterative optimization of the first order derivatives of that function, and took steps that were proportional to the negative of our gradient to update model weights. This is what we call gradient decent. However, since we want to find the maximum of our policy value function, $J(\theta)$, we will perform gradient ascent, which iteratively updates model weights that are proportional to the positive of our gradient. Hence, we can get a deep neural network to converge on optimal policies by evaluating trajectories that are generated by a given policy, instead of individually evaluating the quality of state-action pairs. Following this, we can even make actions from favorable policies have a higher probability of being selected by our agent, whereas actions from unfavorable policies can be sampled less frequently, given game states. This is the main intuition behind policy gradient methods. Naturally, a whole new bag of tricks follow this approach, which we encourage you to read up on. One such example is *Continuous Control with Deep Reinforcement Learning*, by, which can be found at `https://arxiv.org/pdf/1509.02971.pdf`.

An interesting policy gradient implementation to look into could be the Actor Critic model, which can be implemented in continuous action space to solve more complex problems involving high-dimensional action spaces, such as the ones we previously discussed. More information on the Actor Critic model can be found at `https://arxiv.org/pdf/1509.02971.pdf`.

This same actor critic concept has been used in different settings for a range of different tasks, such a natural language generation and dialogue modeling, and even playing complex real-time strategy games like StarCraft II, which interested readers are encouraged to explore:

- **Natural Language Generation and dialogue modeling**: `https://arxiv.org/pdf/1607.07086.pdf`
- **Starcraft II: a new challenge for reinforcement learning**: `https://arxiv.org/pdf/1708.04782.pdf?fbclid=IwAR30QJE6Kw16pHA949pEf_VCTbrX582BDNnWG2OdmgqTIQpn4yPbtdV-xFs`

Summary

In this chapter, we covered quite a lot. Not only did we explore a whole new branch of machine learning, that is, reinforcement learning, we also implemented some state-of-the-art algorithms that have shown to give rise to complex autonomous agents. We saw how we can model an environment using the Markov decision process and assess optimal rewards using the Bellman equation. We also saw how problems of credit assignment can be addressed by approximating a quality function using deep neural networks. While doing so, we explored a whole bag of tricks like reward discounting, clipping, and experience replay memory (to name a few) that contribute toward representing high dimensional inputs like game screen images to navigate simulated environments while optimizing a goal.

Finally, we explored some of the advances in the fiend of deep-Q learning, overviewing architectures like double DQNs and dueling DQNs. Finally, we reviewed some of the challenges that are present in making agents successfully navigate high-dimensional action spaces and saw how different approaches, such as policy gradients, may help address these considerations.

Section 3: Hybrid Model Architecture

This section familiarizes the reader with understanding the current potential and limits of deep learning, and how to get inspired by academia and industry, collating all the resources required to implement an end-to-end deep learning workflow.

This section comprises the following chapters:

- Chapter 8, *Autoencoders*
- Chapter 9, *Generative Networks*

Making some imports

For this exercise, we will be using Keras's functional API, accessible through `keras.models`, which allows us to build acyclic graphs and multioutput models, as we did in Chapter 4, *Convolutional Neural Networks*, to dive deep into the intermediate layers of convolutional networks. While you may also replicate autoencoders using the sequential API (autoencoders are sequential models, after all), they are commonly implemented through the functional API, allowing us to gain a little more experience of using both of Keras's APIs:

```
import numpy as np
import matplotlib.pyplot as plt

from keras.layers import Input, Dense
from keras.models import Model
from keras.datasets import fashion_mnist
```

Probing the data

Next, we simply load the `fashion_mnist` dataset that's contained in Keras. Note that while we have loaded the labels for each image as well, this is not necessary for the task we are about to perform. All we need are the input images, which our shallow autoencoder will regenerate:

```
(x_train, y_train), (x_test, y_test) = fashion_mnist.load_data()
x_train.shape, x_test.shape, type(x_train)
((60000, 28, 28), (10000, 28, 28), numpy.ndarray)
plt.imshow(x_train[1], cmap='binary')
```

Following is the output:

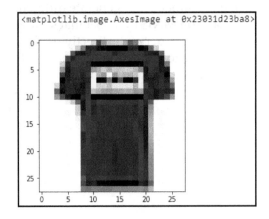

8
Autoencoders

In the preceding chapter, we familiarized ourselves with a novel area in **machine learning (ML)**: the realm of reinforcement learning. We saw how reinforcement learning algorithms can be augmented using neural networks, and how we can learn approximate functions that can map game states to possible actions the agent may take. These actions are then compared to a moving target variable, which in turn was defined by what we called the **Bellman equation**. This, strictly speaking, is a self-supervised ML technique, as it is the Bellman equation that's used to compare our predictions, and not a set of labeled target variables, as would be the case for a supervised learning approach (for example, game screens labeled with optimal actions to take at each state). The latter, while possible, proves to be much more computationally intensive for the given use case. Now we will move on and discover yet another self-supervised ML technique as we dive into the world of **neural autoencoders**.

In this chapter, we will explore the utility and advantages of making neural networks learn to encode the most representative features from a given dataset. In essence, this allows us to preserve, and later recreate, the key elements that define a class of observations. The observations themselves can be images, natural language data, or even time-series observations that may benefit from a reduction in dimensionality, weeding out bits of information representing less informative aspects of the given observations. Cui bono ? You ask.

Following are the topics that will be covered in this chapter:

- Why autoencoders?
- Automatically encoding information
- Understanding the limitations of autoencoders
- Breaking down the autoencoder
- Training an autoencoder
- Overviewing autoencoder archetypes
- Network size and representational power
- Understanding regularization in autoencoders

- Regularization with sparse autoencoders
- Probing the data
- Building the verification model
- Designing a deep autoencoder
- Using functional API to design autoencoders
- Deep convolutional autoencoders
- Compiling and training the model
- Testing and visualising the results
- Denoising autoencoders
- Training the denoising network

Why autoencoders?

While, in the past (circa 2012), autoencoders have briefly enjoyed some fame for their use in initializing layer weights for deep **Convolutional Neural Networks** (**CNNs**) (through an operation known as **greedy layer-wise pretraining**), researchers gradually lost interest in such pretraining techniques as better random weight initialization schemes came about, and more advantageous methods that allowed deeper neural networks to be trained (such as batch normalization, 2014, and later residual learning, 2015) surfaced to the general sphere.

Today, a paramount utility of autoencoders is derived from their ability to discover low-dimensional representations of high-dimensional data, while still attempting to preserve the core attributes present therein. This permits us to perform tasks such as recovering damaged images (or image denoising). A similar area of active interest for autoencoders comes from their ability to perform principal component analysis, such as transformations on data, allowing for informative visualizations of the main factors of variance that are present. In fact, single-layer autoencoders with a linear activation function can be quite similar to the standard **Principal Component Analysis** (**PCA**) operation that's performed on datasets. Such an autoencoder simply learns the same dimensionally reduced subspace that would arise out of a PCA. Hence, autoencoders may be used in conjunction with the t-SNE algorithm (`https://en.wikipedia.org/wiki/T-distributed_stochastic_neighbor_embedding`), which is famous for its ability to visualize information on a 2D plane, to first downsample a high-dimensional dataset, then visualize the main factors of variance that are observable.

Moreover, the advantage of autoencoders for such use cases (that is, performing a dimensionality reduction) stems from the fact that they may have non-linear encoder and decoder functions, whereas the PCA algorithm is restricted to a linear map. This allows autoencoders to learn more powerful non-linear representations of the feature space compared to results from PCA analysis of the same data. In fact, autoencoders can prove to be a very powerful tool in your data science repertoire when you're dealing with very sparse and high-dimensional data.

Besides these practical applications of autoencoders, more creative and artistic ones also exist. Sampling from the reduced representation that's produced by the encoder, for example, has been used to generate artistic images that were auctioned for around half a million dollars at one New York-based auction house (see `https://www.bloomberg.com/news/articles/2018-10-25/ai-generated-portrait-is-sold-for-432-500-in-an-auction-first`). We will review the fundamentals of such image generation techniques in the next chapter, when we cover the variational autoencoder architecture and **Generative Adversarial Networks** (**GANs**). But first, let's try to better understand the essence of an autoencoder neural network.

Automatically encoding information

Well then, what's so different about the idea of autoencoders? You have surely come across countless encoding algorithms, ranging from MP3 compression that's performed to store audio files, or JPEG compression to store image files. The reason autoencoding neural networks are interesting is they take a very different approach toward representing information compared to their previously stated quasi-counterparts. It is the kind of approach you have certainly come to expect after seven long chapters on the inner workings of neural networks.

Unlike the MP3 or JPEG algorithms, which hold general assumptions about sound and pixels, a neural autoencoder is forced to learn representative features automatically from whatever input it is shown during a training session. It proceeds to recreate the given input by using the learned representations that were captured during the session. It is important to understand that the appeal of autoencoders do not come from simply copying its input. When training an autoencoder, we are typically not interested in the decoded output it generates per say, but rather how the network transforms the dimensionality of the given inputs. Ideally, we are looking for representative encoding schemes by giving the networks incentives and constraints to reconstruct the original input as closely as possible. By doing so, we can use the encoder function on similar datasets as a feature detection algorithm, which provides us with a semantically rich representation of the given inputs.

These representations can then be used to perform a classification of sorts, depending on the use case being tackled. It is thus the architectural mechanism of encoding that's employed, and which defines the novel approach of autoencoders compared to other standard encoding algorithms.

Understanding the limitations of autoencoders

As we saw previously, neural networks such as autoencoders are used to automatically learn representative features from data, without explicitly relying on human-engineered assumptions. While this approach may allow us to discover ideal encoding schemes that are specific to different types of data, this approach does present certain limitations. Firstly, autoencoders are said to be **data-specific**, in the sense that their utility is restricted to data that is considerably similar to its training data. For example, an autoencoder that's trained to only regenerate cat pictures will have a very hard time generating dog pictures without explicitly being trained to do so. Naturally, this seems to reduce the scalability of such algorithms. It is also noteworthy that autoencoders, as of yet, do not perform noticeably better than the JPEG algorithm at encoding images. Another concern is that autoencoders tend to produce a **lossy output**. This simply means that the compression and decompression operation degrades the output of the network, generating a less accurate representation compared to its input. This problem seems to be a recurrent one for most encoding use cases (including heuristic-based encoding schemes such as MP3 and JPEG).

Thus, autoencoders have unraveled some very promising practices to work with *unlabeled* real-world data. However, the vast majority of data that's available on the digital sphere today is in fact unstructured and unlabeled. It is also noteworthy that popular misconception assigns autoencoders into the unsupervised learning category, yet, in reality, it is but another variation of self-supervised learning, as we will soon discover. So, how exactly do these networks work?

Breaking down the autoencoder

Well, on a high level, an autoencoder can be thought of as a specific type of feed-forward network that learns to mimic its input to reconstruct a similar output. As we mentioned previously, it is composed of two separate parts: an encoder function and a decoder function. We can think of the entire autoencoder as layers of interconnected neurons, which propagate data by first encoding its input and then reconstructing the output using the generated code:

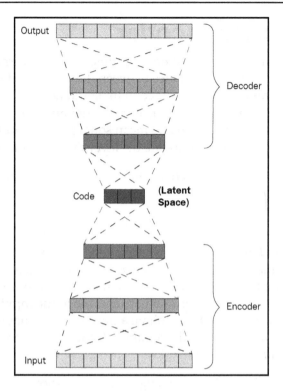

Example of an undercomplete autoencoder

The previous diagram illustrates a specific type of autoencoder network. Conceptually, the input layer of an autoencoder connects to a layer of neurons to funnel the data into a latent space, known as the **encoder function**. This function can be generically defined as $h = f(x)$, where x refers to the network inputs and h refers to the latent space that's generated by the encoder function. The latent space may embody a compressed representation of the input to our network, and is subsequently used by the decoder function (that is, the proceeding layer of neurons) to unravel the reduced representation, mapping it to a higher-dimensional feature space. Thus, the decoder function (formulized as $r = g(h)$) proceeds to transform the latent space that's generated by the encoder (h) into the *reconstructed* output of the network (r).

Training an autoencoder

The interaction between the encoder and decoder functions is governed by yet another function, which operationalizes the distance between the inputs and outputs of the encoder. We have come to know this as the `loss` function in neural network parlance. Hence, to train an autoencoder, we simply differentiate our encoder and decoder functions with respect to the `loss` function (typically using mean squared error) and use the gradients to backpropagate the model's errors and update the layer weights of the entire network.

Consequently, the learning mechanism of an autoencoder can be denoted as minimizing a `loss` function, and is as follows:

$$min\ L(x, g\,(\,f\,(\,x\,)\,)\,)$$

In the previous equation, L represents a `loss` function (such as MSE) that penalizes the output of the decoder function $(g(f(\,x\,)))$ for being divergent from the network's input, (x). By iteratively minimizing the reconstructed loss in this manner, our model will eventually converge to encode ideal representations that are specific to the input data, which can then be used to decoded similar data with a minimal amount of information loss. Hence, autoencoders are almost always trained via mini-batch gradient decent, as is common with other cases of feed-forward neural networks.

While autoencoders may also be trained using a technique known as **recirculation** (Hinton and McClelland, 1988), we will refrain from visiting this subtopic in this chapter, as this method is rarely used in most machine learning use cases involving autoencoders. Suffice it to mention that recirculation works by comparing network activations on given inputs to network activations on the generated reconstruction, instead of backpropagating gradient-based errors that are derived from differentiating the `loss` function with respect to network weights. While conceptually distinct, this may be interesting to read upon from a theoretical perspective, since recirculation is considered to be a biologically plausible alternative to the backpropagation algorithm, hinting at how we ourselves may update our mental models of the world as new information comes about.

Overviewing autoencoder archetypes

What we described previously is actually an example of an **undercomplete autoencoder**, which essentially puts a constraint on the latent space dimension. It is designated undercomplete, since the encoding dimension (that is, the dimension of the latent space) is smaller than the input dimension, which forces the autoencoder to learn about the most salient features that are present in the data sample.

Conversely, an **overcomplete autoencoder** has a larger encoding dimension relative to its input dimension. Such autoencoders are endowed with additional encoding capacity in relation to their input size, as can be seen in the following diagram:

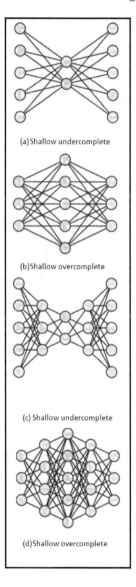

(a) Shallow undercomplete

(b) Shallow overcomplete

(c) Shallow undercomplete

(d) Shallow overcomplete

Network size and representational power

In the previous diagram, we can see four types of basic autoencoding architectures. **Shallow autoencoders** (an extension of shallow neural networks) are defined by having just one hidden layer of neurons, whereas deep autoencoders can have many layers that perform the encoding and decoding operations. Recall from the previous chapters that deeper neural networks may benefit from additional representational power compared to their shallow counterparts. Since autoencoders qualify as a specific breed of feed-forward networks, this also holds true for them. Additionally, it has been noted that deeper autoencoders may exponentially reduce the computational resources that are required for the network to learn to represent its inputs. It may also greatly reduce the number of training samples that are required for the network to learn a rich compressed version of the inputs. While reading the last few lines may incentivize some of you to start training hundreds of layered autoencoders, you may want to hold your horses. Giving the encoder and decoder functions too much capacity comes with its own disadvantages.

For example, an autoencoder with excess capacity may learn to perfectly recreate input images of Picasso paintings, without ever learning a single representative feature related to Picasso's painting style. In this case, all you have is an expensive copycat algorithm, which may be paralleled by Microsoft Paint's copy function. On the other hand, designing an autoencoder in accordance with the complexity and distribution of the data being modeled may well allow an AE to capture representative stylistic features, iconic to Picasso's *modus operandi*, from which aspiring artists and historians alike may learn. In practice, choosing the correct network depth and size may depend on a keen combination of theoretical familiarity with the learning process, experimentation, and domain knowledge in relation to the use case. Does this sound a bit time-consuming? Luckily, there may be a compromise ahead, which can be achieved through the use of regularized autoencoders.

Understanding regularization in autoencoders

On one extreme, you may always try to limit the network's learning capacity by sticking to shallow layers and having a very small latent space dimension. This approach may even provide an excellent baseline for benchmarking against more complex methods. However, other methods exist that may allow us to benefit from the representational power of deeper layers, without being penalized for issues of overcapacity up to a certain extent. Such methods include modifying the `loss` function that's used by an autoencoder so as to incentivize some representational criteria for the latent space being learned by the network.

For example, instead of simply copying the inputs, we may require our `loss` function to account for the sparsity of the latent space, favoring more rich representations over others. As we will see, we may even consider properties such as the magnitude of the derivatives of the latent space, or robustness to missing inputs, to ensure that our model really captures representative features from the inputs it is shown.

Regularization with sparse autoencoders

As we mentioned previously, one way of ensuring that our model encodes representative features from the inputs that are shown is by adding a sparsity constraint on the hidden layer representing the latent space (h). We denote this constraint with the Greek letter omega (Ω), which allows us to redefine the `loss` function of a sparse autoencoder, like so:

- Normal AE loss: $L(x, g(f(x)))$

- Sparse AE loss: $L(x, g(f(x))) + \Omega(h)$

This sparsity constraint term, $\Omega(h)$, can simply be thought of as a regularizer term that can be added to a feed-forward neural network, as we saw in previous chapters.

 A comprehensive review of different forms of sparsity constraint methods in autoencoders can be found in the following research paper, which we recommend to our interested audience: *Facial expression recognition via learning deep sparse autoencoders*: https://www.sciencedirect.com/science/article/pii/S0925231217314649.

This frees up some space in our agenda so that we can give you brief overview of some other regularization methods that are used by autoencoders before we proceed to coding our very own models.

Regularization with denoising autoencoders

Unlike sparse autoencoders, denoising autoencoders take a different approach toward ensuring that our model captures useful representations in the capacity that it is endowed. Here, instead of adding a constraint to the `loss` function, we can actually modify the reconstruction error term in our `loss` function. In other words, we will simply tell our network to reconstruct its input by using a noisy version of that very input.

In this case, noise may refer to missing pixels in a picture, absent words in a sentence, or a fragmented audio feed. Thus, we may reformulate our `loss` function for denoising autoencoders like so:

- Normal AE loss: $L(x, g(f(x)))$
- Denoising AE loss: $L(x, g(f(\sim x)))$

Here, the term $(\sim x)$ simply refers to a version of the input x that has been corrupted by some form of noise. Our denoising autoencoder must then proceed to uncorrupt the noisy input that's provided, instead of simply attempting to copy the original input. Adding noise to the training data may force the autoencoder to capture representative features that are the most relevant for properly reconstructing the corrupted versions of the training instances.

 Some interesting properties and use cases (such as speech enhancement) for denoising autoencoders have been explored in the following paper, and are noteworthy for interested readers: *Speech Enhancement Based on Deep Denoising Autoencoder*: `https://pdfs.semanticscholar.org/3674/37d5ee2ffbfee1076cf21c3852b2ec50d734.pdf`.

This brings us to the last regularization strategy we will cover in this chapter, that is, the contractive autoencoder, before moving on to practical matters.

Regularization with contractive autoencoders

While we will not dive deep into the mathematics of this subspecies of autoencoder network, the **contractive autoencoder** (**CAE**) is noteworthy due to its conceptual similarity to the denoising autoencoder, as well as how it locally warps the input space. In the case of CAEs, we again add a constraint (Ω) to the `loss` function, but in a different manner:

- **Normal AE loss**: $L(x, g(f(x)))$
- **CAE loss**: $L(x, g(f(x))) + \Omega(h,x)$

Here, the term $\Omega(h, x)$ is represented differently, and can be formulated as follows:

$$\Omega(h,x) = \lambda \sum_i \left|\left| \nabla x\, h_i \right|\right|^2$$

Here, the CAE makes use of the constraint on the `loss` function to encourage the derivates of the encoder to be as small as possible. For those of you who are more mathematically oriented, the constraint term $\Omega(h, x)$ is actually known as the **squared Frobenius norm** (that is, the sum of squared elements) of the Jacobian matrix that's populated with the partial derivatives of the encoder function.

 The following paper provides an excellent overview of the inner workings of CAEs and their use in feature extraction, for those who wish to expand their knowledge beyond the brief summary provided here: *Contractive Auto-Encoders: Explicit Invariance During Feature Extraction*: `http://www.iro.umontreal.ca/~lisa/pointeurs/ICML2011_explicit_invariance.pdf`.

Practically speaking, all we need to understand here is that by defining the omega term as such, CAEs can learn to approximate a function that can map inputs to outputs, even if the input changes slightly. Since this penalty is applied only during the training process, the network learns to capture representative features from the inputs, and is able to perform well during testing, even if the inputs it is shown differs slightly from the inputs it was trained on.

Now that we have covered the basic learning mechanism as well as some architectural variations that define various types of autoencoder networks, we can proceed to the implementation part of this chapter. Here, we will be designing a basic autoencoder in Keras and progressively updating the architecture to cover some practical considerations and use cases.

Implementing a shallow AE in Keras

Now, we will implement a shallow autoencoder in Keras. The use case we will tackle with this model will be simple: make an autoencoder generate different fashionable items of clothing by using the standard fashion MNIST dataset that's provided by Keras. Since we know that the quality of network output depends directly on the quality of the input data available, we must warn our audience to not expect to generate the next best-selling clothing item through this exercise. The pixelated 28 x 28 images that the dataset has will be used to clarify the programmatic concepts and implementational steps you must familiarize yourself with when attempting to design any type of AE network on Keras.

We can proceed by checking the dimensions and types of the input images, and then plot out a single example from the training data for our own visual satisfaction. The example appears to be a casual T-shirt with some undecipherable content written on it. Great – now, we can move on to defining our autoencoder model!

Preprocessing the data

As we've done countless times before, we will now normalize the pixel data between the values of 0 and 1, which improves the learning capability of our network from the normalized data:

```
# Normalize pixel values
x_train = x_train.astype('float32') / 255.
x_test = x_test.astype('float32') / 255.

# Flatten images to 2D arrays
x_train = x_train.reshape((len(x_train), np.prod(x_train.shape[1:])))
x_test = x_test.reshape((len(x_test), np.prod(x_test.shape[1:])))

# Print out the shape
print(x_train.shape)
print(x_test.shape)
--------------------------------------------------------------
(60000, 784)
(10000, 784)
```

We will also flatten our 28 x 28 pixels into one vector of 784 pixels, just as we did in our previous MNIST examples while training a feed-forward network. Finally, we will print out the shapes of our training and test arrays to ensure that they are in the required format.

Building the model

Now we are ready to design our first autoencoder network in Keras, which we will do using the functional API. The basics governing the functional API are quite simple to get accustomed to, as we saw in previous examples. For our use case, we will define the encoding dimension of the latent space. Here, we chose 32. This means that each image of 784 pixels will go through a compressed dimension that stores only 32 pixels, from which the output will be reconstructed.

This implies a compression factor of 24.5 (784/32), and was chosen somewhat arbitrarily, yet can be used as a rule of thumb for similar tasks:

```
# Size of encoded representation
# 32 floats denotes a compression factor of 24.5 assuming input is 784
float
# we have 32*32 or 1024 floats
encoding_dim = 32
#Input placeholder
input_img = Input(shape=(784,))
#Encoded representation of input image
encoded = Dense(encoding_dim, activation='relu',
activity_regularizer=regularizers.l1(10e-5))(input_img)
# Decode is lossy reconstruction of input
decoded = Dense(784, activation='sigmoid')(encoded)
# This autoencoder will map input to reconstructed output
autoencoder = Model(input_img, decoded)
```

Then, we define the input layer using the input placeholder from `keras.layers` and specify the flattened image dimension that we expect. As we already know from our earlier MNIST experiments (and through some simple math), flattening images of 28 x 28 pixels returns an array of 784 pixels, which can then be fed through a feed-forward neural network.

Next, we define the dimensions of the encoded latent space. This is done by defining a dense layer that's connected to the input layer, along with the number of neurons corresponding to our encoding dimension (earlier defined as 32), with a ReLU activation function. The connection between these layers are denoted by including the variable that defines the previous layer in brackets, after defining the parameters of the subsequent layer.

Finally, we define the decoder function as a dense layer of equal dimension as the input (784 pixels), with a sigmoid activation function. This layer naturally connects to the encoded dimension representing the latent space, and regenerates the output that's drawing upon the neural activations in the encoded layer. Now we can initialize our autoencoder by using the model class from the functional API, and providing it with the input placeholder and the decoder layer as arguments.

Implementing a sparsity constraint

As we mentioned earlier in this chapter, there are many ways to perform regularization when designing autoencoders. The sparse autoencoder, for example, simply implements a sparsity constraint on the latent space to force the autoencoder to favor rich representations. Recall that neurons in a neural network may *fire* if their output value is close to 1, and refrain from being active if their output is close to 0. Adding a sparsity constraint can simply be thought of as constraining the neurons in the latent space to be inactive most of the time. As a result, a smaller number of neurons may fire at any given time, forcing those that *do* fire to propagate information as efficiently as possible, from the latent space to the output space. Thankfully, implementing this procedure in Keras is fairly straightforward. This can be achieved by defining the `activity_regularizer` argument, while defining the dense layer that represents the latent space. In the following code, we use the L1 regularizer from `keras.regularizers` with a sparsity parameter very close to zero (0.067, in our case). Now you know how to design a sparse autoencoder in Keras as well! While we will continue with the unsparse version, for the purpose of this exercise, you are welcome to compare the performance between these two shallow autoencoders to see the benefits of adding sparsity constraints to the latent space when designing such models first-hand.

Compiling and visualizing the model

We can visualize what we just did by simply compiling the model and calling `summary()` on the model object, like so. We will choose the Adadelta optimizer, which restricts the number of accumulated past gradients to a fixed window during backpropagation, instead of monotonically decreasing the learning rate by choosing something such as an Adagrad optimizer. In case you missed it earlier in this book, we encourage you to investigate the vast repertoire of available optimizers (http://ruder.io/optimizing-gradient-descent/) and experiment with them to find a suitable one for your use case. Finally, we will define a binary cross entropy as a `loss` function, which in our case accounts for pixel-wise loss on the outputs that are generated:

```
autoencoder.compile(optimizer='adadelta', loss='binary_crossentropy')
autoencoder.summary()
```

Following is the output:

```
Layer (type)                 Output Shape              Param #
=================================================================
input_1 (InputLayer)         (None, 784)               0

dense_1 (Dense)              (None, 32)                25120

dense_2 (Dense)              (None, 784)               25872
=================================================================
Total params: 50,992
Trainable params: 50,992
Non-trainable params: 0
```

Building the verification model

Now we have almost all we need to initiate the training session of our shallow autoencoder. However, we are missing one crucial component. While this part is not, strictly speaking, required to train our autoencoder, we must implement it so that we can visually verify whether our autoencoder has truly learned salient features from the training data or not. To do this, we will actually define two additional networks. Don't worry – these two networks are essentially mirror images of the encoder and decoder functions that are present in the autoencoder network we just defined. Hence, all we will be doing is creating a separate encoder and decoder network, which will match the hyperparameters of the encoder and decoder functions from our autoencoder. These two separate networks will be used for prediction only after our autoencoder has been trained. Essentially, the encoder network will be used to predict the compressed representation of the input image, while the decoder network will simply proceed to predict the decoded version of the information that's stored in the latent space.

Defining a separate encoder network

In the following code, we can see that the encoder function is an exact replica of the top half of our autoencoder; it essentially maps input vectors of flattened pixel values to a compressed latent space:

```
''' The seperate encoder network '''

# Define a model which maps input images to the latent space
encoder_network = Model(input_img, encoded)
```

```
# Visualize network
encoder_network.summary()
```

Following is the summary:

```
Layer (type)                Output Shape            Param #
=================================================================
input_1 (InputLayer)        (None, 784)             0
_____
dense_1 (Dense)             (None, 32)              25120
=================================================================
Total params: 25,120
Trainable params: 25,120
Non-trainable params: 0
_____
```

Defining a separate decoder network

Similarly, in the following code, we can see that the decoder network is a perfect replica of the bottom half of our autoencoder neural network, mapping the compressed representations stored in the latent space to the output layer that reconstructs the input image:

```
''' The seperate decoder network '''

# Placeholder to recieve the encoded (32-dimensional) representation as
input
encoded_input = Input(shape=(encoding_dim,))

# Decoder layer, retrieved from the aucoencoder model
decoder_layer = autoencoder.layers[-1]

# Define the decoder model, mapping the latent space to the output layer
decoder_network = Model(encoded_input, decoder_layer(encoded_input))

# Visualize network
decoder_network.summary()
```

Here is the summary:

```
Layer (type)                    Output Shape              Param #
=================================================================
input_2 (InputLayer)            (None, 32)                0
_____
dense_2 (Dense)                 (None, 784)               25872
=================================================================
Total params: 25,872
Trainable params: 25,872
Non-trainable params: 0
_____
```

Note that to define the decoder network, we must first construct an input layer with a shape that corresponds to our encoding dimension (that is, 32). Then, we simply duplicate the decoder layer from our earlier autoencoder model by referring to the index corresponding to the last layer of that model. Now we have all the components in place to initiate the training of our autoencoder network!

Training the autoencoder

Next, we simply fit our autoencoder network, just as we've done with other networks countless times before. We chose this model to be trained for 50 epochs, in batches of 256 images, before weight updates to our network nodes are performed. We also shuffle our data during training. As we already know, doing so ensures some variance reduction among batches, thereby improving the generalizability for our model:

```
1  autoencoder.fit(x_train, x_train,
2                  epochs=50,
3                  batch_size=256,
4                  shuffle=True,
5                  validation_data=(x_test, x_test))
```

```
Train on 60000 samples, validate on 10000 samples
Epoch 1/50
60000/60000 [==============================] - 4s 61us/step - loss: 0.5303 - val_loss: 0.4575
Epoch 2/50
60000/60000 [==============================] - 2s 32us/step - loss: 0.4240 - val_loss: 0.4048
Epoch 3/50
60000/60000 [==============================] - 2s 38us/step - loss: 0.3940 - val_loss: 0.3865
Epoch 4/50
60000/60000 [==============================] - 2s 41us/step - loss: 0.3768 - val_loss: 0.3709
Epoch 5/50
60000/60000 [==============================] - 2s 40us/step - loss: 0.3629 - val_loss: 0.3588
```

Finally, we also defined the validation data using our test set, just to be able to compare how well our model does on unseen examples, at the end of each epoch. Do remember that in normal machine learning workflows, it is common practice to have both validation and development splits of your data so that you can tune your model on one split and test it on the latter. While this is not a prerequisite for our demonstrative use case, such double-holdout strategies can always be beneficial to implement for the sake of achieving generalizable results.

Visualizing the results

Now comes the time to bear the fruits of our labor. Let's have a look at what kind of images our autoencoder is able to recreate by using our secluded test set. In other words, we will provide our network with images that are similar (but not the same) to the training sets, to see how well our model performs on unseen data. To do this, we will employ our encoder network to make predictions on the test set. The encoder will predict how to map the input image to a compressed representation. Then, we will simply use the decoder network to predict how to decode the compressed representation that's generated by the encoder network. These steps are shown in the following code:

```
# Time to encode some images
encoded_imgs = encoder_network.predict(x_test)
# Then decode them
decoded_imgs = decoder_network.predict(encoded_imgs)
```

Next, we reconstruct a few images and compare them to the input that prompted the reconstruction to see whether our autoencoder captures the essence of what items of clothing are supposed to look like. To do this, we will simply use Matplotlib and plot nine images with their reconstructions under them, as shown here:

```
# use Matplotlib (don't ask)
import matplotlib.pyplot as plt
plt.figure(figsize=(22, 6))
num_imgs = 9
for i in range(n):
    # display original
    ax = plt.subplot(2, num_imgs, i + 1)
    true_img = x_test[i].reshape(28, 28)
    plt.imshow(true_img)

    # display reconstruction
    ax = plt.subplot(2, num_imgs, i + 1 + num_imgs)
    reconstructed_img = decoded_imgs[i].reshape(28,28)
    plt.imshow(reconstructed_img)
plt.show()
```

Following is the output generated:

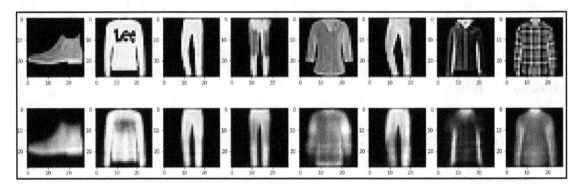

As you can see, while our shallow autoencoder doesn't recreate brand labels (such as the **Lee** tag that's present in the second image), it certainly does get the general idea of human items of clothing, despite having a considerable meager learning capacity. But is this enough? Well, not enough for any practical use case, such as computer-aided clothing design. Far too many details are missing, partially due to the learning capacity of our network and partially due to the lossy compression output. Naturally, this makes you wonder, what can be achieved by deeper models? Well, as the old adage goes, *nullius in verba* (or to paraphrase in more contemporary terms, let's see for ourselves!).

Designing a deep autoencoder

Next, we will investigate how much better reconstructions from autoencoders can get, and whether they can generate images a bit better than the blurry representations that we just saw. For this, we will design a deep feed-forward autoencoder. As you know, this simply means that we will be adding additional hidden layers between the input and the output layer of our autoencoder. To keep things interesting, we will also use a different dataset of images. You are welcome to reimplement this method on the fashion_mnist dataset if you're curious to further explore the sense of fashion that's attainable by autoencoders.

For the next exercise, we will use the 10 Monkey species dataset, available at Kaggle. We will try to reconstruct pictures of our playful and mischievous cousins from the jungle, and see how well our autoencoder performs at a more complex reconstruction task. This also gives us the opportunity to venture out to use cases far from the comforts of preprocessed datasets that are available in Keras, as we will learn to deal with images of different sizes and higher resolution compared to the monotonous MNIST examples: https://www.kaggle.com/slothkong/10-monkey-species.

Making some imports

We will start by importing the necessary libraries, as is tradition. You will notice the usual suspects such as NumPy, pandas, Matplotlib, and some Keras model and layer objects:

```
import cv2
import datetime as dt
import matplotlib.pylab as plt
import numpy as np
import pandas as pd
from keras import models, layers, optimizers
from keras.layers import Input, Dense
from keras.models import Model
from pathlib import Path
from vis.utils import utils
```

Notice that we import a utility module from the Keras `vis` library. While this module contains many other nifty features for image manipulation, we will use it to resize our training images to a uniform dimension, since this is not the case for this particular dataset.

Understanding the data

We chose this dataset for our use case for a specific reason. Unlike 28 x 28 pixelated images of clothing items, these images represent rich and complex features, such as variation in body morphology, and, of course, color! We can plot out the composition of our dataset to see what the class distributions look like, purely for our own curiosity:

```
1  cols = ['Label','Latin Name', 'Common Name','Train Images', 'Validation Images']
2  labels = pd.read_csv("C:/Users/npurk/Desktop/VAE/monkey_labels.txt", names=cols, skiprows=1)
3  labels
```

	Label	Latin Name	Common Name	Train Images	Validation Images
0	n0	alouatta_palliata\t	mantled_howler	131	26
1	n1	erythrocebus_patas\t	patas_monkey	139	28
2	n2	cacajao_calvus\t	bald_uakari	137	27
3	n3	macaca_fuscata\t	japanese_macaque	152	30
4	n4	cebuella_pygmea\t	pygmy_marmoset	131	26
5	n5	cebus_capucinus\t	white_headed_capuchin	141	28
6	n6	mico_argentatus\t	silvery_marmoset	132	26
7	n7	saimiri_sciureus\t	common_squirrel_monkey	142	28
8	n8	aotus_nigriceps\t	black_headed_night_monkey	133	27
9	n9	trachypithecus_johnii	nilgiri_langur	132	26

You will notice that each of the 10 different monkey species has significantly different characteristics, ranging from different body sizes, color of fur, and facial composition, making this a much more challenging task for an autoencoder. The following depiction with sample images from eight different monkey species is provided to better illustrate these variations among species. As you can see, each of them looks unique:

Since we know that autoencoders are data-specific, it also stands to reason that training an autoencoder to reconstruct a class of images with high variance may result in dubious results. Nevertheless, we hope that this will make an informative use case so that you can better understand the potentials and limits you will face when using these models. So, let's get started!

Importing the data

We will start by importing the images of different monkey species from the Kaggle repository. As we did before, we will simply download the data to our filesystem, then access the training data folder using the operating system interface that's built into Python (using the `os` module):

```
import os
all_monkeys = []
for image in os.listdir(train_dir):
    try:
        monkey = utils.load_img(('C:/Users/npurk/Desktop/VAE/training/' +
image), target_size=(64,64))
        all_monkeys.append(monkey)
    except Exception as e:
        pass
    print('Recovered data format:', type(all_monkeys))
print('Number of monkey images:', len(all_monkeys))
--------------------------------------------------------------------
Recovered data format: <class 'list'>
Number of monkey images: 1094
```

You will notice that we nest the image variable in a `try`/`except` loop. This is simply an implementational consideration, as we found that some of the images in our dataset were corrupt. Hence, if we aren't able to load an image using the `load_img()` function from the `utils` module, then we will ignore the image file altogether. This (somewhat arbitrary) selection strategy leaves us with 1,094 images being recovered from the training folder out of a total of 1,097.

Preprocessing the data

Next, we will convert our list of pixel values into NumPy arrays. We can print out the shape of the array to confirm whether we indeed have 1,094 colored images of 64 x 64 pixels. After doing so, we simply normalize the pixel values between the range of $0 - 1$ by dividing each pixel value by the maximum possible value for any given pixel (that is, 255):

```
# Make into array
all_monkeys = np.asarray(all_monkeys)
print('Shape of array:', all_monkeys.shape)

# Normalize pixel values
all_monkeys = all_monkeys.astype('float32') / 255.

# Flatten array
all_monkeys = all_monkeys.reshape((len(all_monkeys),
np.prod(all_monkeys.shape[1:])))
print('Shape after flattened:', all_monkeys.shape)

Shape of array: (1094, 64, 64, 3)
Shape after flattened: (1094, 12288)
```

Finally, we flatten the four-dimensional array into a two-dimensional array, since our deep autoencoder is composed of a feed-forward neural networks that propagates 2D vectors through its layers. Similar in spirit to what we did in Chapter 3, *Signal Processing – Data Analysis with Neural Networks*, we essentially convert each three-dimensional image (64 x 64 x 3) into a 2D vector of dimensions (1, 12,288).

Partitioning the data

Now that our data has been preprocessed and exists as a 2D tensor of normalized pixel values, we can finally split it into training and test segments. Doing so is important, as we wish to eventually use our model on images that it has never seen, and be able to recreate them using its own understanding of what a monkey should look like. Do note that while we don't use the labels that are provided with the dataset for our use case, the network itself will receive a label for each image it sees. The label in this case will simply be the image itself, as we are dealing with an image reconstruction task, and not classification. So, in the case of autoencoders, the input variables are the same as the target variables. As we can see in the following screenshot, the `train_test_split` function from sklearn's model selection module is used to generate our training and testing data (with an 80/20 split ratio). You will notice that both the x and y variables are defined by the same data structure due to the nature of our task:

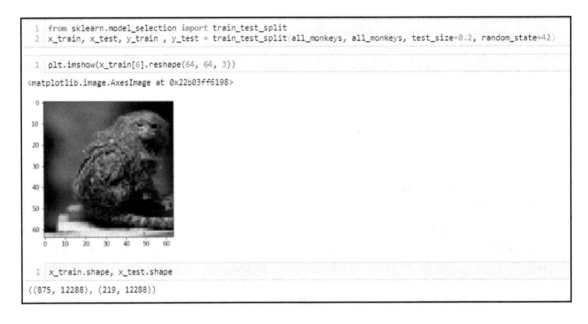

Now we are left with **875** training examples and 219 test examples to train and test our deep autoencoder. Do note that the Kaggle dataset comes with an explicit test set directory since the original purpose of this dataset was to attempt to classify different monkey species using machine learning models. In our use case, however, we do not rigidly ensure balanced classes for the time being, and are simply interested in how deep autoencoders perform at reconstructing images when trained on a high variance dataset. We do encourage further experimentation by comparing the performance of deep autoencoders that are trained on a particular species of monkey. Logic would dictate that these models would perform better at reconstructing their input images due to the latter between training observations.

Using functional API to design autoencoders

Just as we did in the previous example, we will refer to the functional API to construct our deep autoencoder. We will import the input and dense layers, as well as the model object that we will later use to initialize the network. We will also define the input dimension for our images (64 x 64 x 3 = 12,288), and an encoding dimension of 256, leaving us with a compression ratio of 48. This simply means that each image will be compressed by a factor of 48, before our network attempts to reconstruct it from the latent space:

```
from keras.layers import Input, Dense
from keras.models import Model

##Input dimension
input_dim=12288

##Encoding dimension for the latent space
encoding_dim=256
```

The compression factor can be a very important parameter to consider, as mapping the input to a very low dimensional space will result in too much information loss, leading to poor reconstructions. There may simply not be enough space to store the key essentials of the image. On the other hand, we are already aware of how providing our model with too much learning capacity may cause it to overfit, which is why choosing a compression factor by hand can be quite tricky. When in doubt, it can never hurt to experiment with different compression factors as well as regularization methods (provided you have the time).

Building the model

To build our deep autoencoder, we will begin by defining the input layer, which accepts the dimensions corresponding to our 2D vectors of monkey images. Then, we simply start defining the encoder part of our network using dense layers, with a decreasing number of neurons for subsequent layers, until we reach the latent space. Note that we simply choose the number of neurons in layers leading to the latent space to decrease by a factor of 2, with respect to the encoding dimension chosen. Thus, the first layer has (256 x 4) 1024 neurons, the second layer has (256 x 2) 512 neurons, and the third layer, representing the latent space itself, has 256 neurons. While you are not obliged to strictly stick to this convention, it is common practice to reduce the number of neurons per layer when approaching the latent space, and increase the number of neurons for layers occurring after, in the case of undercomplete autoencoders:

```python
# Input layer placeholder
input_layer = Input(shape=(input_dim,))

# Encoding layers funnel the images into lower dimensional representations
encoded = Dense(encoding_dim * 4, activation='relu')(input_layer)
encoded = Dense(encoding_dim * 2, activation='relu')(encoded)

# Latent space
encoded = Dense(encoding_dim, activation='relu')(encoded)

# "decoded" is the lossy reconstruction of the input
decoded = Dense(encoding_dim * 2, activation='relu')(encoded)
decoded = Dense(encoding_dim * 4, activation='relu')(decoded)
decoded = Dense(input_dim, activation='sigmoid')(decoded)

# this model maps an input to its reconstruction
autoencoder = Model(input_layer, decoded)

autoencoder.summary()
```

Layer (type)	Output Shape	Param #
input_1 (InputLayer)	(None, 12288)	0
dense_1 (Dense)	(None, 1024)	12583936
dense_2 (Dense)	(None, 512)	524800
dense_3 (Dense)	(None, 256)	131328
dense_4 (Dense)	(None, 512)	131584

dense_5 (Dense)	(None, 1024)	525312
dense_6 (Dense)	(None, 12288)	12595200

```
=================================================================
Total params: 26,492,160
Trainable params: 26,492,160
Non-trainable params: 0
```

Finally, we initialize the autoencoder by providing the input and decoder layer to the model object as arguments. Then, we can visually summarize what we just built.

Training the model

Finally, we can initiate the training session! This time, we will compile the model with an adam optimizer and operationalize the loss function with mean-squared errors. Then, we simply start the training by calling .fit() on the model object and providing the appropriate arguments:

```
autoencoder.compile(optimizer='adam', loss='mse')

autoencoder.fit(x_train, x_train, epochs=100, batch_size=20, verbose=1)

Epoch 1/100
875/875 [==============================] - 15s 17ms/step - loss: 0.0061
Epoch 2/100
875/875 [==============================] - 13s 15ms/step - loss: 0.0030
Epoch 3/100
875/875 [==============================] - 13s 15ms/step - loss: 0.0025
Epoch 4/100
875/875 [==============================] - 14s 16ms/step - loss: 0.0024
Epoch 5/100
875/875 [==============================] - 13s 15ms/step - loss: 0.0024
```

This model ends with a loss of (0.0046) at the end of the 100th epoch. Do note that since different loss functions have been chosen previously for the shallow model, the loss metrics of each model are not directly comparable to one another. In reality, the manner in which the loss function is defined characterizes what the model seeks to minimize. If you wish to benchmark and compare the performance of two different neural network architectures (such as a feed-forward network and a CNN, for example) it is always advised to use the same optimizer and loss function at first, before venturing to other ones.

Visualizing the results

Now, let's have a look at the reconstructions our deep autoencoder is capable of making by testing its performance on our secluded test set. To do that, we will simply use our separate encoder network to make a prediction on how to compress those images to the latent space from where the decoder network will take up the call of decoding and reconstructing the original image from the latent space that's predicted by the encoder:

```
decoded_imgs = autoencoder.predict(x_test)
# use Matplotlib (don't ask)
import matplotlib.pyplot as plt

n = 6  # how many digits we will display
plt.figure(figsize=(22, 6))
for i in range(n):
    # display original
    ax = plt.subplot(2, n, i + 1)
    plt.imshow(x_test[i].reshape(64, 64, 3))     #x_test
    plt.gray()
    ax.get_xaxis().set_visible(False)
    ax.get_yaxis().set_visible(False)

    # display reconstruction
    ax = plt.subplot(2, n, i + 1 + n)
    plt.imshow(decoded_imgs[i].reshape(64, 64, 3))
    plt.gray()
    ax.get_xaxis().set_visible(False)
    ax.get_yaxis().set_visible(False)
plt.show()
```

We will get the following ouput:

While the images themselves are arguably even aesthetically pleasing, it seems that the essence of what represents a monkey largely eludes our model. Most of the reconstructions resemble starry skies, rather that the features of a monkey. We do notice that the network had started learning the general humanoid morphology at a very basic level, but this is nothing to write home about. So, how can we improve this? At the end of the day, we would like to close this chapter with at least a few realistic looking reconstructions of monkeys. To do so, we will employ the use of a specific type of network, which is adept at dealing with image data. We are speaking of the **Convolutional Neural Network (CNN)** architecture, which we will repurpose so that we can design a deep convolutional autoencoder in the next part of this exercise.

Deep convolutional autoencoder

Luckily, all we have to do is define a convolutional network and reshape our training arrays to the appropriate dimensions to test out how it performs with respect to the task at hand. Thus, we will import some convolutional, MaxPooling, and UpSampling layers, and start building the network. We define the input layer and provide it with the shape of our 64 x 64 colored images. Then, we simply alternate the convolutional and pooling layers until we reach the latent space, which is represented by the second MaxPooling2D layer. The layers leading away from the latent space, on the other hand, must be alternating between convolutional layers and UpSampling layers. The UpSampling layer, as the name suggests, simply increases the representational dimension by repeating the rows and columns of the data from the previous layer:

```
from keras.layers import Conv2D, MaxPooling2D, UpSampling2D

# Input Placeholder
input_img = Input(shape=(64, 64, 3))  # adapt this if using
`channels_first` image data format

# Encoder part
l1 = Conv2D(32, (3, 3), activation='relu', padding='same')(input_img)
l2 = MaxPooling2D((2, 2), padding='same')(l1)
l3 = Conv2D(16, (3, 3), activation='relu', padding='same')(l2)

# Latent Space, with dimension (None, 32, 32, 16)
encoded = MaxPooling2D((1,1), padding='same')(l3)


# Decoder Part
l8 = Conv2D(16, (3, 3), activation='relu', padding='same')(encoded)
l9 = UpSampling2D((2, 2))(l8)
decoded = Conv2D(3, (3, 3), activation='sigmoid', padding='same')(l9)
```

```
autoencoder = Model(input_img, decoded)

autoencoder.summary()
```

Layer (type)	Output Shape	Param #
input_2 (InputLayer)	(None, 64, 64, 3)	0
conv2d_5 (Conv2D)	(None, 64, 64, 32)	896
max_pooling2d_3 (MaxPooling2	(None, 32, 32, 32)	0
conv2d_6 (Conv2D)	(None, 32, 32, 16)	4624
max_pooling2d_4 (MaxPooling2	(None, 32, 32, 16)	0
conv2d_7 (Conv2D)	(None, 32, 32, 16)	2320
up_sampling2d_2 (UpSampling2	(None, 64, 64, 16)	0
conv2d_8 (Conv2D)	(None, 64, 64, 3)	435

```
Total params: 8,275
Trainable params: 8,275
Non-trainable params:
```

As we can see, this convolutional autoencoder has eight layers. The information enters the input layer, from which convolutional layers generate 32 feature maps. These maps are downsampled using the max pooling layer, in turn generating 32 feature maps, each being 32 x 32 pixels in size. These maps are then passed on to the latent layer, which stores 16 different representations of the input image, each with dimensions of 32 x 32 pixels. These representations are passed to the subsequent layers, as the inputs are exposed to convolution and UpSampling operations, until the decoded layer is reached. Just like the input layer, our decoded layer matches the dimensions of our 64 x 64 colored images. You may always check the dimension of a specific convolutional layer (instead of visualizing the entire model) by using the int_shape() function from Keras's backend module, as shown here:

```
# Check shape of a layer
import keras
keras.backend.int_shape(encoded)
```

```
(None, 32, 32, 16)
```

Compiling and training the model

Next, we simply compile our network with the same optimizer and `loss` function that we chose for the deep feed-forward network and initiate the training session by calling `.fit()` on the model object. Do note that we only train this model for 50 epochs and perform weight updates in batches of 128 images at a time. This approach turns out to be computationally faster, allowing us to train the model for a fraction of the time that was taken to train the feed-forward model. Let's see whether the chosen trade-off between training time and accuracy works out in our favor for this specific use case:

```
autoencoder.compile(optimizer='adam', loss='mse')
autoencoder.fit(x_train, x_train, epochs=50, batch_size=20,
                shuffle=True, verbose=1)
Epoch 1/50
875/875 [==============================] - 7s 8ms/step - loss: 0.0462
Epoch 2/50
875/875 [==============================] - 6s 7ms/step - loss: 0.0173
Epoch 3/50
875/875 [==============================] - 7s 9ms/step - loss: 0.0133
Epoch 4/50
875/875 [==============================] - 8s 9ms/step - loss: 0.0116
```

The model reaches a loss of (0.0044), by the end of the 50th epoch. This turns out to be lower than the earlier feed-forward model, when it was trained for half the epochs using a much larger batch size. Let's visually judge for ourselves how the model performs at reconstructing images it has never seen before.

Testing and visualizing the results

It's time to see whether the CNN really does hold up to our image reconstruction task at hand. We simply define a helper function that allows us to plot out a number of sampled examples that are generated from the test set and compare them to the original test inputs. Then, in the code cell that follows, we define a variable to hold the results of our model's inferences on the test set by using the `.predict()` method on our model object. This will generate a NumPy ndarray containing all of the decoded images for the inputs from the test set. Finally, we call the `compare_outputs()` function, using the test set and the decoded predictions thereof as arguments to visualize the results:

```
def compare_outputs(x_test, decoded_imgs=None, n=10):
    plt.figure(figsize=(22, 5))
    for i in range(n):
        ax = plt.subplot(2, n, i+1)
        plt.imshow(x_test[i].reshape(64,64,3))
```

```
        ax.get_xaxis().set_visible(False)
        ax.get_yaxis().set_visible(False)

        if decoded_imgs is not None:
            ax = plt.subplot(2, n, i+ 1 +n)
            plt.imshow(decoded_imgs[i].reshape(64,64,3))

            ax.get_xaxis().set_visible(False)
            ax.get_yaxis().set_visible(False)
    plt.show()

decoded_imgs = autoencoder.predict(x_test)
print('Upper row: Input image provided \nBottom row: Decoded output
    generated')
compare_outputs(x_test, decoded_imgs)
Upper row: Input image provided
Bottom row: Decoded output generated
```

Following is the output:

As we can see, the deep convolutional autoencoder actually does a remarkable job of reconstructing the images from the test set. Not only does it learn body morphology and correct color schemes, it even recreates aspects such as red-eye from a camera flash (as seen on monkey 4 and its artificial doppelganger). Great! So, we were able to reconstruct some ape images. As the excitement soon fades off (if it was even present in the first place), we will want to use autoencoders for more useful and real-world tasks – perhaps tasks such as image denoising, where we commission a network to regenerate an image in its entirety from a corrupted input.

Denoising autoencoders

Again, we will continue with the monkey species dataset and modify the training images to introduce a noise factor. This noise factor essentially changes the pixel values on the original image to remove pieces of information that constitute the original image, making the task a little more challenging than a simple recreation of the original input. Do note that this means that our input variables will be noisy images, and the target variable that's shown to the network during training will be the uncorrupted version of the noisy input image. To generate the noisy version of the training and test images, all we do is apply a Gaussian noise matrix to the image pixels and then clip their values between 0 and 1:

```
noise_factor = 0.35

# Define noisy versions
x_train_noisy = x_train + noise_factor * np.random.normal(loc=0.0,
scale=1.0, size=x_train.shape)
x_test_noisy = x_test + noise_factor * np.random.normal(loc=0.0, scale=1.0,
size=x_test.shape)

# CLip values between 0 and 1
x_train_noisy = np.clip(x_train_noisy, 0., 1.)
x_test_noisy = np.clip(x_test_noisy, 0., 1.)
```

We can see how our arbitrarily chosen noise factor of 0.35 actually affects the images by plotting a random example from our data, as shown in the following code. The noisy image is barely understandable to the human eye at this resolution, and looks just a little more than a bunch of random pixels congregated together:

```
# Effect of adding noise factor
f = plt.figure()
f.add_subplot(1,2, 1)
plt.imshow(x_test[1])

f.add_subplot(1,2, 2)
plt.imshow(x_test_noisy[1])

plt.show(block=True)
```

This is the output that you will get:

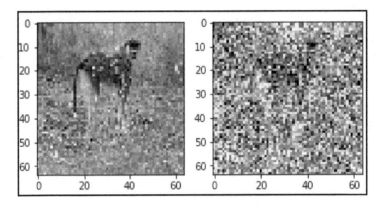

Training the denoising network

We will use the same convolutional autoencoder architecture for this task. However, we will reinitialize the model and train it from scratch once again, this time with the noisy input variables:

```
autoencoder.compile(optimizer='adam', loss='mse')
autoencoder.fit(x_train_noisy, x_train, epochs=50, batch_size=20,
               shuffle=True, verbose=1)
```

```
Epoch 1/50875/875 [==============================] – 7s 8ms/step – loss:
0.0449
Epoch 2/50
875/875 [==============================] – 6s 7ms/step – loss: 0.0212
Epoch 3/50
875/875 [==============================] – 6s 7ms/step – loss: 0.0185
Epoch 4/50
875/875 [==============================] – 6s 7ms/step – loss: 0.0169
```

As we can see, the loss converges much more reluctantly in the case of the denoising autoencoder than for our previous experiments. This is naturally the case, as a lot of information has now been removed from the inputs, making it harder for the network to learn an appropriate latent space to generate the uncorrupted outputs. Hence, the network is forced to get a little bit *creative* during the compression and reconstruction operations. The training session for this network ends after 50 epochs, with a loss of 0.0126. Now we can make some predictions on the test set and visualize some reconstructions.

Visualizing the results

Finally, we can test how well the model actually performs once we give it a more challenging task such as image denoising. We will use the same helper function to compare our network's outputs with a sample from the test set, as shown here:

```
def compare_outputs(x_test, decoded_imgs=None, n=10):
    plt.figure(figsize=(22, 5))
    for i in range(n):
        ax = plt.subplot(2, n, i+1)
        plt.imshow(x_test_noisy[i].reshape(64,64,3))
        plt.gray()

        ax.get_xaxis().set_visible(False)
        ax.get_yaxis().set_visible(False)

        if decoded_imgs is not None:
            ax = plt.subplot(2, n, i+ 1 +n)
            plt.imshow(decoded_imgs[i].reshape(64,64,3))

            ax.get_xaxis().set_visible(False)
            ax.get_yaxis().set_visible(False)
    plt.show()
decoded_imgs = autoencoder.predict(x_test_noisy)
print('Upper row: Input image provided \nBottom row: Decoded output
generated')
compare_outputs(x_test, decoded_imgs)
Upper row: Input image provided
Bottom row: Decoded output generated
```

Following is the output:

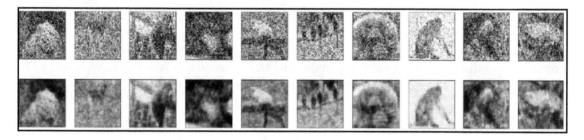

As we can see, the network does a decent job at recreating the images, despite the added noise factor! Many of those images are very hard to distinguish for the human eye, and so the fact that the network is able to recreate the general structure and composition of elements that are present therein is indeed noteworthy, especially given the meager learning capacity and training time allocated to the network.

We encourage you to experiment with more complex architectures by changing the number of layers, filters, and the encoding dimension of the latent space. In fact, now may be the perfect time to practice with some exercises, which are provided at the end of this chapter.

Summary

In this chapter, we explored the fundamental theory behind autoencoders at a high level, and conceptualized the underlying mathematics that permits these models to learn. We saw several variations of the autoencoder architecture, including shallow, deep, undercomplete, and overcomplete models. This allowed us to overview considerations related to the representational power of each type of model and their propensity to overfit given too much capacity. We also explored some regularization techniques that let us compensate for the overfitting problem, such as the sparse and contractive autoencoders. Finally, we trained several different types of autoencoder networks, including shallow, deep, and convolutional networks, for the tasks of image reconstruction and denoising. We saw that with very little learning capacity and training time, convolutional autoencoders outperformed all of the other models in reconstructing images. Furthermore, it was able to generate denoised images from corrupted inputs, maintaining the general format of the input data it was shown.

While we did not explore other use cases, such as dimensionality reduction to visualize main factors of variance, autoencoders have found a lot of applicability in different spheres, ranging from collaborative filtering in recommender systems, to even predicting future patients for healthcare, see *Deep Patient*: https://www.nature.com/articles/srep26094. There is one specific type of autoencoder that we purposefully didn't cover in this chapter: the **Variational Autoencoder** (**VAE**). This type of autoencoder includes a special constraint on the latent space that's being learned by the model. It actually forces the model to learn a probability distribution representing your input data, from which it samples its output. This is quite a different approach than the one we were perusing so far, which at best allowed our network to learn a somewhat arbitrary function. The reason we choose not to include this interesting subtopic in this chapter is because VAEs are, in technical parlance, an instance of generative models, which is the topic of our next chapter!

Exercise

- Make a deep AE with the fashion MNIST dataset and monitor when the loss plateaus. Then, compare it with shallow AE.
- Implement AEs on another dataset of your choice and experiment with different encoding dimensions, optimizers, and `loss` functions to see how the model performs.
- Compare when loss converges for different models (CNN, FF) and how stable or erratic the decrease in loss values are. What do you notice?

Generative Networks

9

In the last chapter, we submerged ourselves in the world of autoencoding neural networks. We saw how these models can be used to estimate parameterized functions capable of reconstructing given inputs with respect to target outputs. While at prima facie this may seem trivial, we now know that this manner of self-supervised encoding has several theoretical and practical implications.

In fact, from a **machine learning** (**ML**) perspective, the ability to approximate a connected set of points in a higher dimensional space on to a lower dimensional space (that is, manifold learning) has several advantages, ranging from higher data storage efficiency to more efficient memory consumption. Practically speaking, this allows us to discover ideal coding schemes for different types of data, or to perform dimensionality reduction thereupon, for use cases such as **Principal Component Analysis** (**PCA**) or even information retrieval. The task of searching for specific information using similar queries, for example, can be largely augmented by learning useful representations from a set of data, stored in a lower dimensional space. Moreover, the learned representations can even be used thereafter as feature detectors to classify new, incoming data. This sort of application may allow us to construct powerful databases capable of high-level inference and reasoning, when presented with a query. Derivative implementations may include legal databases used by lawyers to efficiently search for precedents by similarity to the current case, or medical systems that allow doctors to efficiently diagnose patients based on the noisy data available per patient. These latent variable models allow researchers and businesses alike to address various use cases, ranging from sequence-to-sequence machine translation, to attributing complex intents to customer reviews. Essentially, with generative models, we attempt to answer this question: *How likely are these features (x) present in an instance of data, given that it belongs to a certain class (y)?* This is very different than asking this question: *How likely is this instance part of a class (y), given the features (x) present?*, as we would for supervised learning tasks. To better understand this reversal of roles, we will further explore the idea behind latent variable modeling, introduced in the previous chapter.

In this chapter, we will see how we can take the concept of latent variables a step further. Instead of simply learning a parameterized function, which maps inputs to outputs, we can use neural networks to learn a function that represents the probability distribution over the latent space. We can then sample from such a probability distribution to generate novel, synthetic instances of the input data. This is the core theoretical foundation behind generative modeling, as we are about to discover.

In this chapter, we will cover the following topics:

- Replicating versus generating content
- Understand the notion of latent space
- Diving deeper into generative networks
- Using randomness to augment outputs
- Sampling from the latent space
- Understanding types of Generative Adversial Networks
- Understanding VAEs
- Designing VAEs in Keras
- Building the encoding module in a VAE
- Building the decoder module
- Visualizing the latent space
- Latent space sampling and output generation
- Exploring GANs
- Diving deeper into GANs
- Designing a GAN in Keras
- Designing the generator module
- Designing the discriminator module
- Putting the GAN together
- The training function
- Defining the discriminator labels
- Training the generator per batch
- Executing the training session

Replicating versus generating content

While our autoencoding use cases in the last chapter were limited to image reconstruction and denoising, these use cases are quite distinct from the one we are about to address in this chapter. So far, we made our autoencoders reconstruct some given inputs, by learning an arbitrary mapping function. In this chapter, we want to understand how to train a model to create new instances of some content, instead of simply replicating its inputs. In other words, what if we asked a neural network to truly be creative and generate content just like human beings do?. Can this even be achieved? The canonical answer common in the realm of **Artificial Intelligence (AI)** is yes, but it is complicated. In the search for a more detailed answer, we arrive at the topic of this chapter: generative networks.

While a plethora of generative networks exist, ranging from the variations of the **Deep Boltzman Machine** to **Deep Belief Networks**, most of them have fallen out of fashion, given their restrictive applicability and the appearance of more computationally efficient methods. A few, however, continue to remain in the spotlight, due to their eerie ability to generate synthetic content, such as faces that have never existed, movie reviews and news articles that were never written, or videos that were never actually filmed! To better understand the mechanics behind this wizardry, let's dedicate a few lines to the notion of latent spaces, to better understand how these models transform their learned representations to create something seemingly new.

Understanding the notion of latent space

Recall from the previous chapter that a **latent space** is nothing but a compressed representation of the input data in a lower dimensional space. It essentially includes features that are crucial to the identification of the original input. To better understand this notion, it is helpful to try to mentally visualize what type of information may be encoded by the latent space. A useful analogy can be to think of how we ourselves create content, with our imagination. Suppose you were asked to create an imaginary animal. What information would you be relying on to create this creature? You will sample features from animals you have previously seen, features such as their color, or whether they are bi-pedal, quadri-pedal, a mammal or reptile, land-or sea-dwelling, and so on. As it turns out, we ourselves develop latent models of the world, as we navigate through it. When we attempt to imagine a new instance of a class, we are actually sampling some latent variable models, learned throughout the course of our existence.

Think about it. Throughout our lives, we came across countless animals of different colors, sizes, and morphologies. We reduce these rich representations to more manageable dimensions all the time. For example, we all know what a lion looks like, because we have mentally encoded properties (or latent variables) that represent a lion (such as their four legs, tail, furry coat, color, and so on). These learned properties are a testament to how we store information in lower dimensions, to create functional models of the world around us. We hypothesize that such information is stored in lower dimensions, as most of us, for example, are not able to perfectly recreate the image of a lion on paper. Some may not even come close to it, as is the case for the author of this work. Yet, we are all instantly and collectively able to agree on what the general morphology of a lion would be, just by mentioning the word *lion*.

Identifying concept vectors

This little thought experiment demonstrates the sheer power of latent variable models, in creating functional representations of the world. Our brain would very likely consume a lot more than the meagre 12 watts of energy, were it not constantly downsampling the information received from our sensory inputs to create manageable and realistic models of the world. Thus, using latent variable models essentially allows us to query reduced representation (or properties) of the input, which may in turn be recombined with other representations to generate a seemingly novel output (for example: unicorn = body and face from horse + horn from rhino/narwhal).

Similarly, neural networks may also transform samples from a learned latent space, to generate novel content. One way of achieving this is by identifying concept vectors, embedded in the learned latent space. The idea here is quite simple. Suppose we are to sample a face (*f*) from a latent space representing faces. Then, another point, (*f* + *c*), can be thought of as the embedded representation of the same face, along with some modification (that is, the presence of a smile, or glasses, or facial hair, on top of the original face). These concept vectors essentially encode various axes of disparities from the input data, and can then be used to alter interesting properties of the input images. In other words, we can probe the latent space for vectors that elude to a concept present within the input data. After identifying such vectors, we can then modify them to change properties of the input data. A smile vector, for example, can be learned and used to modify the degree to which a person is smiling, in a given image. Similarly, a gender vector could be used to modify the appearance of a person, to look more female, than male, or vice versa. Now that we have a better idea of what kind of information may be queried from latent spaces, and subsequently be modified to generate new content, we can continue on our exploratory journey.

Diving deeper into generative networks

So, let's try to understand the core mechanics of generative networks and how such approaches differ from the ones we already know. In our quest thus far, most of the networks we have implemented are for the purpose of executing a deterministic transformation of some inputs, in order to get to some sort of outputs. It was not until we explored the topic of reinforcement learning (Chapter 7, *Reinforcement Learning with Deep Q-Networks*) that we learned the benefits of introducing a degree of **stochasticity** (that is, randomness) to our modeling efforts. This is a core notion that we will be further exploring as we familiarize ourselves with the manner in which generative networks function. As we mentioned earlier, the central idea behind generative networks is to use a deep neural network to learn the probability distribution of variables over a reduced latent space. Then, the latent space can be sampled and transformed in a quasi-random manner, to generate some outputs (y).

As you may notice, this is quite different than the approach we employed in the previous chapter. With autoencoders, we simply estimated an arbitrary function, mapping inputs (x) to a compressed latent space using an encoder, from which we reconstructed outputs (y) using a decoder. In the case of generative networks, we instead learn a latent variable model for our input data (x). Then, we can transform samples from the latent space to get to our generated output. Neat, don't you think? Yet, before we further explore how this concept is operationalized, let's briefly go over the role of randomness in relation to generating creative content.

Controlled randomness and creativity

Recall that we introduced an element of randomness in the deep reinforcement learning algorithm by using the **epsilon greedy selection** strategy, which basically allowed our network to not rely too much on the same actions and allowed it to explore new actions to solve the given environment. Introducing this randomness, in a sense, brought creativity to the process, as our network was able to systematically create novel state-action pairs without relying on what it had learned previously learned. Do note, however, that labeling the consequence of introducing randomness in a system as creativity may be the result of some anthropomorphism on our part. In fact, the true processes that gave birth to creativity in humans (our go-to benchmark) are still vastly elusive and poorly understood by the scientific community at large. On the other hand, this link between randomness and creativity itself is a long recognized one, especially in the realm of AI. As early as 1956, AI researchers have been interested in transcending the seemingly deterministic limitations of machines. Back then, the prominence of rule-based systems made it seem as though notions such as creativity could only be observed in advanced biological organisms. Despite this widespread belief, one of the paramount documents that shaped AI history (arguably for the following century to come), the *Dartmouth Summer Research Project Proposal* (1956), specifically mentioned the role of controlled randomness in AI systems, and its link to generating creative content. While we encourage you to read the entire document, we present an extract from it that is relevant to the point at hand:

> *"A fairly attractive and yet clearly incomplete conjecture is that the difference between creative thinking and unimaginative competent thinking lies in the injection of some randomness. The randomness must be guided by intuition to be efficient. In other words, the educated guess or the hunch include controlled randomness in otherwise orderly thinking."*

> *- John McCarthy, Marvin L Minsky, Nathaniel Rochester, and Claude E Shannon*

Using randomness to augment outputs

Over the years, we developed methods that operationalize this notion of injecting some controlled randomness, which in a sense are guided by the intuition of the inputs. When we speak of generative models, we essentially wish to implement a mechanism that allows controlled and quasi-randomized transformations of our input, to generate something new, yet still plausibly resembling the original input.

Let's consider for a moment how this can be achieved. We wish to train a neural network to use some input variables (x) to generate some output variables (y), from a latent space produced by a model. An easy way to solve this is to simply add an element of randomness as input to our generator network, defined here by the variable (z). The value of z may be sampled from some probability distribution (a Gaussian distribution, for example) and fed to a neural network along with the inputs. Hence, this network will actually be estimating the function $f(x, z)$ and not simply $f(x)$. Naturally, to an independent observer who is not able to measure the value of z, this function will seem stochastic, yet this will not be the case in reality.

Sampling from the latent space

To further elaborate, suppose we had to draw some samples (y) from a probability distribution of variables from a latent space, with a mean of (μ) and a variance of ($\sigma2$):

- **Sampling operation**: $y \sim N(\mu, \sigma2)$

Since we use a sampling process to draw from this distribution, each individual sample may change every time the process is queried. We can't exactly differentiate the generated sample (y) with respect to the distribution parameters (μ and $\sigma2$), since we are dealing with a sampling operation, and not a function. So, how exactly can we backpropagate our model's errors? Well, one solution could be to redefine the sampling process, such as performing a transformation on a random variable (z), to get to our generated output (y), like so:

- **Sampling equation**: $y = \mu + \sigma z$

This is a crucial step, as we can now use the backpropagation algorithm to compute gradients of the generated output (y), with respect to the sampling operation itself ($\mu + \sigma z$). What changed? Essentially, we are now treating the sampling operation as a deterministic one that includes the mean(μ) and standard deviation (σ) from our probability distribution, as well as a random variable (z), whose distribution is not related to that of any of the other variables we seek to estimate. We use this method to estimate how changes in our distribution's mean (μ) or standard deviation (σ) affect the generated output (y), given that the sampling operation is reproduced with the same value of z.

Learning a probability distribution

Since we can now backpropagate through the sampling operation, we can include this step as part of a larger network. By plugging this into a larger network, we can then redefine the parameters of the earlier sampling operation (μ and σ), as functions that can be estimated by parts of this larger neural network! More mathematically put, we can redefine the mean and standard deviation of the probability distribution as functions that can be approximated by the parameters of a neural network (for example, $\mu = f(x\,;\theta)$ and $\sigma = g(x;\,\theta)$, where the term θ denotes the learnable parameters of a neural network). We can then use these defined functions to generate an output (y):

- **Sample function**: $y = \mu + \sigma z$

In this function, $\mu = f(x\,;\theta)$ and $\sigma = g(x;\,\theta)$.

Now that we know how to sample outputs (y), we can finally train our larger network by differentiating a defined loss function, $J(y)$, with respect to these outputs. Recall that we use the chain rule of differentiation to redefine this process with respect to the intermediate layers, which here represent the parameterized functions (μ and σ). Hence, differentiating this loss function provides us with its derivatives, used to iteratively update the parameters of the network, where the parameters themselves represent a probability distribution.

Great! Now we have an overarching theoretical understanding of how these models can generate outputs. This entire process permits us to first estimate, and then sample from, a probability distribution of densely encoded variables, generated by an encoder function. Later in the chapter, we will further explore how different generative networks learn by benchmarking their outputs, and perform weight updates using the backpropagation algorithm.

Understanding types of generative networks

So, all we are actually doing here is generating an output by transforming a sample taken from the probability distribution representing the encoded latent space. In the last chapter, we saw how to produce such a latent space from some input data using encoding functions. In this chapter, we will see how to learn a continuous latent space (l), then sample from it to generate novel outputs. To do this, we essentially learn a differentiable generator function, $g(l;\theta(g))$, which transforms samples from a continuous latent space (l) to generate an output. Here, this function itself is what is being approximated by the neural network.

The family of generative networks includes both **Variational Autoencoders (VAEs)** as well as **Generative Adversarial Networks (GANs)**. As we mentioned before, there exist many types of generative models, but in this chapter, we will focus on these two variations, given their widespread applicability across various cognitive tasks (such as, computer vision and natural language generation). Notably, VAEs distinguish themselves by coupling the generator network with an approximate inference network, which is simply the encoding architecture we saw in the last chapter. GANs, on the other hand, couple the generator network with a separate discriminator network, which receives samples both from the actual training data and the generated outputs, and is tasked with distinguishing the original image from the computer-generated one. Once the generator is considered fooled, your GAN is considered trained. Essentially, these two different types of generative models employ different methodologies for learning the latent space. This gives each of them unique applicability for different types of use cases. For example, VAEs perform notably well at learning well-structured spaces, where significant variations may be encoded due to the specific composition of the input data (as we will see shortly, using the MNIST dataset). However, VAEs also suffer from blurry reconstructions, the causes of which are not yet properly understood. GANs, on the other hand, do much better at generating realistic content, despite sampling from an unstructured and discontinuous latent space, as we will see later in the chapter.

Understanding VAEs

Now we have a high-level understanding of what generative networks entail, we can focus on a specific type of generative models. One of them is the VAE, proposed by both Kingma and Welling (2013) as well as Rezende, Mohamed, and Wierstra (2014). This model is actually very similar to the autoencoders we saw in the last chapter, but they come with a slight twist—well, several twists, to be more specific. For one, the latent space being learned is no longer a discrete one, but a continuous one by design! So, what's the big deal? Well, as we explained earlier, we will be sampling from this latent space to generate our outputs. However, sampling from a discrete latent space is problematic. The fact that it is discrete implies that there will be regions in the latent space with discontinuities, meaning that if these regions were to be randomly sampled, the output would look completely unrealistic. On the other hand, learning a continuous latent space allows the model to learn the transitions from one class to another in a probabilistic manner. Furthermore, since the latent space being learned is continuous, it becomes possible to identify and manipulate the concept vectors we spoke of earlier, which encodes various axes of variance present in the input data in a meaningful way. At this point, many of you may be wondering how a VAE exactly learns to model a continuous latent space. Well, wonder no more.

Earlier, we saw how we can redefine the sampling process from a latent space, so as to be able to plug it into a larger network to estimate a probability distribution. We did this by breaking the latent space down by using parameterized functions (that is, parts of a neural network) to estimate both the mean (μ) and the standard deviation (σ) of variables in the latent space. In a VAE, its encoder function does exactly this. This is what forces the model to learn a statistical distribution of variables over a continuous latent space. This process permits us to presume that the input image was generated in a probabilistic manner, given that the latent space encodes a probability distribution. Thus, we can use the learned mean and standard deviation parameters to randomly sample from the distribution, and decode it on to the original dimension of the data. The illustration here helps us better understand the workflow of a VAE:

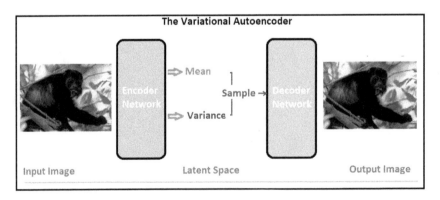

This process is what allows us to first learn, and then sample from, a continuous latent space, generating plausible outputs. Is this still a bit fuzzy? Well, perhaps a demonstrative example is in order, to help clarify this notion. Let's begin by building a VAE in Keras, and go over both the theory and implementational side of things as we construct our model.

Designing a VAE in Keras

For this exercise, we will go back to a well-known dataset that is easily available to all: the MNIST dataset. The visual features of handwritten digits make this dataset uniquely suited to experiment with VAEs, allowing us to better understand how these models work. We start by importing the necessary libraries:

```
import numpy as np
import matplotlib.pyplot as plt
from keras.layers import Input, Dense, Lambda, Layer
from keras.models import Model
from keras import backend as K
from keras import metrics
from keras.datasets import mnist
```

Loading and pre-processing the data

Next, we load the dataset, just as we did in Chapter 3, *Signal Processing – Data Analysis with Neural Networks*. We also take the liberty to define some variables that can be reused later, when designing our network. Here, we simply define the image size used to define the original dimensions of the images (784 pixels each). We choose an encoding dimension of 2 to represent the latent space, and an intermediate dimension of 256. These variables defined here will be later fed to the dense layers of our VAE, defining the number of neurons per layer:

```
(x_train, y_train), (x_test, y_test) = mnist.load_data()
image_size = x_train.shape[1]
original_dim=image_size * image_size
latent_dim= 2
intermediate_dim= 256
epochs=50
epsilon_std=1.0

#preprocessing training arrays

x_train=np.reshape(x_train, [-1, original_dim])
x_test=np.reshape(x_test, [-1, original_dim])
```

```
x_train=x_train.astype('float 32')/255
x_test=x_test.astype('float 32')/255
```

Then, we simply pre-process the images by first flattening them into 2D vectors (of dimension (784) per image). Finally, we normalize the pixel values in these 2D vectors between 0 and 1.

Building the encoding module in a VAE

Next, we will start building the encoding module of our VAE. This part is almost identical to the shallow encoder we built in the last chapter, except that it splits into two separate layers: one estimating the mean and the other estimating the variance over the latent space:

```
#Encoder module
input_layer= Input(shape=(original_dim,))
intermediate_layer= Dense(intermediate_dim, activation='relu',
name='Intermediate layer')(input_layer)
z_mean=Dense(latent_dim, name='z-mean')(intermediate_layer)
z_log_var=Dense(latent_dim, name='z_log_var')(intermediate_layer)
```

You could optionally add the name argument while defining a layer, to be able to visualize our model intuitively. If we want, we can actually visualize the network we have built so far, by initializing it already and summarizing it, as shown here:

```
1  encoder_module= Model(input_layer, (z_mean, z_log_var))
2
3  encoder_module.summary()
```

Layer (type)	Output Shape	Param #	Connected to
input_4 (InputLayer)	(None, 784)	0	
Intermediate_layer (Dense)	(None, 256)	200960	input_4[0][0]
z_mean (Dense)	(None, 2)	514	Intermediate_layer[0][0]
z_log_var (Dense)	(None, 2)	514	Intermediate_layer[0][0]

```
Total params: 201,988
Trainable params: 201,988
Non-trainable params: 0
```

Note how the outputs from the intermediate layer connect to both the mean estimation layer (z_mean) and the variance estimation layer (z_log_var), both representing the latent space encoded by the network. Together, these separate layers estimate the probability distribution of variables over the latent space, as described earlier in this chapter.

So, now we have a probability distribution being learned by the intermediate layers of our VAE. Next, we need a mechanism to randomly sample from this probability distribution, to generate our outputs. This brings us to the sampling equation.

Sampling the latent space

The idea behind this process here is quite simple. We defined a sample (z) simply by using the learned mean (z_mean) and variance (z_log_variance) from our latent space in an equation that may be formulated as follows:

$$z = z\_mean + exp(z\_log\_variance) * epsilon$$

Here, *epsilon* is simply a random tensor consisting of very small values, ensuring a degree of randomness seeps into the queried sample every time. Since it is a tensor of very small values, it ensures that each decoded image will plausibly resemble the input image.

The sampling function presented here simply takes the values (that is, mean and variance) learned by the encoder network, defines a tensor of small values matching the latent dimensions, and then returns a sample from the probability distribution, using the sampling equation defined previously:

```
def sampling(args):
    z_mean, z_log_var = args
    epsilon = K.random_normal(shape=(K.shape(z_mean)[0], latent_dim), mean=0.,
                        stddev=epsilon_std)
    return z_mean + K.exp(z_log_var / 2) * epsilon
```

```
z = Lambda(sampling, output_shape=(latent_dim,))([z_mean, z_log_var])
```

Since Keras requires all operations to be nested in layers, we use a custom Lambda layer to nest this sampling function, along with a defined output shape. This layer, defined here as (z), will be responsible for generating samples from the learned latent space.

Building the decoder module

Now that we have a mechanism implemented to sample from the latent space, we can proceed to build a decoder capable of mapping this sample to the output space, thereby generating a novel instance of the input data. Recall that just as the encoder funnels the data by narrowing the layer dimensions till the encoded representation is reached, the decoder layers progressively enlarge the representations sampled from the latent space, mapping them back to the original image dimension:

```
#Decoder module
decoder_h= Dense(intermediate_dim, activation='relu')
decoder_mean= Dense(original_dim, activation='sigmoid')
h_decoded=decoder_h(z)
x_decoded_mean=decoder_mean(h_decoded)
```

Defining a custom variational layer

Now that we have constructed both the encoder and the decoder modules of our network, there remains but one implementational matter to divert our attention to before we can start training our VAE. It is quite an important one, as it related to how our network will calculate the loss and update itself to create more realistic generations. This may seem a little odd at first glance. What are we comparing our generations to? It's not as if we have a target representation to compare our model's generations to, so how can we compute our model's errors? Well, the answer is quite simple. We will use two separate `loss` functions, each tracking our model's performance over different aspects of the generated image. The first loss function is known as the reconstruction loss, which simply ensures that the decoded output of our model matches the supplied inputs. The second `loss` function is described as the regularization loss. This function actually aids our model to not overfit on the training data by simply copying it, thereby learning ideally composed latent spaces from the inputs. Unfortunately, these `loss` functions are not implemented in Keras as it is, and hence require a little more technical attention to operationalize.

We operationalize these two `loss` functions by building a custom variational layer class, this will actually be the final layer of our network, and perform the computation of the two different loss metrics, and use their mean value to compute gradients of the loss with respect to the network parameters:

```
1   # Custom loss layer
2   class CustomVariationalLayer(Layer):
3
4       def __init__(self, **kwargs):
5           self.is_placeholder = True
6           super(CustomVariationalLayer, self).__init__(**kwargs)
7
8       def vae_loss(self, x, x_decoded_mean):
9           xent_loss = original_dim * metrics.binary_crossentropy(x, x_decoded_mean)
10          kl_loss = - 0.5 * K.sum(1 + z_log_var - K.square(z_mean) - K.exp(z_log_var), axis=-1)
11          return K.mean(xent_loss + kl_loss)
12
13      def call(self, inputs):
14          x = inputs[0]
15          x_decoded_mean = inputs[1]
16          loss = self.vae_loss(x, x_decoded_mean)
17          self.add_loss(loss, inputs=inputs)
18          return x
```

As you can see, the custom layer includes three functions. The first is for initialization. The second function is responsible for computing both losses. It uses the binary cross-entropy metric to compute the reconstruction loss, and the **Kullback–Leibler** (**KL**) divergence formula to compute the regularization loss. The KL-divergence term essentially allows us to compute the relative entropy of the generated output, with respect to the sampled latent space (z). It allows us to iteratively assess the difference in the probability distribution of the outputs different than that of the latent space. The vae_loss function then returns a combined loss value, which is simply the mean of both these computed metrics.

Finally, the call function is used to implement the custom layer, by using the built-in add_loss layer method. This part essentially defines the last layer of our network as the loss layer, thereby using our arbitrarily defined loss function to generate the loss value, with which backpropagation can be performed.

Compiling and inspecting the model

Next, we define our network's last layer (y) using the custom variational layer class we just implemented, as shown here:

```
1   y = CustomVariationalLayer()([input_layer, x_decoded_mean])
```

Now we are ready to finally compile and train our model! First, we put together the entire model, using the `Model` object from the functional API, and passing it the input layer from our encoder module, as well as the last custom loss layer we just defined. Then, we use the usual `compile` syntax on our initialized network, equipping it with the `rmsprop` optimizer. Do note, however, that since we have a custom loss function, the `compile` statement actually does not take any loss metric, where one would usually be present. At this point, we can visualize the entire model, by calling `.summary()` on the `vae` model object, as shown here:

```
1  vae = Model(input_layer, y)
2  vae.compile(optimizer='rmsprop', loss=None)
```

```
1  vae.summary()
```

```
Layer (type)                    Output Shape         Param #    Connected to
==================================================================================================
input_4 (InputLayer)            (None, 784)          0

Intermediate_layer (Dense)      (None, 256)          200960     input_4[0][0]

z_mean (Dense)                  (None, 2)            514        Intermediate_layer[0][0]

z_log_var (Dense)               (None, 2)            514        Intermediate_layer[0][0]

lambda_1 (Lambda)               (None, 2)            0          z_mean[0][0]
                                                                z_log_var[0][0]

dense_5 (Dense)                 (None, 256)          768        lambda_1[0][0]

dense_6 (Dense)                 (None, 784)          201488     dense_5[0][0]

custom_variational_layer_3 (Cus [(None, 784), (None, 0          input_4[0][0]
                                                                dense_6[0][0]
==================================================================================================
Total params: 404,244
Trainable params: 404,244
Non-trainable params: 0
```

As you can see, this architecture takes in the input images and funnels them down to two distinct encoded representations: z_mean and z_log_var (that is, a learned mean and variance over the latent space). This probability distribution is then sampled using the added Lambda layer to produce a point in the latent space. This point is then decoded by dense layers (dense_5 and dense_6), before a loss can be computed by our final custom-built loss layer. Now you have seen everything.

Initiating the training session

Now comes the time to actually train our network. There is nothing out of the ordinary here, except for the fact that we do not have to specify a target variable (that is, y_train). This is simply because the target is normally used to compute the loss metrics, which is now being computed by our final custom layer. You may also notice that the loss values displayed during training are quite large, compared to previous implementations. Don't be alarmed at their magnitude, as this is simply the result of the manner in which loss is computed for this architecture:

```
1  vae.fit(x_train,
2          shuffle=True,
3          epochs=epochs,
4          batch_size=100,
5          validation_data=(x_test, None))

Train on 60000 samples, validate on 10000 samples
Epoch 1/50
60000/60000 [==============================] - 15s 246us/step - loss: 190.8604 - val_loss: 172.9880
Epoch 2/50
60000/60000 [==============================] - 3s 43us/step - loss: 171.1713 - val_loss: 168.7661
Epoch 3/50
60000/60000 [==============================] - 3s 43us/step - loss: 167.3232 - val_loss: 165.9071
Epoch 4/50
60000/60000 [==============================] - 3s 43us/step - loss: 164.7716 - val_loss: 164.0052
Epoch 5/50
60000/60000 [==============================] - 3s 42us/step - loss: 162.9735 - val_loss: 162.5149
```

This model is trained for 50 epochs, at the end of which we were able to attain a validation loss of 151.71 and a training loss of 149.39. Before we generate some novel-looking handwritten digits, let's try visualizing the latent space that our model was able to learn.

Visualizing the latent space

Since we have a two-dimensional latent space, we can simply plot out the representations as a 2D manifold where encoded instances of each digit class may be visualized with respect to their proximity to other instances. This allows us to inspect the continuous latent space that we spoke of before and see how the network relates to different features in the 10-digit classes (0 to 9) to each other. To do this, we revisit the encoding module from our VAE, which can now be used to produce a compressed latent space from some given data. Thus, we use the encoder module to make predictions on the test set, thereby encoding these images the latent space. Finally, we can use a scatterplot from Matplotlib to plot out the latent representation. Do note that each individual point represents an encoded instance from the test set. The colors denote the different digit classes:

```
# 2D visualization of latent space

x_test_encoded = encoder_network.predict(x_test, batch_size=256)
plt.figure(figsize=(8, 8))
plt.scatter(x_test_encoded[:, 0], x_test_encoded[:, 1], c=y_test,
cmap='Paired')
plt.colorbar()
plt.show()
```

Following is the output:

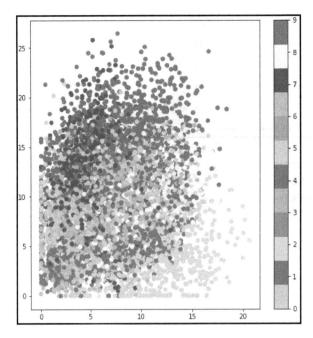

Note how there is very little discontinuity, or gaps between the different digit classes. Due to this, we can now sample from this encoded representation to produce meaningful digits. Such an operation would not produce meaningful results if the learned latent space were discrete, as was the case for the autoencoders we built in the last chapter. The latent space for these models looks much different, when compared to the one learned by the VAE:

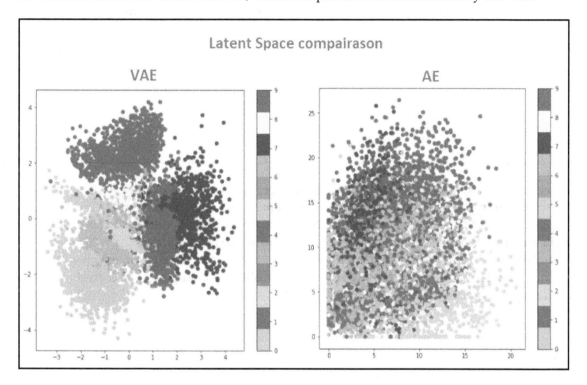

Latent space sampling and output generation

Finally, we can proceed to generate some novel handwritten digits with our VAE. To do this, we simply revisit the decoder part of our VAE (which naturally excludes the loss layer). We will be using it to decode samples from the latent space and generate some handwritten digits that were never actually written by anyone:

```
1  # build a generator network to sample from the learned distribution
2
3
4  decoder_input = Input(shape=(latent_dim,))
5  _h_decoded = decoder_h(decoder_input)
6  _x_decoded_mean = decoder_mean(_h_decoded)
7  generator = Model(decoder_input, _x_decoded_mean)
```

Next, we will display a grid of 15 x 15 digits, each of size 28. To do this, we initialize a matrix of zeros, matching the dimensions of the entire output to be generated. Then, we use the ppf function from SciPy to transform some linearly placed coordinates to get to the grid values of the latent variables (z). After this, we enumerate through these grids to obtain a sampled (z) value. We can now feed this sample to the generator network, which will decode the latent representation, to subsequently reshape the output to the correct format, resulting in the screenshot shown here:

```
1
2
3   # display a 2D manifold of the digits
4   n = 15  # figure with 15x15 digits
5   digit_size = 28
6   figure = np.zeros((digit_size * n, digit_size * n))
7   # linearly spaced coordinates on the unit square were transformed through the inverse CDF (ppf) of the Gaussian
8   # to produce values of the latent variables z, since the prior of the latent space is Gaussian
9   grid_x = norm.ppf(np.linspace(0.05, 0.95, n))
10  grid_y = norm.ppf(np.linspace(0.05, 0.95, n))
11
12  for i, yi in enumerate(grid_x):
13      for j, xi in enumerate(grid_y):
14          z_sample = np.array([[xi, yi]])
15          x_decoded = generator.predict(z_sample)
16          digit = x_decoded[0].reshape(digit_size, digit_size)
17          figure[i * digit_size: (i + 1) * digit_size,
18                  j * digit_size: (j + 1) * digit_size] = digit
19
20  plt.figure(figsize=(10, 10))
21  plt.imshow(figure, cmap='binary')
22  plt.show()
```

Do note that this grid demonstrates how sampling from a continuous space allows us to literally visualize the underlining factors of variance in the input data. We notice that digits transform into other digits, as we move along the *x* or *y* axis. For example, consider moving from the center of the image. Moving to the right can change the digit **8** into a **9**, while moving left will change it into a **6**. Similarly, moving diagonally upward on the right-hand side changes the **8** into a **5** first, and then finally a **1**. These different axes can be thought of as representing the presence of certain properties on a given digit. These properties become accentuated as we progress further and further in the direction of a given axis, moulding the digit into an instance of a specific digit class .

Concluding remarks on VAEs

As we saw in our MNIST experiments, the VAE excels at learning a well-composed continuous latent space, from which we may sample and decode outputs. These models are excellent for editing images, or producing psychedelic transitions where images mould into other images. Some businesses have even started experimenting with VAE-based models to allow customers to try out fashion items such as jewelry, sun glasses, or other apparel completely virtually, using the cameras on customers' phones! This is due to the fact that VAEs are uniquely suited to learning and editing concept vectors, as we discussed earlier. For instance, if you want to generate a new sample halfway between a 1 and a 0, we can simply compute the difference between their mean vectors from the latent space and add half the difference to the original before decoding it. This will produce a 6, as we can see in the previous screenshot. The same concept applies to a VAE trained on images of faces (using the CelebFaces dataset, for example), as we can sample a face between two different celebrities, to then create their synthetic sibling. Similarly, if we wanted to generate specific features, such as a mustache on a face, all we would have to do is find a sample of a face with and without a mustache. Then, we can retrieve their respective encoded vectors using the encoding function, and simply save the difference between these two vectors. Now our saved mustache vector is ready to be applied to any image, by adding it to the encoded space of the new image, before decoding it.

Other amusing use cases with VAEs involve swapping faces on a live feed, or adding additional elements for the sake of entertainment. These networks are quite unique in their ability to realistically modify images and produce ones that never originally existed. Naturally, it makes you wonder whether such technologies can be used for less-amusing purposes; misusing these models to misrepresent people or situations could potentially lead to some dire outcomes. However, since we can train neural networks to fool humans, we can also train them to help us distinguish such forgeries. This brings us to the next topic of this chapter: **GANs**.

Exploring GANs

The idea behind GANs is much more understandable when compared to other similar models. In essence, we use several neural networks to play a rather elaborate game. Just like in the movie *Catch-me-if-you-can*. For those who are not familiar with the plot of this film, we apologize in advance for any missed allusions.

We can think of a GAN as a system of two actors. On one side, we have a Di Caprio-like network that attempts to recreate some Monets and Dalis and ship them off to unsuspecting art dealers. We also have a vigilant Tom Hanks-style network that intercepts these shipments and identifies any forgeries present. As time goes by, both individuals become better at what they do, leading to realistic forgeries on the conman's side, and a keen eye for them on the cop's side. This variation of a commonly used analogy indeed does well at introducing the idea behind these architectures.

A GAN essentially has two parts: a generator and a discriminator. Each of these parts can be thought of as separate neural networks, which work together by checking each other's outputs as the model trains. The generator network is tasked to generate fake data points, by sampling random vectors from a latent space. Then, the discriminator receives these generated data points, along with actual data points, and proceeds to distinguish which one of the data points is real, and which are not (hence the name, *discriminator*). As our network trains, both the generator and the discriminator get better at creating synthetic data and recognizing synthetic data, respectively:

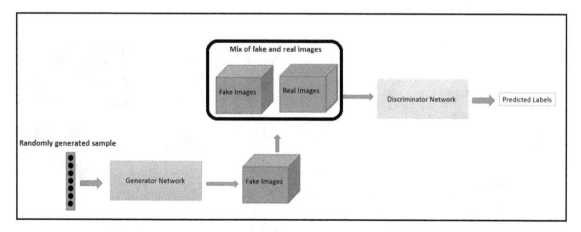

Utility and practical applications for GANS

This architecture was first introduced by Goodfellow and others, 2014, and it has since been popularized by researchers spanning several domains. Their rise to fame was due to their ability to generate synthetic images that are virtually indistinguishable from real ones. While we have discussed some of the more amusing and mundane applications that derive from such methods, more complex ones also exist. For instance, while GANs are mostly used for computer vision tasks such as texture editing and image modification, they are increasingly becoming popular in a multitude of academic disciplines, making appearances in more and more research methodologies. Nowadays, you may find GANs being used for medical image synthesis, or even in domains such as particle physics and astrophysics. The same methodology for generating synthetic data can be used to regenerate denoised images from galaxies far, far away or to simulate realistic radiation patterns that would arise from high-energy particle collisions. The true utility of GANs lies in their ability to learn underlining statistical distributions in data, allowing them to generate synthetic instances of the original inputs. Such an approach is especially useful for researchers when collecting real data, but this may be prohibitively expensive, or physically impossible. Furthermore, the utility of GANs is not limited to the domain of computer vision. Other applications have included using variations of these networks to generate fine-grained images from natural language data, such as a sentence describing some scenery:

https://arxiv.org/pdf/1612.03242v1.pdf

These use cases all show how GANs permit us to address novel tasks, with creative as well as practical implications. Yet, these architectures are not all fun and games. They are notoriously difficult to train, and those who have ventured deep into these waters describe it as more of an art than a science.

For more information on this subject, refer to the following:

- **Original paper by Goodfellow and others**: http://papers.nips.cc/paper/ 5423-generative-adversarial-nets
- **GAN in astrophysics**: https://academic.oup.com/mnrasl/article/467/1/ L110/2931732
- **GAN in particle physics**: https://link.springer.com/article/10.1007/ s41781-017-0004-6
- **Fine-grained text-to-image generation**: http://openaccess.thecvf.com/ content_cvpr_2018/html/Xu_AttnGAN_Fine-Grained_Text_CVPR_2018_paper. html

Diving deeper into GANs

So, let's try to better understand how the different parts of the GAN work together to generate synthetic data. Consider the parameterized function (G) (you know, the kind we usually approximate using a neural network). This will be our generator, which samples its input vectors (z) from some latent probability distribution, and transforms them into synthetic images. Our discriminator network (D), will then be presented with some synthetic images produced by our generator, mixed among real images, and attempt to classify real from forgery. Hence, our discriminator network is simply a binary classifier, equipped with something like a sigmoid activation function. Ideally, we want the discriminator to output high values when presented with real images, and low values when presented with generated fakes. Conversely, we want our generator network to try to fool the discriminator network, by making it output high values for the generated fakes as well. These concepts bring us to the mathematical formulation of training a GAN, which is essentially a battle between two neural networks (D and G), each trying to one-up the other:

$$\min_{G} \max_{D} V(D, G)$$

$$V(D, G) = \mathbb{E}_{x \sim p_{data}(x)}[\log D(x)] + \mathbb{E}_{z \sim p_z(z)}[\log(1 - D(G(z)))]$$

In the given formulation, the first term actually denotes the entropy relating to a data point (*x*) from the real distribution, presented to the discriminator. The goal of the discriminator is to try maximize this term to 1, as it wishes to correctly identify real images. Furthermore, the second term in the formulation denotes the entropy relating to a randomly sampled point, transformed into a synthetic image by the generator, *G(z)*, presented to the discriminator, *D(G(z))*. The discriminator wants none of this, and hence it seeks to maximize the log probability of the data point being fake (that is, the second term), to 0. Hence, we can state that the discriminator is trying to maximize the entire *V* function. The generator function, on the other hand, will be doing quite the contrary. The generator's goal is to try to minimize the first term and maximize the second term so that the discriminator is not able to tell real from fake. And so begins the laborious game between cop and thief.

Problems with optimizing GANs

Interestingly, since both networks take turns to optimize their own metric, the GAN has a dynamic loss landscape. This is different than all other examples we have seen in this book, where the loss hyperplane would remain the same, as we descended it by backpropagating our model errors, converging to more ideal parameters. Here, however, since both networks get a go at optimizing their parameters, each step down the hyperplane changes the landscape a tiny bit, until an equilibrium is reached between the two optimization constraints. As with many things in life, this equilibrium is not easily achieved, and it requires a lot of attention and effort. In the case of GANs, attention to aspects such as layer weight initialization, usage of `LeakyRelu` and `tanh` instead of **Rectified Linear Unit (ReLU)** and sigmoid activation functions, implementing batch normalization and dropout layers, and so on, are but a few among the vast array of considerations that may improve your GAN's ability to attain equilibrium. Yet, there is no better way of familiarizing ourselves with these issues than to get our hands on some code and actually implement an instance of these fascinating architectures.

For more information on this subject, refer to the following:

- **Improved techniques for training GANs:** `https://arxiv.org/pdf/1606.03498.pdf`
- **Photo-realistic image generation:** `http://openaccess.thecvf.com/content_cvpr_2017/html/Ledig_Photo-Realistic_Single_Image_CVPR_2017_paper.html`

Designing a GAN in Keras

For this exercise, suppose you were part of a research team working for a large automobile manufacturer. Your boss wants you to come up with a way to generate synthetic designs for cars, to systematically inspire the design team. You have heard all the hype about GANs and have decided to investigate whether they can be used for the task at hand. To do this, you want to first do a proof of concept, so you quickly get a hold of some low-resolution pictures of cars and design a basic GAN in Keras to see whether the network is at least able to recreate the general morphology of cars. Once you can establish this, you can convince your manager to invest in a few *Titan x GUPs* for the office, get some higher-resolution data, and develop some more complex architectures. So, let's start by implementing this proof of concept by first getting our hands on some pictures of cars. For this demonstrative use case, we use the good old CIFAR-10 dataset, and restrict ourselves to the commercial automobile category. We start our implementation exercise by importing some libraries, as shown here:

```
1   import numpy as np
2   from tqdm import tqdm
3   from pathlib import Path
4
5   import keras
6   import keras.backend as K
7   from keras.datasets import cifar10
8
9   from keras.models import Sequential, Model
10  from keras.layers import Input, Dense, Activation, LeakyReLU, BatchNormalization, Dropout
11  from keras.layers import Conv2D, Conv2DTranspose, Reshape, Flatten
12  from keras.initializers import RandomNormal
13  from keras.optimizers import Adam
14
15  from sklearn.model_selection import train_test_split
16
17  import matplotlib.pyplot as plt
18  %matplotlib inline
```

Preparing the data

We proceed by simply loading up the data through Keras, and selecting only car images (index = 1). Then, we check the shape of our training and test arrays. We see that there are 5,000 training images and 1,000 test images:

```
1  # Load data
2  (x_train, y_train), (x_test, y_test) = cifar10.load_data()
3
4  # Pick the car category
5  x_train = x_train[y_train.flatten() == 1]
6
7  # Check shape
8  x_train.shape, x_test.shape

((5000, 32, 32, 3), (10000, 32, 32, 3))
```

Visualizing some instances

We will now take a look at the real images from the dataset, using Matplotlib. Remember these, as soon we will be generating some fakes for comparison:

```
# Plot many
plt.figure(figsize=(5, 4))
for i in range(20):
    plt.subplot(4, 5, i+1)
    plt.imshow(x_train[i].reshape(32,32,3), cmap='gray')
    plt.xticks([])
    plt.yticks([])
plt.tight_layout()
plt.show()
```

Following is the output:

Pre-processing the data

Next, we simply normalize our pixel values. Unlike previous attempts, however, this time, we normalize the pixel values between -1 and 1 (instead of between 0 and 1). This is due to the fact that we will be using a `tanh` activation function for the generator network. This specific activation function outputs values between -1 and 1; hence, normalizing the data in a similar manner makes the learning process smoother:

```
1  def preprocess(x):
2      return (x/255)*2-1
3
4  def deprocess(x):
5      return np.uint8((x+1)/2*255)
6
7  X_train_real = preprocess(x_train)
8  X_test_real  = preprocess(x_test)
```

We encourage you to try different normalization strategies to explore how this affects learning as the network trains. Now we have all the components in place to start constructing the GAN architecture.

Designing the generator module

Now comes the fun part. We will be implementing a **Deep Convolutional Generative Adversarial Network (DCGAN)**. We start with the first part of the DCGAN: the generator network. The generator network will essentially learn to recreate realistic car images, by transforming a sample from some normal probability distribution, representing a latent space.

We will again use the functional API to defile our model, nesting it in a function with three different arguments. The first argument, latent_dim, refers to the dimension of the input data randomly sampled from a normal distribution. The leaky_alpha argument simply refers to the alpha parameter provided to the LeakyRelu activation function used throughout the network. Finally, the argument init_stddev simply refers to the standard deviation with which to initialize the random weights of the network, used to define the kernel_initializer argument, when constructing a layer:

```
# Input Placeholder
def gen(latent_dim, leaky_alpha, init_stddev ):
    input_img = Input(shape=(latent_dim,))  # adapt this if using
`channels_first` image data format

# Encoder part
x = Dense(32*32*3)(input_img)
x = Reshape((4, 4, 192))(x)
x = BatchNormalization(momentum=0.8)(x)
x = LeakyReLU(alpha=leaky_alpha)(x)
x = Conv2DTranspose(256, kernel_size=5, strides=2, padding='same',
kernel_initializer=RandomNormal(stddev=init_stddev))(x)
x = BatchNormalization(momentum=0.8)(x)
x = LeakyReLU(alpha=leaky_alpha)(x)
x = Conv2DTranspose(128, kernel_size=5, strides=2, padding='same',
kernel_initializer=RandomNormal(stddev=init_stddev))(x)
x = BatchNormalization(momentum=0.8)(x)
x = LeakyReLU(alpha=leaky_alpha)(x)
x = Conv2DTranspose(3, kernel_size=5, strides=2, padding='same',
kernel_initializer=RandomNormal(stddev=init_stddev), activation='tanh')(x)
generator = Model(input_img, x)
generator.summary()
return generator
```

Note the number of considerations taken while designing this model here. For instance, the LeakyReLU activation function is chosen in penultimate layers due to their ability to relax the sparsity constraint on outputs, when compared to the ReLU. This is simply due to the fact that LeakyReLU tolerates some small negative gradient values as well, whereas the ReLU simply squishes all negative values to zero. Gradient sparsity is usually considered a desirable property when training neural networks, yet this does not hold true for GANs. This is the same reason why max-pooling operations are not very popular in DCGANs, since this downsampling operation often produces sparse representations. Instead, we will be using the stride convolutions with the Conv2D transpose layer, for our downsampling needs. We also implemented batch normalization layers (with a moment for moving the mean and variance set to 0.8), as we noticed that this had a considerable effect on improving the quality of the generated images. You will also notice that the size of the convolutional kernels is set to be divisible by the stride, for each convolutional layer. This has been also noted to improve generated images, while reducing discrepancy between areas of the generated image, since the convolutional kernel is allowed to equally sample all regions. Finally, the last layer of the network is equipped with a tanh activation function, as this has consistently shown to produce better results with the GAN architecture. The next screenshot depicts the entire generator module of our GAN, which will produce the 32 x 32 x 3 synthetic images of cars, subsequently used to try fool the discriminator module:

```
Layer (type)                    Output Shape              Param #
=================================================================
input_1 (InputLayer)            (None, 20)                0
_____
dense_1 (Dense)                 (None, 3072)              64512
_____
reshape_1 (Reshape)             (None, 4, 4, 192)         0
_____
batch_normalization_1 (Batch    (None, 4, 4, 192)         768
_____
leaky_re_lu_1 (LeakyReLU)       (None, 4, 4, 192)         0
_____
conv2d_transpose_1 (Conv2DTr    (None, 8, 8, 256)         786688
_____
batch_normalization_2 (Batch    (None, 8, 8, 256)         1024
_____
leaky_re_lu_2 (LeakyReLU)       (None, 8, 8, 256)         0
_____
conv2d_transpose_2 (Conv2DTr    (None, 16, 16, 128)       524416
_____
batch_normalization_3 (Batch    (None, 16, 16, 128)       512
_____
leaky_re_lu_3 (LeakyReLU)       (None, 16, 16, 128)       0
_____
conv2d_transpose_3 (Conv2DTr    (None, 32, 32, 3)         6147
=================================================================
Total params: 1,384,067
Trainable params: 1,382,915
Non-trainable params: 1,152
_____
```

Designing the discriminator module

Next, we continue our journey designing the discriminator module, which will be responsible for telling the real images from the fake ones supplied by the generator module we just designed. The concept behind the architecture is quite similar to that of the generator, with some key differences. The discriminator network receives images of a 32 x 32 x 3 dimension, which it then transforms into various representations as information propagates through deeper layers, until the dense classification layer is reached, equipped with one neuron and a sigmoid activation function. It has one neuron, since we are dealing with the binary classification task of distinguishing fake from real. The `sigmoid` function ensures a probabilistic output between 0 and 1, indicating how fake or real the network thinks a given image may be. Do also note the inclusion of the dropout layer before the dense classifier layer, introduced for the sake of robustness and generalizability:

```
def disc(leaky_alpha, init_stddev):
disc_input = Input(shape=(32,32,3))
x = Conv2D(64, kernel_size=5, strides=2, padding='same',
kernel_initializer=RandomNormal(stddev=init_stddev))(disc_input)
x = LeakyReLU(alpha=leaky_alpha)(x)
x = Conv2D(128, kernel_size=5, strides=2, padding='same',
kernel_initializer=RandomNormal(stddev=init_stddev))(x)
x = BatchNormalization(momentum=0.8)(x)
x = LeakyReLU(alpha=leaky_alpha)(x)
x = Conv2D(256,kernel_size=5, strides=2, padding='same',
kernel_initializer=RandomNormal(stddev=init_stddev))(x)
x = BatchNormalization(momentum=0.8)(x)
x = LeakyReLU(alpha=leaky_alpha)(x)
x = Flatten()(x)
x = Dropout(0.2)(x)
x = Dense(1, activation='sigmoid')(x)
discriminator = Model(disc_input, x)
discriminator.summary()
return discriminator
```

Once again, we encourage you to experiment with as many model hyperparameters as possible, to better get a grip of how altering these different hyperparameters affects the learning and the outputs generated by our GAN model.

Putting the GAN together

Next, we weave together the two modules using this function shown here. As arguments, it takes the size of the latent samples for the generator, which will be transformed by the generator network to produce synthetic images. It also accepts a learning rate and a decay rate for both the generator and discriminator networks. Finally, the last two arguments denote the alpha value for the LeakyReLU activation function used, as well as a standard deviation value for the random initialization of network weights:

```
def make_DCGAN(sample_size,
               g_learning_rate,
               g_beta_1,
               d_learning_rate,
               d_beta_1,
               leaky_alpha,
               init_std):
    # clear first
    K.clear_session()
    # generator
    generator = gen(sample_size, leaky_alpha, init_std)

    # discriminator
    discriminator = disc(leaky_alpha, init_std)
    discriminator_optimizer = Adam(lr=d_learning_rate, beta_1=d_beta_1)
#keras.optimizers.RMSprop(lr=d_learning_rate, clipvalue=1.0, decay=1e-8)
    discriminator.compile(optimizer=discriminator_optimizer,
loss='binary_crossentropy')
    # GAN
    gan = Sequential([generator, discriminator])
    gan_optimizer = Adam(lr=g_learning_rate, beta_1=g_beta_1)
#keras.optimizers.RMSprop(lr=g_learning_rate, clipvalue=1.0, decay=1e-8)
    gan.compile(optimizer=gan_optimizer, loss='binary_crossentropy')
    return generator, discriminator, gan
```

We simply ensure that no previous Keras session is running by calling `.clear_session()` on the imported backend object, K. Then, we can define the generator and discriminator networks by calling their respective functions that we designed earlier and supplying them with the appropriate arguments. Note that the discriminator is compiled, while the generator is not.

Do note that the functions are designed in a way that encourage fast experimentation by changing different model hyperparameters using the arguments.

Finally, after compiling the discriminator network with a binary cross-entropy loss function, we merge the two separate networks together. We do this using the sequential API, which allows you to merge two fully connected models together with much ease. Then, we can compile the entire GAN, again using the same loss and optimizer, yet with a different learning rate. We chose the `Adam` optimizer in our experiments, with a learning rate of 0.0001 for our GAN, and 0.001 for the discriminator network, which happened to work well for the task at hand.

Helper functions for training

Next, we will define some helper functions that will aid us in the training process. The first among them simply makes a sample of latent variables from a normal probability distribution. Next, we have the `make_trainable()` function, which helps us train the discriminator and generator networks in turn. In other words, it allows us to freeze the layer weights of one module (the discriminator or the generator), while the other one is trained. The trainable argument for this function is just a Boolean variable (true or false). Finally, the `make_labels()` function simply returns labels to train the discriminator module. These labels are binary, where 1 stands for real, and 0 for fake:

```
def make_latent_samples(n_samples, sample_size):
    #return np.random.uniform(-1, 1, size=(n_samples, sample_size))
    return np.random.normal(loc=0, scale=1, size=(n_samples, sample_size))
def make_trainable(model, trainable):
    for layer in model.layers:
        layer.trainable = trainable
def make_labels(size):
    return np.ones([[size, 1]), np.zeros([size, 1])
```

Helper functions to display output

The next two helper functions allow us to visualize our losses at the end of the training session, as well as plot an image out at the end of each epoch, to visually assess how the network is doing. Since the loss landscape is dynamically changing, the loss values have much less meaning. As is often the case with generative networks, evaluation of their output is mostly left to visual inspection by human observers. Hence, it is important that we are able to visually inspect the model's performance during the training session:

```
def show_results(losses):
    labels = ['Classifier', 'Discriminator', 'Generator']
    losses = np.array(losses)
    fig, ax = plt.subplots()
```

```
        plt.plot(losses.T[0], label='Discriminator Net')
        plt.plot(losses.T[1], label='Generator Net')
        plt.title("Losses during training")
        plt.legend()
        plt.show()

def show_images(generated_images):
    n_images = len(generated_images)
    rows = 4        cols = n_images//rows

    plt.figure(figsize=(cols, rows))
    for i in range(n_images):
    img = deprocess(generated_images[i])
    plt.subplot(rows, cols, i+1)
    plt.imshow(img, cmap='gray')
    plt.xticks([])
    plt.yticks([])
    plt.tight_layout()
    plt.show()
```

The first function simply accepts a list of loss values for the discriminator and the generator network over the training session, to transpose and plot them out over the epochs. The second function allows us to visualize a grid of generated images at the end of each epoch.

The training function

Next comes the training function. Yes, it is a big one. Yet, as you will soon see, it is quite intuitive, and basically combines everything we have implemented so far:

```
def train(
    g_learning_rate,    # learning rate for the generator
    g_beta_1,           # the exponential decay rate for the 1st moment
estimates in Adam optimizer
    d_learning_rate,    # learning rate for the discriminator
    d_beta_1,           # the exponential decay rate for the 1st moment
estimates in Adam optimizer
    leaky_alpha,
    init_std,
    smooth=0.1,         # label smoothing
    sample_size=100,    # latent sample size (i.e. 100 random numbers)
    epochs=200,
    batch_size=128,     # train batch size
    eval_size=16):      # evaluate size
    # labels for the batch size and the test size
    y_train_real, y_train_fake = make_labels(batch_size)
    y_eval_real,  y_eval_fake  = make_labels(eval_size)
```

```
# create a GAN, a generator and a discriminator
generator, discriminator, gan = make_DCGAN(
    sample_size,
    g_learning_rate,
    g_beta_1,
    d_learning_rate,
    d_beta_1,
    leaky_alpha,
    init_std)

losses = []
for epoch_indx in range(epochs):
    for i in tqdm(range(len(X_train_real)//batch_size)):
        # real images
        X_batch_real = X_train_real[i*batch_size:(i+1)*batch_size]

        # latent samples and the generated images
        latent_samples = make_latent_samples(batch_size, sample_size)
        X_batch_fake = generator.predict_on_batch(latent_samples)

        # train the discriminator to detect real and fake images
        make_trainable(discriminator, True)
        discriminator.train_on_batch(X_batch_real, y_train_real * (1 -
smooth))
        discriminator.train_on_batch(X_batch_fake, y_train_fake)

        # train the generator via GAN
        make_trainable(discriminator, False)
        gan.train_on_batch(latent_samples, y_train_real)

    # evaluate
    X_eval_real = X_test_real[np.random.choice(len(X_test_real),
eval_size, replace=False)]

    latent_samples = make_latent_samples(eval_size, sample_size)
    X_eval_fake = generator.predict_on_batch(latent_samples)

    d_loss  = discriminator.test_on_batch(X_eval_real, y_eval_real)
    d_loss += discriminator.test_on_batch(X_eval_fake, y_eval_fake)
    g_loss  = gan.test_on_batch(latent_samples, y_eval_real) # we want
the fake to be realistic!

    losses.append((d_loss, g_loss))

    print("At epoch:{:>3}/{},\nDiscriminator Loss:{:>7.4f} \nGenerator
Loss:{:>7.4f}".format(
        epoch_indx+1, epochs, d_loss, g_loss))
    if (epoch_indx+1)%1==0:
```

```
        show_images(X_eval_fake)
    show_results(losses)
    return generator
```

Arguments in the training function

You are already familiar with most of the arguments of the training function. The first four arguments simply refer to the learning rate and decay rate used for the generator and the discriminator networks, respectively. Similarly, the `leaky_alpha` parameter is the negative slope coefficient we implemented for our `LeakyReLU` activation function, used in both networks. The smooth argument that follows represents the implementation of one-sided label smoothing, as proposed by Goodfellow and others, 2016. The idea behind this is to replace the real (1) target values for the discriminator module with smoothed values, such as 0.9, as this has shown to reduce the susceptibility of neural networks to fail at adversarial examples:

```
def train(
    g_learning_rate,    # learning rate for the generator
    g_beta_1,           # the exponential decay rate for the 1st moment
estimates in Adam optimizer
    d_learning_rate,    # learning rate for the discriminator
    d_beta_1,           # the exponential decay rate for the 1st moment
estimates in Adam optimizer
    leaky_alpha,
    init_std,
    smooth=0.1,         # label smoothing
    sample_size=100,    # latent sample size (i.e. 100 random numbers)
    epochs=200,
    batch_size=128,     # train batch size
    eval_size=16):       # evaluate size
```

Next, we have four more parameters, which are quite simple to follow. The first among them is `sample_size`, referring to the size of the sample taken from the latent space. Next, we have the number of training epochs and `batch_size` in which to perform weight updates. Finally, we have the `eval_size` argument, which refers to the number of generated images to evaluate at the end of each training epoch.

Defining the discriminator labels

Next, we define the label arrays to be used for the training and evaluation images, by calling the `make_labels()` function, and using the appropriate batch dimension. This will return us arrays with the labels 1 and 0 for each instance of the training and evaluation image:

```
# labels for the batch size and the test size
    y_train_real, y_train_fake = make_labels(batch_size)
    y_eval_real,  y_eval_fake  = make_labels(eval_size)
```

Initializing the GAN

Following this, we initialize the GAN network by calling the `make_DCGAN()` function we defined earlier and providing it with the appropriate arguments:

```
# create a GAN, a generator and a discriminator
    generator, discriminator, gan = make_DCGAN(
        sample_size,
        g_learning_rate,
        g_beta_1,
        d_learning_rate,
        d_beta_1,
        leaky_alpha,
        init_std)
```

Training the discriminator per batch

Thereafter, we define a list to collect the loss values for each network during training. To train this network, we will actually use the `.train_on_batch()` method, which allows us to selectively manipulate the training process, as is required for our use case. Essentially, we will implement a double `for` loop:

```
losses = []
for epoch_indx in range(epochs):
    for i in tqdm(range(len(X_train_real)//batch_size)):
        # real images
        X_batch_real = X_train_real[i*batch_size:(i+1)*batch_size]

        # latent samples and the generated images
        latent_samples = make_latent_samples(batch_size, sample_size)
        X_batch_fake = generator.predict_on_batch(latent_samples)
```

```
# train the discriminator to detect real and fake images
make_trainable(discriminator, True)
discriminator.train_on_batch(X_batch_real, y_train_real * (1 -
smooth))
discriminator.train_on_batch(X_batch_fake, y_train_fake)
```

Hence, for each batch in each epoch, we will first train the discriminator, and then the generator, on the given batch of data. We begin by taking the first batch of real training images, as well as sampling a batch of latent variables from a normal distribution. Then, we use the generator module to make a prediction on the latent sample, essentially generating a synthetic image of a car.

Following this, we allow the discriminator to be trained on both batches (that is, of real and generated images), using the make_trainable() function. This is where the discrimator is given the opportunity to learn to tell real from fake.

Training the generator per batch

After this, we freeze the layers of the discriminator, again using the make_trainable() function, this time to train the rest of the network only. Now it is the generator's turn to try beat the discriminator, by generating a realistic image:

```
# train the generator via GAN
make_trainable(discriminator, False)
gan.train_on_batch(latent_samples, y_train_real)
```

Evaluate results per epoch

Next, we exit the nested loop to perform some actions at the end of each epoch. We randomly sample some real images as well as latent variables, and then generate some fake images to plot out. Do note that we used the .test_on_batch() method to obtain the loss values of the discriminator and the GAN and append them to our loss list. At the end of each epoch, we print out the discriminator and generator loss and plot out a grid of 16 samples. Now all that is left is to call this function:

```
# evaluate
        X_eval_real = X_test_real[np.random.choice(len(X_test_real),
eval_size, replace=False)]

        latent_samples = make_latent_samples(eval_size, sample_size)
        X_eval_fake = generator.predict_on_batch(latent_samples)
```

```
        d_loss  = discriminator.test_on_batch(X_eval_real, y_eval_real)
        d_loss += discriminator.test_on_batch(X_eval_fake, y_eval_fake)
        g_loss  = gan.test_on_batch(latent_samples, y_eval_real) # we want
the fake to be realistic!

        losses.append((d_loss, g_loss))

        print("At epoch:{:>3}/{},\nDiscriminator Loss:{:>7.4f} \nGenerator
Loss:{:>7.4f}".format(
            epoch_indx+1, epochs, d_loss, g_loss))
        if (epoch_indx+1)%1==0:
            show_images(X_eval_fake)
    show_results(losses)
    return generator
```

For more information, refer to the following:

- **Improved techniques for training GANs**: https://arxiv.org/pdf/1606.03498.pdf

Executing the training session

We finally initiate the training session with the respective arguments. You will notice the tqdm module displaying a percentage bar indicating the number of processed batches per epoch. At the end of the epoch, you will be able to visualize a 4 x 4 grid (shown next) of samples generated from the GAN network. And there you have it, now you know how to implement a GAN in Keras. On a side note, it can be very beneficial to have tensorflow-gpu along with CUDA set up, if you're running the code on a local machine with access to a GPU. We ran this code for 200 epochs, yet it would not be uncommon to let it run for thousands of epochs, given the resources and time. Ideally, the longer the two networks battle, the better the results should get. Yet, this may not always be the case, and hence, such attempts may also require careful monitoring of the loss values:

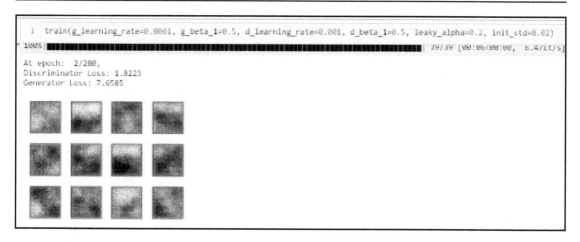

Interpreting test loss during training

As you can see next, the loss values on the test set change at quite an unstable rate. We expect different optimizers to exhibit smother or rougher loss curves, and we encourage you to test these assumptions using different loss functions (RMSProp is an excellent one to start off with, for example). While looking at the plotted losses is not too intuitive, visualizing the generated images across the epochs allows some meaningful evaluation of this exercise:

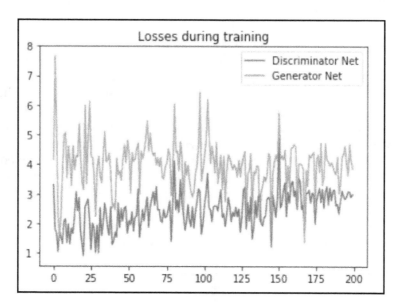

Visualizing results across epochs

In the following, we present eight snapshots of the 16 x 16 grids of generated samples, spread across different times during the training session. While the images themselves are pretty small, they undeniably resemble the morphology of cars toward the end of the training session:

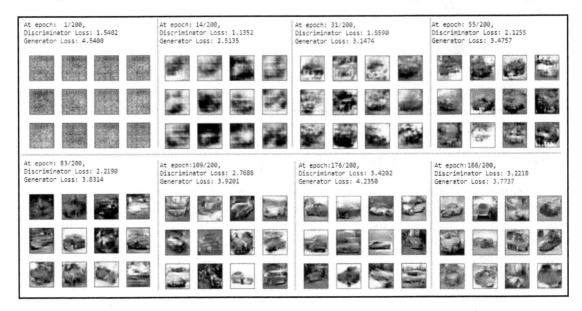

And there you have it. As you can see, the GAN becomes quite good at generating realistic car images after a while, as it gets better and better at fooling the discriminator. Towards the final epochs, it is even hard for the human eye to distinguish real from fake, at least at first glance. Furthermore, we achieved this with a relatively simple and straightforward implementation. This feat seems even more remarkable when we consider the fact that the generator network never actually sees a single real image. Recall that it is simply sampling from a random probability distribution, and uses only the feedback from the discriminator to better its own output! As we saw, the process of training a DCGAN involved a lot of consideration regarding minute detail and choosing specific model constraints and hyperparameters. For interested readers, you may find more details on how to optimize and fine-tune your GANs in the following research papers:

- **Original paper on GANs**: http://papers.nips.cc/paper/5423-generative-adversarial-nets
- **Unsupervised representation learning with DCGAN**: https://arxiv.org/abs/1511.06434

- **Photo-realistic super resolution GAN**: http://openaccess.thecvf.com/
content_cvpr_2017/papers/Ledig_Photo-Realistic_Single_Image_CVPR_2017_
paper.pdf

Conclusion

In this section of the chapter, we implemented a specific type of GAN (that is, the DCGAN) for a specific use case (image generation). The idea of using two networks in parallel to keep each other in check, however, can be applied to various types of networks, for very different use cases. For example, if you wish to generate synthetic timeseries data, we can implement the same concepts we learned here with recurrent neural networks to design a generative adversarial model! There have been several attempts at this in the research community, with quite successful results. A group of Swedish researchers, for example, used recurrent neural networks in a generative adversarial setup to produce synthetic segments of classical music! Other prominent ideas with GANs involve using attention models (a topic unfortunately not covered by this book) to orient network perception, as well as directing memory access to finer details of an image, for example. Indeed, the fundamental theory we covered in this part of the chapter can be applied in many different realms, using different types of networks so solve more and more complex problems. The core idea remains the same: use two different function approximators, each trying to stay ahead of the other. Next, we present a few links for the interested reader to further familiarize themselves with different GAN-based architectures and their respective uses. We also include a link to a very interesting tool developed by Google and Georgia Tech university, that allows you to visualize the entire training process of a GAN using different types of data distributions and sampling considerations!

For more information, refer to the following:

- **Music with C-RNN_GAN**: http://mogren.one/publications/2016/c-rnn-gan/
mogren2016crnngan.pdf
- **Self- attention GANs**: https://arxiv.org/abs/1805.08318
- **OpenAI blog on generative networks**: https://openai.com/blog/generative-
models/
- **GAN Lab**: https://poloclub.github.io/ganlab/?fbclid=
IwAR0JrixZYr1Ah3c08YjC6q34X0e38J7_mPdHaSpUsrRSsi0v97Y1DNQR6eU

Summary

In this chapter, we saw how to augment neural networks with randomness in a systematic manner, in order to make them output instances of what we humans deem *creative*. With VAEs, we saw how parameterized function approximation using neural networks can be used to learn a probability distribution, over a continuous latent space. We then saw how to randomly sample from such a distribution and generate synthetic instances of the original data. In the second part of the chapter, we saw how two networks can be trained in an adversarial manner for a similar task.

The methodology of training GANs is simply a different strategy for learning a latent space compared to their counterpart, the VAE. While GANs have some key benefits for the use case of synthetic image generation, they do have some downsides as well. GANs are notoriously difficult to train and often generate images from unstructured and discontinuous latent spaces, as opposed to VAEs, making GANs harder to use for mining concept vectors. Many other considerations also exist when deciding to choose among these generative networks. The field of generative modeling is continuously expanding, and while we were able to cover some of the fundamental conceptual notions involved, new ideas and techniques surface almost daily, making it an exciting time to be interested in such models.

Section 4: Road Ahead

This section familiarizes the reader with how to use the latest research and developments, reviewed as a plateau to scientifically speculate on the future of deep learning and AI.

We take the perspective of programmers, and scientists, and employ sheer intuition to see how this topic may develop in the future, pointing out potentially new and unexplored paths for research, and business development alike. The implications for generative models and autoencoders will also be used to generate custom artificial images, and topics such as vid2vid, deep fakes, and deep voice, will be examined.

This section only comprises a single chapter:

10
Contemplating Present and Future Developments

Throughout the course of this book, we had the good fortune to explore together an intriguing idea that populates, and currently dominates, the realm of **Artificial Intelligence (AI): Artificial Neural Networks (ANNs)**. On our journey, we had the opportunity to get detailed insight into the functioning of neural models, including the feed-forward, convolutional, and recurrent networks, and thereby **Long Short-Term Memory (LSTM)**. We continued our journey by subsequently exploring self-supervised methods, including **Reinforcement Learning (RL)** with deep Q-networks, as well as autoencoders. We finalized our excursion by going over the intuition behind generative models.

In this chapter, we will cover the following topics:

- Sharing representations with transfer learning
- Transfer learning on Keras
- Concluding our experiments
- Learning representations
- Limits of current neural networks
- Encouraging sparse representation learning
- Tuning hyperparameters
- Automatic optimization and evolutionary algorithms
- Multi-network predictions and ensemble models
- The future of AI and neural networks
- The road ahead
- The problems with classical computing

- The advent of quantum computing
- Quantum neural networks
- Technology and society
- Contemplating the future

Sharing representations with transfer learning

One powerful paradigm that we have not yet had the pleasure of discussing is the notion of **transfer learning**. In our excursions, we saw various methods and techniques that allow neural networks to induct powerful and accurate representations from the data they see.

Yet, what if we wanted to transfer these learned representations to other networks? This can be quite useful if we are tackling a task where not a lot of training data is available beforehand. Essentially, transfer learning seeks to leverage commonalities among different learning tasks that may share similar statistical features. Consider the following case: you are a radiologist who wants to use a **Convolutional Neural Network** (**CNN**) to classify different pulmonary diseases, using images of chest X-rays. The only problem is you only have about a hundred labeled images of chest X-rays. Since you can't go about ordering X-rays for any unsuspecting patient to augment your dataset, you are required to get creative. Maybe you have different images of the same phenomenon (such as MRIs and CT scans), or perhaps you have a lot of X-ray images from different body parts. So, why not use these?

Since we know that earlier layers in CNNs learn the same low-level features (such as edges, line segments, and curvatures), why not simply reuse these learned features from a different task and fine tune that model to our new learning task ? In many cases, transfer learning can save a lot of time, when compared to training a network from scratch, and is a very useful tool to have in your deep learning repertoire. In that spirit, let's explore one very last hands-on example: implementing a simple transfer learning workflow on Keras.

Transfer learning on Keras

In this section, we will explore a very simplistic transfer learning methodology in Keras. The idea behind this is simple: why waste precious computation resources on learning the repetitive low-level features common to almost all images?

We will use the famous CIFAR10 dataset to illustrate our implementation, by making it our task to classify images pertaining to any of the 10 image categories present in the dataset. However, we will augment our learning experience by using layers from pretrained networks and adding them to a network of our own. To do this, we will import a very deep CNN, that has already been trained on expensive **Graphics Processing Units (GPUs)** for hundreds of hours and simply fine-tune it to our use case. The model in question that we will use is the same **VGG net** we used back in Chapter 4, *Convolutional Neural Networks,* to visualize how a neural network sees a cheetah.

This time, however, we will be slicing it open and picking out some of its intermediate layers to splice into our own model, thereby transferring what it has learnt to a new task. We will begin by making some imports:

```
"import numpy as np\n",
"import matplotlib.pyplot as plt\n",
"% matplotlib inline\n",
"\n",
"\n",
"from keras import applications\n",
"from keras import optimizers\n",
"from keras.models import Sequential, Model \n",
"from keras.layers import Dropout, Flatten, Dense, GlobalAveragePooling2D,
Input\n",
"from keras import backend as k \n",
"from keras.datasets import cifar10\n",
"from keras import utils"
```

Loading a pretrained model

We define our image dimensions and load in the VGG16 model with the training weights it achieved on the **ImageNet** classification task (ILSVRC), excluding its input layer. We do this since the images we will train the network on differ in dimension from the original ones it was trained on. In the following code block, we can visually summarize the model object that we loaded in:

```
img_width, img_height = 32, 32
model = applications.VGG19(weights = "imagenet", include_top=False,
input_shape = (img_width, img_height, 3))
model.summary()
```

The output will be as follows:

```
Layer (type)                    Output Shape           Param #
=================================================================
input_1 (InputLayer)            (None, 32, 32, 3)       0
_____
block1_conv1 (Conv2D)           (None, 32, 32, 64)      1792
_____
block1_conv2 (Conv2D)           (None, 32, 32, 64)      36928
_____
block1_pool (MaxPooling2D)      (None, 16, 16, 64)      0
_____
block2_conv1 (Conv2D)           (None, 16, 16, 128)     73856
_____
block2_conv2 (Conv2D)           (None, 16, 16, 128)     147584
_____
block2_pool (MaxPooling2D)      (None, 8, 8, 128)       0
_____
block3_conv1 (Conv2D)           (None, 8, 8, 256)       295168
_____
block3_conv2 (Conv2D)           (None, 8, 8, 256)       590080
_____
block3_conv3 (Conv2D)           (None, 8, 8, 256)       590080
_____
block3_conv4 (Conv2D)           (None, 8, 8, 256)       590080
_____
block3_pool (MaxPooling2D)      (None, 4, 4, 256)       0
_____
block4_conv1 (Conv2D)           (None, 4, 4, 512)       1180160
_____
block4_conv2 (Conv2D)           (None, 4, 4, 512)       2359808
_____
block4_conv3 (Conv2D)           (None, 4, 4, 512)       2359808
_____
block4_conv4 (Conv2D)           (None, 4, 4, 512)       2359808
_____
block4_pool (MaxPooling2D)      (None, 2, 2, 512)       0
_____
block5_conv1 (Conv2D)           (None, 2, 2, 512)       2359808
_____
block5_conv2 (Conv2D)           (None, 2, 2, 512)       2359808
_____
block5_conv3 (Conv2D)           (None, 2, 2, 512)       2359808
_____
block5_conv4 (Conv2D)           (None, 2, 2, 512)       2359808
_____
block5_pool (MaxPooling2D)      (None, 1, 1, 512)       0
=================================================================
Total params: 20,024,384
Trainable params: 20,024,384
```

This is quite a big model. In fact, it has about 20 million trainable parameters!

Obtaining intermediate layers from a model

Thanks to Keras's Lego-like modular interface, we can do some really cool things, such as break apart the aforementioned model and reuse its layers as part of another network. This will be our next step, and it can be easily achieved using the functional API:

```
model2= Model(inputs=model.input, outputs=
            model.get_layer('block3_pool').output)
model2.summary()
```

The result obtained will be as follows:

Layer (type)	Output Shape	Param #
input_1 (InputLayer)	(None, 32, 32, 3)	0
block1_conv1 (Conv2D)	(None, 32, 32, 64)	1792
block1_conv2 (Conv2D)	(None, 32, 32, 64)	36928
block1_pool (MaxPooling2D)	(None, 16, 16, 64)	0
block2_conv1 (Conv2D)	(None, 16, 16, 128)	73856
block2_conv2 (Conv2D)	(None, 16, 16, 128)	147584
block2_pool (MaxPooling2D)	(None, 8, 8, 128)	0
block3_conv1 (Conv2D)	(None, 8, 8, 256)	295168
block3_conv2 (Conv2D)	(None, 8, 8, 256)	590080
block3_conv3 (Conv2D)	(None, 8, 8, 256)	590080
block3_conv4 (Conv2D)	(None, 8, 8, 256)	590080
block3_pool (MaxPooling2D)	(None, 4, 4, 256)	0

```
Total params: 2,325,568
Trainable params: 2,325,568
Non-trainable params: 0
```

Notice that all we had to do is initiate a model object using the functional API and pass it the first 12 layers of the VGG net. This is achieved by using the .get_layer() method on the VGG model object and passing it a layer name. Recall that the name of an individual layer can be verified by using the .summary() method on a given model object.

Adding layers to a model

Now we have retrieved the pretrained intermediate layers from the VGG net. Next, we can connect more sequential layers to these pretrained layers. The idea behind this is to use the representations learned by the pretrained layers and build upon them, thereby augmenting the classification task with knowledge from a different learning task:

```
#Adding custom Layers
num_classes = 10

x = model2.output
x = Flatten()(x)
x = Dense(1024, activation="relu")(x)
x = Dropout(0.5)(x)
x = Dense(1024, activation="relu")(x)
predictions = Dense(num_classes, activation="softmax")(x)
```

To add more layers to our model, we will again use the functional API syntax to create a simple feed-forward network, which takes the output values from the selected VGG net layers and flattens them into 2D arrays, before passing them forward to densely connected layers with 1,024 neurons. This layer then connects to a heavy-dropout layer, where half of the neural connections from the previous layer is ignored while training.

Next, we have another dense layer of 1,024 neurons before reaching the final output layer. The output layer is equipped with 10 neurons, pertaining to the number of classes in our training data, as well as a softmax activation function, which will generate a 10-way probability score for each observation seen by the network.

Now that we have defined the layers we wish to add to the network, we can once again use the functional API syntax to merge the two separate models together:

```
# creating the final model
model_final = Model(input = model2.input, output = predictions)
model_final.summary()
```

You will get this output:

Layer (type)	Output Shape	Param #
input_1 (InputLayer)	(None, 32, 32, 3)	0
block1_conv1 (Conv2D)	(None, 32, 32, 64)	1792
block1_conv2 (Conv2D)	(None, 32, 32, 64)	36928
block1_pool (MaxPooling2D)	(None, 16, 16, 64)	0
block2_conv1 (Conv2D)	(None, 16, 16, 128)	73856
block2_conv2 (Conv2D)	(None, 16, 16, 128)	147584
block2_pool (MaxPooling2D)	(None, 8, 8, 128)	0
block3_conv1 (Conv2D)	(None, 8, 8, 256)	295168
block3_conv2 (Conv2D)	(None, 8, 8, 256)	590080
block3_conv3 (Conv2D)	(None, 8, 8, 256)	590080
block3_conv4 (Conv2D)	(None, 8, 8, 256)	590080
block3_pool (MaxPooling2D)	(None, 4, 4, 256)	0
flatten_1 (Flatten)	(None, 4096)	0
dense_1 (Dense)	(None, 1024)	4195328
dropout_1 (Dropout)	(None, 1024)	0
dense_2 (Dense)	(None, 1024)	1049600
dense_3 (Dense)	(None, 10)	10250

```
Total params: 7,580,746
Trainable params: 7,580,746
Non-trainable params: 0
```

Most important, we must freeze the layer weights of the VGG model, so as to benefit from the representations it has encoded during its previous training session on those nice expensive GPUs.

Here, we only chose to freeze the first four layers and decided to let the rest of the architecture retrain on this new learning task:

```
# Freeze the layers that dont need to train
for layer in model2.layers[:4]:
    layer.trainable = False
```

Other approaches may choose to keep the entire model architecture frozen and only reinitialize the weights of the last layer of the model. We encourage you to try freezing different numbers of layers, and exploring how this changes the network's learning experience, by visualizing the loss convergence, for example.

Intuitively, different learning tasks may require different approaches. It naturally depends on a multitude of factors, such as the similarity between tasks, similarity between the training data, and so on.

A common rule of thumb is to only reinitialize the weights of the last layer if very little data is available on the target learning task. Conversely, if a lot of data is available on the target task, then it is even conceivable to reinitialize weights for the entire network during training. In this case, you would have simply used a pretrained model and reimplemented it for a different use case. As always with deep learning, the answer lies in experimentation.

Loading and preprocessing the data

Next, we preprocess the CIFAR10 images and vectorize the labels, as we have been doing throughout the course of this book. There is nothing special here to note:

```
(x_train, y_train),(x_test, y_test)=cifar10.load_data()
x_train = x_train.astype('float32')
x_test = x_test.astype('float32')
x_train /= 255
x_test /= 255
y_train = utils.to_categorical(y_train, num_classes)
y_test = utils.to_categorical(y_test, num_classes)
```

We first load the images in the first code block. In the second block, we normalize the pixel values to float values between 0 and 1. Finally, in the last block, we one-hot encode our labels. Now, our network is ready to be compiled and trained.

Training the network

Next, we compile our model, with the categorical cross-entropy loss function and the Adam optimizer. Then, we can initiate the training session, as shown here:

```
# compile the model
model_final.compile(loss = "categorical_crossentropy", optimizer =
        optimizers.Adam(lr=0.0001), metrics=["accuracy"])
```

The following will be the output obtained:

```
Train on 50000 samples, validate on 10000 samples
Epoch 1/10
50000/50000 [==============================] - 33s 668us/step - loss: 2.3378 - acc: 0.5036 - val_loss: 0.7967 - val_acc: 0.7214
Epoch 2/10
50000/50000 [==============================] - 30s 607us/step - loss: 0.7708 - acc: 0.7343 - val_loss: 0.6386 - val_acc: 0.7780
Epoch 3/10
50000/50000 [==============================] - 30s 601us/step - loss: 0.6087 - acc: 0.7893 - val_loss: 0.5872 - val_acc: 0.7979
Epoch 4/10
50000/50000 [==============================] - 32s 643us/step - loss: 0.4998 - acc: 0.8269 - val_loss: 0.5339 - val_acc: 0.8184
```

The model was trained in batches of 128 images for 10 epochs. The validation accuracy achieved was about 85%, which was considerably better than the same model trained from scratch. You can try this out yourself, by unfreezing the layers we froze, before training the model. There we have it. Now you have implemented a transfer learning workflow in Keras and are able to reuse neural networks for use cases requiring pretraining or fine tuning

Exercises

1. Experiment with different model depths by retrieving more blocks from the pretrained VGG net. Does the accuracy improve substantially with deeper models? Vary where you pick layers.
2. Change the number of trainable layers; how does this affect the convergence of `loss`?
3. Try out a different model out of the 10 pretrained ones available in `keras.applications` to build a classifier using the notion of transfer learning.
4. Listen to Andrew Ng talk about transfer learning: https://www.youtube.com/watch?v=yofjFQddwHE.

Concluding our experiments

Such accounts bring an end to our explorations and experimentations with various neural network architectures. Yet, there is still a lot more to discuss and discover. After all, while our journey together comes close to fruition, yours has just begun! There are countless more use cases, architectural variations, and implementational details that we could go on to explore, yet doing so will deviate from our initial ambitions for this work. We wanted to achieve a detailed understanding of what neural networks actually do, how they operate, and under what circumstances they may be used, respectively. Furthermore, we want to develop an internal intuition of what is actually happening inside these networks, and why these architectures work as well as they do. The remainder of this chapter will be dedicated to solidifying this notion, allowing you to better relate to the underlying idea of representation learning and applying this notion to any future use cases you may want to address using neural networks. Finally, we will also take this opportunity to address some of the latest developments in the field of ANNs, and how different business and institutions alike have crafted utility for this technology. Finally, we will also attempt to take a step into the future and speculate on how coming developments may affect the scientific, economic, and social landscape, in the advent of phenomena such as big data, and potential technological leaps such as quantum computing.

Learning representations

While we addressed the topic of representations and how this affects the task of learning in Chapter 1, *Overview of Neural Networks*, we can now afford for our discussion to deepen further, given the hands-on practical examples we have executed since.

By now, we are all well aware that the success of any **Machine Learning** (**ML**) algorithm (including deep learning algorithms such as neural networks) is directly dependent on the manner in which we chose to represent the data it is shown. What's the deal here?

To demonstrate the importance of representations and their impact on information processing, recall that we saw a succinct example earlier on in this book. We performed mathematical operations such as long division using Roman numerals, revealing the difficulty of carrying out such a task using suboptimal representations. Indeed, the way we choose to represent information directly impacts the way we process it, the sort of operations we are able to perform on it, and the kind of understanding we may derive.

DNA and technology

Consider another example: the DNA molecule. **Deoxyribonucleic Acid (DNA)** is a molecular structure made up of two intertwined chainlike threads, known as the **double helix formation**. The molecule can be broken down into **simpler monomeric units** (or **nucleoids**), forming base pairs composed of two of the four nitrogen-based building blocks (these being **Adenine (A)**, **Guanine (G)**, **Thymine (T)**, and **Cytosine (C)**).

Many of you may be wondering at this point, *"what does this have to do with the subject at hand?"* Well, as it turns out, this molecular structure holds the blueprints of all lifeforms on this planet. The molecule governs how cells divide, become more complex structures, all of the way up to the preferences and behavior of the flora and fauna here on our home planet.

Needless to say, this quadrinary system for representing information has found a way to encode and copy instructions to produce all life we see around us! No representation format devised by humans so far has ever come close to simulating the grand sphere of life as we know it. In fact, we still struggle to simulate realistically immersive game environments for entertainment purposes. Curiously, by many estimates, the DNA molecule itself can be represented using our own binary system, with about 1.5 gigabytes of data. Think about it, 1.5 gigabytes of data, or one single Blueray disk, is capable of storing all the of instructions for life itself. But that's about all we can do. We can't exactly instruct the Blueray disk to incessantly replicate itself into the complexity we embody and see around us every day. Hardware considerations aside, a paramount reason why we cannot replicate the operations of life in this manner is due to the representation of the data itself! Hence, the way we represent data has severe implications on the kind of transformations we may perform, resulting in ever more complex information-processing systems.

Limits of current neural networks

Similarly, in ML, it is hypothesized that different representations of data allow the capturing of different explanatory factors of variation present therein. The neural networks we saw were excellent at inducing efficient representations from their input values and leveraging these representations for all sorts of learning tasks. Yet, these input values themselves had to undergo a deluge of preprocessing considerations, transforming raw data into a format more palatable to the networks.

Currently, the deficiency of neural networks relates to their heavy dependence on such preprocessing and feature-engineering considerations to learn useful representations from the given data. On their own, they are unable to extract and categorize discriminative elements from raw input values. Often, behind every neural network, there is a human.

We are still required to use our ingenuity, domain knowledge, and curiosity in order to overcome this deficiency. Eventually, however, we will strive to devise systems that require minimal human intervention (in the form of feature engineering, for example) and to truly understand the raw data present in the world. Designing such a system is one of the paramount goals in the field of AI, and one that we hope you can help advance.

For the time being, however, we will cover some useful concepts that allow us to design better representations from raw data, thereby designing better learning experiences for our artificial counterparts.

Engineering representations for machines

The topic of representation learning addresses exactly this. Intuitively, we ask ourselves this: *How can we make it easier for machines to extract useful information from data?* This notion is intrinsically linked to the idea that there exist certain generalizable assumptions about the world that may be applied to better interpret and synthesize the raw data available. These generalized assumptions, in conjunction with experimentative techniques, allow us to design good representations and discard bad ones. They serve as principles of experimentation when designing a preprocessing workflow for learning algorithms such as neural networks.

How should a good representation be?

Intuitively, a good representation should be capable of disentangling the main factors of variation that cause an occurrence. Hence, one approach may be to augment the analytics workflow in a manner so as to make it easier for machines to spot these factors of variance.

Researchers, over the decades, have amassed a set of heuristic assumptions applicable in the field of deep learning that allow us to do exactly this. Next, we will reproduce a subset of such heuristics, or regularization strategies, that are known to augment the learning experience of deep neural networks.

 For a comprehensive technical review of all of the considerations involved in representation learning, please refer to this excellent paper by some of the pioneers of deep learning—*Representation Learning: A Review and New Perspectives* (Y Bengio, A Courville, Pascal Vincent, 2016): https://arxiv.org/pdf/1206.5538.pdf.

Preprocessing and data treatments

As you must already be well aware, neural networks are quite picky eaters. Namely, there are two staple operations that need to be performed before our data can be fed to a neural network: **vectorization** and **normalization**.

Vectorization

Recall that vectorization simply means that all of the inputs and target variables of your data must be in a tensor format, containing floating-point values (or in specific cases, such as the Boston Housing Price Regression example, integers). We previously achieved this by populating a matrix of zeros using indexed values (as in the sentiment classification example), or by one-hot encoding our variables.

Normalization

Besides vectorization, another consideration we had to undertake was normalization of our input data. This was more of a standard practice in most ML workflows and consisted of transforming our input variables into a small, homogeneous range of values. We achieved this in tasks such as image processing by normalizing the pixel values between 0 and 1. In cases where our input variables were on different scales (such as with the Boston example), we had to implement an independent feature-wise normalization strategy. Forgoing such steps may cause gradient updates that do not converge to a global minimum, making it much more difficult for a network to learn. In general, a rule of thumb can be to try independent feature normalization, ensuring a feature-wise mean of 0 and a standard deviation of 1.

Smoothness of the data

Neural networks struggle the least with predictions if they are shown a data distribution that is locally smooth. What does this mean? Simply put, if an input, x, produces an output, y, a point close to this input will produce an output proportionally close to y. This is the property of smoothness and greatly augments learning architecture such as neural networks, allowing them to capture better representations from such data. Unfortunately, however, having this property in your data distribution is not the only criteria for neural networks to learn good representations; the curse of dimensionality, for example, is still one that would need to be addressed, by feature selection or dimensionality reduction.

Adding something such as a smoothening factor to your data, for example, can largely benefit the learning process, as we did when predicting stock market prices with LSTMs.

Encouraging sparse representation learning

Suppose you were training a network to classify pictures of cats and dogs. Over the course of training, the intermediate layers will learn different representations or features from the input values (such as cat ears, dog eyes, and so on), combining them in a probabilistic fashion to detect the presence of an output class (that is, whether a picture is of a cat or a dog).

Yet, while performing inference on an individual image, do we need the feature that detects cat ears to ascertain that this particular image is of a dog? The answer in almost all cases is a resounding no. Most of the time, we can assume that most features that a network learns during training are actually not relevant for each individual prediction. Hence, we want our network to learn sparse representations for each input, a resulting tensor representation where most entries are zero (denoting perhaps the presence or absence of the corresponding features).

In deep learning, sparsity is a very desirable property for learned representations. Not only does this allow us to have a smaller number of neurons active when representing a phenomenon (thereby increasing the efficiency of our network), but it also helps the network to better untangle the main factors of variance present within the data itself.

Intuitively, sparsity allows the network to recognize learned features in data, without being perturbed by small variations occurring in the inputs. Implementation wise, sparsity simply enforces the value of most learned features to zero, when representing any individual input. Sparse representations can be learned through operations such as one-hot encoding, non-linear transformations as imposed by the activation functions, or by other means of penalizing derivatives of the intermediate layers, with respect to the input values.

Tuning hyperparameters

In general, it is assumed that deeper model architectures give access to higher representational power, allowing us to hierarchically organize abstract representations for predictive tasks.

However, as we know, deeper architectures are prone to overfitting, and hence can be challenging to train, requiring keen attention to aspects such as regularization (as seen with the regularization strategies explored in `Chapter 3`, *Signal Processing - Data Analysis with Neural Networks*). How can we assess exactly how many layers to initialize, with the appropriate number of neurons and relevant regularization strategies to use? Given the complexity involved in designing the right architecture, it can be very time consuming to experiment with different model hyperparameters to find the right network specifications to solve the task at hand.

While we have discussed general intuitions on designing more robust architectures, using techniques such as dropout and batch normalization, we can't help but wonder whether there is a way to automate this entire tedious process. It would even be tempting to apply deep learning to this process itself, where it not a discretely constrained optimization problem (as opposed the continuous optimization problems we have so far been solving, using gradient decent).

Automatic optimization and evolutionary algorithms

Fortunately, many tools exist that allow such automatic parameter optimization. **Talos** (`https://github.com/autonomio/talos`) is one such tool built on top of the Keras library, made available as open source on GitHub. It allows you to predefine a set of hyperparameters (such as different number of layers, neurons per layer, and activation functions), after which the tool will automatically train and compare those Keras models to assess which one performs better.

Other solutions such as **Hyperas** (`https://github.com/maxpumperla/hyperas`) or **auto_ML** (`https://auto-ml.readthedocs.io/en/latest/`) allow similar functionalities and can help drastically reduce development time, allowing you to discover what hyperparameters work best for your task. In fact, you can use such tools and make your own genetic algorithms that help you select from a pool of hyperparameters, train and evaluate a network, then select the best of those network architectures, randomly mutate some hyperparameters of the selected networks, and repeat the training and evaluation all over again. Eventually, such an algorithm can produce increasingly complex architectures to solve a given problem, just as evolution does in nature. While a detailed overview of such methods is well beyond the scope of this book, we take the liberty of linking a simplistic implementation of such an approach next, which allows evolving network parameters in order to find ideal configurations.

References

- **Evolutionary algorithms and neural networks**: http://www.weiss-gerhard.info/publications/C22.pdf
- **Implementation of evolutionary neural networks**: https://blog.coast.ai/lets-evolve-a-neural-network-with-a-genetic-algorithm-code-included-8809bece164

Multi-network predictions and ensemble models

Another way to get the best of neural networks is by using ensemble models. The idea is quite simple: why use one network when you can use many? In other words, why not design different neural networks, each sensitive to specific representations in the input data? Then, we can average out their predictions, getting a more generalizable and parsimonious prediction than using just one network.

We can even attribute weights to each network, by pegging each network's prediction to the test accuracy it achieves on the task. Then, we can take a weighted average of the predictions (weighted with their relative accuracies) from each network to get to a more comprehensive prediction altogether.

Intuitively, we just look at the data with different eyes; each network, by virtue of its design, may pay attention to different factors of variance, perhaps ignored by its other counterparts. This method is fairly straightforward and simple to implement and only requires designing separate networks, with good intuition on what kind of representations each network can be expected to capture. After that, it is simply a question of adding appropriate weights to each individual network's prediction and averaging out the results.

The future of AI and neural networks

Throughout the course of this book, we have dived deep into a specific realm of AI, nested within ML, that we call deep learning. This caveat of machine intelligence takes a connectionist approach, combining the predictive power of distributed representations, in turn learned by a deep neural network.

While deep learning neural networks have risen to prominence, since the advent of GPU, accelerated computing, and the availability of big data, many considerations have gone into improving the intuition and implementation behind these architectures, since their re-ascension to popularity, about a decade ago (Hinton et al, 2008). Yet, still, there exist many complex tasks that deep learning is not yet able to adequately tackle.

Global vectors approach

Sometimes, the sequence of mathematical transformations on given input values is simply not enough to learn an effective function mapping them to some output values. Already, many such examples exist, especially in the domain of **natural language processing** (**NLP**). While we restricted our NLP use cases to simple word vectorization, this approach can be limiting for some use cases requiring the understanding of complex dependencies that exist in human language.

Instead, a popular approach is to symbolically attribute properties to words and attribute values to these properties so as to allow comparison with other words. This is the basic intuition behind a technique known as **Global Vectors** (**GloVe**) used as a text-preprocessing vectorization technique, before data is fed to neural networks. Such an approach perhaps alludes to how the use of deep learning will evolve in the future. This specific workflow illustrates the use of principles from both distributed and symbolic representations to discover, understand, and solve complex problems, such as the logical reasoning involved in machine question-answering.

Distributed representation

In the future, it is very likely that we start using principles from various disciplines of AI, in conjunction with the power of distributed representation that deep learning brings to the table, to design systems that are truly and generally intelligent. Such systems can then go about learning tasks in an autonomous manner, with the enhanced capability to tackle complex problems. It could, for example, conduct research following scientific methodology, thereby automating human knowledge discovery. In short, deep learning is here to stay, and will likely be complemented by other subfields of AI, to develop very powerful computing systems.

Hardware hurdles

Yet, before we get to that stage of AI, surely there are other improvements to be made. Recall that deep learning became popular not only because we learned techniques to represent and process data on a higher level, but also because our hardware improved drastically. We now have access to the processing power that would have cost us millions about a few decades ago, for literally a few thousand dollars. Similarly, there may yet be another hardware hurdle for humanity to overcome before we can design truly intuitive and logically superior systems, capable of solving humanity's grand problems.

Many have speculated that this giant leap will materialize in the form of quantum computing. While covering this topic in depth is a bit beyond the scope of this book (and the proficiencies of this author), we could not help but include a short parenthesis to illustrate the benefits and complexities involved in importing neural networks to an emerging computing paradigm, with promising prospects.

The road ahead

While the previous diagram depicting the advances in processing power might make us look back in nostalgia over how far we have come, this same nostalgia will be wiped away quite fast as soon as we realize how far we still have to go.

As we saw in the preceding diagram, the computational power of the systems we have implemented so far are nowhere near that of a human brain. The neural networks that we devised (at least in this book) had a number of neurons ranging anywhere from a million (the equivalent of what you would find in a cockroach) to about ten million (close to what is common for an adult zebra fish).

Attempting to train a network that parallels a human mind, at least in the number of neurons used, is currently beyond the scope of human engineering, as of the date of this book. It simply surpasses our current computing capacity. Moreover, it is important to note that this comparison naturally ignores the detail that the neurons in each of these learning systems (artificial versus biological) are different, both in form and function.

Biological neurons operate much differently than their artificial counterparts and are influenced by quantum systems such as molecular chemistry. The exact nature of information processing and storage in biological neurons is still not fully understood by modern neuroscience. So, how can we simulate what we don't yet fully comprehend? One answer to this dilemma could be to design more powerful computers, capable of representing and transforming information in ways more suited for the domain. This brings us to the phenomenon of quantum computing.

Problems with classical computing

In simplistic terms, quantum mechanics is a field that deals with the study of things that are very small, isolated, and cold. While this may not create an appealing picture at first, consider the problem we are facing currently. Already, the exponential growth of the number of transistors in a chip, as predicted by Moore's law, seems to be slowing down.

Why is this important? These transistors are actually what permits us to compute! From simple data storage to the complex mathematical operations native to neural networks, all data representation in classical computers is by virtue of these semiconductor devices. We use them to amplify and switch electric signals, thereby creating logic gates capable of tracking the presence of charged electrons (1) or absence thereof (0). These switches can be manipulated to create binary digits, or bits, that represent a unit of information. In essence, this binary system forms the basis of all digital encoding, exploiting the physical properties of transistors to store and process information. It is the language of machines, which allows representing and processing information.

From the very first fully digital and programmable computer (Z3, 1938), to the latest supercomputers (IBMs Summit, 2018), this fundamental language of representation has not changed. For all intents and purposes, the lingua franca of machines has remained based on the binary system for about a century.

Yet, as we discussed earlier, different representations allow us to perform different operations. Hence, perhaps it is time for us to revise the fundamental manner in which we represent data. Given the fact that transistors can only get so small, we are slowly but surely reaching the limits of classical computing. Hence, what better place to look for solutions than the infinitesimally small and bizarre world of quantum mechanics.

The advent of quantum computing

While classical computers use binary representations to encode information into bits, their quantum counterparts use the laws of physics to encode information in **Q-Bits**. There are many approaches toward designing such systems. You can, for instance, use microwave pulses to alter the spin momentum of an electron, to represent and store information.

Quantum superposition

As it turns out, this may allow us to leverage interesting quantum phenomena to represent operations that have no known classical counterpart. Operations such as **quantum superposition**, where two different quantum states may be added together to produce a third state, valid on its own. Hence, unlike its classical counterpart, a Q-Bit can have three states: (0), (1), and (1/0,), where the third represents a state only achievable through the property of quantum superposition.

Naturally, this allows us to represent much more information, opening doors for us to tackle problems from higher-complexity classes (such as simulating intelligence, for example).

Distinguishing Q-Bits from classical counterparts

Other quantum properties also exist that distinguish the Q-Bit from its classical counterpart. For example, two Q-Bits can enter an entangled state, where the spin of the electrons of each Q-Bit is set to continuously point in opposite directions.

Why is this a big deal? Well, these two Q-Bits can then be separated by billions of miles, while still seemingly maintaining a link between each other. We know, by virtue of the laws of physics, that the spin of each electron will always point in opposite directions when observed, regardless of the distance between the Q-Bits themselves.

This entangled state is interesting, because there is no classical operation that can represent the idea of two different bits having no specified value, yet always remaining the opposite value of each other. These concepts have the potential of revolutionizing fields such as communication and cryptography, on top of the exponential computing power they bring to the table. The more Q-Bits a quantum computer can leverage, the more non-classical operations it can use to represent and process data. In essence, these are some of the pivotal underlining ideas behind quantum computing.

Quantum neural networks

Many of you may be thinking that all of this is nice, but we ourselves are surely decades away from being able to use a quantum computer, let alone design neural networks on it. While healthy skepticism is always nice, it does not do justice to the efforts of contemporary researchers, scientists, and businesses working around the clock to bring such systems to life. It may surprise you to know, for example, that anybody in the world with an internet connection today has free access to a quantum computer, using the link right here (courtesy of IBM): `https://quantumexperience.ng.bluemix.net/qx/editor`.

In fact, researchers such as Francesco Tacchino and his colleagues have already used this service to implement quantum neural networks for classification tasks! They were able to implement the world's first quantum perceptron, similar in spirit to the perceptron we saw in `Chapter 2`, *A Deeper Dive into Neural Networks*, yet augmented with the laws of quantum mechanics. They used IBM's **Q-5 Tenerife** superconducting quantum processor, which allows the manipulation of up to five Q-Bits, to train a classifier to detect simple patterns such as line segments.

While this may sound trivial at first, the implications of their work are quite significant. They were able to decisively show how a quantum computer allows an exponential increase in the number of dimensions it can process. For instance, while a classical perceptron is capable of processing input values of n dimensions, its quantum counterpart designed by these researchers was able to process 2N dimensions! Such implementations pave the way for future researchers to implement more complex architectures.

Naturally, the realm of quantum neural networks is still in infancy, since quantum computers themselves have a lot of improvements to undergo. However, active research currently focuses on many areas of importing neural nets to the quantum world, ranging from straightforward extensions of connected layers, to quantum optimization algorithms that are better at navigating the loss landscape.

Some have even speculated that quantum phenomena such as tunneling may be used to, quite literally, tunnel through the loss landscape to converge to optimal network weights extremely quickly! This truly represents the dawn of a new age for ML and AI. Once these systems have been thoroughly tried and tested, we may be able to represent truly complex patterns in novel ways, with implications beyond our current imagination.

Further reading

- A paper on quantum neural networks: `https://arxiv.org/pdf/1811.02266.pdf`
- A QNN paper by Google: `https://arxiv.org/pdf/1802.06002.pdf`
- The Google Quantum AI blog: `https://ai.googleblog.com/2018/12/exploring-quantum-neural-networks.html`
- Quantum optimization algorithms: `https://ieeexplore.ieee.org/abstract/document/6507335`

Technology and society

Today, we stand at the intersection of very interesting times. Times that some claim will define the future of humankind and change the way we perceive and interact with the world altogether. Automation, cognitive technologies, AI, and quantum computing are but a few among the sea of disruptive technologies, constantly causing organizations to reassess their value chains and better themselves in the way they impact the world.

Perhaps people will be able to work more efficiently, organize their time better, and devote their lives to activities that uniquely complement their skill sets, thereby delivering optimal value to the society they participate in. Or, perhaps, there is more of a dystopic future ahead of us, where such technologies are used to disenfranchise the masses, observe and control human behavior, and limit our freedom. While the technology itself is simply analogous to any tool previously invented by humans, the way we choose to use these tools will have reverberating consequences for all the involved stakeholders. Ultimately, the choice is ours. Luckily, we are at the dawn of this new era, and so we can still steer the direction of progress in a sustainable and inclusive manner.

Currently, organizations across the globe are rushing to find ways to reap the fruit from such technologies before it is too late for them to adapt, leading to all sorts of concerns spanning from transparency to legality and ethics. These dilemmas surface despite the fact that we are still in the infancy phase of AI. In essence, all the methods and techniques we explored through the course of this book are narrow AI technologies. They are specific systems capable of solving narrow components of a workflow, be it to solve specific computer vision tasks or to answer certain types of questions in natural language. This is very different than the idea of AI, in its literal sense: an intelligence that is autonomous and can learn in a self-sufficient manner, without outsiders directly manipulating its internal learning algorithm. It is an intelligence that can grow and evolve, similar in spirit to the journey of a human baby to an adult, albeit at a different rate.

Contemplating our future

Consider a new-born human baby. At first, it is even incapable of breathing and has to be motivated to do so by a few friendly spanks, delivered by the attending physician. For the first few months, this being does not seem to do anything remarkable and is incapable of independent movement, let alone thought. Yet, slowly, this same baby develops an internal model of the world around it. It becomes better and better at distinguishing all this light it sees and the cacophony of sounds it hears. Soon, it starts recognizing things such as movement, perhaps in the guise of a friendly face, hovering around with deliciously gooey substances. A bit later, it develops a premature internal physics engine, through the observation of the world around it. It then uses these representations to first crawl, then toddle, and eventually even walk, progressively updating its internal physics engine to represent more and more complex models of the world. Soon enough, it is able to perform somersaults, compose elaborate poetry, and peruse causes such as mathematics, history, philosophy, or even AI science.

Do note that nobody is exactly tuning a CNN to make the baby see better, or increasing the size of an LSTM architecture, for the baby to write better poetry. The individual was able to do so without any direct external intervention, by simply observing things around itself, listening to people, and learning by doing. While there are a multitude of things going on under the hood of a human baby as it journeys to adulthood, almost all of which are quite beyond the scope of this work, this example demonstrates how far we still are from creating something that can truly parallel our own intellect.

The same type of baby can eventually learn to drive cars, and with a little bit of help, solve complex problems such as world hunger or interplanetary travel! This is truly an intelligent organism. The artificial counterparts that we explored in our book are not yet worthy of comparison to the former form of intelligence, simply due to their narrow applicability. They are but pieces of a puzzle, a manner of approaching information processing, often for a specific cognitive domain. Perhaps one day, these narrow technologies will be united in a comprehensive system, splicing a multitude of such technologies together, creating something even greater than the components within. In fact, this is currently happening, as we have seen throughout this book already. For example, we saw how convolutional architectures may be merged with other neural network architectures such as LSTMs, for complex visual information processing involving a temporal component, as in making the right moves in a game.

But the question then still remains: will such architectures truly become intelligent? This may be a question for the philosophers of today, but it is also one for the scientists of tomorrow. As these systems evolve, and conquer more and more realms that were previously through attainable only by humans, we will eventually face such existential questions about these machines and ourselves. Are we really that different? Are we just very complex computers, carrying out arithmetic operations through biology? Or is there more to intelligence and consciousness than mere computation? Sadly, we do not have all the answers, yet this does make for an exciting journey ahead for our species.

Summary

In this chapter, we reiterated what we have learned in this book and saw how we can improve the existing techniques. We then moved on to see the future of deep learning and gained insight into quantum computing.

I hope this journey has been informative. Thanks for reading and all the best!

Other Books You May Enjoy

If you enjoyed this book, you may be interested in these other books by Packt:

Advanced Deep Learning with Keras
Rowel Atienza

ISBN: 9781788629416

- Cutting-edge techniques in human-like AI performance
- Implement advanced deep learning models using Keras
- The building blocks for advanced techniques - MLPs, CNNs, and RNNs
- Deep neural networks – ResNet and DenseNet
- Autoencoders and Variational AutoEncoders (VAEs)
- Generative Adversarial Networks (GANs) and creative AI techniques
- Disentangled Representation GANs, and Cross-Domain GANs
- Deep Reinforcement Learning (DRL) methods and implementation
- Produce industry-standard applications using OpenAI gym
- Deep Q-Learning and Policy Gradient Methods

Python Deep Learning - Second Edition

Ivan Vasilev

ISBN: 9781789348460

- Grasp the mathematical theory behind neural networks and deep learning processes
- Investigate and resolve computer vision challenges using convolutional networks and capsule networks
- Solve generative tasks using variational autoencoders and Generative Adversarial Networks
- Implement complex NLP tasks using recurrent networks (LSTM and GRU) and attention models
- Explore reinforcement learning and understand how agents behave in a complex environment
- Get up to date with applications of deep learning in autonomous vehicles

Leave a review - let other readers know what you think

Please share your thoughts on this book with others by leaving a review on the site that you bought it from. If you purchased the book from Amazon, please leave us an honest review on this book's Amazon page. This is vital so that other potential readers can see and use your unbiased opinion to make purchasing decisions, we can understand what our customers think about our products, and our authors can see your feedback on the title that they have worked with Packt to create. It will only take a few minutes of your time, but is valuable to other potential customers, our authors, and Packt. Thank you!

Index

Hands-On Full Stack Web Development with Aurelia

Develop modern and real-time web applications with Aurelia and Node.js

Diego Jose Argüelles Rojas
Erikson Haziz Murrugarra Sifuentes

BIRMINGHAM - MUMBAI

Hands-On Full Stack Web Development with Aurelia

Commissioning Editor: Kunal Chaudhari
Acquisition Editor: Shweta Pant
Content Development Editor: Flavian Vaz
Technical Editor: Vaibhav Dwivedi
Copy Editor: Shaila Kusanale
Project Coordinator: Devanshi Doshi
Proofreader: Safis Editing
Indexer: Pratik Shirodkar
Graphics: Jason Monteiro
Production Coordinator: Shraddha Falebhai

First published: June 2018

Production reference: 1120618

Published by Packt Publishing Ltd.
Livery Place
35 Livery Street
Birmingham
B3 2PB, UK.

ISBN 978-1-78883-320-2

www.packtpub.com

Any success I get is thanks to my family. I would not be who I am without their guidance. Special thanks to my mom, the best person in the world, who is everything in my heart. To my dear J, my friends, and my little dog, you all fill my life with happiness.

– Diego Jose Argüelles Rojas

I dedicate this book to my beloved family. For giving me all the unconditional support and for their constant sacrifice in helping me become the man I am today. I love them with all my heart.

I dedicate it especially to my past self, to that child who fought very hard to achieve his goals. Little Erikson, we did it!

- Erikson Haziz Murrugarra Sifuentes

`mapt.io`

Mapt is an online digital library that gives you full access to over 5,000 books and videos, as well as industry leading tools to help you plan your personal development and advance your career. For more information, please visit our website.

Why subscribe?

- Spend less time learning and more time coding with practical eBooks and Videos from over 4,000 industry professionals

- Improve your learning with Skill Plans built especially for you

- Get a free eBook or video every month

- Mapt is fully searchable

- Copy and paste, print, and bookmark content

PacktPub.com

Did you know that Packt offers eBook versions of every book published, with PDF and ePub files available? You can upgrade to the eBook version at `www.PacktPub.com` and as a print book customer, you are entitled to a discount on the eBook copy. Get in touch with us at `service@packtpub.com` for more details.

At `www.PacktPub.com`, you can also read a collection of free technical articles, sign up for a range of free newsletters, and receive exclusive discounts and offers on Packt books and eBooks.

Foreword

I had my first encounter with web technology in the late 1990s. At that time, and for a number of years that followed, I was knee-deep in native desktop development. The Web, with its static pages and limited interactivity, held no interest for me.

Then, the iPhone came, and everything changed.

Very quickly, the world of one-platform desktop application development was no longer a viable business. Customers demanded rich experiences that worked equally well on iPhone, iPad, Android, Windows, Mac, Linux, and much more. In response, I returned to revisit the Web, hoping to find a way to build native-like experiences in a cross-platform way. In the 10-year span since I first searched, the Web had grown considerably. What was once a world of lifeless text and few images is now a rapidly evolving platform. Styling, animation, layout, SVG, drawing APIs, and many more features were available or soon to be shipped as part of HTML5. JavaScript was also being reborn with built-in primitives for async programming and new language constructs for classes, lambdas, destructuring, and more. All the raw materials for a rich application platform were there, yet something was missing. There was still no way to create components, that is, no built-in concept of an "app," and no mechanism for building multi-screen experiences.

Enter Aurelia.

In early 2015, we shipped the first alpha of Aurelia, a platform with high-performance component rendering rich data-binding, routing, publish-subscribe, data validation, i18n, and more. We took everything we'd learned from building rich desktop applications over the years and reimagined it on top of the modern web. The result is one of the most elegant application frameworks today, and the subject of the book you're holding in your hand.

I'm excited about Full Stack Aurelia Web Development. You're about to embark on an amazing journey that spans the breadth of the modern web. If you haven't looked at HTML, CSS, and JavaScript in a while, don't worry. This book will bring you up to speed on new language standards and browser capabilities. From there, you'll learn how to build applications by thinking in terms of "components." You'll see how to style, test, and debug components; assemble components into screens coordinated by a router; manage data and communication with the server; and even cross-component messaging, modal dialogs, and internationalization.

If you're ready to dive in to modern web development and are looking for a simple and intuitive guide into this exciting new world, you've found it right here. I can't wait to see what you build.

Enjoy the journey!

Rob Eisenberg

Aurelia Project Lead

Contributors

About the authors

Diego Jose Argüelles Rojas is a software developer born in Peru, passionate about technology, music, comics, and beer. He currently works for companies in North America and Europe remotely and simultaneously finishing his professional studies in Brazil. His main objective is to contribute to projects of social impact and to make the world a better place for all.

Erikson Haziz Murrugarra Sifuentes is a computer engineer, scrum master, and DevOps Master with 8 years of experience in building different kinds of software solutions, such as his own programming language, called **Erlan**, and his own Operating System, called **EriOS**. He is an Amazon-certified solutions architect and works as a full stack software engineer at Verizon Enterprise. He is an expert in Big data / Business Intelligence and has implemented complex big data solutions for one of the biggest bank of Peru called BCP.

About the reviewer

Julien Enselme is a young full stack developer from France. He has worked in Switzerland on **Geographic Information System (GIS)** projects with Python and AngularJS. He is currently working in France, mostly on Django-related projects. He stumbled upon Aurelia while the framework was still in the beta stage and immediately loved it. He now uses it on his personal projects and hopes to use it professionally as well. He made several blog posts on Aurelia and has even made some contributions.

Packt is searching for authors like you

If you're interested in becoming an author for Packt, please visit `authors.packtpub.com` and apply today. We have worked with thousands of developers and tech professionals, just like you, to help them share their insight with the global tech community. You can make a general application, apply for a specific hot topic that we are recruiting an author for, or submit your own idea.

Table of Contents

Preface

A few years ago, it was very common to find several IT professionals specialized in just one kind of technology, code language or platform. People dedicated to reviewing all the backend stuff thought that they do not have anything to do with the frontend layer, after all one is developed in Java and C# and the other in HTML and JavaScript. This approach was not good. As times change, we need to start understanding that one application involves not only one part of the business, such as logistic or sales. Your application should involve the entire business and represent it on a binary world with same features, restrictions, and rules. As only a backend developer, your understanding of how data is displayed to the final user is very limited. As just a frontend developer, your knowledge of how many distributed applications interact and retrieve data to be interpreted on the screen is very limited too. As a first consequence, the development time increases and the product quality is not the desired one. Many IT professionals are now leaving their comfort zone and exploring the other side. A full stack developer is not only a developer with knowledge of backend and frontend languages. A full stack developer is a professional capable of understanding and translating each business requirement into application features, knowing the general impact and the changes it could include. Their diagnostic and time duration required to deliver will be always shorter to reality because they know exactly how the current product works, with external dependencies and different platforms.

The microservice revolution came with many changes for the industry. Nowadays, it is not enough to have a good knowledge of just one code language. NoSQL databases changed the relational paradigm, and strict object-oriented languages are now exploring the functional paradigm. These things enforces you to start understanding different programming paradigms, code languages, and frameworks. But there is one language that from its beginning, the only thing it did is grow: JavaScript.

Throughout this book, you will be introduced to the main JavaScript concepts and start understanding how this code language works and why it is so adopted by the community. JavaScript could be used as an object-oriented language or function too. Its flexibility is one of its most awesome features, and the development speed is faster compared with other traditional programming languages. Not only this, JavaScript was empowered with their own runtime platform outside the browser, NodeJS. In this book, you will find that Node is our main partner to develop JavaScript applications, and its simplicity to include external libraries and reuse code is simply awesome.

Tools such as CSS preprocessors, task automation, and testing coverage will be also explained and will give you the knowledge to participate in any development team, understand and propose new features. Our horse battle, Aurelia, will be present in this stage. You must have heard about popular frontend frameworks, such as Angular, or libraries, such as React. Aurelia comes with a very different approach, solving most of the common problems you would find and, of course, making your development process very easy. Forget about configuring the framework and your worries about data binding, AJAX calls, integration with third-party libraries, and so on, Aurelia comes with a big variety of plugins that are ready to help you in any situation, in a very simple way, and allows you to focus only on business code. Aurelia is not just another frontend framework, it is the future of frontend development.

Over the years, JavaScript was used just in frontend layer; with NodeJS, this approach has changed too. The fact that we can execute our JavaScript code in its own runtime environment allows us to start writing backend functionalities to be consumed for the frontend layer. ExpressJS is the backend framework based on NodeJS that will allow us to write our business processing data functionalities in a very simple way, high understandable and just with a few lines of code. To complete your travel through the backend layer, we will show you how to store data in one of the most famous NoSQL databases: MongoDB. Its simplicity and speed to insert and extract data are just amazing.

The IT world changes quickly, and you need to be updated on any change. You will also learn how to secure, test, and prepare your application for the real world and use cloud platforms to deploy your projects that are available worldwide, highly scalable, and secured. Are you ready to start your journey to become a great full stack developer?

Then, we welcome you to the new M.E.A.N. approach (MongoDB, ExpressJS, Aurelia, NodeJS).

Who this book is for

This book is perfect for IT professionals with/without hands-on experience in software development. This book will guide you to create highly scalable applications in AureliaJS by reviewing basic programming concepts and good practices, such as TDD and Security.

By the end of this book, you will become a full-stack programmer with strong knowledge of modern JavaScript frameworks, NoSQL databases, Docker, and cloud technologies.

What this book covers

Chapter 1, *Introducing Aurelia,* explains why JavaScript is a very good code language and how it is changing over time, the common syntax used (ES6), and a brief exploration about other modern frameworks, such as Angular and React, and why Aurelia is the best choice.

Chapter 2, *Styling the User Interface,* introduces you to the modern web development tools, very useful and in demand nowadays. You will learn how to make your stylesheets more friendly and readable and create automated task to execute commands to process your files. Also, you will see the current tendency in web design through the most used CSS libraries in the world.

Chapter 3, *Testing and Debugging* focuses on how to test your Aurelia applications to avoid potential bugs and deliver high-quality apps.

Chapter 4, *Creating Components and Templates,* states that it's time to start abstracting our business components and create isolated pieces that are highly reusable and easy to maintain to build your application. You will learn how to manage events and lifecycles of each part of your application, giving you total control over them.

Chapter 5, *Creating Our RESTful API,* deals with how to implement the backend for your example application using Node.js. Also, you will learn how to design strong APIs.

Chapter 6, *Storing Our Data in MongoDB,* teaches you how to integrate your Node.js backend application to MongoDB to store your application's information.

Chapter 7, *Advanced Features on Aurelia,* shows you more advanced features regarding data binding and other very common scenarios in your day to day work.

Chapter 8, *Security,* explains how to implement Authentication/Authorization and Single-Sign-On in AureliaJS using a common third-party service called Auth0.

Chapter 9, *Running E2E Tests,* is the most important part in the development lifecycle. It's time to test whether all your code work and meet your business requirements, but not as isolated pieces. You will also test whether the functionality of all your components works well together.

Chapter 10, *Deployment,* describes how to deploy your Aurelia applications in your on-premise servers using Docker and NGINX; also, it shows you how to deploy the application to Heroku and Amazon Web Services.

To get the most out of this book

1. You must be familiar with at least the basic principles of one code language. Don't worry if you don't have any professional experience since this book will guide you step by step through each chapter to get the most out of it.
2. We recommend that you start using any Unix-based operative system (Ubuntu, Debian, and macOS). This is because it is more flexible and easy to execute tasks on Terminal.
3. You will need a lot of patience. No one is born with knowledge, so never give up if one concept or example is not clear at the first go.
4. You will also need a lot of practice. It's impossible to cover all the real-world scenarios in a book, so we recommend that you go three steps ahead and modify the examples, add additional features, and research a lot.

Download the example code files

You can download the example code files for this book from your account at `www.packtpub.com`. If you purchased this book elsewhere, you can visit `www.packtpub.com/support` and register to have the files emailed directly to you.

You can download the code files by following these steps:

1. Log in or register at `www.packtpub.com`.
2. Select the **SUPPORT** tab.
3. Click on **Code Downloads & Errata**.
4. Enter the name of the book in the **Search** box and follow the onscreen instructions.

Once the file is downloaded, please make sure that you unzip or extract the folder using the latest version of:

- WinRAR/7-Zip for Windows
- Zipeg/iZip/UnRarX for Mac
- 7-Zip/PeaZip for Linux

The code bundle for the book is also hosted on GitHub at `https://github.com/PacktPublishing/Hands-On-Full-Stack-Web-Development-with-Aurelia`. In case there's an update to the code, it will be updated on the existing GitHub repository.

We also have other code bundles from our rich catalog of books and videos available at `https://github.com/PacktPublishing/`. Check them out!

Conventions used

There are a number of text conventions used throughout this book.

`CodeInText`: Indicates code words in text, database table names, folder names, filenames, file extensions, pathnames, dummy URLs, user input, and Twitter handles. Here is an example: "The source code will be generated in the `src/resources/{type}` folder depending on the type you selected."

A block of code is set as follows:

```
function sum(numberA, numberB){
    return numberA + numberB
}
sum(4,5) //9
sum(5,2) //7
sum(sum(5,1),9) //15
```

When we wish to draw your attention to a particular part of a code block, the relevant lines or items are set in bold:

```
class Example {
    static returnMessage(){
        return 'From static method'
    }
}
let staticMessage = Example.returnMessage() // From static method
```

Any command-line input or output is written as follows:

```
cd my-app
au run --watch --env prod
```

Bold: Indicates a new term, an important word, or words that you see onscreen. For example, words in menus or dialog boxes appear in the text like this. Here is an example: "Create a **New** item, which requires admin."

 Warnings or important notes appear like this.

Tips and tricks appear like this.

Get in touch

Feedback from our readers is always welcome.

General feedback: Email `feedback@packtpub.com` and mention the book title in the subject of your message. If you have questions about any aspect of this book, please email us at `questions@packtpub.com`.

Errata: Although we have taken every care to ensure the accuracy of our content, mistakes do happen. If you have found a mistake in this book, we would be grateful if you would report this to us. Please visit `www.packtpub.com/submit-errata`, selecting your book, clicking on the Errata Submission Form link, and entering the details.

Piracy: If you come across any illegal copies of our works in any form on the Internet, we would be grateful if you would provide us with the location address or website name. Please contact us at `copyright@packtpub.com` with a link to the material.

If you are interested in becoming an author: If there is a topic that you have expertise in and you are interested in either writing or contributing to a book, please visit `authors.packtpub.com`.

Reviews

Please leave a review. Once you have read and used this book, why not leave a review on the site that you purchased it from? Potential readers can then see and use your unbiased opinion to make purchase decisions, we at Packt can understand what you think about our products, and our authors can see your feedback on their book. Thank you!

For more information about Packt, please visit `packtpub.com`.

Introducing Aurelia

1

If you were born in the 80s or 90s, without doubt, you were a witness to the internet evolution. The first web pages were composed only of black text in a white screen; everything they wrote was in pure HTML format, and really, really static. After some years, the first CSS was adding some color to the web, and, after some unsuccessful attempts, JavaScript did appear.

From its first appearance, JavaScript has improved over the years and adapted to build the next generation of web pages. Many companies such as Microsoft were involved in the evolution of this language, adding features and increasing its popularity. This new scripting language allowed the developers to improve the customer experience and application performance and, in a short time, there began to appear the first JavaScript frameworks that made JavaScript the new rock star of web development.

All this sounds great, but, was it always as awesome as the strong language we have today? Uhmm, no it was not. The first JavaScript version was created by *Brendan Eich* in 1995 for the *Netscape Navigator*, named in those times as *Mocha*, then *LiveScript*, and finally, JavaScript.

Let's explore more about the features of this powerful language and how it becomes one of the most used for application development.

In this chapter, we will walk through the following topics:

- JavaScript fundamentals
- The ECMAScript standard
- Setting up our environment
- The Aurelia framework
- The Aurelia command line
- Overview of the example app

JavaScript fundamentals

JavaScript is a programming language used to add custom behavior to your web page by executing code in your web browser side (commonly named client side). So, this allows us to create rich dynamic projects such as games, execute custom code in response to events when the user presses some button, apply dynamic effects to our web page elements, form data validation, and so on.

JavaScript as a single language is very flexible, and there is a big community of developers writing and unlocking additional functionality, big companies working on new libraries and of course, we as empowered developers ready to get all these features and make the web awesome.

There are a few basic characteristics of JavaScript:

- Dynamic typing
- Object oriented
- Functional
- Prototyped
- Event handling

Dynamic typing

In most of the scripting languages, the type is associated with the value, not with the variable itself. What it means? JavaScript and other languages such as Python, called **weakly typed**, does not need to specify which kind of data we will use to store in the variable. JavaScript has many ways to ensure the correct type of an object, including *duck typing*.

 Why duck?
Well, James Whitcomb did a humorous inference explaining the deductive thinking about it—"If it looks like a duck, swims like a duck, and quacks like a duck, then it probably is a duck"

Let's look at an example:

```
1.  var age = 26;
2.  age = "twenty-six";
3.  age = false;
```

In the preceding code, the defined variables accept any data type, because data types will be evaluated at runtime, so, for example, the `age` variable in line 1 will be an integer, will become a string in line 2 and, finally, Boolean. Sounds tricky? Don't worry, think of the variable as an empty vial without a label. You can put anything you want, cookies, milk, or salt. What you will store in the vial? Depending of your needs, if you want to make a breakfast, milk should be the better option. The only thing you must keep in mind, is remember what is containing this vial! We would hate to confuse salt with sweet.

If we need to ensure that the value belongs to some specific type, we can use the `typeof` operator to retrieve the data type of a given variable. Let's have a look at them:

- `typeof "Diego"`: This will **return** `string`
- `typeof false`: This will **return** `boolean`
- `typeof "Diego" == boolean`: This will **return** `false`

The `typeof` operator is very useful, but keep in mind it only gives primary types (`number`, `string`, `boolean` or `object`). Different from other similar operators such `instanceof` of Java, `typeof` won't return the object type.

Object oriented

JavaScript objects are based on associative arrays, improved with the prototyping inclusion. The properties and values can be changed at runtime. Another common way to create objects is using the **JavaScript Object Notation (JSON)** or using functions.

Let's see how an object created by JavaScript code looks, and its JSON representation:

```
// Let's create the person object
function Person(first, last, age) {
    this.firstName = first;
    this.lastName = last;
    this.age = age;
}
var diego = new Person("Diego", "Arguelles", 27);

//JSON representation of the same object
{
    firstName: "Diego",
    lastName: "Arguelles",
    age: 27
}
```

Functional

A function is an object inside itself. They have properties, methods, and can include inner functions. It's a way to encapsulate a functionality you want to reuse in more than one place in your application; you just need to write the function name instead of all the code inside that, just like the following example:

```
function sum(numberA, numberB){
    return numberA + numberB
}
sum(4,5) //9
sum(5,2) //7
sum(sum(5,1),9) //15
```

Prototyped

JavaScript uses prototypes instead of classes for inheritance. It is possible to emulate all OOP characteristics using just prototypes:

```
function Person(first, last, age) {
    this.firstName = first;
    this.lastName = last;
    this.age = age;
}

var diego = new Person('Diego', 'Arguelles', 26)
diego.nationality = 'Peruvian'
console.log(diego)
// Person {firstName: "Diego", lastName: "Arguelles", age: 26, nationality:
"Peruvian"}

Person.prototype.career = 'Engineering'
console.log(diego.career) // Engineering
```

That being said, what is exactly a prototype? Different from objects, one prototype does not have a closed structure. In objects, we define standard properties and we just have these properties for work, since JavaScript is not completely an object-oriented language, we have the advantage to add, remove, or change properties and values of our prototypes depending on our needs.

We can modify prototype attributes at runtime. Note that even if you can modify any prototype, you should only modify yours. If you modify standard prototypes (for example, the array prototype) you will encounter very weird bugs in your application.

Events handling

Events allow you to add the real interaction on your web page. JavaScript allows you to attach event handlers on your HTML pages and execute custom code when they are triggered. For example, the given code will display an alert when the user clicks on your web page body:

```
document.querySelector('body').onclick = function() {
    alert('You clicked the page body!!!');
}
```

The ECMAScript standard

In the beginning, some companies such as Microsoft were trying to develop their own JavaScript implementation, in this case, JScript for Internet Explorer 3.0, in the year 1996. To define a standard, Netscape delivered JavaScript to the **European Computer Manufacturers Association** (**ECMA**), a standards organization for information and communication systems.

The first edition of ECMA-262 was adopted by the ECMA General Assembly in June 1997. Several editions of the language standard have been published since then. The name *ECMAScript* was a compromise between the organizations involved in standardizing the language, especially Netscape and Microsoft, whose disputes dominated the early standards sessions.

So, after all these standardization processes and paperwork, what are we using? ECMAScript, JScript, ActionScript, or JavaScript? Are they the same? Well, basically no. After the standardization, ECMAScript was defined as the main language, and JavaScript, JScript, and ActionScript are dialects of this language, of course, JavaScript being the most known and used.

The ECMAScript Version 5 is supported by most browsers nowadays, released in 2011. Some of the features managed for this version are as listed:

- Support for new Array methods
- Support for manage dates
- Support for JSON

At this point, we've seen pure ES5 syntax, very verbose, sometimes highly coupled with other functionality, and if we are planning to develop a big application, it can become difficult to maintain.

Thank God we won't have to deal with this syntax anymore. The **ECMAScript 6 (ES6)** version came with a lot of changes that simplify the development and understanding of our code.

ES 6

This version arrives with significant changes in the language syntax. Let's review the new features and compare with the ES5 syntax.

In ES5, to make a near representation of an object in JavaScript, we commonly type something like this:

```
function Person(name, age) {
    this.name = name;
    this.age  = age;
}
Person.prototype.sayHi = function() {
    return 'Hi, my name is ' + this.name + ' and i have ' + this.age + '
years old';
}

var Erikson = new Person('Erikson', 26);
Erikson.sayHi(); // 'Hi, my name is Erikson and i have 26 years old'
```

If we want to improve our code, maybe we can do some refactoring, as follows:

```
function Person(name, age) {
    this.name = name;
    this.age  = age;

    this.sayHi = function () {
        return 'Hi, my name is ' + this.name + ' and i have ' + this.age +
' years old';
    }
}
```

That's how **Object-Oriented Programming (OOP)** is done on JavaScript these days, but for programmers with previous experience on Java or PHP, that syntax result is a little difficult to understand, because they are not dealing with real objects, they are dealing directly with the prototypes. ES6 introduces a new syntax to declare objects:

```
class Person {
    // Contructor define properties for our object representartion
    constructor(name, age) {
        this.name = name;
        this.age = age;
    }
    // Class method
    sayHi() {
        return 'Hi, my name is ' + this.name + ' and i have ' + this.age +
' years old';
    }
}
var Erikson = new Person('Erikson', 26);
Erikson.sayHi() // Hi , my name is Erikson and I have 26 years old
```

As you can see, now, the syntax is more readable and understandable, and we can extend from another class, just like other languages, such as Java:

```
class Developer extends Person {

    constructor(name, age, role){
        super(name, age)
        this.role = role;
    }
    sayHi(){
        return super.sayHi() + ' and i am a ' + this.role
    }
}
var Erikson = new Person('Erikson', 26, 'Javascript developer');
Erikson.sayHi() // 'Hi, my name is Erikson and i have 26 years old and i am
a Javascript developer'
```

Also, of course, we can use encapsulation principles to manipulate our object properties. Similar to Java, we can define mutator methods to get the property value or set some value to a property:

```
class Person {

    constructor(name, age) {
        this.name = name;
        this.age = age;
    }
    get checkName() {
        return this.name;
    }
    set giveName(newName) {
        this.name = newName;
```

```
    }
}
var Erikson = new Person('Erikson', 26);
Erikson.checkName() // returns Erikson
Erikson.giveName('Hazis')
Erikson.checkName() // returns Hazis
```

Having these kind of methods does not avoid the fact that you can still be using the JavaScript native syntax to change the values or add properties at runtime. You will still be able to do the following:

```
Erikson.name = 'Diego'
Erikson.name // Returns Diego
```

Like other languages, ES6 allows static methods using the static modifier:

```
class Example {
    static returnMessage(){
        return 'From static method'
    }
}
let staticMessage = Example.returnMessage() // From static method
```

Do you note something? In the last example, we used `let` instead of `var` to declare a variable. ES6 has two new ways of defining a variable: `let` is the direct replacement of `var`, and `const` will be used if we are declaring a constant. Can we still use `var` instead of the new ES6 declaration syntax? Yes, but let's imagine that you are an experienced developer and have two trainees under your supervision. In your code, you can define something like this:

```
var PI = 3.1416
```

Also, of course, we do not want this value changed, for any reason. As this is still a `var`, any trainee developer is able to change the value, directly or indirectly (from a method call, assignation error, bad comparison syntax, and so on), so we are exposed to get errors on our application. To prevent these kind of scenarios, `const` would be a more accurate modifier for this variable.

Does ES6 only improve syntax for objects' declaration? No. At this moment, we only focused on our class definition syntax, because it will be the core of all applications, just like OOP. Now, we will check other improvements that we are pretty sure you will find very useful in your day-to-day work.

A very important note: You must know that different to other code languages, in Javascript you can define `const MY_ARRAY = []` and you will still being able to do `MY_ARRAY.push(3)`. The `const` prefix will only avoid the overwriting, so you cannot do `MY_ARRAY = [1,2]`

Arrow functions

You need to iterate over the elements of an array; normally, you would write something like this:

```
var data = ['Ronaldo', 'Messi', 'Maradona'];
data.forEach(function (elem) {
    console.log(elem)
});
```

With the arrow functions, you can refactor your code and write something as follows:

```
var data = ['Ronaldo', 'Messi', 'Maradona'];
data.forEach(elem => {
    console.log(elem);
});
```

The arrow (=>) operator defines a function in one line, making our code readable and ordered. First, you need to declare the inputs; the arrow will send these params to the function body defined by the operator:

```
// We could transform this
let sum = function(num) {
    return num + num;
};
// Into just this
let sum = (num) => num + num;
```

String interpolation

Do you remember those times when you needed to concatenate a string using the + operator? It won't be necessary anymore. For example, the following code concatenates `string1` and `string2` using the + operator:

```
let string1 = "JavaScript";
let string2 = "awesome";
let string3 = string1 + " " + string2
```

Now, let's look at how interpolation helps us write simpler code:

```
let string1 = "JavaScript";
let string2 = "awesome";
let string3 = `${string1} ${string2}`
```

Destructuring

We have a new way to assign values to objects and arrays. Let's look at some examples:

```
var [a, b] = ["hello", "world"];
console.log(a); // "hello"
console.log(b); // "world"

var obj = { name: "Diego", lastName: "Arguelles" };
var { name, lastName } = obj;
console.log(name); // "Diego"

var foo = function() {
    return ["175", "75"];
};
var [height, weight] = foo();
console.log(height); //175
console.log(weight); //75
```

Setting up our environment

At this point, we are ready to start writing our first functions and methods in JavaScript language. We know how to deal with the new ES6 syntax and how we can use all these new features to improve our application. Let's set up our environment and install Node.js.

Installing Node.js

The first thing you need to do to start using NPM is download Node.js. Node is an asynchronous event-driven JavaScript runtime. It is not a new language or a new syntax; it's just the platform where you can write JavaScript code outside the browser and Node.js will use the power of Google's V8 JavaScript Engine to execute it.

If you're using OS X or Windows, the best way to install Node.js is to use one of the installers from the Node.js download page.

If you're using Linux, you can use your package manager or check the download page to see whether there's a more recent version that works with your system.

To check whether you have a previous version installed, run the following command:

```
$ node -v
```

The Node Package Manager

The **Node Package Manager** (**NPM**) is a complete tool created to help developers share, maintain, and reuse JavaScript code bundled in packages with other developers to reuse it on their own applications. NPM is made up of three distinct components:

- The NPM website
- The NPM registry
- The NPM command-line tool

NPM website

This website serves as the primary tool for users to discover packages; you'll find something like this:

This page describes all the features of the package you want to download, a brief documentation about it, the GitHub URL, and instructions to import them into your project.

NPM Registry

It is a large database of information about each package. The official public NPM registry is at `https://registry.npmjs.org/`. It is powered by a CouchDB database, of which there is a public mirror at `https://skimdb.npmjs.com/registry`.

NPM CLI

A command-line tool for interacting with the registry and allowing the developers to publish or download packages.

Once you have the code downloaded on your machine, NPM will make it very easy to check whether there is an update available and download those changes when they're made. More than two bits of reusable code is called a package. That's just a directory with one or more files in it, along with a file called `package.json`, which contains all the metadata about that package.

Common NPM operations

Like all the command-line tools, it is important to understand the options provided by NPM. The NPM CLI is a powerful tool that will help us in the development cycle of our project.

Updating NPM

The first step is complete! We have the Node runtime on our machine ready to execute our `.js` files, so the last thing we need to start working on is the NPM. Node comes with NPM installed by default, but NPM gets updated more frequently than Node, so we can check the updation of our NPM CLI by executing the following command:

```
$ npm install npm@latest -g
```

Installing NPM packages

NPM is installed and configured; now it's time to start working. There are two ways to install NPM packages. Our choice will depend on how we want to use the package. The options are as listed:

- **Globally:** Install the given package globally as part of our command-line tools
- **Locally:** Install the given package to be available only in our application context

With this in mind, type the following command to install a new package:

```
$ npm install <package-name>
```

This instruction will create a folder called `node_modules`, where we will download all the packages we need. We can ensure that we have the package downloaded, entering the folder and checking the existence of a folder with a name similar to our package name. Run the following command to list all the packages installed in your project:

```
$ ls node_modules
```

Versions

If no package version is specified, we will get the latest. To install a specific version, we need to add the following to the `install` command:

```
npm install <package-name>@<version>
```

The package.json file

We know how to download a package and how to import it into our project. However, we will commonly need more than one package, with some specific versions. Should we memorize them to download manually each time we set up the project? No, now is the moment to create a `package.json` file.

This file is not only to map our dependencies; it must contain all the metadata about our project, and it serves as a quick documentation for which packages your project depends on. As minimal, the `package.json` should contain the following:

- **Name**: Project name, all lowercase with no blank spaces (you can use underscores if needed)
- **Version**: In the form of x.x.x

We can create this file manually, but NPM allows us to create it automatically by executing the following command:

```
$ npm init
```

The preceding command will prompt you with a bunch of questions that will be present in your package.json file. If you don't want to accept the defaults without being prompted any question, run the same command, adding a --yes flag at the end:

```
$ npm init --yes
```

Then, you will get a package.json file, as follows:

```
{
  "name": "my_package",
  "version": "1.0.0",
  "description": "",
  "main": "index.js",
  "scripts": {
    "test": "echo \"Error: no test specified\" && exit 1"
  },
  "repository": {
    "type": "git",
    "url": "https://github.com/package_owner/my_package.git"
  },
  "keywords": [],
  "author": "",
  "license": "ISC",
  "bugs": {
    "url": "https://github.com/package_owner/my_package/issues"
  },
  "homepage": "https://github.com/package_owner/my_package"
}
```

Dependencies and devDependencies

You have all your dependencies installed now. You start working and during the development process, you may need some other dependencies to improve your code. You just need to run the NPM CLI to get the new dependency, but this will not be present in your package.json file! It can be very dangerous, because if you don't have the list of libraries or dependencies you need for your project, when you want to run it in a different machine, your code will fail, because the dependency is not installed in that machine.

We can ensure that the new package name will be added to our dependencies' list, adding the --save or --save-dev flag. The first will add the package name to the dependencies' section of the package.json file. This means that the dependency is mandatory for the application itself and should be installed before running or deploying the application. On the other hand, we have the devDependencies' part, where there will be only the dependencies used for our development process:

```
$ npm install <package_name> --save
```

Now, we are ready to start developing JavaScript applications. In the next section, you will make use of NPM to install the Aurelia command-line tool required to create new Aurelia projects, but let's continue exploring the Aurelia framework.

The Aurelia framework

Before we start working with Aurelia and learning this amazing framework, it is important to have it clear why you should choose Aurelia over other popular frameworks. For that reason, let's explore in detail what a JavaScript framework is and the key differentiator present in Aurelia.

What is a JavaScript framework?

In the last section, we were reviewing all concerns about JavaScript and how we can organize our packages using NPM and Yarn. Now, it's time to review some tools that will improve our development experience; it's time to talk about frameworks.

A framework can be described as a group of tools and methodologies organized to solve common problems in the project development. Those solutions are generic; each one was tested in different environments and allows you to reuse that functionality to save time and cost.

So, based on the previous explanation, we can define a JavaScript framework as a collection of components and libraries (in most cases, interdependent) to fill the needs of the application in browser clients. What are these needs? Let's check some of the most generic ones:

- Routing
- Data sending features and retrieval (XMLHttpRequest)
- Correct DOM management

- Managing and organizing your code in separated functionality
- Defining standard data flows for the application
- Defining lifecycle for some functionality

Why use a JavaScript framework?

In general, a JavaScript framework will help us do the following:

- Organizing your code
- Structuring it in a maintainable and ordered way
- Making separation of concerns
- Implementing tested solutions to the most common problems
- Working on a base structure that any developer can follow

More specifically, a JavaScript framework is particularly helpful for applications where much of the business logic will take place on the client side—routing, templating, first-pass model validation, table building and pagination—pretty much whatever you might have used the server for in the past, but now without the latency and overhead that additional HTTP calls would have incurred.

JavaScript framework comparison

One problem always has more than just one solution, and JavaScript developers know that. Before 2010, developers had very limited options to implement their functionality in their day-to-day work. The most popular option in these times was jQuery, used a lot nowadays too. Although jQuery was not a bad choice, but it has a great weakness. For example, if your project growth and your business code become more complex, jQuery will be really difficult to maintain, your concerns will be mixed, and you will be involved in one of the most common anti-patron—**Spaghetti code**.

In 2010, Google released one of the most popular JavaScript frameworks—Angular. Different from jQuery, Angular comes with a complete set of tools and a new way to organize the JavaScript code, introducing new concepts such as modules, components, routes, and templates. After Angular, many JavaScript frameworks were appearing; some of them became very popular for the company sponsoring them, such as Facebook with React.js, others gained fame by the adoption of the community, such as Meteor and Vue, and others are really new in the neighborhood.

As innovation is the essence of technology, one of the main engineers of Angular 2 project developed a new awesome framework called Aurelia, which, in just three years in the market, is becoming the new rock star in the neighborhood.

Why Aurelia?

Over the last years in our current day-to-day work, we were getting involved with a vast variety of JavaScript frameworks; the most popular was always Angular, but we learned that popularity is not synonymous with quality. For understanding purposes, we will check some of the most used frameworks nowadays and then make a little comparison with our battle horse, Aurelia.

Angular

The component-based framework uses Typescript as the main (and unique) JavaScript platform. Angular is a complete superset of libraries designed for all purposes of **Single Page Applications (SPA)**, very useful for developing applications from scratch. You can link your templates and your `Typescript` code so you `HTML` is updated with values from your code and ready to react on user actions . You need to learn three basic concepts about this framework—directives, modules, and components. Each one involves another, and you need to register each component with one Module to make it available. JavaScript also has its own module system for managing collections of JavaScript objects. It's completely different and unrelated to Angular's module system. Angular has its own implementation to define service classes, routes, double data binding, HTTP requests, and so on, making this framework very heavyweight.

Technical information

- **Size**: 698 Kb
- **Standard compliance**: ES 2016 (TypeScript)
- **Non-compliant**: NG2 Markup and Dart
- **Interoperability**: Average

Dependency injection

The dependency injection framework requires more configuration. In contrast to Aurelia, Angular requires you to specify the HTML `selector` and `template`, increasing the file complexity. Aurelia will detect the template based on a name strategy:

```
@Injectable()
class Ticket { /* */ }

@Component({
  selector: 'ticket',
  providers: [Ticket],
  template: `...`
}) //Configuration code mixed with business class
export class Sale {
    constructor(private ticket: Ticket) {}

    public activate() {
        // do something...
        this.ticket.toast("Sale processed!");
    }
}
```

Component encapsulation

Angular components need more explicit configuration and some (in some cases confusing) characters in the template. You can put the template in a separate file, or for simpler components, you can include the template inline:

```
/* product-list.component.ts */
@Component({
    selector: 'product-list',
    template: `<div><product-detail *ngFor="let thing of things"
[product]="product" /></div>`
})
export class ProductList {
    public products: Product[];
}
```

React.js

Different from Angular, React.js is a library that can be integrated with any JavaScript project. It is used for handling the view layer for the web applications and build reusable UI components. React is component based too, but it mixes the HTML code inside the JavaScript files, in JSX format. JSX is a React syntax very similar to XML format since you can manage your view layer and add some behavior defining some attributes as the state or properties of your component. Sounds a little confusing? Yes, you will need to learn how JSX works and read about some of the new concepts about the tool.

React.js has a great feature—server-side rendering. What does that mean? Common JavaScript frameworks let the render work to the client side, so the browser needs to interpret your JavaScript files and transform it to plain HTML files. It can take time depending on how much data will be displayed on the page. With React.js, you can configure your server to have all those pages processed in the server side, so the browser just needs to call the correct HTML file and of course, the loading time will be less.

Similar to Angular, React.js offers you a complete set of libraries to implement dynamic routing, data binding, HTTP requests, and other React implementations libraries such as Inferno.js, with a rendering algorithm more powerful and optimized.

 One very important note! Aurelia now has its own server side rendering plugin. You can find more info there: https://aurelia.io/docs/ssr/introduction/

Technical information

- **Size**: 156 KB or 167 KB with plugins
- **Standard compliance**: ES 2015
- **Non-compliant**: JSX
- **Interoperability**: High friction

Dependency injection

There is no such dependency injection concept in React.js.

Component encapsulation

A component is *one* JS class. Do you want to include another component in your component? Just import it:

```
import {ProductDetail} from "./ProductDetail";

interface Props {
    products: Product[];
}
export class ProductList extends React.Component<Props, undefined> {
    render() {
        return <div>
            {this.props.products.map(th => <ProductDetail key={th.id}
product={th} />)}
        </div>
    }
}
```

Aurelia

Aurelia is a new JavaScript framework created by one of the team members of Angular 2 project. Different from Angular, Aurelia is composed of a collection of libraries that work together using well-defined interfaces so that it's completely modular. This means that a web application only needs to include the dependencies that it needs, not the complete bundle.

Aurelia's APIs are carefully designed to be consumed naturally by both today's and tomorrow's most useful web programming languages. Aurelia supports ES5, ES2015, ES2016, and Typescript, which are very helpful and give you high flexibility.

Furthermore, writing web applications using ES6 is not a new thing. In fact, there are many solutions out there that can allow you to write Angular apps using ES6 (you need to configure it manually and it's not included in the default Angular configuration).

You don't need to worry about special framework concepts or syntax; Aurelia is a *convention over configuration* framework, encouraging you to use good practices when developing applications, and it allows the developers to focus only on business code.

Technical information

- **Size**: 252 kb minimum, 302 kb with standard plugin

- **Standard compliance**: HTML, ES 2016, Web Components (including the Shadow DOM)
- **Interoperability**: Very interoperable

Dependency injection

All you need is the `@autoinject` annotation. The JS/HTML mapping is performed automatically by the framework:

```
class Ticket { /* class code, properties, methods... */ }

@inject
export class Sale {
    constructor( ticket ) {}

    public activate() {
        // do something...
        this.ticket.toast("Sale processed!");
    }
}
```

For `Typescript` users, the annotation names are very similar. Use `@autoinject` instead of `@inject` and don't forget to specify the visibility and type of object in the constructor : `constructor(private ticket : Ticket)`

Component encapsulation

Component encapsulation uses a separate template file that looks more or less like every other web templating language you've ever used. By convention, if your component class is in `hello.ts`, then its template is in `hello.html` and your component will be `<hello/>`:

```
<!-- product-list.html -->
<template>
    <require from="product-detail"/>
    <div>
        <product-detail repeat.for="product of products"
product.bind="product"/>
    </div>
</template>

/* producty-list.js */
export class ProductList {
    public products[];
}
```

Each JavaScript framework has its own way of working, and we can explore more features about each one, but Aurelia has something special—you don't need to go far away from learning how the framework works, and in extreme cases, in their own way/syntax for developing. With Aurelia, you will feel like writing plain JavaScript and HTML code, highly maintainable, scalable, and focusing only on your business purposes.

Now it's time to start working with Aurelia. So, let's explore the Aurelia command line to start our trip. Keep reading!

Aurelia command-line tool

There are many ways to create an Aurelia project. For this book, we will use the official Aurelia command-line tool, which is supported by the Aurelia team. Although there are other options to configure your Aurelia application, such as Webpack and JSPM, we consider that the CLI is powerful and will help us save valuable time configuring our application skeleton and build tools.

In this section, we will explore in detail the CLI capabilities, and you will convince yourself that this is the best option for our adventure. After this section, you will be a master in using the Aurelia CLI.

Installation

Installing the CLI is not a big deal if you have installed Node.js in the previous section. We just need to open your favorite Terminal and execute the following command, and if you are using a Unix-based operating system, remember to add `sudo` before the command if you have permission issues:

```
npm install -g aurelia-cli
```

The preceding command will install the Aurelia CLI as a global executable command-line tool. This allows us to use the CLI with the `au` command as any other command of our operative system Terminal, for example, the `dir` command.

After the installation is complete, execute the following command:

```
au help
```

This should return the following output that displays the CLI help. As you can see, this command has two main options:

Now that we are sure that it is working as we expected, let's learn how to get the most out of it.

Creating a new application

This is one of the most important options. As its name says, it will create a new Aurelia application with a well-defined application folder structure and all the initial configuration files in just three steps.

Execute the following command and replace my-app with your application's name:

```
au new my-app
```

When the Aurelia CLI wizard is running, we will select the following options to create our application:

1. Select 1 for ECMAScript next generation language
2. Select 1 to create the project
3. Select 1 to install the dependencies

Once you answer the last question, the CLI will install all the dependencies and once everything is complete, you will see the following output in your Terminal window:

```
Congratulations


Congratulations! Your Project "my-app" Has Been Created!


Getting started

Now it's time for you to get
started. It's easy. First, change directory into your new project's folder. You
can use cd my-app to get there. Once in your project folder,
simply run your new app with au run. Your app will run fully
bundled. If you would like to have it auto-refresh whenever you make changes to
your HTML, JavaScript or CSS, simply use the --watch flag If you want
to build your app for production, run au build --env prod.
That's just about all there is to it. If you need help, simply run au
help.


Happy Coding!
```

Running our Application

Next, we will look into the run option. This option allows us to run our application, and it provides us with an option to create a productive development environment by specifying the --watch option, which configures a watcher to detect changes in our source code and update our browser automatically. This cool feature is known as browser-sync or auto-refresh.

The run command also allows us to specify the environment where we want to execute our application; these are the default environments: dev, stage, and prod. By default, the CLI will run our application using the dev environment. Use the --env flag to change it.

What means exactly each environment? Well, in software development, commonly when you are writing your application you test your code on you local development environment (`dev`). Once you think its complete, you send it to a Quality Assurance area to test your application, this tests won't be performed on your machine so you need to export your application and deploy it on another server, it will be called the `test` environment. Finally, once the QA people gives his approval, you code will be deployed in the real world environment (`prod`). Of course, this is a very basic scope, you will find many more environments in other companies such UAT (User Acceptance Test).

For example, let's get into our application (`cd` command) and execute the following command:

```
cd my-app
au run --watch --env prod
```

The following is the output that has two URLs where we can see our application up and running:

```
Writing app-bundle.js...
Writing vendor-bundle.js...
Finished 'writeBundles'
Application Available At: http://localhost:9000
BrowserSync Available At: http://localhost:3001
```

Open the `http://localhost:9000` URL in your favorite web browser, and you should see the following:

Pay attention to the last two lines in the console. Those tell you in which port is running your application, it could be different depending on your operating system and which port you have available.

Now, let's test how auto-refresh works, remember that this feature is enabled by adding the --watch option in the au run command.

Open the app.js file located in the src folder and change the 'Hello World!' string to 'Hola Mundo!':

```
export class App {
  constructor() {
    this.message = 'Hola Mundo!';
  }
}
```

Save it and go back to your browser; the CLI will detect the change you made in the app.js file and will refresh your browser automatically.

To be more productive, you can use two displays—the first with your application running in the browser and the second with your source code editor.

Testing our application

Of course, testing is an important skill all developers need to have. We have a complete chapter to talk about testing and discuss TDD, unit testing, and end-to-end testing.

The test command comes with the --watch and the --env flags. Use the watch option to tell the CLI to detect changes in the test folder and execute the tests again.

In order to run tests, the CLI uses Karma, which is a test runner technology that is configured to use Jasmine testing framework to write all our testing files that should be saved into the test folder.

For example, the preceding command will run the app.sec.js file located in the test/unit folder:

```
au test --watch --env stage
```

The following is the output that has executed one test successfully:

```
Writing app-bundle.js...
Writing vendor-bundle.js...
Finished 'writeBundles'
Starting 'karma'...
10 11 2017 20:00:41.841:WARN [karma]: No captured browser, open http://localhost:
9876/
10 11 2017 20:00:41.856:INFO [karma]: Karma v0.13.22 server started at http://loc
alhost:9876/
10 11 2017 20:00:41.872:INFO [launcher]: Starting browser Chrome
10 11 2017 20:00:43.120:INFO [Chrome 61.0.3163 (Windows 7 0.0.0)]: Connected on s
ocket _caD1N6xnvVAQgH2AAAA with id 52826047
Chrome 61.0.3163 (Windows 7 0.0.0): Executed 1 of 1 SUCCESS (0.002 secs / 0 secs)
```

Building our application

Now is the time to deploy our application, but before we do this, we need to compress and minify our Aurelia code. Aurelia CLI provides us with the build option to generate these ready-to-deploy files that contain all our application code.

As you might want to build your application for different environments (dev, stage, or prod), this build option comes along with the --env flag. For example, execute the following command in your project:

```
au build --env prod
```

The following is a sample output of my-app project:

```
Writing app-bundle.js...
Writing vendor-bundle.js...
Finished 'writeBundles'
```

As the output shows, there are two main files generated: app-bundle.js, which contains our application logic and vendor-bundle.js, which contains third-party dependencies. These two files are generated into the scripts folder in our root application folder.

If you want to run your application and check whether everything is okay with the bundles you recently created, let's install the http-server module using npm. Run the following command in your Terminal:

```
npm install -g http-server
```

Now, create a `dist` folder in your application root folder and copy the `index.html` page and the `scripts` folder that contain our bundles.

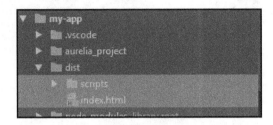

For the last step, get into the `dist` folder in your Terminal and run the following command:

```
cd dist
http-server
```

Use the `cd` command to navigate across your folders in your Terminal.

This command will expose some four URLs where the web server is running; copy the first URL and open it on your web browser, and you should see your application up and running:

```
> http-server
Starting up http-server, serving ./
Available on:
  http://192.168.1.39:8081
  http://192.168.56.1:8081
  http://192.168.99.1:8081
  http://127.0.0.1:8081
```

Generating custom resources

Aurelia, like many JavaScript frameworks, allows you to create reusable components that help you avoid writing duplicated code, reuse your component in multiple parts of your app, and also export them as plugins to reuse them in other projects.

Aurelia allows you to generate the reusable pieces of code utilizing the following templates:

- Components
- Custom elements
- Custom attributes
- Binding-behaviors
- Value-converters

These templates are all located in our project root folder in the `aurelia_project/generators` folder. For example, the following command generates a custom Aurelia element:

```
au generate element my-reusable-element
```

The source code will be generated in the `src/resources/{type}` folder depending on the **type** you selected.

Each type will be discussed in the following chapters, so don't feel bad if you don't understand the differences between them. Keep reading my friend! :)

World Cup app overview

Now it is time to talk about our application we will build together. Apart from our web application written, of course, in Aurelia, we also need a backend service to persist our data. For the backend service, we will be using Node.js with the Express framework to build a robust API and MongoDB as our non-relational data storage. The following diagram explains our World Cup project architecture:

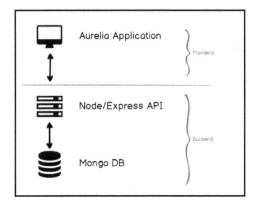

This a very simple architecture; the Aurelia app talks to the Node API directly, and the Node API talks to the database, which is a MongoDB database, using a very popular open source library called Mongoose. This is getting better; keep reading!

Exploring the application features

The app we will develop is the Football World Cup app. We will use an awesome UI framework called Materialize, which, by default, will help us create a responsive web application, so our users can open this app in their mobile and desktop browser with an adaptable user interface.

Although this is a simple application, we will cover the most important concepts of Aurelia that you will find in a real production application. We will improve this app along with the book. Listed are the features we will develop for this app:

- Matches explorer
- Teams explorer
- News
- Admin portal
- Social authentication

So, let's start exploring the features that this application delivers to our users.

Matches explorer

This feature is related to the matches in the entire competition. The users will be able to perform the following actions:

- List the **Matches** activity
- Create a new **Match**, which requires admin

Listing the matches

The user will see the list of matches represented as cards. A calendar is shown to the user to navigate and see the matches scheduled per day. The mock-up is shown here:

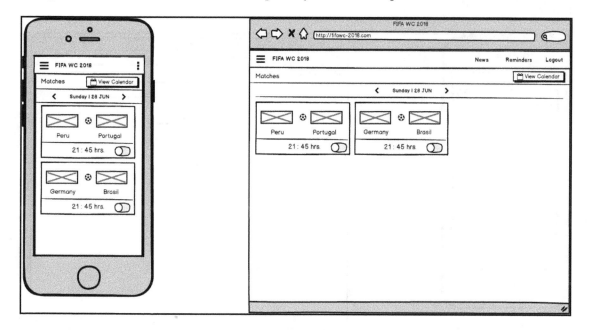

Creating a new Match

To create a new **Match**, an admin account is required. Once the user is authenticated, they can schedule a new **Match** by selecting the teams and the time. The mock-up is shown as follows:

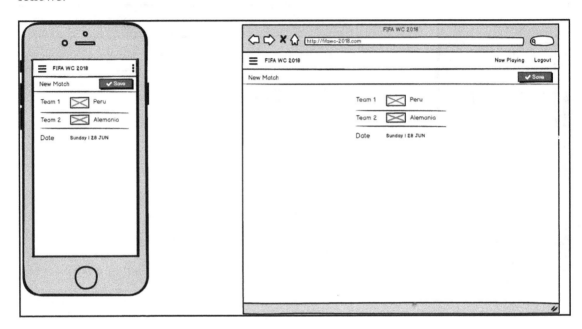

Teams explorer

This feature is related to the matches in the entire competition. The users will be able to perform the following actions:

- List the **Teams**
- Create a new **Team**, which requires admin

Listing the teams

The user will see the list of teams represented as cards. The mock-up is as follows:

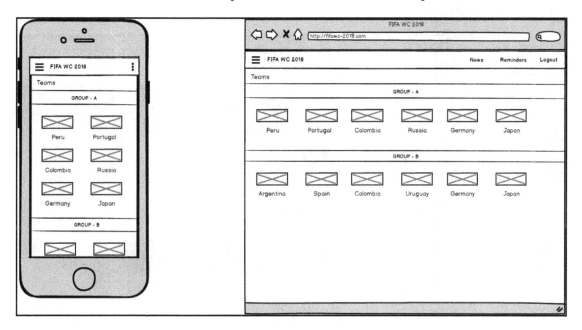

Creating a new team

To create a new **Team**, an admin account is required. Once the user is authenticated, they can create a new team. The mock-up is this:

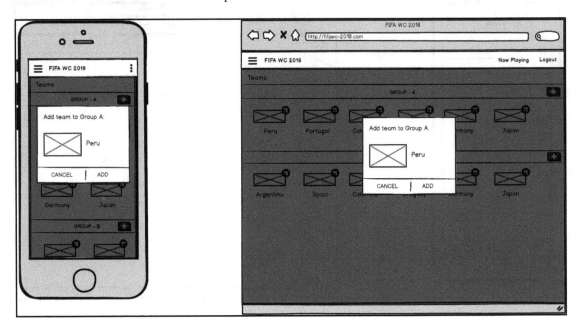

News

This feature is related to the news. The users will be able to perform the following actions:

- List the **News**
- Create a **New** item, which requires admin

Listing the News

The user will see the list of news represented as cards. The mock-up is as shown:

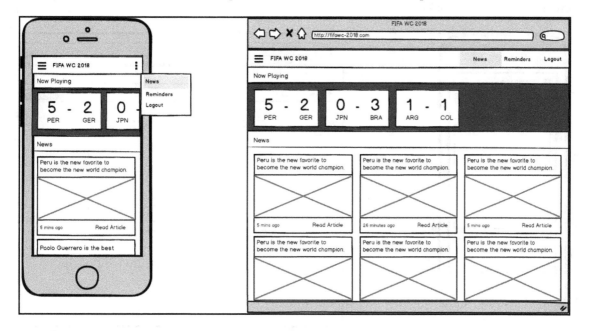

Create a New

To create a **New**, an admin account is required. Once the user is authenticated, they can create a **New**. The mock-up is this:

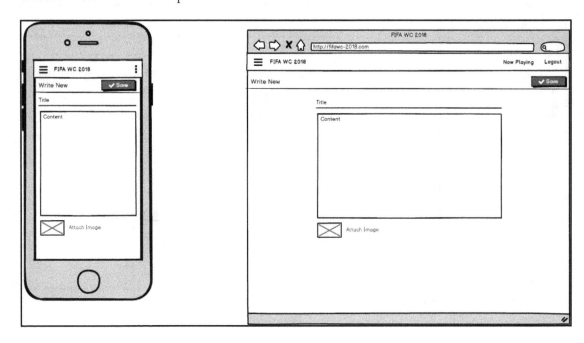

Social authentication

The user will be able to sign in using their Google or Facebook account. The mock-up is this:

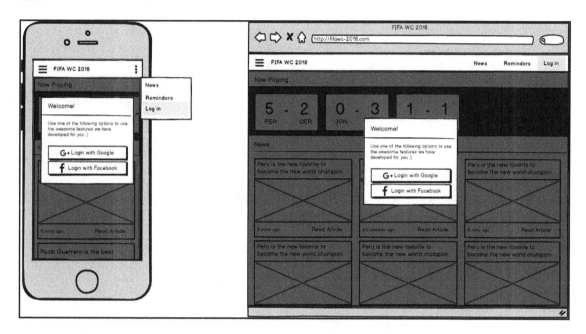

Now that we have an idea of the application we will develop, let's continue creating the initial application project.

Creating our app

Let's start creating our application. If you remember our last section about the Aurelia CLI, we need to use it again to create a new application, so open your favorite Terminal tool and execute the following command:

```
au new worldcup-app
```

Enter the following input in the Terminal:

1. Select 3 to define our custom options for this project
2. First option: Which module loader / bundler would you like to use? RequireJS (Default)

3. **Second option:** `What transpiler would you like to use? : Babel (Default)`

4. **Third option:** `How would you like to setup your template? : Default (No markup processing.)`

5. **Fourth option:** `What CSS processor would you like to use?` In this case, we will choose `Sass (3)`

6. **Fifth option:** `Would you like to configure unit testing?` Of course, we will mark `Yes (Default)`

7. **Sixth option:** `What is your default code editor?` We use WebStorm, but you can choose the most familiar to you.

Now, you will see the main structure of your application on the console:

```
Project Configuration
    Name: worldcup-app
    Platform: Web
    Bundler: Aurelia-CLI
    Loader: RequireJS
    Transpiler: Babel
    Markup Processor: None
    CSS Processor: Sass
    Unit Test Runner: Karma
    Editor: WebStorm
```

8. Finally, select `1` to create the project and then install the project dependencies

This is a custom setup. Our project will be composed with the following features:

- **RequireJS**: Well known file and module loader, with a good browser support. Another option could be SystemJS and Webpack.
- **Babel**: Babel is one of the most used *transpilation* tools nowadays. A `transpiler` is a tool that transforms code written in JavaScript ES6 syntax or later into ES5 code. Why? Because most of the browsers does not have well supported yet the last JavaScript version.
- **Markup processing**: It loads our modules and create the final files which will be interpreted by the browser. We won't use a custom markup processing in this stage.
- **SASS**: A nice preprocessor CSS library, we will review it at more detail in the next chapter.

- **Karma**: A JavaScript test library. We will talk about it in more detail in the Chapter 3, *Testing and Debugging*.
- **WebStorm**: A very nice IDE for JavaScript developers. It is not free but if you have an educational email account from your university or institute, you can get a student license for one year.

Once everything is done, open the `worldcup-app` folder with your favorite editor.

 We know Webpack is a very awesome module loader, but for learning purposes, we prefer to use RequireJS across all this book because is more simple and let us explain better how to configure manually each tool and library we will use in this book.

The project structure

The Aurelia CLI will generate the source code with its base structure, which has everything configured and ready to start writing our application's source code.

The following screenshot shows the root application folder:

Let's start talking about the aurelia_project folder, which contains the main aurelia.json configuration file with all the settings about the dependencies, blunder, build target, loaders, testing run-time tool such as Karma, testing framework, and more. You will modify this file frequently to specify new dependencies our application needs to use.

The next element in the aurelia_folder is the environments folder, which contains three files: dev.json, stage.json, and prod.json. These files contain values depending on the environment you are running on. Do you remember the --env flag in the run option? The CLI will use one of these files to configure our app's environmental values.

The remaining two folders are generators and tasks. They are used to generate Aurelia custom reusable components and to declare gulp tasks, respectively.

The scripts folder contains the bundles generated after we execute the au build command.

As you might guess, the src folder contains our application source code, followed by the test folder, which contains our source code to test our project.

The Bootstrap process

Like many JavaScript frameworks such as Angular and React, Aurelia needs a place in the index.html page to mount the application. This place is known as the entry point. Open the index.html file, and you should see something similar to the following code:

```
<!DOCTYPE html>
<html>
  <head>
    <meta charset="utf-8">
    <title>Aurelia</title>
    <meta name="viewport" content="width=device-width, initial-scale=1">
  </head>

  <body aurelia-app="main">
    <script src="scripts/vendor-bundle.js" data-main="aurelia-
bootstrapper"></script>
  </body>
</html>
```

Aurelia requires an HTML element to load our application. By default, the application is loaded in the body element; we know this because this element uses the aurelia-app attribute, which is used to specify the main JavaScript script file that contains all the configuration for our application, and as you note, by default, Aurelia is configured to use the main file. The following is the content of the main.js file:

```javascript
import environment from './environment';

export function configure(aurelia) {
  aurelia.use
    .standardConfiguration()
    .feature('resources');

  if (environment.debug) {
    aurelia.use.developmentLogging();
  }

  if (environment.testing) {
    aurelia.use.plugin('aurelia-testing');
  }

  aurelia.start().then(() => aurelia.setRoot());
}
```

Let's analyze this file; the first line imports the environment variables from the environment.js file located in the root folder. When you specify the --flag {env} option, the CLI looks for the {env}.json file in the aurelia_project folder and copies its content into the environment.js file.

This file also exports a single configure function, which receives as a parameter the aurelia object that you use to override default configurations and add any code you wish before the app is launched. For example, you can tell Aurelia that you want to declare components as global (features), configure internationalization to manage different languages, and so on.

Once the aurelia object is configured, the last line of code will render our application into the root HTML element, which has the aurelia-app attribute in the index.html page. By default, it renders the app.js component into the root element. Of course, we can override the default values by passing the element you wish to render as the first parameter and the HTML element where you wish to render the app as a second parameter:

```javascript
aurelia.start().then(() => aurelia.setRoot('my-component',
document.getElementById('my-div')));
```

We will be modifying this file along the way; the most important thing to remember is that this file is processed before the app is rendered and apart from the `Aurelia.json` file, this is the second most important file. The following diagram explains the bootstrapping process:

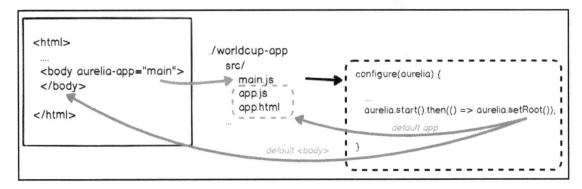

Now you know how the bootstrapping process works. Let's understand how you can create reusable components.

Understanding components

In the last section, we saw that Aurelia requires a component to mount as the root of our entire application and by default, it was the app component. Now let's explore this component.

A **component** is composed of two files, the first written in JavaScript that contains the component's view model and the second one is the markup template written in HTML. They must have the same filename to help the view model resolve its view template. The component's view model is a JavaScript file, which exports a class that contains the component's attributes and functions. For example, this is the content of the `app.js` component:

```
export class App {
  constructor() {
    this.message = 'Hello World!';
  }
}
```

The `App` class declares a constructor that initializes the `message` property. Properties can be declared into the `constructor` or can be defined outside of it. Consider this example:

```
export class App {
  message = 'Hello World!';
}
```

 Use the outside property declaration style when you are declaring simple classes such as **Plain Old CLR Objects (POCO)**, which now implements more logic than simply get and set its property values.

To use the properties defined in our `app.js` view model, we need an HTML template with the same filename. Open the `app.html` file to see its content:

```
<template>
  <h1>${message}</h1>
</template>
```

The first thing to note is that the `message` property declared in the view model is present, but in order to bind the value, we have to use the `${}` string interpolation operator. Finally, when Aurelia renders the component in the web page, the `${message}` declaration will be replaced by `'Hello World!'`.

We can extend our components by adding functions that can be called from the template. For example, let's declare the `changeMessage()` function:

```
export class App {

  constructor() {
    this.message = 'Hello World!';
  }

  changeMessage() {
    this.message = 'World-Cup App';
  }

}
```

From the preceding code, you can see how declaring a function is a simple; we use the same syntax of the `contructor` declaration. If you want to use the properties declared in the App class, you have to use the `this` reserved word to access any property or function.

Now it is time to invoke our `changeMessage` function. First, we will create a button in our template in the `app.html` file and declare a trigger to the `click` event of the button. Open the `app.html` file and apply the following changes:

```
<template>
  <h1>${message}</h1>
  <button click.trigger="changeMessage()">Change</button>
</template>
```

The first thing to note here is that we don't use the default HTML `onclick` event; instead, we use the `click` event with no `on` at the start of the event name. This convention is used only for the Aurelia templating engine. So, we say that we want to invoke the `changeMessage()` functions by binding this function to the `click` event using the `trigger` binding mechanism.

Launch your app by executing the `au run` command in your Terminal, and test this out. When you click on the **Change** button, you should see how the message is changed from `'Hello World!'` to `'World-Cup'` App. The `h1` HTML element is changed because we have previously declared and bound the `${message}` property into its content.

Binding is a big concept we will cover in next chapters in a more detailed way. So, keep reading my friend, it just starting.

Summary

In this chapter, you learned how Aurelia is different from other popular frameworks; we compared Aurelia to ReactJS and Angular. We saw that Aurelia is more lightweight and has better performance, but the most important thing is that Aurelia is based on the ECMAScript 6 standard. So, instead of learning a framework, with Aurelia, you are learning an International Standard.

Also, we installed NodeJS and the NPM; these two open source technologies are extremely important, because Aurelia requires them in order to set our development environment and install our dependencies.

We explored the Aurelia command-line tool in detail, dived into its capabilities, and now you are familiar with it and are able to create, launch, test, and build your apps.

Finally, we talked about the example application we will build—an awesome FIFA World Cup single-page application. You also learned what an Aurelia component is and understood the way they split the view model and the template into two separate files that have to use the same filename with the `.js` and `.html` extensions, respectively.

In the next chapter, you will learn how to apply style and color to our application by installing and configuring the Google Material Design plugin in our app. Enjoy the next chapter!

Styling the User Interface

2

We now have our running Aurelia application and know all the basic principles of JavaScript programming. Our **Hello World!** message appears on screen, but don't you think it is a little simple and static? In this chapter, we will explore how to add style to our application using modern tools such as SASS and LESS. Also, we will talk about the most important styling libraries used nowadays such as Bootstrap, Semantic UI, and Material Design. Finally, with all this previous learning, let's make our application look cool, awesome, and attractive by configuring our project to use the Aurelia-Materialize plugin. Some of the tools we are going to use for this purpose are:

- CSS preprocessors: SASS, LESS
- Task automation tools: Gulp
- CSS libraries: Bootstrap, Material Design, Semantic UI

Sounds exciting? We know yes, first we need to start talking about CSS, have you heard about it before? Don't worry, we will explain it in a brief but consistent way. Just CSS is not so awesome, so we will introduce you to some tools to make your style sheets awesome! Tools such SASS and LESS are very useful to these purposes, but we need to run some commands each time we need to use it, so we will also talk about task automation tools. No more manual repetitive commands! Finally, we don't need to reinvent the wheel. We have CSS libraries with different design templates, each one oriented to different concepts and purposes. Last, but not least, we will practice configuring our previously created application with all these awesome tools to make our development process more friendly and interesting. We are sure you will find this chapter really interesting and useful, so let's start!

Talking about CSS

Basically, CSS is a language structure that describes the style of some HTML file (can also be used for XML), defining how it should be displayed. This structure allows developers to manage the behavior on one or multiple web pages; any change performed on some CSS element will be reflected in all HTML elements linked to it.

How does it work?

CSS is based on rules. These rules are defined on `.css` files, called **style sheet**. Style sheets can be composed of one or more rules, applied to one HTML or XML document; the rule has two parts: selector and declaration:

```
h4 { color : red}
```

The h4 element is the selector, and `{ color : red }` is the declaration.

The selector works as a link between the document and the style, specifying the elements that will be affected by that declaration. The statement is the part of the rule that states what the effect will be. In the previous example, selector h4 indicates that all elements h4 will be affected by the declaration stating that the color property will have the network value (red) for all elements h4 of the document or documents that are linked to that style sheet.

We have three ways to link our style sheet with the HTML file.

The first option is to use the `<link>` element, on the `<head>` section of the HTML file. We just need to specify the absolute or relative path/URL of our style sheet to import into our web page:

```
<!DOCTYPE html>
<html lang="en">
<head>
 <title>Aurelia is Awesome</title>
 <link rel="stylesheet" type="text/css"
href="http://www.w3.org/css/officeFloats.css" />
</head>
<body>
 .

 .
</body>
</html>
```

Next, we can use the `<style>` element of the HTML file, generally in the `<head>` section too. It will be loaded when our file is called by the application:

```html
<!DOCTYPE html>
<html lang="en">
<head>
    <style type="text/css">
        body {
            padding-left: 11em;
            font-family: Georgia, "Times New Roman", serif;
            color: red;
            background-color: #d8da3d;
        }
        h1 {
            font-family: Helvetica, Geneva, Arial, sans-serif;
        }
    </style>
</head>
<body>
 <!--Here the styles will be applied-->
</body>
</html>
```

Alternatively, we can style the HTML directly using the `style` flag:

```html
<!DOCTYPE html>
<html lang="en">
<head>
    <!--Nothing here-->
</head>
<body>
    <h1 style="color: blue">Aurelia is awesome!</h1>
</body>
</html>
```

Ready to add some cool style to our application? This is just the beginning!

Exploring SASS and LESS

We were reviewing some of the most basic CSS concepts, just to refresh our knowledge about the syntax and elements that compose a style sheet. In the real world, a style sheet could have more than 20 classes belonging to one HTML page; in extreme cases, these classes could be one hundred or more. In these cases, maybe you will find CSS syntax very primitive, not auto-explanatory, and incomplete in some cases. It's hard to implement inheritance on big systems and over time, it could become hard to maintain.

You can apply different approaches in order to write better CSS code, you can define different classes for each web page and then import them on one single CSS file, or maybe you could define parent classes and apply inheritance to child elements, but, in both cases, you will need to deal with maintainability problems.

It's just for the reason that in order to write better CSS code, reuse code in an effective way, and add some extra approaches to make it more dynamic and understandable to any developer, CSS preprocessors become a very used tool for any developer, increasing their productivity and drastically reducing the amount of code in our style sheets.

As we can expect, each CSS preprocessor has its own syntax, not too different and not hard to learn. All of them support classic CSS; the extra features will be explained as we move on using the two most used tools nowadays—SASS and LESS.

Variables

Imagine that you are coding the web page for your company; you define the style sheet, and, of course, you have a font standard color for all titles, body text, and so on. You are writing your CSS classes and notes that you need to repeat the same color value on more than one class definition. Okay, it's not so hard to copy and paste the same value across my entire file. You finally present that web page to your UX designer and oh, surprise! That red doesn't have to be so deep. You need to correct to the new color code. What does that mean? You will need to dive into your style sheet and manually change each color value for the new one.

Like other programming languages, with CSS preprocessors, we can define variables to reuse them across our style sheet, avoid repeating the same value, and save time when we need to adjust or change that same value. Let's look at an example:

SASS syntax:

```
$my-height: 160px;

div {
  height: $my-height;
}
```

Then, LESS syntax:

```
@my-height: 160px;

div {
  font-size: @my-height;
}
```

They're pretty similar right? Let's explore other features!

Nesting

Nesting elements in pure CSS are a bad deal. They are not friendly, are hard to read, and make us write and repeat a lot of code. Using a CSS preprocessor, you will provide a more friendly reading to any developer; the code auto explains what the CSS is doing and how the classes inherit from others. Look at the magic:

Using the SASS syntax:

```
$my-link-color: #FF0000;
$my-link-hover: #00FFFF;

ul {
  margin: 0;

  li {
    float: left;
  }

  a {
    color: $my-link-color;

    &:hover {
```

```
        color: $my-link-hover;
      }
    }
  }
```

Using the same in LESS:

```
@my-link-color: #FF0000;
@my-link-hover: #00FF00;

ul {
  margin: 0;

  li {
    float: left;
  }

  a {
    color: @my-link-color;

    &:hover {
      color: @my-link-hover;
    }
  }
}
```

One thing you need to know is that the browser does not directly interpret the SASS or LESS syntax. Do you need to convert your code to normal CSS syntax, how could you perform it? In the case of SASS, just type the following command:

```
$ sass --watch app/sass:public/stylesheets
```

They both export the same CSS output:

```
ul { margin: 0; }
ul li { float: left; }
ul a { color: #999; }
ul a:hover { color: #229ed3; }
```

As you can see, CSS preprocessors provide us a more friendly readability and quick understanding of what the code is doing.

Extends

Sometimes, you define various classes that share a common definition. With the `@extend` feature, you can define a common class and make others extend from it instead of copying the same code in each one:

SASS example:

```
.block { margin: 25px 58px; }

p {
  @extend .block;
  border: 3px solid #00FF00;
}

ol {
  @extend .block;
  color: #FF0000;
  text-transform: lowercase;
}
```

LESS:

```
.block { margin: 25px 58px; }

p {
  &:extend(.block);
  border: 3px solid #00FF00;
}

ol {
  &:extend(.block);
  color: #FF0000;
  text-transform: lowercase;
}
```

CSS output:

```
.block, p, ul, ol { margin: 10px 5px; }

p { border: 1px solid #eee; }
ul, ol { color: #333; text-transform: uppercase; }
```

If/else statements

Oh, please, this is a really awesome feature! With this feature, you will be able to control the aspect of your page in a reactive way, based on determined conditions.

SASS example:

```
@if lightness($my-color) > 90% {
  background-color: #FF0000;
}

@else {
  background-color: #00FF00;
}
```

In LESS, the things are not similar. You need to use CSS guards:

```
.mixin (@my-color) when (lightness(@my-color) >80%) {
  background-color: #00FF00;
}
.mixin (@my-color) when (lightness(@my-color) =< 80%) {
  background-color: #FF0000;
}
```

These are not all the preprocessor features, but at this moment, they're enough to start working on our FIFA World Cup application!

Automating tasks with Gulp

In the previous section, we learned how to use a CSS preprocessor and how to compile this SASS/LESS code into pure CSS to be interpreted by the browser. Note that each time you make a change, you will need to recompile the entire file, which means that you will need to type the same command and do the same task one, two, and several times. Yes, it's really boring. Fortunately, we have task automation tools. What does that mean? Some other tool will do the dirty job for us.

Understanding Gulp

Gulp is an open source JavaScript-based task runner, which uses code-over-configuration approach to define its tasks. These could be the following:

- Bundling and minifying libraries and style sheets

- Refreshing your browser when you save a file
- Quickly running unit tests
- Running code analysis
- LESS/SASS to CSS compilation
- Copying modified files to an output directory

This tool uses the stream module of Node.js; first of all, we need to define what a stream is. It can be defined as a tool that allows data reading on one file and takes it to another place through pipes methods. The principal feature of Gulp.js is that it does not write files/folders into the hard drive, like other automation tools. That's a good feature, because we can configure several tasks, and it won't impact our computer performance.

How does Gulp.js work?

As we said before, Gulp does not write anything on the hard drive. So, all operations are performed at the filesystem level. It observes the file preconfigured to check for any change (read) and after some edition, it will rewrite the compiled content linked with another file, or execute some preconfigured command.

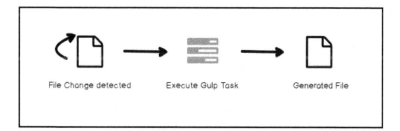

File Change detected   Execute Gulp Task   Generated File

Installing Gulp

Gulp is available on Windows, Linux, and macOS. The installation process is very similar in any of these operating systems, and the only difference is that you need to run the installation command as administrator on UNIX-based platforms. You need to have already installed Node and NPM on your PC. To install, type the next command:

```
$ npm install –g gulp
```

Let's wait some minutes after the installation process finishes and then verify that all its okay:

```
$ gulp -v

CLI Version 3.9.0
```

That's all! We now have Gulp installed and ready to automate tasks!

First of all, you need to ensure that your web project is already configured to import npm modules; if no package.json file exists, you must create one with the npm init command. To start working with Gulp, just type the following command:

```
$ npm install --save-dev gulp
```

This will install gulp node module locally on your project. Remember that the --save-dev flag lets npm update its package.json file in the devDependencies section to be resolved only on development time.

The next step is to create the gulpfile. This file will act as manifest to define the tasks we want to execute. All of them should be defined in this file; let's go through an example:

```
// gulpfile.js
var gulp = require('gulp');

gulp.task('hello-world', function(){
    console.log('hello world');
});
```

require is a node function to add a reference to a module. Since we are referencing the gulp module, we are able to use this task automation method.

Now, when we run the gulp hello-world command from the command line, the task automation tool will search on the gulpfile the task matching by name and execute it.

Gulp provides three primary task methods:

- gulp.task: To define a new task with a name, array dependencies, and the function to execute
- gulp.src: It sets the folder where the source files are located
- gulp.dest: It sets the destination folder where build files will be placed

Gulp can be configured to execute any task, such as image transformation, JavaScript files transpiling, concatenation, and case processing. Let's see some more advanced examples.

JavaScript task

We will configure an automated task to transform our created SCSS files into CSS. This code can be implemented in any web project (with gulp dependencies preconfigured, of course):

```
$ npm install gulp-sass --save-dev
```

gulp-sass is a customized plugin for gulp to work with SASS files.

After importing the npm modules into our project, let's reference them into our gulpfile:

```
var gulp = require('gulp');
var sass = require('gulp-sass');
```

Then, we need to create a new task. Let's call it process-styles:

```
// SCSS processing
gulp.task('process-styles', function() {gulp.src('sass/**/*.scss')
        .pipe(sass().on('error', sass.logError))
        .pipe(gulp.dest('./css/'));});
```

Note that we use the pipe() method to call any extra plugins between the .src() and the .dest() sections. The code is so self-explanatory, we are just passing the route where the gulp task will find the files to be converted, then configuring a fault behavior if some error is raised and if everything is okay, we just specify the route of our generated files.

Automating tasks

At this point, we have some task compressed into a single file. All this compression will be performed when we run the gulp command. We can group the preconfigured task to be run into one single command. Suppose we have three tasks already defined: process-styles, other-task, and some-other-task. Now we just need to define all these tasks into a single new task:

```
// run all tasks
gulp.task('run', ['process-styles', 'other-task', 'some-other-task']);
```

Save and press *Enter* the gulp run command line to execute all the tasks defined.

That's great, but we still need to enter commands manually. Rumpelstiltskin, that was not part of the deal! Don't worry, we have one last surprise for you—gulp.watch(). With this method, you could monitor your source files and execute some task when a change is detected. Let's configure watch task into our gulpfile:

```
// watch for changes in code
gulp.task('watch', function() {
  // some example tasks
  // detect image changes
  gulp.watch(folder.src + 'img/**/*', ['images-task']);

  // detect html changes
  gulp.watch(folder.src + 'html/**/*', ['html-task']);

  // detect javascript changes
  gulp.watch(folder.src + 'js/**/*', ['js-task']);

  // detect css changes <--- Our created task
  gulp.watch(folder.src + 'scss/**/*', ['process-styles']);
  .
  .
  .
  // And so many task as we need to watch!

});
```

Finally, rather than running gulp watch task manually, let's configure a default task:

```
gulp.task('default', ['run', 'watch']);
```

Save, and then just run the command gulp into your terminal. You will note that a gulp observer is always looking if any change is performed in the files preconfigured! Of course, it includes all your .scss files! Now you can change and add new styles and view it automatically reflected in your browser, without the need to execute some command by yourself. If you want to terminate this watch process, just type *Ctrl* + *C* to abort monitoring and return to the command line. Now you really have a strong task automation tool configured and ready for use! The Aurelia CLI preconfigures gulp task activities for you, but it's very important to know how it works behind the scenes; also, you are able to modify this configuration and add custom behavior if you consider it needed.

Exploring CSS frameworks

We are ready to start writing our first HTML elements and add style to the application. There are common elements that can be repeated in more than one application: tables, grids, input tags, select, and so on. We can define our own, but you should keep in mind that all of these elements need to be standardized, and defining it from zero can become a difficult task. Today, we have many HTML libraries and templates to start developing our view layer and add custom behavior to satisfy our own needs. Let's explore the three most used HTML, JS, and CSS libraries.

Bootstrap

Bootstrap is one of the most popular and complete frontend libraries. It is composed of HTML templates, predefined CSS classes, and JavaScript files to add a more dynamic behavior to each component. Created by Mark Otto and Jacob Thornton at Twitter and then released as open source project in August 2011, Bootstrap was one of the first libraries providing custom elements and a grid system to design responsive webs. What does responsive mean? Responsive web design is about creating websites that automatically adjust themselves to look good on all devices, from small phones to large desktops.

The grid is the most important aspect of this framework. It defines the bases in which the layout is created. Bootstrap implements five tiers or scales based on the screen width. Customize the size of your columns on extra small, small, medium, large, or extra large devices, however you see fit. For grids that are the same from the smallest of devices to the largest, use the `.col` and `.col-*` classes. Specify a numbered class when you need a particularly sized column; otherwise, feel free to stick to `.col`. Let's look at an example for a small screen:

Here, keep the following in mind:

- .col-sm-1 will fit 1/12 of the screen width
- .col-sm-2 will fit 1/6 of the screen width
- .col-sm-4 will fit 1/3 of the screen width
- .col-sm-6 will fit 1/2 of the screen width
- .col-sm-12 will fit the entire screen width

In the same way, Bootstrap includes a vast variety of preconfigured classes to simplify the alignment of our HTML elements, making our web application look ordered and attractive. Another thing we really like about bootstrap is the high customization level. We can transform all their components, adding custom behavior or style, and it will not generate any conflict with the existing library. An advanced design with some elements customized could look like this:

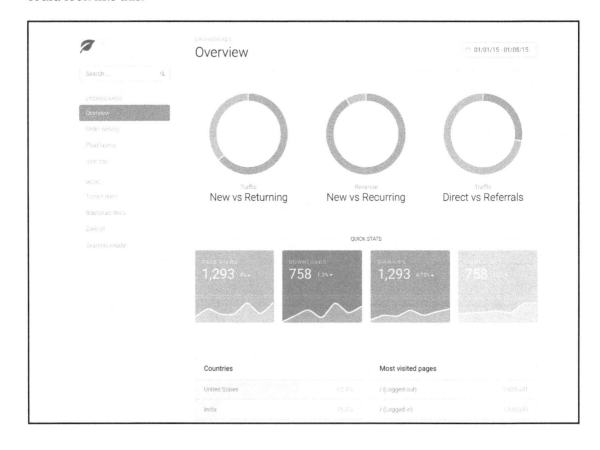

Doesn't care the purpose, Bootstrap is created to provide a highly customizable solution for any business need you might have. Let's explore more libraries!

Material Design

Powered by Google, Material Design is more than just a CSS/JS library. It's a complete philosophy design, based on shapes, shadows, and transitions. Material Design is based on three main principles.

Material is the metaphor

Consider all the space around you as a motion system. You can touch it, you can feel it, and see how it can change their aspect when you interact. Plain surfaces, paper, and colors are common in our daily lifestyle, and Material uses these attributes to create an intuitive and familiar interface to the final user, providing a big superset of animations without breaking the rules of physics.

Bold, graphic, and intentional

Pleasing to the eyes, Material Design is not intrusive or aggressive. It implements a hierarchy meaning based on colors, scales, and white spaces, inviting the user to interact with the web interface.

Motion provides meaning

Motion respects and reinforces the user as the prime mover. Primary user actions are inflection points that initiate motion, transforming the whole design. Action and reaction rules, serving to focus attention and maintain continuity.

As we said before, Material is not a library, but many libraries are based on Material, and one of the most used nowadays is Materialize. This library provides all features like others, such as grid systems, prebuilt components, and custom behavior, with the difference that all of it is created by following Material Design principles. Let's look at an example of web pages developed using Materialize:

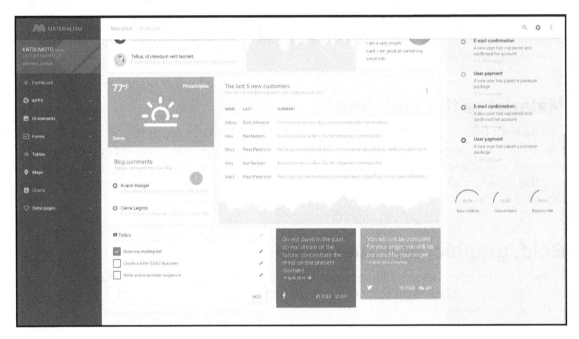

As you can see, the Material interface is simple, clean, and self-explanatory.

Semantic UI

The new guy in the neighborhood, Semantic comes with tons of unique new features based on modals, accordion elements, 3D transformations, even ratings, and so on.

> *"Semantic empowers designers and developers by creating a shared vocabulary for UI."*
>
> *- Semantic UI Team*

Why *Semantic*? It's because it provides class names that sound really natural in common English language instead of random class names, and, of course, it describes what the CSS classes are doing to the HTML element.

Let's see how the implementation differs from other frontend libraries; on Bootstrap, the names of CSS classes are very friendly for humans to read:

```
<div data-role="header">
    <a href="#"
        class="ui-btn-left ui-btn ui-btn-inline ui-mini ui-corner-all ui-
btn-icon-left ui-icon-delete">Cancel</a>
    <h1>My App</h1>
    <button class="ui-btn-right ui-btn ui-btn-b ui-btn-inline ui-mini ui-
corner-all ui-btn-icon-right ui-icon-check">
        Save
    </button>
</div>
```

Using the Semantic UI library, classes use human words. That's very friendly! Coding is more like writing regular text:

```
<div class="ui stackable inverted divided equal height stackable grid">
```

Semantic UI comes with a lot of themes, and they are easy to configure. For example, the following screenshot shows a web page developed using Semantic UI:

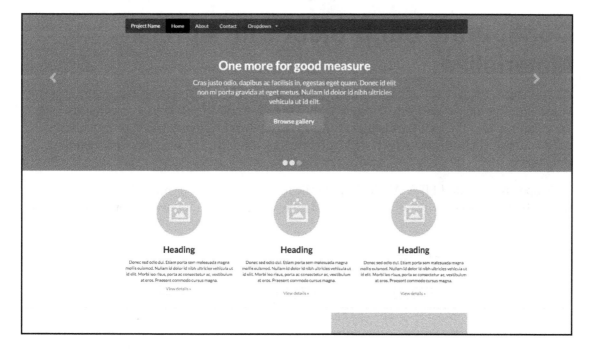

You can read more about this awesome library at `https://semantic-ui.com`.

All the mentioned libraries are mobile-first based. What does that mean? Let's keep exploring!

The mobile-first approach

Mobile-first is a relatively new way to design web pages, facilitating the responsiveness starting always by the small screen devices, such as mobile phones or tablets. When you start designing, you must have a close idea of where your product will be displayed.

Now, it's time to choose a frontend library to start creating our first project components. In our opinion, Material Design can give a more natural feel to the final user and looks great on mobile devices (Android UI is based on Material). Bootstrap can be a good option too, still looking like a common web page on small screens. The same goes for Semantic UI, but this one has transitions and animations that we will really miss. So, let's start configuring our project with Materialize library.

Configuring our project with Aurelia-Materialize

As we said in the last section, Material Design is not a library. However, many libraries are based on Material philosophy, so we will choose Materialize CSS. Their components look very natural, and the best part is that Aurelia has its own implementation of this library called Aurelia-Materialize, which will facilitate us a lot in the development process and integration.

Let's open our created FIFA World Cup application and set the Terminal into the root folder; then we need to install some dependencies. Execute the following commands in the next order:

- `$ au install jquery`
- `$ au install tslib`
- `$ au install materialize-amd`
- `$ au install aurelia-materialize-bridge`

In our `index.html` file, lets include the Material Design icons to be imported into our project:

```
<link href="https://fonts.googleapis.com/icon?family=Material+Icons"
rel="stylesheet">
```

Next, in our `main.js` file, we need to configure our new plugin:

```
aurelia.use.plugin('aurelia-materialize-bridge', b =>
b.useAll().preventWavesAttach());
```

The `b => b.useAll()` script allows us to load all Aurelia-materialize components into our project. If you only need a few of them, you can specify each one in the next way:

```
.plugin('aurelia-materialize-bridge', bridge => {
    bridge
        .useButton()
        .useCollapsible()
        .useModal()
        .useTabs()
        .useWaves().preventWavesAttach();
});
```

Then, we need to add our generated `.css` to the `index.html` file:

```
<link rel="stylesheet" href="styles/css/materialize.min.css">
```

 Since we have the Aurelia CLI installed from the previous chapter, we are using this feature to get the new dependencies. Make sure you have at least the `0.32.0` version.

You are done! We are finally ready to start developing our generated, configured, and running web application.

At this point, your application folder should contain the following (or similar) project structure:

If you are using an earlier version of `Aurelia-CLI` (`0.33.1`), please read the following recommendations:

- Add `node_modules/jquery/dist/jquery.js` to the `prepend` section of the `vendor-bundle.js` configuration in the `aurelia.json` file and remove `jquery` from dependencies section.
- Add `node_modules/materialize-amd/dist/js/materialize.amd.js` at the end of `prepend` section of the `vendor-bundle.js` configuration in the `aurelia.json` and remove the `materialize-amd` configuration from dependencies section.

Summary

In this chapter, we learned how to style our Aurelia application using CSS. Also, we explored the two most popular CSS preprocessors—LESS and SASS. We saw how these preprocessors help us develop more powerful style sheets using variables and extensions.

We explored how to automate tasks using Gulp. Gulp is used by the Aurelia CLI to execute all the tasks related to it.

Lastly, we went through different CSS Frameworks and explored and configured Google's Material Design Framework. We used Material Design to create our example application and take advantage of the most common UI elements.

In the next chapter, we will see how to apply testing in our code by adopting Test-Driven-Development in our development process. Keep reading!

3
Testing and Debugging

Testing is one of the most important phases of the development process. Whatever type of project you are working on, testing is key if you want to deliver applications with high quality and make your users happy.

Just imagine what would happen if your favorite taxi application makes your driver take you to the wrong place or the price of your trip is higher than it's supposed to be? This embarrassing bug will undoubtedly produce a series of catastrophic events that will damage the reputation of the application and, worse still, the company reputation.

Learning how to test our Aurelia applications and how to correctly apply the **Test-Driven Development** (**TDD**) approach will improve the quality of your applications, avoid embarrassing bugs, make your users happier, and make you a better developer. So, in this chapter, we will cover the following topics:

- Benefits of testing
- TDD
- Aurelia testing framework

- Practicing testing
- Debugging our code

Benefits of testing

Making *testing* part of our development process comes with a lot of benefits in every layer of our project. Before we start writing code to test our application, let's review the benefits that good testing brings to:

- The development team
- The project
- The organization
- The users

For the development team

If you work in a team with multiple members, you might have experienced that bad moment when a member pushes some changes and the application does not work as expected. Not only that, if the team does not have a mechanism to avoid changes that can break, someone else's code might cause conflict and decrease the quality of our applications.

Applying testing enables a mechanism that helps us avoid potential bugs in the code. It is recommended that you write test scripts for all the components into the application. The code coverage percentage is an indicator of how much testing the development team has written for the application. It is recommended to have a 100 percent coverage; with this, you ensure that every time someone else changes the code, you are not breaking someone else's code.

For the project

If you are working in an *agile* team, you might be familiar with sprints of two weeks or maybe one month. When you work in agile teams, it is important to automate as much as you can, and automating the testing phase will help your team deliver deliverables quickly.

Automating testing without the need for human intervention requires your team to write tests in all the phases of the application, such as these:

- Unit test
- Integration test
- UI test
- End-to-end test

For Aurelia applications, you will learn how to write unit-test scripts and end-to-end tests. Writing tests and automating them will increase the development speed of our team.

For the organization

It is important to protect the reputation of the organization in which you are working. Testing projects in our organization as much as possible will improve its reputation and make it more reliable.

There are many cases where big companies have lost a large amount of money because of failures in software. All these mistakes could have been avoided if the applications had been tested before they were published to the users. For that reason, understanding the importance of good testing is key in every aspect of the organization.

For the users

Nothing is worse than delivering an application to your users that does not satisfy their needs, and even worse is an application infested with bugs and is of a generally poor quality. Think carefully about what you deliver to your users. The more you code, the more satisfied your users will be.

Test-Driven Development

This is a development approach that changes the way developers test the code of their applications. Previously, developers implemented all the business logic of their applications and once everything was coded, they wrote the tests.

Writing test scripts is not an easy task; just imagine the time it takes to code all the business logic of your application, and the fact that you have to write tests for all the possible scenarios requires a lot of knowledge about the system itself and the level of complexity only increases if you are the sole developer who maintains the code. However, thankfully, there is a better way to test things out. TDD is composed of three simple phases:

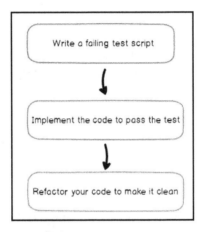

Always remember these three colors: red, green, and blue; they represent the TDD cycle. Being in the red phase means that you have written what your piece of code is supposed to do, but the functionality is not implemented yet and the test will fail. Being in the blue phase, it means that you have implemented the code and the test now passes without any problem, but the code might be refactored. Lastly, being in the green phase means that both the code and tests were implemented and passed successfully, and the code is well formatted and easy for any developer to read.

Let's cover each step in further detail to get a close look at TDD phases by coding a simple example.

Making our code fail

It is important to know that we won't use any testing framework at this point. The main goal in this section is to understand how TDD works; we have a complete tour of testing technology in the following sections in this chapter.

We will use TDD to create an additional function called `sum`, which will return the sum of two numbers that are passed as parameters. First, using an editor of your choice, create a new file called `testing.js` and add the following code:

```
const assert = require('assert');

function add(n1, n2) {
  return 0;
}
```

First, we import the `assert` module to use its `equal` function. The `equal` function expects three parameters:

- The current value or expression to be analyzed
- The expected value
- The message that should be thrown in case the current and expected value are not equal

If the assertion *fails*, the program will be *finished* and you will see the reason why the assertion fails in your Terminal.

Once we import our `assert` module, we proceed to create our `add` function. However, this function does not perform any operation; this is because our intention is to first write the test and make it fail, and after that we will implement the logic itself in the next point. In the same `testing.js` file, append to the following code with the testing case right below the `add` function:

```
let result = add(5, 5);
assert.equal( result, 10, "Should be 10");

console.log("Test passed!!");
```

Now we have our test case, which will compare the current value—add(5, 5)—housed into the result variable against the expected value—10, and if they are not equal, the `Should be 10` error message will be displayed and as the program is complete, the next expression—`console.log`—won't be executed.

It's time to execute our test. Using your Terminal, get into your folder where you have created the `testing.js` file and execute the following command:

```
$ node testing.js
```

If everything went wrong, you should see the following output:

```
assert.js:81
  throw new assert.AssertionError({
   ^

AssertionError: Should be 10
  . . .
```

Cool! Now it's time to implement the code and pass our test.

Implementing the code

Now, let's implement the code in the add function. We will declare a result variable into the function to house the addition between the two parameters passed to it. Open the testing.js file and apply the following changes:

```
const assert = require('assert');

function add(n1, n2) {
    const result = n1 + n2;

    return result;

}

var result = add(5, 5);
assert.equal(result, 10, "Should be 10");

console.log("Test passed!!");
```

Now that we have implemented the logic for our add function, the next time we run the test, we expect that the assertion.equal function won't fail and the Test passed!! message will be displayed. Let's try it out. Execute the following command:

```
$ node testing.js
  Test passed!!
```

As you can see, the test passed and now the Test passed!! message is displayed. By using this strategy to write the test first and then implement it, we can be 100 percent sure that our application is doing what it's supposed to do.

Let's follow the last step to finish our TDD flow.

Refactoring our code

At this point, everything is okay; we have our test and implementation written, the code is doing what we expect, and it seems that there's nothing left to do. But, as a good developer, we should look for ways to make our code more readable and reduce the lines of code. Also, the refactoring phase is used to change some weird variable names and, if possible, add comments to our code if needed.

Open your `testing.js` file and apply the following changes to make it more readable:

```
var assert = require('assert');

function add(n1, n2) {
  return n1 + n2;
}

assert.equal(add(5, 5), 10, "Should be 10");

console.log("Test passed!!");
```

The first change is in the `add` function. As this is a simple addition operation, declaring a `result` variable is not necessary, so we return the addition result in the `return` function to make it more readable.

Finally, we are passing the results of the call to `add(5, 5)` into the `assert.equal` function, so it is easier to know what you are trying to test.

As you might see, TDD is easy to implement but a little bit hard to adopt; we (the authors :D) encourage you to adopt and use it at work. This will make your life easier and will help you become a better programmer who knows how to deliver quality software.

Now it's time to see what Aurelia has to offer. Keep reading!

Aurelia testing frameworks

Aurelia is powered by other open source testing technologies which together help us set up a very productive development environment. Understanding the fundamentals of these technologies will give us a clear idea of how things work and will give you the knowledge to tackle any problem that may appear in the future.

Before we write our first Aurelia tests, let's learn about JasmineJS and KarmaJS, the most awesome frameworks that the JavaScript ecosystem could provide us for testing, and let's use the example implemented in the TDD section to understand how to write testing scripts using the Jasmine syntax and assertions helper functions.

Learning JasmineJS

As is detailed in its website, Jasmine is a behavior-driven development framework for testing JavaScript code: it does not depend on any other JavaScript frameworks, it does not require a DOM, and it has a clean, obvious syntax so that you can easily write tests. Jasmine is an easy-to-learn framework, and it comes with its own assertion functions, so we don't need to install any additional assertion library, such as Chai. Let's start installing it and exploring the building blocks—suites and test cases.

Installation and configuration

We will use the NPM tool to install Jasmine. Open your favorite Terminal and execute the following command:

```
$ npm install jasmine --global
```

The preceding instruction will install Jasmine as an executable program that you can invoke in any folder in your Terminal. We achieve this using the `--global` flag in the `npm install` command.

Once Jasmine is installed, we need to create our project example skeleton to practice with Jasmine. For this, we need to do the following:

1. Create a new folder called `practice-jasmine`
2. Initialize a new Jasmine project by executing the `jasmine init` command
3. Write our test script

So, having the steps clear, open your Terminal and execute the following commands:

```
$ mkdir practice-jasmine
$ cd practice-jasmine
$ jasmine init
```

Once the `jasmine init` command is executed, it will create the following folder structure for our project:

```
└──────spec
    └──────support
        └──────jasmine.json
```

You can get the preceding tree list by installing the `tree` program and executing it into your `practice-jasmine` folder with the `tree` command.

As you can see in the root of the project's folder, there is a `spec` folder, where we will save all our test scripts. Right in the `spec` folder, there is a `support` folder where a `jasmine.json` file has been created for us. This file contains all the configuration that Jasmine will use to find our test scripts and then execute them. Using the editor of your choice, open the `jasmine.json` file:

```
{
  "spec_dir": "spec",
  "spec_files": [
    "**/*[sS]pec.js"
  ],
  "helpers": [
    "helpers/**/*.js"
  ],
  "stopSpecOnExpectationFailure": false,
  "random": true
}
```

The important properties to consider in this file are `spec_dir`, which points to the folder that hosts our test scripts, and `spec_files`, which declares a regular expression that tells Jasmine that the files containing `spec.js` or `Spec.js` at the end of their names have to be considered as test scripts and have to be processed.

To validate that everything is configured correctly, execute the following command in the root `practice-jasmine` directory:

```
$ jasmine

Started


No specs found
Finished in 0.002 seconds
```

You should see the message `No specs found` displayed which means that as we didn't write any test yet, Jasmine was not able to process any test case. Also, you can see how much time Jasmine takes to execute your tests.

Test suites

Following the best practices, you have to separate your tests that are similar to be grouped in suites. For example, in our application, we will write code to manage football matches and information about teams. Both matches and teams are different domains and for that reason, we should group the tests related to the matches in a suite and repeat the same for teams.

Following the example where we created an `add` function, we might be implementing this function for a Calculator application, so let's use this as an example to understand Jasmine. In the `specs` folder, create the `calculator.spec.js` file and write the following code:

```
describe("Calculator", function() {

    ...

});
```

We have created our test suite; for that, we are using the `describe` function and we pass the name of our suite as the first parameter, in this case `Calculator`, and as the second parameter, we pass a function that will contain the code for our test cases.

Test cases

To write the test for our applications, we need test cases that should basically consider all the possible scenarios that your app can afford. For our Calculator example, we will create test cases for the four main arithmetic operations—addition, multiplication, subtraction, and division. Test cases are created using the `it` function, as follows:

```
describe("Calculator", function() {

    it("should return the addition ", function() {
        ...
    });

    it("should return the substraction ", function() {
        ...
    });
```

```
    it("should return the multiplication ", function() {
        ...
    })

    it("should return the division ", function() {
        ...
    })

});
```

Before we continue on our trip, we should have something to test. So let's create a Calculator object to test out. In the same calculator.spec.js file, add the following code at the very beginning, before the suite declaration, as follows:

```
var Calculator = {
  add: function(n1, n2) {
    return n1 + n2;
  },
  substract: function(n1, n2) {
    return n1 - n2;
  },
  multiply: function(n1, n2) {
    return n1 * n2;
  },
  divide: function(n1, n2) {
      return n1 / n2;
  }
}
```

```
describe("Calculator", function() {
...
```

Now that we have something to test, let's learn about how we can write assertions in our test file.

Expects

We test the functionality of our code by writing expects that are no more than simple assumptions that we have for our code if everything was implemented correctly. In the file we are working on, apply the following changes:

```
...

describe("Calculator", function() {
```

```
it("should return the addition ", function() {
    expect(Calculator.add(1, 2)).toEqual(3);
});

it("should return the substraction ", function() {
    expect(Calculator.substract(1, 2)).toEqual(-1);
});

it("should return the multiplication ", function() {
    expect(Calculator.multiply(1, 2)).toEqual(2);
})

 it("should return the division ", function() {
    expect(Calculator.divide(1, 2)).toEqual(0.5);
})

});
```

We have created the expectations that we have for our code. For example, for the additional test case, we expect that the result of add(1, 2) returns 3. We specify the match operation using helper functions, such as the toEqual function, that as its name says, won't raise any exception in case the result of calling the add function is the same as the expected value.

Now that we have our test script fully implemented, let's execute it and see what we get in the console. Run the following command:

```
$ jasmine

Started
. . . .


4 specs, 0 failures
Finished in 0.006 seconds
```

Now the output displayed is that 4 specs were found and executed without failures. It is time to see what will happen if we force a test case to fail. Replace the expect statement in the addition test case for the following expects:

```
...

it("should return the addition ", function() {
        expect(Calculator.add(1, 2)).toEqual(30);
});

...
```

Once the changes are applied, run the following command to make our test fail:

```
$ jasmine

Started
F...
Failures:
1) Calculator should return the addition
  Message:
    Expected 3 to equal 30.
  Stack:
    Error: Expected 3 to equal 30.
        ...
4 specs, 1 failure
Finished in 0.011 seconds
```

Let's analyze the output. The first thing to note is the following F... string, this means that the first test has failed and the other 3 (dots) are correct. You can also read the Expected 3 to equal 30 message giving the reason why our test fails, and finally the test resume that shows that 4 specs where found but just 1 failure occurred.

 The output for this test displays the failing test at the beginning of the F... string. This might be at the beginning or in another order. That is because the random property in the jasmine.json file is configured to be true, which means random executions. If you want to execute your tests sequentially, change the random property to false.

You have seen how easy it is to use the Jasmine framework to test our code. Of course, you have to learn more about it; we would really like to teach you everything about Jasmine, but that is beyond the scope of this book. We recommend you visit the official site at https://jasmine.github.io/.

Learning KarmaJS

We have explored Jasmine, which basically is a testing framework powered with a cool syntax and functions that help us write the test scripts for our application; in order to execute our test, we had to execute them manually and wait until this finished to see how many tests passed and how many failed.

Karma is a test runner. A test runner is a tool that is configured to look for the test scripts of our application, execute the tests automatically, and export the result of our testing. As we are creating web components with Aurelia, we will need to test our application in different browsers with different characteristics, and as web browsers are different in many ways, we need a way to test our web application in all possible browsers to ensure that our users won't face any problem with our app.

Karma is able to use any testing framework to implement tests. As we have learned Jasmine, we will be using it to write our test scripts, and we will be using Karma to pick up the test files, execute them, and export the results. The following illustrates the flow:

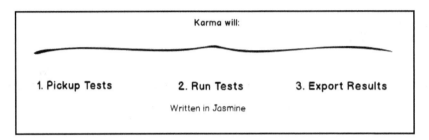

We will see the power of KarmaJS later in this chapter; just keep in mind that Aurelia uses Karma as its test runner for all the projects that you create using the Aurelia CLI, as discussed in `Chapter 1`, *Introducing Aurelia.*

Installing karma

We will use the NPM to install Karma and other dependencies. Let's start creating a practice folder called `practice-karma` and initializing our project. Run the following command:

```
$ mkdir practice-karma
$ cd practice-karma
$ npm init
```

We use `npm init` to create a new module; this will prompt you a bunch of questions and will create a `package.json` file similar to this:

```
{
  "name": "practice-karma",
  "version": "1.0.0",
  "description": "",
  "main": "index.js",
  "scripts": {
```

```
    "test": "echo \"Error: no test specified\" && exit 1"
  },
  "keywords": [],
  "author": "",
  "license": "ISC"
}
```

Up to now, you should have the following folder structure:

```
practice-karma/
 └── package.json
```

Now it's time to install Karma and the dependencies that we require to use Karma and Jasmine. In the `practice-karma` folder, run the following command:

$ npm install karma karma-jasmine jasmine-core karma-chrome-launcher --save-dev

The preceding command will install the dependencies required to use Karma and Jasmine, and also will add the dependencies to our `package.json` file into the `devDependencies` attribute. Open your `package.json` file, and you should see something similar to this:

```
{
  "name": "practice-karma",
  "version": "1.0.0",
  ...
  "devDependencies": {
    "jasmine-core": "^2.8.0",
    "karma": "^1.7.1",
    "karma-chrome-launcher": "^2.2.0",
    "karma-jasmine": "^1.1.1"
  }
}
```

 As we have to use the `--save-dev` flag, the dependencies are listed in the `devDependencies` attribute; if you use `--save` instead, it will list the dependencies in the `dependencies` attribute.

Configuring Karma

Now that Karma is installed, we need to configure the following:

- Jasmine as testing tool
- Folders with the app code

- Web browser launcher
- Reporters

Setting up all the preceding parameters might result in a very time-consuming task, so we will use the Karma executable to configure everything automatically. In the `practice-karma` folder, run the following command:

```
$ karma init
```

This will prompt you a bunch of questions; just press enter to accept all the default configuration, and once everything is done, a `karma.conf.js` file will be created:

```javascript
module.exports = function(config) {
  config.set({
    basePath: '',
    frameworks: ['jasmine'],
    files: [
    ],
    exclude: [
    ],
    preprocessors: {
    },
    reporters: ['progress'],
    port: 9876,
    colors: true,
    logLevel: config.LOG_INFO,
    autoWatch: true,
    browsers: ['Chrome'],
    singleRun: false,
    concurrency: Infinity
  })
}
```

We need to specify a pattern for the files to be utilized in the testing process. To do this, apply the following changes to the `files: []` property:

```javascript
...
files: [
  'specs/*.spec.js'
],
...
```

Now we have specified that every file that ends with .spec.js in its name will be processed by karma. Let's create the specs folder and inside, create the calculator.spec.js file:

```
$ mkdir specs
$ touch calculator.spec.js
```

You should have a project structure similar to the following:

```
.
└── node_modules
├── package.json
├── karma.spec.js
└── specs
    └── calculator.spec.js
```

Now it's time to test things out by creating a testing example.

Testing example

For the Calculator app example, let's create the *src* folder in the root project's folder and create the calculator.js file inside:

```
$ mkdir src
$ touch src/calculator.js
```

As you can see, we are not saving our calculator.js file inside the specs/ folder, so we need to configure karma to load the files present in the src/ folder. Apply the following changes in the karma.conf.js file:

```
...
files: [
        'specs/*.spec.js',
        'src/*.js'
],
...
```

Now, Karma will load all the files from the specs and src folder when testing is running.

Let's implement the code of our `calculator.js` file. Using your editor of choice, open the `src/calculator.js` file and apply the following code:

```
window.Calculator = {

  add: function(n1, n2) {
    return n1 + n2;
  },

  multiply: function(n1, n2) {
    return n1 * n2;
  }

}
```

 If you want to make a variable accessible globally, simply create it as a property of the window object. In this case, we made the `Calculator` object **global**.

Now, let's write our test case. Open the `specs/calculator.spec.js` file and apply the following code:

```
describe("Calculator Tests", function() {

  it("should return 10", function() {

    expect(window.Calculator.add(5, 5)).toBe(10);
  });

});
```

The preceding code should be familiar to you if you note that we are using the Jasmine testing framework to write our tests. Now that we have everything set up and our code implemented, let's continue by launching the tests.

Launching the test runner

Now that we have our test code and a Calculator object, it's time to launch Karma to execute our test. Open the command line and in the `practice-karma` root folder, execute the following command:

```
./node_modules/karma/.bin/karma start karma.conf.js
```

The preceding command will output a bunch of logs, while it opens a new window in your Chrome web browser and executes your test into the web page recently started. This page is opened in Chrome because it is configured in the `karma.conf.js`. Consider this example:

```
$ ./node_modules/karma/bin/karma start karma.conf.js

10 12 2017 12:12:43.049:WARN [karma]: No captured browser, open
http://localhost:9876/
10 12 2017 12:12:43.059:INFO [karma]: Karma v1.7.1 server started at
http://0.0.0.0:9876/
10 12 2017 12:12:43.060:INFO [launcher]: Launching browser Chrome with
unlimited concurrency
10 12 2017 12:12:43.086:INFO [launcher]: Starting browser Chrome
10 12 2017 12:12:44.628:INFO [Chrome 62.0.3202 (Mac OS X 10.12.6)]:
Connected on socket 8n0My3AYk-xKfu9sAAAA with id 38155723
Chrome 62.0.3202 (Mac OS X 10.12.6): Executed 1 of 1 SUCCESS (0 secs /
0.002 secChrome 62.0.3202 (Mac OS X 10.12.6): Executed 1 of 1 SUCCESS
(0.007 secs / 0.002 secs)
```

Note in the last lines that our test was executed with a successful result. The web page launched looks similar to this:

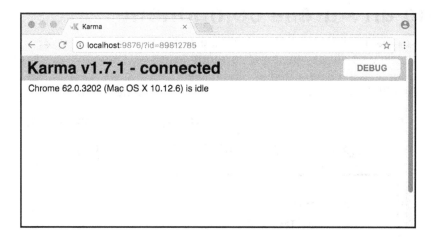

As you might have noted, running the previous command might be too long to remember; to make our life easy, let's configure our `package.json` file to configure the `test` script to execute this command for us. Open the `package.json` files and apply the following changes:

```
{
    "name": "practice-karma",
```

```
...
"scripts": {
  "test": "./node_modules/karma/bin/karma start karma.conf.js"
},
"keywords": [],
"author": "",
"license": "ISC",
"devDependencies": {
  ...
}
}
```

Once configured, execute the following command to run the tests:

```
$ npm test
```

That's it. Using Karma and Jasmine will give us all the enablers we need to write robust tests for our applications. Both technologies are not limited to web development. You can use them in any Javascript project such as a backend written in Node.js. So now, it's time to see an example with a real Aurelia component. Keep reading!

Testing an Aurelia component

In order to see a real testing example, we will create a simple application. This app will merely greet a user and display the topic currently learning. These two pieces of data, the username and topic, will be persisted as bindable entities and we will call this component info-box. We will develop an application similar to the following mock-up:

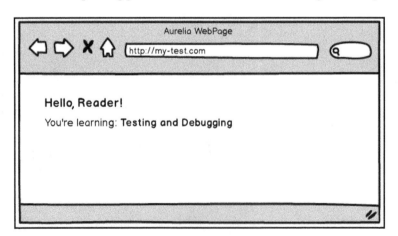

Coding the application

We will use the Aurelia CLI to generate our Aurelia application. Aurelia configures the project to work with the Karma test runner and the Jasmine testing framework and uses Chrome as the default web browser.

Creating the application

To create our application, open your Terminal and in the working directory you prefer, run the following command and accept the defaults:

```
$ au new aurelia-testapp
```

The preceding command will create a new directory called `aurelia-testapp`; let's get into this folder and launch the application by running the following command:

```
$ cd aurelia-testapp
$ au run --watch

. . .
Finished 'writeBundles'
Application Available At: http://localhost:9000
BrowserSync Available At: http://localhost:3001
```

The preceding command will output a bunch of logs while the development server is starting and Aurelia is getting started. Head over to `http://localhost:9000`; and you should see something similar to the following:

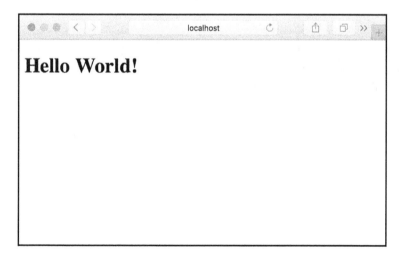

Creating our component

To create our `info-box` component, we will use the Aurelia CLI. Stop the running application and execute the following command. This will ask you for the destination folder; press *Enter* to use `src` as default:

```
$ au generate component info-box


What sub-folder would you like to add it to?
If it doesn't exist it will be created for you.

Default folder is the source folder (src).

[.]>
Created info-box in the 'src' folder
```

This command will create two files that together define the `info-box` component; these files are as listed:

- `info-box.js`: Contains the component's view model
- `info-box.html`: Contains the HTML view template

Let's implement our `info-box` component.

Implementing the info-box view model

Open the `info-box.js` file and apply the following changes to declare the `username` and `topic` attributes:

```
export class InfoBox {
  constructor() {
    this.username = 'Reader';
    this.topic = 'Testing and Debugging';
  }
}
```

Implementing the info-box view HTML template

Open the `info-box.js` file and apply the following changes to bind our attributes to the HTML template:

```
<template>
  <h1>Hello, ${username}!</h1>
  <p>You are learning: <b>${topic} </b></p>
</template>
```

Rendering the info-box component

To load and render our component, we need to import the component into the app component. Open the `app.html` file and apply the following changes:

```
<template>
  <require from="info-box"></require>

  <info-box></info-box>
</template>
```

First, we import the `info-box` component and then use it using the `<info-box>` tag syntax. With changes done, launch the application again by running the `au run --watch` command:

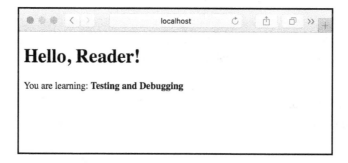

Writing the test

Before we start writing our test, let's clean up the `test` folder by removing the `app.spec.js` file in the `unit` folder. Once completed, you should have something similar to folder tree:

```
.
├── aurelia-karma.js
└── unit
    └── setup.js
```

In the `unit` folder, create the `info-box.spec.js` file and add the following code:

```
import {StageComponent} from 'aurelia-testing';
import {bootstrap} from 'aurelia-bootstrapper';

describe('Info-Box', () => {

  it('should render the username and topic', () => {

  });
});
```

First, we import two objects from the Aurelia framework that we will use to initialize our `info-box` component. Then, we declare our `Info-Box` test suite and we declare one test case.

Note that we are using a special syntax; instead of using `function() {}`, we are using `() => {}` ECMAScript syntax. To unit test our component, we will need to perform the following steps:

1. Bootstrap the component
2. Test the component

Bootstrapping the component

We will need to create the component so that Jasmine will use it to apply the test. Apply the following changes in the `info-box.spec.js` file:

```
import {StageComponent} from 'aurelia-testing';
import {bootstrap} from 'aurelia-bootstrapper';

describe('Info-Box', () => {
```

```
it('should render the username and topic', done => {

    let component = StageComponent
                .withResources('info-box')
                .inView('<info-box></info-box>');

    component
    .create(bootstrap);
  });

});
```

Before we bootstrap the component, it has to be created. We use the `StageComponent` object to instantiate an Aurelia component; we specify the component by passing its name as a param of the `withResources` function. Lastly, we specify a view using the `<info-box>` element in the `inView` function.

Once we have the component skeleton defined, we call its `create` function and pass the `bootstrap` object. The `bootstrap` object contains the default configuration specified in the `main.js` file, as discussed in `Chapter 1`, *Introducing Aurelia.*

Testing the component

Now that we have our component created, we need to test it. To do this, we rely on the done callback passed to the test function to notify Jasmine that the test is done. If we don't specify the done parameter, our test won't be executed because we execute our assertions in a promise and if we don't call it, we will get a timeout error since Jasmine won't be able to know when our test completed. Let's apply the following changes to the `info-box.spec.js` file:

```
import {StageComponent} from 'aurelia-testing';
import {bootstrap} from 'aurelia-bootstrapper';

describe('Info-Box', () => {

  it('should render the username and topic', done => {
    let component = StageComponent
                .withResources('info-box')
                .inView('<info-box></info-box>');

    component
    .create(bootstrap)
    .then(() => {
```

```
const h1 = component.element.querySelector('h1').innerHTML;
const pa = component.element.querySelector('p').innerHTML;

expect(h1).toBe('Hello, Reader!');
expect(pa).toBe('You are learning: <b>Testing and Debugging </b>');

done();

})
.catch(e => console.log(e.toString()));
});
});
```

You should be aware that if you are using Webpack, you might need to import PLATFORM from the `aurelia-pal` module in order to load the `info-box` resource as follows—`.withResourceS(PLATFORM.moduleName('info-box'))`. For additional Webpack considerations, visit the official site at https://aurelia.io/docs/build-systems/webpack.

In the `then` function, we pass our callback that will use the `component.element.querySelector` function to access the HTML elements into the `info-box` component, and we use the `innerHTML` property of the elements to access the element's values.

Next, we compare the values of the elements by the expected values and when all the `expect` statements are executed, we call the `done()` function to tell Jasmine we have finished this test case.

Lastly, a `catch` callback is passed to print any error detected in the test process. Once everything is complete, run the following command in your Terminal:

```
$ au karma
```

If everything went right, the Chrome web browser should be opened and you should see the following output in your Terminal window:

```
. . .
Starting 'karma'...
. . .
Chrome 62.0.3202 (Mac OS X 10.12.6): Executed 1 of 1 SUCCESS (0 secs /
0.105 secChrome 62.0.3202 (Mac OS X 10.12.6): Executed 1 of 1 SUCCESS
(0.109 secs / 0.105 secs)
Finished 'karma'
```

That's it! Now you know how to test Aurelia components. A little challenge for you is to apply everything learned in a TDD cycle. Have fun!

Debugging our code

Debugging tools are extremely important for a developer. It does not matter which programming language or framework you are using, or if you are working on either frontend or backend project. Debugging will always be present in your development process.

Nowadays, the web browser does more than just server pages, caching content, saving favorites, and so on. They are complete web development tools that provide awesome tools to debug our code and application performance.

Let's see how we can debug our code using our favorite web browser. We will use Chrome Developer Tools as an example.

Refactoring our application

First, we need to start our application and open it in a web browser. Let's use our `aurelia-testapp`:

```
$ cd aurelia-testapp
$ au run --watch
```

With the application up and running, head over to `http://localhost:9000` to see the application. We will add a button and when the button is pressed, we will debug some dummy code. Open the `info-box.html` file and apply the following change:

```
<template>
  <button click.trigger="debugme()"> Debug Me!</button>

</template>
```

Open the `info-box.js` file and apply the following changes:

```
export class InfoBox {
  debugme() {
    alert("YOU PRESSED THE DEBUGME BUTTON")

  }

}
```

Go back to your browser application, click on the **Debug Me!** button, and you should see the following on the screen:

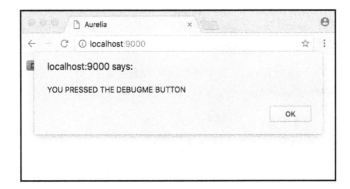

Debugging with Chrome Developer Tools

We need to open the Chrome Developer Tools. To do this, go to the **View** | **Developer** | **Developer tools** option in the menu or press *F12*. You should see something like the following:

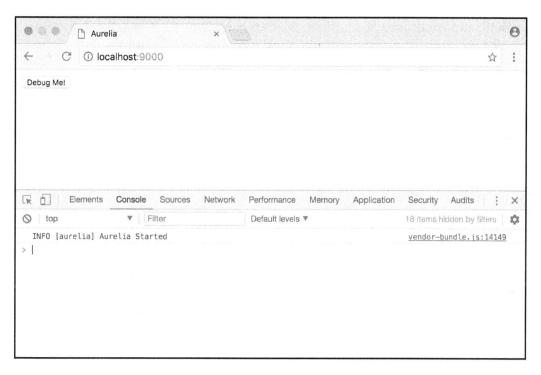

With this window open, let's apply a little change to our `info-box` file to tell the browser that we want to stop and debug our code:

```
export class InfoBox {
  debugme() {

    debugger;

    alert("YOU PRESSED THE DEBUGME BUTTON")

  }

}
```

Go back to your application and click on the **Debug Me!** button. The `debugger;` instruction will stop the browser execution and enter into the browser debugging mode:

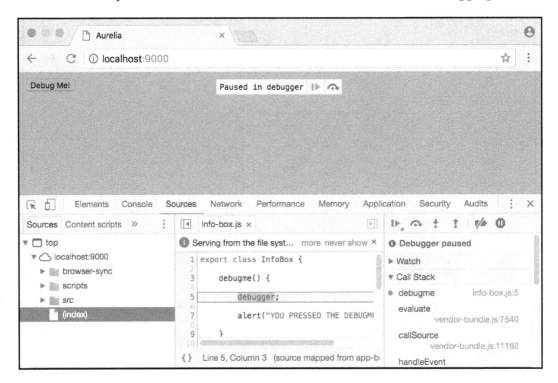

You can use the Developer Tools options to navigate your code, analyze variables values, add breakpoints, and so on. I personally prefer to debug my code in this way. You can try debugging code using the Node.js command line or another type of debugging. Debugging tools will vary depending on the web browser you are working on.

Now that we are in good shape and we know how to style and test Aurelia applications, it's time to learn how to create awesome Aurelia components. Keep reading!

Summary

In this chapter, we explored the benefits that good testing brings to our company, team, products, and users. Good testing will always make our products better and our users happy.

We learned how to apply TDD to our software development process and the importance and impact it has on the quality of our apps. You should always remember that TDD is composed of three colored phases: the red phase, which makes your test fail; the blue phase, which makes your test pass; and lastly, the green phase, which refactors and cleans your code.

We also learned about the testing technologies that Aurelia uses for development and learned how to use them independently. Jasmine is the testing framework and Karma is used as the test runner.

We practiced with a real testing example of an Aurelia component and we explored some debugging options.

Now that we are in good shape and know how to style and test Aurelia applications, it's time to become real experts in creating Aurelia components. So, keep reading!

4
Creating Components and Templates

Welcome to the second part of this book and congratulations for coming here! Now that you know the basic principles and techniques of programming in JavaScript, it's time to go deeper and know much better about some advantages offered by the wonderful framework that is Aurelia. Our starting point in this chapter will be to understand what is a component and how we can manage its life cycle through events that are taking place in our application. Then, we will explore the dependencies injection, a well-known design pattern used by most popular frameworks such as Java EE, Spring, and Aurelia! Our main focus will be to explain how we can manage our DOM and dynamically display the data on the screen, configure routes to access certain functionalities in our application, and, of course, apply everything learned in our FIFA World Cup application. This chapter will cover a lot of very useful concepts, some of them are:

- Creating components
- Dependency Injection pattern
- Component's life cycle/events
- Data binding
- Aurelia router
- Testing components

Let's start!

Lego components

Most modern frontend JavaScript frameworks provide some sort of support for component-based development. This is an incredibly important step in the direction of development for the web. Components provide a way to write small parts with a consistent API that can easily be orchestrated as part of a larger screen, application, or system. Imagine each component as a Lego piece—you can use it wherever you want and it will keep the same shape and behavior.

A component can be an HTML part, a JavaScript piece of code, a service, and so on. Any reusable part should be interpreted as a component.

A little puzzle

Let's practice a little how to think and abstract one application into a few components. Here's some web template with some sections:

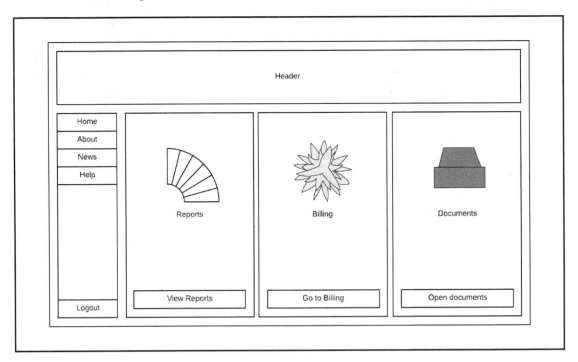

Now, it's time to think.

How many sections are similar?

- Buttons are very similar; just the text/color can change
- Menu options can be a reusable single component
- Main page sections are the same; just the content changes
- The header can be decoupled from the application main section

Which sections do you think can be reused across application pages, take a look:

- Main page sections can be used as a container for other options
- The buttons can be shared across all the application sections

Last, but not the least, do you think you need to refresh the entire page when you submit or just some sections?

A better option can be to refresh only what really needs to be refreshed. Each section can independently manage their data and the way it's retrieved.

Of course, all these answers depend on the business rules of the application, but the principles are always the same. If you find some section of your application that can be reused, reloaded, managed, and maintained independently of other sections, you should decouple it into a single component.

Once you have defined what parts of your application will be a component, it's time to organize. You must identify which components will be used just for some page in particular (maybe an Item component for a shopping cart page), how many of them will be shared across the entire application (a common table to be used into many reports of your application) and finally, organize them by separated groups:

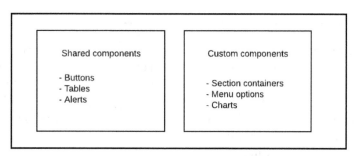

Now, let's create one folder per component; you should keep in mind that if some component will be *parent* of another component, the *child* folder should be created inside the parent, to specify ownership. Remember always that as a programmer, your main goal is to make your code readable and understandable to other developers—that's a good quality measure!

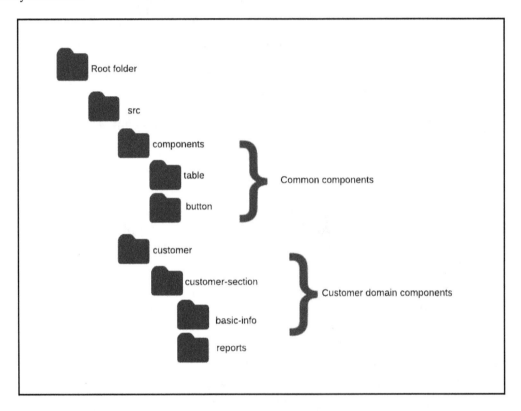

At this point, we now have our folder structure created for our components. An Aurelia component is basically composed of two files: the HTML template, called **view**, is rendered into the DOM. The .js file, called **view model**, is written in ES Next, and it defines the behavior and provides data for the view. The templating engine, along with **dependency injection (DI)**, that we will explain in detail in the following sections, is responsible for creating and enforcing a predictable life cycle for the component. Once the component is instantiated, Aurelia's data binding links the two pieces together, allowing changes in your view model to be reflected in the view and vice versa. This separation of concerns allows us to work/collaborate with designers and improve our product quality. Let's create one component as an example:

```
/**card-component.js**/

export class CardComponent {

  cardTitle;

  constructor(){
    this.cardTitle = 'Card component example'
  }

}
```

```
<!--card-component.html-->

<template>
  <div class="card" >

    <div class="card-header">
      <h2>${cardTitle}</h2>
    </div>
    <div class="card-body">
    </div>

  </div>
</template>
```

You should remember some good practices about naming your components:

- Use dashes for naming your components. For example, <my-component> and <my-other-component> are valid name syntax, while <my_component>, <myComponent> and <my_other_component> are not. You must keep this notation, because the HTML parser will differentiate between custom and regular elements.
- You can't register an already existing tag.
- Custom elements are not self-closing. Only native HTML attributes allows this feature. Ensure that you write a closing tag (<my-component></my-component>).

Our first component is created, hard coded, and works. Wait a second... how does the .html template know that my .js file is correct for retrieving data? Aurelia works under one premise: convention over configuration. What does that mean? If we use the same name for both files, the framework automatically will map that JavaScript file managing the .html template, we do not write any configuration code (different from other frameworks). Now, it's time to integrate it into our main page.

We just need to import the filename with the <require> tag. For other reasons, this tag will be in the top section of the page. Then, we just call the component:

```
<!--main-template.html-->

<template>
 <require from="./components/card-component"></require> //Remember to add
the close tag

 <div class="main-content">
    <card-component></card-component>
 </div>

</template>
```

Launch your application, and you will see your component in action. In this case, we just defined one single property to be rendered from the .js file to our template. This is a very basic example, so don't worry, the action is coming!

Learning how DI works

DI is based on the Inversion of control pattern. Let's explain that.

Imagine that we create a web application without Aurelia. You will have to manually implement something like this:

1. Load/instantiate a view model
2. Load/instantiate a view
3. Bind the view to the view model
4. Append the view to the DOM
5. Handle click on a link by user.
6. Parse the URL hash, determine which view model to load/instantiate, check whether the current view can be deactivated, and more
7. Rinse and repeat

Again, and many more times. Without Aurelia, you are implementing the logic that controls the application life cycle instead of your application business logic and features.

Now, let's create one using Aurelia. You won't work on any configuration code at the application level because the framework does that job for you. Instead, you focus on writing the views, view models, behaviors, and routes that embody your application's custom logic and appearance. Aurelia inverts the control, handling the application life cycle while allowing you to define your own features and behavior of the application. How? Through life cycle hooks.

Life cycle hooks are optional methods you attach to view models. Aurelia's router and the templating engine will invoke these methods at the appropriate time, allowing you to control specific life cycle steps.

We will explore all these methods deeper in the following sections; at the moment, we will focus only on **Inversion of Control (IoC)** and DI features.

Aurelia uses the IoC pattern to reduce the work required to build applications. You can specify and control them however you want using overridable conventions and hooks when the application starts/ends.

DI uses the same pattern for resolving dependencies. A dependency is an object that can be used, or more specifically, a service. Using this pattern, you made that service a part of the state of the client object, because you are passing that entire service rather than allowing the client to build or find the service.

DI needs an injector. This injector is responsible to provide and construct the service object and define that inside the client's state. The client is not allowed to directly call the injector code. It only waits until all its dependencies are satisfied.

Two modules are the key enablers for the DI pattern's application in Aurelia:

- **dependency-injection**: An extensible and very lightweight DI container for JavaScript
- **metadata**: Provides a consistent way of accessing type, annotation, and origin metadata across a number of languages and formats

To illustrate how the DI works, let's define a typical view model class with some external services injected. The code should be something like this:

```
import CustomerService from './services/customer-service'

@inject(CustomerService)
export class CustomerComponent {
```

```
constructor(customerService){
  this.customerService = customerService
}

}
```

Now, let's analyze that code. How is this view model created at runtime?

Aurelia takes care of the creation order of each element, but how does it work? Well, first of all, Aurelia uses the DI container to instantiate all view models. As we said earlier, the client object doesn't instantiate or locate their own dependencies. They rely on Aurelia to supply the dependencies as constructor arguments.

How are these dependencies discovered?

In an object oriented language (such as Java), the DI container can identify each dependency by its type. In the case of Aurelia, the dependencies, implementations are determined using the constructor arguments order list. In JavaScript, we can store a variety of information about our components or application as metadata. We don't have the chance to define a type-based constructor to define our objects. To deal with this situation, we must embed this information on the class itself, as *metadata*.

We can use decorators to add a customized constructor signature to our classes, based on types to be consumed by the Aurelia's DI container. This is exactly what the annotation @inject (CustomerService) performs in the view model file. If you are a TypeScript user, you can use the emitDecoratorMetadata flag, used for the same purpose of adding a constructor info to our classes. Just add the @autoInject() decorator to your class; in this case, the constructor parameter types are not needed.

View models written in this way are easy to test and modularize. You can split a big class into small components and inject them to achieve the goal. Remember that large classes are hard to maintain and are very vulnerable to rely on the anti-pattern *spaghetti code*.

Dependency resolution is a recursive process. Let's explain that—our customer view model has a dependency on the CustomerService file. When the DI container instantiates the CustomerComponent class, it first needs to retrieve the CustomerService instance or instantiate one if it doesn't already exist in the container. The CustomerService may have dependencies of its own, which the DI container will recursively resolve until the full dependency chain has been identified.

You can have as many injected dependencies as you need. Simply ensure that the inject decorator and the constructor match one another.

In case you are not using Babel or TypeScript decorator support, you can provide the inject metadata using a static method in your class:

```
import {CustomerService} from 'backend/customer-service';
import {CommonAlerts} from 'resources/dialogs/common-dialogs';
import {EventAggregator} from 'aurelia-event-aggregator';

export class CustomerProfileScreen {

  static inject() { return [CustomerService, CommonAlerts,
EventAggregator]; }

  constructor(customerService, alerts, ea) {
    this.customerService = customerService;
    this.alerts = alerts;
    this.ea = ea;
  }

}
```

Static methods and properties are supported. The inject decorator simply sets the static property automatically. Why use it? Just to make our syntax more elegant and understandable.

Managing a component's life cycle

As we said earlier, Aurelia provides very complete life cycle event methods to customize and improve the behavior of our application. Here's a list with these methods:

```
export class ComponentLifecycleExample {

  retrievedData;

  constructor(service) {
    // Create and initialize your class object here...
    this.service = service;
  }

  created(owningView, myView) {
    // Invoked once the component is created...
  }

  bind(bindingContext, overrideContext) {
    // Invoked once the databinding is activated...
  }
```

```
attached(argument) {
  // Invoked once the component is attached to the DOM...
  this.retrievedData = this.service.getData();
}

detached(argument) {
  // Invoked when component is detached from the dom
  this.retrievedData = null;
}

unbind(argument) {
  // Invoked when component is unbound...
}

}
```

Let's explore each method presented in the script:

constructor(): This is the first method that is called. It's used to set all view model dependencies and values required for its instantiation.

The constructor method can be used for instantiating and initializing attributes to your component, and they should not necessarily be declared previously:

```
constructor(){
  this.customerName = 'Default name'
  this.placeholderText = 'Insert customer name here'
}
```

Also, you can initialize variables using class methods:

```
constructor(){
  this.date = this.getCurrentDate()
}

getCurrentDate(){
  //Method implementation
}
```

created(owningView, myView): Next, the created method is called. At this point, the view has been created and belongs to the view model; they are connected to the controller. This callback will receive the view declared inside of the (owningView) component. If the component itself has a view, it is passed as second parameter, (myView).

`bind(bindingContext, overrideContext)`: At this point, the binding has started. If the view model has the `bind()` callback overridden, it will be called at this time. The first argument represents the binding context of the component. The second parameter is used for adding additional contextual properties.

`attached()`: The `attached` callback is executed once the component is ready for use. It means instantiated and has its properties set and computed correctly.

This method is perfect for retrieving data or set properties if you are using injected service methods. You can configure different ways to load your data, show loading alerts for the user, and increase the user experience. Let's see a quick example:

```
export class ComponentExample {

  dataList
  constructor(){
    // Constructor's code
  }
  attached(){
    this.showLoader(true);
    this.service.retrieveAllData()
                .then( data => {
                    this.dataList = data.getBody()
                    this.showLoader(false)
                    this.showAlert('Data retrieved correctly!!!')
                })
                .catch( error => {
                  console.log(error)
                  this.showLoader(false)
                  this.showAlert('Oops! We have some errors retrieving
data!')
                })
  }
}
```

As you can see, we can define fallback alerts or methods to ensure that we are handling errors correctly (just if needed).

`detached()`: Called when the component will be removed from the DOM. Different from the previous methods, this method is not executed when the application starts.

The same as the previous example, we can define this method to restore the data to a previous state, delete local storage data, and so on.

`unbind()`: Called when the component is unbound.

You should remember that each of these life cycle callbacks is optional. Just override what you really need. The execution order is the same as the list order mentioned earlier.

Managing events with Aurelia

We were explaining how to override and catch determined events and methods in the component life cycle, but what if we want to write our own methods and execute them when the user clicks on some button or moves the mouse for one section? We will start to *delegate* events.

The event delegation concept is a useful concept where the event handler is attached to one single element instead of multiple elements on the DOM. What implies that? Memory efficiency. It drastically reduces the number of event subscriptions by leveraging the *bubbling* characteristic of most DOM events.

On the other hand, we have the trigger concept. Similar, but not equal. You should use trigger binding when you need to subscribe to events that do not bubble (blur, focus, load, and unload).

Some examples are as listed:

- You need to disable a button, input, or another element
- The element's content is made up of other elements (reusable component)

In code words, it can be explained like this:

```
<select change.delegate="myEventCallback($event)" ></select>
```

In your view model, you should have the method implemented with the correct number of params, so each time the `<select>` element changes, the event will be delegated to your custom function to handle it:

```
export class TriggerAndDelegateExample {

  myEventCallback(event){
    console.log(event)
  }

}
```

Now, let's `trigger` the same method:

```
<div class="option-container"
focus.trigger="myEventCallback($event)"></div>
```

Note that we are using `trigger` binding to catch a not bubbling event.

In your daily work, maybe `delegate` and `trigger` could be enough for managing events, but there are some situations where you will need to know a little more advanced features to deal with it. Imagine that you are integrating a third-party plugin and need to interact with this content. Normally, `trigger` or `delegate` should do the work, but this won't be the case.

Let's look at an example:

```
<div class='my-plugin-container' click.delegate='onClickPluginContainer()'>
    <plugin-element></plugin-element>
</div>
```

But why? Remember that you are dealing with a third-party plugin, so this will manage its events independently of the `container` component. That being said, the inner plugin will call `event.stopPropagation()` on any click events.

So what can we do in that case? Don't worry, you have another option—the `capture` command:

```
<div class='my-plugin-container' click.capture='onClickPluginContainer()'>
  <plugin-element></plugin-element>
</div>
```

Now, the method will be executed correctly. Again, the most important question, why? It's because with the `capture` command, the `onClickPluginContainer()` event is guaranteed to happen irrespective of whether `event.stopPropagation()` is called or not inside the container.

Now, at this point, maybe you are wondering "So...what command should I use? Which of these is better?" The answer is simple—it depends on what you need. We recommend that you use `delegate`, because you will improve your application performance. Then, use `trigger` only if the event requires this, and finally, use `capture` if you will deal with third-party plugins or elements that you can't control, but remember that this last one is not commonly used and is not how you should normally work with browser events.

You can find more info about delegate and trigger in the official docs: `https://aurelia.io/docs/binding/delegate-vs-trigger/`

Data binding

Aurelia has its own data binding system. Let's explain that with an example.

You know that you need to define a view and a view model file for each Aurelia component. Binding is the process that reflects the view model data into the view, and vice versa. As we said earlier, one of Aurelia's most beautiful features is double-binding framework, so you won't have to worry about updating the data on the view or view model.

Aurelia supports HTML and SVG attributes to JavaScript expressions. The binding attribute declaration is composed of three parts:

```
attribute.commamnd = "expression"
```

Let's explain each one:

`attribute`: Refers to the HTML/SVG attribute we will apply to the binding. For example, one input tag could have defined the following attributes:

```
<input  value="someValue" id="inputId"  />
```

`value` and `id` will be the attributes we could refer.

`command`: Here, you will use one of Aurelia's binding commands:

- **one-time**: Flows data to one direction, from view model to view, just once.
- **to-view / one-way**: Flows data in one direction, from view model to view.
- **from-view:** Flows data in one direction, from view to view model.
- **two-way**: Default behavior, flows data from view model to view and vice versa.
- **bind**: Automatically chooses the binding mode. It uses two-way binding for form controls and to-view binding for almost everything else.

Let's use the same input element defined earlier as an example:

```
<input  value.from-view="userInputValue" id.bind="editableId"  />
<input  value.one-time="defaultInputValue" id.one-way="generatedId"  />
```

The first `input` element uses the `from-view` command to bind anything the user writes in the `input` element, but this value cannot be changed and reflected from the `view-model` into the `view`. The `id` attribute uses the `two-way` binding, so this `id` can be updated in the view layer and reflected in the view model. The second binds the `value` attribute just once, then any update to this value will be ignored. In the case of the `id` attribute, it is generated by the `view-model` file, and any modification from `view` won't be reflected on `view-model`.

`expression`: The last part. Commonly a JavaScript expression used to reflect `view-model` attributes, computed properties, and so on. Again, let's use the same `input` element for example purposes:

```
<input   value.from-view="modelValue" id.bind="formName + randomNumber"   />
```

The `value` attribute just reflects the `modelValue` property into the view. The `id` attribute is performing an operation to attach a random number generated in the view model into one predefined property and use it as a single value to bind.

The same way that as event managing part, there could be some situations that you will need to use a little more advanced features to get the expected results. Commonly, you may deal with situations where you have `@bindable` properties while developing custom elements/attributes. These properties expect a reference to a function, so just use the `call` binding command to declare and pass a function to the bindable property. The `call` command is superior to the `bind` command for this use case, because it will execute the function in the correct context, ensuring that this is what you expect it to be:

```
<custom-element go.call="doSomething()"></custom-element>
```

`go` is the `@bindable` attribute, and `doSomething()` is your `view-model` function.

One more feature you can add to your application is string interpolation. These expressions enable interpolating the result of an expression with text. The best way to demonstrate this capability is with an example. Here are two `span` elements with data-bound `textcontent`:

```
<span textcontent.bind="'Hello' + name"></span>

<span>Hello ${name}</span>
```

At this point, we know the basic concepts about Aurelia's binding engine. Now, let's use this great feature in more advanced ways to improve our application!

We have explored in Chapter 2, *Styling the User Interface*, some ways to add CSS to our application and make it look great. However, in your daily work, you can find some common situation that will make you 'mix' some features.

Here's one:

You are writing a dashboard page and depending on user status (active, inactive), the **Submit** button should look colorful or just disabled with a different shape.

You can bind an element's class attribute using string interpolation or with .bind/.one-time:

```
<template>
  <button class="btn ${isActive ? 'btn-active' : 'blocked-btn'}
submit"></button>
  <button class.bind="isActive ? 'btn-active' : 'blocked-btn'"></button>
  <button class.one-time="isActive ? 'btn-active' : 'blocked-
btn'"></button>
</template>
```

Using ternary operations, you can say to your view which class should be rendered into the view. Let's analyze the first:

- isActive refers to a boolean property defined in view model.
- ? is the ternary operator. If the condition is true, the first argument will be used, in this case, the 'btn-active' class.
- : represents the else element of the condition. If it's evaluated to false, the second argument after the : will be used.

Aurelia allows you to use external JavaScript libraries. It supports, on its binding system, only adding or removing the specified classes in the binding expression.

In this way, classes added by other code (for example, classList.add(...)) are not removed. This behavior implies a small cost, noticeable only in benchmarks or some critical situations like iteration of large lists. Replace the default behavior by binding directly to the element's className property using class-name.bind="....", or class-name.one-time="..." can be a better option; so much faster.

Similar to classes, you can bind style attributes directly into the DOM. Remember that defining styles directly into the element is not wrong, but using classes, you can add more standardization to your elements and make this easy to maintain. Like other HTML attributes, you can use style.bind to retrieve style definitions from your view-model.

For example, let's define one array of styles:

```
export class StyleExample {
  constructor() {
    this.styleAsString = 'color: red; background-color: blue';

    this.styleAsObject = {
      color: 'red',
      'background-color': 'blue'
    };
  }
}
```

Then, in the view file, we just need to bind the predefined properties:

```
<template>
    <div style.bind="styleAsString"></div>
    <div style.bind="styleAsObject"></div>
</template>
```

You can use string interpolation too:

```
<div style="width: ${width}px; height: ${height}px;"></div>
```

However, if you need to add compatibility with Internet Explorer and Edge, this syntax will be illegal. In those cases, you must use the css attribute:

```
<div css="width: ${width}px; height: ${height}px;"></div>
```

Binding computed properties

Sometimes it is desirable to return a dynamically computed value (post-processed value) when accessing a property, or you may want to reflect the status of an internal variable without requiring the use of explicit method calls. In JavaScript, this can be accomplished with the use of a getter function:

```
export class Developer {
  firstName = 'Erikson';
  lastName = 'Murrugarra';

  get fullName() {
    return `${this.firstName} ${this.lastName}`;
  }
}
```

There's no trick here, you just need to bind the `fullName` property. The binding system will analyze the property and how we are referring to a function; it will process the required info before rendering the computed value. This is also called **dirty checking**; it will be constantly observing if some property changes its value, and if it has some repercussions on the computed element, it will be re-evaluated and reprocessed. Sounds like a multiple execution of the same method? Yes, your getter function will be called so many times, approximately once every 120 milliseconds. That's not an issue, but if we have a lot of computed properties or if our getter functions are a little complex, you should consider indicating to the binding systems which properties you want to observe; at this point, dirty checking is avoided. This is where the `@computedFrom` decorator comes in:

```
import {computedFrom} from 'aurelia-framework';

export class Developer {
  firstName = 'Erikson';
  lastName = 'Murrugarra';

  @computedFrom('firstName', 'lastName')
  get fullName() {
    return `${this.firstName} ${this.lastName}`;
  }
}
```

`@computedFrom` will tell the binding system which properties need to be observed. When those expressions change, the binding system will reevaluate the property (execute the getter). This eliminates the need for dirty checking and can improve performance.

Value converters

As we explained before coming across this topic, user interface elements in Aurelia are composed of two files: view and view model pairs. The view is written in pure HTML and is rendered into the DOM. The view model is written in JavaScript and provides data and behavior to the view. Aurelia links the two files together, as one single element using its powerful data binding engine, allowing changes in your view model to be reflected in the view and vice versa. Sometimes the data showed by your view model is not in a good or understandable format for displaying in the UI. Dealing with date and numeric values are the most common scenarios:

```
export class Example {
  constructor() {
    this.showRawData();
  }
```

```
showRawData() {
  this.currentDate = new Date();
  this.someNumber = Math.random() * 1000000000;
  }
}
```

Our view should look like this:

```
<template>
        ${currentDate} <br/>
        ${someNumber}
</template>
```

This code will give us the current date and some random number; well, that's what we are expecting and that's okay, but let's see how this data is displayed:

```
Sun Dec 31 2017 18:04:45 GMT-0500 (-05)
936693540.3380567
```

That's definitely not friendly for user reading. A cool solution to this problem can be to compute the formatted values and expose them as properties of the `view-model` file. This is a valid approach, but remember that we are overloading our model with extra properties and methods; it can be a little messy in the future, especially when you need to keep the formatted values in sync when the original property value change. Fortunately, Aurelia has a feature to help us deal with these situations.

The most common option will be to create value converters to translate the model data into a readable format for the view. All okay at this point, but what happens if it is the view that needs to convert the value for sending it into a format acceptable for the `view-model`?

Aurelia value converters are quite similar to other value converters of another languages, such as XAML. The nice thing is that Aurelia comes with some notable improvements:

- The Aurelia `ValueConverter` interface uses two methods: `toView` and `fromView`. These methods define the direction the data is flowing in.
- Aurelia value converter methods can accept multiple parameters.
- Aurelia allows you to use multiple value converters in one single property, just using pipes (|).

Let's look at an example to convert our date property into a more friendly readable value:

```
import moment from 'moment';

export class DateFormatValueConverter {

  toView(value) {
    return moment(value).format('M/D/YYYY h:mm:ss a');
  }

}
```

Our `view-model` file won't change:

```
export class Example {
  constructor() {
    this.showRawData();
  }

  showRawData() {
    this.currentDate = new Date();
    this.someNumber = Math.random() * 1000000000;
  }
}
```

However, our `view-model` file will look quite different at this time:

```
<template>
    <require from="./date-format"></require>
    ${currentDate | dateFormat} <br/>
    ${someNumber}
</template>
```

With this value converter, we'll see this value on the screen:

```
12/31/2017 6:25:05 pm
```

This looks much better. Again, it's time to ask the more important question—why? Let's examine what we did. First, we created our value converter class called `DateFormatValueConverter` and implemented the `toView` method. Aurelia will execute this method and apply to the model values before displaying the data on screen. For converting purposes, we are using MomentJS. Next, we've updated the `view` file and added `<require>` tags to import our value converter class into the view that will use it.

When the framework processes the resource, it examines the class's metadata to determine the resource type (custom element, custom attribute, value converter, and such). Metadata isn't required, and in fact, our value converters didn't expose any. If you are curious, you must note something—we used the `ValueConverter` postfix to name our converter class. Again, why? It's because you must remember that one of the Aurelia bases is convention over configuration. In this way, the name ending with `ValueConverter` will be assumed to be one value converter.

Now we will show you a little more advanced example. Let's apply some changes to our class converter:

```
import moment from 'moment';

export class DateFormatValueConverter {
  toView(value, format) {
    return moment(value).format(format);
  }

}
```

The `view-model` file is still the same. Now, our template file will change again:

```
<template>
      <require from="./date-format"></require>

      ${currentDate | dateFormat:'M/D/YYYY h:mm:ss a'} <br/>
      ${currentDate | dateFormat:'MMMM Mo YYYY'} <br/>
      ${currentDate | dateFormat:'h:mm:ss a'} <br/>
</template>
```

Now we can use the same value converter class to render data in different formats, according to our view demands.

Without any doubt, we have covered some of the most important features of Aurelia's binding behavior, but, for sure, there are more methods and commands that we will see in practice. For the moment, we are ready to pass to another important concept—routing.

Routing and resources

Routing is one of the most important parts of a web application. We already have our application deployed in `http://localhost:9000`, but it's time to start defining names and addresses for our resources. First, we need to define what a resource is. Conceptually, a resource is every related data belonging to one single object or element. For example, a person resource can have fields such as name, address, birthday, and more. So, expanding this, a resource can be a list of persons too. We will talk deeply about how your resources should be named, organized, and called, but at this moment, you just need to know the basics. In a web application, every resource has its own address. Let's look at an example:

We have an address book with some contacts:

- `http://localhost:9000/` is the server URL, the base of all resources, the father path. Generally related to the home/welcome page, or first you define the user's view. The page has a button to see all our contacts.
- `http://locahost:9000/persons` is a URL related to the person list resource. Here, we will show a list of persons of our address book. You are able to pick one to see its contact details.
- `http://locahost:9000/persons/p001` will refer to the person with the p001 ID. Here, we will be able to see its details. If you give this URL to another user, they should be able to see the same data as you, because this URL belongs to one single contact—the p001.
- `http://locahost:9000/persons?search=p001` is a little different. Imagine that our contact list is composed of more than 500 people. Don't you think it could be easier for the user search them by ID, name, or the most generic parameter? Here, we are using a query-param to express our search criteria; of course, we're still working with our friend p001.

Now, let's configure our application to be ready for routing.

At this point, we have already created some components in our application. If not, don't worry, we will have enough time to practice that in the last part of this chapter.

Now, let's add some code to our `app.js` file. Remember that this file should be located in the base `src` folder of our application, since now it will represent our base route for all the applications:

```
export class App {
  configureRouter(config, router) {
    this.router = router;
    config.title = 'Aurelia';
```

```
config.map([
    { route: ['', 'home'],          name: 'home',          moduleId:
'home/index' },
    { route: 'users',               name: 'users',         moduleId:
'users/index', nav: true,           title: 'Users' },
    { route: 'users/:id/detail',    name: 'userDetail', moduleId:
'users/detail' },
    { route: 'files/*path',         name: 'files',         moduleId:
'files/index', nav: false,   title: 'Files', href:'#files' }
  ]);
  }
}
```

Let's analyze the properties and methods used to define our routes:

- `configureRouter(config, router)` is a reserved method that the framework will evaluate in the base `view-model` when the application starts. The parameters are referencing to the `Router`, `RouterConfiguration` from `aurelia-router` package. If they are not provided, the framework will inject them automatically.

- `this.router = router` is a reference to the router element, just to allow us to access this from the view layer (`app.html`), allowing us to build navigation menus dynamically.

- `config.title` refers to our application title displayed in the browser window. Technically, it's applied to the `<title>` element in the `<head>` of the HTML document.

- `config.map()` adds route(s) to the router. Although only route, name, moduleId, href, and nav were shown earlier, there are other properties that can be included in a route. The interface name for a route is `RouteConfig`. You can also use `config.mapRoute()` to add a single route.

- route is the pattern to match against the incoming URL fragments. It can be a string or array of strings. The route can contain parameterized routes or wildcards as well.

Now, let's analyze the routes we've created:

- In the first `route` element, the first flag, `route`, is making reference to the base path (`''`) and the `home` path. If we directly access `http//:localhost:9000/` or `http//:localhost:9000/home`, the application will display the same page. The `name` flag is the URL identifier to call directly from one link or `href` element. Finally, we need to reference which file we are referencing with the `route`; in this case, the component is located in `home/index` and will be represented inside the `moduleId` flag.
- The second URL is referencing to the `users` resource, but it has some variations. The `nav` flag can be a Boolean or number property. When set to true, the route will be included in the router's navigation model. When specified as a number, the value will be used in sorting the routes; this makes it easier to create a dynamic menu or similar elements. Finally, the `title` flag will show the page title appended to the page title in the browser window.
- The third is a little different. We can see a weird param in the middle of the route, the `:id`. This means that this part of the URL signature will be dynamic, do you remember our person `p001`? The `:id` parameter will be used to represent the `p001` code and make the URL unique for this resource. Also, in the `view-model` file, we will be able to consume that parameter and retrieve some data related to it.
- Lastly, we are seeing `'files/*path'`. Wildcard routes are used to match the *rest* of a path. The `href` flag is a conditionally optional property. If it is not defined, `route` is used. If `route` has segments, `href` is required as in the case of files, because the router does not know how to fill out the parameterized portions of the pattern.

There can be some situations where you will need some extra features to deal with them.

For example, case-sensitive routes; Aurelia has that problem solved too:

```
config.map([
            { route: ['', 'home'], name: 'home',  moduleId: 'home/index' },
            { route: 'users',        name: 'users', moduleId: 'users/index',
nav: true, title: 'Users', caseSensitive: true }
]);
```

The `caseSensitive` flag will be used in these cases.

Another situation, very common, can be the unknown routes; Aurelia has a nice way to deal with it:

```
config.map([
            { route: ['', 'home'], name: 'home',  moduleId: 'home/index' },
            { route: 'users',        name: 'users', moduleId: 'users/index',
nav: true, title: 'Users' }
        ]);

config.mapUnknownRoutes('not-found');
```

The `config.mapUnknownRoutes()` method will make a reference to the `'not-found'` component module. Another way is representing it as a function:

```
const handleUnknownRoutes = (instruction) => {
    return { route: 'not-found', moduleId: 'not-found' };
}

config.mapUnknownRoutes(handleUnknownRoutes);
```

Other common scenario could be redirected routes. This is very simple—you just need to add the `redirect` flag and specify the reference to the module you want to show:

```
config.map([
    { route: '', redirect: 'home' },
    { route: 'home', name: 'home', moduleId: 'home/index' }
]);
```

At this point, we know how to configure the routing at the `view-model` level, but what about the view? Don't worry, this will be our next topic.

All this configuration was performed in the `app.js` file, so now we need to go to our `app.html` file. You must consider some things before adding the routing property to your template.

Commonly, most web applications use a base layout. This can be composed by the header, a lateral menu, and the view content. That being said, the only element that should be refreshed and reloaded with the router is the view content; the header and the menu will always be the same for the entire application, so we need to define our router element inside that container; let's look at the code:

```
<template>
  <div class="header">
    <header-component></header-component>
  </div>
  <div class="menu">
```

```
    <menu-component></menu-component>
  </div>
  <div class="main-content">
    <router-view></router-view>
  </div>
</template>
```

The `<router-view></router-view>` is the HTML flag that Aurelia router will use to render the components we've configured as routes. Graphically, the representation is as follows:

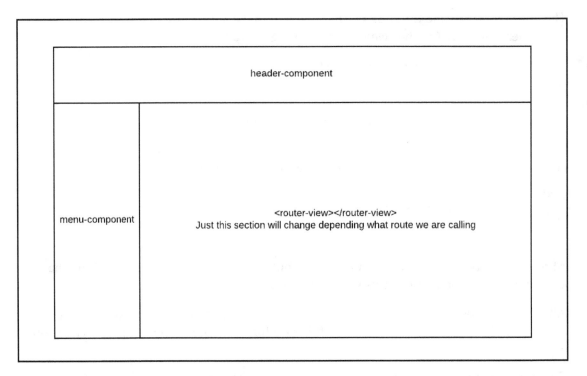

At this point, everything is okay. However, this is a very basic approach; let's explore some advanced way to make our layout more flexible and configurable. We know that the `router-view` element defined in HTML is always associated with one or more views referenced in a router configuration method defined in its parent view's view model.

To specify a layout on the `router-view` HTML element, we use the following attributes:

- `layout-view`: Specifies the layout view to use through the filename (with path)
- `layout-model`: Specifies the model parameter to pass to the activate function of view model
- `layout-view-model`: Specifies the `moduleId` to use with the layout view

To explain that, we will implement a custom layout page totally decoupled from our `app.html` file:

```
<template>
    <div>
       <router-view layout-view="layout.html"></router-view>
    </div>
</template>
```

We are referencing a file called `layout.html`. This file will contain our basic layout distribution:

```
<template>
    <div class="left-content">
       <slot name="left-content"></slot>
    </div>
    <div class="right-content">
       <slot name="right-content"></slot>
    </div>
</template>
```

Also, note the `<slot>` tag. This is a mechanism to associate parts of the layout to part of some view referencing its name; in this case, let's create a `home` component with custom layout:

```
<template>
    <div slot="left-content">
       <home-header></home-header>
    </div>
    <div slot="right-content">
        <home-menu></home-menu>
    </div>
</template>
```

Any content outside of the slot declared won't be rendered. We just have one more task to do—configure the router:

```
config.map([
        { route: '', name: 'home', moduleId: 'home' }
]);
```

We just need to declare the route and reference it to the home module. The layout will *read* the slot tags defined inside and will render to the main template. In this way we can customize the layout according to the route we are accessing the application, one use case could have custom menu options while displaying some routes.

There is one more thing we need to cover to have our router ready for work—the fallback route. Imagine that your application is based on roles. If the user is not allowed to access some resource, he should be redirected to the previous location. What if there's no previous location? The fallback route comes to the rescue!

Let the code show the magic:

```
export class App {
    configureRouter(config, router) {
        this.router = router;
        config.title = 'Example';
        config.map([
            { route: ['', 'home'], name: 'home',  moduleId: 'home/index' },
            { route: 'users',        name: 'users', moduleId: 'users/index',
nav: true, title: 'Users' }
        ]);

        config.fallbackRoute('users');
    }
}
```

Now you know the most important characteristics about Aurelia router and how to configure it to improve your application. We are almost ready to start creating components to our FIFA WC App. In the last chapter, we learned about testing, TDD, and debugging. Now, it's time to apply the learned concepts and test our components. Let's code!

Testing our components

Testing is one of the most important steps when you develop software applications. At this point, we are ready to start creating components, defining binding behaviors, and configuring our routes. All is okay, but how do we ensure that our components work as expected? We need to test each component before marking it as complete and ready for QA/Production environment.

With Aurelia's component tester, you'll be able to test your component in an isolated way, like on a mini Aurelia application. What to do when testing a component? Evaluate the expected data, and assert a response to data binding and behavior through the life cycle.

First of all, we need to install the `aurelia-testing` package:

```
npm install aurelia-testing
```

This library is based on Jasmine, the popular BDD JavaScript testing framework that provides the test structure and assertions. If you generated your application with the Aurelia CLI, Jasmine should be included.

Once installed, you can start writing your first unit test. We are going to start with a simple component that returns the customer name.

First, let's define our `View` template:

```
<template>
    <div class="custName">${custName}</div>
</template>
```

And in the `ViewModel` file:

```
import {bindable} from 'aurelia-framework';

    export class CustomerComponent {
      @bindable custName;
}
```

Our component should work. Let's verify that. We need to create our test file:

```
import {StageComponent} from 'aurelia-testing';
import {bootstrap} from 'aurelia-bootstrapper';

describe('CustomerComponent', () => {
  let component;

  beforeEach(() => {
```

```
      component = StageComponent
        .withResources('customer-component')
        .inView('<customer-component cust-name.bind="custName"></customer-
component>')
        .boundTo({ custName: 'Diego' });
    });

    it('should render first name', done => {
      component.create(bootstrap).then(() => {
        const nameElement = document.querySelector('.custName');
        expect(nameElement.innerHTML).toBe('Diego');
        done();
      }).catch(e => { console.log(e.toString()) });
    });

    afterEach(() => {
      component.dispose();
    });
  });
```

Okay, that looks fine; it should pass. What are we doing?

First, we import the `StageComponent` from `aurelia-testing`:

```
import {StageComponent} from 'aurelia-testing';
```

The `StageComponent` just creates a new instance of the `ComponentTester` class, which does all the work. Next, the `StageComponent` factory will stage the component:

```
      component = StageComponent
        .withResources('src/customer-component')
        .inView('<customer-component cust-name.bind="custName"></customer-
component>')
        .boundTo({ custName: 'Diego' });
```

The `StageComponent` has one property—`withResources()`—and it allows you to start off the staging with a fluent API. The class method `withResources` is very useful to specify which resource or resources you will use and register. If you need more than one single resource, just use an array of string to register all of them. Then, `inView` method allows us to provide the HTML code we need to run. This is a standard view where you can define properties and other stuff just like in our application's real components. Finally, `boundTo` method provides a test `viewModel` with the predefined data configured in `inView`.

In this first part, the staging is performed by Jasmine's `beforeEach()` method in order to reuse the same setup in case we have multiple tests:

```
component.create(bootstrap).then(() => {
    const nameElement = document.querySelector('.custName');
    expect(nameElement.innerHTML).toBe('Diego');
    done();
}).catch(e => { console.log(e.toString()) });
```

Next, we enter the test itself, the `create()` method. Create will kick everything off and bootstrap the mini Aurelia application (it's receiving the `bootstrap` component imported from the `aurelia-bootstrapper` library imported earlier); this method will configure the test using `standardConfiguration`, register provided resources as global resources, start the application, and, finally, render your component so that you can assert the expected behavior. In this case, we want to ensure that our `custName` property gets rendered correctly in the HTML by selecting the div tag via its class name. We use `document.querySelector('.custName')` to get the element value and assert that its `innerHTML` is Diego. Next, we call Jasmine's `done` function to tell Jasmine that the test is complete. Calling done is needed since the create method is asynchronous and returns a `Promise`. If the test raises some error, the `catch()` method will be triggered and will print the error log in console:

```
component.dispose();
```

Finally, we call `dispose` on our `ComponentTester` instance. This will clean up the DOM so that our next test starts out with a clean document.

Our first test is complete and guess what...it passed! That was a very basic example, but we've learned the basic parts of a component test and how we can include it in our application. Now, let's explore more advanced features.

Testing component life cycle

We need to ensure that our data is retrieved as expected, and the same way, we need to assert that our component behavior is going well too. To do this, we can tell the component we created that we will manually handle the life cycle methods; you will find the code very self-explanatory:

```
import {StageComponent} from 'aurelia-testing';
import {bootstrap} from 'aurelia-bootstrapper';

describe('CustomerComponent', () => {
```

```
    let component;

  beforeEach(() => {
    component = StageComponent
      .withResources('src/customer-component')
      .inView('<customer-component cust-name.bind="custName"></customer-
component>')
      .boundTo({ custName: 'Diego' });
  });

  it('can manually handle life cycle', done => {
    let nameElement;

    component.manuallyHandleLifecycle().create()
      .then(() => {
        nameElement = document.querySelector('.custName');
        expect(nameElement.innerHTML).toBe(' ');
      })
      .then(() => component.bind())
      .then(() => {
        expect(nameElement.innerHTML).toBe('Foo bind');
      })
      .then(() => component.attached())
      .then(() => {
        expect(nameElement.innerHTML).toBe('Foo attached');
      })
      .then(() => component.detached())
      .then(() => component.unbind())
      .then(() => {
        expect(component.viewModel.custName).toBe(null);
      })
      .then(() => component.bind({ custName: 'Bar' }))
      .then(() => {
        expect(nameElement.innerHTML).toBe('Bar bind');
      })
      .then(() => component.attached())
      .then(() => {
        expect(nameElement.innerHTML).toBe('Bar attached');
      })
      .then(done)
      .catch(done);
  });

  afterEach(() => {
    component.dispose();
  });

});
```

The imported libraries still being the same, the create() method of our component element will bootstrap the application and provide us with an easy way to check for our life cycle method responses; just ensure that you call them in the order they are executed.

What about components depending on external services? Don't worry, you just need to add some extra lines to the test code and create a class "mocking" the service.

First, our Mock class:

```
export class MockService {
    firstName;

    getFirstName() { return Promise.resolve(this.firstName);
}
```

Our test class will look like this:

```
describe('MyComponent', () => {
    let component;
    let service = new MockService(); //Our created Mock

    beforeEach(() => {
        service.firstName = undefined;

        component = StageComponent
            .withResources('src/component')
            .inView('<component></component>');

        component.bootstrap(aurelia => {
            aurelia.use.standardConfiguration();
            aurelia.container.registerInstance(Service, service); //Register
    our mock service instance to the current container instance
        });
    });

    it('should render first name', done => {
        service.firstName = 'Diego';

        component.create(bootstrap).then(() => {
            const nameElement = document.querySelector('.first-name');
            expect(nameElement.innerHTML).toBe('Diego');

            done();
        });
    });

    afterEach(() => {
```

```
            component.dispose();
        });
    });
```

First of all, we are declaring our mock service as a global variable. This will be used for injecting it into Aurelia's container context; this way, the component won't detect any difference between the real service class and our mocked service. Another thing you should pay attention to is that at the `beforeEach()` method level, we are declaring the `firstName` property as `undefined`; this is just to make it reusable and customizable for each test depending on their own needs. Remember that this method is executed independently for each unit test.

What if I need to define a more complex view, evaluating containers for my component? Easy, you are allowed to use template literals:

```
import {StageComponent} from 'aurelia-testing';
import {bootstrap} from 'aurelia-bootstrapper';

describe('MyAttribute', () => {
  let component;

  beforeEach(() => {
    //Literal HTML syntax
    let view = `
          <div class="row">
            <div class="col-xs-12">
              <div my-attribute.bind="color">Diego</div>
            </div>
          </div>
        `;
    component = StageComponent
      .withResources('src/my-attribute')
      .inView(view)
      .boundTo(viewModel);
  });
  //...
});
```

What do you think? It's easy right? That's good! Now, we are completely ready for the best part of this chapter; let's put everything in practice!

Time to practice!

It's time to start coding! At this point, we have our application created and running, preconfigured to use SASS as CSS preprocessor, and integrated with the Aurelia Materialize library to follow good design practices of Material Design. Now we need to define our layout. It will be very basic at this time and across the application growing, our developed components can be improved and refactorized.

First, we need to access our root folder application; once inside, we just need to type the following command:

```
au run --watch
```

Next, we open our favorite browser's window, which should look something like this:

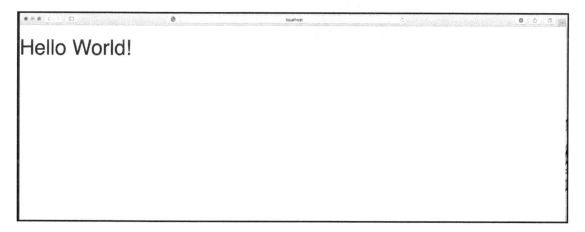

Now, let's create our main layout. Inside the `src` folder, we will create a folder named layout. Inside this folder, to subfolders: header and menu:

- `./src > layout > header >`: Here, we will create an HTML file for view and JS file for view-model. Both files are called `app-header`
- `./src > layout > menu >`: Same way as the header, both files will be called `app-menu`

Our folder structure should look like this:

First, we'll create the `app-header` component. Let's open the HTML file and create our `navbar` header. It's at this point that we will see the Aurelia Materialize features:

```
<template>
  <md-navbar>
    <div class="margin-content">

      <ul class="hide-on-med-and-down right">
        <li md-waves><a href="#about">About</a></li>
        <li md-waves><a href="#map">Login</a></li>
      </ul>

    </div>
  </md-navbar>
</template>
```

`<md-navbar>` tag refers to the `navbar` element of Aurelia Materialize. This is very helpful because the components are already created; we just need to call them and start defining how we want to show to our user. We won't create any CSS class at this point. Inside our `nav-bar`, we are creating two navigation options just to see how it looks on the browser.

With our first component created, it's time to integrate it with our main page, `app.html`. First, we need to call the created component using the `<require>` tag:

```
<require from="./layout/header/app-header"></require>
```

Then, we just need to call the created component by its filename:

```
<app-header></app-header>
```

Now just reload your browser's window and... an error is raised! What to do in that case? What happened? Our best friend, the console, will tell us the truth:

```
DEBUG [templating] importing resources for app.html Array [ "materialize-
css/css/materialize.css", "layout/header/app-header" ]
vendor-bundle.js:14222:8 TypeError: target is undefined[Learn More]
```

Let's pay attention to the last parts of each line. First, the error occurred when the Aurelia bootstrapper was importing and configuring our created component. The last message tells us the error cause: undefined target.

Think for a few minutes, what could have happened? We know you have enough knowledge to tell us what the error was.

Ready? If you note, our recently created view-model file for app-header.js is completely empty. So we have the view, but that view is not pointing to anything, and the target is undefined! To solve this error, we just need to declare the component name and export it:

```
export class AppHeader {

}
```

Now, let's reload our browser:

Awesome, right? Relax, this is just the beginning. Now it's time to create our menu.

Our chosen Materialize component is the fixed sidenav. However, to integrate this into our application, we will merge some of the techniques and concepts learned until now. First, let's code our component:

```
<template>

  <md-sidenav view-model.ref="sideNav" md-fixed="true" md-edge="left">
    <ul>
      <li md-waves><a>Option A</a></li>
      <li md-waves><a>This is better</a></li>
```

```
            <li md-waves><a>I want this</a></li>
            <li md-waves><a>Oops!</a></li>
        </ul>
    </md-sidenav>

</template>
```

Similarly, using the `<require>` tag, we will import it into our `app.html` file. If we just call the `sidenav` menu, we will get the following result:

Of course, we don't want to hide our main application content! It's time to start using CSS to make the `app-menu` play for our team.

First, let's add some container order to our app.html page. It should be something like this:

```
<template>
    <require from="materialize-css/css/materialize.css"></require>
    <require from="./layout/header/app-header"></require>
    <require from="./layout/menu/app-menu"></require>

    <app-header></app-header>
    <main>

        <div class="row">
            <div class="col s12 m12 l12">
                <h1>${message}</h1>
            </div>
        </div>

        <app-menu></app-menu>
    </main>

</template>
```

We are just involving our main content, in this case, the message property, into one container that fills the entire screen no matter the resolution.

If we run the application, we'll still be seeing the same result. We need to apply some custom CSS modifications to our sidenav component. It's time to start using SASS!

We have SASS on our dependencies path, and it's ready for use in our application, but let's add some modifications just to make our files distribution a little more understandable for us.

Go to the `aurelia_project` folder and open the task called `process-css.js`.

If you remember the Gulp task automation from the previous chapters, you'll find the code very familiar. We just need to add one single line:

```
export default function processCSS() {
  return gulp.src(project.cssProcessor.source)
    .pipe(sourcemaps.init())
    .pipe(sass().on('error', sass.logError))
    .pipe(gulp.dest('./')) //THIS LINE
    .pipe(build.bundle());
}
```

Why this line? We want to see the generated CSS file into our project and import it from our `index.html` file. Again, why? It's because using this file directly into your browser, your style modifications and debugging will be easier in case you need to modify or maintain the style sheets.

Then, let's create our `styles` folder. This should be located directly in our `src` folder. Could it be located in a different location? Sure, but we recommend that you first check your `aurelia.json` file.

If you search the `cssProcessor` task, you will find this:

```
"cssProcessor": {
  "id": "sass",
  "displayName": "Sass",
  "fileExtension": ".scss",
  "source": "src/**/*.scss"
},
```

The source property is indicating the level at which our scss files will be located, and guess where they are by default? Yes, the `src/*whatever*/*.scss` location. You can modify it, but for our current purpose, we don't need to.

Then, inside our folder, let's create our first .scss file called _mainlayout.scss. Remember that the _ prefix is to indicate that this style sheet will be used as part of another style sheet. We just need to add the following code:

```
header, main, footer {
  padding-left: 300px;
}

md-navbar[md-fixed="true"] nav {
  padding-right: 300px;
}

md-sidenav {
  div {
    collapsible-body {
    }
    padding: 0;
  }
}
```

We are just telling our header and application main body to stay 300 px right from our app menu. Now, it's time to reload our browser:

Our base layout is done! Guess what? Yeah, its time to add routing!

Let's decouple the welcome message of the `app.js` file. Create a home component to render a custom message; we called it `app-home`. Now, instead of the `<h2>` tag in your `app.html` file, put the `<router-view>` tag.

In the app `view-model` file, delete the `constructor` method; we won't use it this time. Then, just add the following code:

```
configureRouter(config, router) {
  this.router = router;
  config.title = 'FIFA WC 2018';
  config.map([
    { route: ['', 'home'],        name: 'home',        moduleId: 'home/app-
home' },
  ]);
}
```

Now, let's reload our browser. Pay attention to the window title; it now reflects our application name!

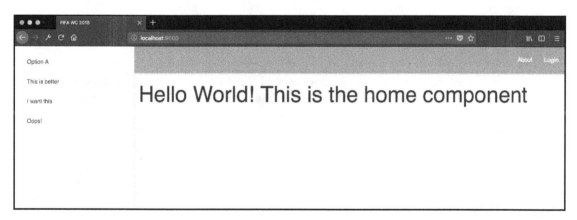

For practice purposes, we are done by this time! If you note, we're mixing a lot of concerns in just some basic approaches to our application. Now, let's add the extra value to our code. Do you remember our hard-coded menu options? Don't you think it should be dynamic? Yes, we are talking about adding dynamic binding to our practice! What are you waiting for, open your `app-menu` view and `view-model`!

Let's create an array of string in the `view-model` layer. We will use the same options used in the image:

```
export class AppMenu {

  menuOptions = [
```

```
      'Option A',
      'This is better',
      'I want this',
      'Oops!',
   ]

}
```

Next, the magic. The `repeat` command will do the dirty work for us. Okay, we know that we didn't mention it before; do you remember when we said we'll review a lot of new concerns when implementing a real application? This is one of those:

```
<template>

  <md-sidenav view-model.ref="sideNav" md-fixed="true" md-edge="left">
    <ul>

      <li repeat.for="option of menuOptions" md-waves><a>${option}</a></li>

    </ul>
  </md-sidenav>

</template>
```

That was very easy. Now we are really done. Our FIFA WC 2018 App is ready to start writing our business services and components! One more thing is pending and that's the tests part. We won't cover it in practice, because in the next chapter, we will find some more complex components created for our application, and we will be nice to apply testing to real-life components.

Summary

Your knowledge about Aurelia at this moment is just amazing! We wanted to cover every aspect regarding component creation and how you can abstract your business scenario into one digital application. You learned that each component is part of an everything, is reusable, and allows you to separate your application concerns. Since a component is an isolated piece of your application, it manages his own life cycle; Aurelia allows us to have complete control and configure events such as data loading or some custom behavior when the components is destroyed. Another very interesting thing is that we can create our own events, and we can trigger them from the view layer.

Also, you must remember that one component can inherit from other components, and they all have properties. Remember that Aurelia is a double-way binding framework, so all these properties are synchronized between the view and view model files. We also learned how to implement value-converters and some other binding behavior to improve our application performance and reduce the amount of code, making our application more lightweight and maintainable. Once our components are created and we have our application scenarios, it's time to link all of them through dynamic routing, defining user workflows and passing dynamic properties to each template. Last but never least, we went through how to test our application components, ensuring their functionality and life cycle behavior.

You can start creating components and exploring the Aurelia Materialize's library to customize your application. In subsequent chapters, you will find our app very advanced, but don't worry, there won't be anything we haven't explained. Keep practicing!

Creating Our RESTful API

5

A web application is composed of different layers; upto now, you have been developing the client-side layer of the FIFA World Cup project. However, just presenting a user interface to the user is not enough. We need to process some business logic in order to provide an appropriate user experience to our users, such as subscribing to the next matches, retrieving the roaster for the user's favorite team, managing login, and more.

In order to have a full web application, we should implement the following server-side missing pieces in our project:

- The RESTful API layer
- Database layer

Once upon a time, developers used to implement all the layers in a single project, and this was because of the adoption of popular open source web platforms such as XAMPP, which configures a PHP/MySQL environment in just a few seconds. So, developers used to write the client-side web pages in PHP and add HTML code in the same file, mixing server-side with client-side code.

With the passing of the years, new techniques were introduced. Now, developers separate client side and server side in different projects, and in addition to separating the project, these layers are deployed in different domains. All of this was possible thanks to the introduction of new client-side and server-side frameworks. All this brings a new challenge—communication—so having separate projects now requires a way to exchange information with each other. RESTful APIs become the right solution to communicate between the client side and backend using the HTTP protocol as the mean of data transportation between these layers.

The following illustration depicts the new way to create web apps:

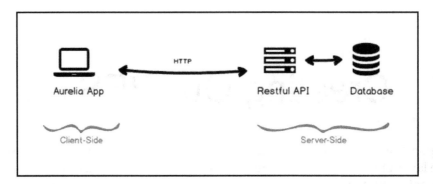

In this chapter, we will implement the RESTful API layer. For this, we will use Node.js and JavaScript to build a robust RESTful API. You will also learn the concepts and how to design robust APIs using an open source framework on top of Node.js called ExpressJS. We will also explore the new MEAN stack and learn about the technologies behind it and why we decided to baptize it as the new MEAN stack. Lastly, you will learn how to improve your RESTful APIs using new techniques to improve the developer experience in your team.

So, we will cover the following topics:

- Understanding RESTful
- Designing APIs
- Creating an API with Node.js
- Improving our API with ExpressJS
- Coding our project

Understanding RESTful

In this section, we will go through the components HTTP and **CRUD** (**Create, Retrieve, Update** and **Delete**), which form the basic building block of RESTful. These components together make possible the communication between different applications over the internet in a distributed environment via a well-defined API.

Understanding HTTP

Every time you are navigating on the internet, you are using the HTTP. Even when you are booking a ride on Uber, you are using HTTP. In fact, HTTP is present in almost all the applications that you use on a daily basis.

HTTP is based on the principle of client-server communication. It means that every time you want to access an information or resources, you have to send a request object and the server will send you all the requested information into a response object. The following diagram explains this communication:

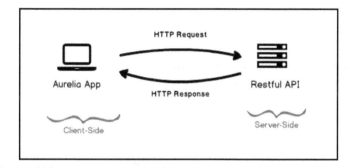

So, in order to really understand how to design a robust HTTP RESTful API we need to know how URLs works and learn about the HTTP protocol.

URLs

URLs are the way how applications give access to their information assets by defining well-structured endpoints. For example, if you want to search about Peru, you would probably access from a web browser the following URL: https://www.google.com/search?q=Peru. Let's divide the previous URL into parts and analyze it in details:

From the diagram, we see that there are basically four parts:

- **Protocol**: This is the HTTP for non-secure connections or HTTPS for secure connections
- **Domain**: The registered domain that will be translated to the server IP, which contains this resource
- **Path**: This allows us to separate our resources into segments
- **Query String**: This is optional but allows us to provide additional data

We will always use URLs to access resources hosted on another server.

Verbs

The HTTP verbs are the magic behind RESTful APIs. Let's use an example to understand how HTTP verbs works. We want to create an API to manage products; our first version might look like this:

Endpoint	HTTP verb	Goal
`http://myapp/api/createProduct`	POST	To create a product
`http://myapp/api/updateProduct/P1`	POST	To update an existing product
`http://myapp/api/listProducts`	GET	To retrieve the complete list of products
`http://myapp/api/viewProductDetails/P1`	GET	To retrieve a single product
`http://myapp/api/deleteProduct/P1`	POST	To delete a product

From the preceding table, you can note that we need to remember five endpoints, and we are using two HTTP verbs: POST and GET. It might be understood that every time we want to retrieve information, a GET verb is used, and to perform operations that will modify the existing information in our system, a POST verb is used.

So, let's make our endpoints easy to remember using HTTP verbs. After applying a simple refactor, now our table might look as follows:

Endpoint	HTTP verb	Goal
`http://myapp/api/products`	GET POST	To retrieve the full list of products. To create a new product.
`http://myapp/api/products/P1`	GET DELETE PUT	To retrieve a single product. To delete an existing product. To modify an existing product. In this case, you must send the full document, not just the fields that have changed.

Now, we are using the HTTP verbs, and we have reduced from five endpoints to just two. HTTP verbs are sent with every request to the server, so servers can use them to identify what operation a user wants to perform, sending the correct endpoint and verb.

Headers

The headers contain additional information about every request that we send to the server. The headers that you will use more frequently during development are these:

- **Content-Type**: To tell the server which type of response you are waiting for
- **Accept**: To tell the server which type of content the client can process
- **Authorization**: To send a piece of information to validate the identity of the information consumer

Of course, there are more headers. Refer to `https://developer.mozilla.org/es/docs/Web/HTTP/Headers` to learn more about the HTTP headers.

Body

The body is present in the request and response objects. Every time you want to create a new entry in your database, you have to pass the information in the body section of your HTTP Request. The data in the body section is known as **payload**.

CRUD over HTTP

As you might have noted when we talked about HTTP verbs, every verb is related to a CRUD operation. Basically, these four operation refers to the basic functions that all the database engines perform.

So, mapping each HTTP verb with its respective CRUD operation, we will have the following table:

HTTP Verb	CRUD Operation	GOAL
POST	Create	Create or Insert a new element in our app
GET	Retrieve	Retrieve or Read elements from our app
PUT	Update	Update or Modify any existing element into our app
DELETE	Delete	Delete or Remove any existing element into our app

Designing APIs

Now that we are clear about what HTTP is and the building blocks behind it, we need to design a friendly and robust API. Another advantage of this is that we will improve the developer experience in our organization by having a well-defined API.

API documentation is another key practice that you have to apply in every API development you will do. With documentation, the development team and API consumers are aware of the full functionality of the API, because they are defined in an easy-to-read format. For example, the financial team and the logistics team in an organization can share their API documentation between them and start working on a possible integration solution immediately because they now know the full details of the APIs.

Let's learn how to design robust APIs by understanding the API first movement and other design concepts.

API first

API first is one of the most important concepts you should keep in mind while developing a new product or a service, you have to think of it as if it were the user interface for programmers. In fact, APIs are the way how you can expose the functionalities of your products in a distributed big system.

Nowadays, techniques and approaches such as cloud applications and microservices are becoming adopted everywhere, and they suggest a new way to develop software. With microservices, you have to split your application into different independent services; each service contains a specific set of related features of your application, such as taking some Amazon APIs as an example, we can have something like the following:

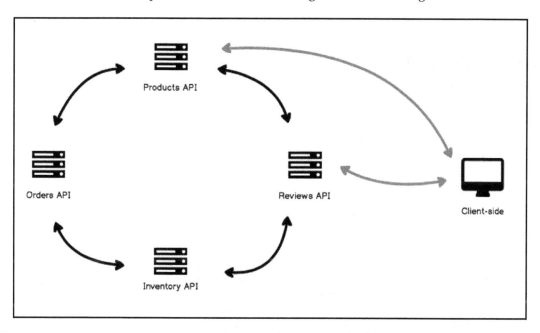

As you can see, there are different services that need to exchange information and functionalities. All of those have to define a consistent and self-explained API that the other services have to use in order to either perform an operation in another service that it is not able to do or a client-side application will invoke the APIs directly to access some information.

The main understanding behind API first is that before you implement any code or UI design in your system, you should design your API in such a way that even if you don't have any user interface, developers should be able to navigate and access the information and functionality into your application data.

API design

To design a robust, self-explained, friendly, and easy-to-use API, we will follow the set of best practices that have been used and implemented over the years by the internet gurus. Thankfully, some great developers and architects had defined a set of rules that we will cover in this section.

Nouns as paths

Have you ever seen some API endpoints that contain a full sentence to access a resource? Some examples might be the following:

```
http://myshop.com/createNewProduct
http://myshop.com/deleteProduct
http://myshop.com/updateProduct
http://myshop.com/getProductDetail/P01
http://myshop.com/getProductComments/P01
```

The first thing to keep in mind is that you should never use verbs in your endpoints. Instead, use nouns in plural to refer to a resource into your API Endpoint. For example, the preceding example can be refactored to this:

The Rest way - Not recommended	The RESTful way - Recommended
http://myshop.com/createNewProduct http://myshop.com/deleteProduct http://myshop.com/updateProduct	http://myshop.com/products
http://myshop.com/getProductDetail/P01	http://myshop.com/products/P01
http://myshop.com/getProductComments/P01	http://myshop.com/products/P01/comments

A good practice is not to extend the path depth higher than three paths. For example, use this:

```
http://myshop.com/products/P01/comments
```

Do that instead of the following:

```
http://myshop.com/products/details/P01/comments/today
```

If you want to extend your API to perform additional operations such as getting the first 10 messages published today, use query strings instead of paths. Consider this example:

```
http://myshop.com/products/P01/comments?day=today&count=10
```

HTTP verbs for CRUD

Now that you have designed clean endpoints for your API, it is time to take advantage of what we learned about HTTP verbs. You might be asking yourself how do you differentiate when you want to create, update, or delete a product if you are using the same endpoint, /products? This is the case where we use HTTP verbs. For example, for the /products endpoint, we will have something like the following verbs:

Endpoint	HTTP Verb	Goal
/products	POST	To create a new product
/products	PUT	To update an existing product
/products	DELETE	To delete an existing product

So from the preceding table, you can note that the key differentiator is the HTTP Verb. In short, an endpoint is composed by one path and an HTTP Verb.

API documentation

When you are working on a real project, the number of endpoints you will need to design will be higher. You will need a way to remember all your endpoints and the reason they were designed. Similarly, we are confident that documenting software is extremely important for us to remember what a piece of code is supposed to do; API documentation allows us to tell the API consumers how they can use our API by documenting the endpoints and other additional metadata, such as the ones listed:

- Endpoint path
- HTTP verbs
- The expected headers
- The expected body structure
- The expected results

 There is an awesome open source tool that helps you document and share the documentation with your APIs called **Swagger**. We encourage you to visit the official site and play with it at https://swagger.io.

A possible documentation might be just a simple table that contains the data used in the request and responses. For example, the documentation to create a new product might be this:

Path	Products
HTTP method	POST
Expected Results	**HTTP 200 OK** status code
Expected Input Headers	Content-type: `application/json`
Expected Input Body	{id: `Integer`, name: `String`, price: `Decimal`}
Goal	Use this endpoint to create a new product
Authorization	Required Authorization Token

Having the knowledge of how to design self-explained APIs and how to use HTTP to create endpoints, let's move forward to implement a RESTful API with Node.js.

Creating an API with Node.js

It's time to start having fun and code our RESTful API. Until now you have seen the theory behind APIs and that knowledge is very important to understand the following sections. So, you might be wondering, why Node.js? The short answer is because it is cool! Haha, just kidding. Node.js has evolved since its creation in 2009 by *Ryan Dahl*. Node.js is used for leading companies over the world, such as LinkedIn, Facebook, Amazon, and more.

Node.js is not limited to API Development. In fact, you might create any kind of project from command-line tools to **Internet of Things (IoT)** applications. So, let's start learning about the advantages of Node.js and coding our API.

Node advantages

Node.js has a lot of advantages; we will explore the more important ones in the following subtopics.

Asynchronous

In most programming languages, I/O operations are performed synchronously. Synchronous execution will block the program flow until the blocking operation finishes its execution. For example, the following Python code is executed synchronously and blocks the execution:

```
file_content = open("my_file.txt") // takes 10 seconds
file_content_2 = open("my_other_files.txt") // takes 20 seconds
print file_content
print file_content_2
```

The total execution time will be approximately 30 seconds. That is because of the I/O Blocking operation. If we represent the synchronous execution as a timeline:

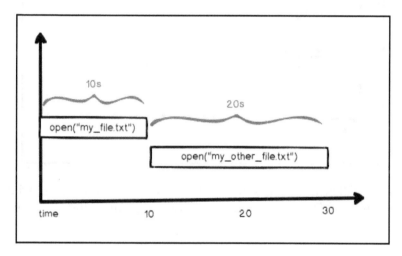

Now if we execute the same operation in an asynchronous way using JavaScript:

```
open("my_file.txt", (file_content) => {
  console.log(file_content)
})

open("my_file_2.txt", (file_content_2) => {
  console.log(file_content_2)
})
```

From the previous code, you can note that we use a callback to process the content of the file. Callbacks are functions that are invoked after some events occur. For example, `(file_content) => {}` will be called once the content of `my_file.txt` is ready to use.

The two `open()` statements will be executed at the same time. Executing the statements in parallel will help us reduce the execution time. For example, let's see the timeline execution for this asynchronous code:

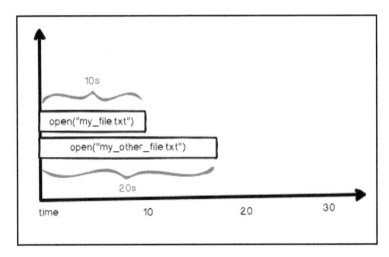

Now the execution will be just 20 seconds, and, with this, we have improved our application performance. This is one of the key advantages that Node.js brings up to the game.

Single-thread

Every time a new user request arrives at the backend server it will create a new thread for the request, this is the classic behavior for backend servers that don't use Node.js. Once the server sends the response to the user, it releases the thread. Handling just a few threads is not an issue but, imagine what would happen if you need to handle millions of users at the same time? Let's graph this issue:

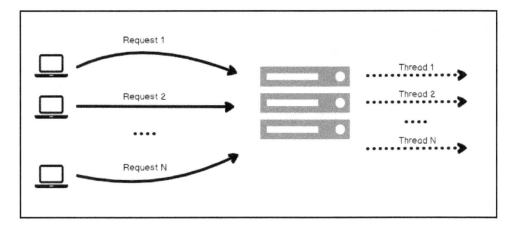

Node.js does not have this issue because of its single-thread strategy. Instead of starting a new thread for each request, it will use the same main thread to handle all the requests and will be supported by the event-loop. The following diagram depicts this scenario:

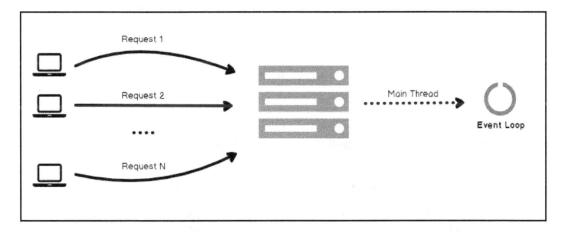

This scenario is better for CPU utilization; multiple threads allow NodeJS to take advantage of multi-core CPUs. However, we need more than a simple chapter to talk about them. We strongly encourage you to visit the official Node.js site at `https://nodejs.org/en/`.

Now it's time to code a simple HTTP Server and start the fun part!

Simple HTTP Server

It is time to start coding and see how we can implement a simple HTTP Server using Node.js. So, open your Terminal and in the working directory of your choice, go ahead and create a new folder called `my-server`:

```
$ mkdir my-server
$ cd my-server
```

Once you move into the `my-server` folder, we will need to initialize an NPM module, so run the following command:

```
$ npm init -y

{
  "name": "my-server",
  "version": "1.0.0",
  "main": "index.js",
  "scripts": {
    "test": "echo \"Error: no test specified\" && exit 1"
  },
  "keywords": [],
  "author": "",
  "license": "ISC",
  "description": ""
}
```

Now it's time to create the `server.js` file by executing the `touch server.js` command in your Terminal. This file will contain the code for our server. We will start importing the HTTP module:

```
const http = require('http')
```

We import any module using the `require` built-in function, and we define the `http` variable to house the module reference. Let's implement a simple handler by writing the following code:

```
const myRequestHandler = (request, response) => {
    response.end('Hello From our Node.js Server !!')
}
```

As you can see, a handler is just a function that declares two parameters:

- `request`: Used to read the information sent by the client
- `response`: Used to send information to the client

Our handler is using the `response` parameter to send our friendly message to the client. Now it's time to create a server instance using the `http` reference we declared earlier:

```
const server = http.createServer(myRequestHandler)
```

We are creating an empty server that does not perform any operation. To make our server useful, we pass the `request` handler we declared earlier, `myRequestHandler`. With this, our server is able to send our `Hello` message every time some client sends an HTTP request to our server. To finish our server implementation, we need to listen to the client request:

```
server.listen(5000, () => {
    console.log("server is running on port 5000")
})
```

That's all! Now that we have a simple HTTP, execute the `node server.js` command to run the server. Let's test things out. Head over to `http://localhost:5000` and you should see something like the following:

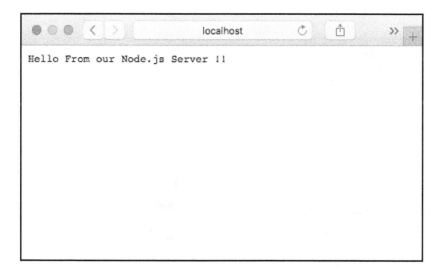

Now you know how to create a simple HTTP server using the native HTTP module that comes along with Node.js. However, in order to create a powerful RESTful backend, we need to use a more sophisticated framework.

In the next section, we will enhance our simple server using Express.js.

Improving our API with Express.js

Express.js is an open source web framework created on top of Node.js. We can implement our REST API using the Node.js HTTP module, but we will have to write a lot of code to handle a simple user request. Express.js is very flexible and provides a set of features that will allow us to create robust APIs.

Coding our server

It's time to create our FIFA backend folder and start working on the API development. Open your Terminal and run the following command:

```
$ mkdir wc-backend
$ cd wc-backend
$ npm init -y

{
  "name": "wc-backend",
  "version": "1.0.0",
  "description": "",
  "main": "index.js",
  "scripts": {
    "test": "echo \"Error: no test specified\" && exit 1"
  },
  "keywords": [],
  "author": "",
  "license": "ISC"
}
```

Once the initialization is done, let's install Express.js. Execute the following command:

```
$ npm install --save express
```

Next, create the `server.js` file in the root folder and write the following code:

```
const express = require('express')
const app = express()

app.use((req, res) => {
    res.send("Hello!")
})

app.listen(3000, () => {
    console.log('running on port: 3000')
})
```

We start importing the `express` module and instantiation of an express application into the `app` variable. Next, we use the application instance to configure a simple request handler using the `app.use` function. Into this function, we pass another function as a parameter that has two parameters for the request and response: `req` and `res`. To send a simple message, we use the `res` parameter.

Once the server application instance is configured, we bring it to life by calling its `listen` function and passing the HTTP port where it will listen to new HTTP requests:

```
$ node server.js
```

 We strongly recommend you to use **nodemon** in development. The nodemon will restart your node application every time it detects a change in your source code automatically. To install nodemon, just execute the `npm install -g nodemon` command. To run your server, use the `nodemon server.js` command.

Let's test it by opening `http://localhost:3000` in your browser or using an HTTP client command-line tool. Consider the given example:

```
$ curl http://localhost:3000

Hello!
```

So far so good! Let's define a route path to make a self-explanatory API. Apply the following change to the `server.js` file:

```
...
app.use('/hello', (req, res) => {
    res.send("Hello!")
})
...
```

Now, head over to `http://localhost:3000/hello` and you should see the same `Hello!` message. You can navigate to `http://localhost:3000` to see what you get after the change:

```
$ curl http://localhost:3000/hello

Hello!
```

Using routes

Routes are the magic behind our RESTful API. If you remember when we talked about HTTP verbs, RESTful is composed by combining CRUD operations with the HTTP verbs. Express.js makes easy the definition of these RESTful way. For example, open the `server.js` file and apply the following change:

```
. . .
app.get('/hello', (req, res) => {
    res.send("Hello!")
})
. . .
```

As you can see, we changed use for `get`. As you are so smart, you know that `get` refers to the GET HTTP verb, so let's define our RESTful routes for our Teams API. In the `server.js`, apply the following changes:

```
. . .

app.get('/teams', (req, res) => {
    res.send("To retrieve the list of teams")
})

app.post('/teams', (req, res) => {
    res.send("To create a new team")
})

app.put('/teams', (req, res) => {
    res.send("To update an existing team")
})

app.delete('/teams', (req, res) => {
    res.send("To delete an existing team")
})

. . .
```

Once we apply these changes, it's time to test them. Run the following commands in your Terminal:

```
$ curl -X POST http://localhost:3000/teams
   To create a new team
```

```
$ curl -X GET http://localhost:3000/teams
   To retrieve the list of teams
```

Cool! our RESTful API is responding correctly. Note that we use the `-X [HTTP Verb]` to tell curl which HTTP verb we want to use for the given request. Now that we are ready with the main skeleton of our API, we need to structure our project in a consistent way because we will create a group of files and should always organize our source code. Keep reading!

Coding our project

Here we are! We will implement the code of our project. Our application is composed of three domains:

- **Teams**: To manage the information of all the teams that participate in the World Cup competition
- **Matches**: To manage the information of all the Matches during the competition
- **Security**: To manage the information of the users and permissions

The teams and matches follow the same implementation with a few variants. For that reason, in this section, we will write the code to implement the `Team` domain and then expose it via our API, and you will be able to implement the code for the `Match` domains yourself. Of course, the complete source code is available in the `https://github.com/Packt-Aurelia-Fullstack-Book/worldcup-app` GitHub repository.

So, having said that. Let's start!

Our project structure

Let's start by creating the Project structure for our source code. Create the following directories and files in your working directory, as shown in the following screenshot:

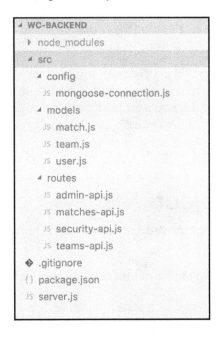

The `src` folder contains three subfolders: `models`, `routes`, and `config`. In this chapter, we will just use the **routes** folder and the `teams-api.js` file. The other two will be explored in the next chapter when we talk about Databases and MongoDB.

The goal of the routes folder is to host all the API Routes declaration. We have declared our routes in the `server.js` file; it might be a good idea if we are working on a small project, but it is not a good idea for a big project, which will have a lot of routes declarations. For that reason, a good strategy is to separate the routes per API functionality; for example, teams-API, matches-API, and auth-API. With this, we will have more easy-to-read and easy-to-maintain code.

Implementing the Teams API

Before we start coding, we have to design our API first. The following table contains the documentation for the API we will implement:

Route	HTTP Verb	Goal	Responses
/teams	GET	List all the teams	Http 200 - OK
/teams	POST	Create a new team with body {name: String}	Http 201 - Created
/teams/:id	GET	Get a single team	Http 200 -OK Http 404 - Not Found
/teams/:id	PUT	Update an existing team	Http 200 -OK Http 404 - Not Found
/teams/:id	DELETE	Delete an existing team	Http 200 -OK Http 404 - Not Found

Keeping this in mind, let's begin with the fun part!

Configuring the JSON Parser

We will start by configuring our server to be able to parse JSON. This means that Express.js will automatically parse the data that flows in and out of the HTTP Request. The following diagram explains this:

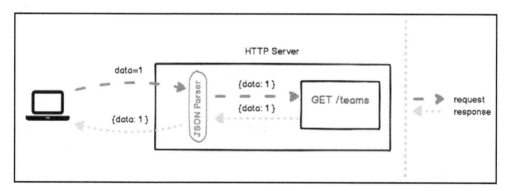

As you can see, all the requests will be intercepted by the **JSON Parser**. The **JSON Parser** is better known as a **middleware**. A middleware is just a simple function that is processed before another function. For example, the **GET /teams** function is supposed to be the only function that should be called in every request, but as we have configured the **JSON Parser**, the **GET /teams** will be invoked once the **JSON Parser** function is completed.

To configure this in our code, first we need to install it. Run the npm install --save body-parser in your terminal and apply the following changes:

```
const express = require('express')
const bodyParser = require('body-parser')
const app = express()

app.use(bodyParser.json())

app.get('/teams', (req, res) => {

    const teams = [{ "name": "Peru" }, {"name": "Russia"}]

    res.json(teams)
})
...
```

First, we import the body-parser module. Then, we configure the application to use our bodyParser.json() using its app.use function. All the middleware are configured by calling this function.

Lastly, to test whether the JSON Parser is working, we define the teams variable containing two teams with their respective names. To send the teams, we use res.json instead of res.send. Let's check the results by executing the following command:

```
$ curl -X GET http://localhost:3000/teams

[{"name":"Peru"}, {"name":"Russia"}]
```

Now that our API is able to receive and send JSON, let's move our routes to its own file.

Refactoring routes

We previously created the teams-api.js file in the routes folder. Open that file and apply the following changes:

```
const express = require('express')
const api = new express.Router()
```

```
let teams = [
    { id: 1, name: "Peru"},
    { id: 2, name: "Russia"}
]
```

First, we import the `express` module. From this module, we are declaring the `api` variable, which is an instance of `express.Router`. A `teams` variable has been created in order to host some fake data for the teams. We will use this router to configure our CRUD/HTTP handlers, as follows:

```
api
  .route('/teams')
  .get((req, res) => {
    res.json(teams)
  })
  .post((req, res) => {
  })

app.listen(3000, () => {
...
```

Using the `api` route variable, we define the `'/teams'` path as root for the HTTP handlers. In the `get` handler, we are just sending the list of teams as the response.

Lastly, we need to export the `api` route to be used in the `server.js` file:

```
...
module.exports = api
```

Once we are ready, open the `server.js` file to apply the following changes that will configure the server to use this route:

```
const express = require('express')
const bodyParser = require('body-parser')
const teamsApi = require('./src/routes/teams-api')
const app = express()

app.use(bodyParser.json())
app.use(teamsApi)

...
```

First, we import the Teams API module from the relative path into our project and use the `app.use` function to configure our routes. Let's test things out; run the following command in your Terminal:

```
$ curl -X GET localhost:3000/teams

[{"id": 1, "name":"Peru"},{"id": 2, "name":"Russia"}]
```

Cool! Now we have our code clean and everything is working as we expect. It's time to write some code to implement the POST, PUT, and DELETE handlers. We will use the fake `teams` variable to add data in memory until we learn how to use a real database in the next chapter.

Creating a team

To create a team, we need to implement the POST handler. The data to the new team will be sent into the `body` parameter into the HTTP Request. Apply the following changes to the `teams-api.js` file:

```
...
api
  .route('/teams')
  ...
  .post((req, res) => {
    let team = req.body

    teams.push(team)

    res.status(201).json(team)
  })
  ...
...
```

First, we read the data from the `req.body` property. Then, we insert the new element into the `teams` array. Lastly, we send the `teams` array with the new team added and specify the HTTP status **201**, which means **Resource Created**.

 You can find the full list of HTTP statuses at `https://en.wikipedia.org/wiki/List_of_HTTP_status_codes`.

To test things out, we will call our API using the following command:

```
$ curl -X POST -H "Content-Type: application/json" -d '{"id":3, "name":
"Brasil"}' localhost:3000/teams
```

Our command is a little weird this time. As we are using JSON, we have to explicitly tell the HTTP Request that we are sending JSON data, so we use the -H header option. To send the information, we use the -d data option. That's all! It looks difficult but it is not.

Now you can use the GET method to list all the teams and see the new team added to our list.

Retrieving the list

We already have the list handler, but the listing is not enough. Apart from retrieving the full list, we will need to retrieve a single team. To do this, we will need to add a new GET route and learn how to use params. Apply the following changes into the teams-api.js:

```
...
api
  .route('/teams')
...

api
  .route('/teams/:id')
  .get((req, res) => {
      const id = req.params.id

      for(let team of teams) {
          if (team.id == id)
              return res.json(team)
      }

      return res.status(404).send('team not found')
  })

module.exports = api
```

First, we declare a new route, which now contains a dynamic param—/teams/:api. We said dynamic because, of course, it can take any value that will be available as an attribute of the req.params object. Note that the name you use for your param will be created as a property, for example, req.params.id in this case.

Next, we create a simple `for` loop that iterates across the full list of teams and looks for the team that has the same `id` we passed in the route param. If a team is found, we send the team by calling the `res.json(team)` statement. As we want to quit the handler immediately after we send the response, we use `return` to exit the handler. If a team is not found, we send an error message and mark the response with the HTTP `status` 404, which means **Resource not found**.

Lastly, to test our implementation, execute the following command:

```
$ curl http://localhost:3000/teams/1
  {"id":1,"name":"Peru"}

$ curl http://localhost:3000/teams/2
  {"id":2,"name":"Russia"}
```

 Keep in mind that by default, curl always sends a -X GET request if no HTTP verb has been explicitly defined.

Let's continue with our last two implementations for PUT and DELETE.

Updating a Team

The update process is a combination of two processes—the search for a team and the update process itself. In the previous implementation, we wrote the code to look up an existing team. So, let's reuse the same code by defining a function that can be used for retrieve, update, and delete. Open the `teams-api.js` file and apply the following changes:

```
...
let teams = [
    { id: 1, name: "Peru"},
    { id: 2, name: "Russia"}
]

function lookupTeamIndex(id) {
    for(var i = 0; i < teams.length; i++) {
        let team = teams[i]
        if (team.id == id)
            return i
    }
    return -1
}
```

```
api
  .route('/teams')
...
```

We created the `lookupTeam` function, which expects for the `id` as a param and will return a valid team index if it is found. Otherwise, it will return -1. Now we need to refactor our handle to retrieve a Team:

```
...
api
  .route('/teams/:id')
  .get((req, res) => {
      let id = req.params.id
      let index = lookupTeamIndex(id)

      if (index !== -1)
        return res.json(teams[index])

      return res.status(404).send('team not found')
  })
...
```

Having done that, let's implement our update handler. Apply the following changes in the same `teams-api` file:

```
...
api
  .route('/teams/:id')
  .get((req, res) => {
      ...
  })
  .put((req, res) => {
      const id = req.params.id
      const index = lookupTeam(id)

      if (index !== -1) {
        const team = teams[index]

        team.name = req.body.name
        teams[index] = team

        return res.json(team)
      }

      return res.status(404).send('team not found')
  })
...
```

So we define a `.put` route and look up for a team by passing the `id` param. If a valid index is returned, we save the team instance in the `team` variable and apply the change to its `name` property by reading the data from the `request.body` object and finally, we send the updated team. If there is not a valid index for the ID passed, we return a Not Found message.

Execute the following command to test things out:

```
$ curl -X PUT -H "Content-Type: application/json" -d '{"name": "Brasil"}'
localhost:3000/teams/999

Team not found
```

Deleting a Team

The `delete` process is similar to the `update`. First, we need to retrieve a valid index from the `teams` array and then remove it from there. Open the `teams-api.js` file and apply the following changes:

```
...
api
  .route('/teams/:id')
  .get((req, res) => {
    ...
  })
  .put((req, res) => {
    ...
  })
  .delete((req, res) => {
    const id = req.params.id
    const index = lookupTeam(id)
    const team = teams[index]

    if (index !== -1) {
      teams.splice(index, 1)
      return res.send(team)
    }

    return res.status(404).send('team not found')
  })
...
```

So we define a `.delete` route and look up for a team by passing the `id` param. If a valid index is returned, we save the team instance in the `team` variable. Next, we delete the element from the array using the `splice(index, 1)` expression. Lastly, we return the deleted `team` just for the information purposes.

We are done! We have implemented a RESTful API that exposes HTTP handlers for our Teams feature. We need to apply security to our routes and other advanced features. We will learn all about that in subsequent chapters. Keep reading!

Summary

In this chapter, we explored the API's world and understood how APIs are implemented using the HTTP Protocol and CRUD operations. This great combination enables the exchange of information easier than before.

We also learned how to create an API using Node.js and saw how easy it is to build a RESTful API using one of the most popular open source web frameworks—Express.js.

In the next chapter, we will integrate our API with MongoDB in order to save information in a real database instead of sending fake data. It's getting better.

Storing Our Data in MongoDB

6

All the applications that you use on a daily basis store their information in databases. Databases allow you to provide the best experience to your users. Just imagine how hard it might be for your users without a database. For example, imagine you have bought a new iPhone and need to have all your contacts from your Instagram account added to your new phone. If databases did not exist, you would need to copy all of your contact information and add it locally to your new device. This may sound ridiculous, but this is how a world without databases might be.

It is important to learn how to create applications that are able to connect and store information into a database. So, now you will learn how to use MongoDB as your NoSQL database and how to integrate our backend with it using one of the most popular libraries called Mongoose.js.

In this chapter, we will cover the following topics:

- NoSQL databases
- Introducing MongoDB
- MongooseJS
- Integrating our API with MongoDB

NoSQL databases

Big companies around the globe are using NoSQL Databases to provide the velocity that the users expect when using their applications; companies such as Facebook, Amazon, and Google all use them. However, why are these databases so special? To answer this question, let's see what is the difference between SQL and NoSQL databases:

SQL databases	NoSQL databases
Table-based and hard structured	Not table-based
Encourage normalization	Encourage denormalization
Require a schema	Are schema-less
Fast	Superfast
Scalability is difficult to achieve	Scalability is extremely easy to achieve

Of course, there are more differences and benefits, but talking about all the advantages and the science behind them is beyond the scope of this book.

It is important to know that there are different types of NoSQL databases to solve different types of challenges. Let's learn about them.

Document databases

This is one of the most popular databases, thanks to MongoDB and CouchDB. This type of database stores the information in a JSON-based document. As this is a key-value store, you can save complex objects that contain arrays, nested documents, and other different data types. For example, you can save the following *person* in the JSON document:

```
{
  "identification" : "PE0022458197",
  "name": {
    "firstName": "Jack",
    "LastName": "Ma"
  },
  "age": 45,
  "addresses": [
    {"country": "Peru", "address": "MyTown PE#32"},
    {"country": "China", "address": "OtherTown CH#44"}
  ]
  ...
}
```

As you can see, you don't need to store the addresses in a different document (or a table in SQL databases); you can perfectly store them in the same document (or a table in SQL databases).

Introducing MongoDB

As stated on its official website, MongoDB is an open source document database with the scalability and flexibility that you want and the querying and indexing that you need.

MongoDB uses collections to persist a set of JSON documents, and the schema for the documents can change over time without affecting the other documents stored in the collection. The schema-less feature is great when you are working on applications that have different kind of roles and users. A user might utilize some fields, while other users might require some other fields but without the need to fill the unused fields with null values. Instead, fields that are not required are not persisted in the JSON document.

Installing MongoDB

You can learn how to install MongoDB on its official site at `https://www.mongodb.com`. We strongly recommend you to use Docker for your development environment instead of installing MongoDB on your local machine. So, let's see how you can install MongoDB using Docker containers.

First, you will need to download Docker from its official site, `https://www.docker.com`. Once the download is completed, go ahead and install it. If you are working on MacOS or Windows, Docker will also install another tool called **Kitematic**. When the installation is done, look for **mongo** in the **Containers** section. Then, hit **CREATE**. Take a look at the following screenshot:

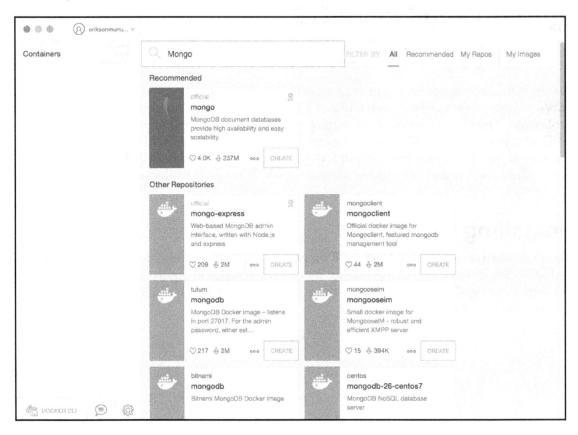

The tool will download the image and once it is done, it will run the MongoDB container and provide us the host and port where MongoDB is running, as illustrated:

For users who are using Linux, execute the following command to create a MongoDB container:

```
> docker run -p 27017:27017 -v $(pwd)/data:data/db mongo
```

The previous command will start a new container and exposes its internal port `27017` and will share a directory called `data` from your host to the container. By doing this, we can persist the container information into our host file system.

Once we have our MongoDB database running on top of Docker, we need to practice a little bit with MongoDB.

CRUD operations

Before we integrate our API with MongoDB, it is important to learn how to interact with MongoDB directly. So, let's learn how to perform the basic CRUD operations using the MongoDB command-line tool. To do this, we will need to access the MongoDB container Terminal, but it is extremely easy using Kitematic. In the container's toolbar, click on the **exec** options. This will launch a Terminal window connected to the MongoDB container Terminal.

When it is launched, type `mongo` to get into the MongoDB CLI. Take a look at the following screenshot:

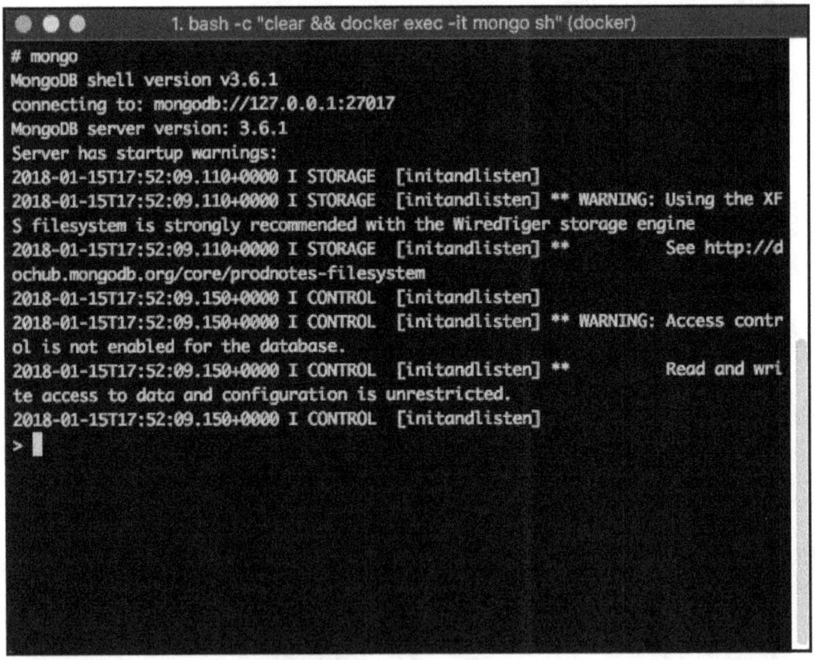

For users who are using Linux. You can get into the container by running the following command:

```
$ docker exec -it mongo sh
```

Cool! Now we are ready to play with MongoDB.

Creating a document

To insert a document, first we specify the `collection` name and pass the JSON document by calling the `insert` method as the following syntax:

```
> db.collection_name.insert(JSON_Object)
```

Let's insert the first team to our `teams` collection:

```
> db.teams.insert({"code": "PER",
... "name": "Peru",
... "ranking": 11,
... "captain": "Paolo Guerreo",
... "Trainer": "Ricardo Gareca",
... "confederation": "Conmebol"})

WriteResult({ "nInserted" : 1 })
```

The three dots at the beginning of the lines refer to new lines or the *Enter* key.

If the insertion was executed correctly, you should receive the `writeResult` response that contains the number of documents inserted into its `nInserted` property.

Retrieving documents

To retrieve the list of documents, we use the `find` method. For example, run the following query to retrieve the full list of teams:

```
> db.teams.find()

{ "_id" : ObjectId("5a5cf1419afc8af268b9bb21"), "code" : "PER", "name" :
"Peru", "ranking" : 11, "captain" : "Paolo Guerreo", "Trainer" : "Ricardo
Gareca", "confederation" : "Conmebol" }
```

As you can see, a new `_id` property has been added automatically. This property is known as the primary key of the JSON document. This is an autogenerated value, so you will have a different value when you run the command.

The teams' collection over time will have more than just a single team. So, how could we retrieve a single team from the collection? Do you remember the { } JSON object we passed to the find method? This JSON object is used to query the collection. So, if we want to retrieve the Peru team, we have to execute the following query:

```
> db.teams.find({"code": "PER"})

{ "_id" : ObjectId("5a5cf1419afc8af268b9bb21"), "code" : "PER", "name" :
"Peru", "ranking" : 11, "captain" : "Paolo Guerreo", "Trainer" : "Ricardo
Gareca", "confederation" : "Conmebol" }
```

Note that we can pass any field used in the JSON document. For example, you can use name, ranking, captain, and so on.

Updating documents

To update a document, we use the updateOne or updateMany methods. For example, let's update the ranking property of the Peru team. Execute the following code:

```
> db.teams.updateOne({"code": "PER"}, {$set: {"ranking": 1}})

{ "acknowledged" : true, "matchedCount" : 1, "modifiedCount" : 1 }
```

The syntax looks a little weird, but it is not. The first question you might have is why do we need $set? We need $set to specify the fields that we are interested to update. Otherwise, you will replace the document. Consider this example:

First, let's list our teams' collection to see the first update reflected:

```
> db.teams.find({"code": "PER"})

{ "_id" : ObjectId("5a5cf1419afc8af268b9bb21"), "code" : "PER", "name" :
"Peru", "ranking" : 1, "captain" : "Paolo Guerreo", "Trainer" : "Ricardo
Gareca", "confederation" : "Conmebol" }
```

Also, yes, the ranking field has been updated to 1. Now let's try to update this document without the $set operator:

```
> db.teams.updateOne({"code": "PER"}, {"ranking": 1})

[thread1] Error: the update operation document must contain atomic
operators :
```

Note that an error is thrown and no changes have been made. That is helpful for us because we are using the `updateOne` method, but there is another method called `update`, which will give us headaches if we don't use it properly. For example, run the following code:

```
> db.teams.update({"code": "PER"}, {"ranking": 1})

WriteResult({ "nMatched" : 1, "nUpserted" : 0, "nModified" : 1 })
```

At this moment, when you note that you forgot the `$set` operator, you have lost your team's data. Try to find the Peru team:

```
> db.teams.find({"code": "PER"})
```

No results are shown. Now a tear might be rolling down your cheek. Funny, right?

Be careful when you are updating or deleting documents. A production error of this type can cost you the post.

Deleting documents

Lastly, to delete a document, we use the `deleteOne` or `deleteMany` methods. For example, again insert the Peru team and run the following code:

```
> db.teams.deleteOne({"code": "PER"})

{ "acknowledged" : true, "deletedCount" : 1 }
```

Cool! Now we are in a good shape to learn about Mongoose and how to integrate our API with MongoDB. Keep reading!!

> We recommend that you use a GUI tool to explore your MongoDB data. We use **Robo 3T** or Robomongo. You can download it from its official page at `https://robomongo.org`.

MongooseJS

Mongoose.js is one of the most popular NPM modules to integrate a Node.js application with a MongoDB database. It provides an easy way to model our application data and comes along with different built-in features to validate, cast, and query our database, avoiding boilerplate code.

We will use our MongoDB container that we installed in the previous section. The two pieces of information that we need are the host and port where MongoDB is running. That information is shown in the Kitematic tool in the `Home/IP & Ports/Access URL` section. For example, in my case, these are `localhost` and `32768`:

Installing Mongoose

To install Mongoose, we will use NPM. So, in your Terminal, navigate to the `wc-backend` project and run the following command:

```
$ npm install --save mongoose
```

Once the installation is done, we need to get into the `src` folder and create a new folder called `config`. In the `config` folder, now create a new file called `mongoose-connection.js`:

```
$ cd src
$ mkdir config
$ touch config/mongoose-connection.js
```

Now that we have Mongoose installed and we have created our configuration file, it is time to write some code to establish the connection to MongoDB.

Configuring Mongoose

This is where the best part starts. So, we will need to create a connection to the *database*; to do this, open the `mongoose-connection.js` file and apply the following changes:

```
const mongoose = require('mongoose')

mongoose.connect('mongodb://localhost:32768/wcDb')

mongoose.Promise = global.Promise

mongoose.connection.on('connected', () => {
  console.log('connection is ready')
})

mongoose.connection.on('error', () => {
  console.log(err)
})
```

First, we import the Mongoose module and host it into the `mongoose` constant. Then, we call the `connect` function and pass the connection URL using the *host* and *port* that points to our MongoDB docker container. Lastly, we tell mongoose that our database name will be wcDb. If the connection was successful, the `connected` event will be called and the `connection is ready` message should be printed. Let's test things out; execute the following command:

```
$ node src/config/mongoose-connection.js

connection is ready
```

Cool! Our Node.js module is able to establish a successful connection with MongoDB using Mongoose. Now we will need to define schemas, models, and collections. Keep reading!

Defining schemas

To store information in our database we need to create a model, this model is created based on a initial schema definition. This schema definition contains the attributes and datatypes of the information we want to store. Let's define the schema for our collections of teams. In the same `mongoose-connection.js` file, add the following code:

```
...
const TeamSchema = new mongoose.Schema({
  name: String,
  ranking: Number,
  captain: String,
  trainer: String,
  confederation: String
})
```

As you can see, defining schemas is straightforward. We use the `mongoose.Schema` object and define the fields we want for our schema as a JSON object.

Data types

As in other database engines, the fields should be defined with a data type. The following are all valid types:

- `String`
- `Date`
- `Number`
- `Boolean`
- `Array`
- `ObjectId`
- `Buffer`
- `Mixed`

Perhaps, you are familiar will almost all the data types listed. The `Mixed` data type basically allows you to define a field whose value can be of any data type. Personally, we don't recommend the use of this data type because maintaining a `Mixed` field can become hard, and you may want to write boilerplate code to use it.

Validation

Mongoose comes with several built-in validators. Some validators are present in all data types and some are exclusive for a data type. For example, a `String` field will have the `min` and `max` validators but a `Boolean` type will not.

Let's add some validations to our `Team` schema. Open the `mongoose-connection.js` file and apply the following changes:

```
...
const TeamSchema = new mongoose.Schema({
  name: {
    type: String,
    min: 3,
    max: 100,
    required: true,
    unique: true
  },
  ranking: {
    type: Number,
    min: 1
  },
  captain: {
    type: String,
    required: true
  },
  Trainer: {
    type: String,
    required: true
  },
  confederation: {
    type: String,
    required: true,
    uppercase: true
  }
})
```

Now, our schema looks more professional and will help us validate the data before it is persisted in MongoDB. Most of the validators are self-explanatory. As you might have noticed, when you want to apply validators, the syntax to declare a field changes a little bit; in this case, a JavaScript object should be passed to define the data type and validators. To find more information about validators, visit `http://mongoosejs.com/docs/validation.html`.

Creating models

Now that we have our schema, it is time to tell Mongoose that we want to use that Schema to create new objects in order to send them to MongoDB. To do this, we need to create a model by passing the schema already defined. Open the `mongoose-connection.js` file and add the following code:

```
...
const Team = mongoose.model('team', TeamSchema)
```

Believe it or not, we just need this line to interface our schema to MongoDB. In this line, we tell Mongoose that we want to call our collection as `team`. The result of calling `mongoose.model` will be an object that is the model; we will use this object to create new instances. The `Team` object also contains built-in CRUD methods, so we will use them to create CRUD operations to the database.

To test things out, let's create the `Peru` team and save it in our database. In the same file, add the following changes:

```
...
const peruTeam = new Team({
  name: 'Peru',
  ranking: 11,
  captain: 'Paolo Guerrero',
  Trainer: 'Ricardo Gareca',
  confederation: 'Conmebol'
})

peruTeam.save((err, data) => {
  if (err)
    throw err

  console.log("Team was created with the Id", data._id)
})
```

First, we create the `peruTeam` object using the `Team` model instance we created earlier. Each new instance contains built-in functions. The `save` built-in function is called to save the `peruTeam` in the database. A callback is defined to process the result of the operation. If everything goes right, a message showing the new generated ID will be shown. So, execute the following command to test things out:

```
$ node src/config/mongoose-connection.js

connection is ready
Team was created with the Id 5a5f8e5c34a28e049c026ed6
```

Cool! Now we are ready to start the integration between our database module and our
RESTful API. Keep reading!!

Integrating our API with MongoDB

Here we are! It's time to implement our Teams Rest controller. To do this, we will start
decoupling the Team model that has all the logic to communicate with the MongoDB
database. Once the Team model is refactored, we will start implementing the code in the
Team Rest Controller to implement the CRUD operations to do the following:

- List all the teams
- Create new teams
- Update the existing teams
- Delete teams

Let's get our hands dirty!

Decoupling the Team Model

We have created a `models` folder in the root project directory. In this folder, we will create
all the models for our application. Start creating the `team.js` file in the `src/models`
folders:

```
$ touch src/models/team.js
```

Remember that we use the `touch` command to create a new file. Then, open this file, and
from the `src/config/mongoose-connection.js` file, cut the following lines and copy
them into the `src/models/team.js` file, as follows:

```
const mongoose = require('mongoose')

const TeamSchema = new mongoose.Schema({
    name: {
      type: String,
      min: 3,
      max: 100,
      required: true,
      unique: true
    },
    ranking: {
      type: Number,
```

```
    min: 1
  },
  captain: {
    type: String,
    required: true
  },
  Trainer: {
    type: String,
    required: true
  },
  confederation: {
    type: String,
    required: true,
    uppercase: true
  }
})
```

```
module.exports = mongoose.model('team', TeamSchema)
```

We just need to isolate the TeamSchema definition, and we are exporting the model created by mongoose to be accessed later by the Rest Controller. Be sure that your src/config/mongoose-connection file looks like the following:

```
const mongoose = require('mongoose')
mongoose.connect('mongodb://localhost:32768/wcDb', { useMongoClient: true
})
mongoose.Promise = global.Promise

mongoose.connection.on('connected',() => {
  console.log('connection is ready')
})

mongoose.connection.on('error', err => {
  console.log(err)
})
```

Cool! So far, so good. Now it is time to implement our Rest Controller.

Implementing the Rest Controller

Isolating the business logic is always a good practice; for that reason, we won't be calling the model directly from the Rest Controller.

Connecting the app

Let's start by calling the mongoose-connection module to open a connection to MongoDB. Open the server.js file and apply the following changes:

```
const express = require('express')
const bodyParser = require('body-parser')
const teamsApi = require('./src/routes/teams-api')
const mongooseConfig = require('./src/config/mongoose-connection')
const app = express()

app.use(bodyParser.json())
app.use(teamsApi)
...
```

That's all we need to establish a new connection. The mongoose-connection file contains the logic to open a connection to MongoDB, so we don't need to type more code.

Creating a new team

To create a new team, we need to call the model's built-in methods provided by Mongoose. The save function is used to create and update the fields for any model. So, first we will start importing the Team model into the src/routes/teams-api.js file, as follows:

```
const express = require('express')
const api = express.Router()
const Team = require('../models/team')

let teams = [
    { id: 1, name: "Peru"},
    { id: 2, name: "Russia"}
]
...
```

Now that we have imported the module with the require function and stored it into the Team constant, we can use it to create a new team. Let's modify the POST HTTP method of the Rest Controller:

```
...
api
  .route('/teams')
  .get((req, res) => {
    res.json(teams)
  })
  .post((req, res, next) => {
```

```
        let team = new Team(req.body)

        team.save()
        .then(data => res.json(data))
        .catch(err => next(err) )
    })
...
```

The first change to note is the next param into the function. This param is used to throw an error to express in case Mongoose is not able to create a new team. Then, we create a new team, passing the body param from the req object and calling the save function. The save function returns a Promise that is just an asynchronous call, which, when finished successfully, will return the information of the new team saved into the then method. Once we have the data, we send the information as a JSON type to the client.

Let's test things out. First, we need to get the server up by executing node server.js and then we will use cURL to test this endpoint. Open your Terminal and run the following command:

```
$ curl -X POST -H 'Content-type: application/json' -d '{"code": "GER",
"name": "Germany", "ranking": 8, "captain": "Paolo Guerreo", "Trainer":
"Ricardo Gareca", "confederation": "Conmebol"}' http://localhost:3000/teams

{"__v":0,"name":"Germany","ranking":8,"captain":"Paolo
Guerreo","Trainer":"Ricardo
Gareca","confederation":"CONMEBOL","_id":"5a662fbf728726072c6298fc"}
```

If everything went right, you should see the JSON object responding with the autogenerated _id attribute. Let's see what happens if we run it again:

```
$ curl -X POST -H 'Content-type: application/json' -d '{"code": "PER",
"name": "Peru", "ranking": 11, "captain": "Paolo Guerreo", "Trainer":
"Ricardo Gareca", "confederation": "Conmebol"}'

http://localhost:3000/teams

MongoError: E11000 duplicate key error collection: wcDb.teams index: name_1
dup key: { :\"Peru\" }
...
```

Now we receive an ugly error that says we are falling in a duplication key error. Why is this happening? Let's get answers from the model schema that we defined earlier. Open the `src/models/team.js` file:

```
const mongoose = require('mongoose')

const TeamSchema = new mongoose.Schema({
    name: {
      type: String,
      min: 3,
      max: 100,
      required: true,
      unique: true
    },

    ...
```

Hot dog! You have the answer. The error we are facing, is because we defined the name property as `unique:true`.

We will need to fix something in the message. We expect a JSON response from the REST API, so let's configure a global exception handler in our backend to send the error as a JSON object instead of an ugly and incomprehensible HTML page. Open the `server.js` file and apply the following change:

```
const express = require('express')
const bodyParser = require('body-parser')
const teamsApi = require('./src/routes/teams-api')
const mongooseConfig = require('./src/config/mongoose-connection')
const app = express()

app.use(bodyParser.json())
app.use(teamsApi)

app.use((err, req, res, next) => {
    return res.status(500).send({ message: err.message })
})


app.listen(3000, () => {
    console.log('running on port: 3000')
})
```

We defined a global middleware, which is a function that expects four params:

- `err`: Contains null if no error is thrown; otherwise, it's an instance of error or another value
- `req`: The source request sent by the client
- `res`: The response property
- `next`: The reference to the next action that Express.js will call

As is expected, all the errors return an HTTP status different than 200. Until we define the correct status of the other CRUD operations, let's leave it with `status(500)` by default. Now, let's run it again and see what happens:

```
$ curl -X POST -H 'Content-type: application/json' -d '{"code": "PER",
"name": "Peru", "ranking": 11, "captain": "Paolo Guerreo", "Trainer":
"Ricardo Gareca", "confederation": "Conmebol"}' http://localhost:3000/teams

{"error":"E11000 duplicate key error collection: wcDb.teams index: name_1
dup key: { : \"Peru\" }"}
```

As you can see, we receive a JSON object with a single `error` attribute. Cool! Let's continue and learn how to retrieve the full list of teams.

Listing the teams

To retrieve the full list of teams, we will make use of the GET HTTP method. Let's start by cleaning up our code a little bit. Until now, we have been using an array of teams; we won't need it anymore, so let's remove it. In `src/routes/teams-api.js`, apply the following changes:

```
...

api
  .route('/teams')
  .get((req, res) => {
    // TODO
  })
  .post((req, res, next) => {
    let team = new Team(req.body)
    team.save()
      .then(data => res.json(data))
      .catch(err => next(err) )
  })

api
```

```
.route('/teams/:id')
.get((req, res) => {
    // TODO
})
.put((req, res) => {
  // TODO

})
.delete((req, res) => {
  // TODO
})
```

...

Now that we have our code cleaned, add the following change to implement the logic to retrieve the full list of teams:

```
...
api
  .route('/teams')
  .get((req, res, next) => {
    Team.find()
      .then(data => res.json(data))
      .catch(err => { next(err) })
  })
  .post((req, res, next) => {
    let team = new Team(req.body)
    team.save()
      .then(data => res.json(data))
      .catch(err => { next(err) } )
  })
...
```

First, we call the `find` method to return a `Promise` as the `save` function used to create new teams. As it is a `Promise`, we will receive the data returned from the database into the `then` function and if something goes wrong, it will return an error in the `catch` function. Let's test it:

```
$ curl http://localhost:3000/teams

[{"_id":"5a662fbf728726072c6298fc","name":"Peru","ranking":11,"captain":"Pa
olo Guerreo","Trainer":"Ricardo
Gareca","confederation":"CONMEBOL","__v":0}]
```

Awesome! Now we are able to retrieve the list of teams using the `api` we just implemented. Let's continue!

Finding a single team

To find a single team, we will make use of the `findById` built-in method, and we will pass a valid ID to it. So, apply the following changes:

```
api
  .route('/teams/:id')
  .get((req, res, next) => {
      let id = req.params.id

      Team.findById(id)
        .then(data => res.json(data))
        .catch(err => next(err))
  })
  .put((req, res) => {
    // TODO

  })
  .delete((req, res) => {
    // TODO
  })
```

First, we extract the ID from the `req.params` object. Note that we are not using the `/teams` route. Instead, we are using the `/teams/:id` route. It means that Express.js will inject the `id` attribute as an element of the `params` object. Then, we call the `findById` method and send the response to the client. Let's test it:

```
$ curl http://localhost:3000/teams/5a662fbf728726072c6298fc

{"_id":"5a662fbf728726072c6298fc","name":"Peru","ranking":11,"captain":"Pao
lo Guerreo","Trainer":"Ricardo Gareca","confederation":"CONMEBOL","__v":0}
```

Cool! It is working. Note that we are using an existing ID—5a662fbf728726072c6298fc. This value will be different for you. To get a valid value, just call the `/teams` endpoint to list all your teams, and copy and replace it with the value in the `_id` attribute.

Now, what would happen if we pass an invalid ID? Let's test it:

```
$ curl http://localhost:3000/teams/5a662fbf728726072c629233

null
```

A `null` value is retrieved now. According to our API Documentation, we have to return the `HTTP 404` status to represent a **Not found** response. So, to do this, we need to validate the result from the `findById` method and raise an error if we receive a null as a response. Go ahead and apply the following changes:

```
...
api
  .route('/teams/:id')
  .get((req, res, next) => {
      let id = req.params.id
      Team.findById(id)
        .then(data => {
          if (data === null) {
            throw new Error("Team not found")
          }

          res.json(data)
        })
        .catch(err => { next(err) })
  })
...
```

Now with this implementation, if we receive a `null`, we will raise an error that will be handled by our global error handler, which will send a JSON object with the error message. Let's test it:

```
$ curl http://localhost:3000/teams/5a662fbf728726072c629233

{"error":"Team not found"}
```

Lastly, we need to modify our error handler to change the HTTP status code to `404`. In the `server.js` file, apply the following change:

```
...
app.use((err, req, res, next) => {
    let status = 500

    if (err.message.match(/not found/)) {
        status = 404
    }

    return res.status(status).send({ error: err.message })
})
...
```

First, we declare the STATUS variable and assign 500 as its default value. Then, we apply a regular expression validation to check whether the message contains the not found string. If so, STATUS is changed to 404. So, let's test it again, adding the -v flag in the curl command to see the HTTP status:

```
curl http://localhost:3000/teams/5a662fbf728726072c629233 -v
...
>
< HTTP/1.1 404 Bad Request
...
{"error":"Team not found"}
```

That's it! Now with this, we are ready to learn how to update a team.

Updating teams

To update our teams, first we will need to look for an existing team in our database using the ID provided in the path. If a team is found, we apply the changes to the team object. So, let's start adding the following code:

```
api
  .route('/teams/:id')
  .get((req, res, next) => {
    ...
  })
  .put((req, res, next) => {
    let id = req.params.id

    Team.findById(id)
      .then(data => {
        if (data == null) {
          throw new Error("Team not found")
        }
        return data
      })
      .then(team => {
        // We found the team.
        // Code to update goes here!
      })
      .catch(err => next(err))

  })
  .delete((req, res) => {
```

```
        // TODO
    })
  . . .
```

First, we extract the `id` passed in the endpoint. Then, we call the `findById` method to look for an existing team. If a valid team is found, we will have a `team` object as a parameter. Otherwise, an error will be thrown.

As you can see, there are more lines of code to add to our logic. Now it's time to extract the values from the `req.body` object and modify the `team` found:

```
    . . .
        .put((req, res, next) => {
          let id = req.params.id
          let teamBody = req.body

          Team.findById(id)
            .then(data => {
              if (data == null) {
                throw new Error("Team not found")
              }
              return data
            })
            .then(team => {
                team.code = teamBody.code || team.code
                team.name = teamBody.name || team.name
                team.ranking = teamBody.ranking || team.ranking
                team.captain = teamBody.captain || team.captain
                team.trainer = teamBody.trainer || team.trainer
                team.confederation = teamBody.confederation || team.confederation

            })
            .catch(err => {
              next(err)
            })

        })
    . . .
```

We have created a `teamBody` variable to host the `req.body` data. Then, we change the values into the `team` object. We are using the `||` operator; this operator will assign `teamBody.code` if this value is sent in the body object. Otherwise, it will assign the same value to the `team` object. With this, we are able to change the values only if they are sent.

Now, to save it to the database, we will call the save method as we did when we coded the logic to create a new Team:

```
...
.put((req, res, next) => {
    let id = req.params.id
    let teamBody = req.body

    Team.findById(id)
      .then(data => {
        if (data == null) {
          throw new Error("Team not found")
        }
        return data
      })
      .then(team => {
        team.code = teamBody.code || team.code
        team.name = teamBody.name || team.name
        team.ranking = teamBody.ranking || team.ranking
        team.captain = teamBody.captain || team.captain
        team.trainer = teamBody.trainer || team.trainer
        team.confederation = teamBody.confederation || team.confederation

        return team.save()
      })
      .then(result => res.json(result))
      .catch(err => next(err))

})
...
```

Cool! Now we have implemented the logic to update our Team entities. Let's test things out. Execute the following command:

```
$ curl -X PUT -H 'Content-type: application/json' -d '{"ranking": 1}'
http://localhost:3000/teams/5a662fbf728726072c6298fc

{"_id":"5a662fbf728726072c6298fc","name":"Peru","ranking":1,"captain":"Paol
o Guerreo","Trainer":"Ricardo Gareca","confederation":"CONMEBOL","__v":0}
```

Excellent! Now we are able to update Team entities. However, have you noticed that our code is a little difficult to organize? We are using multiple Promise entities to find and save a product. What will happen if we need to perform more asynchronous operations? Sooner or later, we will end up having code that contains a lot of then instructions that might be difficult to maintain and understand. However, don't worry! The async/await comes to save the day! Keep reading.

The async/await instruction

The async and await are two instructions that come to save our life from the `Promise` chaos. This will allows us to write asynchronous code using asynchronous syntax. Let's organize our code to see how this works!

First, we will need to create a new function for the update process, as follows:

```
...
const Team = require('../models/team')

const updateTeam = async (id, teamBody) => {
  try {
    let team = await Team.findById(id)

    if (team == null) throw new Error("Team not found")

    team.code = teamBody.code || team.code
    team.name = teamBody.name || team.name
    team.ranking = teamBody.ranking || team.ranking
    team.captain = teamBody.captain || team.captain
    team.trainer = teamBody.trainer || team.trainer
    team.confederation = teamBody.confederation || team.confederation

    team = await team.save()
    return team

  } catch (err) {
    throw err
  }
}

api
  .route('/teams')
...
```

The first thing to note in the preceding code is the `async` keyword. This keyword will wrap the returning result into a `Promise` and will allow us to use the `await` keyword. You cannot use `await` keyword in a non-async function. The `await` keyword will wait for the asynchronous call `Team.findById(id)` to end and will return the result. The same happens when we call the `team.save()` method.

Using async-await helps us avoid the `Promise` chaos. It provides us with an execution flow that might look like an asynchronous execution.

Once we have defined the `updateTeam` async function, we need to modify our PUT endpoint to call this new function:

```
...
  })
  .put((req, res, next) => {
    updateTeam(req.params.id, req.body)
      .then(team => res.json(team))
      .catch(err => next(err))

  })
  .delete((req, res) => {
    // TODO
  })
...
```

We said that `async` will wrap the result into a `Promise`, so to use the result, we will need to use the `then` and `catch` methods to process the returning `Promise`.

That's it! Now we are ready to learn how to delete an existing object.

Deleting teams

Deleting a team is extremely easy. To do this, we will call the remove built-in method of the `Team` model. Add the following code:

```
...
.delete((req, res, next) => {
    let id = req.params.id

    Team.remove({_id: id})
      .then(result => res.json(result))
      .catch(err => next(err))
  })


module.exports = api
```

Now, let's test things out. Execute the following command:

```
$ curl -X DELETE http://localhost:3000/teams/5a662fbf728726072c6298fc

{"n":1,"ok":1}
```

The output is a bit different now; we received a JSON object with two params:

- n: The number of documents removed
- ok: 1 if the operations were successful or 0 if not

Awesome! Now we have our Rest API to manage our teams ready, but there is a key missing piece in our API that we did not take care of, and that is security. We will make our API secure by adding an authentication and authorization layer in subsequent chapters. Keep reading!

Summary

In this chapter, you learned what a database is and the difference between SQL and NoSQL databases. Also, we implemented the API to manage teams that is able to persist the information into a MongoDB database.

You also learned about async/await, and we were able to code a more easy-to-read and maintainable asynchronous logic.

In the next chapter, we will explore advanced features of Aurelia to integrate our REST API with our Aurelia web application.

Advanced Features on Aurelia 7

Congratulations! Finally, we are here. Welcome to the last chapter of the second section of this book! At this point, we are really sure that you know how to plan and develop, and now we will add some cool features to make our application more interesting and scalable. Maybe you were thinking about how to share some properties or trigger events across all the components, or make your application understandable for people from different countries speaking different languages. Well, internationalization is a great concept that you are going to meet in this chapter. What if you need to perform operations to convert dates, numbers, or currency? Well, these kinds of situations (and so much more) are very common in a real application, so you need to be prepared to deal with it. You know what? We have good news! Aurelia is prepared with a great solution for every case (and so much more too!). In this chapter, you will learn the following topics:

- Event Aggregator
- Internationalization
- Logging
- Aurelia dialog
- Value converters
- Custom binding behaviors
- Validators
- Custom attributes
- Computed properties

Let's start with this awesome chapter; I assure you that you will find it very useful and interesting. We promise.

Subscribing and publishing events – Event Aggregator at the rescue!

In our current application, we have different components and views. Some of them need to retrieve data from the server, others just need to process data provided for other components, and yet others just help our user interface be more elegant and understandable. Okay, all looks good at this point. Note that at this point, our application supports different kinds of processing—data load, transformation, and how this is displayed. Each one implies a different cost of performance, and because of that one could take longer than others. That being said, let's describe a common scenario—the user enters our application and navigates to the page listing all the matches for this month. There is a lot of data to be retrieved, and you need to calculate the time between today and the match date (for each one).

The time remaining for the cost of all of this operation will depend on the amount of data returned by the server, so you need to remember something—when you design an application, design it while taking into consideration the most extreme cases.

Getting back to our application case, we can find two scenarios:

- The most convenient one is where the user knows that the application is retrieving data and waits patiently until the page is completely loaded. Honestly, based on our experience, this scenario represents 5% of the common user behaviors with digital applications.
- The second and most probable scenario is an impatient user, who thinking that their internet connection is lost, refreshes the page constantly, or presses some button, or, worse yet, leaves our application forever.

We need to take action to tell the user "Hey! I'm working on something, please wait!" and at the same time, block every button that can trigger an event causing more waiting time. We are sure you know the answer, the famous loading bar icon.

We have two options to implement it:

- Put a loading bar icon on every view/component and manage its behavior inside each one
- Put just one loading bar icon in our main application template and call it from other components

Maybe you are wondering, how can I call one event from another child component? Well, without Aurelia, of course, it could be a hard task to perform, but luckily, it won't be that case. Aurelia comes with an incredible and easy-to-learn/understand feature—Event Aggregator.

Like choosing to use anything, the decision to use the Event Aggregator module should be dictated by your application requirements. In most cases, it's for dealing with *cross-cutting concerns*.

Let's take an over view of what cross-cutting concerns are.

If there is some method that should be triggered at some event of the application/components lifetime and not have any relationship with it, we are talking about a cross-cutting concern. Some generic examples are as listed:

- Application loading
- Session validation
- Logging

Configuring Event Aggregator

The Event Aggregator class is not hard to understand. Incredibly, it just has three exposed methods. Like any other Aurelia module, you just need to import and inject it into your view model before using it:

```
import { inject } from 'aurelia-framework';
import { EventAggregator } from 'aurelia-event-aggregator';

@inject(EventAggregator)
export class ExampleClass {
    constructor(EventAggregator) {
        this.ea = EventAggregator;
    }
}
```

Now, let's explore the Event Aggregator methods in detail.

publish(event, data)

This method allows you to fire events. Remember that our `EventAggregator` will be placed in some parent component, so you know which components will be subscribed to it. So, because of that, this method does not have a specific target; they are just events triggered to space and doesn't matter if they have zero or more subscribers.

The first argument is the event name. You can choose any name for this, as it is your custom event. It will be used as an identifier to call it from external components across our application. In this case, you can use `EventAggregator` to configure our loading bar, so it would be right to name our event according to it. We will call it `dataRetrievingEvent`.

The second argument is the data you want to pass to the event (to supply some data, for example) and it's completely optional. Most of the time, it will be an array or an object of data. You can even pass through a string value if you like. However, not all events need to receive new data.

We will call this method using our class definition variable for `EventAggregator`:

```
this.ea.publish('dataRetrievingEvent', {message: 'Loading...don't close the
window!'
```

That was very easy. We have our first custom event configured and ready to be called from any component in our application.

subscribe(event, callbackFunction)

If we published an event at the first method, now it's time to listen to it. The first parameter is the event name we want to subscribe, and the second is a callback function that can be used to get the value sent by the event publisher. This data can be a simple string, or, like in our case, an object.

Like the preceding example, we can access this method through our `EventAggregator` class instance in our component:

```
let subscription = this.ea.subscribe('dataRetrievingEvent', response => {
    console.log(response);
    // This should yield: Object {message: "Loading...don't close the
window!"}
});
```

We have defined a `subscriber` object which is basically a method call. This object will make a direct reference to the subscribed event and allows us to execute directly a child function called `dispose`. This function is used to delete the existing subscription, generally used when our component is destroyed. Keep in mind that even the Event Aggregator is a great feature; a little cost in performance will be paid, so don't abuse it.

Here's an example of a subscription that is removed when the view model is detached:

```
import { inject } from 'aurelia-framework';
import { EventAggregator } from 'aurelia-event-aggregator';

@inject(EventAggregator)
export class ExampleClass {
    constructor(EventAggregator) {
        this.ea = EventAggregator;
    }

    attached() {
        this.subscriber = this.ea.subscribe('dataRetrievingEvent', response
=> {
            console.log(response.message);
        });
    }

    detached() {
        this.subscriber.dispose();
    }
}
```

This is a garbage collection measure and ensures that your app does not use resources that it no longer requires.

subscribeOnce(event, callbackFunction)

This method is exactly the same as the `subscribe()` method, but with just one difference—it automatically unsubscribes the event once the callback is raised. Maybe in some cases, you will find some situations that just require a *one-time* subscription, such as our loading bar. The example is very similar to the `subscribe()` method example:

```
attached() {
    this.subscriber = this.ea.subscribeOnce('dataRetrievingEvent',
response => {
        console.log(response.message);
    });
}
```

We are sure that you will find this feature really useful. This is just the beginning! Let's explore other awesome APIs!

Adding more languages to our application – Internationalization!

One of the more interesting (and useful) features for every web application is internationalization. We are developing an application for the FIFA World Cup Russia 2018, so, based on that, it would be awesome if our application supported multiple languages for all the users worldwide.

For this purpose, we will use the official `aurelia-i18n` plugin; this will be used to get the current app location. This plugin is based on the `i18next` library, with some very interesting characteristics such as those listed:

- Translation loaders
- Language detection
- Product localization
- Flexibility and scalability

The last one is the most important feature. With scalability in mind, you can implement internationalization with just one configuration file for smaller projects, and if you need to implement it on a bigger project, just create multiple translation files and load them according to the user's need.

Installation and configuration

Depending on which build tool you've chosen to create and configure your application, you will find many ways to install and get ready with the `aurelia-i18n` plugin. At this point, we've used the Aurelia CLI, but let's explore how to configure it in case we had chosen a different option, remember them?

- Webpack
- JSPM
- Aurelia CLI

For Webpack users

We need to retrieve the plugin from the npm repository, so just type the following command to get the latest:

```
npm install aurelia-i18n --save
```

It will download and save the plugin in your project dependencies. As we said earlier, aurelia-i18n is based on i18n framework, so you should install a backend plugin. One of the most famous is i18next-xhr-backend, a simple i18next backend to be used in the browser. How does it work? Easy, using XHR, it will load resources from some backend server. Yes, your translation files! If you want to use the built-in aurelia-loader backend, the same plugin Aurelia use to get resources, it's okay, you can ignore the next step.

You know what to do now.

```
npm install i18next i18next-xhr-backend --save
```

We are almost ready. In your Webpack configuration file, you must add aurelia-i18n to your project's Aurelia bundles list (on the Aurelia section):

```
const coreBundles = {
    bootstrap: [/* many options here */],
    aurelia: [
      /* many options here too*/
      'aurelia-i18n' // add aurelia-i18n to the array
    ]
  }
```

JSPM users

Similar way as the first two steps, but instead of using the known NPM, we will use JSPM. First, we will download the aurelia-i18n plugins:

```
jspm install aurelia-i18n
```

For the backend, type this:

```
jspm install npm:i18next-xhr-backend
```

Since we will use the built-in aurelia-i18n-loader, we don't need to add any additional configuration.

Aurelia CLI users

Almost the same as we explained in the Webpack user section, we need to retrieve the `aurelia-i18n` plugin and backend server from the `npm` repositories:

```
npm install aurelia-i18n --save
npm install i18next i18next-xhr-backend --save
```

Now, we need to tell our project that we have new dependencies to be configured. Open your Aurelia configuration file (`aurelia.json`) and look for the `dependencies` section. You must add the following entries:

```
{
    "name": "i18next",
    "path": "../node_modules/i18next/dist/umd",
    "main": "i18next"
},
{
    "name": "aurelia-i18n",
    "path": "../node_modules/aurelia-i18n/dist/amd",
    "main": "aurelia-i18n"
},
{
    "name": "i18next-xhr-backend",
    "path": "../node_modules/i18next-xhr-backend/dist/umd",
    "main": "i18nextXHRBackend"
}
```

 If your application was created using the `Aurelia CLI 0.33.1`, you can omit this last step.

Finally, we are done with the plugins. Now, let's configure it to our application!

Configuring and defining our first translation files

Our application is ready to start using the `i18n` framework. There are some steps to get ready with the plugin, so let's explore them.

The first thing we need is to locate our `index.html` file. This should be located in our main root application folder. Ensure that your `<body>` section is the same as the following:

```
<body aurelia-app="main">
    /* Some content */
</body>
```

 If you are a `Webpack` user, locate the `index.js` file instead of `index.html`.

Then, in your root app location, create a folder called `locales`. It will be used to store all your location files. Create one folder per language you want to support. Then, inside each folder, create a file called `translation.json`. This file will contain all your text translation structures, depending on your application.

Your application folder structure must look like this:

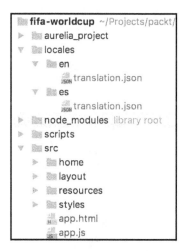

`i18next` works based on a predefined transaction-file schema. Look at the following example of our en-EN transaction file:

```
{
    "welcome": "Welcome to FIFA WC 18!",
    "user_male": "Mr.",
    "user_female": "Mss.",
    "time_remaining": "Time Remaining : {{time}}"
}
```

Now, one for es-ES language support:

```
{
    "welcome": "Bienvenido a FIFA WC 18!",
    "user_male": "Sr.",
    "user_female": "Sra.",
    "time_remaining": "Tiempo pendiente : {{time}}"
}
```

So these are simply for example purposes and very useful to understand how this plugin works. Now, it's time to configure the plugin backend. Do you remember that we created the `src/main.js` file to define our configuration function? Well, it's time to open this file and add some new configuration. If you haven't created this file yet, this is a good time to do that.

For those who have chosen the `i18next-xhr-backend` support, first of all, open the `main.js` file and find the Aurelia's configuration section. In the first lines of the file, you must import the following files:

```
import {I18N, TCustomAttribute} from 'aurelia-i18n';
import Backend from 'i18next-xhr-backend';
```

Then, create a new plugin pipe:

```
aurelia.use
  .standardConfiguration()
  .plugin('aurelia-materialize-bridge', b => b.useAll())
  .plugin()/* <<<< You must create a new plugin pipe*/
  .feature('resources');
```

Now, inside the new plugin pipe, add the following configuration:

```
.plugin('aurelia-i18n', (instance) => {
        let aliases = ['t', 'i18n'];
        TCustomAttribute.configureAliases(aliases);
        instance.i18next.use(Backend);

        return instance.setup({
          backend: {
            loadPath: './locales/{{lng}}/{{ns}}.json',
          },
          attributes: aliases,
          lng : 'es',
          fallbackLng : 'en',
          debug : false
        });
});
```

Let's explain a little of what are we doing in this file.

First, we need to configure our i18n aliases, so just declare them on a simple string array and pass it as a parameter to the static configureAliases() method. This will map the defined values in our <html> tags to call the correct values. It may sound a little confusing at this time, but don't worry, you are very near to seeing the whole picture:

```
let aliases = ['t', 'i18n'];
TCustomAttribute.configureAliases(aliases);
```

Next, we register the imported backend plugin (i18next-xhr-backend) into our aurelia-i18n instance:

```
instance.i18next.use(Backend);
```

Finally, we need to add some configuration. This is completely based on the i18n configuration documents, so you can find more information about this at http://i18next. com/docs/options. That promise configuration must be returned; because of that, we are adding the return statement before the instance.setup() declaration:

```
backend: {  // <-- configure backend
    loadPath: './locales/{{lng}}/{{ns}}.json', // <-- Our location files
path
},
```

The last options are used to map fallback language, default language and so on:

```
attributes: aliases, <<-- Predefined aliases
lng : 'es', // <<-- Default language to use (overrides language detection).
fallbackLng : 'en',// <<-- Language to use is current location language is
not available
debug : false // <<-- Log info level in console output
```

We are ready to start using the plugin. Good job!

If your are a Webpack user, don't forget to put the PLATFORM prefix before the plugin name. Example:
.plugin(PLATFORM.moduleName('aurelia-i18n'), (instance) => {......});

Using the plugin – Multilanguage support!

To start using our files, you must tell your ViewModel components which language to use. We will perform this operation at constructor method; check out this example:

```
import {I18N} from 'aurelia-i18n';
import { inject } from 'aurelia-dependency-injection';

@inject(I18n) export class WelcomePageComponent { constructor(i18n) {
this.i18n = i18n; this.i18n
  .setLocale('es-ES')
  .then( () => {}); } ... }
```

What if you want to get the active locale? Easy, change the configuration file to look like this:

```
import {I18N} from 'aurelia-i18n';

@inject(I18n)
export class WelcomePageComponent {
    constructor(i18n) {
      this.i18n = i18n;
    }
    ...
}
```

Similar to setLocale(), we have the getLocale() method. You can retrieve the active locale by typing the following:

```
console.log(this.i18n.getLocale());
```

Now, on the HTML file, we just need to call our translation aliases to map the properties we have defined in our translation.json files:

```
<h2 t="welcome">Welcome to FIFA WX 18</h2>
```

Optionally, we are able to use our second alias to map values:

```
<h2 i18n="welcome">Welcome to FIFA WX 18</h2>
```

Now you are ready to start adding multiple language support for your application! There are so many other advanced hints to get the best results using this plugin. We will show you one of them up next.

Imagine that you need to map <html> tags in your translation files. Is that possible? Yes. Imagine you need to render some long test (a product description, for example) and need to bold just a few words like price or discount. What do we need to do? Very easy, just add the HTML tag you need:

```
"time_remaining": "Time remaining : <b>{{time}}</b>"
```

Now, let's use this in our View file:

```
<label t="time_remaining">Time remaining : {{time}}</label>
```

If you look at your window, you'll see something like <b>bold</b>; don't be scared, it's normal. It's because we didn't set the correct markup to make our HTML tag correctly interpreted. You must know that there are four main attributes to add custom behavior to our translation file variables:

- [text]: Default attribute, escapes the tag value as simple text
- [html]: Tells our translation file "Hey, this contains HTML tags, render it as them!"
- [append]: Appends the translation to the current content already present in the element (allows HTML)
- [prepend]: Prepends the translation to the current content already present in the element (allows HTML)

This attribute has to be before our translation identifier key. You know what to do next:

```
<label t="[html]time_remaining">Time remaining : {{time}}</label>
```

Awesome? Yes, it is. It's up to you to research about other more advanced features; we are very sure you will enjoy all the options that i18n offers. That's all for this chapter? Of course, no. Let's keep exploring!

Tracking method calls and user actions – Logging

As a developer, you know how important it is to know what is happening in your application. Some information about the user clicks, event triggers, or error messages, having a good logging tool by your side telling you whether your application is okay (or really bad) is good practice. Commonly, developers use the common `console.log()` statement and when it's time to deploy it to UAT or production, they comment all these lines.

Aurelia knows how important this feature is, and guess what—yes, it has its own plugin for this purpose. Let's explore!

Configuring your log manager

By default, Aurelia has the logging API already in their dependencies, so you don't need to run any `npm` command at this point. Of course, if for some reason that library is missing, you know how to deal with it.

First, we need to create a file to configure our log levels. In the `resources` folder, create a file called `custom-log-appender.js`. This name is completely optional; you can name it in the most convenient way.

First, let's configure all our log levels:

```
export class CustomLogAppender {

  constructor(){}
  debug(logger, message, ...rest){
    console.debug(`DEBUG [${logger.id}] ${message}`, ...rest);
  }
  info(logger, message, ...rest){
    console.info(`INFO [${logger.id}] ${message}`, ...rest);
  }
  warn(logger, message, ...rest){
    console.warn(`WARN [${logger.id}] ${message}`, ...rest);
  }
  error(logger, message, ...rest){
    console.error(`ERROR [${logger.id}] ${message}`, ...rest);
  }
}
```

We are almost ready. Now, open the main configuration file (`main.js`) and import the logging dependencies from Aurelia:

```
import {LogManager} from 'aurelia-framework';
```

Also, import our recently created `CustomLogAppender`:

```
import {CustomLogAppender} from './resources/custom-log-appender';
```

Now, configure the Aurelia's `LogManager` with your created `CustomLogAppender`:

```
LogManager.addAppender(new CustomLogAppender());
LogManager.setLevel(LogManager.logLevel.debug);
```

Look for the `configure()` function. Just need to add one single line:

```
export function configure(aurelia) {
  aurelia.use
    .standardConfiguration()
    .developmentLogging() // <-- Logging activated for development env!
    .plugin('aurelia-animator-css');
```

Note that this kind of configuration will apply for all the environments (dev, test, prod). Commonly, logging is most used to detect error on development phase, so let's add some improvement to the previous configuration:

First, let's create a file called `environment.js`. This file will contain our current activated environments:

```
//environment.js
export default {
  debug: true,
  testing: false
};
```

Then, we need to import that file into our `src/main.js` file:

```
import environment from './environment';

export function configure(aurelia) {
 aurelia.use
    .standardConfiguration()
    .plugin('aurelia-anumator-css');

if (environment.debug) {
    aurelia.use.developmentLogging();
}
```

```
        .
        .
        .
    }
```

You are ready to start using the logger! Let's open one `ViewModel` file and start recording what is happening inside:

```
import {LogManager} from 'aurelia-framework';
let logger = LogManager.getLogger('homePage');
logger.debug('me');

export class HomePage() {
    activate(){
        logger.debug("Enter to home page!!!");
    }
}
```

This is so easy and so useful. Of course, we have so many more special features to show you. Keep reading man!

Modal configuration – Aurelia dialog at rescue!

Every application needs to show different kinds of information to the final user. Does that information need to be displayed on one page? Not necessarily. The final user is very familiarized with the bootstrap dialog (commonly called `Modal`), which is a custom JavaScript `alert()` element. More elegant and more friendly to add custom behavior, it could now be used only to show alerts information, also you can configure entire forms or confirmation dialogs. In our FIFA World Cup application, the `Aurelia-materialize` plugin has already configured this feature for the modal component, but let's explore how this works and how we can improve it. Let's go!

Getting the Aurelia-dialog plugin

If you are using JSPM manager, type the following command:

```
jspm install aurelia-dialog
```

Else, for Webpack / Aurelia CLI users, use the known npm install command:

```
npm install aurelia-dialog --save
```

Remember to save this dependency into your project dependencies section. It's very important, because it will be used in the final application build.

Now, let's tell our application that we have a new plugin. Like other plugins seen earlier, open your Aurelia configuration file (aurelia.json) and add a new plugin section:

```
{
    dependencies: [
    // Some content here
      {
        "name": "aurelia-dialog",
        "path": "../node_modules/aurelia-dialog/dist/amd",
        "main": "aurelia-dialog"
      }
    // Some content here too
    ]
}
```

We have already configured our index.html file to use manual bootstrapping; if not, just ensure that it has the <body> element with the aurelia-app="main" tag inside:

```
<body aurelia-app="main">
</body>
```

In your application config file (main.js), add a new plugin() entry:

```
export function configure(aurelia) {
    aurelia.use
      .standardConfiguration()
      .developmentLogging()
      .plugin('aurelia-dialog'); // <<-- Add this plugin!
```

Also, if you want to add a more customized behavior to your `modal`, you can implement some configuration inside this `plugin()` pipe. Optionally, you can configure the `aurelia-dialog` plugin as follows:

```
.plugin(PLATFORM.moduleName('aurelia-dialog'), config => { // <<--
PLATFORM.moduleName is mandatory if you are using webpack
        config.useDefaults();
        config.settings.lock = true;
        config.settings.centerHorizontalOnly = false;
        config.settings.startingZIndex = 5;
        config.settings.keyboard = true;
});
```

You are ready! Now, it's time to listen to our plugin!

Adding dialog components to our application

Let's create a `UserRegister` modal for our application. This will look something like this:

```
import { inject } from 'aurelia-framework'
import { DialogController } from 'aurelia-dialog'

@inject(DialogController)
export class UserForm {
  user = { firstName: '',
           lastName: '',
           age: 0
  };

  activate(user){
    user = user;
  }
}
```

This is very simple by now. Remember that this component will be the modal itself. The modals are displayed over the main content, so now we will configure this behavior into our `Home` component. Pay attention to this section; it's a little tricky, but we are sure that you will find it easy to implement.

First, let's import `DialogService` from our recently imported `aurelia-dialog` plugin:

```
import {DialogService} from 'aurelia-dialog';
```

Also, let's import our recently created `UserForm` component:

```
import {UserForm} from './user-form';
```

Now, let's configure the dialog behavior:

```
export class HomeComponent {
   static inject = [DialogService]; // <<-- Same as use the @inject
annotation

   user = { firstName: 'Diego', lastName: 'Arguelles', age: 26 }

   constructor(dialogService) {
      this.dialogService = dialogService; <<-- We need to inject the service
into our component
   }

   openModal(){
      this.dialogService.open({ viewModel: UserForm, model:
this.user}).whenClosed(response => {
         if (!response.wasCancelled) {
            console.log('good - ', response.output);
         } else {
            console.log('bad');
         }
      });
   }
}
```

In addition, the `<template>` file needs to contain one `<button>` to trigger the `openModal()` method:

```
<template>
   <button click.trigger = "openModal()">New user</button>
<template>
```

Let's explain the `openModal()` method:

First, we need to open the modal. We will set some default values for our recently created user object. This method will return a `promise` object. Why? So simple, with this `promise`, we will be able to handle any event triggered inside the modal:

```
this.dialogService.open({ viewModel: UserForm, model: this.user}).then();
```

Inside the `then()` statement, our `promise` will be defined in such a way:

```
response => {
    //We will get the response value returned by the modal
    if (!response.wasCancelled) {
        console.log('All OK - ', response.output); //Should output the
recently created user info
    } else {
        console.log('Something get wrong!');
    } console.log(response.output);
}
```

Now, let's look at our `<template>` file:

```
<template>
    <ux-dialog>
        <ai-dialog-body>
            <h2>User registration</h2>
            <input placeholder="User name" model.bind="user.firstName" />
            <input placeholder="User last name" model.bind="user.lastName" />
            <input placeholder="User age" model.bind="user.age" />
        </ai-dialog-body>
        <ai-dialog-footer>
            <button click.trigger = "controller.cancel()">Cancel</button>
            <button click.trigger = "controller.ok(message)">Ok</button>
        </ai-dialog-footer>
    </ux-dialog>
</template>
```

Of course, we can customize how our modal is displayed. For example, bootstrap by default adds 50% opacity in the modal background. To get the same result, include this CSS class in an existing or new style sheet. Depending on which CSS preprocessor you are using, don't forget to import it if necessary:

```
ai-dialog-overlay.active {
    background-color: black;
    opacity: .5;
}
```

 Remember that we are overwriting an existing class from Aurelia dialog, so you don't need to specify this class in the `<html>` component.

Now, you are ready to add a more user-friendly behavior to your application with the use of dynamic dialogs.

Dynamic value converters – Less code, more functionality

As we said at the beginning of this chapter, our application should be available for all the users worldwide. You are completely free to model the application according to your own purposes. Maybe you want to implement premium features that would need you to pay to access them, so you will need to express the cost in the user currency. Another good thing could be to have a custom formatted date, or simply add some number conversion, decimal rounds, and so on.

You already know how to bind and interpolate values between Aurelia `View` and `ViewModel` components. Now we will see how to improve that data binding. Come on!

The problem – Data is not exposed as we need

One of the common problems we could have is the date formatting. In other code languages such as Java, you have a utility class like `SimpleDateFormat`, which converts the `Date()` object to a more friendly human reading format. In JavaScript, we have some libraries to do that job, but they are not so simple to call. Let's see an example.

You get the current date in your `ViewModel` component; then, you pass that value to the `View` layer:

```
export class Example {
    constructor() {
      this.changeDate();
      setInterval(() => this.changeDate(), 3000); //<<-- This method will
be executed each 3 seconds
    }

    changeDate() {
      this.currentDate = new Date(); //<<-- Get the current date
    }
}
```

In our `View` file, we map the `currentDate` value to be displayed:

```
<template>
    ${currentDate}
</template>
```

When you run the example, you will be displayed in your screen the following output:

```
Sun Feb 25 2018 14:06:37 GMT-0300 (-03)
```

Okay, we can do better; it's time to call our value-converters, but exactly, what is a value converter? The Aurelia documents explain it really good:

> *"A value converter is a class whose responsibility is to convert view-model values into values that are appropriate to display in the view and vice versa."*

That being said, let's create one value-converter file just for example purposes. Since we are working with a `Date()` value, we will work with the `moment` plugin.

If you don't have it in your dependencies tree, just import it from `npm` repositories:

```
npm install moment --save
```

Then, first of all, import this library in our value-converter file:

```
import moment from 'moment';

export class DateFormatValueConverter {
    toView(value) {
        return moment(value).format('M/D/YYYY h:mm:ss a');
    }
}
```

Okay, now let's explain how this works:

- You know that Aurelia is a convention over configuration-based framework. With that being said, if you name this class terminating it `ValueConverter`, the framework will use this class as a custom value converter without any more configuration.
- The `toView()` method is inherited from the Aurelia `ValueConverter` interface. It defines the data flow direction, if it comes to `ViewModel` to `View`, or vice versa, you have the `fromView()` method.
- Those value-converter methods could receive more than one parameter.

Now, we just need to import this value-converter in our `View` file like any other dependency, using the `<require>` tag:

```
<template>
    <require from="./date-format"></require> <<-- Path to your value
converter
```

Now, we need to add the converter to our binding syntax:

```
<template>
    <require from="./date-format"></require>
    ${currentDate | dateFormat} <br/> <<-- Name mapped for our value
converter
</template>
```

Now, refresh your browser window:

```
2/25/2018 2:25:36 pm
```

So much better, right? Well, this same dynamic can be applied to number format converters, currency, and so on. Let's make the example a little more advanced—what if we need to show multiple date formats across our entire application? Should we define a value-converter file per format we need? It's a valid option, but not the most effective. Do you remember when we said that value-converter interface methods can receive more than one parameter? Well, what if we send the date format as parameter too? Let's try to see what happens:

```
toView(value, format) {
    return moment(value).format(format);
}
```

You can specify a default format in case no one was provided:
`toView(value, format = 'M/D/YYYY'){ ... }`

Nice, our formatter now accepts the `format` pattern as a parameter. It's not the magic of Aurelia; it's because we are using `moment.js` a nice JavaScript library, which allows us to perform this kind of operations.

Now, in our `View` file, we can add as many time formats as we need:

```
${currentDate | dateFormat:'h:mm:ss a'} <br/>
${currentDate | dateFormat:'M/D/YYYY h:mm:ss a'} <br/>
${currentDate | dateFormat:'MMMM Mo YYYY'} <br/>
```

Now, look at your browser window:

```
2:33:11 pm
2/25/2018 2:33:11 pm
February 2nd 2018
```

That was very nice. Now it's time to take a look at a little more complicated example but with a more common usage—arrays order.

You know how to retrieve data from one backend service; often this data is retrieved as an `array` object and shown as a list in the `View` file. That's all okay, but what if we need to order these values according to some property? Look at the code example:

```
export class ArraySortingValueConverter {
    toView(array, config) {
        let sorter = (config.direction || 'ascending') === 'ascending' ? 1
: -1;
        return array.sort((a, b) => {
            return (a[config.propertyName] - b[config.propertyName]) *
sorter;
        });
    }
}
```

What are we doing? Let's explain.

We are receiving two parameters, one array, and one config property. The config property is an object with two values: `config.direction`, which can be one of these two options: ascending or any other string. Depending on that, the sorter can order the list incrementing values 1, or decreasing with -1 in descending order. Then, in the return statement, we are using the sort function of the array itself, and we are sending as parameter the anonymous function to compare the mapped `config.propertyName` values in the config object.

This is how we are retrieving the data from some backend service:

```
import {HttpClient} from 'aurelia-http-client';

export class Example {
    users = [];
    activate() {
        return new HttpClient()
            .get('https://api.ourorganization.com/users')
            .then(response => this.users = response.content);
    }
}
```

There's nothing weird at this point. Now, let's check the `View` file:

```
<template>
    <require from="./array-sort"></require> <<-- Import your value
converter
```

```
    <div class="row">
      <div class="col-sm-3" repeat.for="user of users | arraySorting: {
propertyName: 'code', direction: 'descending' }">
          ${user.firstName}
      </a>
    </div>
  </div>
</template>
```

It's beautiful. We don't need to add any JavaScript function or weird configuration to start using this very useful functionality.

Binding custom behaviors to our application

Let's continue with our Aurelia special features exploration. In the last section, we saw value-converters, and it's impossible to not make a relationship between this feature and the binding engine of Aurelia framework. Maybe you think that both features have much in common, well, not so much really. Let's start explaining how the binding engine works.

The view resources in Aurelia framework can be divided into four categories:

- Value converters
- Custom attributes
- Custom elements
- Binding behaviors

We will focus only on the last one. It's not because the others are less important but because it will be better for us to understand how this works first and then explore the other categories. Don't worry, value-converters are already covered, and you will have a clearer idea about the difference between both features.

The value-converter acts just as a bridge interceptor between View and ViewModel (or vice versa). The binding behavior goes beyond—it has full access to the binding instance across the complete component life-cycle. This allows us to make changes in the binding behavior, such as modifying the binding throttle time, or adding customization to how the values are updated.

Remember that Aurelia is a two-way binding framework, so you don't need to worry about the data synchronization between `View` and `ViewModel`. How is this performed? Aurelia has a predefined throttle mechanism that updates values each 200 ms, by default. Could it be updated? Yes, Aurelia left us free to manage this value according to our needs. Similar to the `value-converters` syntax, we need to call the binding behavior in the `<template>` file, where we need it:

```
<input type="text" value.bind="query & throttle:850">
```

Did you note the `&` symbol? It's the first difference with the already covered value-converters. When we need to define a binding behavior, we tell this to the framework using the `&` wildcard. Another thing you must note is that we can send parameters to the binding behaviors. Just need to add the `:` symbol after the behavior declaration and send the value. Its possible to send multiple params? Yes. How? Look at the example:

```
<input type="text" value.bind="query & customBehavior:arg1:arg2:arg3">
```

Also, you are allowed to declare more than one behavior in one element:

```
${value | upperCase & throttle:800 & anotherBehavior:arg1:arg2}
```

In the same way, you can define the updating time period between `View` and `ViewModel`; you have another interesting binding behavior called **debounce**. We can refer to this behavior in the same category of *throttle*, but the difference is that instead of calculating updating time, it prevents the binding from being updated until a specified interval has passed without any changes.

Maybe you will find this feature more useful; let's explain it through a real use case.

In our FIFA World Cup application, one of the most demanded features could be a search input, more specifically, an autocomplete. You already know that autocomplete component should retrieve data according to the users' input value. The big question when you develop this feature is "when should we trigger the `searchByKey()` method of the autocomplete? On every keypress? When the input length is greater than 2 or 3?". Really, this is a hard question; your application performance is directly compromised.

This is a good moment to think about *debounce*. Instead of triggering the `searchByKey()` method each time the user enters a value, trigger it some time after the user enters their search key:

```
<input type="text" value.bind="teamCountry & debounce:1000">
```

Other really useful binding behavior you can use is `oneTime`. By default, Aurelia set the preconfigured two-way binding to each `ViewModel` property. The big question is "do we really need this two-way binding activated for each property in our components?". Most of the time, the answer is no. Here's where `oneTime` comes and becomes our performance optimization partner. Really, it has a direct impact on application performance? Yes. To enable double binding, Aurelia needs to implement multiple observers looking for any changes in your component properties. With `oneTime`, we just tell the app—map this property to my view and forget it:

```
<span>${score & oneTime}</span>
```

Of course, there are many more predefined binding behaviors to explore, but if you remember, we used one binding behavior defined as `customBehavior` in our first example. Did you note that? Guess what, Aurelia allows you to define your own binding behavior, and now it's time to learn how.

Similar to custom value-converters, you can create custom binding behaviors. Check the following example:

```
export class DynamicExpressionBindingBehavior {

  bind(binding, source, rawExpression) {
    console.log('Binding : '+rawExpression)
  }

  unbind(binding, source) {
    console.log('Unbinding ')
  }
}
```

Like the last examples, let's explain what the code is doing.

First, you must know that similar to the `toView()` and `fromView()` methods from value-converters, custom binding behaviors need to implement two methods: `bind(binding, src, expressions...)` and `unbind(binding, src)`.

On the `bind()` method, we are manipulating the user input value passed as a parameter. Something you must know is that on the `bind()` method, the first two parameters are sent by Aurelia. The other params can be one or more custom parameters; in this case, `rawExpresions`.

The `unbind()` method just ensures that our binding behavior returns to normal when our data processing ends.

Looks simple? Yes, the example looks easy, but a real implementation will be harder to understand. Don't worry, the predefined set of binding behavior commonly provided by Aurelia framework is enough for every application's purposes.

Improving our application forms – Validators

We know how the binding engine of Aurelia works. Also, we know how to intercept and customize that binding behavior. We know too how to transform data between View-ViewModel layer according to our needs. Just some things are pending, and the `aurelia-validation` plugin is one of them. When you need data provided by the user, you have to expect anything. The user didn't know your app. He will do anything he wants, and you need to be prepared for that. You need to ensure that data provided by the user is, at least, in the right format your back service is expecting. You need to filter just the right values and send alerts to the user telling which values are wrong and how they can fix it. We often need to put ourselves on the user's side. Software development is more than just programming, more than just creating forms and storing/retrieving data. We need to make our application fault-tolerant and as we said earlier, think always in the worst case. Just imagine something like this—you are developing an application that needs to perform some calculations. You have three inputs: a, b, and c; you need to calculate the sum. Well, that sounds easy, right? We have two users who type the following:

```
User 1 : value for a)33; b)23; c)32
```

You press the **Submit** button and get the correct sum—88. Fine, the application accomplished their purpose. Let's see what second user puts:

```
User 2: value for a)49 b)34j c)12
```

As you can see, the last user presses by error the j character. Will it rely on an application error? No. Our operation will be performed, JavaScript is not a typed language, so it will operate in the following way:

```
49 + "34j" + 12 = "4934j12"
```

The user will see that value, and we are sure they will never use your application again.

Preparing for war – Getting the validation plugin

Like other plugins we could have installed, the installation and configuration steps are very similar. If this is the first time you are performing this operation, just carry out the following steps:

If you are using NPM as package manager, use this:

```
npm install aurelia-validation --save
```

Alternatively, if you are a JSPM user, use this:

```
jspm install aurelia-validation
```

Now, open your `main.js` file where we had configured our application plugins. In the `configure()` function, add the new plugin:

```
export function configure(aurelia) {
    aurelia.use
      .standardConfiguration()
      .developmentLogging()
      .plugin('aurelia-validation'); // <<-- Add this plugin!
```

Finally, open your `aurelia.json` file and add the following plugin declaration:

```
{
  "name": "aurelia-validation",
  "path": "../node_modules/aurelia-validation/dist/amd",
  "main": "aurelia-validation"
}
```

We are ready. Let's go!

First steps – Defining our rules

The Aurelia validation plugin is based on standard rules. We need to define our own set of rules using the `ValidationRules` class. This class has some static methods that receive our values and verify that the input value meet our requirements. Also, one validation rule must have one predefined format. The first method we will explain is `ensure()`:

```
ValidationRules.ensure('myValidatedProperty')
```

This method accepts one argument that will be our property name that we want to validate. Also, in case you were validating an object, you are allowed to pass anonymous functions as a parameter:

```
ValidationRules.ensure(u => u.firstName)
```

The second method we will explain is `displayName()`. This is not required but is useful if you need to show this property in one predefined format in your validation messages; consider this example:

```
ValidationRules.ensure(u => u.firstName).displayName('User name')
Error message: The user name is required.
```

Finally, we need to define our set of rules that will apply to that field; some of the most used are as follows:

- `required()` prevents the user from submitting null or blank values
- `matches(regex)` helps us ensure that the input value meets a predefined format, and is common on date fields
- `email()` is an easy way to ensure that the email is in the right format
- `minLength(length)` and `maxLength(length)` validate the length of string properties

If our user's first name should never be null, the validation rule will be this:

```
ValidationRules.ensure('u => u.firstName').displayName('First name')
    .required().withMessage(`\${$firstName} cannot be blank.`);
```

Did you note something different? Yes, we are using the `withMessage()` method to customize our validation error message. The thing becomes more interesting.

What if you need these validation rules to apply just for one object? Don't worry, Aurelia has the problem solved. You need to tag the object you want to apply the rule on; the example is self-explanatory:

```
// User.js class inside our models folder
 export class User {
    firstName = '';
    lastName = '';
 }

export const UserRules = ValidationRules
    .ensure('firstName').required()
    .ensure('lastName').required()
    .on(User);
```

We are almost ready. Now, we need to configure our form controller with the recently created validation rules:

```
import { inject, NewInstance } from 'aurelia-dependency-injection';
import { ValidationController } from 'aurelia-validation';
import { User, UserRules } from '../models/User'

@inject(NewInstance.of(ValidationController))
export class UserRegisterForm {
    constructor(userValidationController) {
      this.user = new User(); // 1
      this.formValidator = userValidationController; //2
      this.formValidator.addObject(this.user, UserRules); //3
    }
}
```

Maybe you are wondering why we need this `NewInstance.of()` statement? Well, for each validation rule we are applying, we need a single controller to validate it. So, with this statement, we just ensure that a new `ValidationController` instance is created.

Now let's explain what is occurring inside our constructor method:

- Line 1: We are creating a new instance of the `User` object to use his properties in our form.
- Line 2: We are assigning the new `ValidatorController` instance into our `formValidator` object.
- Line 3: We are saying to our `formValidator` that the evaluated object is our user instance, and will use the imported `UserRules`.

Other way to configure our `formValidator` is defining the properties and rules inside the `validate()` method:

```
formValidator.validate({ object: user, propertyName: 'firstName', rules:
myRules });
```

In our `submit()` method, we just need to add the following:

```
formValidator.validate()
      .then(result => {
        if (result.valid) {
        // validation succeeded
        } else {
```

```
        // validation failed
    }
});
```

Lastly, we need to tell our template where the validators will be placed:

```
<input type="text" value.bind="user.firstName & validate">

<input type="text" value.bind="user.lastName & validate">
```

The first value will be passed as a parameter to the ensure() function. Hey, wait a second! We need to specify where our error messages will be placed! Well, that's really simple, we would implement an error list like this:

```
<form>
    <ul if.bind="formValidator.errors">
      <li repeat.for="error of formValidator.errors">
        ${error.message}
      </li>
    </ul>
</form>
```

Alternatively, if you want to display the message beside the wrong input element, you can use the <span> tag and other very interesting custom attribute: validation-errors

```
<div validation-errors.bind="firstNameErrors">
    <label for="firstName">First Name</label>
    <input type="text" class="form-control" id="firstName"
            placeholder="First Name"
            value.bind="user.firstName & validate">
    <span class="help-block" repeat.for="errorInfo of firstNameErrors">
      ${errorInfo.error.message}
    </span>
</div>
```

The validation-errors attribute contains all validation errors regarding to the specified element (in this case firstNameErrors).

Now, start putting validation rules across your application forms! See you in the next section!

Manipulating the DOM – Custom attributes

We are almost done with the most used advanced features of Aurelia. Now, it's time to explore other categories belonging to binding engine plugins—what exactly are custom attributes? Let's explain that in a very easy way—you know the HTML tags, such as <div>, <input>, and <span>. Also, you know that each element has attributes such as class, type, and style. Well, now we can add more attributes to make the element more customizable and add a more advanced behavior. Let's look at an example.

We had also seen the value-converters, but don't you think it would be awesome if we implement a custom attribute to perform this operation on any element? Consider something like this:

```
<label datetime="format:YYYY-MM-DD HH:mm">${match.date}</label>
```

Also, match.date will be a simple Date() JavaScript object without any format. Why do we need to accomplish this? Pay attention, we are sure that at this point, knowing the basic binding concepts, you will find it very easy.

First, create a class to configure your customAttribute:

```
import {customAttribute, bindable, inject} from 'aurelia-framework';
import moment from 'moment';

@inject(Element, moment); <<-- We already know how moment js works
@customAttribute('datetime'); <<-- The attribute name to refer it
@bindable('format'); <<-- The property we pass as parameter
export class Datetime {

    constructor(element, moment) {
        this.element = element;
        this.moment = moment;
    }

    bind() {
        this.element.innerHTML =
moment(this.element.innerHTML).format(this.format);
    }
}
```

What is Element doing? That's simple—it helps us point to the right element we want to apply the custom attribute to. Next, we just need to call our file into the template we need.

Another very interesting way to define your custom attribute is using the already known convention over configuration feature:

```
import {bindable, inject} from 'aurelia-framework';
import moment from 'moment';

@inject(Element, moment);
export class DatetimeCustomAttribute {

    @bindable format; // <<-- The value property can also be placed inside
the class declaration

    constructor(element, moment) {
        this.element = element;
        this.moment = moment;
    }

    bind() {
        this.element.innerHTML =
moment(this.element.innerHTML).format(this.format);
    }
}
```

Now, in our `View` file:

```
<require from="./datetime"></require>
<label datetime="format:YYYY-MM-DD HH:mm">${match.date}</label>
```

What if we need this custom attribute available for all my application components? Well, we have a very good news—you can configure it as a global resource into your application configuration file (`main.js`).

Identify the `configure` method and add a global resource pointing to our recently created custom attribute:

```
export function configure(aurelia) {
    aurelia.globalResources(
        "./datetime"
    )
}
```

At this time, you must find all these features very easy to learn, and this is because you know more advanced features that helped us understand how the framework works. See you in the last section!

Understanding how computed properties work

Welcome to the last section of this chapter! You can consider yourself a full stack programmer with strong knowledge on frontend technologies. If you note, the concepts that Aurelia uses to implement the different features are based on common problems that every web application needs to deal with, no matter which framework it is using. Also, as open source tools, the different plugins are based on other tools that actually give support to other framework plugins, such as Angular.

Now, the last feature that we will explain is about computed properties. We can resume it in a single line:

Computed properties are those that are preprocessed on the `ViewModel` layer in a JavaScript function.

Let's see a very simple practical use—you are developing a page that shows the `${firstName}` and `${lastName}` as a single value—`${completeName}`.

A common solution should create a JavaScript function to concatenate both values and map it into a `ViewModel` property. This is valid, but Aurelia comes with a better solution—the `aurelia-computed` plugin. This improves the efficiency of data-binding computed properties.

Do you remember the `getter/setter` function we mentioned in the first chapter? Well, it's time to use them.

This plugin uses Aurelia's JavaScript parser to parse the body of the property's getter function and check the result for observability purposes. If the getter function is observable, a specialized observer is returned to Aurelia's binding system. The observer publishes change events when properties accessed by the getter function change.

Let's look at an example:

```
// "firstName" and "lastName" will be observed.
get completeName() {
  return `${this.firstName} ${this.lastName}`;
}
```

There's nothing special yet. This function is using `dirty-checking` to bind the `completeName` computed property.

Why dirty? It's because the observer strategy wont be waiting for any change performed in the two values needed to retrieve the `completeName` property. It means the getter function will be executed many times across your component life cycle. Should we consider it as an issue? Really no, but if your application is becoming bigger and you have many computed properties, your performance could be directly impacted. So, what's Aurelia's solution? Just one annotation—`@computedFrom`:

```
import {computedFrom} from 'aurelia-framework';

export class User {
  firstName = 'Diego';
  lastName = 'Arguelles';

  @computedFrom('firstName', 'lastName')
  get completeName() {
    return `${this.firstName} ${this.lastName}`;
  }
}
```

Aurelia's binding system will observe the specified properties and reevaluate bindings when any of the properties change. The `aurelia-computed` plugin simply automates the dependency identification and is able to support more complex scenarios such as observing property paths.

Another common use for this feature is to retrieve the current logged user data. We can define a Boolean property to tell our component whether the user is logged in or not, and based on this, show the real username or just `Visitor`:

```
// "isLoggedIn", "user" and "user.userName" will be observed.
@computedFrom('userName')
get userName() {
  return this.isLoggedIn ? this.userName : '(Visitor)';
}
```

Summary

Definitely this was a very extensive chapter. We recommend to have a second read in the topics you consider more important, also as be said before, remember that if you want a complete understanding of each feature explained, you must research and do proof of concept to get the best option and experience. Due to the nature of our application, the FIFA World Cup is a worldwide event, so you need to make it available for all countries, i18n help us a lot to deal with internationalization with a very easy implementation. If you need to share properties or trigger events between your components, EventAggregator is the best choice. Aurelia offers a very usable variety of binding behaviors, making your code more clean, understandable and maintainable. Value converters, validators, computed properties are just a few binding behaviors that allows developer to reduce code. Remember that many of these features have dependence on third party libraries, so don't forget to download them and configure it into your project bundle.

We are really sure that this chapter was the most interesting...until this moment! See you in the next chapter!

8
Security

Security is crucial for every application that you plan to build. Security is a very complex topic that should be analyzed and implemented considering best practices and standards. The **Open Web Application Security Project (OWASP)** organization is a worldwide non-profit organization focused on improving the security of the applications.

All the applications implement at least a simple security layer known as the authentication and authorization layer, which is responsible for restricting some access and features according to the permissions granted to a user based on the credentials provided to the application. Although this chapter is focused on how to secure our Aurelia applications, we will implement a simple authentication and authorization API as an example to integrate with our Aurelia web application.

In this chapter, we will be covering the following topics:

- Understanding JSON Web Tokens
- Custom authentication and authorization
- Introducing Auth0
- Social login with Auth0
- Single sign-on

Understanding JSON Web Tokens

We have implemented a RESTful API that serves the information to be displayed into our Aurelia web app. This API doesn't have any security mechanism, so if any malicious users get the endpoint URL, they can run malicious scripts against our application and ruin our application. For that reason, we should reject any management operations performed by unauthorized users.

Our app should implement a mechanism to manage user's access and privileges. There are many ways to implement authentication and authorization. For our application, we will be using an open standard in the industry called **JSON Web Token (JWT)**.

JWT

JWTs are an open, industry standard, RFC 7519 (`https://tools.ietf.org/html/rfc7519.html`) method for representing claims securely between two parties. The way we use them is simple. First, we authenticate to the backend server by providing a username or password. If our credentials are correct, the backend server will generate a token that will contain the user information that should be persisted in the client side using a local storage mechanism. This JWT should be passed to the server in every request so that the server can recognize who the user is and what permissions this user has; with this information, the server allows or denies the user request.

Let's understand how this works. Navigate to `https://jwt.io/`; scroll down a little, and you will find the example section similar to the following image:

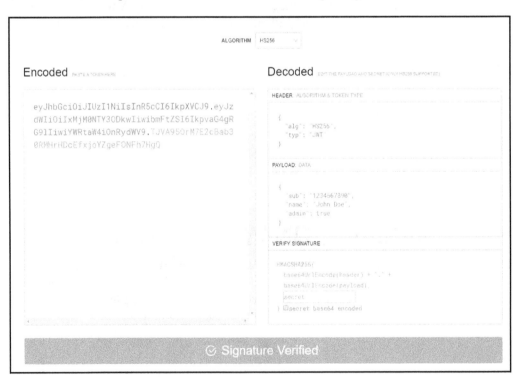

Let's read the information from right to left. On the right, we have the **Decoded** section that has three sections:

- **HEADER**: Contains the information about the **algorithm** used to **encrypt** the token
- **PAYLOAD**: The piece of **information** that we will define and use in our application, for example, user information
- **VERIFY SIGNATURE**: The signature of the token; we will define a **secret value** to encrypt our token

In the left **Encoded**, we can see the result of the final token encrypted based on the information of these three sections mentioned earlier.

As you might guess, this encrypted value is calculated in our backend server. This token is delivered to the user every time they log in to the application. They save this token on the client side and then send it on every request using the `Authorization` HTTP header. Let's see how all this works.

Custom authentication and authorization

Let's now understand the two main concepts behind application security that you have to implement in all your projects.

Implementing authentication

Authentication is the process where we validate the identity of a given user and check whether the user has valid credentials to access our application or backend API. With authentication, we restrict the access to users who are not members of our application.

We will create a basic authentication API as the goal of this book is to show you how you can secure your Aurelia application. We won't go into further details about the backend implementation. We will create a hard-coded authentication flow, but you can integrate it with a database using Mongoose, as described in `Chapter 6`, *Storing Our Data in MongoDB*.

So, let's get our hands dirty. Open the backend project, create a new file in the `routes` folder called `security-api.js`, and write the following code:

```javascript
const express = require('express')
const api = express.Router()

const logIn = (username, password) => {
    // Logic Here
}

api
  .route('/auth')
  .post((req, res, next) => {
    // Logic here
  })


module.exports = api
```

First, we import `express` and create an instance of the `Router` class. Secondly, we define a function called `logIn`, where we will implement the logic to authenticate the user and generate the JWT. Then, we will define a `/auth` route to process a `POST` endpoint. Finally, we export the API to be used in the main `server.js` file.

The authentication logic

Let's create a simple authentication logic. The backend expects a username and password with the value of the administrator. If these values are provided, it will return a valid token; otherwise, it will return `null`. Apply the following changes to the code:

```javascript
const express = require('express')
const api = express.Router()

const logIn = (username, password) => {
    if (username === 'admin' && password === 'admin') {
        const userData = {
            name: "Admin"
        }
        return generateToken(userData)
    }
    return null
}

api
...
```

The code is very straightforward. First, we compare the value in a simple `if` conditional, and we created a `userData` object, which will contain the user information, in this case just a name value is provided. Finally, we will call a `generateToken` function and pass `userData` to return a valid token.

Let's implement the `generateToken` function.

Generating the token

We will use an NPM module to generate JWT called `jsonwebtoken`. Open a new console and write the following command into the `wc-backend` folder to install the module:

```
$ npm install jsonwebtoken --save
```

Once the installation is finished. Open `security-api.js`, and let's import our library, as follows:

```
const express = require('express')
const jwt = require('jsonwebtoken')
const api = express.Router()

. . .
```

With our dependency imported in our file, let's implement the `generateToken` function. Apply the following changes:

```
. . .
const logIn = (username, password) => {
    if (username == 'admin' && password == 'admin') {
        let userData = {
            name: "Admin"
        }
        return generateToken(userData)
    } else {
        return null
    }
}

const generateToken = userData => {
    return jwt.sign(userData, "s3cret", { expiresIn: '3h' })
}

. . .
```

That's all! Let's understand the code. We call the sign function of the `jwt` object to create our token. We pass the following information to the function:

- `userData`: The piece of information we want to tokenize
- `secret`: A secret value that is used to encrypt and validate the token
- `expiration`: The expiration date of the token

Now we are ready with the authentication logic. To finish our implementation, we have to make this logic available via our REST Controller.

The authentication REST controller

We have already defined the route that will be responsible to make our logic available as a REST endpoint, so the only step required is to call our `logIn` function. Go ahead and apply the following change:

```
...

const generateToken = (userData) => {
    return jwt.sign(userData, "s3cret", { expiresIn: '3h' })
}


api
  .route('/auth')
  .post((req, res, next) => {
    let { username, password } = req.body
    let token = logIn(username, password)
    if (token) {
        res.send(token)
    } else {
        next(new Error("Authentication failed"))
    }
  })


module.exports = api
```

First, we extract the `username` and `password` from the `req.body` object. After that, we call the `logIn` function and host the result in the `token` variable. If the `token` is not null, we respond with a successful response by calling the `res.send` function. If the token is null, we pass an `Error` object into the next parameter, which will raise a global exception along with a failed response.

Lastly, we have to modify the `server.js` file to register our API to express, as follows:

```
const express = require('express')
..
const seurityApi = require('./src/routes/security-api')
const mongooseConfig = require('./src/config/mongoose-connection')
const app = express()

app.use(bodyParser.json())
app.use(teamsApi)
app.use(seurityApi)
...
```

Now we are ready to test our implementation. In a new Terminal window, run the following `curl` command:

```
$ curl -X POST -H "Content-type: application/json" -d '{"username":"admin",
"password":"admin"}' localhost:3000/auth

eyJhbGciOiJIUzI1NiIsInR5cCI6IkpXVCJ9.eyJuYW1lIjoiQWRtaW4iLCJpYXQiOjE1MTk1Nz
YwMDEsImV4cCI6MTUxOTU4NjgwMX0.4cNGYgz_BZZz5GEfN6MS3pkreGTkUBqJS1FZVC3_ew
```

If everything is well implemented, you should receive an encrypted JWT as a response.

Cool! It's time to play with authorization. Keep reading!

Implementing authorization

With authentication, we ensure that our application is being used by an authorized person with valid credentials. In most of the applications that you will build in the future, you will find that there are users who have different permissions on the application. For example, a given student might have the permissions to see their grade, but a student is not able to modify the grades. Otherwise, a user who is a teacher can update grades and access other features that a student cannot.

We will implement authorization using another NPM module `express-jwt-permissions`. By using this module, we will be able to implement authorization in a very simple way. Open the `security-api.js` file and apply the following changes:

```
const logIn = (username, password) => {
    if (username == 'admin' && password == 'admin') {
        let userData = {
            name: "Admin",
            permissions: ["admin:create:match", "admin:update:scores"]
        }
        return generateToken(userData)
    } else {
        return null
    }
}
```

That's all! The previous library will look into the JWT and check whether it has the `permissions` attribute defined. If so, we will extract this information and restrict access to users who do not have the admin permission. In the next section, we will implement the admin REST controller and see how we restrict the access to more details.

Having said that, we are ready to start the Admin API implementation!

Creating the Admin API

In order to understand how authorization works, let's implement a basic Admin API that will be accessed only by the administrator of our site. Our application has two principal types of users:

- **Normal**: This user is able to see the featured matches and the score
- **Admin**: This user is responsible to create new matches and update the score

We will use two open source NPM modules to manage the restriction workflow in our backend. The following diagram explains this flow in more detail:

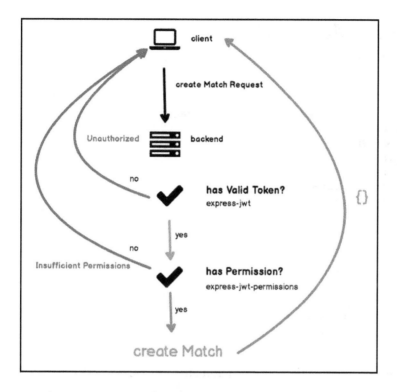

Everything starts with a user request that tries to access a restricted endpoint. The backend first validates whether a valid token is present in the HTTP request; this validation is performed by the `express-jwt` module. Secondly, if the request has a valid token, the flow will check whether the token has valid permissions to access the restricted endpoint; this validation is performed by `express-jwt-permissions`. If the request has a valid token and has permissions, the user request will be able to access the restricted endpoint and perform the action.

Managing matches

To create a match, we will need to create a valid Match database schema. We already know how to do it using Mongoose. Let's do it.

Creating the Match schema

Create the `match.js` file in the `src/models` folder. Then, add the following code:

```javascript
const mongoose = require('mongoose')

const MatchSchema = new mongoose.Schema({
    team_1: {
       type: String,
       min: 3,
       max: 100,
       required: true
    },
    team_2: {
       type: String,
       min: 3,
       max: 100,
       required: true
    },
    score: {
       team_1: Number,
       team_2: Number
    }
})
module.exports = mongoose.model('match', MatchSchema)
```

We have defined three attributes, the first two—team_1 and `team_2`—will store the information of the two teams playing. The `score` of the match. That's all we need for our model.

Creating the REST controller

Let's start by creating a new file in the `src/routes` folder named `admin-api.js`. Then, write the following code:

```javascript
const express = require('express')
const api = express.Router()

api
  .route('/admin/match/:id?')
  .post((req, res, next) => {
     // logic to create Match
  })
    .put((req, res, next) => {
```

```
    // logic to update Scores
  })
```

```
module.exports = api
```

You are very familiar with this code structure. First, we import the modules required to define our REST controller. Secondly, we create a /admin/match/:id? route and define the POST method to create a new match and another PUT method to update the scores.

Pay attention to the route definition; we are declaring an optional path variable called :id. To make a path optional, we add the ? operator after its name.

So far so good. Let's implement them.

Creating Matches

Creating a new Match is simple. We just need to import the Match model and call its built-in save method, as follows:

```
const express = require('express')
const api = express.Router()
const Match = require('../models/match')

api
  .route('/admin/match/:id?')
  .post((req, res, next) => {
      const match = new Match(req.body)
      match.save()
        .then(data => res.json(data))
        .catch(err => next(err) )
  })
    .put((req, res, next) => {
      // logic to update Match
  })
```

```
module.exports = api
```

First, we import the Match model. Then, in the POST method, we create a new Match object and call the save function. If the operation is successful, we send the new Match via the res.json method. To test our creation logic, we need to configure the server.js to use our new Admin API, as follows:

```
const express = require('express')
```

```
. . .
const adminApi = require('./src/routes/admin-api')
const mongooseConfig = require('./src/config/mongoose-connection')
const app = express()

app.use(bodyParser.json())
app.use(teamsApi)
app.use(seurityApi)
app.use(adminApi)

app.use((err, req, res, next) => {
```

Once we have applied the previous change, open a new terminal to test things out:

```
$ curl -X POST -H "Content-type: application/json" -d '{"team_1": "Peru",
"team_2": "Chile", "score": { "team_1": 20, "team_2": 0} }'
localhost:3000/admin/match/

{"__v":0,"team_1":"Peru","team_2":"Chile","_id":"5a94a2b8221bb505c92d801c",
"score":{"team_1":20,"team_2":0}}
```

Cool! Now we have our creation logic up and running with a great real example.

List Matches

To list our matches, we won't need security, because all the users should be able to get the full list of matches in the applications. So let's implement the matches API.

So, create a new file called matches-api.js into the src/routes folder and apply the following code:

```
const express = require('express')
const api = express.Router()
const Match = require('../models/match')

api
  .route('/matches')
  .get((req, res, next) => {
    Match.find().exec()
        .then(matches => res.json(matches))
        .catch(err => next(err))
  })

module.exports = api
```

Next, we have to configure the `server.js` file to map our `Match` APIs. In the `server.js` file, apply the following change:

```
...
const adminApi = require('./src/routes/admin-api')
const matchesApi = require('./src/routes/matches-api')
const mongooseConfig = require('./src/config/mongoose-connection')
const app = express()

app.use(bodyParser.json())
app.use(teamsApi)
app.use(seurityApi)
app.use(adminApi)
app.use(matchesApi)

...
```

Cool! Let's test things out. Open a Terminal window and execute the following command:

```
$ curl localhost:3000/matches

[{"_id":"5a949f982c1fda05b8c5c00a","team_1":"Peru","team_2":"Chile","__v":0
,"score":{"team_1":20,"team_2":0}}]
```

That's it! We have our public `Match` API.

Updating the Scores

To update the `score`, we will require the ID of the match to look up for an existing one. If a valid match is found, we will apply the updates. If no match is found, we have to respond with a `404 not found` HTTP response. Otherwise, we respond with a `Success 200` HTTP response.

Let's start by creating the `updateScore` function, as shown:

```
...
const Match = require('../models/match')

const updateScore = async (matchId, teamId) => {
  try {
    let match = await Match.findById(matchId)

    if (match == null) throw new Error("Match not found")

    if (teamId == 'team_1') {
      match.score.team_1++;
```

```
    } else {
      match.score.team_2++;
    }

    match = await match.save()
    return match

  } catch (err) {
    throw err
  }
}


api
  .route('/admin/match/:id?')
...
```

Now, let's call our function in the PUT HTTP verb, as illustrated:

```
...
api
  .route('/admin/match/:id?')
  .post((req, res, next) => {
    ...
  })
api
  .route('/admin/match/scores/:id')
  .post((req, res, next) => {

    const matchId = req.params.id
    const teamId = req.body.teamId

    updateScore(matchId, teamId)
      .then(match => res.json(match))
      .catch(err => next(err))
  })
...
```

Cool! Let's test things out. Execute the following `curl` command to update the match we created earlier:

```
$ curl -X POST -H "Content-type: application/json" -d '{"teamId": "team_1"
}'  localhost:3000/admin/match/scores/5a94a2b8221bb505c92d801c

{"_id":"5a94a2b8221bb505c92d801c","team_1":"Peru","team_2":"Chile","__v":0,
"score":{"team_1":21,"team_2":0}}
```

Note that the team_1 (Peru team) now has 21 goals in its score, and the Chile team has 0.

Awesome! Now we are able to create a new Match and update the scores. Let's use express-jwt and express-jwt-permissions to secure our APIs. Keep reading!

Securing the REST controller

Now it's time to secure our API. To do this, let's start by installing our two NPM modules. Open a Terminal window and run the following command:

```
$ npm install --save express-jwt express-jwt-permissions
```

Once the installation is done, let's validate our token.

Validate token

Every HTTP request has to send the JWT in its authorization header. The express-jwt middleware will check whether a valid token has been passed. If so, the request will continue its flow, otherwise the backend will respond with an unauthorized exception.

Go ahead and apply the following changes to the admin-api.js file:

```
...
const Match = require('../models/match')
const auth =require('express-jwt')

const updateScore = async (matchId, teamId) => {
  ...
}

api
  .route('/admin/match/:id?')
  .post(auth({ secret: 's3cret'}),
  (req, res, next) => {
    ...
  })
...
```

First, we start importing the express-jwt module and instantiate a new constant called auth. Secondly, we use the auth function and pass a JSON object that has the secret attribute; we will use the same secret value we used to sign our tokens in security-api.js:

```
return jwt.sign(userData, "s3cret", { expiresIn: '3h' })
```

The `auth` function is responsible for checking whether a valid token has been passed in the authorization header. Let's try to create a new `Match` entity without passing a valid token. Open the Terminal window and execute the following command:

```
$ curl -X POST -H "Content-type: application/json" -d '{"team_1": "Peru",
"team_2": "France", "score": { "team_1": 5, "team_2": 5} }'
localhost:3000/admin/match/

{"error":"No authorization token was found"}
```

As you can see, this time we are receiving an error message that says that our backend API is waiting for a valid token and none has been provided. So, to tackle this situation, we will need to create a valid token first. Let's create a valid token by calling our security API and logging in as admins. Execute the following command:

```
$ curl -X POST -H "Content-type: application/json" -d '{"username":"admin",
"password":"admin"}' localhost:3000/auth

eyJhbGciOiJIUzI1NiIsInR5cCI6IkpXVCJ9.eyJuYW1lIjoiQWRtaW4iLCJpYXQiOjE1MTk2OT
gyMjksImV4cCI6MTUxOTcwOTAyOX0.HQiz-NbBDBc9kVyBRNUeMsrDexEsk92WXoRyijNp1Rk
```

A new valid token has been created for me. Be aware that this token has a random value, so the token generated for you will be completely different.

Once we have a valid token, let's try again; however, this time we will pass the token using the `Authorization` HTTP headers, as follows:

```
$ curl -X POST -H "Content-type: application/json" -H "Authorization:
Bearer
eyJhbGciOiJIUzI1NiIsInR5cCI6IkpXVCJ9.eyJuYW1lIjoiQWRtaW4iLCJpYXQiOjE1MTk2OT
gyMjksImV4cCI6MTUxOTcwOTAyOX0.HQiz-NbBDBc9kVyBRNUeMsrDexEsk92WXoRyijNp1Rk"
-d '{"team_1": "Peru", "team_2": "France", "score": { "team_1": 5,
"team_2": 5} }'  localhost:3000/admin/match/

{"__v":0,"team_1":"Peru","team_2":"France","_id":"5a94c2559e11b6089b2b265e"
,"score":{"team_1":5,"team_2":5}}
```

Cool! Now we are able to create a new `Match`. Pay attention to the syntax that we have used to pass the token. We have used the `Authorization: Bearer <token>` syntax.

We have protected our API, but what about if we have two different types of administrators? Let's say that one group of administrators can be limited to only add `Match` entities, and the other group of administrators is limited to only update the scores. We need a way to manage this separation of roles. Let's learn how permissions work.

Validate permissions

Permissions allow us to limit the access to a group of resources. You should be aware that authentication is not enough if we want to secure our backend APIs. To implement permissions, open the `admin-api.js` file and apply the following changes:

```
...
const auth =require('express-jwt')
const guard = require('express-jwt-permissions')()

const updateScore = async (matchId, teamId) => {
  ...
}

api
  .route('/admin/match/:id?')
  .post(auth({ secret: 's3cret'}),
    guard.check('admin:create:match'),
    (req, res, next) => {

      ...

  })
...
```

First, we start by initializing a `guard` constant. Secondly, we call `guard.check`; this function will look for the `admin:create:match` permission in the JWT. Remember that these permissions have to be present in the token. If the user has permission, the flow will continue and the new `Match` will be created. Otherwise, we will receive a `Could not find permissions` error.

Let's try to create a new `Match`; execute the following command:

```
$ curl -X POST -H "Content-type: application/json" -H "Authorization:
Bearer
eyJhbGciOiJIUzI1NiIsInR5cCI6IkpXVCJ9.eyJuYW1lIjoiQWRtaW4iLCJpYXQiOjE1MTk2OT
gyMjksImV4cCI6MTUxOTcwOTAyOX0.HQiz-NbBDBc9kVyBRNUeMsrDexEsk92WXoRyijNp1Rk"
-d '{"team_1": "Peru", "team_2": "Brasil", "score": { "team_1": 80,
"team_2": 5} }'  localhost:3000/admin/match/

{"error":"Permission Denied"}
```

That's interesting! Although we are authenticated and are passing a valid token, why are we not able to create the `Match`? Let's look at the user token generation logic. Open the `security-api.js` file:

```
...
const logIn = (username, password) => {
    if (username == 'admin' && password == 'admin') {

        let userData = {
            name: "Admin"
        }

        return generateToken(userData)

    } else {
        return null
    }

}
...
```

As you can see, our token doesn't have the permissions defined. Let's fix this by adding the right permissions:

```
...
    let userData = {
        name: "Admin",
      permissions: ["admin:create:match"]
    }
...
```

That's all. Let's generate a new token by logging in again, and let's test things out.

First, execute the following command to generate a valid token:

```
$ curl -X POST -H "Content-type: application/json" -d '{"username":"admin",
"password":"admin"}' localhost:3000/auth
```

eyJhbGciOiJIUzI1NiIsInR5cCI6IkpXVCJ9.eyJuYW1lIjoiQWRtaW4iLCJpYXQiOjE1MTk2OT
k4MzIsImV4cCI6MTUxOTcxMDYzMn0.cVTtJHcbQ2J76s6uRjuySCWq4dKX1NzAfIn10ZLgri

Cool! this new token contains the permissions. Next, let's try to create the new `Match` again by passing this new token:

```
$ curl -X POST -H "Content-type: application/json" -H "Authorization:
Bearer
eyJhbGciOiJIUzI1NiIsInR5cCI6IkpXVCJ9.eyJuYW1lIjoiQWRtaW4iLCJpYXQiOjE1MTk2OT
gyMjksImV4cCI6MTUxOTcwOTAyOX0.HQiz-NbBDBc9kVyBRNUeMsrDexEsk92WXoRyijNp1Rk"
-d '{"team_1": "Peru", "team_2": "China", "score": { "team_1": 5, "team_2":
5} }'  localhost:3000/admin/match/

{"__v":0,"team_1":"Peru","team_2":"China","_id":"5a94c87987d2820a0d1931e7",
"score":{"team_1":5,"team_2":5}}
```

Hot dog! We are now able to manage authentication and authorization in our backend API. Of course, you can improve this security authentication by saving a collection of users in a MongoDB database and create different users with different roles. Also, implement `log out` using `express-jwt-blacklist` and in another fashion, but for the purpose of this book, we are good with this basic implementation. Keep reading!

Introducing Auth0

Managing authentication and authorization by ourselves might become a really difficult task to do. Imagine that you need to implement security logic for web applications, mobile applications, and desktop apps. Even your customer might ask you to integrate their applications to social networks and use multifactor authentication or use a password-less method. Although we have implemented the security for our application, we encourage you not to write security code yourself unless you are creating a really simple application.

So, in this section, we will implement authentication and authorization using one popular service called Auth0 (`https://auth0.com`). This service will help us empower our authentication flows, such as these:

- Social login
- Single sign-on
- Email authentication

- Multifactor
- Password-less authentication
- Fingerprint login
- LDAP integration

Also, Auth0 provides monitoring and other out-of-the-box services that will help us manage our user's information.

A simple example

Although we use our custom implementation for the world cup application, we have prepared a simple example to show you how to use Auth0 with Aurelia. You can download the code from `https://github.com/EriksonMurrugarra/AureliaAuth0`.

Auth0 implements JWT; this should ring a bell for you, because we have implemented our custom Auth0 implementation using JWT. Let's start by creating a free account on Auth0.

Creating an account

First, navigate to the official Auth0 site, `https://auth0.com`, and click on the **SIGN UP** button:

Then, fill the form with your email and password, and click on the **SIGN UP** button or use your social network accounts:

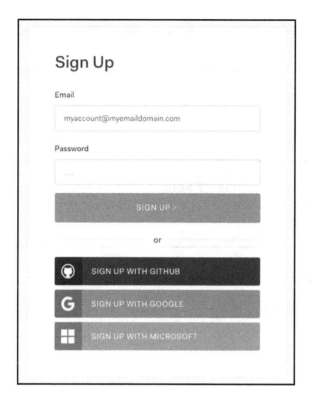

Once the sign-up process is complete, you should be redirected to your administration dashboard. The administration dashboard will allow you to configure the different security mechanisms that you can implement in just a few seconds. Let's continue by registering an application to generate some valid configuration values to connect our Aurelia application to Auth0.

Registering an Auth0 client application

If you have previous experience of working with third-party service providers, you might have noted that in order to use their services, you have to register an application in order to get some private keys that you will use to access your third-party provider's resource. The same happens with Auth0; we should first register an application and then use the keys generated to configure our apps.

On the dashboard page, go ahead and select the **Applications** menu and click on the **CREATE CLIENT** button:

After clicking on the **CREATE CLIENT** button, fill the following form with your application's name and select **Single Page Application** for the client type; then, click on **CREATE**:

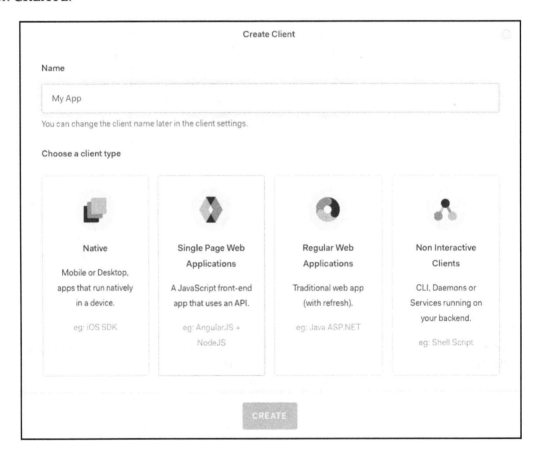

Once we create the client, a new configuration page will be displayed. Navigate to the **Settings** tab and you will see the following configuration values:

- **Name**: The name of our application
- **Domain**: The domain you previously registered in the sign-up process
- **Client ID**: A unique ID that makes your application unique
- **Client Secret**: The secret value used to sign the JWT that Auth0 will generate
- **Allowed Callback URL**: The list of URL that Auth0 will redirect when the authentication is a success

That's it. Before we explore the application's code, let's start understanding how Auth0 manages authentication by analyzing the following diagram:

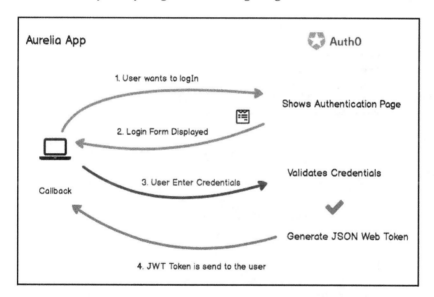

The flow begins when the **User** wants to log in to the application. You might have a kind of Navigation bar with a button that when clicked on will trigger a JavaScript function that will call an Auth0 JavaScript login function. Secondly, the user will be redirected to a built-in **Auth0 Login Form** and will have to enter their credentials to sign up. The credentials entered by the users are validated by Auth0; if the Auth0 finds a valid user with the provided credentials, it will generate a valid JWT that will be sent to the user/Aurelia app. This JWT will be used to access your backend resources. Remember that you can use the **Client Secret** property to decrypt the token in the backend.

Exploring our example application

First, we will need to download the source code from the GitHub repository at `https://github.com/EriksonMurrugarra/AureliaAuth0`. Let's open a Terminal window in the folder of your preference and run the following command:

```
$ cd /some/path
$ git clone https://github.com/EriksonMurrugarra/AureliaAuth0
```

Once the source code is downloaded, we will need to install the dependencies and run the application. Let's get into the source code folder and execute the following commands:

```
$ cd AureliaAuth0
$ npm install
...
$ au run --watch

Writing app-bundle.js...
Writing vendor-bundle.js...
Finished 'writeBundles'
Application Available At: http://localhost:9000
BrowserSync Available At: http://localhost:3001
```

Let's open a new browser and navigate to `http://localhost:9000`, which will display a simple home page with a **Log In** option in the Navigation bar:

Cool! We have our application up and running, but we will need to configure it first before we can log in successfully. Go ahead and open the following `auth-service.js` file located in the `src` folder. We will need to replace the values for the configuration values that we got when we created our client application on Auth0. In our case, the values are the following:

```
...
auth0 = new auth0.WebAuth({
    domain: 'eriksonmurrugarra.auth0.com',
    clientID: 'LBmldq5OOXHPYz4SAyMr03ThgfMOiHs7',
    redirectUri: 'http://localhost:9000/callback',
    audience: 'https://eriksonmurrugarra.auth0.com/userinfo',
    responseType: 'token id_token',
    scope: 'openid'
})
...
```

It's important to mention that the `redirectUri` should be registered in Auth0 in the application settings in **Allowed Callback URLs**.

Cool! Save the changes and click on the **LOG IN** button to be redirected to the following page:

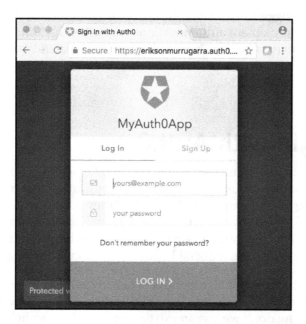

The previous page is provided by Auth0; you might note that the URL has changed. It means that every time that our users are asked to log in, they will be redirected to Auth0. As you haven't created any user account yet, you will need to sign up first. Once you are done with the registration process, you will be redirected to the home page:

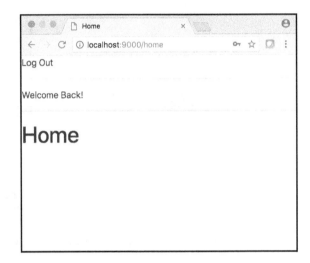

That's it! Now you are logged in to the application using a more secure strategy. Remember that you should never implement authentication and authentication yourself. It is best practice to use a third-party service. The developers who created the services such as Auth0 will definitely have had years of experience creating the most secure authentication and authorization mechanism than you.

Social Login with Auth0

There is an important truth behind the human behavior when they are in front of any registration form. Most of your users will hate your application if you make them waste their valid time asking for personal information that they have already filled in their favorite social network. Even if you try to create the best user experience for your **SIGN UP** form, they will avoid them. So, how do we make our users happy and avoid them having to do this horrible sign-up process? Social Login integration to the rescue!

Implementing Social Login might be repetitive work in case you have multiple social networks that you need to integrate into your application. Instead of implementing everything yourself, why don't we use an existing service that can help us in this process? Auth0 to the rescue!

Let's implement Social Login in just 3 minutes. Yeah! you read well, just 3 minutes. Go ahead and navigate to your Auth0 dashboard at `https://manage.auth0.com` and navigate to the **Connections/Social** menu. Then, go ahead and activate the social networks that you want to integrate with your authentication flow, as follows:

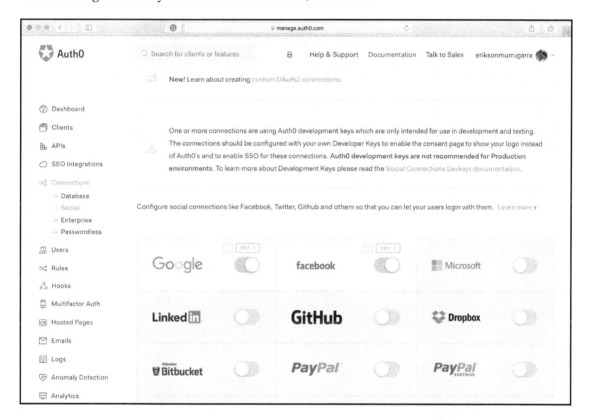

As you can see, I have enabled **Google** and **Facebook** for the authentication flow. Remember that you will need to register an application on Facebook and Twitter first and then use the keys generated to configure the Social Login methods.

We are almost done. To finish the process, we just need to tell our client application that we want to enable social login. To do this, let's navigate to the **Clients** menu and get into the **MyAuth0App** client application. Then, navigate to the **Connections** tab and enable **Facebook** and **Twitter** in the **Social** section, as demonstrated:

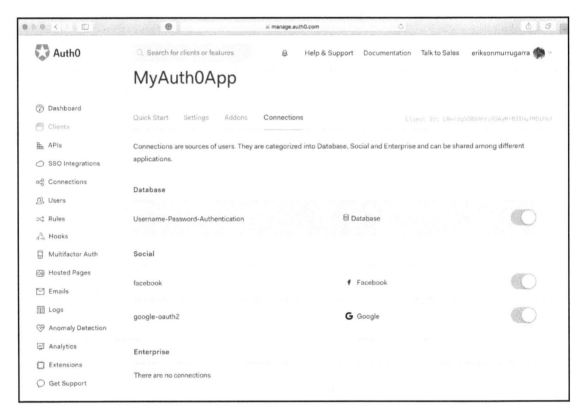

Once we have everything configured, the next time when your users try to log in to the application, they will see the following form:

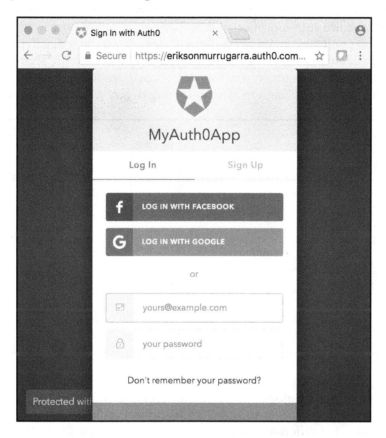

Cool! Now we know how to integrate our applications to allow our users to sign in to our application, allowing them to use their favorite social network accounts.

Single sign-on

If you are implementing a big enterprise solution that consists of different distributed applications that require authentication and authorization but require to use the same user's database, you will need to implement a different flow to manage the authentication in all these independent applications. This mechanism is called **single sign-on** (**SSO**), which will basically ask for login once in any of your applications and will reuse the same generated token in all the applications. The following diagram explains this flow:

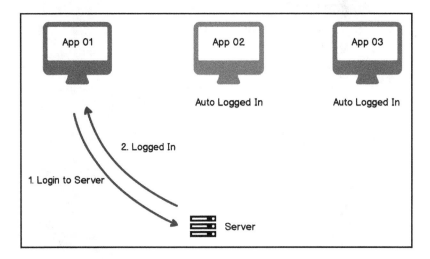

In the preceding illustration, there are three applications. Let's suppose that these three different applications are developed by the same company and the employees use the three applications. Imagine that in order to access each application, the employees have to log in to each application using different credentials, or they can choose to use the same username and password for the three apps.

Why should our users log in again to another application if these applications share the same user information? First, a user will log in to the server and retrieve a valid token. Once the first application is logged in to, it can save the token as cookies or in `LocalStorage` in the browser. When the user accesses Application 02, the app should detect that there is an existing token and should use it to access the server without asking for credentials.

Now that you know how SSO works, You are free to implement SSO by yourself or use an external service. Auth0 has an awesome support for SSO.

Summary

In this chapter, we created a custom implementation to manage authentication and authorization in order to protect the use of our API from unauthorized users. You have seen that implementing Auth0 on your own might be a difficult task and will require more security layers than the ones we have implemented. A good practice is to use an external service to implement authentication and authorization in your projects. We created a simple application that uses one of the most popular third-party services, called Auth0.

We also covered how to integrate social login to our application, but we implemented this feature using Auth0 built-in social connection features. You can implement social authentication on your own, but again, it is better to spend energy on your application login rather than wasting time implementing features that can be achieved in no time using a third-party service.

We looked at how SSO works in theory and learned that it is a simple process reusing the user token in all your different applications.

That's it! In the next chapter, you will learn how to apply end-to-end tests on your Aurelia applications. Keep reading!

Running E2E Tests

9

Congratulations! You are just one step away from becoming a full stack application developer! For now, we will stop talking about Aurelia; you know the framework and have a high level of knowledge of how JavaScript works as a programming language. Now, it's time to expand our knowledge about full-stack application development. We have our FIFA WC 2018 application running on our localhost and have some unit testing implemented. Is it enough to ensure that it will work in a QA or production environment? Of course, no.

Unit testing is very important, but it only ensures the correct functionality of one single service. How can we ensure that all our applications (database, backend, frontend, and any other external services) are working correctly as one single application? This is what we will learn in this chapter.

Testing is one of the highly demanded skills for all developers nowadays. Why? It's because programming is no longer just writing code and to ensure that it works on your own PC, you need to create code that ensures this functionality and also be able to automate the testing process to create a continuous delivery pipeline.

We can divide the testing phase into four different levels, and we will cover each one through this chapter. Look at the following image:

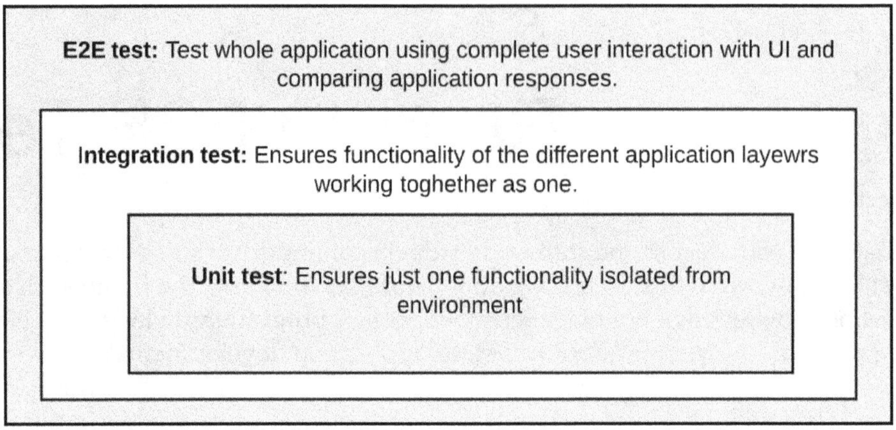

We can refer to these layers as basic tests. Once we have covered all three layers, we can commit and push our code. Is that all? No. We have more advanced testing layers that should be performed using tools completely external to our application:

- **System testing** ensures that all our business use cases are resolved and satisfied. It's like black box testing where we don't know how each method or operation is performed; we just care about the input and output. This kind of testing starts in the frontend layer, emulating common user operations and expecting some data already processed through the backend APIs and external services. You must know that system testing can be automated in your CI cycle.
- **Acceptance testing** is performed by real end users. They ensure that your system will support all user interactions, evaluating time, performance, and one very important aspect—your app's user experience. Commonly, this test is performed by the product owner first in an external environment called **user acceptance testing (UAT)**.

So, we can resume the testing phase in the following illustration:

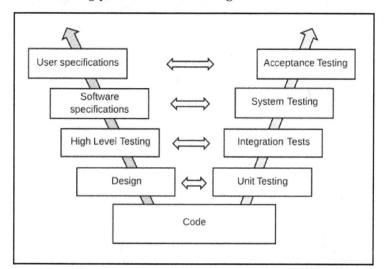

We will cover each testing phase through this chapter. We've already reviewed the unit testing in the last section of `Chapter 4`, *Creating Components and Templates*, which is useful to ensure the functionality of a single component, but how can we evaluate the complete interaction between our components and other external services? It's time to go one step ahead and learn about integration testing. But even one step ahead is not enough for us, so let's go deeper and evaluate one very important but often ignored aspect of every web application: we can ensure our application functionality, but is it simple to use by our final users? UI testing will give us the answer. Finally, let's add some cool documentation to each endpoint we are exposing to be consumed by some client, even if it's web or mobile. We will show you how Swagger works and how it can generate a nice readable documentation about your API. The topics covered in this chapter are these:

- Integration testing
- UI testing
- API testing – Swagger

Do not pass through this chapter; testing is a very important part of the application development life cycle. Ready? Go!

Integration testing – Multiple services, one application

We have all our functionalities already tested. We know that our services work correctly but what about our database connection? What about our SSO? Can you confirm these services/dependencies work correctly?

Integration testing plays an important role in the application development cycle by verifying the correct behavior of the system. Let's explore our current application architecture:

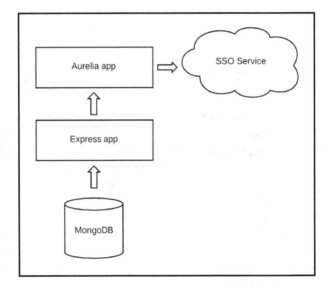

Integration tests ensure the correct interaction across our different application layers, in this case, database connection, SSO service, and frontend application.

Why should you do integration tests? Well, if it's not clear yet, there are a few reasons to consider:

- Easy integration with daily builds in your **Continuous Integration (CI)** cycle. Your progress will be testable at any time.
- Easy to test in dev/QA/UAT/Production environment. It's easy, just like running your application.
- Tests run faster as compared to end-to-end tests.

- Allows you to detect system-level issues. Communication between services, database connection, and so on.

Now, let's add some integration tests to our existing express application.

Configuring applications for integration testing

The only prerequisite you need is the Node runtime environment running correctly. In JavaScript, we have some tools to make integration tests, such as the following:

- **SuperTest**: The best feature is its strong documentation; easy to understand and implement, you just need to write a few lines of code to start testing your application.
- **Mocha**: A simple JavaScript test framework. It can be executed in the web browser or in your Node environment. Since Mocha is based on JavaScript, it can execute asynchronous tests and generate very useful reports.

We will use both tools together for our testing purposes.

With SuperTest, you gain advantages such as the following:

- You can simulate a multiple user interaction, storing different credentials (tokens) to switch between users.
- You don't need to worry about delete or add mock data. SuperTest will perform the operations to clean or add data to your store.
- The most useful feature—all these tests can be automated and integrated in your CI pipeline.

SuperTest is a big help for productivity; also, it offers a natural way to write and test your code at the same time; it is very intuitive and human readable. Let's go over how to quickly set it up for something like user retrieving data.

Where can you run SuperTest tests? Basically, you can run them in any server you want. No matter whether you are deploying on local `dev` servers or cloud providers, SuperTests can be executed from any of them, but you must know something—SuperTest includes its own express server. This server should not be running all the time, but using some external tools like nodemon, you can automatically restart your server each time we have a change and need to test it. If you don't want to run all the tests, Mocha's only specifier is a nice solution too.

First, we need to download our dependencies:

```
npm i supertest mocha chai -s
```

Chai allows us to choose any of the following prefixes: should, expect, or assert. Just like other test tools, they are all available here too.

We already have our server.js file, so you won't need to add any code there. Yes, you don't need to run any server, and this is the most beautiful advantage of SuperTest!

Remember that our test files should be separated from the application files. Next, create your tests file with the touch tests.spec.js command, and let's add some code:

```
const app = require('./server');
const chai = require('chai');
const request = require('supertest');

var expect = chai.expect;

describe('API Tests', () => {
  it('should return football teams', function(done) {
    request(app)
      .get('/teams')
      .end(function(err, res) {
        expect(res.statusCode).to.equal(200);
        done();
      });
  });
});
```

Let's explain what the code is doing.

We are importing our server, Chai and SuperTest. SuperTest includes its own .expect(), but we are using Chai's syntax. The code sets a group of API Tests and creates one test to check whether the /teams endpoint returns **200 (OK)** as status code. Note that the done() function is important to declare our asynchronous tests are complete. Of course, this is a very high-level test, and we can add more assertions such as evaluating the response's content and more. For example purposes, this is very simple to understand and know how SuperTest works.

Now, let's see if it works. Run the following command:

```
npm test
```

You should get this:

```
> npm test

> integration-tests@1.0.0 test /Projects/worldcup-app
> mocha '**/*.spec.js'

  API tests
    ✓ should return football teams

  1 passing (41ms)
```

 Make sure you have correctly configured the `test` command in the script section on `package.json` file.

Mocking external dependencies

Okay, you can write some integration tests. Is it enough? Not yet. Let's think. We really need to connect to external services? What if they're down? Of course, our test will fail but not for some application error. To avoid this, we will use Mocks.

Mocking is the technique used to simulate some object/service/component and return a predefined response when its called. We'll not connect with real services, so we'll be using `sinon.mock` to create a mock model for our Teams schema, and we'll test the expected result:

```
// Test will pass if we get all teams
        it("should return football teams", (done) => {
            var TeamMock = sinon.mock(Team);
            var expectedResult = {status: true, team: []};
            TeamMock.expects('find').yields(null, expectedResult);
            Team.find(function (err, result) {
                TeamMock.verify(); //Verifies the team and throws an
exception if it's not met
                TeamMock.restore(); //Restore the fake created to his
initial state
                expect(result.status).to.be.true;
                done();
            });
        });
```

All okay at this point. Now, let's evaluate another very important aspect of testing, code coverage.

 Make sure that `sinon` is downloaded in your project and imported in your current test file to make the example work, same as any external model you may need. You can find more info about `sinon` at http://sinonjs.org.

Calculating code coverage

With our integration test already written and running, we have one thing pending to do. It would be an awesome thing if we could see how our tests are doing with respect to our app in terms of test coverage.

Let's add code coverage to the app!

Istanbul is a very famous JavaScript code coverage tool that computes different metrics such as statement quality, lines of code, function use, and branch coverage with module loader hooks to analyze all our code and add coverage when running tests, giving us real-time information about our application. It supports all kinds of JavaScript coverage use cases, from unit tests to functional and browser tests. The best part about this is that it is scalable.

Fortunately, we just need to install Istanbul and `nyc` (this last one in the command line client for `istanbul`). We just do this:

```
npm install istanbul --save-dev
```

```
npm install nyc --save-dev
```

Then, we modify our `package.json` file. This is to add test with coverage to our `script` object:

```
"test-coverage": "nyc mocha ./spec.js"
```

Then, run the following:

```
npm run test-coverage
```

You should be able to see the coverage summary of your application in the console.

Does our app meet our business requirements? UI testing

Don't be confused, we won't test frontend application functionality. This is already tested with our unit test, so what is really UI testing? Well, it is a very long discussion. We can have many test suites configured to be executed at any time, and this will ensure that our E2E meets the business requirements already programmed. What do we mean by this? Unit and integration testing cannot evaluate all areas of a complete application, specifically the areas related to workflow and usability. Basically, all our automated tests can only verify code that exists. They cannot evaluate functionality that is maybe missing or issues related to visual elements of our application and how easy our product is to use. This is the real value of GUI testing, which is performed from the perspective of a user instead of the practical point of view of the developer. By analyzing an application from a user's perspective, GUI testing can provide enough information to the project team to decide whether the application is ready to deploy or we need to reorganize some features to accomplish the user needs.

So, that being said, will I always will need a person who should be verifying a functionality manually? Yes and no. This theme is really hard to explain, because different points of view can be referenced and in some cases, contradicted. For these cases, we will focus on some very useful testing techniques in the next section.

Scripted testing

Just like its name, scripted testing based on prescripts elaborated by software testers to detect whether there are some functionalities not covered for the application at that moment. For example, a script doing a login, saving some data, and then retrieving it from another screen. The script defines the predefined data that the tester will use to evaluate each screen and the expected output. Then, the tester analyzes the results and reports any found defects to the application development team. Scripted testing can be performed manually by humans or can be supported by test automation through CI tools.

The advantage is that you can divide the work between your most experienced developers to write the scripts and the entry-level developers to run the script and analyze the data, giving maintenance and learning the business requirements.

The disadvantage is that it's hard to maintain if your UI changes frequently. This kind of testing is highly coupled with your business code so if it changes, the entire test should change too.

Exploratory testing

In this kind of testing, we won't use any automated script. It enforces the tester to use the application as a common user and evaluate aspects such as design, how easy our product is for the final users, how is the user experience, alternative workflows, and more. The tester may identify any failure regarding these aspects and provide valuable feedback to developers.

Since explanatory tests do not use scripts, there is still pre-planning. In real-life situations, commonly in session-based exploratory testing, the testers team sets goals for the planned tests and defines a time frame to perform exploratory testing in focused areas. All this information is introduced in a document called test-charter. Sessions and results of exploratory testing are documented in a report and reviewed in the daily meeting with the entire team.

The advantage is that testers have more time to focus on the actual testing, because the time to prepare test cases and look at boring documentation is reduced, becoming a constant challenge to find more issues and increase their business knowledge.

The disadvantage is that this kind of test is not auto-executable and of course, cannot be repeated to be used as a regression test. Also, you will need testers with a deep understanding of your business requirements that most of the time are hard to find. In addition, in real-time scenarios, it may be impractical to try to cover an entire application with exploratory testing since we won't find enough testers with the required knowledge about the product.

UX testing

In user experience testing, actual end users (or user representatives) evaluate an application for its ease of use, visual appearance, and ability to meet their needs. The users will explore all the applications in an isolated environment called UAT, which can be configured in a local server or some cloud provider. You must keep in mind that it does not matter where the product is deployed, it should represent the same conditions as your production environment.

Don't confuse user experience testing (UX) with user acceptance testing (UAT). UAT is a testing level that verifies that a given application meets demanded requirements focusing only on business use cases. For example, in UAT, you can ensure that your **Retrieve Teams** button works correctly and returns the correct data well formatted. So, it's not enough? Of course no, because you don't know yet whether your button is well placed or whether it's difficult to find from the end user's perspective.

Okay, now that we understand how this kind of testing works, which one should we apply? All taken decisions regarding testing should target to maximize the value of the product for its final users, even by detecting bugs or unexpected features, and by ensuring functionality and usability. To achieve this goal, in real-time situations, we will need a combination of all different test techniques reviewed at this time.

Planning our tests – Time for the truth

Planning is a very important phase of any project, and this won't be an exception. It is important to have a test plan that identifies the resources available for testing and that prioritizes areas of the application to be tested before we start writing our cases. With this information, the testing team will be able to create test scenarios, test cases, and test scripts for scripted testing, documented in the test charter.

This is an example of the structure that our test plan should contain:

- Defined dates for each test
- Required testers
- Required resources such as servers, environments, tools, and cloud providers correctly configured to start testing
- Target application environments, such as different screen resolutions, mobile devices, and supported browsers
- User workflows/navigation to test
- Testing techniques to be used, including scripted testing, exploratory testing, and user experience testing
- Goals for testing, including the acceptance criteria to determine if a test passes or fails

Also, we can add some more sections according to our own needs:

GUI Test Plan Template

Overview

Application Name	
Version	
Description	
Target Release Date/Sprint	

Target Test Platform	Browser /App	Start Version	End Version	Physical Devices	Virtual Devices / Emulators
Desktop					
Mac O/S					
Windows O/S					
Other					
Mobile					
Android					
iOS					
Windows					
Other					

Testing Scope	In Scope	Out of Scope
Visual Design		
Functionality		
Performance		
Security		
Usability		
Accessability		
Compliance		

Target User Personas	In Scope	Out of Scope

Test Resources and Strategy

Scripted Testing	Target	Review Level	% Complete	% Remaining	On Schedule
Test Start Date					
Test End Date					
Number of Testers					
Hours per Day					
Total Testing Hours					
Scripts Written	10		60 %		
Scripts Executed					
Scripts Passed					
Scripts Failed/Blocked					
	Critical	High	Medium	Low	Total
Defects Identified					

Exploratory Testing	Target	Review Level	% Complete	% Remaining	On Schedule
Test Start Date					
Test End Date					
Number of Testers					
Hours per Day					
Total Testing Hours					
Scenarios Written					
Scenarios Failed/Blocked					
	Critical	High	Medium	Low	Total
Defects Identified					

User Experience Testing	Target	Review Level	% Complete	% Remaining	On Schedule
Test Start Date					
Test End Date					
Testers per Persona					
	Critical	High	Medium	Low	Total
Defects Identified					

Test plans can be text documents, excel tables, or a test management tool to develop the test plan to support analysis and reporting. There are many tools available, some of them to download into your private server and others to be used on a cloud provider.

Our GUI test plan should not be considered as a full system test plan. You can also consider other aspects such as load testing, security, backup, fault tolerance, and recovery.

Done, we have our plan! What's next? Identify our testing priorities. For example, first of all, we need to ensure the following:

- Visual design
- Security
- Usability
- Compliance
- Functionality
- Performance

Now, it's time to represent it in a mental map to be understood by the entire team and perform the required tests. Check out this example:

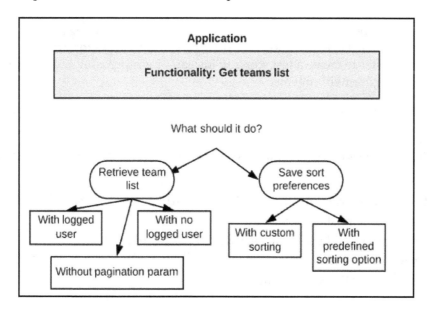

The most common areas to test when we are navigating on a web application are these:

- Compatibility with different versions of most used browsers
- Behavior when the user clicks on the back or refresh button (in browser)
- Behavior after a user returns to the page using a bookmark or their browser history
- Behavior when the user has multiple browser windows open on the UAT at the same time

Defining common scenarios

We can define a test scenario as a brief statement describing how an application will be used in specific real-life situations, for example, "the user will be able to log in with a valid username and password." Commonly, test scenarios are written from development documents such as requirements or user stories, each one with the required acceptance criteria to accomplish that. If these documents are not created yet, product owners should write them and define the different scenarios and acceptance criteria to mark the product as complete.

Scenarios are useful because they can guide exploratory testing, giving a good understanding of a GUI event, without restricting the testing team to a specific procedure. Since it is much faster to create a test scenario instead of writing a full test case, scenarios are most used in agile environments.

If scenarios are used in scripted testing, they can be used as the base from which test cases can be written.

For example, the *login scenario* mentioned earlier can have test cases for GUI events such as the following:

- User enters a valid username and password
- User enters invalid username
- User enters valid username but invalid password
- User tries to reset the password
- User presses the **Submit** button repeatedly

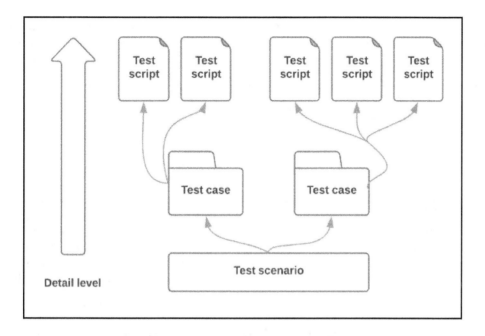

Writing test cases

Commonly, this document starts with a brief description of a GUI event to be tested, we will still use the example about the login attempt. We should specify conditions and steps for executing the test. Finally, we need to evaluate the expected result of the test and define the acceptance criteria for determining whether the test succeeds or fails.

You must keep in mind some considerations such as the ones listed here:

- How often the user interface changes
- How much freedom end users will have when navigating through the application
- If you have testers with less experience, they may need more detailed procedures

What to include? Good question. Similar to our planning template, we need to put our acceptance criteria organized in a document where we can check and save the evolution of each test case. Here's a very basic example:

Test Case ID	Title	Test Scenario ID	Procedure	Data Source	Expected Result	Actual Result	Use for Regression
1							
2							
3							
4							
5							
6							
7							

It's important that you have separated your test data for test cases. Most of the time, issues are products of validation errors in the project, so the development teams must know which parameters caused this error. Always remember that application development is a team work, so you must give all the facilities to your colleagues to get the best product.

Organizing our test – Creating scripts

This is the most detailed part of our test. Here, we will define the steps and procedures to execute our test. Create sufficient test scripts to verify paths that users will take through the UAT.

Always remember to document the input data and the expected output; it will be very important when we have to deal with unexpected events.

API test with Swagger

In the last section, we were centered in the E2E testing of our entire application starting from the frontend, but what about our API itself? Remember that one API can be used to serve many client types such as web or mobile. So, don't you think it would be awesome to ensure this functionality independently from the entire application life cycle? Sure, we know you agree, and we have in mind a very nice solution to accomplish this objective—Swagger.

Swagger is a specification and a nice group of tools to write RESTful APIs. Based on their own web page definition:

"Swagger is the world's largest framework of API developer tools for the OpenAPI Specification (OAS), enabling development across the entire API life cycle, from design and documentation, to test and deployment."

In the group of tools we have in Swagger, we can find these:

- Swagger Editor: This tool will allow us to view the updated document in real time.
- Swagger Codegen: A template-driven engine to generate interactive documents.
- Swagger UI: Allows to visualize the RESTful API, and check input and responses. So, *Swagger UI* takes an existing JSON or YAML document and creates interactive documentation.

Installing Swagger

Let's start getting our most important dependency, Swagger. Remember that we will use NPM to download Swagger, because we will use it on a ExpressJS API. Swagger has its own implementation depending on the platform you need to document.

There are two very famous swagger implementations to integrate with an ExpressJS application:

- `swagger-node-express`
- `swagger-ui-express`

The `swagger-node-express` is the official *Swagger* module for *Node*. Some of the most interesting (and not so) characteristics of this library are as follows:

- Official distribution of the Swagger API. We are fully supported by an organization working actively on the development of the product.
- It is open source.
- Comes with *Swagger Editor* and Swagger Codegen.
- *Swagger UI* needs to be inserted inside the code where we are adding documentation.
- Since documentation is quite poor, you need to read the source code of some different libraries to learn and understand each argument used to configure Swagger.

The `swagger-ui-express` is supported by the community, another great open source option. How does it work? This library adds a middleware to your Express.js application that serves the Swagger UI bound to your Swagger document. It's really easy to configure; the only thing you will need to perform is add one route to host Swagger UI, without need to copy anything manually. Documentation is really good, and we think everything you need should be there.

Given the functionality and simplicity of this tool, we've decided to use this library instead of any other option to achieve our main goal of documenting our application.

To get started, we need to add the library to our current project:

```
npm install -save swagger-ui-express
```

Once the library is added to our project, we need to configure a route to host Swagger UI. Also, we need to load the Swagger API definition of our application. In our application, the Swagger API definition is a single file containing information about our application represented in a JSON object.

To create the Swagger API definition, we have used Swagger Editor. Remember that you are free to use JSON or YAML notation. Let's look at an example of the same definition in different formats:

In JSON it is done as follows:

```json
{
    "swagger": "2.0",
    "info": {
        "version": "1.0.0",
        "title": "WorldCup API",
        "description": "A simple API to learn how to write FIFAWC
Specification"
    },
    "schemes": [
        "http"
    ],
    "host": "localhost:3000",
    "basePath": "/",
    "paths": {
        "/teams": {
            "get": {
                "summary": "Gets team list",
                "description": "Returns a list containing all teams of the
WorldCup.",
                "responses": {
```

```json
        "200": {
            "description": "A list of Teams",
            "schema": {
                "type": "array",
                "items": {
                    "teams": {
                        "country": {
                            "type": "string"
                        },
                        "trainer": {
                            "type": "string"
                        }
                    }
                }
            }
        }
    }
}
```

In YAML:

```yaml
swagger: "2.0"

info:
  version: 1.0.0
  title: WorldCup API
  description: A simple API to learn how to write FIFAWC Specification

schemes:
  - https
host: simple.api
basePath: /doc

paths:
  /teams:
    get:
      summary: Gets teams list
      description: Returns a list containing all Teams of the WorldCup.
      responses:
        200:
          description: A list of Teams
          schema:
            type: array
            items:
              properties:
```

```
country:
    type: string
trainer:
    type: string
```

Both are very human readable.

Even if our specification file is a text that can be edited with any text editor, nowadays we have many specialized tools to achieve this, giving us some useful features such as syntax validation, format, autocomplete parameters, and more. The best option to write specification file is Swagger Editor (yes, its own tool), a powerful set of static files that allows you to write and validate Swagger specification in YAML syntax and see how your file will look rendered.

The created Swagger API definition will be stored in our application as a JSON object inside the `swagger.json` file. At this moment, our setup script should look like this:

```
const swaggerUi = require('swagger-ui-express')
const swaggerDocument = require('./swagger.json'); //Our specification file

app.use('/api-docs', swaggerUi.serve, swaggerUi.setup(swaggerDocument));
```

As you can see, first middleware is setting up our Swagger server. This middleware will return static files that are needed for hosting Swagger UI. Second middleware is our setup function that will set up Swagger UI to use our predefined users parameters in the `json/yml` file.

Also, of course, our documentation URL is `http://localhost:3000/api-docs`.

Summary

You are now just one step away from getting the maximum knowledge about full-stack applications and all the stuff it concerns. As we said earlier, one of the most important parts, and the one that makes the difference between just a programmer and a full-stack application developer, is testing. This chapter was meant to be easily understandable and highly applicable in your day-to-day work, giving you the most modern concepts and tools used in application testing.

You need to remember that integration tests are the assurance process of all components working well together, such third-party systems, external databases, and asynchronous processes. Depending on which platform you use, you will have a complete ecosystem to accomplish this and get the best value from your application. The best part is that you can automate all the tests at this layer and make your deployment process safer. One thing you cannot test using script is the usability of the application. You will need real humans to interact with your product and in this layer different UI testing techniques come to the rescue. Remember that user experience is one differential when you need to offer your products to the market.

Finally, all the different tests need to be documented to be used by other developers to improve more features of your application. Swagger is a very nice and simple tool to generate a detailed documentation and share with your team.

Now we have completely covered the testing phase! You know what time it is... Let's deploy! See you in the next chapter!

10
Deployment

Now that we know how to create Aurelia applications, we should be able to deploy them in our own servers or if you want to take advantage of other big companies resources, why don't use cloud providers to deploy our apps?

In this chapter, you will learn how to deploy your applications on your own self-managed servers using Docker and NGINX. Also, you will learn how to deploy applications on Heroku and one of the best cloud providers on the planet—**Amazon Web Services** (**AWS**).

We will use Docker to deploy locally, because this will make our deployment portable so that you can deploy your application in your own data center or in the cloud.

Having said that, in this chapter, we will cover the following topics:

- Configuring our web for production
- Deploying on your own server
- Deploying on Heroku
- Deploying on AWS S3 buckets

Configuring our web for production

Before we deploy our application to production, we should prepare and configure it. Let's create an example Aurelia application and deploy it. Open a new Terminal window and run the following command to start a new `deployme` project:

```
$ au new deployme
  ...
  ...
  Happy Coding!

$ ls deployme/aurelia_project/environments
  dev.js   stage.js   prod.js
```

Let's navigate to the `aurelia_project/environments` folder. In this folder, you will find the following files that map to a specific development environment:

- `dev.js`: Contains the configurations for the development phase.
- `stage.js`: Contains the configuration for the staging phase. This phase is also known as **Quality Assurance (QA)**.
- `prod.js`: Contains the configuration for the production phase. In this phase, our application is being used by our final users.

Let's open the `dev.js` file and check the content of the configuration for the development phase:

```
export default {
  debug: true,
  testing: true
};
```

A configuration file is a simple JSON file. As you can see in the `dev.js` file, the `debug` and `testing` attributes are true. It means that while we are developing our application, we will be able to debug and test the application. Let's add a new attribute to see how this works. In the `dev.js` file, apply the following changes:

```
export default {
  debug: true,
  testing: true,
  appTitle: 'DeployMe [dev]'
};
```

Now, let's go ahead and open the `prod.js` file and see how the application should be configured for production:

```
export default {
  debug: false,
  testing: false
};
```

In production, we don't need to debug anything, and we don't test our application, so we have to disable debugging and testing and set the value as `false`. Let's create the `appTitle` attribute, but this time with the correct value for production:

```
export default {
  debug: false,
  testing: false,
  appTitle: 'DeployMe'
};
```

Now let's apply the following changes to the `app.js` file to read the `appTitle` from the environment `environment.js` configuration file:

```
import environmentConfig from './environment'

export class App {
  constructor() {
    this.appTitle = environmentConfig.appTitle;
  }
}
```

Now, let's apply the following changes to the `app.html` file:

```
<template>
  <h1>${appTitle}</h1>
  <p>
    Hello :)!
  </p>
</template>
```

Once the changes are applied, let's run the application, but this time let's specify the environment in order to see how the application's title changes depending on the environment. Go ahead and run the following command for the development environment:

```
$ au run --watch --env dev
...
Application Available At: http://localhost:9000
```

Navigate to the `http://localhost:9000` in your browser and you should see something similar to the following image:

Cool! Now let's run the application, but this time let's change the (--env) environment flag from dev to prod in order to create the production version:

```
$ au run --env prod
...
   Application Available At: http://localhost:9000
```

Navigate to the http://localhost:9000 in your browser and you should see something similar to the following image:

Cool! We are almost done with the production version. Before we deploy our application, we will need to create a minified version of our code. To do so, execute the following command:

```
$ au build --env prod
```

The preceding command will generate the build scripts into the scripts folder, which will contain the JavaScript files ready for production. These files are minified in order to improve the load performance in the client browser. We will take the dist folder and index.html for the deployment process. Basically, an Aurelia application deployment has the following files architecture:

```
./
   - index.html
   - dist/
     - app-bundle.js
     - vendor-bundles.js
```

Details of the JavaScript files are provided in further details in the Aurelia CLI section of `Chapter 1`, *Introducing Aurelia*.

Cool! Let's learn how to deploy our application. Keep reading!

Deploying on your own server

Upto now, we have the production files ready to be deployed. The typical deployment scenario is when you want to deploy your web application on your local server, local computer, or internal corporate server. This is a common practice for big companies that want to manage and have full control on their servers. So, let's learn how to do that using Docker and NGINX as our best allies.

Creating our NGINX configuration file

The only role that NGINX will play in our deployment is to serve as a web server, so we will write a simple configuration file for our server. Go ahead and create the `default.conf` file in the project root folder:

```
server {
    listen 80;
    server_name localhost;

    location / {
        root /usr/share/nginx/html;
        index index.html index.htm;
    }

    error_page 500 502 503 504 /50x.html;
}
```

Let's understand what this configuration file does. First, we tell NGINX to `listen` on port `80`. It means that when we want to access our application, we should call to this port. Secondly, we define the path where NGINX will find our application files. We will have to copy the `scripts` folder and `index.html` file into this folder.

Cool! We have the NGINX configuration file for our application web server. Let's continue with the `Dockerfile` file setup.

Creating our Dockerfile

Our `Dockerfile` contains the receipt to build a Docker image with all the configuration we need to start our NGINX web server and also will contain the web application that has to be copied inside the container. Go ahead and create the `Dockerfile` file in the project root folder:

```
FROM nginx:alpine

COPY default.conf /etc/nginx/conf.d/default.conf

COPY index.html /usr/share/nginx/html/index.html
COPY dist /usr/share/nginx/html/scripts
```

Yeah, that's all! This is a simple Docker file that uses `nginx:alphine` as its base image. We `COPY` the `default.conf` file, which contains the NGINX configuration file, and, finally, we `COPY` our web application files.

That's it! let's build our Docker image and run our very first container.

Running our application on Docker

Before we can run our application, we will need to create a Docker image using our `Dockerfile`. Open a new Terminal and navigate to the project root folder. Once you are there, run the following command to build our Docker image:

```
$ cd /some/path/deployme
$ docker build -t mydeploymeapp .

Sending build context to Docker daemon 130.9MB
Step 1/4 : FROM nginx:alpine
Digest:
sha256:17c4704e19a11cd47545fa3c17e6903fc88672021f7f907f212d6663baf6ab57
Status: Downloaded newer image for nginx:alpine
 ---> 91ce6206f9d8
Step 2/4 : COPY default.conf /etc/nginx/conf.d/default.conf
 ---> 0e744f0e2556
Step 3/4 : COPY index.html /usr/share/nginx/html/index.html
 ---> 092ad92d0d5c
Step 4/4 : COPY scripts /usr/share/nginx/html/scripts
 ---> 6d097542eec5
Successfully built 6d097542eec5
Successfully tagged mywebapp:latest
```

We use the `docker build` command to build a new image. The `-t` option allows us to give our image a name, in this case, our image is called `mydeploymeapp`. Pay attention to the period (`.`) in the last command argument; the `docker build` command uses a `Dockerfile` to build the new image. We specify the path of this `Dockerfile` in the last option of the command; as this file is in the root folder where we are running `docker build`, we should use the *period* symbol to specify the current folder, which in this case contains the `Dockerfile`.

Once the build process is finished, we will have the `Successfully built` message.

Now we are ready to start our application. Go ahead and run the following command to start a new `mydeploymeapp` Docker container:

```
$ docker run -p 8000:80 mywebapp
```

We used the `docker run` command to start a new container and pass the `-p` option to map our host `8000` port to the NGINX `80` port, which is listening inside the container. The last argument is the Docker image that we want to create, in this case, our application's image.

Cool! Our application is up and running. Let's navigate to `http://localhost:8000` and you should see the following page:

That's it! We have successfully deployed our Aurelia application on our local server using Docker and NGINX. You can install Docker on your remote server and follow the same steps we did in this section to install any Aurelia application.

Let's learn in the following sections how to deploy apps to the cloud. Keep reading!

Deploying on Heroku

It's time to take advantage of the cloud and start looking for new approaches. In this section, we will see how to deploy our Aurelia example application to Heroku. We will follow the next steps in order before we start the deployment process:

1. Create a Heroku account
2. Prepare our application
3. Deploy

Let's start with the very first step.

Creating a Heroku account

Navigate to `https://heroku.com` and click on the **SIGN UP FOR FREE** button. Then, fill the form with your account information. Once you are ready, we will need to install the Heroku CLI. This CLI will provide us with an easy-to-use command-line tool that we will use to deploy our applications and perform other administration operations on our applications.

To download the Heroku CLI, navigate to `https://devcenter.heroku.com/articles/ heroku-cli`. Select your operating system and follow the installation instructions. Once the installation finished, go ahead and open a new Terminal window and execute the following command to log in to your Heroku workspace:

```
$ heroku login

Enter your Heroku credentials:
Email: erikson.murrugarra@gmail.com
Password: ****************
Logged in as erikson.murrugarra@gmail.com
```

The preceding command will ask you for your `email` and `password` that you used in the signup process. Provide your credentials and if everything is correct, you will receive the `Logged in as ...` message.

Preparing the application

Heroku, just like other cloud providers, does not offer any way to deploy static HTML files, so we will need to deploy our application using another strategy. We will create a simple PHP file that will serve as the entry point that will have one line of code to import our `index.html` file:

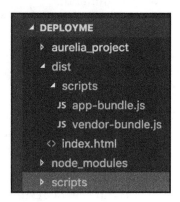

Now, in the `dist` folder, go ahead and create the `index.php` file with the following content:

```
<?
    include_once("index.html");
```

We use the `invoke_once` function to import the `index.html` page as the main page.

Deploy

Once we have our application static files and our `index.php` entry point file, let's create a new Heroku application. Navigate to the `dist` folder and `init` a new Git repository running the following commands:

```
$ cd dist
$ git init
$ git add .
$ git commit -m "My Application commit"
```

We use git add following by a period (.) to add all the files to the staging area. It means all the changes will be candidates to commit.

Once we have our local git repository, let's create a new Heroku application named `mydeploymeapp`. Execute the following command:

```
$ heroku apps:create deploymeapp

  Creating • deploymeapp... done
  https://deploymeapp.herokuapp.com/ |
https://git.heroku.com/deploymeapp.git
```

We use the Heroku CLI tool and call the `apps:create` option to create a new application. You have to change the application's name, because they should be globally different from other app's names. Once created, Heroku will respond with the application's URL.

Now that we have our application created, let's push the code to the Git repository created by Heroku to host our application's code and see the results. Execute the following command:

```
$ git push heroku master

Counting objects: 3, done.
...
remote:
remote: -----> PHP app detected
remote:
...
done.
To https://git.heroku.com/mydeploymeapp.git
   15cb66e..72d4d2a master -> master
```

As you can see, Heroku will recognize automatically that we are deploying a PHP application, and it will deploy our application. Let's go ahead and navigate to your application's URL; mine is `https://mydeploymeapp.herokuapp.com`:

Awesome! Now that we know how to deploy our application on the *cloud* using Heroku, let's explore how can we do this with another very popular cloud provider. We will learn how to deploy our website using **Amazon Simple Storage Service** (**Amazon S3**). Keep reading!

Deploying on AWS S3 Buckets

AWS is one of the biggest cloud providers across the globe. We will learn how to deploy our Aurelia application using AWS S3. Yes, I am not crazy! We will deploy our application without installing any server or **Elastic Cloud Compute** (**EC2**) virtual machine instance.

Uploading files

Before we start the process, you will need to have an account on AWS. Navigate to the following URL to create your free account—`https://aws.amazon.com`.

Once you are done with the registration process and are logged in to the AWS console, go ahead and navigate to the S3 service dashboard, as shown:

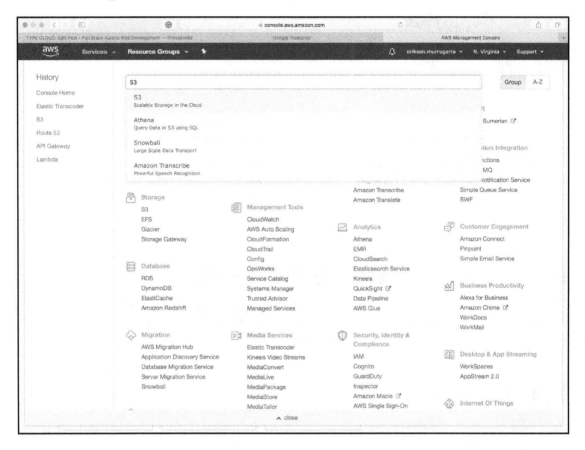

Once the S3 dashboard is loaded, you will see the list of all the your AWS buckets that you created before. If not, you will see an empty list. Click on the **Create Bucket** button to create a new bucket and name your bucket with your application's name and click on the **Next** button to accept the defaults:

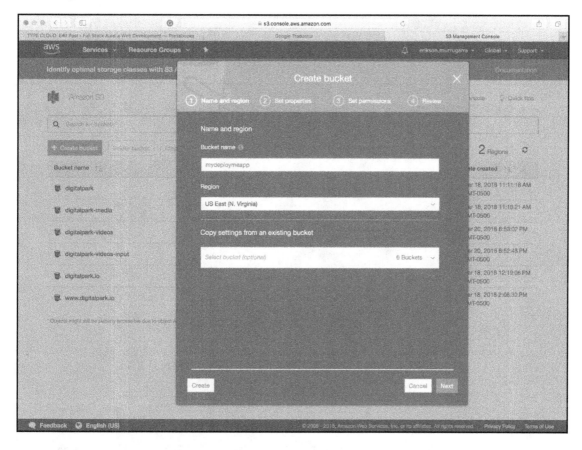

Once created, you should see the new S3 bucket in the list:

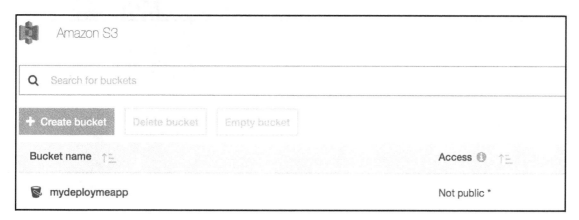

Now get into your bucket, and let's upload the `index.html` file to the bucket by clicking on the **Add files** button and selecting the file. Don't forget to grant public read permission when you are submitting the files:

Once we have selected our web application files that we want to deploy in S3, we should make these files public so that S3 will be able to serve the file publicly, otherwise our users won't be able to access our web application files. To do so, select the **Grant public read access to this object(s)** option in the **Manage public permissions** drop-down list, as illustrated:

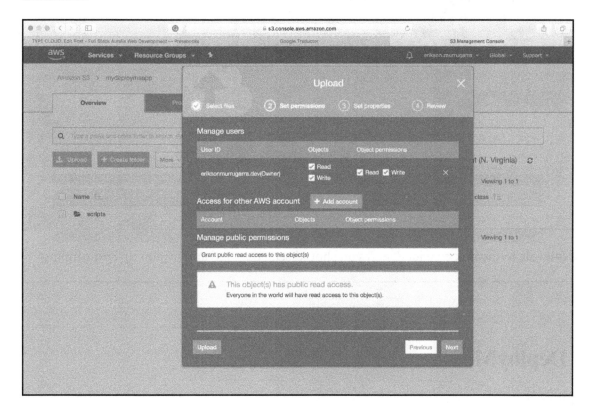

Cool! To upload the contents into the `script` folder, you will need to create a folder for scripts in the bucket. To do this, just click on the **Create Folder** button. Once you have the folder created, go ahead and upload the `app-bundle.js` and `vendor-bundle.js` files into the S3 scripts folder (don't forget to grant public permission).

Configuring our S3 Bucket for the web

Let's configure our bucket to act as a website bucket. Before we do that, let's access our `index.html` file from our web browser. To do this, select the `index.html` page and let's copy the URL besides **Link** that appears in the object settings panel:

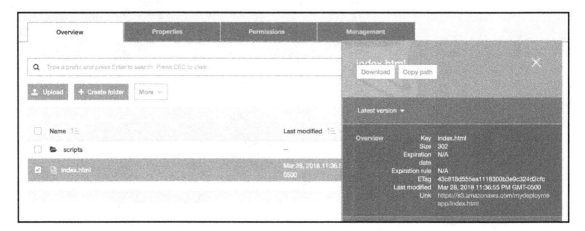

Navigate to the link provided, and you should see your web application up and running:

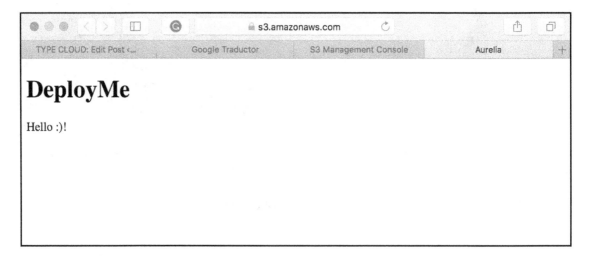

There is one last step we should do. First, note that the URL is not friendly, and we are accessing our web using the `index.html` file. This is not the right way to deploy a web application on Amazon S3. Let's configure our bucket to explicitly make it a web bucket.

Let's navigate to the **Properties** tab in our bucket and select the static web hosting option. Select the **use this bucket to host a website** option, type `index.html` as the index page, and click on **Save:**

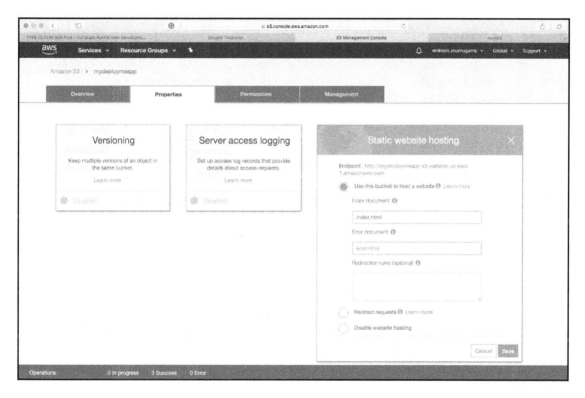

Cool! Now we are ready. Copy the new URL provided by AWS and navigate to it to see the web application up and running:

Awesome! You are ready to deploy your applications on AWS using S3 buckets without the need to provide any virtual server. Congratulations!

Summary

In this final chapter of the book, you learned how to deploy web applications on self-managed or on-premise servers and also how to take advantage of the cloud.

You learned how to use Docker to deploy applications. Using Docker will help you in all the phases of development, so we strongly encourage you to buy a Docker book and start learning about it right now!

We also covered how to deploy applications on top of Heroku. Heroku is a **Platform as a Service (PaaS)** that will manage and monitor your applications for you. So you don't have to worry about infrastructure; you just need to worry about creating awesome applications.

Finally, you came across how to deploy applications using AWS S3 buckets to deploy applications without any virtual server configuration.

Aurelia is becoming very popular and is being adopted by important organizations; this is the right time to become an expert and be ready for the revolutionary future in which Aurelia will play a very important role. On the other hand, you only have a little bit of knowledge about Docker and cloud computing. We encourage you to explore more about these technologies, which are extremely important in the IT world.

Having said that, we wish you the best in your next adventure.

Other Books You May Enjoy

If you enjoyed this book, you may be interested in these other books by Packt:

Full-Stack Web Development with Vue.js and Node
Aneeta Sharma

ISBN: 9781788831147

- Build an application with Express.js
- Create schemas using Mongoose
- Develop a single-page application using Vue.js and Express.js
- Create RESTful APIs using Express.js
- Add test cases to improve the reliability of the application
- Learn how to deploy apps on Heroku using GitHub
- Add authorization using passports

Learning Aurelia
Manuel Guilbault

ISBN: 9781785889677

- Build a modern single-page web application
- Understand the workflow of an Aurelia application
- Design reusable web components, which can be shared and integrated into various frameworks and libraries
- Write clean, modular, and testable code that will be easy to maintain and evolve
- Use all the latest–and even future–web standards, so the application gathers minimal technical debt

Leave a review - let other readers know what you think

Please share your thoughts on this book with others by leaving a review on the site that you bought it from. If you purchased the book from Amazon, please leave us an honest review on this book's Amazon page. This is vital so that other potential readers can see and use your unbiased opinion to make purchasing decisions, we can understand what our customers think about our products, and our authors can see your feedback on the title that they have worked with Packt to create. It will only take a few minutes of your time, but is valuable to other potential customers, our authors, and Packt. Thank you!

Index